D1129736

Inside Today's Home

Ray Faulkner
STANFORD UNIVERSITY
Sarah Faulkner

Inside

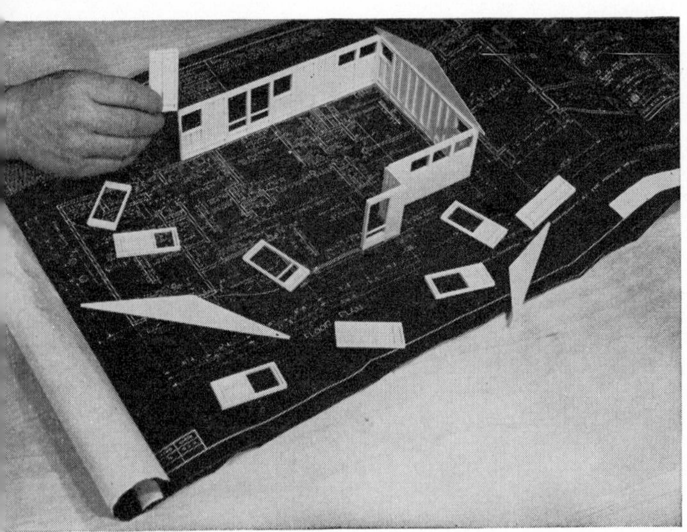

NEW YORK

Today's Home

REVISED EDITION

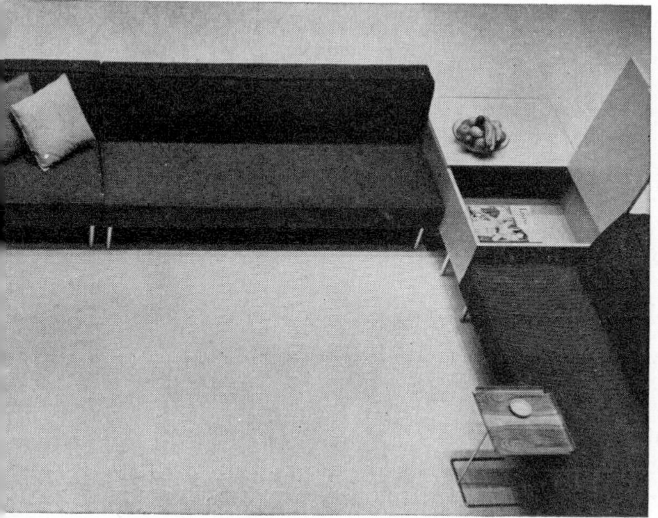

HOLT, RINEHART AND WINSTON

Library of Congress Catalog Card Number: 60-10134
22754-0610
Printed in the United States of America

January, 1962

Preface to Revised Edition

INSIDE TODAY'S HOME was written to help you make a home appropriate to the kind of family life you want. This is not a matter of following fads and fashions, or formulas and rules, obediently. It demands active, individualized thinking about many matters.

House planning, furnishing, and landscaping—three closely related parts of one problem—are all involved. Solving this problem well means planning from "inside out," not merely from inside the house to the exterior and the yard but from inside yourself to your home as a whole. It requires, first of all, a realistic appraisal of your own and your family's personality and desired way of living, esthetic preferences, and resources. Then it demands an understanding of the basic facts about design and color, the materials and furnishings now available, and the many ways in which these can be adapted to your own situation. In all of this, the ways in which other persons have handled their problems is an invaluable inspiration but never a ready-made blueprint. We have, therefore, attempted to stimulate you to analyze your own needs and preferences, to explain alternative means of achieving your goals, and to introduce basic principles and useful information.

So many persons have contributed to this book, knowingly or otherwise, that it is impossible to mention them by name. First are the students whose questions and comments have kept us alert to the interests as well as to the areas of ignorance of those just beginning to think about home planning. Then there are the readers of the first edition who have called our attention to possible improvements, and the many persons who have helped us obtain illustrative materials. Finally, our four boys continue to remind us that planning and keeping a home suited to today's family living is far more than "decoration"—and is also a never-ending activity.

R. F.
S. F.

Stanford, California
February 15, 1960

Contents

In Locust Valley, New York, architect Jose Luis Sert remodeled an old stable for his home. Free-standing bookshelves hide a compact kitchen. Furniture against the walls leaves maximum open space to be used as the family wishes. (*Photograph by Gottscho-Schleisner*)

PART I

Our Activities, Space, and Equipment

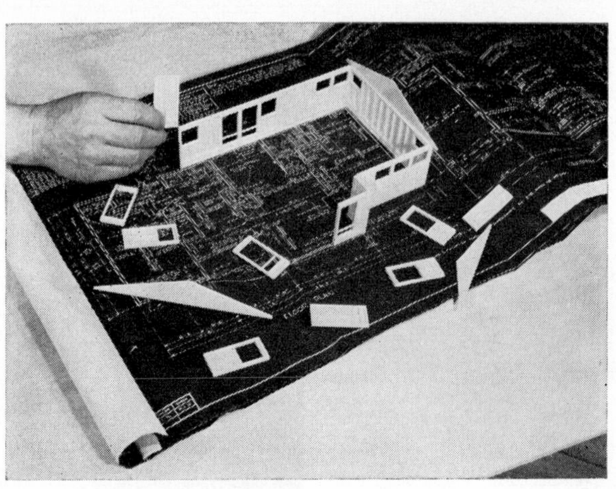

1. A Beginning

Never before has there been such widespread interest in home planning or such varied materials from which to choose. That no styles or rules restrict your choices constitutes a great challenge. Fortunately, there are many publications on the subject and there are experts ready to share their experience. BUT if a home is to be really your own, active participation in its planning and furnishing is in order. Among the first questions to be answered are: How do you want to live? What activities give greatest satisfaction? Which forms, colors, and materials give lasting pleasure? What will all this cost in time, energy, and money?

In planning a living room, for example, the logical beginning is an analysis of the group activities for which the room is intended, and then a consideration of the size, shape, character, and cost of the space and equipment needed for these activities. But you cannot wisely treat the living room as an isolated unit. How does it relate to other areas in the home, to the sun and wind, to the view and outdoor living space? Piecemeal planning is seldom successful.

Above. There is no better investment than thoughtful planning. (*National Plan Service*)

Contemporary needs and contemporary ways of meeting these needs are far less a matter of a "modern style" than a way of analyzing and solving today's problems directly. Not long ago modern homes and modern furniture were regarded by many as another passing fad. In some ways these people were right, for today's homes differ markedly from some of their stripped-down, cold, and angular predecessors.

Trends change as does the life from which they grow. In this century the modern movement has had three overlapping phases. The "modernistic" phase, which came in the 1920's, was a clumsy but sincere attempt to cease aping the past. Bulbous chairs and sofas, skyscraper bookcases, and angular tables and lamps were used with textiles and wallpapers of nervous, aggressive design. "Machine modern" came to prominence in the 1930's and still persists. It is a serious attempt to take full advantage of machine production and to simplify homes and furnishings. Many of the results are beautiful in a pure, precise way; others seem cold and mechanistic.

"Naturalism" is perhaps the best word to describe the leading trend today. It begins with our own natures and extends to a sympathetic understanding and modification of the nature that surrounds us. Wood for houses and furniture has come back into its own. Fabrics with naturelike textures and colors are favored for their lasting beauty and ease of maintenance while houses are integrated with the landscape. Naturalism is a trend in which rigid prescriptions have no place and in which well-founded individualism flourishes. It is today's way of living—and it is a very happy solution.

Some of the characteristics of this trend are illustrated in the house shown in Figures 4A to 5B.* It is a modest house on a typical subdivision lot, but it is not commonplace. It was designed by an ingenious architect (who was responsible for some of Hollywood's most lavish homes), and it was economically built along with several hundred similar but not identical houses. Thus quality was kept high and costs low.

Every foot of space was thoughtfully planned for livability, economy of time and energy, attractiveness, and a degree of individuality rare in tract houses. The plan shows a carport and covered walk that give protected access to both "service" and "guest" entrances. In days past these would have been the "back" and "front" doors; now both are on the front, the shortest distance from street and carport. The service entrance opens logically into the laundry-storage area and kitchen. The main entrance brings us into a vestibule from which every room in the house can be reached easily. Straight ahead is a combined living-dining room, which opens onto

* Figure numbers for the illustrations are the same as the page numbers on which they appear throughout this book.

A

B

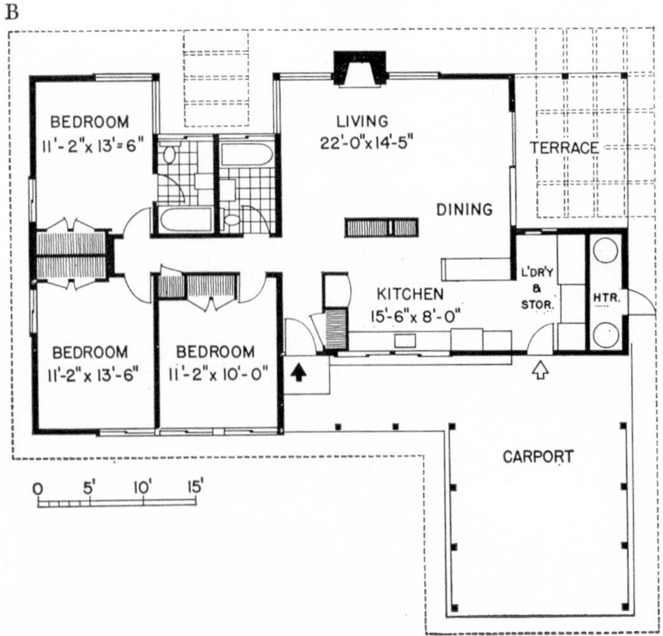

A "tract" house, when well designed, can be handsome, individual, and yet inexpensive. Burton A. Schutt, architect.

Above. The living room has drama in its high ceiling, large windows, impressive fireplace; tranquillity in its balanced furniture placement and plain walls and floors; sparkle in its contrasts of dark and light, accents of patterns, painting, and sculptural driftwood. (*Photographs by Julius Shulman*)

Left. The plan shows unusually well-organized space, compact but not boxy, with patterns of circulation, grouping of rooms, and furniture arrangement integated into a gracious setting for home life.

A

Above. The living area can be extended visually by opening the curtains over the wide expanse of glass, physically by opening the sliding doors onto a protected terrace.

Below. Unified by a strong roof line, projecting bays and sheltered courts relate the exterior to the interior and the site.

B

a livable terrace. To the right are the kitchen and laundry. To the left, three bedrooms and two baths are arranged compactly and with desirable privacy from the rest of the house.

Many devices make the living-dining area attractive and seemingly spacious far beyond its moderate size. The free-standing cabinet that shields the kitchen also creates a logical space for living and another one for dining. In three directions, outdoor space is borrowed through window walls that flood the room with balanced daylight. A large, sliding glass door near the dining table opens onto a terrace designed for use in many kinds of weather. Sheltered by the walls of the house on two sides, the terrace is enclosed on the other two sides by latticework fences that are in effect the boundary walls of the living area. The ceiling, too, actively stretches the space because it is high, elongated by dark beams, and continues visibly beyond the glass walls as overhanging roofs and protective trellises. The cork floor is at the same level as the concrete terrace floor that gives solid, dry footing for people and outdoor furniture. In contrast to this openness and movement are the solid block of the fireplace and the warmly enclosing plywood walls.

The furnishings, like the shell of the house, are mass-produced and moderately priced. More important, they are comfortable and pleasing, and they are sufficiently distinctive to differentiate this home from its neighbors. Arranged around the fireplace and window walls, the major furniture group provides comfortable, congenial seating for six to eight people. (Dining chairs and outdoor furniture are at hand for larger groups.) These simple, well-proportioned pieces are similar in basic shape but varied in their coverings. The sofa and cushion on the bench are light tan; the lounge chair, ottoman, and a pillow on the sofa are sparkling red. Plaid upholstery on the occasional chair brings together the tan, brown, and red used elsewhere. Unpatterned beige curtains and rug further unify the room. A piece of driftwood above the fireplace, a reproduction of one of Paul Klee's paintings, and the very important views into the garden complete the furnishings.

The exterior perfectly expresses the interior, for it has the same character and similar materials. Redwood, scored vertically in random-width grooves, gives a quiet pattern of light and shadow and a sense of scale consistent with the size of the house. It becomes a foil for the large areas of glass and rugged textures of the masonry chimney. A broad band of wood at the roof's edge makes the house seem wider and lower. Trellises and openings in the roof lighten the structure and relate the building to the space around it.

We turn our attention now from a whole house to an analysis of two chairs (Figs. 7A and B). Both are examples of contemporary Scandinavian design. The modern version of the eighteenth-century Windsor chair gives

A

B

Two chairs, both by Scandinavian designers sensitive to the qualities of wood, illustrate two of the trends in furniture design today.

Left. Morgens Lasser's chair has an informal naturalism that sturdily expresses the nature of wood and exploits its beauty. (*Pacific Overseas Inc.*)

Right. Finn Juhl has combined the same basic appreciation of materials with a refined elegance to produce a chair of sculptured grace. (*Baker Furniture, Inc.*)

as comfortable support as can be expected of an all-wood chair: height and depth of the shaped seat, angle and height of the back, and the design of the arms suit most people. Because it can be made easily from minimum materials, the original price is low. Upkeep is minimal. The forthright expression of structure is a first step in this chair's claim to beauty. Next there is the brisk yet harmonious relationship of back to seat and to legs, the subtle tapering of the legs and spindles, and then the grain and color of the wood. In spite of close adherence to the "typical" Windsor chair, this example is individualized in its sensitive proportions and the craftsmanlike shaping of each part. It would seem at home in an unpretentious room, such as that shown in Figure 13A, for a family that valued simplicity combined with sensitiveness above ornateness or elegance.

Carrying forward a long tradition of Scandinavian skill in working wood, the second chair offers greater comfort with its resilient seat and back that conform to each sitter. Although costlier to buy and to maintain, it is not an extravagance. Here, too, the structure is the essence of the design, but the structure has been handsomely refined. Four uprights, two standing vertically and two angled to buttress the weight, support the frame. Careful study shows that these verticals are thinner at top and bottom, but notice that the thickest part of each set is at a different height. This is not whimsy. Logically, the front supports are thickest where they join the seat, the back where they join the stretchers. Then notice the arms. They develop from the front supports in a complex way—the top of this joint is a softened right angle while the underside is a smooth curve. As the arms approach the rear supports, they broaden in a downward curve and then resolutely rise to support the chair's back. Such refinements may or may not be appreciated at a glance but they contribute to the chair's lean, elegant beauty. Also they give the chair a pronounced character that is nearly as difficult to imitate as it was to create. As you read this book, you might decide to which homes each of these chairs would be most completely suited.

From this discussion, we can define home design as the organization of space and equipment for satisfying living. But what makes a piece of furniture, a room, a whole house "good"? A chair, for example, is good if it

- Gives comfortable support, thereby fulfilling its requirements of *use.*
- Is worth the original cost, plus the time, energy, and money required to keep it clean and in good repair; in short, it is *economical.*
- Gives pleasure when seen or touched; then it is *beautiful.*
- Has a character of its own and also suits the family so well that it "belongs" in their home; then it gains *individuality.*

Home planning and furnishing, then, has four goals: *use, economy, beauty,* and *individuality.* Underlying all of these is appropriateness.

Use is a central concept in creating today's homes. We want homes that serve their purposes, that "work" effectively—space that is planned for all family activities; chairs that earn the space they take; storage that is convenient and accessible; lighting, heating, and plumbing that do their jobs. Overemphasis on the utilitarian can, of course, lead to a laboratory-like coldness, but such excesses in no way diminish the primary importance of having our homes serve us well.

Economy refers to the management of human, material and monetary resources.

A

B

Economy takes many different forms, all of which can be rewarding.

Above. With a unique blending of individuality and beauty with economy and usefulness, Virginia Stanton planned her kitchen with complete, not merely mechanistic, functionalism as an aim. (*Photograph by Maynard Parker. Courtesy of* House Beautiful)

Left. A workshop planned for economy of time, space, and effort can also be a visually pleasant space in which to enjoy a hobby. (*Courtesy of* Popular Home Magazine. *United States Gypsum Co.*)

Human resources consist of abilities plus time and energy. Each person has a complex of abilities peculiarly his own, and his productivity is in part determined by encouragement to do what he does best. It is sound economy, as well as an effective way to promote individuality, to give a good cook a suitable kitchen (Fig. 9A), to give a mechanic shop space (Fig. 9B), or a musician the needed instruments and space to use them. Time and energy for such enriching activities have been greatly increased by labor-saving devices, for example, automatic furnaces and washing machines. More fundamental, though, than the purchase of such equipment is planning every part of the home for maximum efficiency. If you are building, buying, or renting space for living, check carefully the size, shape, and location of rooms, the durability of the materials, and the finishes used for walls and floors. If you are furnishing a home, think of the time you will have to spend on housekeeping and maintenance. How much do you want for other activities?

Material resources are all the things that have been purchased or received as gifts, and few persons realize how many they own. It is surprisingly easy to forget some of them and to rush unthinkingly to buy a new object when something already owned would do as well. Possibly a little repair or adaptation is indicated, but that costs far less than a replacement.

A system of using your money is well worth the little time it takes to plan and follow, especially since few families can afford everything they want. Each purchase should contribute its share to the total plan. It should be worth what you pay and not cost more than you can comfortably afford. Remember, too, that cost is both original and continuing. First cost must be balanced with the total upkeep cost over the life of the object. Unfortunately, most things that are beautiful, durable, and economical to maintain have a high price tag. For example, wool or leather upholstery for furniture costs considerably more than cotton. But many cottons are not easy to keep clean, may soon become shabby and have to be replaced. Over the years, cotton may be a poor investment; yet it may be all you can afford. This example illustrates the interrelationships of time, energy, and money.

One kind of economy is remodeling an old house, an example of which is shown in Figure 11. This was a good house built in Illinois two decades ago, but the single window in the back wall of the living room did little to light the room or open it to the pleasant garden. To gain a sense of spaciousness as well as to integrate the indoors with the outdoors, the owners took out the entire end wall and replaced it with insulating glass. A small window near the corner was converted into a door that gives pleasant access to a terrace and lawn. At comparatively small expense, the room was transformed from a darkish interior to a space flooded with light.

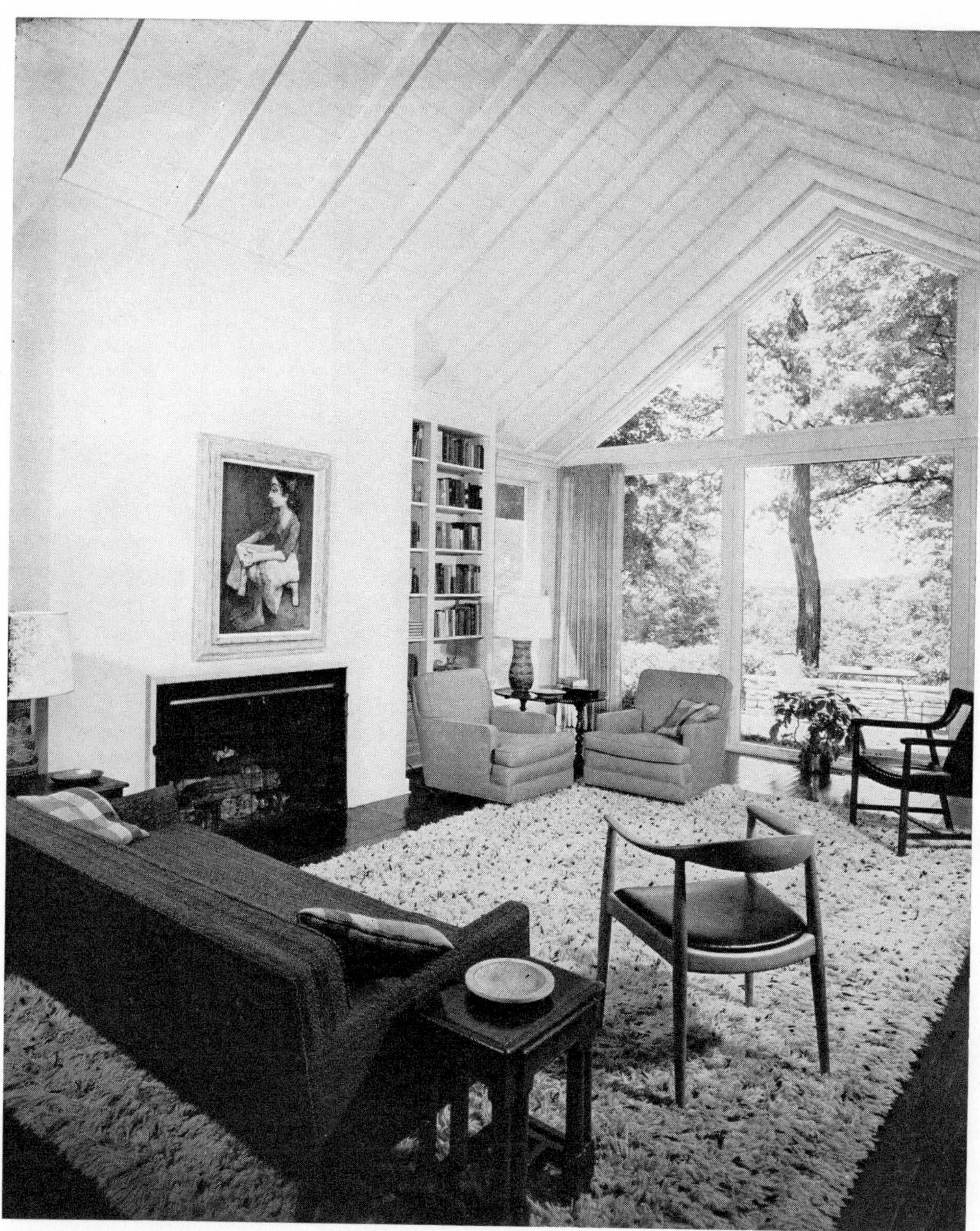

That remodeling can be worth while is evident in this Illinois room that has been made light and spacious by a window wall and simplified fireplace, an invigorating color scheme, and a few new furnishings. Milton Schwarz, architect. (*Photograph by Bill Hedrich, Hedrich-Blessing. Courtesy of* Better Homes and Gardens)

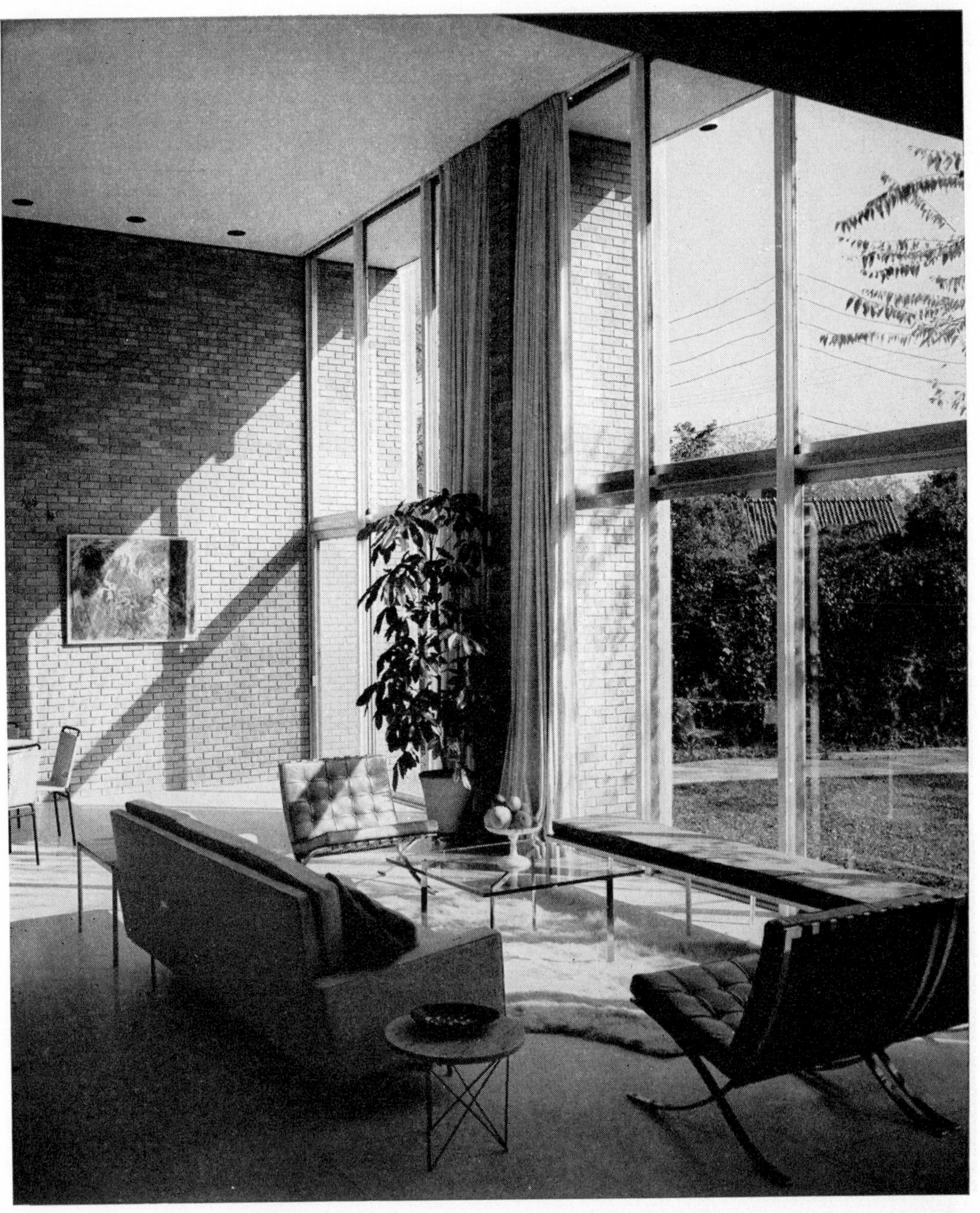

In Houston, Texas, the Gerald S. Gordons' living room seems cool and open. A sense of space and refinement of detail in both structure and furniture build up to a climax in the soaring windows. Bolton and Barnstone, architects. (*Photograph by Fred Winchell*)

A

B

Above. In the Winston Eltings' living room, Libertyville, Illinois, the massive fireplace is an anchor for a furniture group. Large windows lighten the space; a storage wall houses the miscellaneous objects used in this area. Schweikher and Elting, architects. (*Photograph by Bill Hedrich, Hedrich-Blessing*)

Left. Travel posters, inexpensively famed and easily changed, and a large jug holding flowers, personalize a wall space. (*Dunbar Furniture Co.*)

Beauty is that quality which pleases the senses and lifts the spirit. The elements of beauty—form, line and texture, space, light, and color—can be put together in myriad combinations to achieve the desired effect. Although beauty, in a very real sense, is centered as often in the eyes of the beholder as it is inherent in the object itself, there are guiding aims and principles (discussed in Chapter 5) that may be of use in capturing this elusive quality. In addition, sensitively selected and used materials contribute to beauty—as well as to use, economy, and individuality. Each material has its own special potentialities and limitations, which are discussed in Chapters 8, 9, and 10.

Beauty submits to no quick and easy recipes or inviolable laws, as can be seen in a living room from Texas and one from Illinois (Figs. 12 and 13A). In the Gordons' Texas home, it is the space that demands first consideration. This two-story volume that expands beyond its confines is geometrically defined by planes of varied materials. A pinkish brick wall and pillar project beyond the spectacular window walls on one side, the opposite side is a storage wall with wood doors below high windows. Off-white floor and ceiling add to the cool spaciousness desirable in Texas. The furniture is as precisely and rigorously disciplined as is the architecture. For conversation, there is an almost symmetrical arrangement of furniture in an uninterrupted sweep of space. With no demanding center of interest, this furniture group is held together by its geometric disposition and the harmony of the individual pieces. This segment of space is further defined, but very subtly, by a large rug of tawny fur and the spectacular bank of windows it faces. In general character, the living room is formal, dignified and elegant, an urbane city house—restrained to the point of understatement. The owners' words are illuminating: "We feel that we are living in a piece of sculpture, unique in that it is spacious, comfortable, sparkling, and above all—beautiful."

There is no understatement in the living room architect Winston Elting designed for his family. A massive fireplace of concrete with a few exposed, split-granite boulders is the dominating focus of an informal furniture arrangement and sets the keynote of a rustic house in harmony with its site. Here, as in the Gordons' home, an "area" rug suggests partial definition of this part of a long living-dining space. Also similar to the Gordon living room is the frank exposure of the house structure, but here fir and redwood take the place of steel and brick. In spite of a construction system as geometrically regular as that in the Gordons' home, this house seems as natural as its setting of fields and oak trees.

Each of these houses is beautiful in its own way. Both of them were designed in whole and in part with great sensitivity to all the guiding

A

B

The quietly handsome drapery fabric at the left is more durable and less expensive than the highly spirited, colorful print at the right. (*Edwin Raphael Co., Inc.*)

principles and factors to be discussed later. They differ because their owners differ. One wanted lofty, serene spaciousness and smooth surfaces with a minimum of pattern. The other sought a more rugged sense of enclosure for a less formal way of living.

Individuality—the quality that differentiates your home from those of your friends and makes you and them feel that it is really yours—is important. No one wants his home to have the generalized character of a hotel lobby or bedroom that, necessarily, aims at the common denominator of many diverse personalities. Usually, however, if a home is the natural outgrowth of a family's interests and preferences, individuality will develop as naturally as the personalities of those who have made it. Individuality at its best is an outgrowth, not something superimposed from outside; and it grows most convincingly out of fundamentals, not accessories. In a mass-production age, the quest for individuality is often overdramatized: the result is a shallow, self-conscious desire to be different—often in a different way every few years—and it may lead to nothing more than a house full of impersonal, but fashionable, decorator's touches. Far better to be just yourself, making the most of your strengths and weaknesses, and let your homes shape themselves easily and naturally.

Use, beauty, economy, and *individuality* are as closely related as the warp and woof of a textile. None can be completely dissociated from the others and retain full significance. On the other hand, you cannot consider all these factors simultaneously. In selecting draperies for a window wall (Figs. 15A and B), for example, you might first focus attention on utility

—how well the material controls the transmission of light and extreme outdoor temperatures, the privacy it affords, and its sound-absorbing qualities. Then you might look at the price tag while thinking about ease of upkeep and life expectancy. Color, texture, and pattern are highly important considerations. Finally, there are your own preferences as well as the character of the room in which it will hang. All this will probably raise difficulties: genuinely beautiful drapery fabrics are likely to be costly and are not always durable or easily cleaned; those that catch your eye first may grow tiresome or be inappropriate for the room. That leads to the challenge of balancing each factor against the others so that your choice will be wise, not whimsical, and your satisfaction lasting.

► APPROACHING THE PROBLEM

No two individuals face the problem of home planning and furnishing in identical ways. The following six steps indicate one approach—but by no means the only possible one—that you might take when planning your home.

1. Inventory your present possessions; then list expected additions.

Listing in an orderly way all that you now own is an easy but strategic first step. Such a list is a surprising index both of personality and of resources.

Equipment for eating is a good example. A critical look at dishes, glassware, silver, and table linens tells quickly what type of meals can be well served. Informal buffet suppers are feasible only if suitable trays, plates, and tumblers are on the shelves. Accumulated glass stemware, seldom used, may represent a big investment in money and storage. Those who do not yet have households can start thinking about what they want. Perhaps some of the desired things are remote probabilities. Distinguishing between these and the more likely possibilities will save time and future disappointment.

Table settings, of course, are only a fraction of home furnishings. Furniture, lamps, rugs, and draperies are more basic. Then comes the miscellany related to a family's interests—books and magazines, musical instruments, sports gear, or painting and sculpture. Making a careful inventory, perhaps at three- or five-year intervals, alerts you to what and how much you possess, where and how often each object is used, how deeply it is enjoyed, and where it is stored. Possessions help make home life more satisfying. They should be used and cherished but not allowed to mold an artificial way of living.

2. List favored activities.

Individuals differ markedly in the hobbies or work they enjoy, and good homes reflect this diversity. Some activities, such as conversation or reading, require no special equipment other than comfortable seats, appropriate illumination, and protection from disconcerting noise. Other activities, of which furniture-making and weaving are examples, make more demands.

Listing your possessions and activities is the groundwork for the next stages of planning.

3. Decide on the general character of your home.

Each room, chair, and textile illustrated in this chapter has a definite personality. Each not only expresses but leads toward a way of living. Beyond these are an almost infinite number of personalities, basic ideas, or themes around which a home can be planned.

It is a provocative exercise to think about the varied ways of providing for possessions and activities so that the family's individuality will be evident. Beware, though, of some of the major pitfalls. Choosing a theme merely because it is the fashionable trend may be simply playing into the hands of those whose job is to make people dissatisfied with what they had last year. Also, trying to copy what your friends have achieved seldom leads to long-term satisfaction. Another path to almost certain failure is to decide on a theme and then force all family life to conform to it —space for children's play, for example, may well differ in character from that planned for adult group living. Then, too, it is risky to decide too quickly on your home's character before all the factors that can make home life pleasant are understood. Finally, the importance of individuality can be greatly exaggerated, and the quest to be different can lead to a keyed-up theatricalism suited to very few families.

4. Learn the ways and means of achieving the desired character.

You can start by simply looking, listening, and touching. Then ask questions and make comparisons to help develop a vocabulary, a reservoir of ideas, and some guiding principles. Sources of inspiration and enlightenment are legion: stores, museums, motion pictures, and television; your own home, those of friends, and exhibition houses; and books, magazines, and newspapers.

A good beginning is to investigate a single aspect of the total problem with some thoroughness. It matters not a bit with what you start, but it is more fun to begin with something of special interest. Seating equipment is a good illustration. One of the first steps is to learn what kinds of chairs, stools, davenports, and benches are available. The variety is amazing, for seating can be for one person or for two or more; fixed or movable; hard or soft, high or low, with or without backs or arms; of wood, cane, metal, plastic, or stone. It can be cheap or costly, easy or difficult to maintain, sturdy or fragile in construction. Its shape can be rectangular, curved, even triangular, and it can be ornamented or plain. Size, actual and apparent, ranges from small to big, while weight goes from heavy to light. Character ranges from formal to informal, relaxing to activating, and unusual to commonplace. This list might be continued for several pages if materials are considered. Wood, for example, can be hard or soft, fine or coarse grained, light or dark, red or brown, yellow or black. Upholstery can be of wool, cotton, silk, leather, fur, or plastic and each of these materials can be had in many colors and textures.

You might prefer to begin this study with tables or chests, textiles or floor coverings, dishes or glassware, house plans or landscape design. Whatever the field, though, keep asking these questions: How well does this object meet the human needs for which it was produced? What would it cost in money, time, and energy? What degree and kind of beauty does it have? Does it have desirable individuality?

5. *Consider finances.*

Costs, original and continuing, are factors never to be ignored. How much is available for spending? Over what period of time? What expenditures will give greatest satisfaction?

The financial resources of the young and unmarried, about to be married, or just married are usually modest and every penny must count. Furthermore, there is likelihood of one or more moves before permanent settling. Family life often begins in small, rented, possibly furnished quarters. Then, as family and finances increase, there is usually a move to a larger, unfurnished, rented space or to a home of one's own. Thus, planning and spending for an only partially predictable future is in order.

Although there is no single way to solve the problem of wise initial spending, the following suggestions have merit.

- Get a few good basic objects, such as a bed, comfortable sofa, and storage chests that are durable, pleasing in character, and can be used flexibly. Concentrate spending on these.
- Fill in with frankly inexpensive, perhaps temporary things, such as Chinese split cane chairs, fiber rugs, and unbleached muslin draperies.
- Tend to avoid the moderately expensive things that are not quite what is wanted—not really excellent in design, structure, or material—but which cost too much to be discarded easily later.

In short, hit high and low in the beginning, fill in the scale as you go along. As tastes mature and needs become more definite, the general character of a home often changes. While avoiding the commonplace, also think twice about those pieces so aggressively individualistic that they fit in only one environment.

6. Continually remember the desired goal.

It is surprisingly hard to keep clearly in mind what you set out to achieve, surprisingly easy to alter your course without realizing it. Irresistible bargains, impulse buying of any kind, or simply failing to remind yourself what is wanted can over the years lead you far from the intended route and into an uncongenial environment.

To be sure, it may be necessary to change ideas. One may move from California to Maine, from city to country. Economic conditions may change and the family may increase or decrease. Tastes may evolve in new directions. When such changes occur, make intelligent, considered modifications, but do not let the accidental or the incidental shift the course.

Achieving a good home is far more than deciding on a color scheme and selecting and arranging furniture. The roots of a good home are in the family's needs and wishes, and its major expression is the plan and architectural shell that shape space for living. Its full development takes us out into the landscape and to the community beyond. For several decades technologists and homemakers have given more concentrated attention to home design than ever before. Time-motion studies and technical advances at first took center stage. Although these important studies are being continued, attention is also being given to spiritual factors. Concern with the effects on human happiness of new ways of heating and lighting, of shaping and coloring homes is catching up with technical advances. With an unparalleled array of potentialities at our command, we can create homes that are, in the words of architect Richard Neutra, "soul anchorages." In the next three chapters we will consider how living with others, private living, and housekeeping can be pleasant as well as efficient.

2. Living with Others

Living with one's family and entertaining friends are enterprises as rewarding as they are diversified. Some of the activities—conversation, games, making music, and small children's play—are as old as man himself. Widespread reading is comparatively new, while experiencing television or *hi-fi* music is only a decade or two old. Quite recently, home hobbies have enjoyed a great revival. Design is only beginning to catch up with what families actually do in homes today.

The emphasis given to each group activity varies from individual to individual and from one family to another. Furthermore, changes are inevitable for individuals and families as the years pass. Because none but the very wealthy can provide equally well for all, most of us must decide carefully which group activities give greatest satisfaction, then plan accordingly. A logical first step is to consider specific group activities, the environment and equipment desirable for each, and then to find suggestions and principles helpful in solving specific and general problems.

Above. A tea cart simplifies serving food to family or guests. (*Dunbar Furniture Co.*)

► GROUP ENTERTAINMENT AND LEISURE

Conversation

Conversation is the major group activity, pervading all parts of the home but reaching greatest intensity in the living and dining spaces. Basic needs are:

- *Space* sufficient for the normal number of persons. Each person in an easy chair, for example, needs at least 3′0″ by 2′4″ but with his feet stretched out he may take up to 5 feet.
- *Comfortable* seats for each participant; a minimum of one good seat for each permanent member of the family and additional ones to accommodate guests.
- *Arrangement* of seats and tables in a generally circular or elliptical pattern so that each person can look at others easily and talk without shouting; arrangement should be ready for group conversation without moving furniture. A diameter of 8 to 10 feet is desirable.
- *Light* of moderate intensity with highlights at strategic points.
- *Surfaces* (tables, shelves, etc.) on which to put things.

Conversation thrives in a warm, friendly room if the architecture, furnishings, and accessories are spirited but not overpowering, distractions are minimized, and sounds are softened. This kind of environment has been created in the Arthur Bergers' home (Figs. 22A and B). Handsome old and new furniture are sensitively brought together and reveal their character against a background of mellow brick and wood. A light-colored rug, contrasting with the deep brown concrete floor, defines the conversation area in which sofa, chairs, and tables are arranged for a friendly interchange of ideas and sentiments. Although strictly rectangular, this living-dining space is far from boxy. As the plan (Fig. 23) shows, the entrance to the house is an ample gallery with glass walls on the long sides. A broad opening leads to the L-shaped space with a dining area at the kitchen end. Firmly anchored by the substantial fireplace, window walls in the dining and living space open on two sides to sheltered terraces. A wood ceiling with substantial exposed beams warms the room visually and tempers sound. Finally, the room is enhanced by a few distinctive Oriental objects, while several large plants add a decorative quality as well as relate the enclosed space to the garden.

A

The Arthur Bergers' living room in Dallas, Texas, is warmly welcoming, discriminatingly combines the old and the new. O'Neil Ford, architect.

Above. A simple but sensitively proportioned fireplace and a light-colored area rug stabilize the furniture group, which has been set away from the walls.

Below. Brick walls on two sides visually extend the room into the yard. Large windows, thinly curtained and protected by overhanging roofs, give an airy spaciousness without glare or undue exposure. (*Photographs by Ulric Meisel. Courtesy of* Interiors. *Copyright 1956, Whitney Publications, Inc.*)

B

The Bergers' group-living space is simple but interesting in shape. A glass-walled gallery and two open courts clearly separate the private bedroom area to the left from living, dining, and kitchen space.

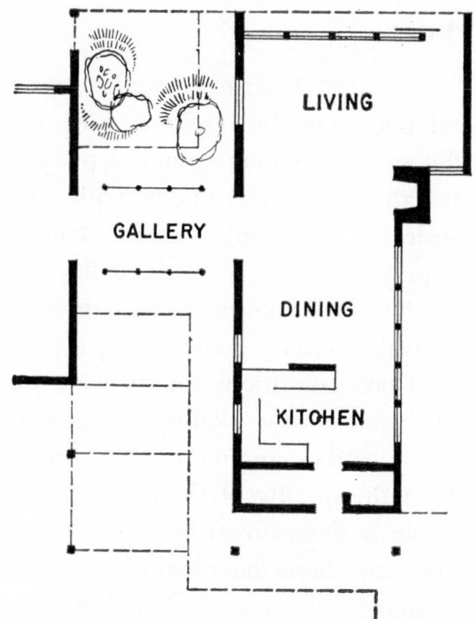

Group conversation is also the normal accompaniment of meals because the furniture and its arrangements afford ideal conditions for an hour or so (Figs. 33A and D). Terraces and patios become natural conversation centers when they offer good seating and some shelter as illustrated in Figure 27A.

Reading

Members of a literate culture enjoy reading if the reading material is stimulating and the reading conditions good. Minimum essentials are:

- *Seating* which gives adequate support to the back (to the neck, arms, and back for maximum comfort); resilient but not soporific.
- *Light* coming over one shoulder; moderately strong daylight or artificial light that illumines the room and concentrates fairly intense but diffused light on the reading material.
- *Security* from distracting sights, sounds, and household traffic.

Desirable additions are a chairside table, accessible shelves to hold books and magazines, and enough space to stretch your eyes occasionally. Such conditions, good for more or less casual reading, can be easily achieved in typical living rooms. If, however, one or more members of the family do concentrated reading, greater seclusion is needed, and bedrooms or a study should be appropriately planned.

Music

In most American families, music is limited to radio, record player, and television, but quite a few people enjoy creating their own music. This usually centers around a piano placed flat against a wall that is large enough for the instrument with space for the participants. More serious musicians may want a "music center," preferably in a corner or alcove that keeps all needed paraphernalia together and out of the way of other activities. An intermediate step is to place the piano at right angles to the wall, thereby demarcating a partially segregated area.

Good conditions for listening to music are similar to those for group conversation—a workable arrangement of seats and tables, moderate illumination, and a minimum of distractions—except for more serious concern about the quality of the sound. Although the quality of musical sounds is primarily determined by the instruments and performers, the room's materials and shape have critical effects. Acoustically, materials are classified as sound-reflecting or "live" if they bounce the sound, as does wood, plaster, or glass; and as sound-absorbing or "dead" if they soak up sound, as do heavy draperies, books, cork, or other acoustical materials. An excess of live materials gives excessive amplification and reverberation while too many dead surfaces rob music of its brilliance. It has also been found that live surfaces should be opposite dead surfaces. Then, too, experts have long known that musical sounds are best in those rooms in which opposite surfaces are not parallel to each other or in which the space is broken up in some way.

Happily, many devices that improve acoustics are favored for other reasons. The varied materials used in many contemporary rooms range from live to dead besides adding color and texture interest. If properly balanced and located, they temper music pleasantly. Free-standing cabinets (Fig. 25A) and deviations from boxiness create stimulating spatial patterns. The sloping ceiling in the Havens' house (Fig. 25A), the alcove and beamed ceiling in the Bergers' home (Fig. 22A), give visual as well as aural satisfaction.

Hi-fi radio or phonograph speakers perform best when mounted in or placed against a live wall facing a dead one; better yet is to put them in the corner of two live walls opposite two that absorb sound. Many experts recommend placing speakers at or above ear level, slanting them down slightly, and keeping them at least 10 feet from the listeners. For convenience, separate the tuner and record player from the speaker so that the operator can get the desired balance of sound, a feat next to impossible if his ear is too near the speaker. Then, too, placing tuner and player in an accessible

A

B

Planning architecture and furnishings for conversation, reproduced music, and television demands ingenuity.

Above. A symmetrical conversation center for a man who enjoys friends, books, and recorded music. A radio-phonograph is accessibly housed in the case at the left. The room's shape, the books, upholstered furniture, and floor covering improve acoustics. Both natural and artificial light come through ceiling panels of translucent glass. Harwell Hamilton Harris, architect. (*Blue Ridge Glass Corporation. Photograph by Maynard Parker*)

Left. Radio tuner and record player with record storage, conveniently near the major seating, comprise the control center. The speaker and a swiveling television set are placed in a wall between living room and kitchen. Raphael Soriano, architect. (*Photograph by Julius Shulman*) part of the room is better than having them in a hard-to-get-at corner. Notice that in the Shulmans' house (Fig. 25B) these have been placed inconspicuously yet accessibly while the speakers are in the walls some distance away.

Television

Bringing the theater and movie house, concert hall, sports field, and even the classroom into the heart of the home was bound to alter patterns of home leisure drastically. In many households television holds the attention of one or more persons for several hours daily, and it has become a potent force in bringing the whole family together for inexpensive home entertainment. It can also be a distraction difficult to escape. Major considerations are efficient seating, control of light and sound, and protection for those who are not amused.

- *Seating* requirements are much like those for conversation, except that everyone must be able to see the screen. Since few persons can or wish to devote one room entirely to TV, easily movable or collapsible chairs give welcome flexibility to room arrangement and use; backrests or cushions on the floor enlarge the capacity.
- *Location of screen* should be at approximately eye level and permit all to see it well.
- *Lighting* is best when it is of low intensity and shines neither on the screen nor in the viewers' eyes.
- *Acoustical control* is similar to that for music.

Although cumbersome, especially in depth, TV receivers can be put in many places. Living rooms, or better, family rooms, are typical locations. If mounted in walls, TV receivers can be treated as part of the whole design or they can rotate to face either living room or kitchen (Fig. 25B). In rooms without fireplaces, the receivers can be built up into a center of interest with pictures or mirrors, screens or accessories. Finally, they can be mounted on portable stands and pushed from place to place.

Quiet Indoor Games

Cards, checkers, and chess require concentrated effort. They are most relaxing when played on a well-illuminated table about 2′3″ high while the players sit on moderately high, straight hard chairs in a spot free from distractions. Folding card tables, or the new lower dining tables, and dining chairs set up in the living, dining, or family space suffice for most families. Serious gamesters, however, may want table and chairs permanently and suitably placed.

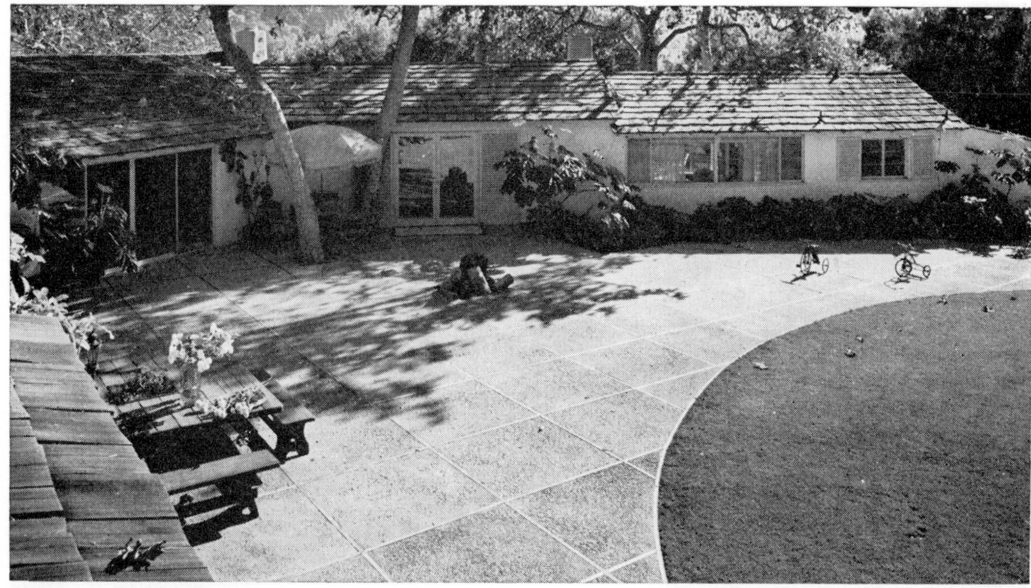

A

Planned outdoor space adds a physical and an emotional dimension to home life.

Above. A large paved terrace offers sun and shade, space for children and adults. Douglas Baylis, landscape architect; Cliff May, architect. (*Photograph by Julius Shulman*)

Below. Well-designed house walls and overhanging roofs treble the usefulness of outdoor areas, let each person choose his climate. Wurster, Bernardi, and Emmons, architects. (*Photograph by Roger Sturtevant*)

B

A

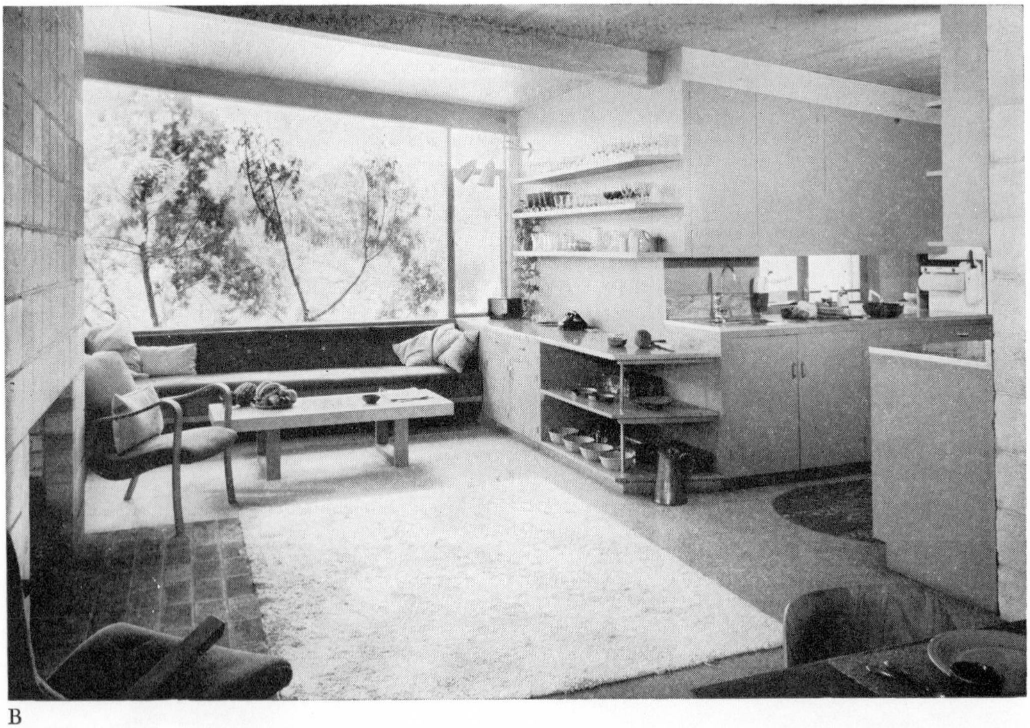

B

In Sarasota, Florida, the Russells' house for a family with five children has space planned for parents and offspring. Twitchell and Rudolph, architects.

Left above. Widening a bedroom hall into a 7'4" lanai transforms it into a children's play area.

Left below. Adjacent to the kitchen is an informal family gathering place. A fireplace, built-in lounge, and storage facilities give a sense of permanence in contrast to the flexibility of the play space. (*Photographs by Ezra Stoller*)

Below. The plan is well zoned for diverse activities, admirably suited to Florida's climate.

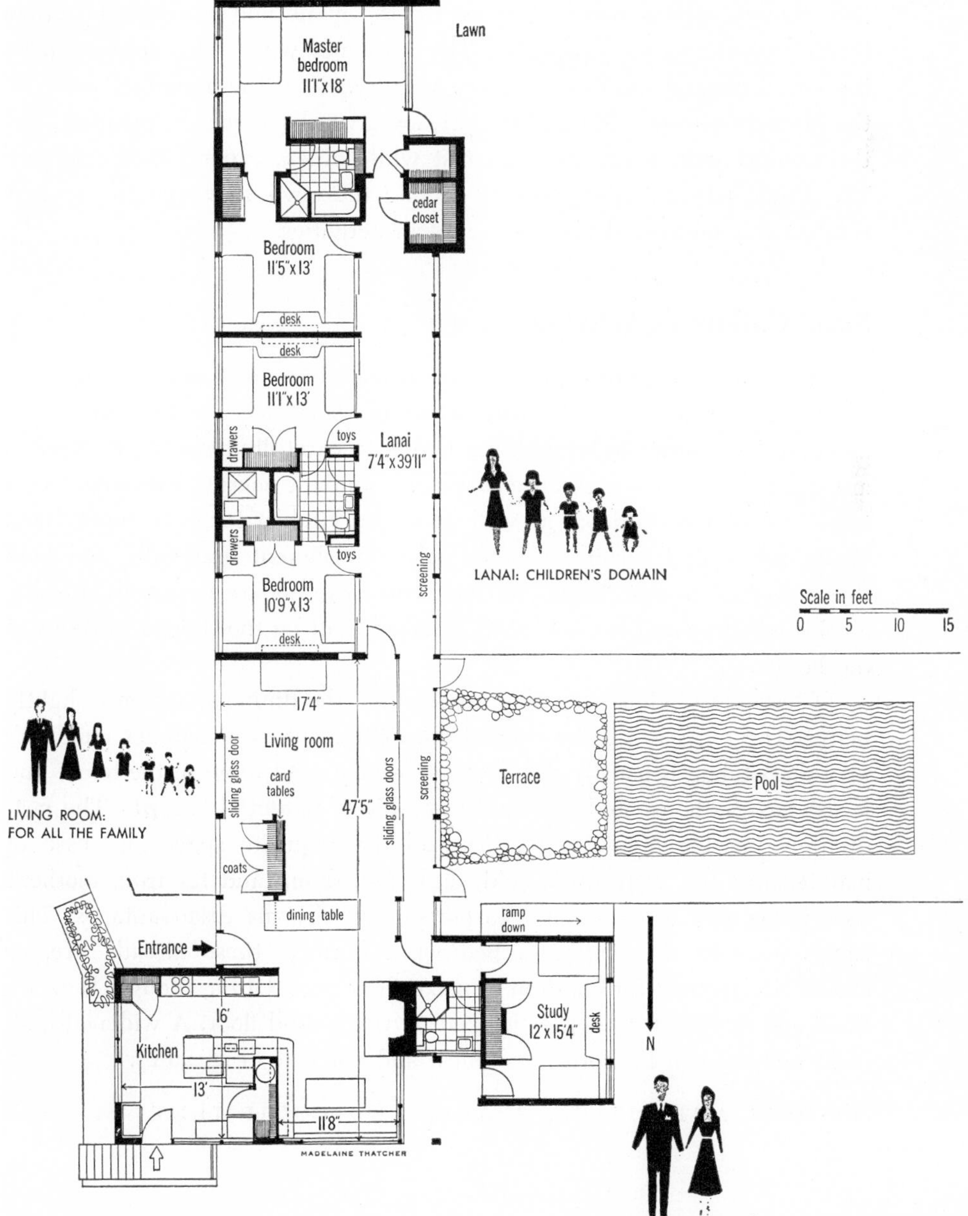

Active Indoor Entertainment

Dancing, charades, and other active games require plenty of space, a durable floor, and furniture easily pushed out of the way. Experience has shown that family rooms, discussed on pages 38 to 42, are a good solution.

Outdoor Games

Croquet, badminton, and Ping-pong as well as the less rigidly ruled outdoor sports should not be minimized. They will not give much satisfaction, though, unless sufficient space for the game and convenient storage for the necessary gear is provided. The frequency with which outdoor space is enjoyed depends on the durability and dryness of the underfoot surfaces, the protection from wind and the privacy given by fences or planting, and the comfort with which one can rest while others expend their energies. The ample paved terrace curving around the lawn shown in Figure 27A is admirably conceived for many outdoor activities.

Small Children's Activities

The needs of small children range from active noisy play to quiet moments, from eagerness to be with others of their own age to desire to be alone, from wanting to be with the family to carefully avoiding it. Needed are space adequate for the discharge of abundant energy, convenient to a toilet and to the outdoors as well as to the kitchen for easy supervision. Walls, floors, and furniture should take punishment gracefully and lend themselves to change. Light, warmth, and fresh air are requisites. Ideally, all this is segregated from what, it is hoped, will be the quieter portions of the house.

Clearly the living room is unsuitable and the dining space only slightly better. The kitchen has the needed durability, but even without children's play the kitchen is usually the most intensively used room in the house and it also has the household's greatest assembly of potential hazards. The fast-disappearing basements and attics had the requisite space and ease of maintenance but were often cold, dark, and damp and far from mother's supervising eye. Garages and carports have obvious disadvantages. This leaves us with the children's bedrooms, because these already are, or should be, planned for children to make their own. Often, though, they are small and in two-story houses located on the second floor. A widened bedroom hallway can be both economical and efficient (Fig. 28A).

These factors, together with adult needs for informal space, have led to the "family room." Because this space is often used for eating, we will withhold discussion of it until we have considered the diverse ways in which families eat today.

► EATING WITH FAMILY AND FRIENDS

Eating is a lively part of group living, for meals are one of the few daily events that brings an entire family together with a single purpose. Here, too, have been marked changes in the last few decades. Gone for most of us are the days when a good-sized room was furnished and reserved specifically for those three hours a day spent in eating. As house size shrank, household help became scarce, and food costs rose, there was a short-lived trend to minimize the importance of eating together, to accent efficiency rather than pleasantness. When you are planning dining situations, it pays to look at the requirements for meals in general, then at specific requirements for meals of different types. In general, you need:

- *Surfaces* on which to put food and utensils, usually 27 to 30 inches high but variable in size, shape, and type—tables that seat all or serve only one; counters, arms of chairs, and the like.
- *Seats* giving comfortable, upright support, such as chairs, stools, built-in or movable benches.
- *Light,* natural and artificial, which illumines food and table without glare.
- *Ventilation* without drafts.

To these essentials we quickly add that *convenience to kitchen and dish storage* saves energy, *freedom from excessive noise* saves nerves and helps digestion, and *pleasant surroundings and table settings* raise spirits.

Family sit-down meals deserve first attention. For these there ought to be one adequately large, relatively permanent space planned so that the table can be prepared, the seating arranged, the meal served and eaten, and the table cleared with minimum interference to and from other activities. A few of the many ways of planning dining space are shown on pages 32 and 33. Chapter 4 includes illustrations of well-planned facilities for eating in the kitchen.

Holiday celebrations are important family events but occur so seldom that the necessary space can seldom be reserved for them alone. This suggests a dining area with at least one end opening into the living or activity space, thereby permitting the celebration to extend as the number of participants demands. Figures 29 and 32D are excellent examples.

A

Left and below. A **change of level** and a two-way fireplace unmistakably differentiate a living from a dining room without loss of visual spaciousness. The bedroom balcony above creates additional vistas but can be closed for privacy. Contrasting materials, each used in large simple areas, handsomely enrich and diversify the rigorously geometric design. Breuer and Noyes, architects. (*Photograph by Ben Schnall*)

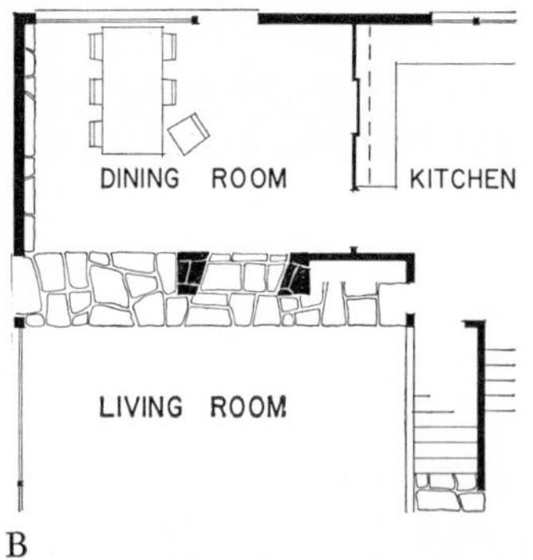

B

C

Left and below. An **L-shaped space** for living and dining, related to a patio, can be completely opened for large informal gatherings; but sliding doors create a segregated dining room for more formal meals. Such flexibility is a boon in small houses. Thornton Abell, architect. (*Photograph by Julius Shulman*)

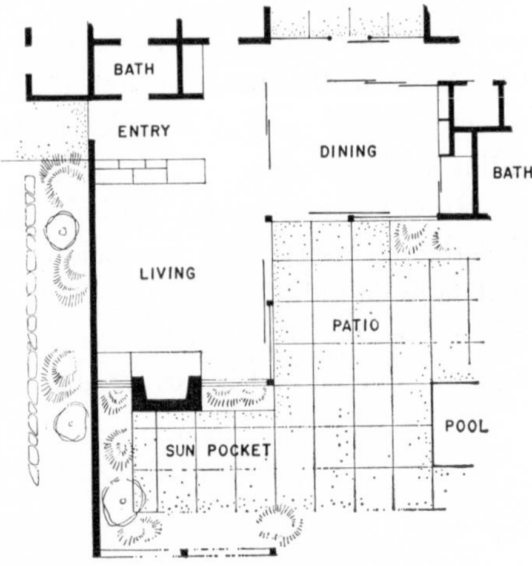

D

A

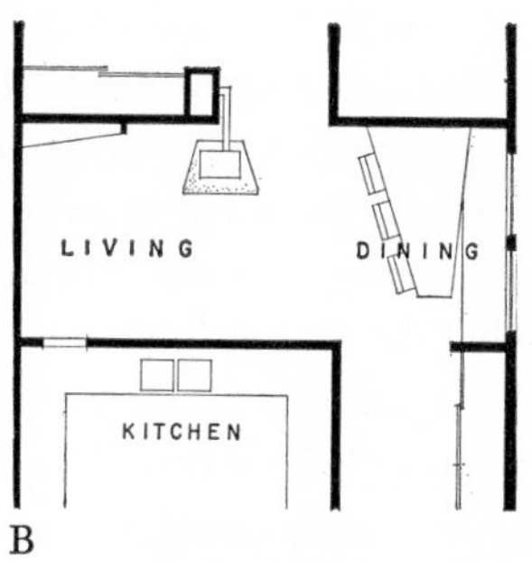

B

Left and above. A **corner of the living room** with a built-in and cushioned bench and table angled to allow easy passage forms an inviting spot for conversation. Although quite efficient for eating, it avoids the "dining room look." Gordon Drake, architect. (*Photograph by Morley Baer*)

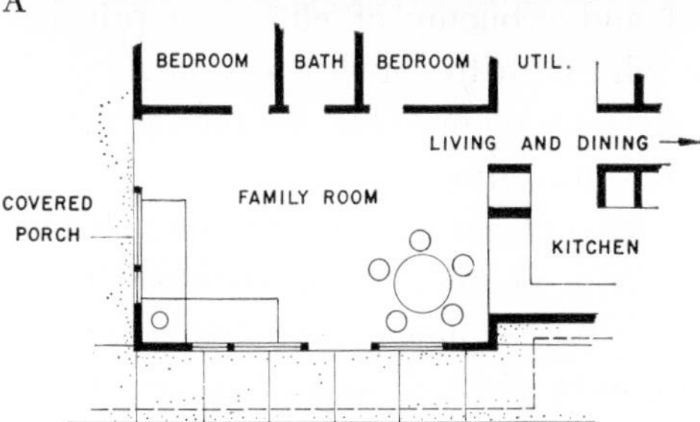

C

Left and below. Dining in the family room has much to recommend it in terms of economy of time and space. A big round table, useful for many purposes other than meals, is just beyond a cooking, barbecuing, and serving counter. Here everything is conducive to lively living and in one big, open room. George Rockrise, architect. (*Photograph by Ernest Braun. Courtesy* SUNSET Magazine.)

D

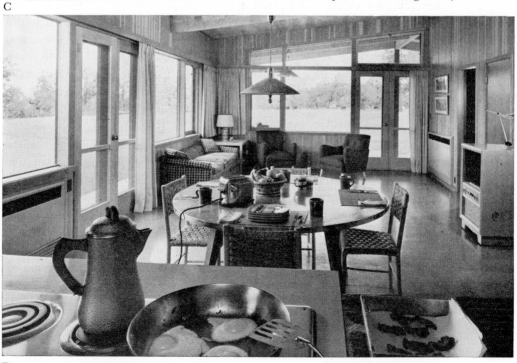

Formal meals in the home have become rare because of their cost in space, equipment, and time. Well-segregated dining space (Figs. 32A and C) is almost a necessity in order to set the table in advance, give the guests a pleasant surprise with the table setting and allow them to enjoy a meal uninterrupted by other activities, and then to get out of sight of the table when the meal is over.

Buffet meals, like self-service grocery stores and cafeterias, permit one to see what he is getting and distribute the labor of serving food. Also, they make it possible to use all the group living space for eating and usually lead to a lively informality. If such meals are to be handled often and successfully, you might emulate cafeterias where good carrying trays and not-too-precious dishes and glassware are provided, food is served from counters near the kitchen, traffic is directed so that tray-laden people do not collide, and when dinner is in hand a place to rest body and food is near by. The serving bars and furnishings in Figures 28B and 33D are thoughtfully designed for buffet meals.

Hurry-up meals in which speed and economy of effort are primary goals have a few advantages. Those who wish to eat this way might look at lunch counters where a counter with stools on one side and food preparation center on the other function with a dispiriting efficiency.

Outdoor meals can punctuate eating routines with a refreshing change of surroundings, a different type of food, another eating pattern. In all parts of the country outdoor eating could be much more frequent if it were planned for with the same attention given to indoor meals. At its best outdoor eating takes place in an appropriately furnished space near the kitchen or barbecue. Firm paving, a protecting roof, solid enclosure on two or three sides and screen on the others (all of which are illustrated in Figures 27B and 4B) are well worth their cost. But, of course, even without all this, picnics and barbecues can be happy family or guest affairs in which all can participate, actively or as spectators, in what can be the fun of cooking, serving, eating, and even after-meal cleanups.

Small children's meals are a vital part of home life and an aspect of the educational process often poorly handled. We might as well acknowledge that eating is both an adventure and problem for small children. They will play, experiment, and make mistakes. Common sense suggests providing a place, preferably in the kitchen, play space, or family room, where children can spill or scatter food on durable, easy-to-clean surfaces. But at an early age children want to eat with adults and quite rightly object to conditions midway between those for adults and those for household pets. Here, again, the plan of the house, the way it is finished and furnished, strongly affects the manner of family living.

► PLANNING FOR GROUP LIVING

After considering the character and demands of specific group activities, we can formulate several generalizations useful in planning.

- Each group activity occurs in more than one part of the house and yard. Eating takes place in dining or living spaces, kitchens or family rooms, or patios. Conversation is enjoyed everywhere and music, willy-nilly, often pervades the remotest corners of the home. Thus, planning today is more a matter of organizing space for activities than of arranging "rooms."
- In terms of noise and movement, group pursuits are notably diverse but they fall into three general categories. The full development of each type is best realized when homes are appropriately zoned.

  Quiet, sedentary activities, such as reading and quiet games, involve little physical movement. They produce minimum noise but suffer greatly from distractions, which suggests grouping them in a quiet zone of the dwelling.

  Noisy, sedentary activities, which include eating and music, deserve an acoustically controlled part of the group living space more or less separated from those areas where quietness is desirable.

  Noisy, active activities take as much space as can be found. They interfere with other home pursuits and give furnishings, floors, and walls considerable drubbing. Play or family space and the outdoors are logical centers.
- Planning for group living demands the concerted endeavor of the whole family. Each member has a right to express his desires and to realize them in so far as feasible. The six steps suggested in Chapter 1 for **Approaching the Problem** (pp. 16-19) are directly applicable.

Although planning is discussed more fully in Chapter 18, a few basic points are worth introducing here.

- There is no "best" shape for group living space, for each type has its merits and demerits determined in good part by specific conditions. They can be variously shaped, combined or separated as shown in the plans on pages 36-37 as well as in other illustrations in this book.
- Locating group living space near the main entrance, outdoor living space, and kitchen has advantages.
- Orientation is determined by several factors, chief of which are sun and wind, protected view, and public streets.

Group-living areas can be one large space divided for varied activities in many ways:

A simple rectangle relies on **furniture arrangment,** which can be changed easily. Curtis and Davis, architects.

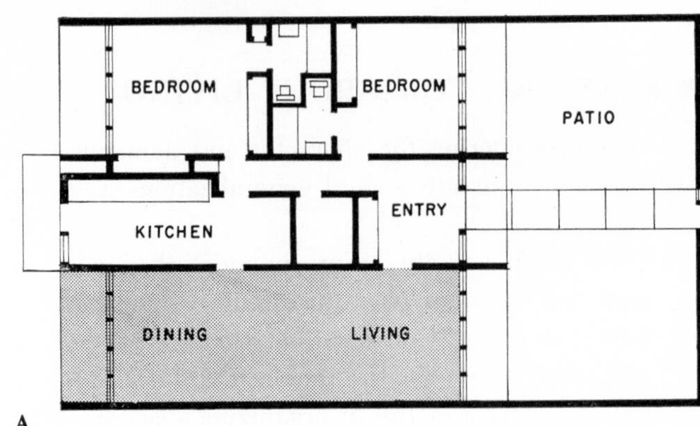

A

The **shape** of the space suggests rather than enforces zoning. Charles M. Goodman, architect.

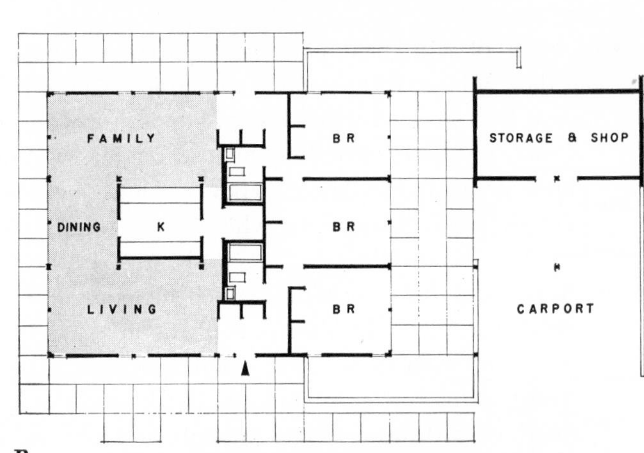

B

Different levels again are suggestive rather than rigid. John Portman, architect.

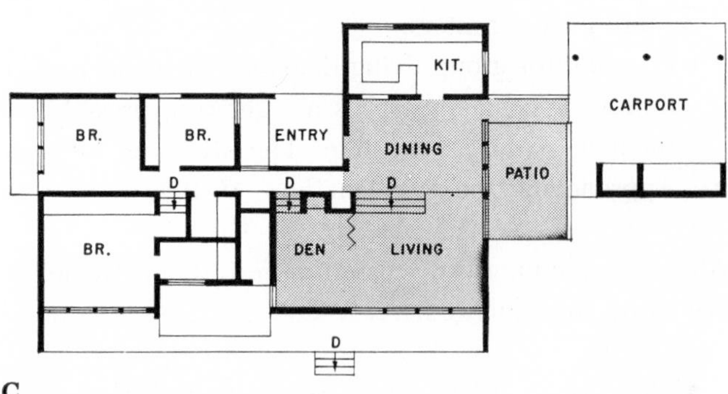

C

Movable walls or sliding doors open or close off space as required. Edward L. Barnes, architect.

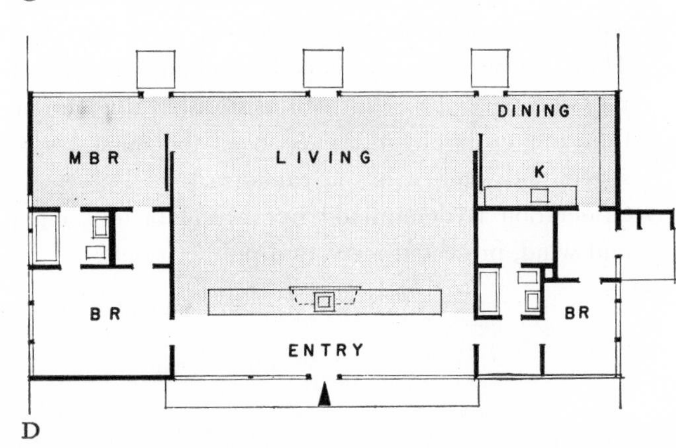

D

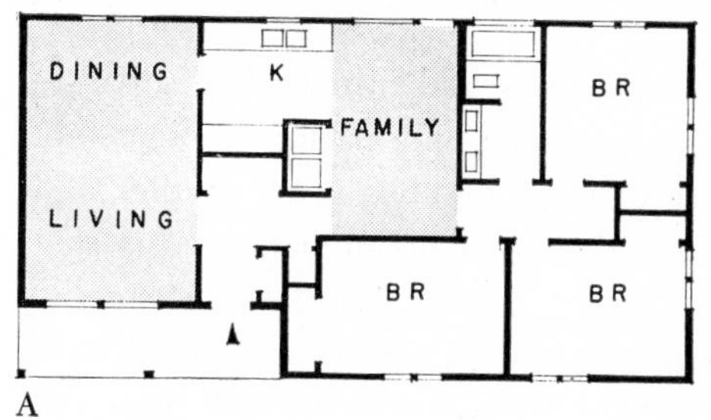

A

Or the area can be divided into separate rooms. In addition to the living room there can be a family room or a seclusion room or study.

A family room open to the kitchen has often proved successful. Auburn Construction Company.

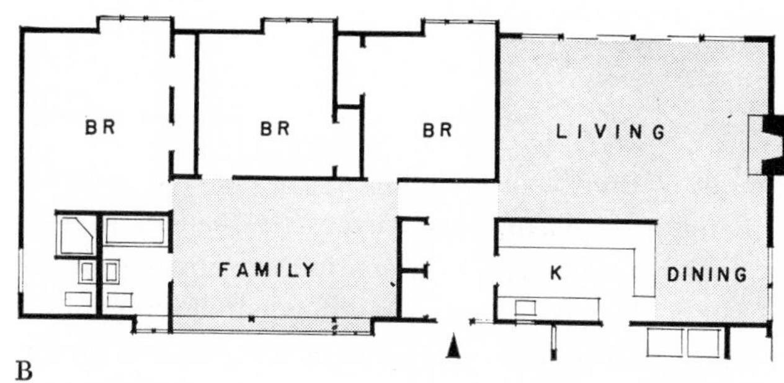

B

A family room adjoining children's bedrooms minimizes some kinds of conflicts. Anshen & Allen, architects.

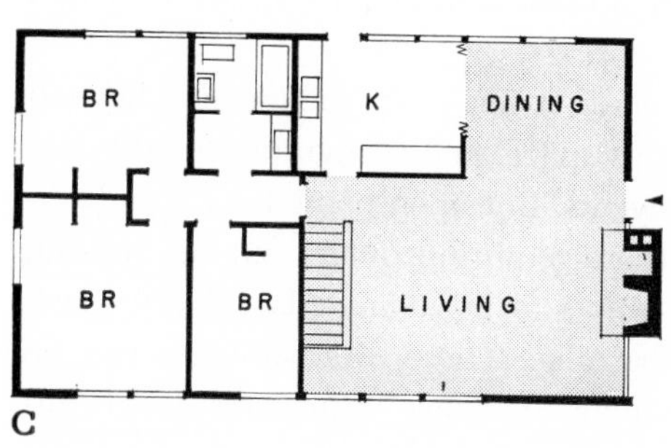

C

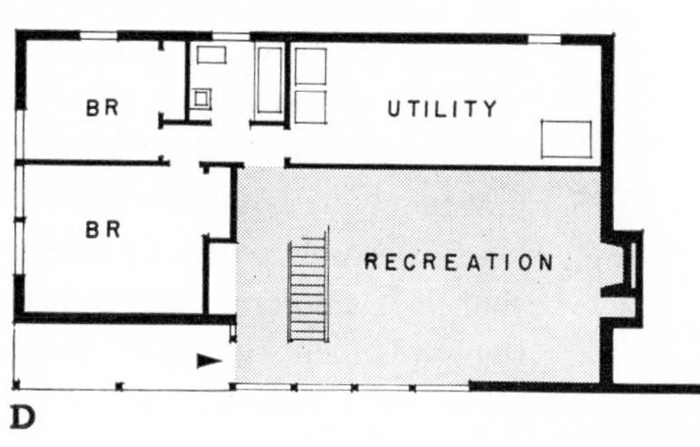

D

Above. Putting a family room on another floor gives near maximum isolation, for better or for worse. Smith, Keyes, Satterlee & Lethbridge, architects.

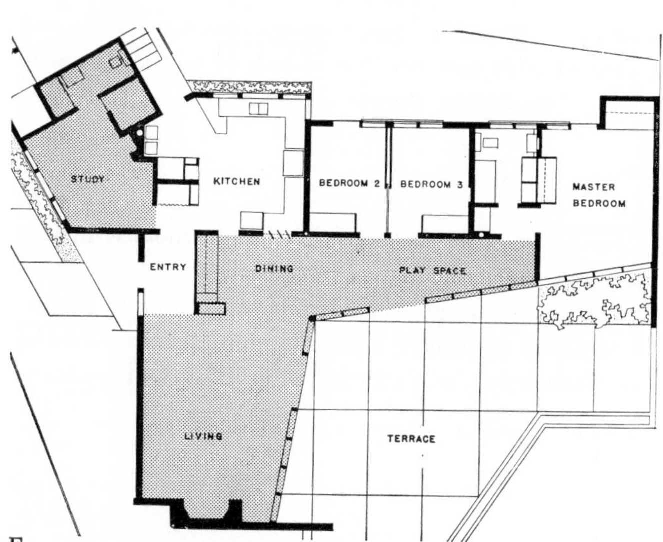

E

A study, or seclusion room, can provide a welcome retreat. Spencer and Ambrose, architects.

Fifty to seventy-five years ago many houses had four or five separate rooms of ample size for group living—an entrance hall, parlor, living room, dining room, and possibly a library or den. As families grew smaller and entertainment less home-centered, as building and maintenance costs skyrocketed and household help became scarce, group living space shrank. Parlors disappeared first and then separate dining rooms. Entrance halls contracted to vestibules; and dens became a rarity. Costs are still high and help is hard to find—but families are getting larger and home entertainment is an active force. These conditions have led to renewed interest in *open plans*, *family rooms*, and *seclusion rooms*.

Open Plans

Homes with a minimum of fixed floor-to-ceiling partitions and a maximum of flexible group living space have many virtues. Instead of tightly enclosed, boxlike rooms, space is organized as a continuing, flowing entity designed for diverse purposes. A striking example, shown in Figures 40A and B, combines maximum flexibility with economy. In this home a group living area measuring 13′6″ by 40′ can be quickly rearranged with movable, free-standing cabinets. Other examples of open planning are shown on pages 4, 22-23, 28-29, 32, 36, 37, and 39.

The advantages of open plans include a sense of spaciousness beyond actual dimensions, diversified use of this space, and recognition of the fact that family activities are not isolated events. But open plans have disadvantages: noisy activities interfere with those requiring quiet, and the retiring soul finds minimum refuge when he wants to be alone. Also, if not sensitively planned, the space may seem barnlike. These disadvantages can be overcome in several ways. First is shaping the space with walls and furniture so that different functions are segregated. L-shaped rooms, furniture at right angles to walls, and flexible screens or movable walls as illustrated in this and other chapters are some of the major design possibilities. Second is planning for noise control with surfaces that absorb or break up noise. Third are family rooms and fourth are the areas segregated for seclusion.

Family Rooms

Often called the "newest room in the house," a family room is in fact the oldest with a continuous history wherever man has lived. To mention but a few instances, cave dwellers and lake dwellers had family rooms; Pompeian atriums and medieval great halls sheltered multifarious activities, and farm kitchens have often been the center of family life. Contemporary

A

In contemporary open planning, entrance areas and hallways often merge with each other and with adjacent rooms. Here a cabinet behind the built-in sofa is the only separation between entrance and living room, but the brick floor and trellis overhead define without enclosing space for circulation. The fireplace, open on three sides, both separates and unites the living room with the dining space beyond it. Carl Maston, architect. (*Photograph by Julius Shulman*)

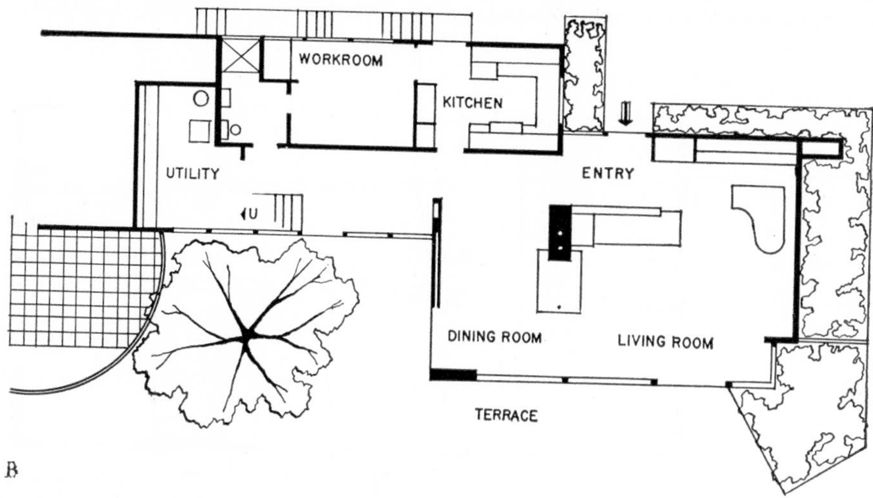

B

A

An open-plan living-dining-play space, measuring 13′6″ by 40′, can be flexibly partitioned by moving the caster-mounted cabinets for differing needs. George Rockrise, architect. (*Photograph by Ernest Braun. Courtesy of* SUNSET Magazine)

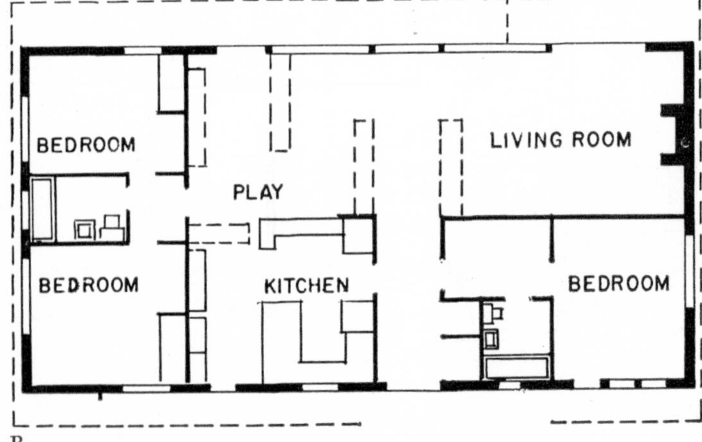

B

A

HEATER
CLOSET
UP
KITCHEN & DINING AREA
WORKSHOP
CHILDREN'S AREA
STUDIO AREA
TV AREA

B

The Cleo Hovels of Hopkins, Minnesota, transformed a little-used basement into a family room. Through sensible planning and wise selection of furniture, it now accommodates a variety of interests and relieves pressure on the rest of the house. (*Photograph by Warren Reynolds, Infinity, Inc. Courtesy of* Better Homes and Gardens) examples show great variety as illustrated in Figures 28A and B, 29, 41A and B. The converted basement in Minneapolis incorporates a kitchen and eating area, space for children's play and television plus a studio. In Figure 1, the living room is in reality a family room where a large space is kept open and flexible by furniture fitted against the walls or used to subdivide space. The Russells' home shows a continuous space with one end primarily for adults, the opposite end for children, and an area for eating logically located between the two.

Typical family rooms include eating space for children, grownups, and company; comfortable furniture for sitting or lying down; space for small children's activities and possibly for adult hobbies. They are ideal locations for television, radios, and phonographs as well as for homemade music. They help keep living rooms quiet and most of the family together in an informal, durably furnished, easily maintained area. Although family rooms can have varied locations, they are usually most successful when directly adjoining the kitchen. Easy access to livable outdoor areas is almost as imperative.

Seclusion Rooms

Seclusion rooms are as important for some individuals as are family rooms. They are much like the older studies or dens except that they belong to no one person. In contrast to family rooms, those designed for seclusion are typically small. The degree of insulation from distractions is a matter of preference. Figure 43A is an eyrie with an expansive view of the landscape and several degrees removed from group activities. At the other extreme, seclusion rooms can be completely private, in which case they can double as guest rooms (Fig. 43B).

Most persons want as much space for group living as is possible, but such space is seldom wisely achieved by reducing bedrooms, kitchens, baths, and storage to cramped cubbyholes. In small houses, group living space may range from a meager minimum of 300 square feet to a more ample 500 square feet or better. In larger houses, the space is limited only by needs and resources. The decision depends on how much space is wanted and can be afforded, but apparent size can be greatly increased by the ways and means detailed in Chapters 5, 6, and 7. The illusion of space, however, is only a palliative for space-hungry families.

The many details discussed in the preceding sections are important but they should not obscure major goals. The social quarters of any home should give every person a sense of security in the family group and

A

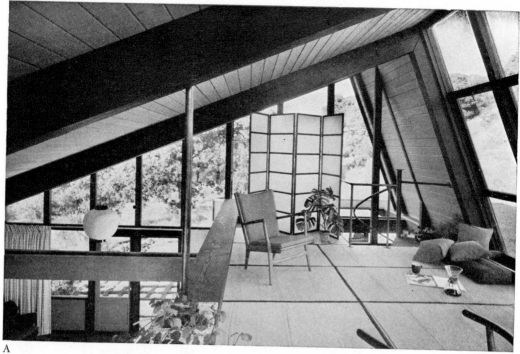

Getting away from group activities is as important as being part of them.

Above. Hung halfway between floor and roof, the chief reason for this balcony is simply delight—a place to loaf and dream, read, listen to records, or exchange confidences. Kolbeck and Petersen, architects. (*Photograph by Ernest Braun*)

Below. A seclusion room or study can be small but restful and adequate for homework or an overnight guest if the furnishings are simple and compactly related to the walls. (*Photograph by Robert C. Cleveland*)

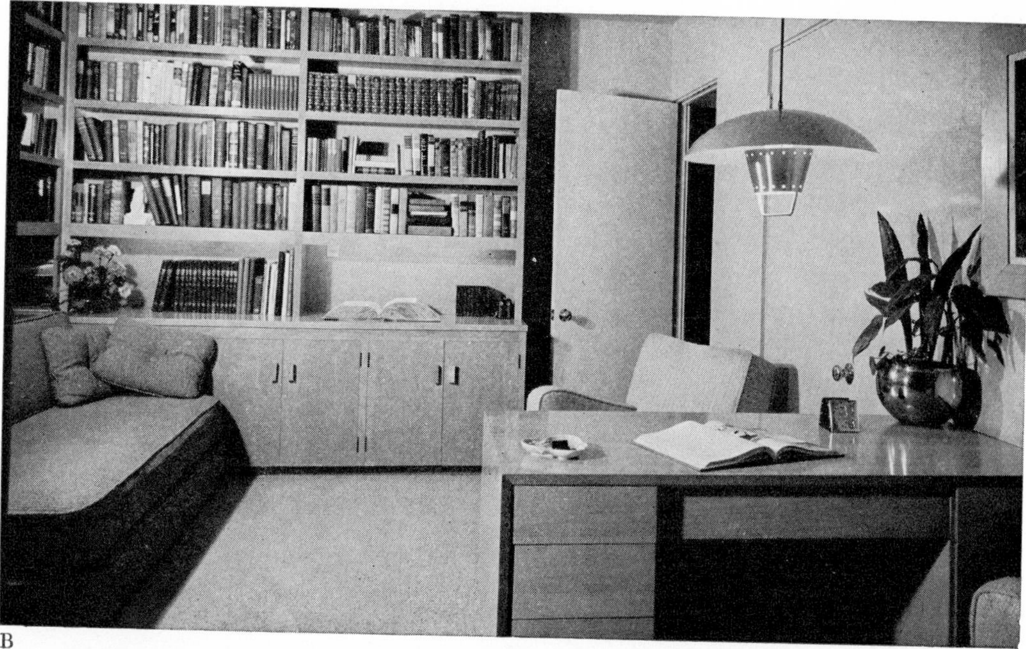

B

encourage each to play his best role in the family pattern. Each individual deserves opportunity to express his own feelings and to do at least some things the way he wants. In short, group living space ought to promote the security, self-realization, and socialization of each member of the family.

"We had these alcoves built so we wouldn't interfere with the children playing." (By permission of NEA Services, Inc.)

3. Private Living

Individuals need varying degrees of privacy for sleeping, napping, or just stretching out to relax, for dressing and undressing as well as keeping clean. Other facets of private living are introduced when overnight guests are entertained or when hobbies or work which demand seclusion are done at home. Finally, members of the family need not only time but space in which to collect their thoughts or pursue their dreams—in short, to get to know themselves as individuals again.

► SLEEPING AND DRESSING

Primitive man slept on the ground, on rock ledges, in caves, or in trees, seeking only protection from the elements and his enemies. As civilization advanced and man began to build sheltering structures, he usually reserved in them a place for sleeping although this was not always separated from other areas. Historically, man was late

Above. Sculptural fittings for lavatory basins are delightful departures from the ordinary. (*P. E. Guerin, Inc.*)

in isolating sleeping from other functions and then he did not do so continuously. From the decline of the Roman Empire until the Renaissance, it was fairly common practice for all persons in the household to sleep in one room, often on the floor. Today we assume that seldom will more than two persons sleep in one room and that care will be taken to make their sleep effective.

Recent investigations have indicated that the rest given by seven or eight hours of sleep can be equalled in five or six hours if the room is absolutely dark and quiet, the air is pure and its movement moderate and uniform, and the temperature is constant and high enough so that only light coverings are needed. This has led some to recommend sleeping in a cubicle with air, light, and sound precisely and automatically controlled.

Such conditions are efficient, but human beings are not quite this single-minded. Sometimes it is pleasant to go to bed early and read, occasionally glancing up at a picture or a textile. It is fun to wake up in a room, not a cubicle, and to lie in bed looking through a window or listening to the call of a bird or the burbling of a baby. It is relaxing to curl up or stretch out on your bed in the afternoon. Often bedrooms offer the best conditions in the home for concentrated reading or study. For these reasons, for the past few centuries sleeping has taken place in a moderately sized, multipurpose, segregated space. Today with larger families in smaller houses bedrooms require careful planning.

The requisites for **sleeping** and **napping** are:

- A *bed* or *beds* long and wide enough for one or two persons.
- A *bedside table* or built-in storage headboard for what is needed near the bed.
- A *light source* over the bed for reading or emergencies.
- *Control of natural light* by draperies or blinds. If the room is moderately dark in color, reducing the intensity of natural light is easier to achieve.
- *Ventilation,* best with windows or ventilators in opposite walls, next best in adjacent walls, least good when confined to one. Being able to let hot air out through windows at ceiling height greatly reduces summer heat.
- *Quietness,* achieved by locating bedrooms away from, or insulating them against, noisy areas and by using sound-absorbing materials in the room.

Dressing and **undressing,** involving varied movements, indicate conditions quite different from those best for sleeping.

- *Space* sufficient to stand, stretch your arms, turn around, bend over, and also to see yourself in a

- *Mirror,* full length if possible.
- *Seating* for dealing with hosiery and shoes.
- *Storage* for all type of clothes within the reach of an arm or the step of a foot; a minimum of 5 feet of hanging space per person is desirable.
- *Dressing table* with a well-lighted mirror and storage space.
- *Lighting,* artificial or natural, so that you can find what is wanted and see how you look in it.

Ideally, all this takes place in a separate dressing area adjoining sleeping quarters and bath, but too often it is sandwiched into whatever space the bed and other furniture leave in the bedroom. Under these conditions, it becomes less frustrating if a "dressing area" is planned for each occupant of the room, possibly in a corner where *all* his clothes are conveniently stored. Certainly, each person deserves his own closet including or near his chest of drawers (Figs. 50B and 52B). Adding a mirror, good lighting, and a chair makes such dressing centers adequate.

► PLANNING BEDROOMS

Bedrooms vary in terms of the number of persons sharing them, the accommodations they offer, and the relative emphasis placed on each activity carried out in the room. At one extreme is the sleeping cubicle found in inexpensive hotels, summer camps, trains, or ships. Then come those with adequate space for the bed, chest of drawers, and a chair plus just enough room in which to dress. Better are those somewhat larger that are planned and furnished for reading or relaxation in a comfortable chair and writing or working at a desk or sewing table.

The number of sleeping areas in a house is conditioned by the family's size and economic status. Since two-bedroom houses are adequate for only a few families, three bedrooms have become the norm. Surveys, though, indicate that almost one third of those seeking homes want four bedrooms. A room for each child is desirable but often not feasible for large families.

Four ways in which bedrooms and baths can be fitted into house plans are shown on page 48. Ideally, each person should be able to go directly from a convenient outside entrance to his bedroom without going through other rooms. This means either a bedroom hall leading off the entrance area or outside doors to each room.

Location of doors and windows is at least as critical in bedrooms as in any part of the house. If there is more than one, the doors should be as close together as is compatible with other requirements. Since the most frequently used traffic path is between the door leading into the room and

A

Location and arrangement of bedrooms and bathrooms is a first step toward good private living.

Left. Bedrooms and bathrooms are typically grouped together in the quietest part of the house. In this plan, three bedrooms and two bathrooms can be reached from a secluded hall. The bathroom near the hall entrance is convenient for guests and the occupants of the master bedroom. Palmer and Kreisel, architects.

Below. In two-story or split-level houses, the bedrooms and baths are usually upstairs, as in this house designed by James G. Durham. On some sites, however, it may be preferable to have them on the lower level or they can be divided between the two levels, as illustrated in Chapter 18.

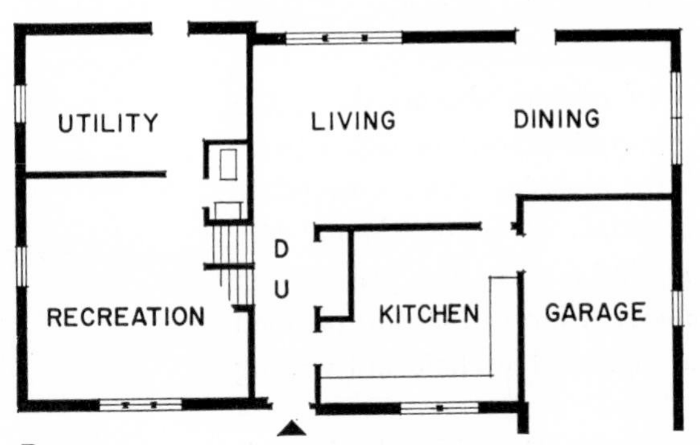

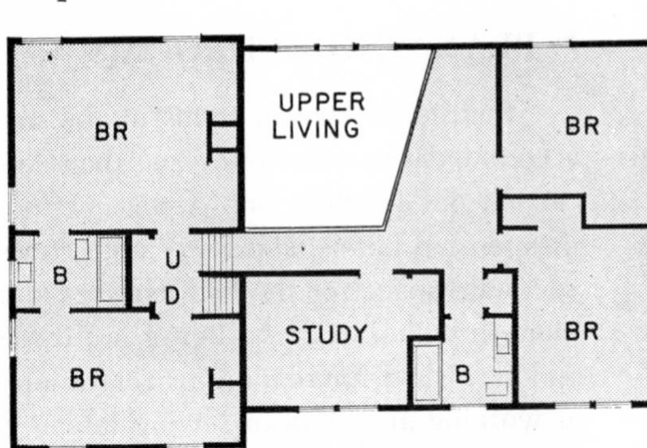

B

Below left. In more complex plan shapes, bedrooms and baths can be in a segregated wing remote from household noises. Richard Pollman, architect.

Below right. Both parents and children may find greater peace if their bedrooms and baths are separated. Dreyfuss and Blackford, architects.

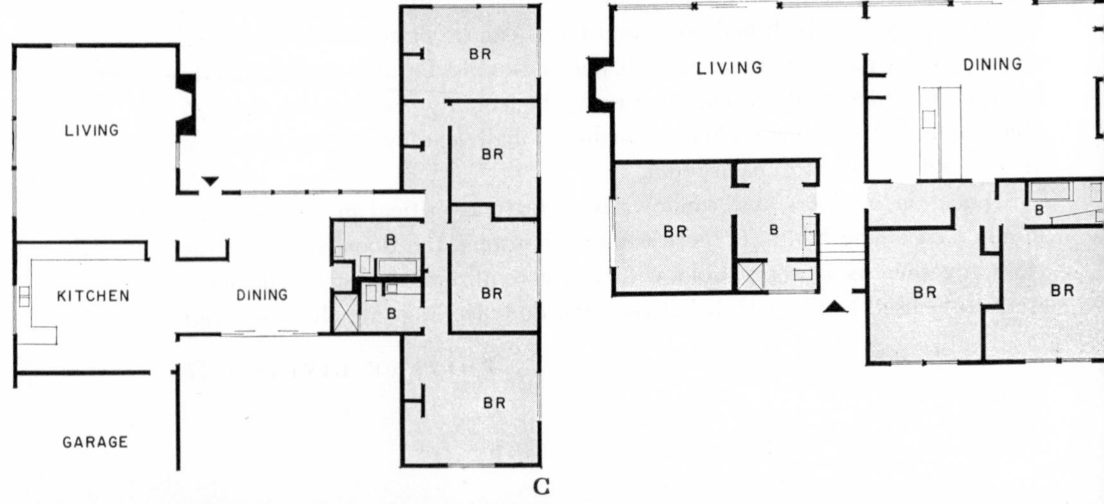

C

the closet or dresser, it is sensible to keep this path short and direct. If the door is not directly in line with the bed or dressing area, some privacy is afforded even when the door is open. Grouping the windows makes rooms seem larger and gives more usable wall space, although the need for ventilation suggests windows in two or more walls.

The need for convenient storage in bedrooms is exceeded only by the same need in kitchens. Basic principles are designing the storage space for what it is to hold, keeping all space for each person's clothes together, and having this space near the door. The storage in the boy's bedroom (Fig. 50A) is an enlightened application of these common-sense principles.

Bedrooms are potentially one of the most appropriate places in the home to indulge your individuality. Perhaps bright, light colors are not quieting, but if you yearn for them and the rest of the family does not, your bedroom is a good place to satisfy your urge. Photographs with sentimental appeal or cherished collections differentiate your bedroom from those belonging to others. Even in small rooms, there is usually adequate cubic footage for such indulgences if bookcases, shelves, and cupboards are arranged against walls that will not be harmed by hooks and thumbtacks.

Boys enjoy rough and ready rooms with as much free floor space as possible, surfaces on which treasures can be displayed, and drawers in which they can be kept—all of which can be seen in Figure 50A. Girls typically like soft colors and floral patterns as illustrated in Figure 50B. Movable partitions in or between children's bedrooms permit the freedom of large open spaces or quiet seclusion at will (Fig. 51).

When man and wife share a bedroom, a different situation arises: it should suit and express both, as does the room in Figure 52A. Walls and furniture of fir, a harmoniously textured carpet, a bedspread subtly echoing the parallel lines and textures of both walls and carpet, and a bamboo window shade for control of light and privacy set the character of quiet naturalism. Natural light is diffused by the glass curtains, artificial light is provided by fixtures mounted on or built into the walls to save space and ease maintenance. Through careful planning this bedroom of average size and shape becomes much more than sleeping space, chiefly because the trim built-in furniture unifies equipment designed for many purposes. At the right is the husband's desk with drawers beside it and an easily moved chair. In the center are two chests of drawers. The left corner with its compact, convenient, around-the-corner combination of dressing table, desk, and bedside table belongs to the wife. Notice, too, how the well-illumined mirror continues the line of the windows and greatly enlarges the apparent size of the room.

A

Boys' bedrooms often differ markedly in character from those for girls.

Left. A boy's bedroom designed for rugged use. Concrete floor, wood walls and ceiling, plastic-surfaced desk and counter, and pegboard for displays are all durable and easily maintained. Anshen and Allen, architects.

Below. A girl's bedroom appropriately feminine and delicate. Light blue wallpaper with a floral pattern sets off the old brass bedstead; the other walls are painted white. The rug, on a brown cork floor, repeats the wallpaper's color. Morgan Stedman, architect. (*Photographs by Maynard Parker. Courtesy of* House Beautiful)

B

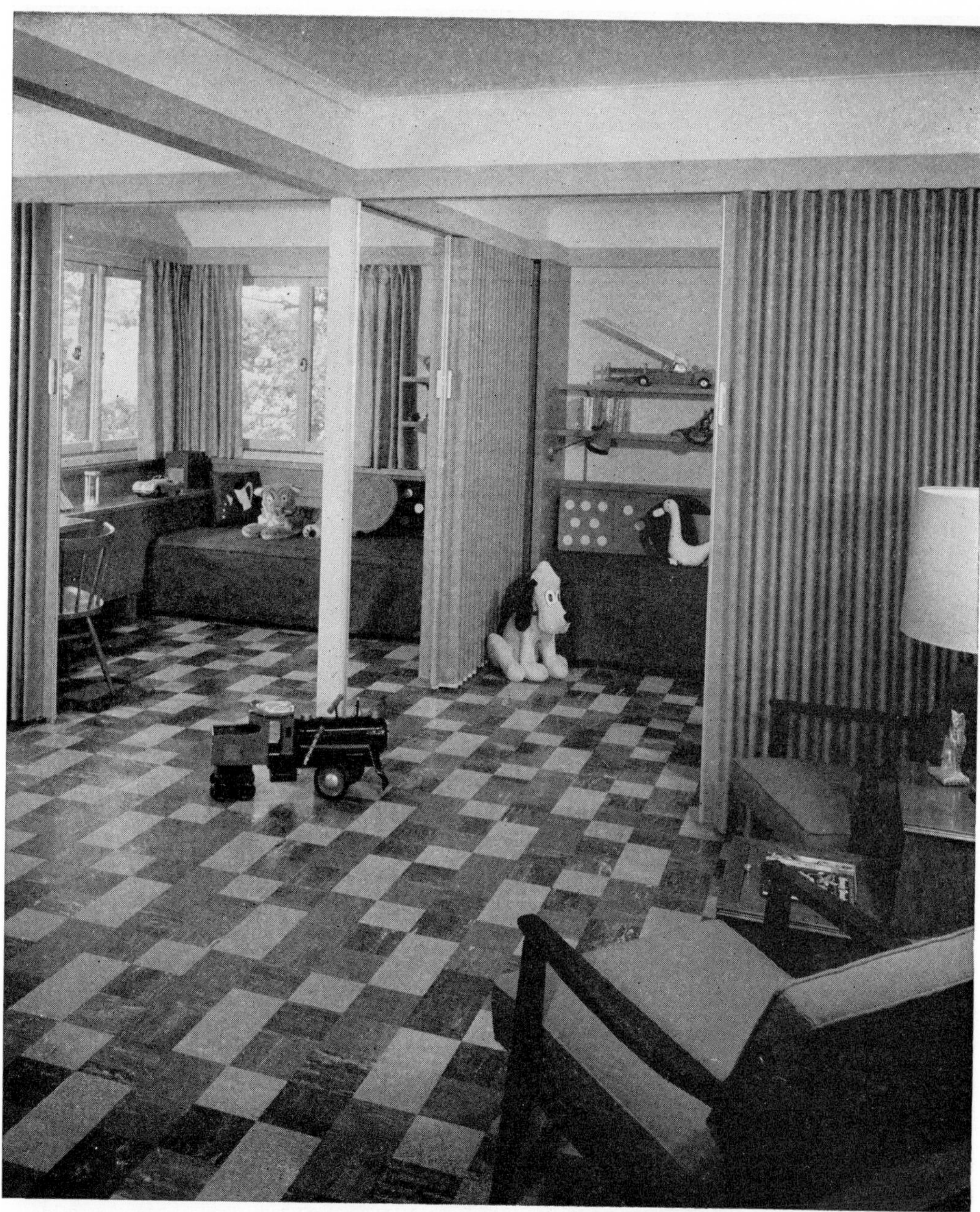

Folding walls between two small bedrooms and a play area can be pushed back to make one large space or closed for the privacy needed for sleeping or study. Fehr and Granger, architects. (*Photograph by William Howland. Courtesy of* House Beautiful)

A

The master bedroom can be a personalized haven.

Above. A simple, restful bedroom thoughtfully planned with ample, well-organized storage, dressing, and desk space in a minimum area. Willard Hall Francis, architect.

Below. No one would ever mistake this for a hotel bedroom because the owners have expressed themselves in a spirited way. The contrasts are strong, the harmony richly complex. Burton Schutt, architect. (*Photographs by Julius Shulman*)

B

► HYGIENE

For several decades, bathrooms were the home's most standardized room, and until recently we took for granted the three unrelated white fixtures conspicuously standing out from the walls of the smallest room in the house. Walls were invariably plaster or tiles, timidly pastel in color. Windows were small and frequently hard to reach. Such bathrooms promised little beyond a dispiriting efficiency and often failed to live up even to that minimum essential.

Surveys indicate that people want more, larger, and better bathrooms with big basins and counter tops. Bigger medicine chests as well as extra shelf and clothes-hamper space are invariably mentioned. People ask for lots of light, rapid and effective ventilation, quick heat, and sound-absorbing materials. Color and texture are not overlooked by these homemakers who have found that cheerful bathrooms help get everyone's day off to a good start.

In a small but uncrowded bathroom in the Eltings' home (Fig. 54A) redwood walls and cabinets bring the same informal warmth already illustrated in the living room of this home (Fig. 13A). High windows combine privacy with good light and ventilation. Sliding, mirrored doors, far more efficient than the typical swinging type, cover the medicine chest. In a larger family bathroom (Fig. 54B), the two wash basins are part of the counter in an area separated from the tub and toilet by sliding doors. Tile is used in these compartments where needed, but the rest of the room is warmed by wood and cork surfaces.

Location of bathrooms is primarily a matter of convenience, privacy, and cost (Figs. 55A through E). In a one-bathroom house, you should conveniently be able to reach this important room from the bedrooms without going through or getting in sight of group living space, but the bathroom should also be as near the kitchen and living space as feasible. This tough assignment is well handled in the plan shown in Figure 55C. The desire to multiply bathrooms is checked only by their cost. Ideally, a home for three or more persons should have at least two bathrooms, as should one with sleeping quarters on two floors. As the family increases so should the plumbing. The ideal number can be decreased, however, if the tub or shower and the toilet are in separate compartments, or if wash basins are put in bedrooms.

Size and location of doors and windows, the arrangement of fixtures, provision for storage, and finishes for walls, floors, and ceilings are important considerations.

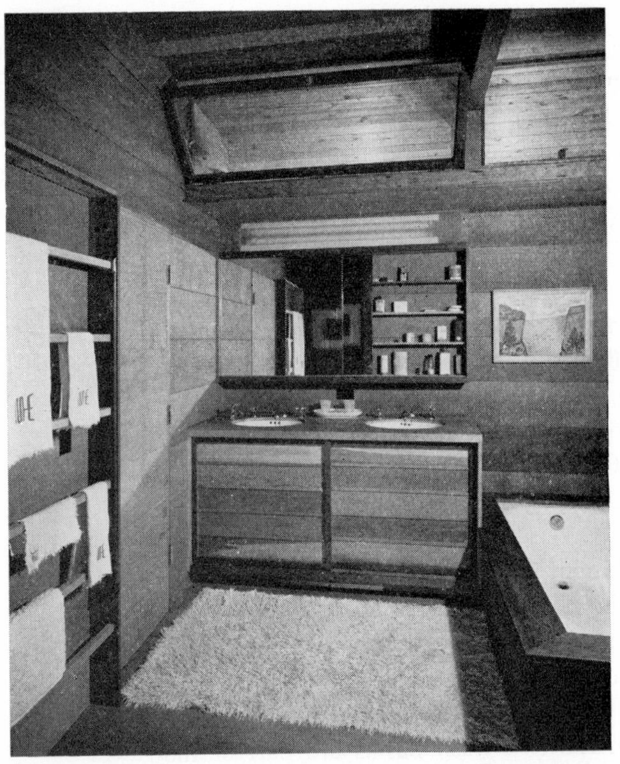

A

Left. In the Eltings' home, wood is liberally used in bathrooms. Durability is assured by special treatment of the wood, efficiency by placing two wash basins in a commodious sliding-door cabinet with an ample medicine chest above. A wide wooden rim around the tub and the tier of towel rods are unusual but workable details. Schweikher and Elting, architects. (*Photograph by Hedrich-Blessing*)

Below. Bathrooms planned for family use can be economical, efficient, and attractive. Tub and toilet are in separate compartments with sliding doors. Two wash basins are joined by a counter and mirrored wall concealing twin medicine chests. Tile walls and concrete floor make the tub area waterproof. Plastic coated wood, wallpaper, and cork give warm color and texture to the remainder. (*Crane Company*)

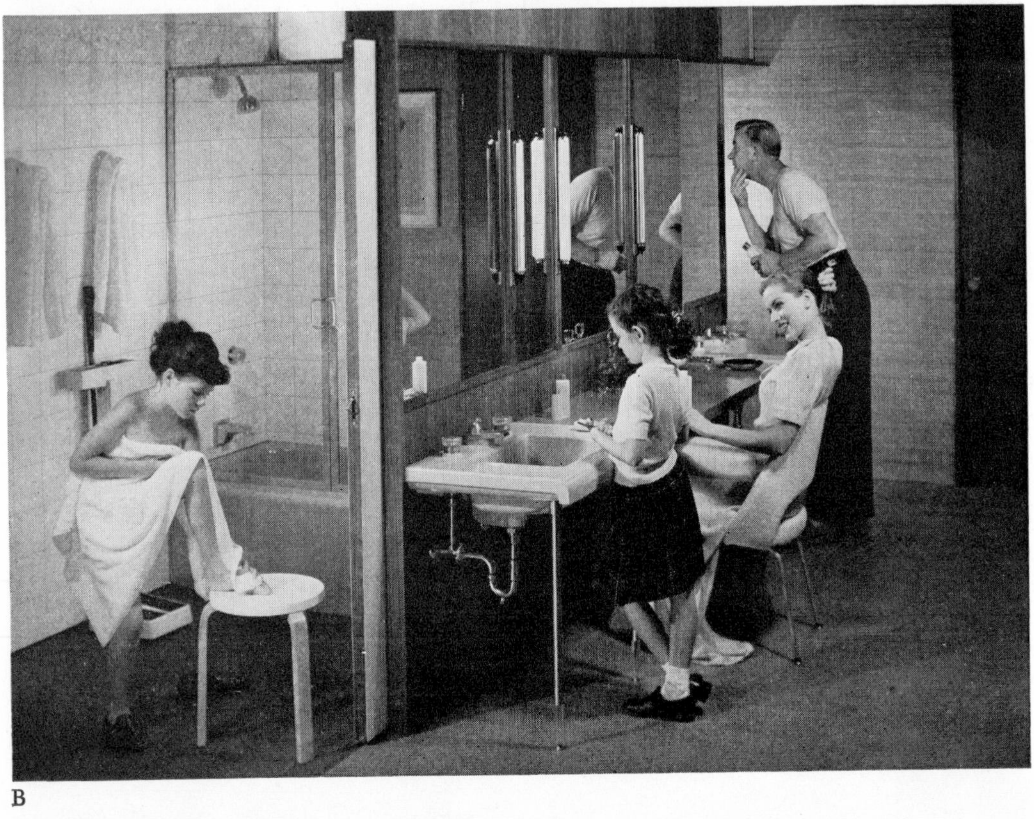

B

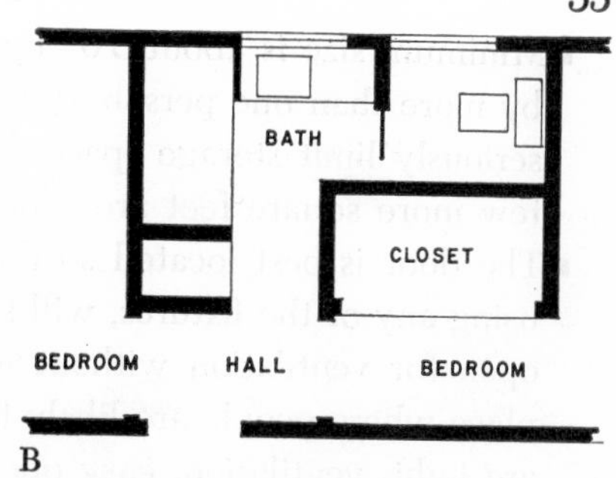

Location of bathrooms is dependent on the type and cost.

Above left. **Private** bathrooms for one or two persons entered only through the bedroom or dressing room. **Plumbing costs are lowest if all fixtures are on one wall.**

Above right. **Semiprivate,** planned for two or three members of the family, located near the bedrooms but entered from the bedroom hall. **Plumbing costs increase if fixtures are on two walls.**

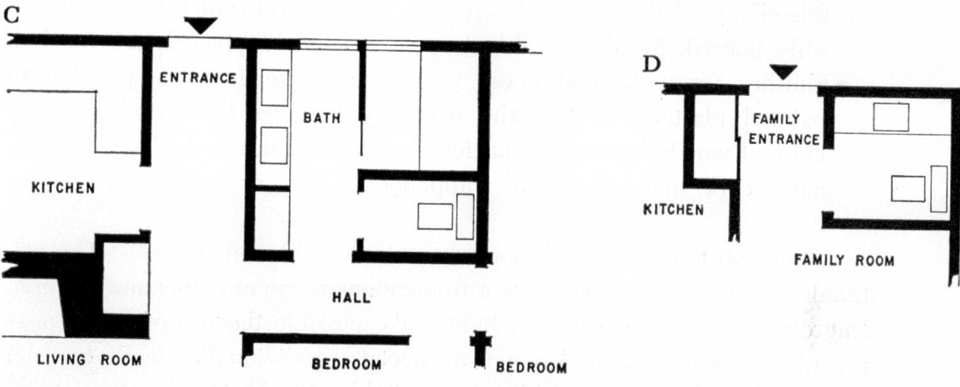

Above left. **Family** type which serves all should be large and compartmented, centrally located but out of sight of the group living space. **Plumbing costs are highest if fixtures are scattered.**

Above right. **Powder** rooms near the guest entrance or **wash-up** rooms near the family entrance and play space keep either guests or dirt out of the other bathrooms.

Right. **Concentrating** all plumbing including that of kitchen and laundry reduces construction costs but takes very careful planning to be successful. **The costs differences, however, are almost negligible if convenience is affected.**

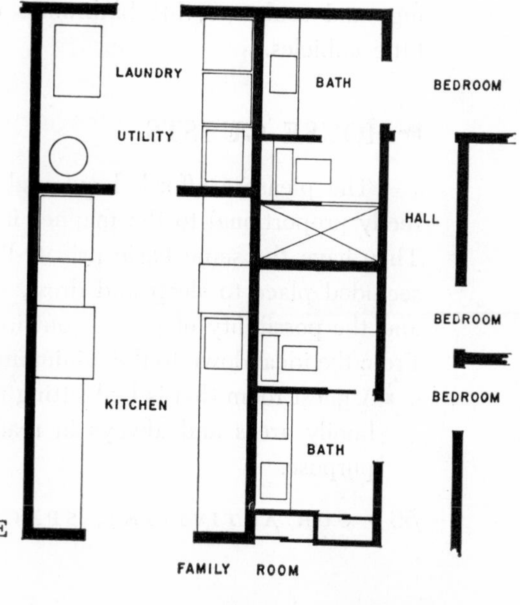

- A secluded room or study that doubles as a guest room, a sensible solution because a room well planned for seclusion has most of the qualities of a good guest room (Fig. 43B).
- A quiet alcove off the group living space that can readily be made private by folding or sliding doors, curtains, or screens.
- An extra bed in one or more of the bedrooms, perhaps a bunk as shown in the boy's room (Fig. 50A) or a bed that folds into the wall (Fig. 57B).
- A sofa bed in the living room, one type of which is shown in Figure 57A.

Few can afford a spare guest room, but if a family expects to have house guests with any frequency, it should direct its efforts toward making their visits as pleasant as possible.

► INDIVIDUAL WORK AND HOBBIES

With today's emphasis on individuality, personal expression, and self-realization, space and equipment for satisfying such urges are becoming increasingly important—and at a time when both space and equipment are very expensive. Solving this problem is possible but not easy, now that spare rooms, basements, attics, and backyard sheds are becoming scarce.

Writing necessitates a desk, in or around which the needed paraphernalia can be conveniently kept. A desk in the living space, especially if in a secluded corner (Fig. 59A) can provide for the needs of a small family. In larger families it is far more satisfactory to have a desk for the housewife in the kitchen or master bedroom, one for each child in his bedroom, and to give some thought to where the man of the house can readily put pen on paper.

Knitting and crocheting can be done wherever one can read, but mending and sewing, whether as work or a hobby, are not so easily disposed of. The collection of needles, scissors, and "findings" seems to invite disorder and the fingers of small children to which they are a definite hazard. Adding a sewing machine and space for sewing brings further complications. In order of desirability are a special sewing room, which is nowadays a luxury; space in the master bedroom; or a spot in the already overcrowded kitchen or laundry. Wherever sewing is fitted in—and regrettably that is usually just the way it is handled—well-planned storage is a requisite (Fig. 59B).

Such handcrafts as weaving or woodworking not only require space and specialized equipment but make almost as much noise as does music.

A

Individual work and hobbies are too important to be neglected in planning.

Above. Built-in bookshelves and a desk at right angles to the wall make a compact, pleasant study or writing corner which is separated but not isolated from the rest of the living room. Harwell Hamilton Harris, architect. (*Photograph by Julius Shulman*)

Right. A closet can house and hide all the paraphernalia needed for dressmaking. This closet has a drop-down table hinged to the inside of one door, a full-length mirror on the other. The sewing machine can be rolled out. All supplies are easily accessible. (*Photograph by Charles H. Pearson. Courtesy of* Better Homes and Gardens)

B

A really comfortable chair set off in a well-lighted bedroom corner invites relaxed reading. Inexpensive India prints and hemp rugs add color and texture to an ordinary old room. (*Courtesy of* LIVING for Young Homemakers)

Important as these may be to the individual, such interests can quickly and seriously endanger the composure of the rest of the family unless they are somewhat isolated in a family room or completely segregated in a special room or the garage.

► SOLITUDE

For parents raising families—as well as for the children being raised—solitude is a rare and precious state. Recent studies of what people want and do not have in contemporary houses indicate that for many persons, especially housewives, this need is acute. Too often the bathroom is the only haven—and this leads to many complications. Much importance is given to the two-week vacation during which one "gets away from it all." Good as this is, it is no substitute for the half-hour vacation most individuals need every day. This brings us back to the real need for planning multi-use bedrooms (Figs. 60 and 61) and to the desirability of seclusion rooms.

Designed as a "studio-library" in which to do serious studying and art work, this room with its two studio couches might also be used as a multi-purpose bedroom or for an occasional visiting couple. Keck and Keck, architects. (*Photograph by Hedrich-Blessing*)

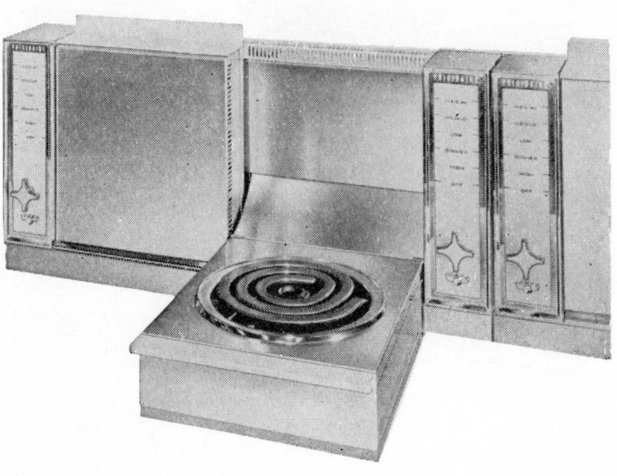

4. Housekeeping

HOUSEWIVES HAVE HAD MUCH TO SAY on the subject of making homes easier to manage. Among their suggestions are garages that are convenient for toting groceries from cars to kitchens and kitchens with space for dining tables and chairs. They want more appliances than ever in kitchens plus well-planned automatic laundries, but if necessary most housewives would give up gadgets for more space. Also high on their lists are "decontamination rooms" where children can clean up before infiltrating the rest of the house. Built-ins are favored throughout the home to save on original furniture costs, upkeep, and space. Quite rightly, though, housewives do not want these efficiencies at the sacrifice of individuality or beauty. Today all these qualities can be combined in the areas planned primarily for leisure or for work.

Keeping the home clean, in order, and in good repair are wholesome aspects of home life that can be invigorating family enterprises. The

Above. Surface cooking units can be attached to the back of the counter top, folded back when not in use. (*Frigidaire*)

greatest labor-saving possibility at our command is sensible planning of the whole house and yard. This includes:

- Putting together functionally related areas, such as dining space, kitchens, and carports.
- Storing objects conveniently and accessibly at points of use.
- Selecting materials and forms that are easy to maintain.
- Having no more furniture and accessories than are used or enjoyed.

To this can be added the long list of appliances designed to minimize effort. All these expedients do not lead to a home that takes care of itself, but each labor-saving device can contribute toward a home life in which there is time and energy for hobbies or cultural pursuits.

Although most home work is concentrated in the kitchen, laundry, garage, or basement, some of it must be done throughout every part of the structure and landscape. This kind of home work includes such miscellaneous projects as "straightening up" and housecleaning, sewing, miscellaneous repairs, and yard and garden work.

► GETTING MEALS

Few home activities have received such intensive study as has meal preparation, with the result that kitchens have changed rapidly and drastically. Home economists have studied every phase of the problem while manufacturers produce new equipment yearly. Neither is an accident or whim: both grow directly from the observation that keeping a family well fed is a large-scale order which takes many hours each day seven days a week.

Analysis of Activities

In chronological sequence, getting a meal involves planning and shopping, receiving and storing supplies, preparing food and serving it, and cleaning up after the meal is over. A thorough study of these operations by Mary Holl Heiner and Helen E. McCullough * has provided a basis for planning kitchens of many types. It should be underlined that this study deliberately did not conclude with "the perfect kitchen," for these experts knew that no single kitchen would suit all situations. Their findings are basic but generalized to cover only how the work centers should be planned, not how they should look (pages 64-65).

* Conducted at the College of Home Economics, Cornell University, and reported in *Architectural Forum,* February and March 1946.

DESIGN OF KITCHEN WORK CENTERS HAS BENEFITED FROM MUCH STUDY BUT NEED NOT BE STANDARDIZED

Below. The **Mixing Center,** sometimes called the Preparation Center, is for all kinds of mixing—salads, breads, and pastries or desserts. It should have:

A

A **counter** at least 36 inches long and not more than 30 to 32 inches high, in contrast to the standard 36-inch height, to lessen fatigue.

Wall cabinets to store condiments, packaged foods, and cookbooks.

Base cabinets with drawers for small tools and drawers or sliding shelves for pans and heavy items used in mixing.

The **Mixing Center** is best located near the refrigerator, in which many mix-first items are stored, and also convenient to the sink. Because much time is spent here, knee space and a stool could be included.

Below. The **Cooking Center** becomes the busiest area for half an hour or so prior to eating, and it is also the danger spot. Efficiency is increased by:

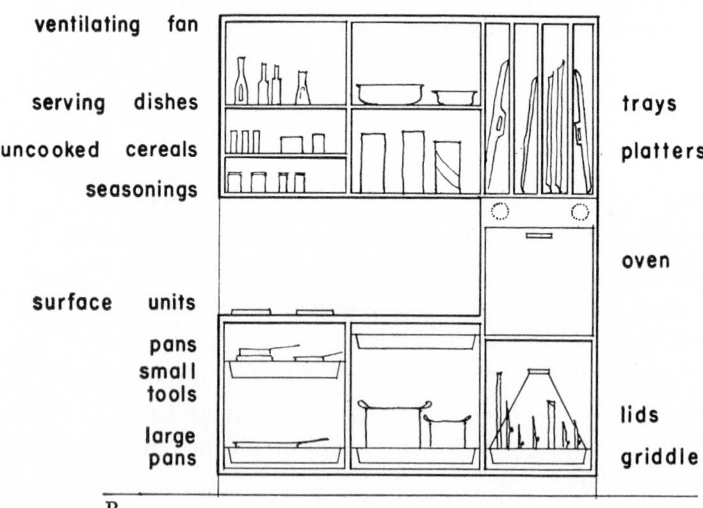

B

Heat-resistant counters on both sides of surface units and on at least one side of built-in ovens.

Wall cabinets near by for small cooking utensils and seasonings.

Base cabinets for larger, heavier items.

Ventilation with a quiet exhaust fan over cooking surface.

Near the Sink and Mixing Centers, and convenient to the eating space, describes the most desirable location for this center.

Below. The **Sink Center** is indeed multipurpose, serving as it does for washing fruits and vegetables, dishes and children's hands and providing water for mixing, cooking, freezing, and drinking. It may spread into storage for tableware although that is sometimes better at the Serving Center. The Sink Center needs:

Counters at both sides, at least one a waterproof drainboard.

Storage space for such sink-first items as utensils for food cleaning, cutting, and straining; dish cloths and towels, and soaps. It is convenient to store foods that need peeling and/or water first, a miscellany ranging from coffee and dried fruits to potatoes and onions, in or near this center.

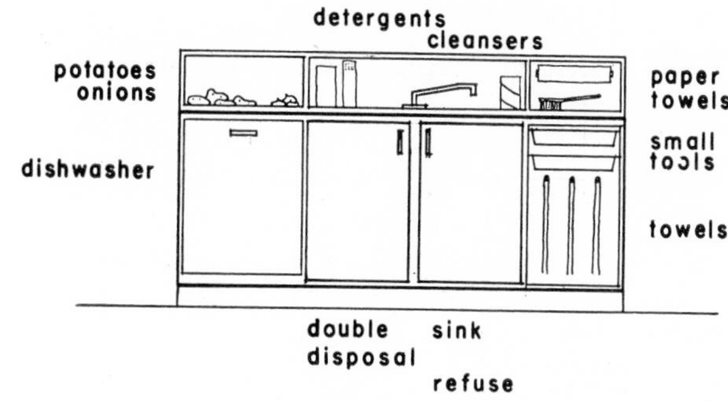

A

A **stool** and **knee space** would ease labor of cleaning vegetables and dishes.

Provision for **trash** and **garbage.**

Because it is desirable to have the Sink Center near both Cooking and Mixing Centers, it is often located between them. Double sinks, or two separated sinks, have much to recommend them.

Below. The **Serving Center** is used for storing those items that go directly from storage to table—most tableware, linens and accessories, such foods as sugar and catsup, and toasters. Often located between food preparation and eating areas, the Serving Center should have:

Ample cupboard space designed for the items to be stored. If between cooking and eating areas, these can be accessible from either side.

A durable counter with or without a pass-through to facilitate serving.

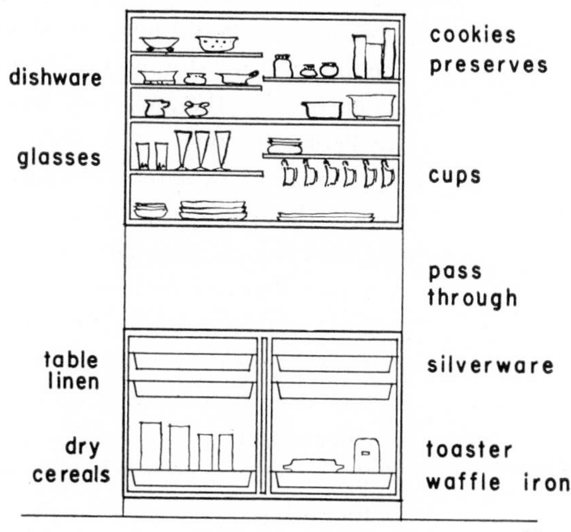

B

Since the Serving Center is used heavily during setting and clean-up times, close proximity to the eating table is desirable.

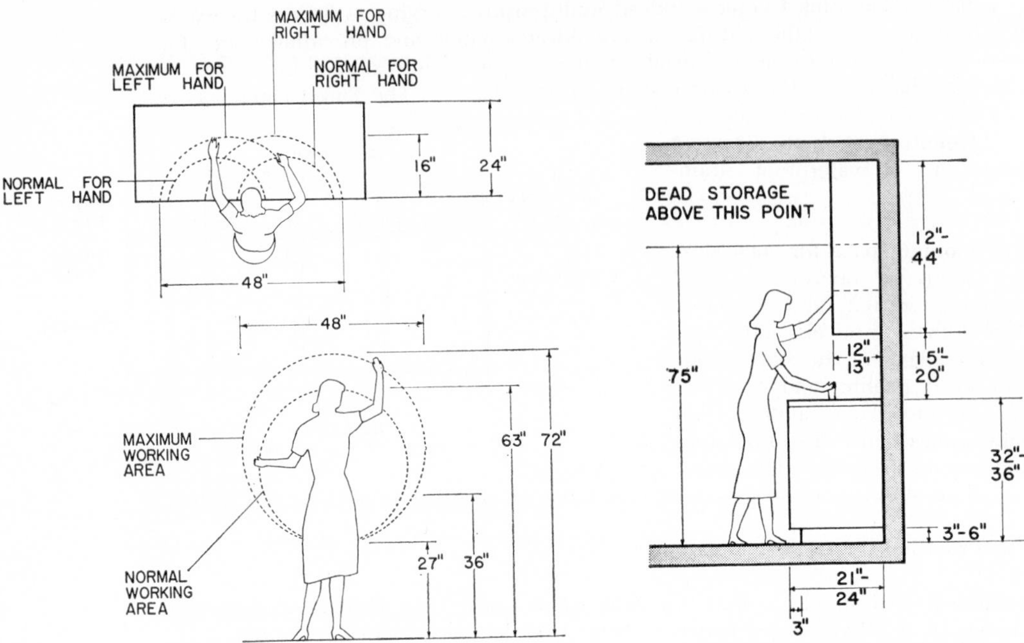

Kitchen dimensions should be based on the height and reach of the persons using that room. These are for average women.

Kitchen planning starts with some important facts.

- The housewife's physical limitations vary with her height, but generally work curves should not exceed 48 inches wide and 16 inches deep, and the top shelf for storage should not be more than 72 inches high. Energy is conserved if the most used storage is between 27 and 63 inches above the floor (Fig. 66).
- Storage deserves careful thinking about objects in relation to their use and to those who use them.

  Convenience—time and energy are conserved if items are stored where they are first used rather than putting all similar things—pots and pans or sharp knives, for example—in one place.

  Visibility—storing items (except for such identical articles as tumblers) only one row deep facilitates finding them.

  Accessibility—logic indicates putting most frequently used items at the most convenient height, heavy objects below, and those seldom used above.

  Flexibility—adjustable shelves and drawers with removable dividers adapt to changes in needs of families and design of kitchen tools.

  Maintenance—open shelves are efficient for items used daily, but enclosed storage for those used less often reduces cleaning.

- The number and variety of items stored even in a modest kitchen is startling: for example, 75 to 80 packaged foods and 40 to 50 utensils are used in mixing operations.
- Kitchen procedures indicate four work centers: *Mixing, Cooking, Sink,* and *Serving.*

The designs for these centers shown on pages 64 and 65 are for typical kitchens. They could be easily assembled in varied kitchen layouts, could have interchangeable parts, and could include built-in appliances. Individualized habits and preferences might, however, lead to different arrangements and allocation of space.

Placement of Work Centers

The cardinal principle of work-center organization is appropriateness to the individuals using the kitchen most intensively. For most situations, however, the following generalizations hold:

- Traffic in and around the work centers should be limited to that connected with getting meals. Miscellaneous traffic should be diverted elsewhere.
- Distances between work centers should be as short and the routes as direct as possible and still allow for the necessary counters and storage. This usually means that the "work triangle" formed by Cooking, Sink, and Mixing Centers measures more than 12 but less than 20 feet in length.
- Standard kitchen arrangements fall into four categories as illustrated on page 68. Although most kitchens are basically related to one of these four types, those designed to solve special problems or to meet individual needs may differ markedly from standard practice.

Planning the Kitchen

Designed as an energy-saving kitchen-workroom,* the example shown in Figures 70A and B and Figures 71A, B, and C is the result of extensive research. Study of the plan reveals that this ample, almost square, space measuring 18′ by 17′6″ is divided by an "island" into two zones, one for food preparation and eating and the other for laundry and storage. The food preparation zone is a "Broken U" shape. Before getting into specifics, notice that large windows in two walls, over the sink and beside the dining

* Developed by the Agricultural Research Service, U. S. Department of Agriculture.

Almost all kitchen plans are related to one of these basic types.

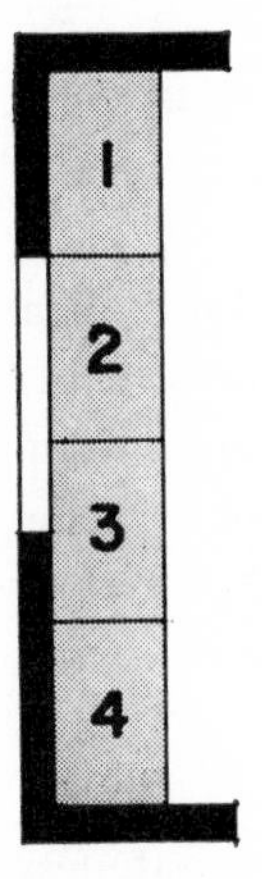

A. STRAIGHT LINE

A. **Straight-line** kitchens can be fitted into alcoves and concealed when not in use. They are available in complete prefabricated units and economically concentrate plumbing and wiring. They are, however, suitable only for "kitchenettes" because if equipment and storage are normal size, many steps are wasted.

B. **Right-angle** kitchens have less distance between centers, leave room for eating or laundry, and divert miscellaneous traffic a little.

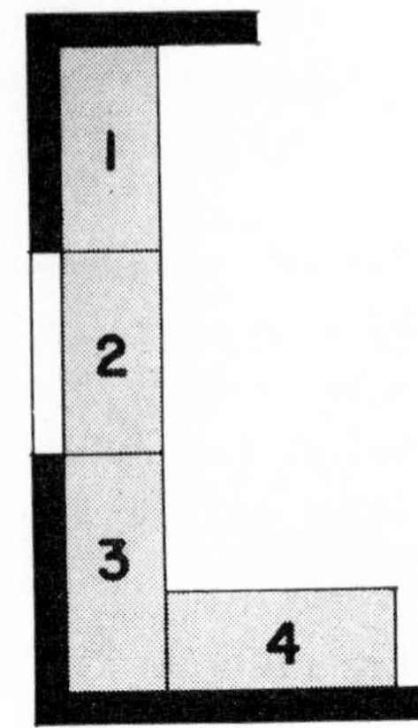

B. RIGHT ANGLE

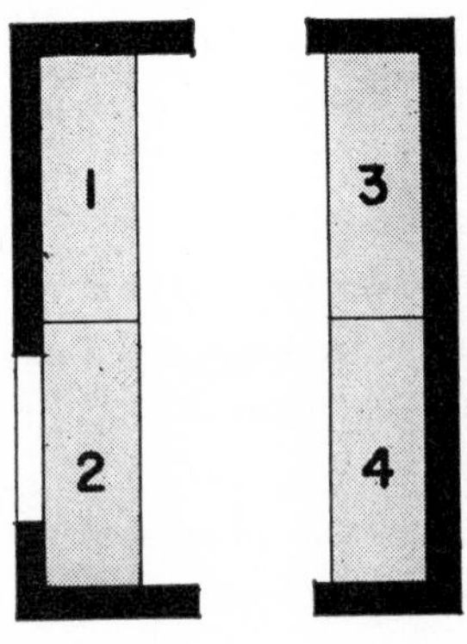

C. OPPOSITE WALLS

C. **Opposite-wall** kitchens further reduce distances between work centers but invite traffic if doors are at both ends.

D. **U-shaped** kitchens are the most compact and efficient and have the further grace of minimizing traffic.

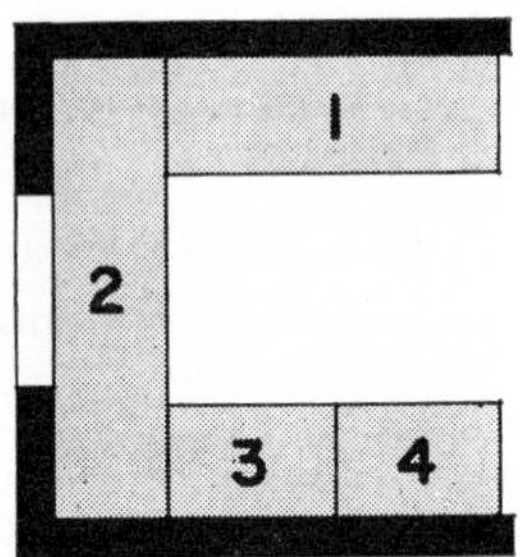

D. "U"- SHAPED

table, give excellent daylight. Circulation is equally well planned: the three doors have been arranged in the laundry-storage area to minimize circulation in the space for food preparation. The work triangle falls within the limits stated earlier.

A masterpiece of design, the refrigerator island has on the cooking side a wall-hung refrigerator that facilitates seeing and reaching food. Behind the shallow counter on which items taken from the refrigerator can be rested are cabinets for beverage cartons. In addition to multi-use drawers and towel-drying racks, the base has space to keep the very important serving cart. The opposite side has a planning desk with telephone and radio. Shelves above hold cookbooks, lower shelves are for children's toys.

The Cooking Center, with surface units arranged so that pans on each can be tended without reaching over others, has a pegboard wall at the sides for pots, pans, lids, and oven mitts. In the wall at the right, the oven is mounted with its bottom at the energy-conserving height of 32″ above the floor. Space above designed for vertical storage of platters and trays plus drawers below makes this a complete center.

The Mixing Center is adjacent to the sink and just around the corner from that for cooking. A floor-to-ceiling corner cabinet with revolving shelves, graduated in width for visibility, holds the foods and utensils most frequently used at this point. Flour and sugar bins are within easy reach at the back of the counter, mixing tools are accessibly mounted on a pegboard wall. A mixer, mounted on casters, pulls out from behind a door at a touch. An adjustable posture stool, stored in the knee space under the counter, can readily be moved to the sink.

The Sink Center has knee space so that cleaning operations can be performed while sitting. Vegetable bins and cupboards for soap as well as slots for knives are within easy reach at the back of the sink below the windows.

The Serving Center adjoins the sink counter and the eating areas. An accordion-type door can be open so that the housewife, if seated on a swivel chair, can reach almost everything behind it. Flatware is in drawers, linens on pull-out shelves. Another pull-out shelf brings toaster and coffeemaker conveniently near. Even bread, cake, and cookies are kept in vented drawers.

The rest of this kitchen-workroom space, devoted to laundry and storage, will be discussed later in this chapter.

Maintenance is lessened and illumination improved by light-colored, laminated plastic tops on counters, cart, and table. White paint inside the cupboards gives stimulating contrast to the greenish-blue walls and cabinets. Vinyl flooring in a grayed tan terrazzo pattern makes minor spots inconspicuous.

Totally different in intent and character is the living-kitchen illustrated in Figures 72A and B and Figure 73, even though it has an island and major equipment is arranged in a "Broken U." Although efficient, the goal was a common space to keep the family happily together. The space-dividing island, 4 feet high, obscures most of the kitchen clutter yet allows the housewife to participate in group activities while preparing meals. The food preparation zone has the Cooking Center in the island, while the opposite wall not only integrates Sink and Mixing Centers but offers a view of the outdoor play yard. The family-room side of the island has a built-in bench

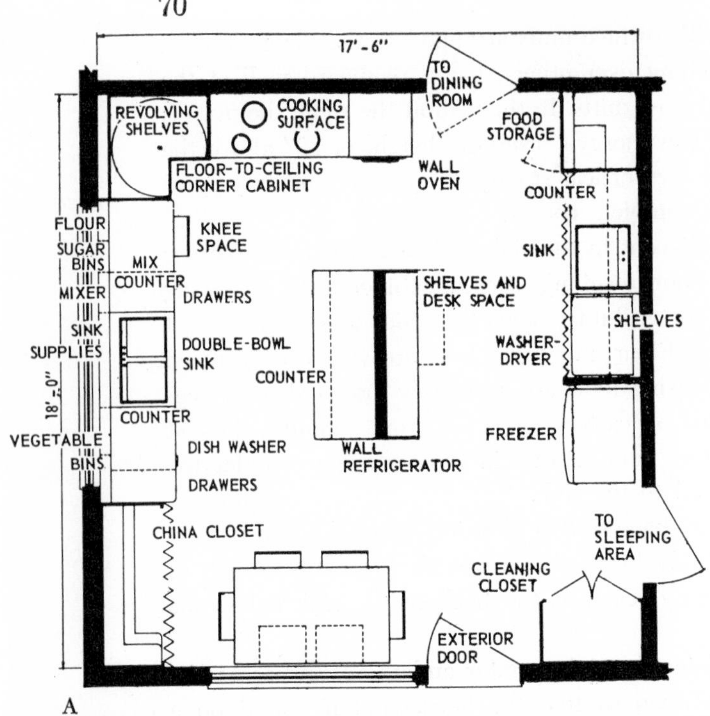

A

Left. The kitchen-workroom plan shows equipment, workspace, and storage arranged for maximum efficiency. (*U. S. Department of Agriculture, Agricultural Research Service*)

Below. The central island divides a traffic-free kitchen area from a laundry-storage passageway to other parts of the house.

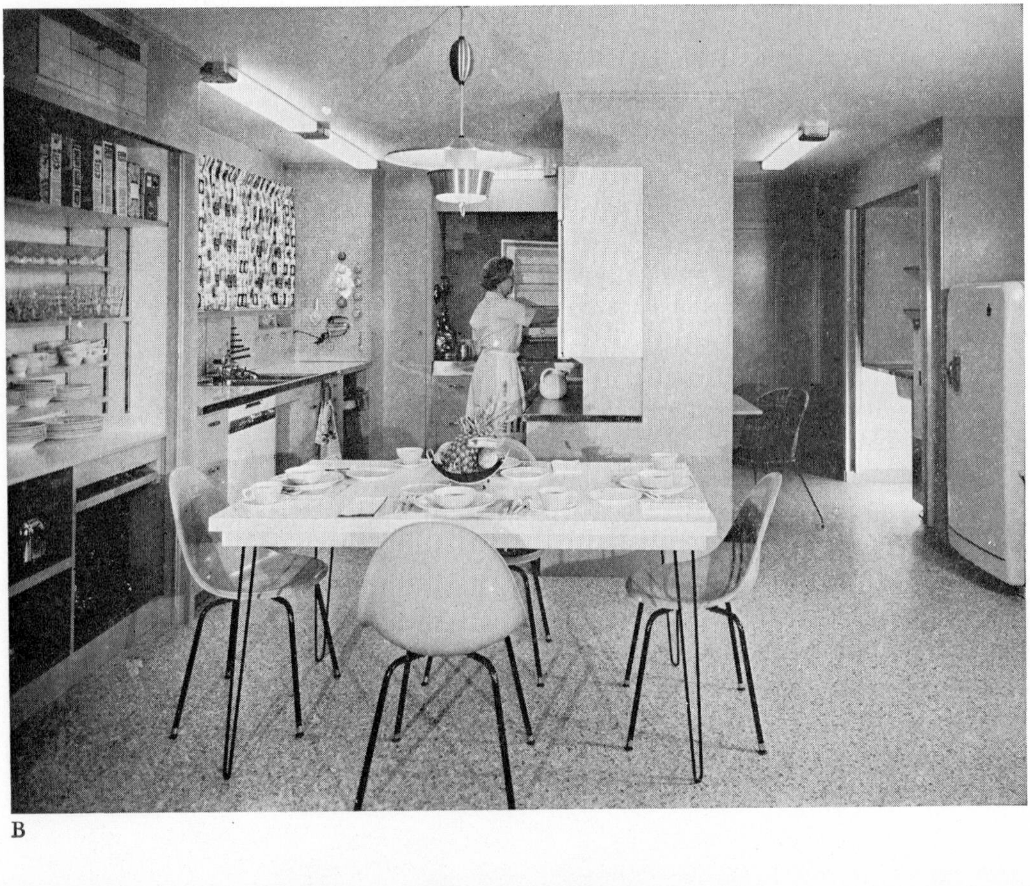

B

A

Above. The wall-hung refrigerator makes foods easily visible, is convenient to all work centers, the breakfast table, and dining room. The Cooking Center has oven and surface units at good working heights.

Below left. Sitting at the Mixing Center, the homemaker has needed tools and ingredients within reach.

Below right. Cleaning up after meals is simplified by a cart on wheels, a dishwasher and double sink, a revolving stool, and sufficient knee space. (*U. S. Department of Agriculture photographs*)

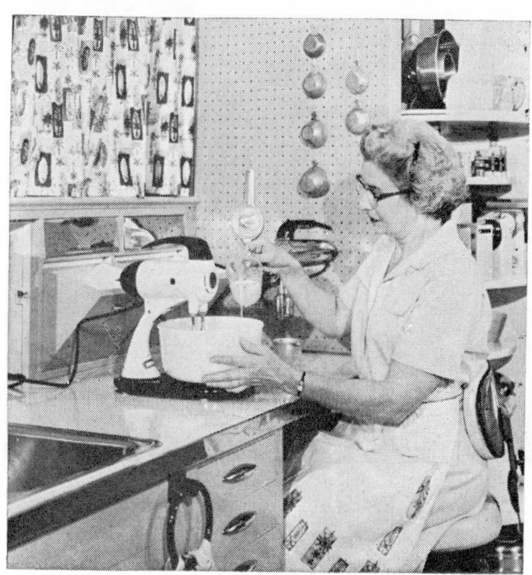

B

A

B

to provide comfortable seats for several persons while eating or doing any of the other things best done at a table. One end of the island contains family-room storage, the other end holds dishes. The bench faces a raised fireplace nicely related to a seating ledge and bookshelves at the left and to a sofa, desk, and music storage at the right. Interest in the utilitarian should certainly not cause one to overlook the liberating shape of the room and the divider, the intimately lowered ceiling over the relaxation area, the welcome surprise of light from high windows, or the congenial combination of knotty wood and brick. This is not only an island kitchen but an open kitchen, frankly acknowledging that preparing meals is good fun in a family setting.

Kitchens that open as fearlessly to the outdoors as some do to group living spaces are becoming popular in all parts of the country. Their possibilities are legion, but those conducive to outdoor eating have these characteristics: ease in getting food from kitchen to terrace and a comfortable place in which to enjoy the meal. In Minneapolis, the Petersons' kitchen (Fig. 75A) is united with a protected porch and walled garden through a glass door in a window wall that stretches from floor to the pitched ceiling. With planning of this caliber, the times in which eating outdoors can be enjoyed is greatly increased. In a high-ceilinged kitchen (Fig. 75B) compactness and efficiency may dictate the use of all wall

The Morgan Evans' family-room kitchen, efficient in details but with emphasis on warmth and congeniality. Frederick Barienbrock, architect.

Left above. The cooking island of knotty pine and red tiles separates and hides the clutter of meal preparation from the more social dining and lounging side.

Left below. On the family-room side, the angled island makes an inviting recess for a built-in bench and for a table whose shape was suggested by the space. (*Photographs by Julius Shulman*)

Right. An irregular hexagon, a refreshingly different but workable shape, individualizes the plan of the Evans' kitchen.

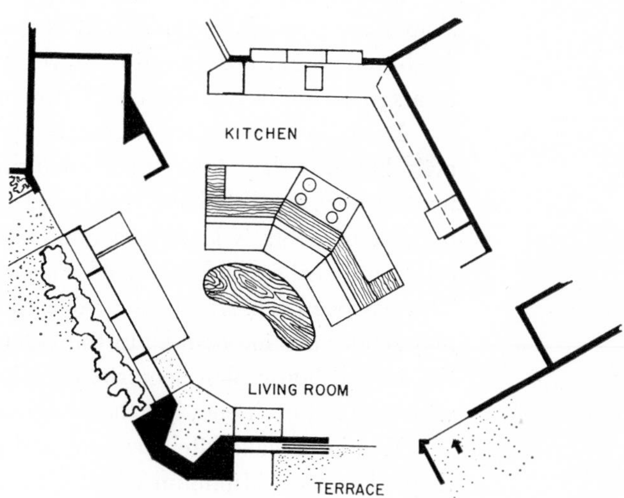

space for equipment, counters, and cupboards yet allow views through open shelves or windows above convenient storage heights.

These kitchens designed for efficiency and integration with family life or the out-of-doors are only a few examples of what personal needs may indicate. There are minimum alcove cooking centers off living rooms in small apartments and farm kitchens large enough for the family and helpers. Some kitchens are planned with children foremost in mind, others for gourmets, and there are kitchens for families in which servants do the work. Kitchen planning is successful only when it satisfies the users' needs, because, as with every other part of the home, a kitchen takes on full meaning only when used.

Generalizing about the several important aspects of kitchens is risky in view of the diverse functions that kitchens may perform. *Size,* for example, is determined not only by the number of persons using the kitchen and the amount of food prepared for family or guests but also by the kind and number of other activities that take place in the kitchen areas. The space needed in small homes for food preparation alone may vary from around 60 to 130 square feet, but in larger homes more space may be needed. The addition of laundries or eating space, hobby and relaxation centers may raise the total to 300 square feet or more. As we mentioned earlier, a majority of families want ample kitchens, but efficiency and pleasantness are determined by shape, doors and windows, and location in the house plan as well as by size.

Shape has no ready-made rules. Although typically rectangular, other shapes are possible (Fig. 73). It is generally agreed, though, that a small food-preparation area requires fewer steps if its shape falls between that of a square and a rectangle with proportions of 2 to 3.

Doors in kitchens are necessary evils—necessary as entrances and exits, evils because they take space, determine location of work centers, and invite traffic. Experts have concluded that efficiency is increased when the number of doors is kept to a minimum, when doors are as close to each other as feasible, and when no major work center comes between them. This has been achieved in the research kitchen, but elsewhere other factors may render this impossible. In the Petersons' home (Fig. 75A), for example, the lot and house plan necessitated a long narrow kitchen and utility room with doors at each end, but the designers avoided making it a thoroughfare.

Windows make kitchens light and pleasant and provide ventilation but they take space. Minimum window area should equal at least 10 percent of the floor area, but 15 to 20 percent is better. If possible, at least one counter

A

Kitchens in many climates can be pleasant and well lighted with large areas of glass.

Above. In Minnesota, the Peterson's opposite-wall type kitchen is efficient because it is not a passageway. It is also cheerful because of the pleasant views of the porch and enclosed, tree-shaded terrace beyond. Carl Graffunder, architect. (*Photograph by Reynolds, Infinity, Inc. Courtesy of* Better Homes and Gardens)

Right. In California, a U-shaped kitchen gains light and spaciousness from the dramatic high windows and sloping ceiling. Open shelves above the sink allow the cook to see the dining area and the view beyond. Henry Hill, architect. (*Photograph by Morley Baer*)

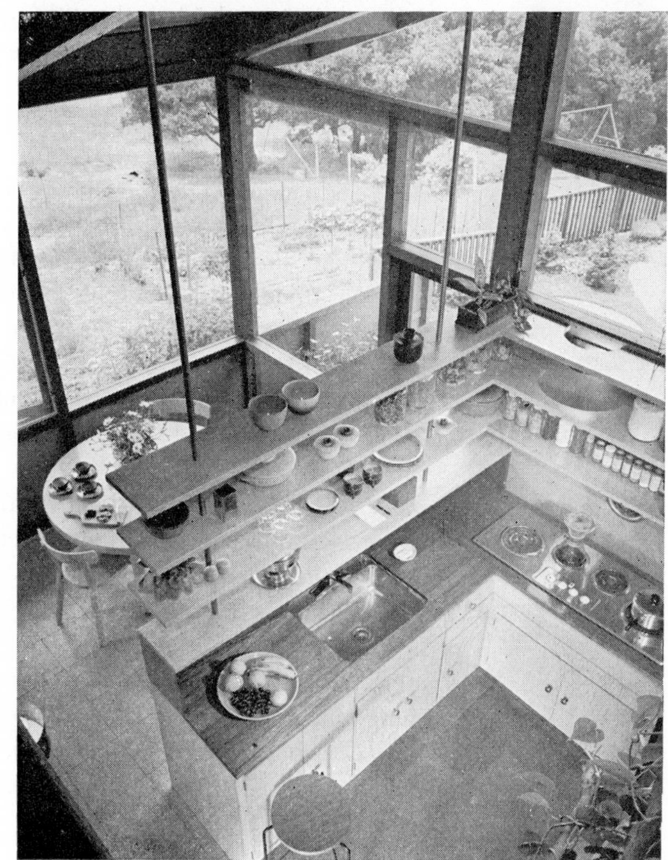

B

should have ample daylight and afford an outlook. Contemporary architects have developed many ingenious ways of daylighting kitchens without sacrificing wall space. In the Petersons' kitchen a skylight and small windows between counters and wall cabinets maximize use of walls. High windows (Fig. 75B) flood the food preparation area with daylight and let the housewife enjoy an expansive view without taking an inch of usable space.

Location of kitchens is a matter of critical importance, but there are many good solutions as shown on page 77.

Kitchens take the greatest drubbing of any room in the house and have to be cleaned most often. They are noisy—and the center of the housewife's work. These factors suggest selecting shapes and materials for floors, counters, cupboards, walls, and ceilings for *wear-resistance, cleanability, sound-control,* and *pleasantness* to sight and touch.

New ways of living, new concepts of planning, and technological advances have brought kitchens that are handsome and efficient. In a later section of this chapter ways of reducing housework in the kitchen and elsewhere will be discussed. Chapters 5, 6, and 7 deal with design and color, while Chapters 8, 9, and 10 analyze the qualities of materials. In these chapters are many facts and ideas applicable to all phases of kitchen design.

► LAUNDRY

Every week many millions of pounds of clothing and household linens are washed in American homes. But two factors have changed the way in which this is done: first, the development of automatic washers and dryers; and second, the trend toward getting laundry equipment out of dark, inconvenient basements. Provisions for home laundering range from using the sink or washbasin for rinsing out little things to having a fully equipped, separate laundry. The size and age distribution of the family, the size of the house, and the attitude toward sending laundry out are factors in laundry planning.

Laundry activities, like meal-getting, fall into four categories:

- **Receiving, sorting,** and **preparing,** which require a counter, a cart, or simply the top of the washer.
- **Washing** which necessitates laundry trays and/or a washer plus storage for supplies.
- **Drying** in an automatic dryer or convenient drying yard.
- **Finishing** and **ironing** for which an ironing board or ironer is needed plus space to put finished laundry and, ideally, space and equipment for mending.

Kitchens can be placed in almost any part of the house, but steps will be saved if they are the shortest feasible distance from indoor and outdoor eating spaces and from the garage and service area. Further, they ought to be convenient to the main entrance and not far from a lavatory. As long as these requirements are considered, they can be:

A

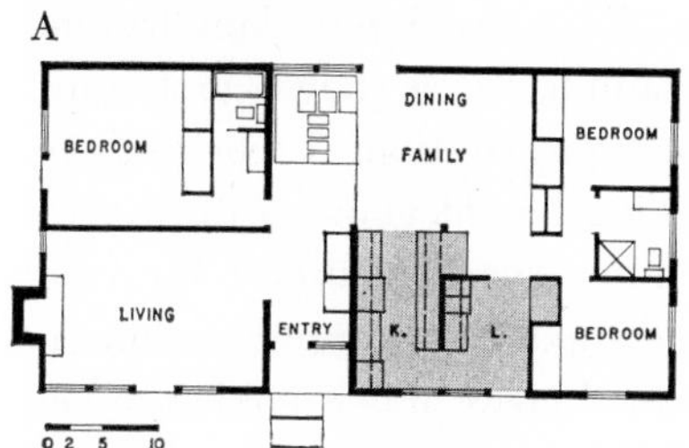

B

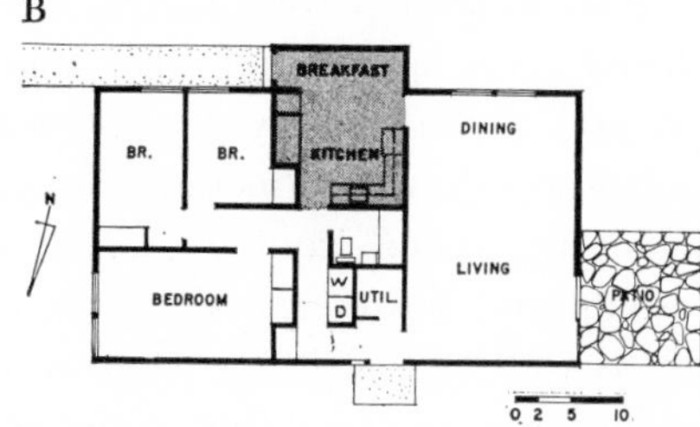

Above left. At the *front,* as in this Idaho house designed by architects Grider and La Marche.

Above right. At the *back,* a solution illustrated by Robert Engelbrecht's plan for a home in New York state.

C

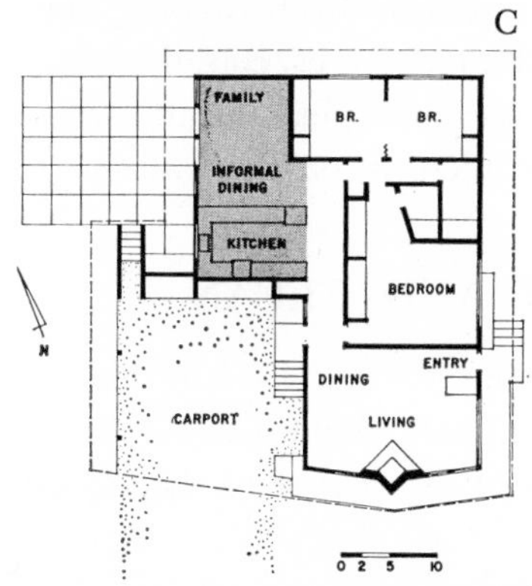

D

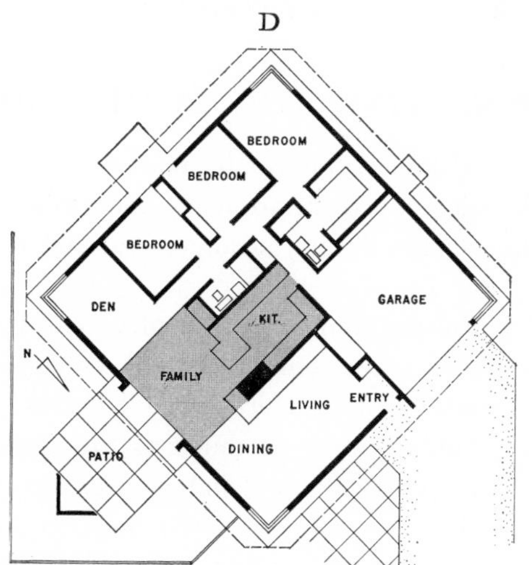

Above. At the *side,* as shown in a California home planned by Paderewski, Mitchell, and Dean.

Right. In the *center,* as in R. Duane Conner's compact plan for Oklahoma City.

Below. On the *first floor* of a two-story house, a typical solution well handled by Louis F. Bodkin III for a home in Oregon.

Right. On the *second floor* of a two-story house when, as in this Florida plan by George Ely and Glenn Johnson, the view and the climate make the upper floor more desirable.

E

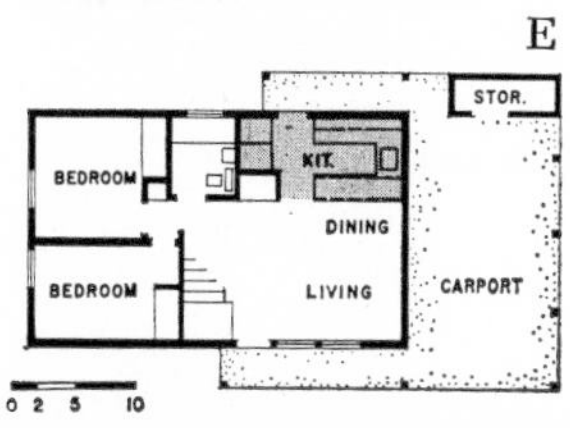

F

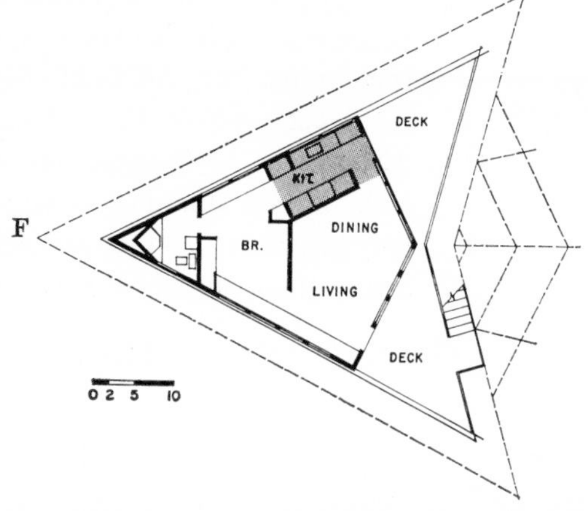

In small houses, laundry space is often reduced to a minimum and compacted into the utility room, the kitchen, basement, or garage. Utility rooms segregate the clutter and noise of laundry work. Those with laundry trays or deep sinks and which serve as family entrances are also good places to clean up after play or garden work (Fig. 77A). Combining laundry and kitchen saves space, time, and steps. The laundry area shown in Figures 70A and B is desirably separated from food preparation. A combination washer and dryer are mounted at good working height above a drawer for clothes that need ironing. A sink with counter space is useful for hand washing and flower arranging. Below is knee space for storing a laundry cart as well as for sitting while working, and shelves above hold supplies. Folding doors conceal this equipment when not in use.

Basements and garages, having little in their favor, are to be avoided if possible. One other location, however, has been successfully tried in some houses and that is the bedroom wing, in some space usually adjoining the bathroom. Since most laundry originates and returns to bedrooms and laundering is seldom done at night, this location deserves consideration. Washing and ironing, wherever they are done, are more pleasant in a well-lighted place made cheerful with color or even pictures on the wall.

► KEEPING THE HOME ORDERLY AND CLEAN

Families, but chiefly housewives, spend many hours a week in housekeeping, but there are many ways to reduce this work. One is careful attention to the design, arrangement, and materials of every part of the home.

Putting things back in place can be speeded in several ways.

- Plan conveniently located centers for each major activity with every needed item near at hand. If this planning is applied to reading and hobbies quite as much as to laundry work, things are more likely to be put away immediately after use and to be found easily when needed.
- Have a well-considered location for each object—chairs, tables, and lamps placed so that they seldom need to be moved, convenient storage for everything not in continuous use. In short, a workable furniture arrangement plus adequate storage.
- Have a maximum of fixed objects. Built-in seating, tables, and lighting fixtures stay where they belong despite the whims of children and adults. Alternatives to built-ins are furniture units (Fig. 80A) designed to look and act almost as though they were integral parts of the house—they fit tightly together and against the wall to save space—and lighting fixtures that can be fastened to walls.

- Select movable objects with movability in mind. These should be lightweight, easy to grasp, and resistant to the wear that moving brings. For example, pull-up and dining chairs ought to be sturdy yet easy to lift, not the kind that demand a floor-scraping shove (Fig. 80B).
- Store or discard everything not often used or enjoyed. Households have a tendency to become cluttered with objects no longer important to the family. The time and space they require can be used for more satisfying purposes.

Cleaning, too, can be much less of a chore if forms, colors, and materials are chosen with maintenance in mind and if there is good storage for cleaning materials, as in Figure 70A.

Dust and dirt are unpleasant to see and touch, unhygienic, and tend to shorten the life of anything on which they remain. They are most harmful and difficult to dislodge if they become embedded in the material. This suggests:

- Forms that are broad and simple with a minimum of separate parts, moldings, or crevices into which dust and dirt settle and from which they are hard to remove. This applies to walls, furniture, tableware, indeed to everything.
- Furnishings that either come to the floor or are supported on a minimum number of legs high enough to make it easy to clean under them.
- Surfaces that are smooth and impenetrable, such as well-sealed wood or concrete, ceramic or plastic tile. Almost everyone, to be sure, also wants the richness and warmth of textured fabrics. These are hard to keep really clean but compensate by not showing "matter foreign to the article in its pure state," as dirt has been defined. Fibers that do not absorb dirt and textiles treated to resist soil and stain, however, are easily maintained.
- Colors that are grayed and neither extremely light nor dark. These are the colors in which nature abounds. They are also the colors on which a little dust or dirt passes unnoticed.
- Surfaces that are patterned rather than plain. Color-varied surfaces are easier to maintain than are those of solid colors but those easiest to keep looking well have small, irregular patterns as in Figures 80D, E, and F.
- Surfaces that are dull rather than glossy. Mirrors and shiny metals bring brilliance and accents but they show fingerprints, water spots, and dust. Mat surfaces with their lack of luster and gloss take such inevitables in their stride.

Many home furnishings are economical of money, energy, and space.

Left. Unit furniture is versatile, flexible, and saves space. (*Country Workshop*)

A

Left below. Chinese cane chairs are comfortable, easy to move, and inexpensive. (*Calif.-Asia*)

Below. Glass mosaic and polished brass make a beautiful, easy-to-keep table. Margot Stewart, designer. (*Helga Photo Studio, Inc.*)

B

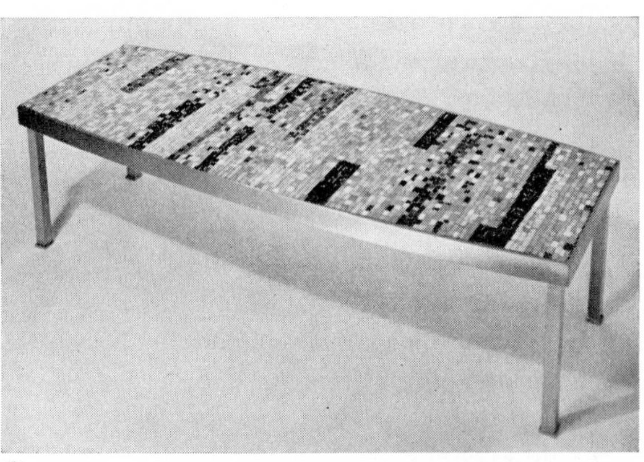

C

Left below. Saran plastic fibers woven in small pattern take everyday hard use, indoors or out, with nonchalance. (*Bolta Products*)

Center. Spun silk and Bemberg woven in an intricate pattern is richly handsome but easily cared for. (*Boris Kroll Fabrics, Inc.*)

Right. Plastic floor covering can be strikingly decorative yet mask the effects of hard use. (*Armstrong Cork Company*)

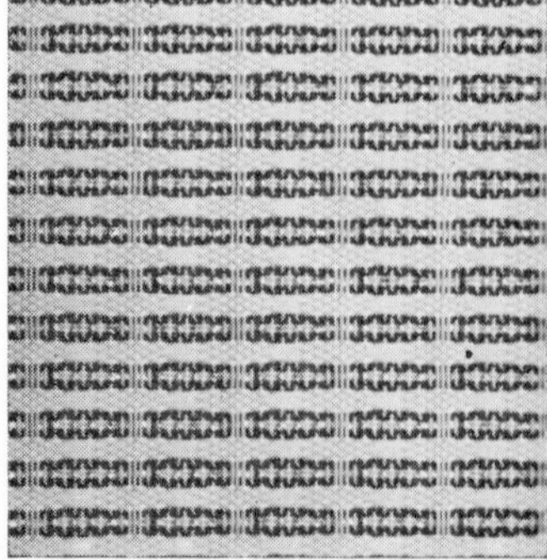

D

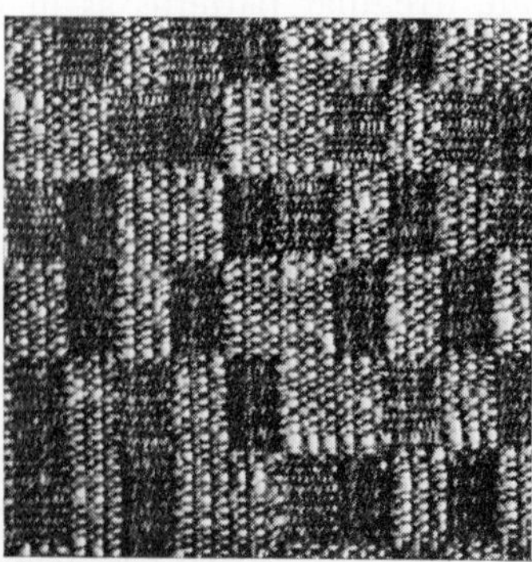

E

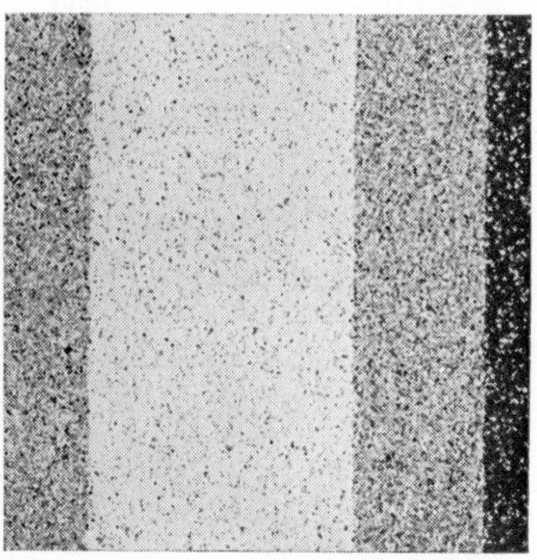

F

That this drive for efficiency need not lead to dullness is well exemplified by the mosaic coffee table (Fig. 80C), which not only meets the requisites listed above but is liquid-proof, durable, and handsome. All this applies equally well to the textile (Fig. 80D) that refuses to absorb stains or dirt.

Spilled and spattered liquids constantly threaten the housekeeper. Water is the most common but least serious, while other liquids, from beverages to ink, may stain or bleach porous, noncolorfast materials. To economize on work and possible replacement use:

- Waterproof materials wherever feasible. Especially needed in kitchens, laundries, and bathrooms, they also merit consideration where food is served, especially to children, and in family rooms. Glass, metal, and glazed ceramics are history's chief waterproof surfaces to which have been added a host of plastics and synthetics (Figs. 80D and F) that are opening the way to easier housekeeping.
- Materials that do not show water marks. In general, plain shiny surfaces whether glass, metal, plastics, or painted wood show water spots removable only by polishing. On surfaces that are dull or patterned, such as the mosaic table and plastic flooring, they are scarcely noticeable.
- Colorfast materials. Here science has made many and mighty contributions of which the Saran textile is one example.

Even in the most careful households, surfaces get scratched and dented. Here, again, knowledge of materials in terms of use is valuable.

- Resilient materials, such as rubber, cork, or cane, take blows or scratches with scarcely a record of the event.
- Rigid materials, such as masonry, metal, and some plastics, are seldom affected by moderate abuse but will crack, break, or dent under heavy blows. If and when this happens, repair is difficult, sometimes impossible.
- Wood, especially the harder types, ages gracefully if finished to reveal its color and grain. Like sterling silverware, it grows richer with use. It seems to make minor scratches and blemishes part of itself. Dents can be sanded or filled. If split, wood can be glued back together.
- Glossy finishes almost always resist scratching and abrasion better than those that are dull. *But* the blemishes are more conspicuous.
- Patterns, especially those that are small and indistinct, conceal blemishes quite as much as they camouflage dust, water marks, and stains.

If carried to an extreme, the above suggestions could lead to a home monotonously medium brown and gray with a profusion of little texture patterns everywhere and no plain bright, dark, or light colors, no sparkling surfaces. This, of course, is not intended. But for easy housekeeping and informal living the suggestions can be advantageously applied to the *big surfaces of walls, floors,* and *furniture.*

Use, economy, beauty, and individuality have been happily united in the living room shown below. Because it was planned with people and furniture in mind, there is a satisfactory place for every object. Much of the furniture—the book and storage cases, sofa, end and dining tables—are built in as is the concealed lighting. The few movable pieces, such as the coffee table and chairs, are easy to grasp and lift. All pieces either come to the floor or stand vacuum cleaner height above it. The forms are broad and simple but neither monotonous nor dull. Because the major surfaces show natural colors and patterns, they get along with little maintenance. Were it not that this chapter emphasizes housekeeping we would discuss, rather than merely mention, the interest achieved in the ceiling variations, the band of high glass that brings light and lets one see the sky without demanding curtains for privacy, the lively contrast of textures, the painting that is large enough for the space it occupies, the high degree of unity and individuality, and the promise of good living that even a black and white photograph extends.

The living and dining space in a small house that integrates to a remarkable degree use, economy, beauty, and individuality. Gordon Drake, architect. (*Photograph by Julius Shulman*)

(McGuire Furniture Co.)

PART II

Design and Color

5. Design: Aims and Principles

THE WORD DESIGN has several meanings: purpose, aim, or intention; plan or scheme; and selection and organization. When these definitions are put together, they describe the total design procedure of deciding on one's aim, developing a plan or approach, and selecting and organizing the forms and materials best suited to the purpose.

In art, however, design is often limited to the selection and organization of form, space, color, and texture to create beauty and individuality. In this chapter we will focus attention on design in this limited sense, considering use and economy only when they are particularly vital aspects of a design problem.

Design for beauty has no laws, recipes, or rigid standards to trouble or comfort us because beauty and creative individuality are close partners. Design is a living, not an arbitrary, matter. At its best, each object and each epoch seeks and finds its own appropriate order. There are,

Above. Crisp, lively rhythms distinguish a printed textile designed by Alexander Girard. (*Herman Miller Furniture Co.*)

however, useful observations and guides that may be approached by looking at two exceptionally beautiful living rooms. The Port Royal parlor (Fig. 86A) is a consummate example of eighteenth-century American design that is equalled by Frank Lloyd Wright's own living area in Taliesin, Wisconsin (Fig. 86B).

Although different in every detail, these two rooms have many basic characteristics in common. Both are planned and furnished for group use. Their space is adequate in size and appropriate in shape. Comfortable sofas and chairs, tables, or ledges are arranged for family leisure or entertaining. Both rooms, however, go well beyond merely satisfying our physiological requirements. Materials have been chosen, shaped, or ornamented to please our senses and extend a hospitable welcome with no sacrifice of utility. Notice, too, that in each paintings, china or vases, patterned textiles, flowers and plants are used solely for esthetic satisfaction or sentimental attachment. In short, these rooms express and fulfill their utilitarian and esthetic purposes.

Each room seems all-of-a-piece, holds together cohesively because architecture and furnishings have a dominant character. One is formal and refined, the other informal and vigorous. Interest is held in each by two seemingly paradoxical qualities, namely, a forceful unity and a stimulating diversity. The Port Royal parlor is a contrapuntal union of the strictly rectangular architectural background and the curvilinear forms in the furnishings. Shunning monotony, these curves range from the strong, sculptural legs of the chair in the left foreground to the intricate tracery in the Oriental rug. Mr. Wright's room has relatively few curves but an ingeniously diversified oganization of horizontals, verticals, and diagonals. As basic materials, he chose wood and stone, both of which have an organic variety of color, grain, and texture.

Each of the two rooms is balanced in ways appropriate to its general character. Typical of eighteenth-century design, the symmetrical placement of fireplace, furniture, and accessories brings unquestioned equipoise to the Port Royal parlor, but the lively forms activate what might have been an inert arrangement. The asymmetrical placement of the fireplace, painting, and furniture in Mr. Wright's room is a sensitive balancing of visual weights without exact repetition from side to side.

An all-pervading beat or pulse brings to every part of these rooms a rhythmic expectedness, but here the similarity ends. Crisp and delicate, the rhythms in the Port Royal parlor remind us of Mozart whereas the vigorous, almost martial beat favored by Mr. Wright recalls the powerful energy of Beethoven or Brahms. Although graceful and flowing, the eighteenth-century rhythmic pattern has a Classic quality of self-contain-

A

Left. The Port Royal parlor (1762) is a formal eighteenth-century American room. Philadelphia Chippendale furniture, Oriental rugs, French silk draperies and upholstery, and English cut-glass chandeliers and wall lights combine to produce hospitable elegance. (*Photograph by Gilbert Ask. Courtesy of the Henry Francis du Pont Winterthur Museum.*)

Below. The living room in Frank Lloyd Wright's Wisconsin home (1911-1925) is ruggedly informal. Furnishings and structure are dynamically united in bold, richly varied, interpenetrating planes. (*Photograph by Maynard Parker. Courtesy of* House Beautiful)

B

ment quite different from the expanding, interpenetrating planes that open Mr. Wright's alcove to the space beyond.

A constant human need is to have attention held by intricate or robust forms, then released by simple or quiet ones. These rooms are keyed up to their fireplaces as dominant elements. Designers in the eighteenth century knew well that an element gains emphasis if it is large and centrally located, but they did not stop at this point. Carved pilasters and moldings together with the richly veined marble facing of the fireplace are a handsome setting for a fire, crystal candleholders and china, and the painting. Oriental rugs, made more emphatic by plain wood floors, bring warmth and richness to furniture groups. Mr. Wright's fireplace is also large and prominently placed, and its importance is strengthened by the arrangement of furniture, plants and flowers, a painting, and a photograph.

This analysis demonstrates that a few aims and principles are basic in good interior design. It also should make clear that these aims and principles open many paths to individualized results.

► TWO AIMS OF ORGANIZATION

Form follows function and **variety in unity,** constant aims in historic and contemporary art, apply directly to home design.

Form Follows Function

That the design of anything should grow out of its intended purposes seems obvious, but countless inefficient kitchens, poorly illuminated bathrooms, depressing living rooms, and dining tables with leg-entangling supports prove that design is too often illogical or arbitrary. Nearly everything in the home has its utilitarian aspects and these ought to be basic considerations in its design.

Utility, though, is not the only factor in design, for all objects represent expenditures of money, time, and energy, and they are possible sources of esthetic pleasure and individual expression. A spoon or a sofa is *completely* functional only when it is useful, economical, and beautiful to an individual. This lifts the design and selection of silverware or seating, for example, well above the mere supplying of equipment that fits its user's anatomy. Then there are those objects intended only for the spirit—paintings, sculpture, and accessories whose claim on us is their beauty. These are at the opposite end of the scale from the primarily utilitarian furnace and garden hose, but they are of great significance to the whole man living a full life.

A

B

Two of many solutions to the problem of opening a door—knobs and a lever.

Left. Three possibilities in glass for lighthearted rooms. Paolo Venini, designer. *Right.* Philip Johnson's handle of brushed aluminum. (*Yale & Towne*)

Designing or selecting for all functions is complex. Detailed analysis of specific and general requirements is essential. Factor must be weighed against factor and usually compromises have to be made. Suppose, for example, that you are looking for a coffee table to put in a contemporary living space where adults relax and children want to play. It is easy to find many that are suitable in size, shape, and height; it is not easy to locate a coffee table that is also moderately priced and easy to maintain, that has some storage space and no dangerously sharp corners, and that is pleasing in itself and appropriate to the home. The major difficulty centers around the fact that several of the criteria are contradictory. When this happens, it is sensible to give up the qualities of lesser importance and buy or make a table having those deemed most important.

Form follows function is often misinterpreted as meaning "utility dictates shape." That this is not the case should be clear from the discussion of the Port Royal parlor and Mr. Wright's living area. These rooms and their furnishings show that utility is only *one* of several functions basic to design and that there is more than one way to solve any design problem. Far from being restricting, a study of the functions of any object can inspire quite different solutions as is illustrated by the door handles above.

Variety in Unity

All nature and all art show variety in unity, our own bodies with their unified diversity being the examples best known to us. Our hands, for example, are amazing units in which each part differs from the others yet is coherent with the whole. The Port Royal parlor demonstrates a happy union of American furniture, Oriental rugs, French draperies, and English cut glass. Each has its own distinctive flavor, but they have in common such qualities as refinement and elegance.

Unity may be defined as oneness, or as formed of parts that constitute a whole. It is most successfully achieved out of the strength and clarity of a motivating idea. In home design, this is the general character discussed in Chapter 1. Why should a home be unified? Because a unified home satisfies the desire for wholeness and brings a welcome peace and security not found in a furniture store or a home that resembles one.

Unity may be achieved by several specific means.

- Sameness or repetition is the surest, most obvious, and least interesting means. Having all walls the same color and texture forcefully establishes a unified background. Having all furniture of the same material and design, as in Figure 91A, also makes for oneness (and often monotony as well).
- Similarity and harmony are but one step removed from repetition and lead directly toward unity while introducing some variety. The walls in a home might be of one hue, blue or green for example, but some could be lighter or darker, warmer or cooler, stronger or weaker, or different in texture.
- Emphasizing those parts that most forcefully express the basic character strengthens unity. Much can be done with miscellaneous furniture by putting in noticeable spots those pieces that have the desired qualities, relegating to secondary positions the other pieces that contribute less to the unity of the home.
- Enclosures help unify parts of a home by separating them from their surroundings. Hedges or fences around gardens and frames around pictures are examples.

Variety may be defined as diversity or many-sidedness. It arouses and holds interest as well as bringing vitality through friendly differences. Diversity introduces welcome surprises and heightens the total effect. If carried too far, unity is destroyed because variety can lead to anarchy just as unity can lead toward monotony.

Diversity of materials, forms, colors, or textures and contrasts of all sorts are some of the major ways and means of attaining variety. Variety can be as subtle as a scarcely noticeable difference in the textures of two pillows on a sofa or as clamorous as a polished copper hood on a rough stone fireplace wall. Because variety draws and fixes attention, it should be used full strength only where you want people to look hard and long, in dilution where you want simply to relieve monotony in subordinate places.

Variety has been discussed separately from unity for the sake of clarity. In practice, though, the two are inseparable partners, but the exact relationship between the two is a matter of opinion. Some experts find it advisable to begin with variety and work toward unity. Others, including the writers, believe that variety should grow out of unity as a development of basic ideas, much as an oak tree develops from an acorn. It seems more effective to start with an idea or purpose from which unity and variety grow together than with a series of ideas which have to be "pulled together."

Rarely do homes have too much unity, and for those few that do the simple remedy of introducing some marked variety suffices to give them life. For example, the living room in Figure 91A has good furniture well arranged, but there is too much of the same thing. One yearns for at least one piece of furniture not supported by tubular metal, for some pronounced enrichment, for a few more nonmetallic accessories. Many homes sacrifice unity for variety, and here too the solution is simple—eliminate some of the not-needed variety. The living room in Figure 91B has, for the writers, too much variety, especially of pattern. With furniture, textiles, and accessories as diversified as this, the whole effect could be greatly improved by plainer walls and one appropriate picture in scale with the fireplace.

One way of keeping unity and variety hand in hand is to have a single dominant theme pervade a home, accompanied by a secondary one. Looking back at the Port Royal parlor we see an example of this approach. The basic theme, *rectangularity,* is forcefully expressed in the larger elements—the shape of the room and the rugs, the design of the windows and fireplace. In strong contrast is the second theme of fanciful *curves* seen in the shapes of the furniture and the patterns of rugs and other textiles, the draperies, chandelier, plates, bowls, and flowers. In contemporary homes, a major theme might be informal simplicity coupled with a minor theme of intricately enriched accessories, or the major theme might be formal precision sparked by unexpectedly whimsical accents. Unity is not synonymous with sameness, nor does unity limit anyone completely to one kind of furnishings.

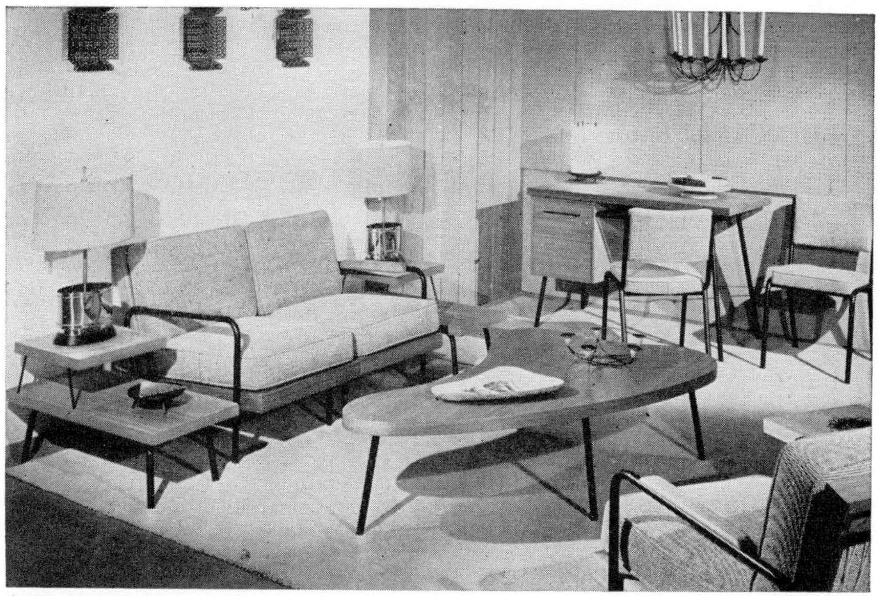

A

Both unity and variety can be pushed too far.

Above. Even well-designed furniture loses its effectiveness when monotonously repeated. Significant unity is not achieved by repetition alone. (*Vista Furniture Company*)

Below. Too much variety and too little dominance confuse the eyes and overwhelm the spirit, substituting busyness for a satisfying wholeness. (*Curtis Companies Service Bureau*)

B

▶ PRINCIPLES OF DESIGN

In the search for ways to create beauty, man has evolved principles based on observation of nature and study of worthy art. Balance, rhythm, and emphasis are a simple but inclusive trio of principles useful in achieving the basic aims of **form follows function** and **variety in unity.**

Balance

Defined as equilibrium, balance is a major principle in all phases of living—from furniture arrangements to bank accounts. Through balance we get a sense of equipoise, but this may range from static permanence through repose and suspended animation to actual motion. It is achieved when interplaying forces, attractions, or weights tend toward resolution.

There are many examples of divergent kinds of balance in nature. The Rock of Gibraltar typifies static permanence with changes too slight to be noticed. Sand dunes, in contrast, are continuously shifting but without loss of equilibrium. Trees, too, are always in a changing equilibrium because their shape changes as they grow and as winds or the seasons affect them. Thus we learn that balance can be an always-changing resolution of forces as well as a dead-weight-against-dead-weight equalization. It is also evident that balance exists in four dimensions—time as well as length, breadth, and width.

In balancing an interior, we deal with the "visual weights" of architecture and furnishings. The visual weight of anything is determined by the psychological impact it makes on us. Objects of large size or of such physically heavy material as stone command respect. Bright colors or strong contrasts of all sorts are quickly noticed and vividly remembered. Elaborate detail arouses interest while anything unusual or unexpected has an importance beyond its size. At the other pole, the small, somber, harmonious, or typical usually settle into the background. Everything in the home is a psychological factor in design, but the forcefulness of each item varies markedly. For example, a small spot of bright color can balance a large grayed area; visually, a significant painting may be as heavy as many square feet of plain wall. Well-balanced interiors hold this interplay of forces in poise.

The balance in a home is as ever-changing as is nature's equilibrium but in different ways. People are the first factor, for a room is never complete except when being used. As people move about, they not only see a home from different angles but actually change the equilibrium by the areas to which they go and the clothes they wear. The second factor is light. Natural illumination is altering every minute of the day and changes markedly with sky conditions and the seasons. Only within small limits can its effects be controlled, yet it affects our homes drastically. For example, subtle nuances of color and very fine detail can be readily appreciated in moderately bright light, but they are all but obscured in very strong sunlight or dusk. Artificial light can be precisely controlled but has to be flexible to meet a number of needs, and flexibility brings variance. The third factor is the composite of all the little things that happen in the course of a day—the reading material and other portable paraphernalia brought in and left—as well as the modifications that come with the months and years—the scarcely noticed fading of textiles and mellowing of wood, to say nothing of the replacement of outworn or unwanted objects. What does all this mean? Simply that in view of these inevitable changes, many of them beyond our strict control, the fundamental pattern of equilibrium had better be strong enough to take these onslaughts in stride, to absorb rather than be destroyed by them.

Three Types of Balance. It is customary to differentiate three types of balance: **symmetrical**, **asymmetrical**, and **radial.**

Symmetrical balance (Fig. 94), also known as formal or passive balance, is achieved when one side of the object is the exact reverse (or mirror image) of the other half. Our clothes, furniture, and household equipment are nearly all symmetrical to fit our symmetrical bodies. Classical architecture, including American eighteenth-century work, is also based on symmetry because of the implied stateliness and reserve that are qualities admired by Classicists. It is easy to appreciate because we can see quickly that, since one side is the reversed replica of the other, the two must be in equilibrium. The effect is typically quiet and reposed, perhaps because it demands little effort from the observer. Its overtones of stateliness and dignity are not easy to explain, but certainly people stand or sit as symmetrically as they comfortably can when they wish to appear dignified. Symmetrical balance tends to stress the center, creating a logical focal point for something one wishes to emphasize. But the resultant division into two equal parts usually reduces apparent size.

Although the above observations are generally true of symmetrical balance as typically used in homes, it is important to note that totally different effects are possible. Violent rhythms or swirling curves, regardless of symmetrical arrangement, will not seem quiet or reposed. Shapes or colors that lead the eyes away from the middle weaken the focal point at the center.

Symmetrical balance usually seems formal and static. (*George McLean*)

At a commonplace level, symmetrical balance is as simple as *a b a*, the formula from which it is derived, and this simplicity contributes to its popularity. Do not assume, though, that because symmetrical balance is basically simple and easy it cannot be subtly and imaginatively handled as in the Port Royal parlor. Although few entire homes or even single rooms are completely symmetrical (utility and the need for variety rule this out), many have such symmetrical parts as centered fireplaces (Figs. 86A and B) or a sofa with identical tables and lamps at both ends (Fig. 91A). Often, however, symmetry is forced arbitrarily, or comes out of habit or laziness, when there is no real need for it. Frequently then symmetry interferes with convenience. For example, doors in centers of walls are seldom logical because they leave two equal areas that may be difficult to furnish unless the room is very large, and they bring traffic into the room's center.

Symmetry is indicated *but not dictated* when:

- formal or reposed effects are wanted;
- focusing attention on something important is desirable;
- use suggests symmetry;
- contrast with natural surroundings is sought.

Symmetry is a good way to achieve unmistakable order. Use it when it comes naturally but do not force it because of the false assumption that symmetry is "correct." For variety and utility, combine it with asymmetrical balance, but with one or the other dominant.

Asymmetrical balance, also referred to as informal, active, or occult balance, is achieved when the visual weights are equivalent but not identical (Fig. 95). This is the principle of the lever or seesaw—weight multiplied by distance from center. Both physical and visual weights follow

Asymmetrical balance suggests informality and movement. (*George McLean*)

similar laws in that heavy weights near the center counterbalance lighter ones farther away. This type of balance is often found in buildings or gardens designed to harmonize with their natural surroundings and to use space most efficiently as well as in furniture arrangements planned for convenience.

The effects of asymmetrical balance differ markedly from those of symmetry. Asymmetry stirs us more quickly and vigorously, and it suggests movement, spontaneity, and informality. Because it is less obvious than formal balance, it arouses our curiosity to see how equilibrium was found. Subject to no formula, asymmetry allows full freedom and flexibility in arrangements for utility as well as for beauty and individuality.

Asymmetrical balance is indicated when:

- informality and flexibility are desired;
- an effect of spaciousness is sought;
- use suggests asymmetry;
- harmony with nature is a goal.

Contemporary trends toward informal, relaxed living find apt expression in homes planned asymmetrically just as those of the eighteenth century favored symmetry as an environment for the formality of their occupants.

Radial balance results when all parts are balanced and repeated around the center as in the spokes of a wheel or the petals of a daisy. Its chief characteristic is a circular movement out from, toward, or around a center. In homes it is found chiefly in such circular objects as plates and bowls, lighting fixtures, flower arrangements, and textile patterns. Although of lesser importance than the two preceding types, radial balance makes its own distinctive contribution in many small objects.

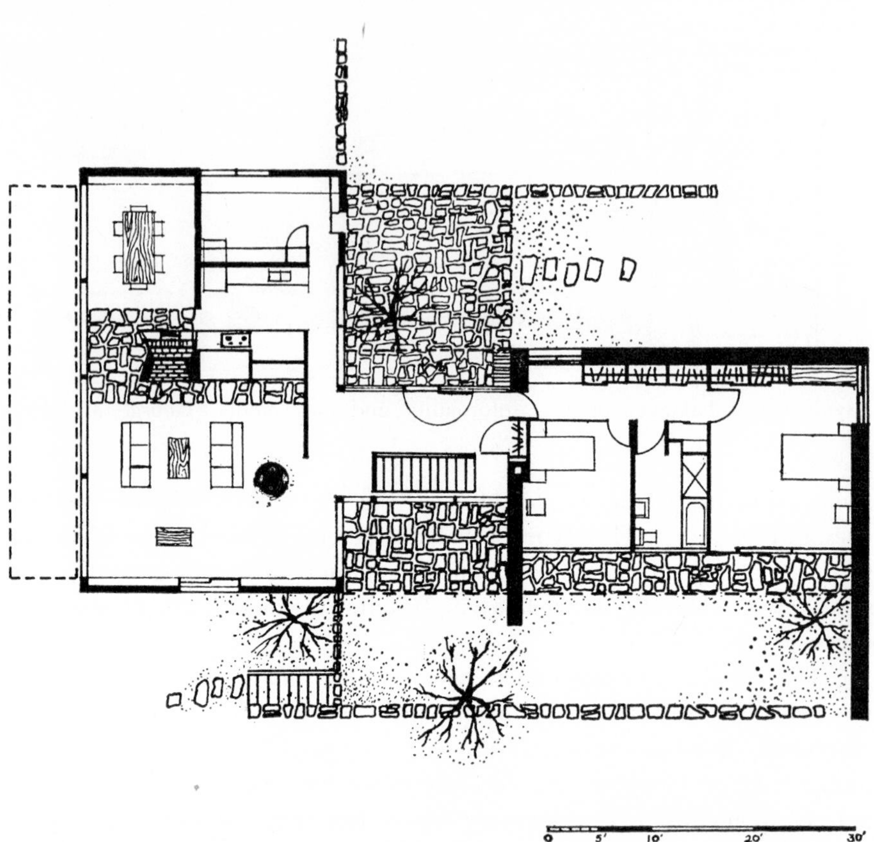

A sensitive example of asymmetrical balance in a Connecticut house plan. The larger size of the group living wing (*left*) has been counterbalanced by the greater weight of the thick, projecting bedroom wing walls. Areas of flagstone paving, indoors and out, set up an interdependent resolution of visual weights. Marcel Breuer, architect.

Earlier in this section we stated that balance applies to all aspects of living. Figure 96 demonstrates that house plans, quite as much as living rooms or abstract paintings, can be sensitively equilibrated. In this binuclear plan, two wings of different size and shape are asymmetrically disposed and joined by a somewhat off-center hall and two paved terraces. Interior partitions subdivide the wings into spaces counterbalanced in size and shape not only for use but for esthetic satisfaction. This aspect of design is seldom noticed until you walk through, or live in, a house. Then it may become even more important than the composure of a painting on a wall, for it consciously or subconsciously affects us all of the time. A well-balanced house plan gives a continuing sense of assurance and order, a feeling that things are as they ought to be.

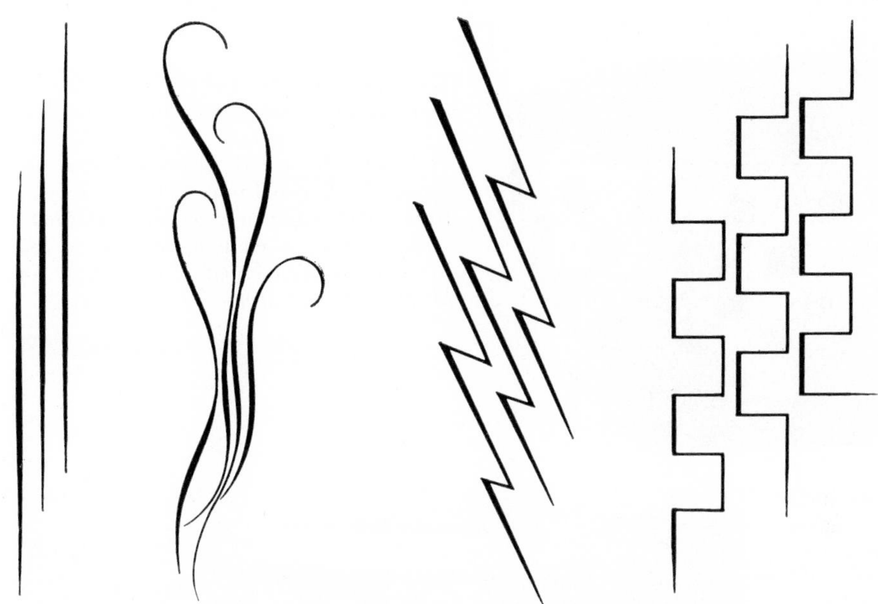

Rhythm is one of the most expressive potentialities at our command. Even lines alone can suggest dignified poise, fanciful freedom, agitated energy, or syncopated variations. (*Walter Zawojski*)

Rhythm

Defined as continuity, recurrence, or organized movement, rhythm is a second major design principle and is one through which an underlying unity and evolving variety can be gained. It is exemplified in time by the **repetition** of our heartbeats, the **alternation** of day and night, and the **progression** of one season into another. In form and space it is seen in the more or less repetitive character of the leaves on a tree, the alternating light and dark stripes of a zebra, and the sequences and transitions of curves in a river.

Rhythm contributes to the beauty of homes in several ways. Unity and harmony are consequences of rhythmic repetition and progression. Character and individuality are in part determined by the fundamental rhythms —gay and light in the Port Royal parlor, dynamic and rugged in Mr. Wright's living room, and precise and serene in the Gordons' home (Fig. 12). Lastly, homes gain a quality of "aliveness" through the implied movement and direction that rhythm induces. This, however, is fully achieved only when a consistent pattern of rhythms prevails. For proof, compare Figures 91B and 100A.

A

The fundamentals of rhythm are simple, their inspired realization another matter.

Left. Repeated black squares, arranged in diagonal rows that can be read from left to right or vice versa, alternate with lines in a contemporary bowl by Marguerite Wildenhain. (*Courtesy of M. H. deYoung Memorial Museum*)

Right. Exuberant, progressing lines make a Chinese jar from the Sung Dynasty seem almost to move as one looks at it. (*Los Angeles County Museum*)

B

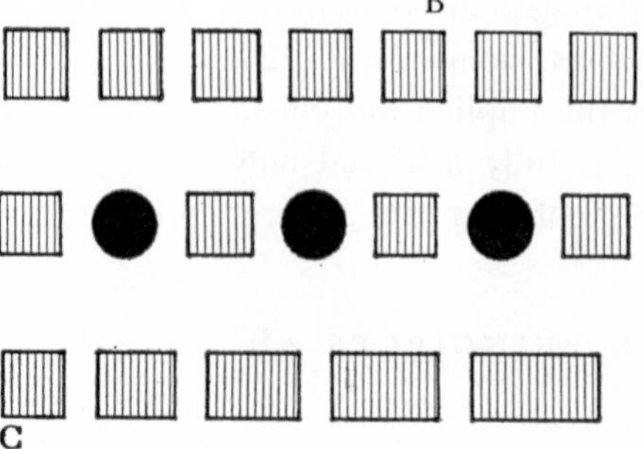

C

Left. Identical squares at regular intervals establish a strong, stable rhythm through *repetition.* Putting black circles between gray squares develops a strongly accented rhythm through the *alternating* repetition of two contrasting shapes and weights. A simple *progression* from square to narrow rectangle produces a more complex, evolving rhythm. (*George McLean*)

Repetition and **progression** are the two primary ways of developing rhythm. **Repetition** is as simple as repeated rectangles or curves, colors or textures; but it can be given more intriguing complexity by **alternating** shapes, colors, or textures. Even the most commonplace home is full of repetition, evidence of its universal appeal and also of the fact that simply repeating anything anywhere is not very stimulating. Some useful guides are:

- Repeat strongly and consistently the forms or colors that underline the basic character.
- Avoid repeating that which is ordinary or commonplace.
- Too much repetition, unrelieved by contrast of some sort, leads to monotony.
- Too little repetition leads to confusion.

Progression is a sequence or transition produced by increasing or decreasing one or more qualities. It is ordered, systematic change. Because progression suggests not only movement but changing movement toward a goal, it is more lively and dynamic than is repetition. It is also a little more difficult to manage and more likely to attract notice, which suggests that it be used in important parts of the home.

Progressions of size, shape, and direction are handsomely dealt with in the dominant portion of the living room in Figure 100A. Above the fireplace is a horizontal rectangle that is the largest expanse of uninterrupted wall. Next comes the wall to which the vine clings, smaller in size and moderately vertical in feeling. This progression is brought to a conclusion by the smallest unit, the definitely vertical pier behind the built-in end table. Accompanying these size and shape changes is a change of direction, for these walls show an angular progression of location. Notice, too, how

Much of the visual appeal of Windsor chairs lies in their surprisingly complex rhythmic patterns. The equal spacing of the spindles in the back together with the shape repetition of the arm supports and legs stabilizes the design. Within this framework of regular recurrence are many kinds of progression—all the curves, the direction and slight tapering of the spindles, and the heights of those above the arm rests—which vitalize the forms. (*Matt Kahn*)

A

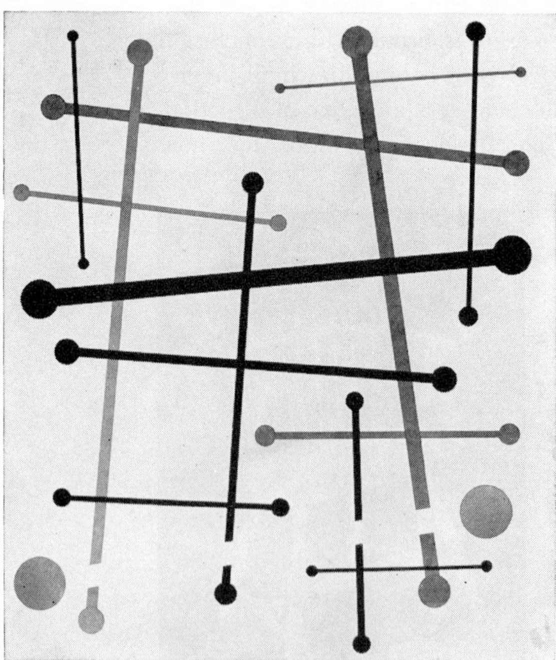

B

Above. The walls in an Arizona living room have a pronounced progression from large to small size, from horizontal to vertical shape, and in their angular placement. The uniform concrete blocks generate a steady, quiet repetition. Blaine Drake, architect. (*Photograph by Julius Shulman*)

Left. Progressions from long to short, thick to thin, black to medium gray enliven a variations-on-a-theme textile design by Angelo Testa.

the lowered ceiling seems to originate in the fireplace wall, just touches the middle wall, and appears to carry through the vertical pier to the wall beyond. Also observe that the ledge and seat begin by paralleling the center wall, then angle out into the room to add one more step to the angular sequence of position of the walls behind. The repeated grid pattern of the concrete blocks emphasizes each change much more than would walls of smooth plaster. Progressions of several kinds are also illustrated in "Stirs" (Fig. 100B). Fifteen similar shapes, none duplicating any other, progress, but not with perfect consistency, from large near the center to small toward the edges. There is also transition, again not monotonously regular, from dark to lighter values. This pattern equally well demonstrates some of the possibilities of variations on a theme, a kind of diversity in oneness, and a lively asymmetric balance.

Emphasis

The third design principle, emphasis, is often referred to as dominance and subordination. Emphasis is concerned with giving just significance to each part and to the whole, calling more attention to the important parts than to those of lesser consequence and introducing variety that will not become either frittery or chaotic. It has to do with focal points, "rest areas," and progressive degrees of interest in between. Without emphasis, homes would be as monotonous as the ticking of a clock, and without subordination, as clamorous and competitive as New York City's Times Square.

Many homes suffer from lack of appropriate dominance and subordination. Such homes include the room in which everything has about the same dead-level, dispirited quality of nonimportance as well as the room in which too many things shout loudly for attention (Figs. 91A and B). Neither room is satisfying. Regrettably less frequent are those rooms in which intentness is directed to a few important elements—a substantial fireplace, a fine large piece of furniture or a painting, a window with an outlook shown to advantage by quieter areas. In these rooms, you are neither bored nor overstimulated. Attention is held and relaxed at many levels.

Two steps are involved in creating a pattern of emphasis: deciding how important each unit is or should be and then giving it the appropriate degree of visual importance. This is not so simple as the superficial concept of "centers of interest and backgrounds" because you are dealing with a scale of degrees, not two categories, of significance. Although this too is an oversimplification, you might start by thinking in terms of four levels, such as emphatic, dominant, subdominant, and subordinate. It might be worth while to list everything in a room under one of these headings.

Emphatic	*Dominant*	*Subdominant*	*Subordinate*
Fireplace	View of garden	Wall treatment	Floor
	Major furniture group: sofa, chairs, end and coffee tables, lamps, large picture	Desk and smaller pictures	Ceiling
		Plants and flower arrangements	Draperies
			Radio-phonograph

If this were your list, your next step might be consideration of such ways of making the fireplace emphatic as size, position, design, and materials. A large, unobtrusively curtained window could key up the view of an attractive garden. The major furniture group might be arranged to direct attention toward the fireplace but also permit one to see the garden. Its size would automatically make it important, but this could be built up, or lessened, by the design of the furnishings together with the color and pattern of the upholstery. Walls of wood or of plaster painted a subdued but not lifeless color are possibilities. Placed in an out-of-the-way location, the desk might be enlivened with small pictures. Plants and flowers could be disposed where needed. Presumably the floor would have little if any pattern and be a neutral color while painted plaster suggests itself for the ceiling. The radio-phonograph could be subordinated by building it into the wall or incorporating it with bookshelves or an end table.

Other conditions and desires would lead to different solutions. An extensive view might become the room's emphatic feature. Fine antique furniture might justify concentration on it or distinctive Oriental rugs might become the center of attention.

Many people, however, do not have an impressive fireplace or a noteworthy collection of furniture or rugs. In such circumstances a wise procedure might be to concentrate spending on one large, important piece of furniture or on a painting, to locate it prominently and augment its attractiveness by grouping smaller furniture and accessories near by. Funds permitting, one or two other good articles not quite so emphatic as the major piece might be secured and made the centers of secondary groups. Still less costly is an out-of-the-ordinary color scheme achieved by painting walls, ceiling, furniture, and maybe even the floor so that the color harmonies become noteworthy. That these do not exhaust the possibilities is illustrated in the four rooms shown on pages 103 and 104. In each of these rooms, dull areas have been transformed into lively ones that afford our naturally roving eyes an interesting focus. They also demonstrate that the whole can be greater than the sum of its parts.

Emphasis in a room lacking a natural focus can be built up by concentrating furniture and accessories into large units.

Right. A stool, bench, and wall shelf plus easily changed prints and accessories make an ordinary wall eventful. (*Dunbar Furniture Company*)

Below. Two daybeds, a corner storage unit and distinctive lamp, and a line of framed prints join their individualities to make a corner of a room worth attention. (The Stylist Magazine)

A

B

A

Walls, made visually interesting with large decorations or furniture, become important.

Left. In a Chicago apartment, a large wall map lifts to significance a simple furniture group without overshadowing it. (*Marshall Field & Company*)

Below. A wall lined with book-filled shelves teamed with a library table, a settle, and two chairs gives consequence to one end of a room. Henry Hill, architect. (*Photograph by Morley Baer*)

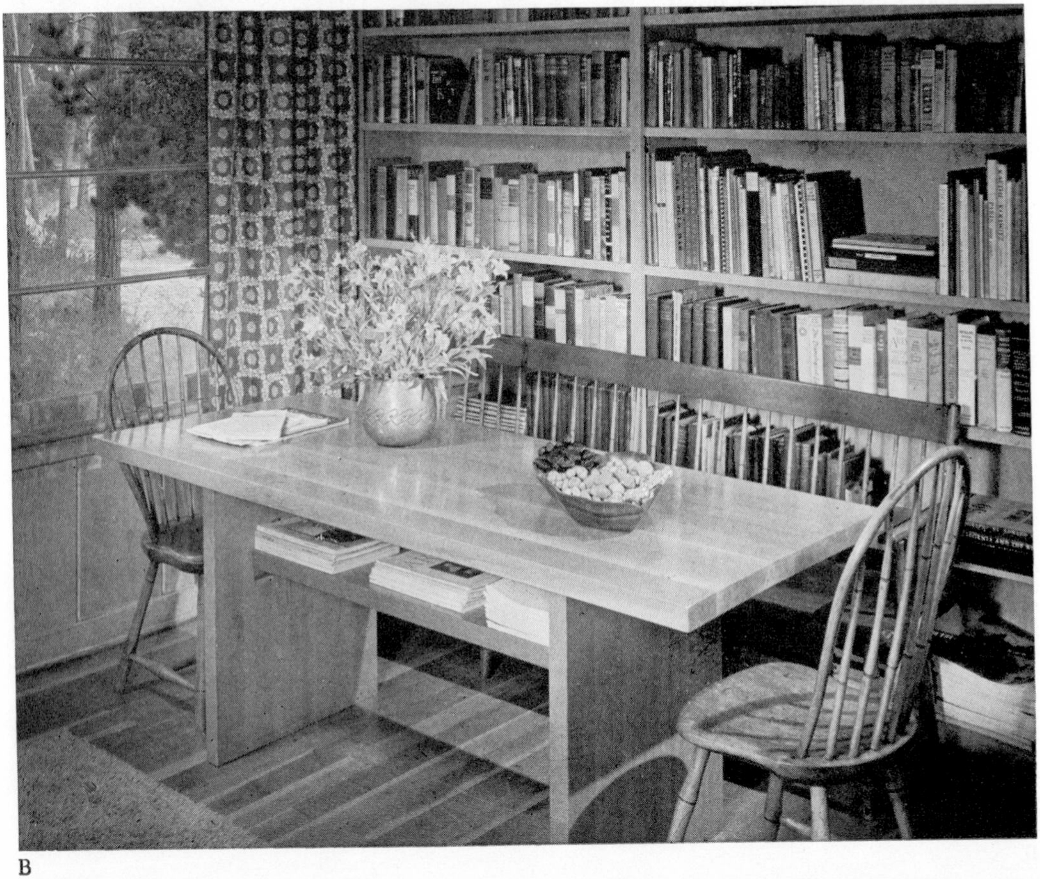

B

In thinking about dominance in your home:

- Decide on the levels of importance of different parts of the home. Play up each according to its significance.
- Limit the number of interesting centers. One dominant and two or three subdominant are about as much as a typical room can take.
- Arrange the parts in proportion to their import. Central positions, for example, are conspicuous. Also, an object gains if "built up" with others less important, a practice widely followed (for beauty as well as use) in relating tables, chairs, lamps, and pictures to a sofa.
- Use the attraction of visual weights thoughtfully. Large forms, intense colors, bright lights, contrast or opposition, and anything off the beaten path compels attention.
- Elimination of the superfluous, of that which obscures or confuses, is often one of the best and least expensive ways to emphasize basic character.

► OTHER PRINCIPLES

Harmony, proportion, and scale are important concepts but not quite so comprehensive as the three major principles discussed earlier.

Harmony, defined as consonance, concord or agreement among the parts, is one facet of unity. It springs from the same sources, such as emphasizing a single motivating idea and making good use of repetition and similarity.

Proportion is generously defined by Webster as "the relation of one portion to another, or to the whole . . . ; symmetry; harmony; balance. . . ." If used to include relationships of all types, proportion is undoubtedly the most significant of all principles, but it attains this significance by becoming so all-inclusive that it is difficult to use. As is often done in art discussions, its meaning can be delimited to *shape relationships.*

Relationships of forms, one to another, can range from the repetitive harmony of identical shapes progressively to the dissonance of a square allied with a jagged "free form." (*George McLean*)

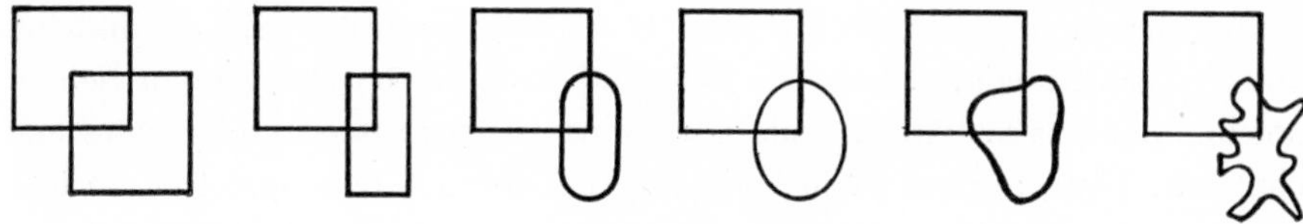

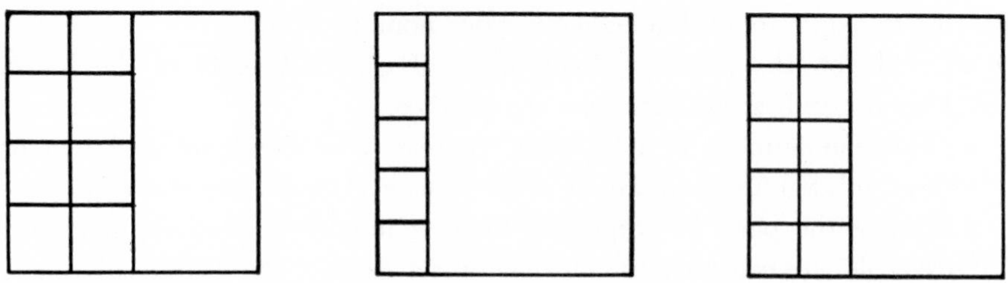

The proportions of shapes affect their expressive qualities. *Left.* A square divided into two equal parts seems logical but not very interesting. *Center.* Markedly unequal division produces contrast and emphasis. *Right.* Some persons find proportions approximating those of the "Golden Section" especially satisfying. (*George McLean*)

In spite of enormous expenditure of time and energy, no foolproof system of proportioning that holds good in all cases has been devised. The so-called "Golden Section" which often gives safe, pleasing results comes nearest. It consists of dividing a line or form so that the smaller portion has the same ratio to the larger as the larger has to the whole. The progression 1:2:3:5:8:13:21 . . . , in which each term is the sum of the two preceding ones, approximates this relationship. For those in need of formulas this is as good as any, but its applications are limited.

All efforts to define "perfect proportions" fall into their true insignificance when one deals with real problems involving use, economy, individuality, and materials. Few persons complain that a fork or floor-lamp stand is poorly proportioned because it is long and thin, that a soup bowl or a sofa is ugly because it is low and broad: they are shaped that way for very good reasons which all recognize. Should we discard the whole concept of proportion because some writers have ossified it? No, but it does cast suspicion on any formulas.

Scale, referring to *size relationships* between parts or between parts and the whole, is closely allied to emphasis. In home design, scale is based on the physical dimensions of our bodies and on our spiritual needs: it is expressed in the actual or apparent size of objects (Fig. 107) and the size and character of their detail.

A vital consideration is "human scale." Physically, typical persons are between 5 and 6 feet tall and weigh between 100 and 200 pounds. These figures act as a yardstick for sizes of rooms, furniture, and equipment. Suitably scaled homes make us look and feel like normal human beings, not like midgets or giants. Scale also helps us appreciate size by clues and contrasts. Thus, a great plain looks larger if there is even one tree on it, a sandy beach if there are a few rocks. These are said to give it "scale." Homes need this too. Draperies and upholstery, for example, can give scale to windows and furniture.

Rising costs have made today's houses considerably smaller than the houses of fifty years ago, and to compensate for their reduction in size they are smaller in scale. So is most contemporary furniture. Massive, bulbous, heavily carved chairs and sofas are rapidly giving way to those that are light in weight and small in bulk, held above slender unadorned wood or metal supports. It is a normal process of suiting the scale of our homes to their size.

We can, though, adapt ourselves to a wide range of different scales if *all major elements are consistent.* The two rooms for contemporary Americans in Figures 108A and B could hardly be less alike, yet each is excellent in its own way for its intended purpose. The difference in scale is startling. One fireplace, small in size and recessed in the wall, is made small in scale by the delicately detailed tile border, the charming little firescreen, and the refined wood panels and moldings. The other is a massive block jutting boldly out into the room. Large, textured concrete blocks and vigorously rough stonework stand for what they are without any distracting detail. Almost every component of each room is consistent, even the bouquet of tulips in one and the coarse-leaved banana plant seen through the glass wall of the other. Imagine—if possible—the lamps or coffee table from the first room placed in the second. Without some contrast, however, the effect of any kind of scale is weakened. In the first room, the large-patterned textile used for walls and draperies alerts us to the smallness of everything else but remains consistent through the intricacy within the pattern. The normal-sized pillows, books, and pottery in the second emphasize the boldness of other elements.

Scale is a matter of detailing as well as of size. Two chairs can be the same size but one looks smaller because the parts are slender and refined. (*George McLean*)

A

Above. A sitting room cozily small in scale, consistent in basic forms and elaboration of detail but accented by the bold wall covering. (*Gump's*)

Below. An exceptionally vigorous living room in Mexico. Almost everything is large in scale, striking in its bold forms, open and uncluttered. Anshen and Allen, architects.

B

Scale, however, is only one of the factors that so sharply differentiate these two rooms. Some of the others are tabulated below:

	Sitting Room	*Living Space*
Form Follows Function	Small, intimate, secluded, formal room for a few persons.	Large, free, open, informal space for groups.
	Forms are delicate, refined, richly detailed.	Forms are large, vigorous, rough, and without ornament.
Variety in Unity	Unity through consistent, small-scale, curvilinear refinement.	Unity through large areas of a few materials treated naturally; straight lines predominate.
	Pronounced variety of size, shape, material, and ornament. Decided contrast of scenic wall pattern.	Limited diversity—but strong and compelling. Strong contrast of solidity and openness.
Balance	Symmetrical.	Asymmetrical.
Rhythm	Easy, graceful, and flowing but self-containing.	Strong and direct, angular, continuing from one object to another and beyond.
Emphasis	Many emphatic areas and small spots.	Emphasis is on whole or large units, almost no concentration in small areas.
Harmony	Consistency of all parts.	Consistency of all parts.
Proportion	Slender.	Blocky.
Scale	Small.	Large.

Design is a matter of relationships, and the aims and principles discussed are all concerned with the relationships among all the parts and the whole of the house. *Form follows function* describes the relationship between total design and purpose; *variety in unity* deals with diversity as related to oneness; *balance, rhythm,* and *emphasis* refer to the ways in which various components are selected and related as means to equilibrium, continuity, and dominance and subordination. Considered together, they help us achieve beauty and, since they are guides rather than rules, offer ample opportunities to express individuality. At one time beauty was regarded as being closely akin to uselessness, individuality was associated with freakishness. Utility and economy, substantial practical partners, were on the other side of the fence. We realize now that such thinking was unsound, that no one of our goals is at odds with the others, that the design of our homes can relate utility, economy, beauty, and individuality—if the problem is grasped and solved realistically. But in this chapter we have consciously concentrated on design for beauty.

6. Space and Form

WRITERS USE WORDS, mathematicians use numbers, and musicians use sounds to express their verbal, mathematical, and musical ideas. In home design the vocabulary is called the plastic elements. These include *space* and *form,* which together with the somewhat less important *line* and *texture,* will be emphasized in this chapter. *Light* and *color* will be treated in Chapter 7. Much as such chemical elements as oxygen and carbon form the compounds of the physical world, the plastic elements comprise our visual environment. And they are the means through which designers, in accord with the aims and principles of design, create expressive beauty.

When architect Willis Mills designed his own home in New Canaan, Connecticut (Figs. 112A and B, 113A and B), he chose what many would call an unbuildable site, because there is a 45-foot drop between relatively level areas at the top and bottom. No ordinary house could have been built

Above. Tapio Wirkkala's crystal vase is vigorously free in form. (*Karhula*)

on this rocky hillside, which challenged him to design an exceptional house on three levels. Topography dictated that garage and entrance hall be on the top floor, which also seemed a logical level for a secluded bedroom-and-study-unit high among the treetops. The living-dining area, kitchen, and another bedroom were placed on the middle level with good indoor-outdoor relationship provided by a large terrace toward the southeast and a small deck on the northwest. A game and a heater room are in the "basement" that emerges above the ground toward the south.

Space, as far as the eye can see, is the chief element in the design and it is fully exploited in the relationship of architecture to environment. As approached from the road, the house is seen as an unpretentious, one-story block. That this "block" is not a solid mass but a series of planes enclosing space is quietly stated: the side walls and roof project beyond the end wall and the recessed end wall is painted in a contrasting color. This calm horizontality heightens the effect of what happens as one goes along a flagstone walk to a narrowing deck. In contrast to the security of stone set in the ground, this light wooden deck boldly projects into space as a series of planes. It becomes a movement into space inviting exploration. From it one's eyes can freely roam through the trees, up to the sky or down to the terrace and rocky hillside. Carrying through a transparent plane of glass at a right angle, the deck becomes an entrance hall which offers a momentary glimpse down into the two-story living room. Then comes a securely enclosed stairway. Near the bottom one can pause on a landing opening to the southwest deck, then turn and go down two steps to receive the full impact of the lofty living area. From here the spatial drama of the site is heightened by a two-story window wall facing the southeast terrace and an unexpectedly tall window offering a close-up study of the trees to the south. The one-story dining alcove, recessed under the entrance hall, emphasizes through contrast the living room's height. Thus anyone coming into this home experiences a carefully planned sequence of spaces contrasting in size, shape, and direction, enclosed by opaque walls and expanded through glass to terraces and the landscape.

With the exception of the three diagonal decks and terrace, the space and form of this home are precisely rectangular. These accentuate the irregularities of the site and carry forward a New England tradition of building on the square. The hillside suggested predominantly vertical forms but these are counterbalanced by the horizontal decks and terraces. Although no detail imitates historical work, the forms are as simple and forthright as vernacular architecture in this region. No jogs or ornament breaks the quiet unity of the flat enclosing surfaces. Here, though, similarity ends, for the

A

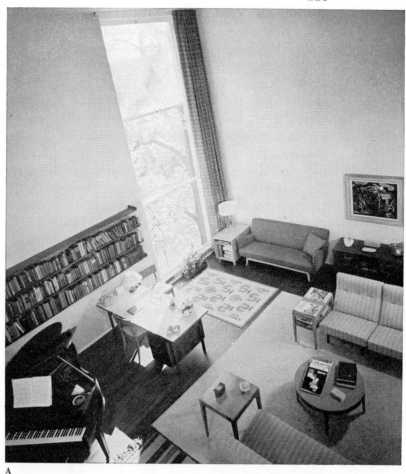

Strict rectangularity unifies architect Willis Mills' own home.

Left above. At the top of a steep site, the garage is firmly anchored to the ground. Along the left side, a walk and wood deck lead to the entrance.

Left below. Precise detailing heightens the drama of two-story windows, boldly cantilevered deck, and the plunging slope beyond.

Above. In the living room, the excitement of the hillside has been exploited by making its two-story height apparent from the entrance balcony and by the very tall window. (*Photographs by Joseph W. Molitor*)

Right. The uncomplicated rectangles of the plan, in keeping with the orderliness of the whole design, burrow into the rock and extend out into space.

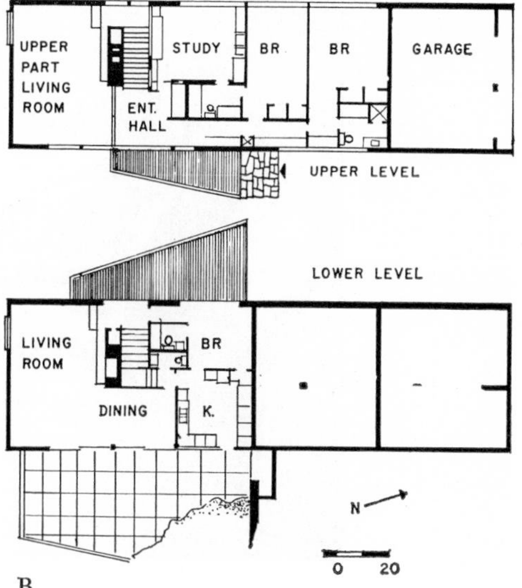

B

disposition of forms is calculated to make space a free-flowing continuity rather than a series of rooms separated from each other and the site.

Line plays an active part in that it accentuates the dominant directions of the planes with which it is integral. One might first notice the pronounced vertical grooves in the natural redwood exterior, the linear thinness of wood and metal between planes of glass, which echo the slender vertical trunks of the surrounding trees. Strips of wood dividing the concrete terrace into squares perform numerous esthetic functions: relieve the monotony and humanize the scale of a large plane of concrete; echo the rectangularity of the house; and throw into relief the free curve of the flower bed, the natural shapes of rocks and plants.

Textures are sensitively employed. Basically, they show a limited range of varying degrees of smoothness—sanded redwood and white wood trim, glass in sliding aluminum sashes on exterior, evenly surfaced plaster walls and wood floors inside. There are, however, contrasts. The smooth, precise restraint of the exterior is a foil for rocks and trees. Inside, textured rugs and upholstery plus shelves filled with books are sufficient punctuation in view of the landscape textures made integral with the interior through large areas of glass.

A screen, a desk, and a low table have been economically joined in one unit. Intersecting and projecting planes, clearly defined, allow space to flow through and around what might have been a bulky mass. (*Photograph by William Howland. Courtesy of* House Beautiful)

That refreshing organizations of space are not limited to new houses on acreage sites is illustrated in Figure 114. The problem faced by the occupants of this one-room apartment was that of segregating sleeping from living space without making confining cubicles. Their solution was a free-standing screen of perforated Masonite. On the bedroom side, a stock door veneered with Philippine mahogany makes an ample desk while on the other side a similar door, at lower height, forms a coffee table. In addition to its multiple usefulness, this piece of furniture activates a monotonous room. It is, in fact, almost a diagram of the visual and emotional impact possible to achieve with intersecting hovering planes, undisguised materials, and structure.

► SPACE

Defined as the emptiness, void, or interval between things, space is the most vital plastic element in home design. Geoffrey Scott has described its importance in these words.

> . . . Architecture alone of the Arts can give space its full value. It can surround us with a void of three dimensions; and whatever delight may be derived from that is the gift of architecture alone. Painting can depict space; poetry, like Shelley's, can recall its image; music can give us its analogy; but architecture deals with space directly; it uses space as a material and sets us in the midst. . . .
>
> But though we may overlook it, space affects us and can control our spirit; and a large part of the pleasure we obtain from architecture—pleasure which seems unaccountable or for which we do not trouble to account—springs in reality from space. Even from a utilitarian point of view, space is logically our end. To enclose a space is the object of building; when we build we do but detach a convenient quantity of space, seclude it and protect it, and all architecture springs from that necessity. But aesthetically space is even more supreme. . . . He designs his space as a work of art; that is, he attempts through its means to excite a certain mood in those who enter it.*

Space suggests the possibility of change, freedom to move bodily, visually, or psychologically until we collide with or are averted by a barrier. For this reason, space, the least tangible plastic element, nonetheless is preeminent. We live *with* and move *around* form, but we live and move *in* space. As we move through such sensitively designed space as in the Mills' house, we participate in its expansion and contraction as naturally as we breathe. As we look at or walk around such furnishings as the space-divider,

* Geoffrey Scott: *The Architecture of Humanism;* Doubleday, 1954, pp. 168-169. Reprinted by permission of the publisher.

our eyes, or maybe our hands and feet, explore what is open and what is closed. Anyone who has ridden in a crowded car to a beach knows the sense of release afforded by getting out into expanses of sand, water, and sky. And no one can forget the deep breath and bodily stretch evoked by a larger segment of space after a long telephone conversation in a crowded booth. We adapt ourselves as well as we can to the space that envelopes and includes us. In doing so, we share in its triumphs or its failures.

Many contemporary ways of enclosing space economically, usefully, of satisfying the spirit, and of making it seem larger than its actual dimensions are illustrated in an inexpensive tract house (Figs. 117A and B).

First is an unmistakable ordered unity of large surfaces, strong and clear enough to be appreciated at once yet with enough surprises to keep it interesting. Neither rigid nor static, this order emphasizes spatial continuity by encouraging one's eyes to roam freely in many directions—through the south window wall or the high and low glass to the west, up to the sloping ceiling, through and under the furniture.

Second, enclosing forms have been treated as planes, not solid masses, except for the sturdy brick fireplace. These planes preserve their independence through differing size and shape, direction, and material. From wall to wall, the floor is covered with soft-textured carpet that is in friendly opposition to the surface qualities of glass, plaster, wood, and brick. It maintains its position as a stabilizing element. The ceiling, in contrast, expresses movement gently in its two sloping planes, dynamically in the ridge beam that accentuates the room's longer dimension. These rhythmic continuities are emphasized by the lively interplay of glass and wood in the west wall. The design of the west wall deserves special attention because it shows one of the most effective devices for opening interior space and relating indoors to outdoors. It is a screen against weather and visual intrusion rather than a wall in the conventional sense. Instead of filling the space from top to bottom and corner to corner, it stops short of one corner and the ceiling but interpenetrates the window wall and continues as a protection for the living terrace. Its independence is strengthened by its material—redwood used vertically with pronounced grooves and stained like driftwood. The carefully calculated yet unexpected high and low glass gives surprise and contrast of dark and light, up, across, and down movements, which add up to a "sequence of unfolding visual experience." The difference from conventional planning is illustrated in the diagram at the top of page 118. Space is not only borrowed from outdoors, but the planes become active esthetic forces rather than merely enclosing backgrounds.

A

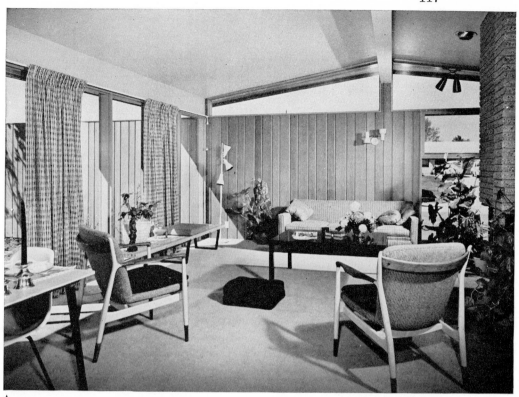

Many devices make this small Kansas house designed by Harold Himes seem large.

Above. In the living room, glass at the right and above the redwood screen wall allows sight lines to travel beyond it. Continuing the wall as a fence sheltering an outdoor terrace doubles the living space, visually and usably. (*Photograph by Julius Shulman*)

Right. The plan, efficiently zoned, joins two protected outdoor living areas to their enclosed counterparts.

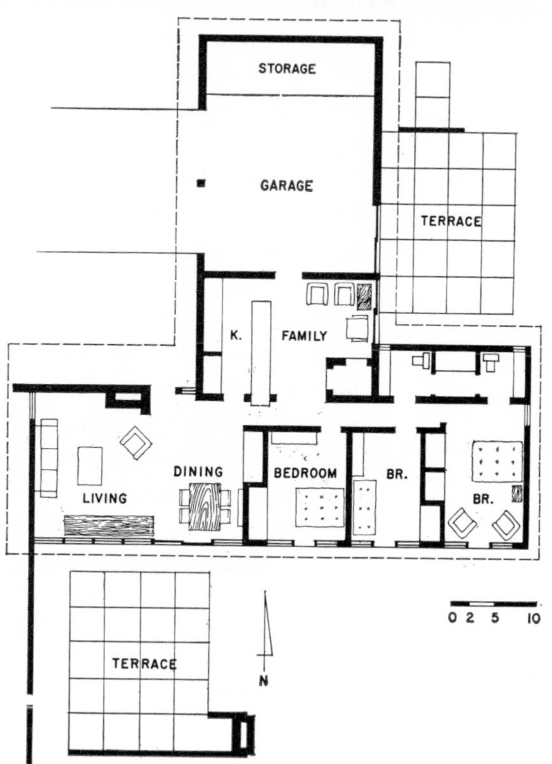

B

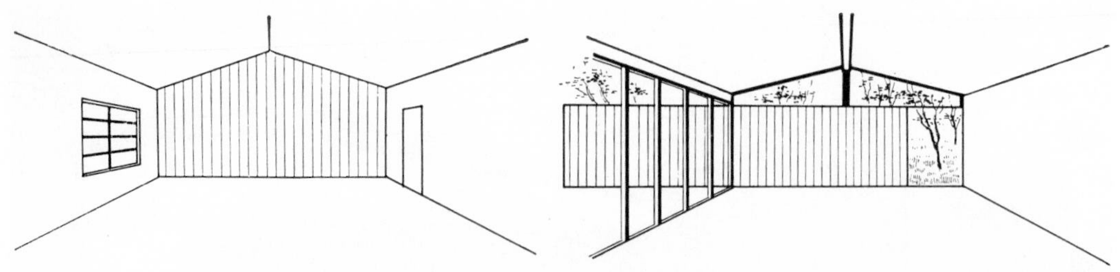

A room seems small and confining when openings are small and corners are tight. (*Right*) The same room if space is borrowed from outdoors or adjoining rooms. (*Walter Zowajski*)

Third, furniture selection and arrangement contribute handsomely to the whole effect. Furniture has been limited to a minimum to avoid an overcrowded feeling. Moderately small in size and in scale, chairs, tables, and the bench are simple but spirited in form. The coffee table is as steady and severely rectangular as the floor. The bench against the window wall is lighter and more active as befits its location: the top is of spaced slats in keeping with the alternating solids and voids of the window wall, while the angles of the supports are similar to those in the ceilings. Showing their sculptural structure frankly, the chairs combine straight, angled, and curved forms. They were specifically designed to stand free in a room and, consequently, to be good looking from any angle. All the furniture mentioned so far stands well off the floor on slender supports to allow unimpeded vision underneath. Only the sofa is bulky and enclosing. Appropriately placed against a solid wall, it contrasts with the airy furniture as the fireplace does with the areas of glass.

Unprecedented in its imaginative boldness and still unsurpassed in its beauty, the Robie house (Figs. 119A and B) designed by Frank Lloyd Wright and built in Chicago in 1907 remains one of the greatest of contemporary homes. Although suffering the early ridicule that is the fate of most important advances in the arts, it has inspired and influenced domestic architecture as much as any building of this century. Long before most architects and home builders had awakened to the fact that they were living in the twentieth century, Mr. Wright demonstrated a full realization of ways to create space-form relationships beautiful in themselves, expressive of modern technology, and, most important, of the life of the people who live in them.

This conquest of space, as vital to man as any in the sciences, resulted from an analysis and dissection of the stereotype house, a sorting out and evaluating of its many components, and then a reorganization of them with

A

The Robie House in Chicago, designed by Frank Lloyd Wright and a magnificent work of art in itself, demonstrated many concepts in planning and construction that are still being explored fifty years later.

Above. A superb statement of his ideas of space-form organization, the exterior gains vitality through planes projecting out into space, repose and solidity from the substantial central mass. (*Photograph by Bill Engdahl. Hedrich-Blessing*)

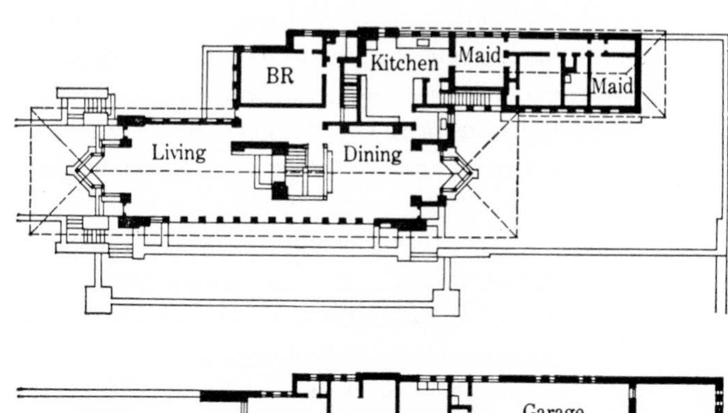

B

Right. The plan of the living and dining, billiard and play areas, flowing around the fireplace-stairwell core in the center, exemplifies Mr. Wright's belief in unconstrained, fluent, constantly varied spatial relationships.

expansive vitality. The open plan makes the space flow as one room intersected by vertical planes for use and for the esthetic pleasure afforded by advancing and retreating planes. This spirited sequence of movement pervades every part of the house because Mr. Wright treated plan, interior, exterior, and landscape as an organic unity. Windows in continuous bands become transparent planes for light and outlook rather than holes punched in walls. In design and material, the walls unite inside and out to underscore the relationship of the building to space around and beyond it. Roofs projecting varied distances beyond supporting walls temper the light, shelter terraces, and stretch the house out into its site.

► FORM

Defined as three-dimensional shape or structure, or as intrinsic character, *form* is the counterpart of space. Except for purposes of analysis and clarification, the two are inseparable since form gives space whatever shape it has. Form, though, is one of the most basic and unchanging elements in the visual world whereas space implies the possibility of change. Furthermore, form typically suggests solidity and enclosure while space makes us think of boundlessness.

Three other terms associated with form deserve definition. *Area* refers to the two-dimensional extent of a shape, such as the floor area of a house or the wall area of a room. *Plane* is closely related to area, for it also implies a flat shape, but in contemporary usage it has come to imply a shape that is an active directional force, as the roof planes of the Robie house, rather than merely the square footage of a surface. Although *line* theoretically has but one dimension, the word is frequently used to describe the dominant directions or the outlines of a shape or space as when the "lines" of furniture or houses are said to be pleasing, or horizontal.

That forms can be causative forces affecting our feelings is demonstrated in the living-room corner shown in Figure 121. The horizontal sofa and tables establish a dominant easy repose. A markedly different kind of eye movement, and of feeling, is induced when one looks at the counterbalancing, subordinate verticals. The folds of the draperies stand straight and tall as does the sculpture in the corner. Less emphatically, the slender legs of sofa and nested tables, the flowers in the vase, express an upright stabilized resistance to gravity. A few diagonals and curves introduce needed diversity with their special expressive qualities. The most conspicuous diagonal is in the sofa, which is strengthened by the table behind it. Less immediately noticeable are the triangular, diagonally mounted legs of the

A corner of a living room designed by Bertha Schaefer in which varied forms, each suited to its purposes, are sensitively combined. (*M. Singer and Sons*)

coffee table, the outline of the lamp, the slight tilt of the sofa's end, and the casual placement of the book, magazine, and pillows. In varying degrees, these diagonals bring a greater feeling of activity than do either horizontals or verticals. The circular coffee table with its rounded accessories and the lamp bring the poised, unified fluidity inherent in circles and spheres. More active are the canoe-shaped braces supporting the glass table top. One has only to imagine this room with all possible forms horizontal or vertical, diagonal or curved to begin appreciating what each type of shape can contribute.

► DESIGN IN SPACE, FORM, LINE, AND TEXTURE

Forms, planes, and lines shape the space in which we live by defining its physical limits, texture adds to its character. Over and above their fundamental work in making our environment livable, these plastic elements have qualities that add to or detract from the beauty and individuality of homes. From these qualities, all parts of our homes derive much of their character,

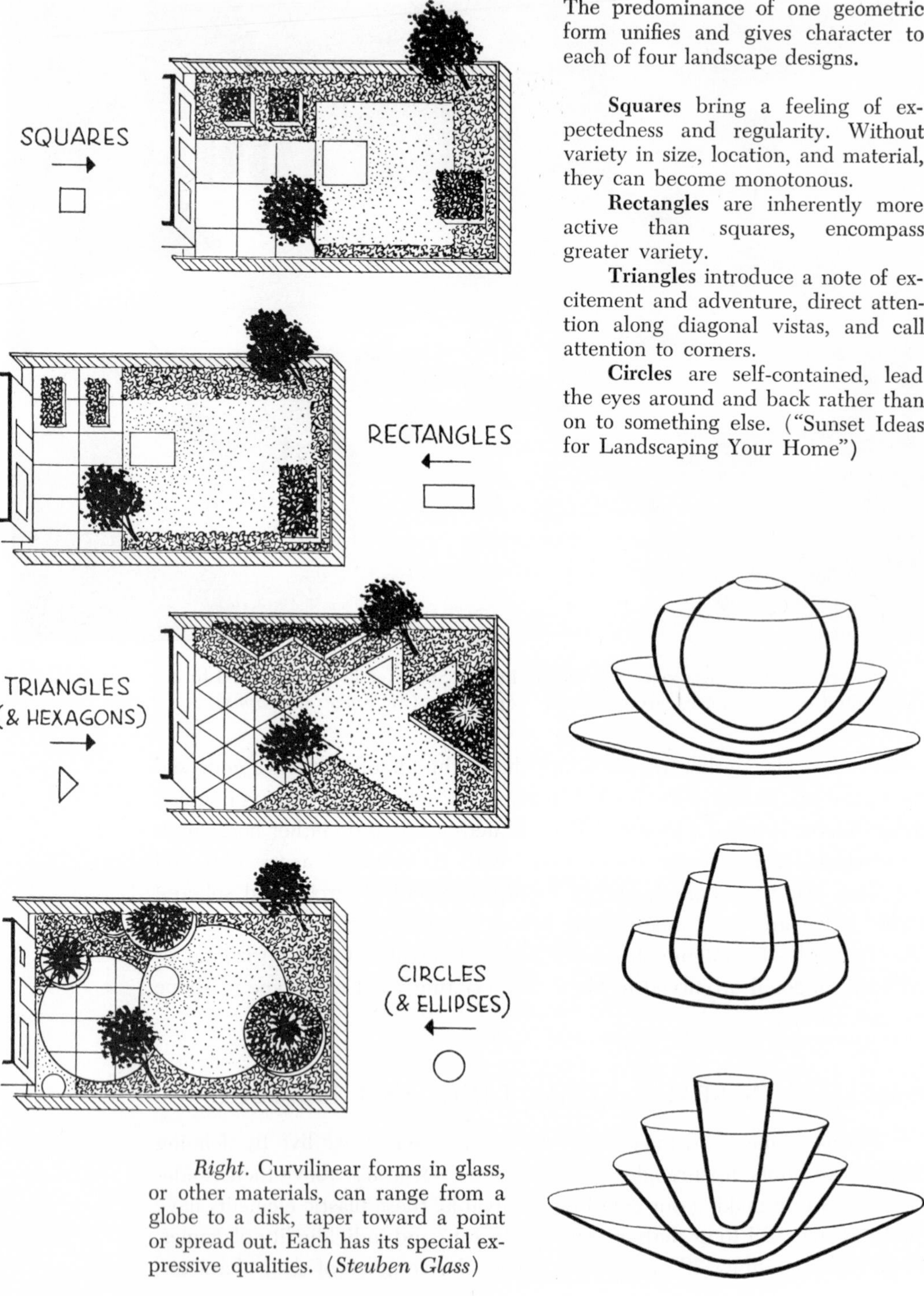

The predominance of one geometric form unifies and gives character to each of four landscape designs.

Squares bring a feeling of expectedness and regularity. Without variety in size, location, and material, they can become monotonous.

Rectangles are inherently more active than squares, encompass greater variety.

Triangles introduce a note of excitement and adventure, direct attention along diagonal vistas, and call attention to corners.

Circles are self-contained, lead the eyes around and back rather than on to something else. ("Sunset Ideas for Landscaping Your Home")

Right. Curvilinear forms in glass, or other materials, can range from a globe to a disk, taper toward a point or spread out. Each has its special expressive qualities. (*Steuben Glass*) their emotional impact or mood (Figs. 122A, B, C, and D). We shall look first at the expressive powers of shape, then of size and direction, and finally at a few of the effects produced by different relationships.

Shape

Stripped to essentials, space and form may be described as rectilinear, angled, or curved. Although each of these categories has its own identity, there are no limits to the ways in which they can be varied (Fig. 122E) and combined for specific desired effects. They are fundamental in the "language of vision," as consequential in home design as in painting or sculpture.

That rectangularity is typical of the larger spaces and forms in homes today is evident in all but an outstanding few of the illustrations in this and preceding chapters. So general is this boxlike shape that we can only wonder why there is no single term to describe it unless the word *room* has come to take on this meaning. It is prevalent not only in whole houses and rooms but in such furniture as beds, tables, storage units, phonographs, and television sets as well as in many sofas, chairs, and benches. Among the reasons for this widespread acceptance, we might note that rectangles:

- Are easily handled on designers' drafting boards, by carpenters and masons on the site, and by machines in factories.
- Fit snugly together—an important factor when multitudinous parts of buildings coming from many sources are assembled on the job and when space is becoming increasingly expensive.
- Have a sturdy secure relationship of exactly 90 degrees, which gives a sense of definiteness and certainty.
- Establish an incipient unity and rhythm when repeated.

In spite of its definiteness, rectangularity can encompass great diversity. Cubes can vary in size, color, or texture, and they can rest stably on one side, insecurely on one edge, or precariously on one corner (Fig. 124A). Each of these positions calls forth a different emotional response. Rectangular forms can do all this and also range in shape from a linear thinness, as in the window frames of the Mills' house, to the almost cubical fullness typical of television receivers. If you want motionless stability, cubes are indicated; for a feeling of movement directed along one line, a slender rectangle may be your solution as it was in the ceiling beam of the Kansas tract house.

The qualities of clarity, stability, and certainty that combine to make rectangular forms favored also can give a harsh, boxy monotony that many persons want to alleviate with other shapes and some wish to avoid insofar

A

Above. Cubes can rest stably on one side, insecurely on one edge, or precariously on one corner. (*Matt Kahn*)

Right. Actually rigid, triangles seem flexible and active. (*Matt Kahn*)

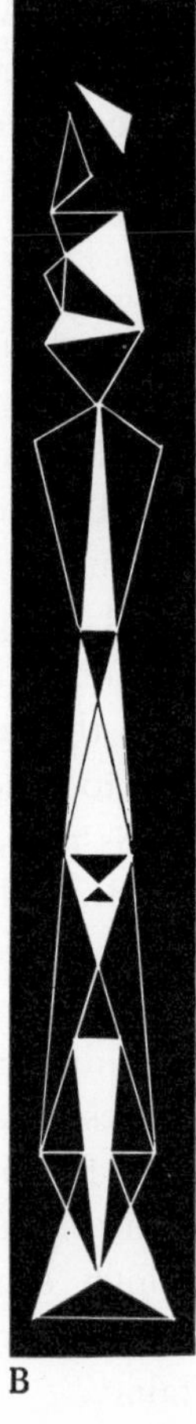

B

C

Above. Curves are the most variable of all forms. (*Matt Kahn*)

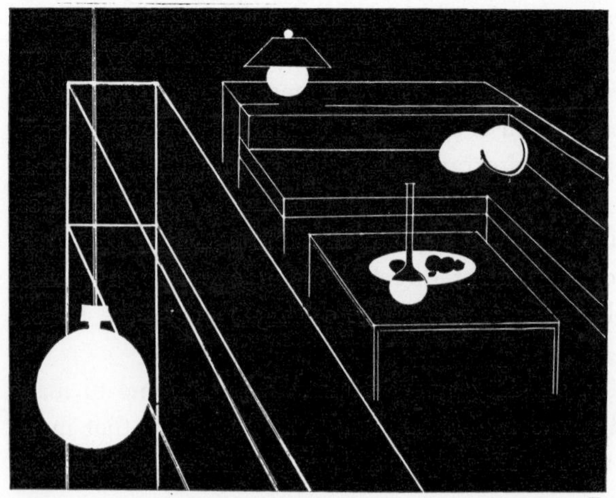

D

Left. True circles and spheres ordinarily serve as small accents—but they can also be large, dominant forms. (*Matt Kahn*) as possible. The right angle, though, has a pure, strong, absolute character, its own quality of beauty.

Pyramids and triangles differ from rectangles in their pointed, dynamic character (Fig. 124B) as do hexagons and octagons to a lesser degree. This difference can be readily seen in the garden plans or by comparing the Mills' and Reifs' living rooms (Figs. 113A and 140B). Although from a structural point of view triangles are one of the most stable forms known (their shape cannot be altered without breaking or bending one or more sides), they express greater flexibility than do rectangles because the angles can be varied to suit the need.

Used with discretion and at large size as in the ceiling of a living room (Fig. 117A) or the gable end of a pitched-roofed house (Fig. 11), they are secure yet dynamic. Small repeated triangles or diamond shapes in textiles, tiles, or wallpaper (Chapters 8 and 11) add briskness to interiors, while a three-sided table between two chairs sets up a congenial relationship. In gardens, diagonals markedly increase apparent size. Because these angular shapes imply motion and are relatively uncommon, they usually attract and hold attention beyond what their dimensions suggest.

Curved forms bring together the lively combination of continuity and constant change (Fig. 124C). They remind us sympathetically of flowers, trees, clouds, and our own bodies. Circles and spheres have a unique complex of qualities.

- They are man's and nature's most conservative and economical forms since they not only enclose the greatest area or volume with the least surfacing but strongly resist breakage or other damage.
- They are as rigidly defined geometrically as squares or cubes but they do not seem so static, probably because we cannot forget that balls and wheels roll easily.
- They have an unequalled unity because every point on the edge or surface is equidistant from the center which, especially when accented, is a natural focal point.

Inside our homes, circles and spheres are usually most noticeable in plates, bowls and vases, lampshades and pillows (Fig. 124D) plus a few tables and stools (Fig. 135). They are also the basic motif in some textiles, wallpapers, and floor coverings. At present, building costs, and perhaps a preference for angles, tend to rule out the circular rooms or bays, curved stairways, and domed ceilings that grace many historic homes. There are,

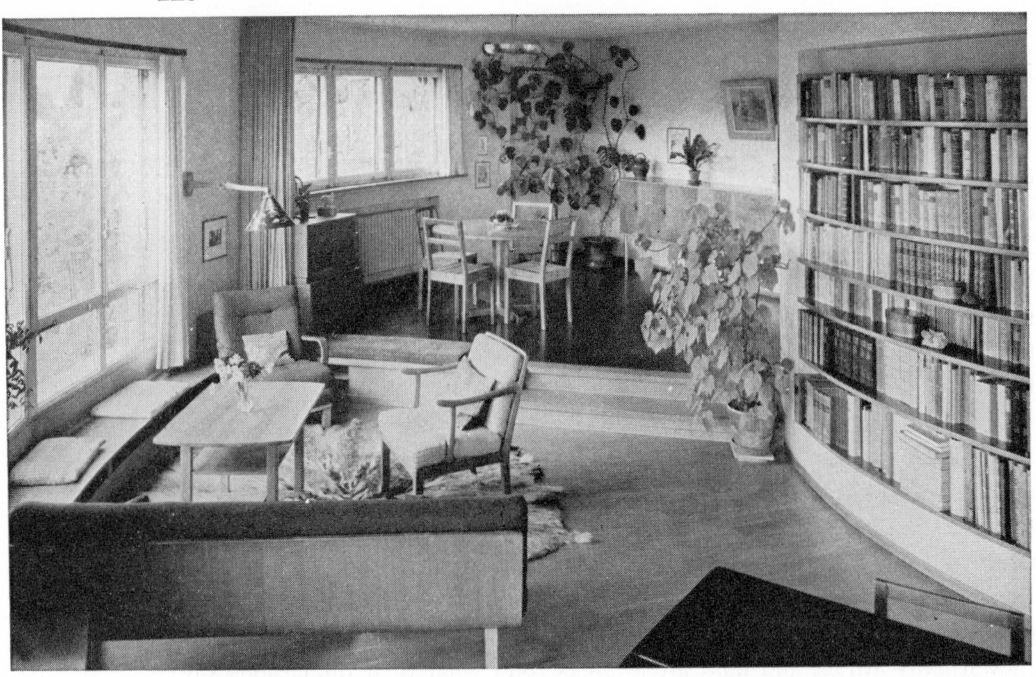

A

Large curved forms are regrettably rare in houses but are often used in landscape design.

Above. In his own home in Switzerland, architect Karl Sherrer decided on a semicircular plan to take full advantage of the sun and views. (*Courtesy of Verlah Girsberger. Photograph by Foto Koch*)

Below. A serpentine flower border harmonizes with the plants it contains, contrasts happily with the many angular forms. Thomas Church, landscape architect. (*Photograph by Rondal Partridge*)

B

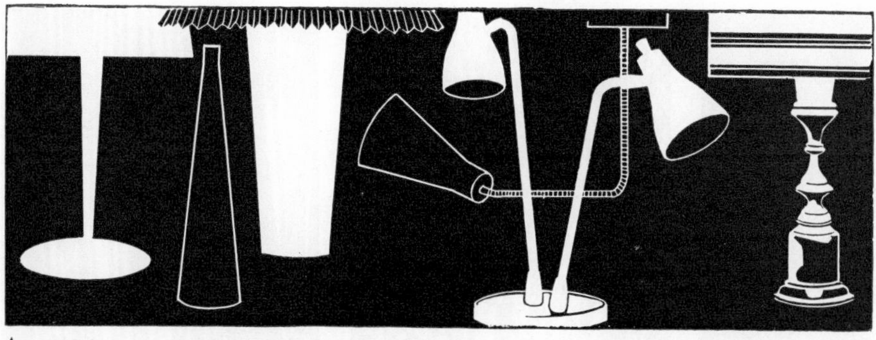

A

Cones and cylinders are often seen in lamp bases and shades. (*Matt Kahn*)

however, such notable exceptions as the Swiss living area (Fig. 126A) and Frank Lloyd Wright's concrete block house illustrated in Chapter 8. For the future, new developments give promise that people may again enjoy the beneficent atmosphere of large curved forms, such as the plastic house in Chapter 9 and Eduardo Catalano's home in Chapter 13.

Cones and cylinders both imply a dynamic, directional movement not found in circles or spheres. Much as cones and cylinders resemble each other, they differ in an important way. Cones, like pyramids, reach a climactic terminal peak whereas cylinders, like rectangles, could continue forever. Thus, cones are more emphatic and direct attention to a focal point.

Both are familiar because they are similar to the trunk, arms, and legs of our bodies. They are also the basic shapes of the arms and legs on most furniture. Furniture legs of wood are often truncated cones, tapering toward the bottom and top for visual lightness and grace (Fig. 127B). Metal cylinders for furniture supports are also favored because they are strong in relation to their weight and size, durable and easy to clean, and can be bent into pleasing curves (Fig. 91A). Cylinders and cones are found in the bases of table lamps and in vases.

Furniture legs, too, are usually cones or cylinders, pure or modified. (*Matt Kahn*)

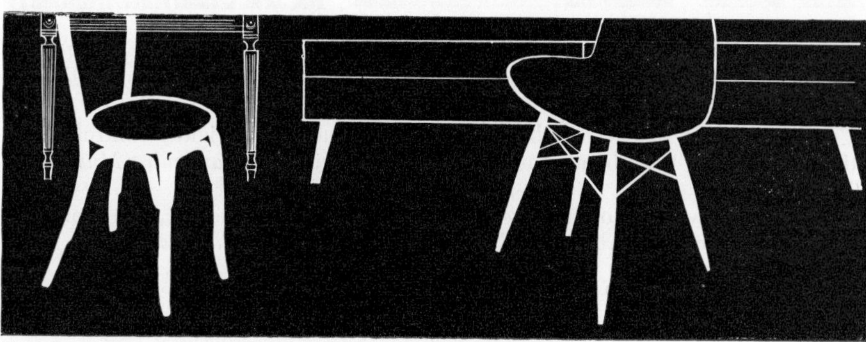

B

A B C

Left. The graceful outlines of "River Ferns" floating on a sheer synthetic textile are reminiscent of the fluid sway of ferns beside a stream. (*J. T. Thorp & Company*)

Center. On a heavier silk brocade, the curves are more rigidly controlled but still indicative of the pliant character of the material. (*Scalamandre Museum of Textiles*)

Right. Flowing smoothly over the surface of a linen textile, the elongated sinuous curves of "Divertissement" invite draping. (*Greeff Fabrics*)

Beyond the geometric curves are those inspired by nature and with these the range of expressiveness is without limit as suggested by the three textiles in Figures 128A, B, and C. Reminiscent of the luxuriant, delicate tracery of plants growing in deep shade, "River Ferns" has sensitive relaxed curves. When hung in folds, this translucent textile elusively half-reveals the patterns behind. The silk brocade is a sturdy cloth appropriately enriched with a vigorous, structural sequence of interlocking forms in tension. More formal and systematic in its clear-cut repetition and progression, it is no less subtle than "River Ferns." Nearly parallel lines that open and then close into dark areas give "Divertissement" a linear flowing character.

There are, of course, many other materials to which nongeometric curves are appropriate. They seem natural in landscape design (Figs. 27A and 126B), are well suited to ceramics and glass (Figs. 98A and B and 110), and to some kinds of furniture (Figs. 60 and 80B).

Size and Direction

The character of any form or space in the home is most obviously determined by its basic shape, but this is only one of a complex of interrelated factors, an observation that is proved by the different treatments of the same shape in Figures 130A through F. Scientists and artists in studying the expressiveness of line and form have come to such generalizations as the following:

- Vertical forms and lines express a stabilized resistance to gravity, a poised uprightness. If high enough, they evoke feelings of aspiration and ascendancy as they do in the Port Royal parlor or the Texas living room (Figs. 86A and 12).
- Horizontals tend to be restful and relaxing, especially when long. If short and interrupted, they become a series of restless dashes.
- Diagonals are as active as a runner's body. Unless sensitively counterbalanced, as they are in the Reifs' home (Figs. 140B and 141B), they seem to be in a never-ending search for equilibrium.
- Big upward curves suggest power and uplift, horizontal curves connote gentleness and quietness, and large downward curves express a range of feelings including sadness and seriousness.
- Small upward curves manifest playfulness, merriment, or agitation.

Emphasize verticals—high ceilings, tall doors and windows, or upright furniture—if you want to have people feel like standing straight and tall or enjoy a suggestion of loftiness. Emphasize horizontals—low ceilings,

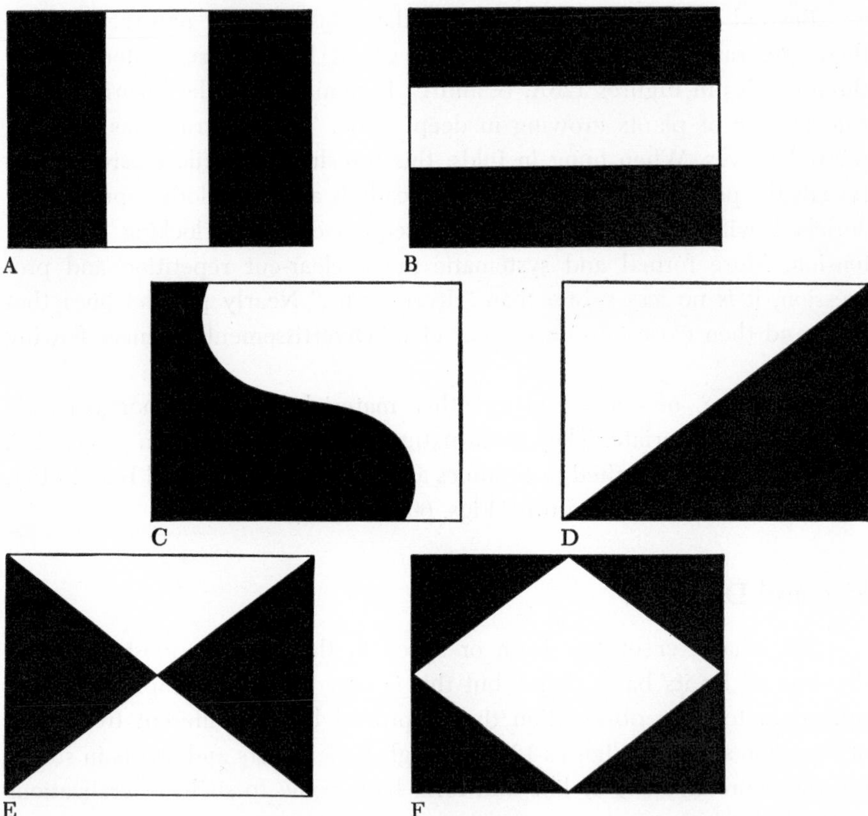

That the character as well as the apparent size and shape of any form is determined by what happens within its outlines is demonstrated by six treatments of the same rectangle. The upper right rectangle looks much longer and lower than its companion, an observation applicable to many phases of home design. (*Julia Pearl*)

broad openings, and stretched-out furniture—if you want them to lounge comfortably, relax, and act informally. Emphasize diagonals—sloping ceilings, oblique walls or furniture, and textiles with diagonal lines—if you want a home environment suggesting activity.

Relationships

Seldom is any form, space, or texture seen in isolation, and its context strongly affects its character. One of the clearest examples is apparent size. The same furniture, for example, will look larger in a small room than it will in one of ample size (Figs. 131A and B). It will also be more conspicuous, and usually seem larger, if there is a strong texture and value contrast between furniture and background.

A

A sofa and table crowded into one end of a small room will seem larger than the same furniture in a less confining space. (*Walter Zawojski*)

B

Shapes gain consequence in many ways, as through inherent interest, size, and position. They also assume importance in two seemingly contradictory ways as illustrated in Figures 131C and D.

Textures undergo similar apparent change in different surroundings, as illustrated in Figures 132A and B.

Of all these relationships the most important is the organization of form to shape space. Planes can be arranged to produce the illusion of a flat surface, an enclosed box, a volume with sloping top and holes, or a dynamic integration of continuing form and space (Figs. 133A through F).

A large triangle gains importance when set against a contrasting background. Placing it against many small triangles makes it far less noticeable but reinforces the "idea" of triangularity. (*Julia Pearl*)

C

D

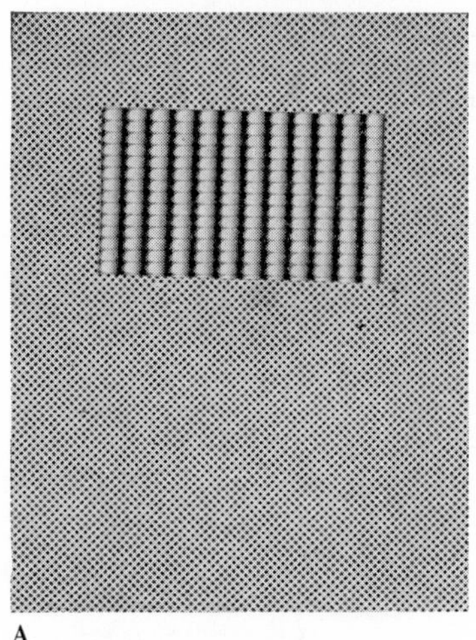

A

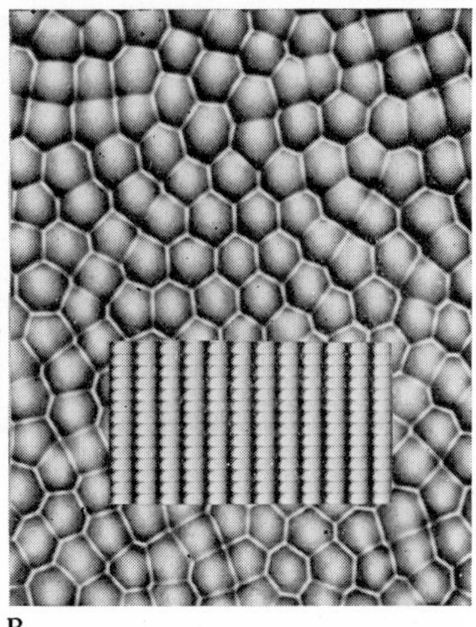

B

The apparent fineness or coarseness of a texture is greatly affected by its background. (*Rigidized Metals Corporation*)

Examples of this sort could be continued as indefinitely as they occur in our homes, but these few suffice to stress the tremendous consequence of relationships.

► ENRICHMENT OF FORM AND SPACE

So far our discussion has centered on pure, unadorned form for good reason: basic structural form (and its counterpart, space) is the taproot of beauty in homes. Man, however, has usually felt a need to enhance basic structural form beyond the call of use, economy, or structure, an observation to which the illustrations in this chapter are no exception. The living room corner (Fig. 121) shows the major means to this end. First you might notice that *basic structure is revealed,* insofar as is feasible and esthetically satisfying. The outstanding example is the circular table, which shows its sculptural supports through a glass top. The nested tables also let us see the essentials of their structure. Advisedly, the lamp and sofa do not reveal their inner complexity of wire and rubber but neither do their shapes deny them. Second, all *shapes are refined* simply to please the senses. This is evident in the handsome proportions of lamp and sofa, the sensitively scaled nest of tables, and the subtly shaped supports of the coffee table. Third, *materials* were chosen that have inherent beauty or have been handled so that they become beautiful. The wood in the tables is an example of the first, the weave of the sofa upholstery of the second. Finally, there is the enrichment deliberately *applied* to the vase holding the tulips.

The way in which planes are organized determines their spatial effect. (*Walter Zawojski*)

Right. Six rectangles laid out in a flat pattern are static and two-dimensional.

Far right. If they overlap one another, a slight three-dimensional effect results.

B

A

C

D

E

When put together as a box (*left*), they make a solid enclosing form with little feeling of space. Bending the top plane into a double-pitched roof (*center*) gives more variety of form and space. Pulling the box apart (*right*) lets space flow in and around the solids.

The Robie house illustrates the possible dynamic complexity of spatial relationships.

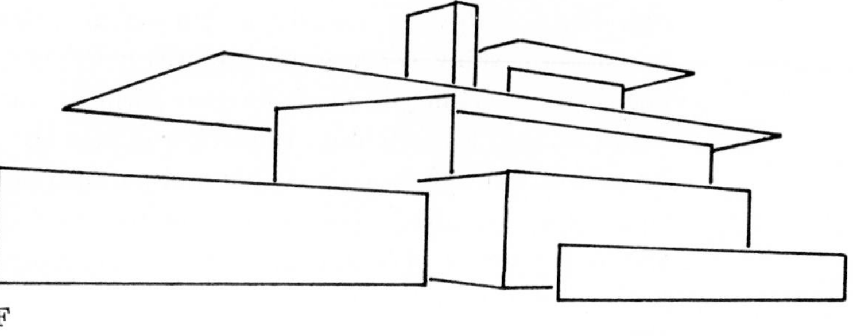

F

Texture

Referring to the surface qualities of materials, we may say that texture describes how they feel when we touch them and how they affect the light that strikes them. Essentially, texture is a kind of ornament but one that deserves special discussion because of its universality and the strategic contributions it makes to contemporary homes. A distinction is often made between *actual* textures in which the three-dimensional surface qualities can be felt, as in bricks and woolen tweeds, and *visual* (also called illusionary or simulated) in which a material reveals a textural pattern under a smooth surface. Sanded wood, polished stone, and many synthetic floor coverings exemplify the latter.

Trying to imagine how the living room in Figure 135 would look if all the textures were eliminated gives some idea of the vitality injected by surface quality. A wide range of textures enhances the design. The smoothest is in the window glass (not seen in this view); the roughest is in the rug. Between these extremes is a full scale—smoothly polished tables; walls, floors, and ceiling sanded and finished but not to a glossy sleekness; varied soft-surfaced upholstery; brick and metal-mesh fireplace screen; textured pottery, bronze urns, and books; and the flower arrangement, which, although not rough, gives a bold textural effect. Predominant in area are the walls and ceiling with their moderately smooth surface but lively visual texture against which the very rough and very smooth are accents.

Texture affects us in a number of ways, all of which are illustrated in this room. *First,* it affects us physically in everything we touch. Upholstery fabrics, for example, if coarse and harsh can be actually irritating. If too sleek and shiny, they look and feel slippery and cold. Those most generally liked are neither excessively rough nor smooth. *Second,* texture affects light reflection and thus the appearance of any form. Very smooth materials—polished metal or satin—reflect light brilliantly, attracting attention and making their colors look clear and strong. Moderately rough surfaces, such as the brick at the fireplace or the pottery on the table, absorb light unevenly; hence their colors look less bright and darker. Very rough surfaces set up vigorous patterns of light and dark, as can be seen in the bands on the rug. *Third,* texture is a factor in household maintenance. Remember that the smooth, shiny surfaces of brightly polished metals are easy to clean but show everything foreign; rougher surfaces, such as bricks or rugs with high pile, call less attention to foreign matter but are harder to clean; and smooth surfaces with a visual textural pattern, of which naturally finished wood is an example, combine most of the good qualities of both. *Finally,* texture is a source of both beauty and individuality, a point well exemplified in the room under discussion.

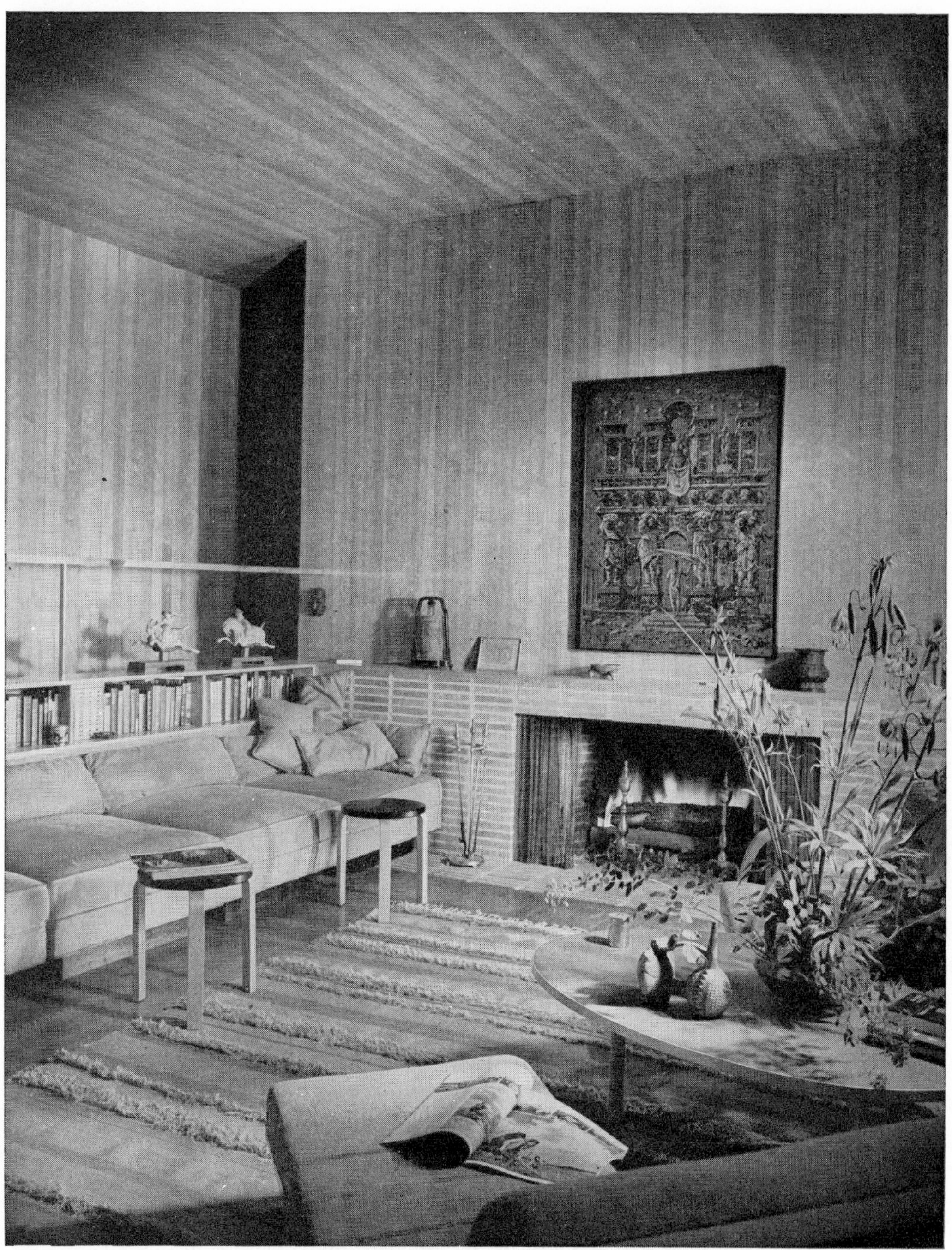

A room in which textures take an active part. John Yeon, architect. (*Photograph by Maynard Parker. Courtesy of* House Beautiful)

Types of Ornament

There are two major types of enrichment, each having subtypes: *

Structural Ornament	*Applied Ornament*
Fortuitous	Naturalistic
Factitious	Stylized
	Abstract

Each type has its special piece to speak in our homes.

Structural Ornament comes from the materials or processes employed in making an object.

- *Fortuitous* (or *by chance*) ornament comes from the materials, as the grain of wood or the veining of marble.
- *Factitious* (or *brought about by effort*) ornament comes from the process, such as the patterns of textiles originating in the weaving process.

Structural ornament is integral with the object it enriches, seems natural and fundamental. Usually it is less subject to physical deterioration, such as breakage or fading, and it is less likely to go out of fashion than is applied ornament. Its range, though, is comparatively limited. Generally, structural ornament is quiet and unobtrusive, qualities that make it appropriate for such large areas as floors, walls, drapery and upholstery materials.

Applied Ornament is that added to an object—patterns printed on cloth, plates, or wallpaper; carved in wood or stone, or etched in glass. Its range is limited only by the nature of materials and the imagination of designers. It can be precisely suited to an object's use, form, and material—or it can be distressingly inappropriate.

- *Naturalistic* ornament closely imitates natural, less frequently man-made, forms.
- *Stylized* or *conventionalized* ornament modifies the appearance of natural or artificial objects to increase appropriateness to form and materials as well as expressiveness and lasting beauty of design.
- *Abstract* ornament shows a minimum if any specific relation to the forms around us.

Three treatments of one motif shown in Figures 137A, B, and C point up the differences between naturalistic, stylized, and abstract ornament.

* This classification follows that devised by Sir Herbert Read and presented in *Art and Industry,* Faber and Faber, 1947.

A

B

C

Naturalistic ornament, like much painting and sculpture, is representational, as illustrated by "River Ferns" (Fig. 128A). It arouses associations with the subject matter—flowers, fish, landscapes, etc.—and the subject matter becomes a major source of pleasure or displeasure. Also the subject matter largely determines the ornament's character: it is difficult to make fish formal and impressive but easy to get that effect with iris or roses.

Stylized ornament relies on such devices as simplification and exaggeration, conventionalization and rearrangement to make natural rhythms more pronounced, emphasize what is most important to the ornament's purpose, and bring all into equilibrium (Fig. 128B). Stylized designs usually "wear better" than do the naturalistic type because they have been consciously planned to give lasting satisfaction. At best, stylized ornament penetrates the superficial surface aspects of nature to reveal more fundamental qualities; at worst, it merely substitutes smooth curves or meaningless angles for nature's complex richness.

Abstract ornament has been used throughout history whenever people wanted patterns that did not remind them strongly of something else (Fig. 128C). It is liked by many today because it is frankly what it is: man-made design for man's enjoyment. Also, abstract ornament is an excellent foil for natural forms—people, views into gardens, and live flowers.

Criteria for Ornament

The most satisfying ornament (including texture) fits the functions, form, size, and material of which it is a part, and is worth while in itself. More specifically:

- Ornament frequently touched should be pleasant to feel. Resting arms or back against sharp carving on a chair or handling sharp-cornered silverware can be physically uncomfortable.

- Ornament should enhance form. The textural pattern of the upholstery on the sofa in Figure 121 strengthens the form. Often, however, the patterns of upholstery fabrics seem at odds with the basic form they cover.
- Ornament should be related to the size and scale of the form. Large pieces of heavy pottery are suited to bold ornamentation; after-dinner coffee cups of porcelain are not.
- Ornament should be appropriate to the material. Fine, linear decoration can be effective on smooth, light-reflecting metal or glass (Figs. 219 and 226C) whereas on wood it might look merely scratchy.
- Ornament should be vital in itself. Spirit and character are as crucial in ornament as they are in the design of form and space.

Attitudes toward ornament, especially applied ornament, have shifted frequently in the past century and have gone from one extreme to the other. To many Victorians, ornament was synonymous with art and, in satisfying their craving for decoration, they reduced space and form to minor roles. Toward the end of the nineteenth century a few architects and designers introduced unelaborated forms associated with simple handcraft traditions that were referred to as the Craftsman style in architecture and as Mission furniture. In a continued search for essentials, the leaders of the Bauhaus Institute in Germany experimented with the precision and simplicity deemed most expressive of twentieth-century technology. Today we recognize that there is need for some kind and some degree of ornamentation, that both structural and applied ornamentation have their place. This has resulted in a growing trend away from stark simplicity but with ornament regarded quite rightly as secondary to space and form.

► SPACE, FORM, AND TEXTURE IN A SMALL HOUSE

The problems put before architect Aaron Green by the Reif family were notably dissimilar from those faced by Willis Mills as discussed at the beginning of this chapter. A long, narrow and almost flat city lot, measuring 50 by 100 feet and hemmed in by neighbors, offered little beyond a convenient location and a few trees. A modest budget added to the challenge of designing a house that seems much larger than its 1,650 square feet of enclosed space. Mr. Green's ingenious solution (Figs. 140A and B and 141A and B) has a richness of interest that belies its basic simplicity.

Access to main and service entrances is afforded by an integrated walk, driveway, and carport. Economically and interestingly planted with ground cover, the front yard is the first step in a sequence of scale from the street into the house. The entrance walk, paralleling driveway and carport but differentiated from both by two planting beds, goes between kitchen and bedroom wings directly to the center of the house. Although straight, it is not dull. A few feet from the public sidewalk several steps introduce the diagonal motif which runs through house and landscape. It also modestly introduces the rhythmic, four-dimensional, organically expanding and contracting treatment of form and space. The unassuming front yard contracts to a small entrance garden as one is passing under an extension of the low carport roof. Briefly, then, one sees the sky through a trellis which brightens the narrowed space, then the entrance garden widens for a few feet.

Once the main door is opened, three vistas appear (but none of these destroys the privacy of any room). Straight ahead one's eyes can travel through the loggia to within a few feet of the back property line. To the right a glass door leads diagonally to a dining terrace. To the left, windows above low bookshelves let one enjoy the tiny garden court, important far beyond its 9 by 17 foot dimensions. The glass-walled, skylighted loggia is more than a hallway, serving as it does for book storage and then widening into a music center as it nears the living room and terrace.

The kitchen, imaginatively planned for convenience and pleasantness, has a laundry and "decontamination" area near carport and service yard, widens into the food-preparation zone and space for dining adjacent to an outdoor eating terrace. The compact master bedroom gets light and air from two opposite sides without sacrificing seclusion and has a private door into the efficiently compartmentalized bathroom. The second bedroom, illumined and ventilated from four directions, provides two corners for bed-sofas integrated with desks, bookshelves, and storage. Dressing areas for each person are segregated by the indented bay, which also added shape interest to the entrance garden.

The living room seems spaciously elastic yet intimate and secure, a paradoxical combination of qualities produced by the subtle handling of form, line, space, and texture. First, and most important, is the room's shape. The asymmetric, hexagonal plan is less constricting than the typical rectangularity yet gives a sense of trustworthy security. The slope of the ceiling opens the room upward, a movement that is both accentuated and steadied by the heavy beams. Second is the way in which the walls are opened with glass and closed with masonry. The massive fireplace wall, joined with built-in sofas and tables around three sides of the space, is a solid haven that contrasts with the four views of different magnitude and character that the room offers. The northeast window wall reveals a small segment of the yard secluded by a fence, which is a continuation of the room's north wall. A larger expanse of glass facing southeast is

A

B

A

Diagonals and triangles open up and expand a small house on a narrow lot, create interesting angles and long vistas. Aaron Green, architect.

Left above. The entrance loggia, with glass and planting on both sides, leads into the living room and out onto the terrace. Although small and in the center of the house, it seems large because space has been borrowed from all sides.

Left below. The living room has been boldly conceived from the commanding mass of the fireplace to the delicacy of the mitered window corner bringing unexpected light and color into the space.

Above. The terrace is another room of the house—private, pleasant and weather-wise. It is roofed partly by sky and trees, partly by an extended roof of the house; walled by a diagonal fence and the living room's window-wall; and paved with concrete. (*Photographs by Maynard Parker. Courtesy of* House Beautiful)

Right. The plan is an ingeniously unified complex of diagonals and right angles, compact but not restricting and, above all, beautiful.

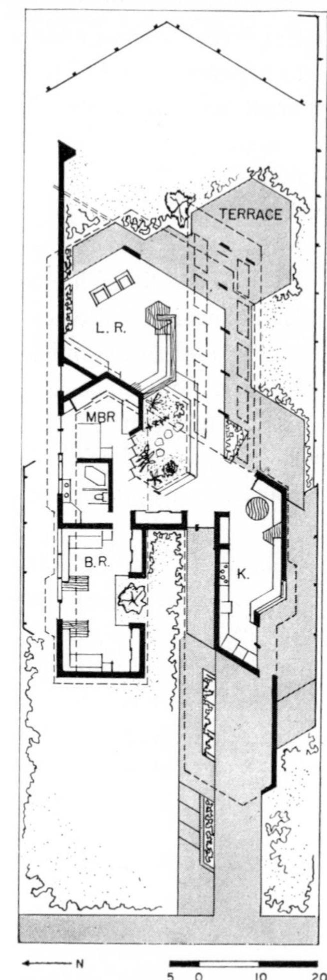

B

oriented toward the living terrace and a far corner of the property. Over the sofa you can see the yard on the south through the loggia, and around the corner is an intimate glimpse into the garden court. Third, line and texture underscore the organization of form and space. Notice how the grooves in the ceiling and the joints in the mortar emphasize the shape and direction of ceiling and fireplace, how the smooth concrete floor and band above the fireplace opening key up the masonry textures.

► CONCLUSION

How to enclose space inexpensively and well has always been a fundamental problem of architecture, and it has seldom been more acute than today with the current high construction and maintenance costs. This has focused attention on ways of increasing the apparent size of homes, a matter that has been detailed in relation to specific examples but which deserves a brief summary. In general a sense of spaciousness is gained if you:

- Establish a strongly ordered unity accentuated by purposeful surprises, such as the tall window in the Mills' living room.
- Emphasize spatial continuity with many and varied vistas for the eyes to explore, as in the Reifs' home.
- Treat form as planes, simple and continuous, carrying beyond expected stopping points, and of contrasting materials to maintain their independence.
- Accentuate the major direction of shapes—the vertical siding of the Mills' house, the ceiling beam in the tract house, and the pattern of brick in the Reifs' fireplace.
- Limit furnishings to those really needed, select pieces moderately small in size and scale, and arrange the larger against walls.
- Keep a dominance of small-scale, unobtrusive textures and patterns with a few marked contrasts.
- Employ such illusionistic devices as mirrors, paintings with deep perspective, or appropriate scenic wallpapers.

The Reifs' home and the other examples shown in this chapter demonstrate the union of order and imagination that characterizes the best contemporary design in space with form. Each has a clearly expressed systematic and structural unity growing out of the specific human needs it serves, the environment in which it stands, and the materials from which it was constructed. Equally significant, each expresses the sensitivity and individuality of its designer and owner more fundamentally through relationships of space and form than through any other aspect.

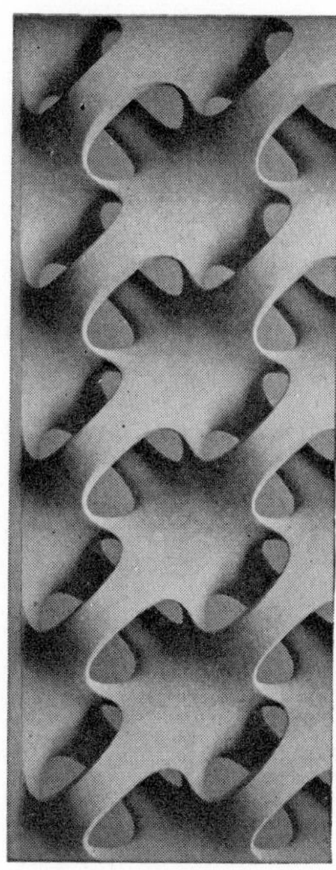
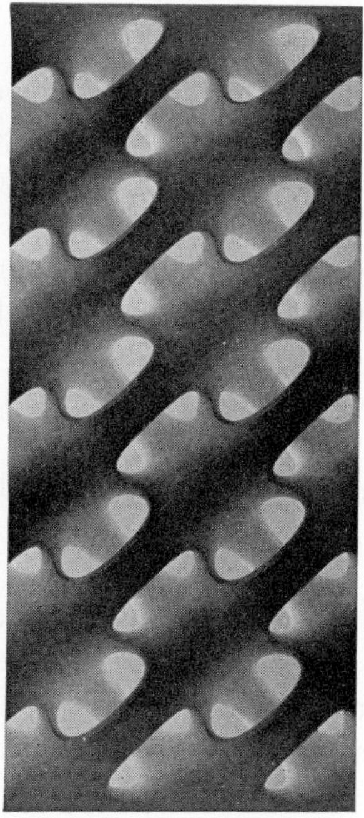

7. Light and Color

LIGHT AND COLOR are as inseparable as space and form. Without light there is no color, and light is always colored. The world is made visible through light entering our eyes, and from sight most persons derive more of their understanding than from all other senses combined.

Although color has long been considered a fundamental of home design, only recently have we become fully aware of its potentialities beyond mere pleasantness or unpleasantness, important as these may be. Even more revolutionary are the developments in home lighting—but we are anticipating the discussion of natural lighting in Chapter 12 and of artificial illumination in Chapter 15. Here we simply introduce the subject of light to emphasize its importance as one of the major plastic elements.

Above. One of Erwin Hauer's grilles shows how different lighting can change appearance dramatically.

► LIGHT

Light is a form of energy, a force to which we react immediately although often subconsciously. Our reactions are a complex of physical and psychological responses as yet imperfectly understood. Physicists, though, know these facts:

- Light varies amazingly in brightness, the light from strong sunlight being approximately 400,000 times that from the full moon, 1,000,000 times that from a star.
- White or apparently colorless light is composed of all the hues of the spectrum.
- Light travels in straight lines until it hits something.

What happens when light hits something varies.

- It may be reflected, absorbed, or allowed to pass through. Usually all three of these happen but in differing amounts depending on the degree of transparency or opacity of the material and its surface qualities.
- Light reflected from smooth surfaces is bright and sharp, diffuse when reflected from rough surfaces.

The appearance of objects is greatly affected by the kind of light that makes them visible.

- Objects illumined by small, sharp light-sources show strong contrasts of light and dark, less contrast if the light source is broad and diffuse, and almost no contrast if evenly lighted from all sides.
- Shadows from objects lighted by small, sharp beams are usually hard, sharp and dark; soft and spread-out if the light source is broad and diffuse; and multiple and overlapping if the light comes from more than one direction.

Perhaps most important is: how does lighting affect us?

- Strong contrast of brightness and darkness are emphatic and dramatic but may be fatiguing to the eyes; uniform lighting is unexciting to the spirit but easy on the eyes (Fig. 143).
- Bright light is stimulating, low levels of illumination are quieting.
- Good light illuminates what we want to see, but the light source does not intrude on our vision.

► COLOR

Like design, color is important only as it affects our living. That it can be influential, for better or for worse, has been proved countless times. Such phrases as "functional color" and "color conditioning" describe its use in business for increased pleasantness and efficiency. In the theater the emotional effects of color have long been exploited. Color can work similar magic in homes. With receding colors or appropriate contrasts, the apparent size of a room can be markedly increased. Ceilings can be made to seem higher or lower with a coat of paint. Where there is no sunlight, its effects can be simulated with yellow walls, and excessive brightness or glare can be reduced with cool, darkish surfaces. Some or all of our furnishings can be brought into prominence or allied with their background by our uses of color. In short, color can markedly alter the appearance of form and space.

The color of an object that we see results from two factors: the way in which the object absorbs and reflects light, and the kind of light that makes the object visible. When light strikes an opaque object, some of its hues are absorbed and others reflected. Those that are reflected give the object its color quality. Lemons and yellow paint, for instance, absorb almost all rays except yellow. White objects reflect almost all the colors in light, while black objects absorb most of them. We say *almost* because pure colors are very seldom found. The true color quality of anything is revealed when it is seen in white light. Usually, however, light is not completely colorless.

The color of light depends on its source and whatever it passes through before coming to our eyes. White (or apparently colorless) light, such as that from the noon sun, contains all the spectrum's hues—violet, indigo, blue, green, yellow, orange, and red—balanced and blended so that the effect is colorless. Light from the moon is bluish while that from open fires and candles is yellowish. Typical incandescent electric light bulbs also give yellowish light if the glass is colorless; but if the glass is blue, some of the yellow rays are filtered out and the light becomes white. In our homes we take advantage of this second factor when we choose incandescent or fluorescent bulbs that produce colored light or when we alter the color of daylight with thin, colored curtains or of artificial light with translucent shades that are not white.

Color Theory

Organizing facts and observations on color into a systematic theory is a first step in understanding color relationships and effects. Three different kinds of theories have been developed: physicists base theirs on

This listing shows, for example, that "artillery" differs from "baby pink" primarily in *value* but that it differs from "Harvard crimson" in both *value* and *intensity*. Similarly, "golden glow" and "cream" differ principally in value, but both value and intensity distinguish "cream" from "olive green." Unless we use an accepted term, such as "cream," that is pegged to one color, it is necessary to describe the three dimensions of a color precisely.

▶ HUE

Hues are often classified as primary, secondary, and tertiary.

- *Primary* hues are yellow, blue, and red and are labeled (1) on the Color Wheel. They are called primary because they cannot be produced by mixing other hues, but mixtures of them will produce nearly every hue.
- *Secondary* hues are green, violet, and orange and are labeled (2) on the Color Wheel. Each results from mixing approximately equal amounts of the two primaries between which it stands.
- *Tertiary* hues are yellow-green, blue-green, blue-violet, red-violet, orange-red, and yellow-orange. Labeled (3) on the Color Wheel, these are produced by mixing a primary with either of the nearest secondaries.

The manner in which secondaries and tertiaries are created demonstrates that hues are changed by adding neighboring hues. Red, for instance, became red-violet when it was combined with violet. If more violet were added, the hue would be changed again. The twelve hues on the Color Wheel are only a beginning because there can be an almost infinite number of hues.

Two other terms need definition.

- *Complementary* hues are those directly opposite each other on the Color Wheel. Yellow and violet, green and red, orange and blue are examples.
- *Analogous* hues are those next to each other, such as yellow, yellow-green, and green; or red, red-violet, and violet-blue.

Effects of Warmth and Coolness

Each hue has its own "temperature," an important characteristic in home design. Reds, yellows, and oranges seem warm. Blue, green, and violet look cool. Yellow-green and red-violet are intermediate.

Good use can be made of the warmth and coolness of hues. A too-cold north room can be cheerfully warmed with yellow walls, tan or brown rugs, and dull orange or red upholstery. Blues, greens, and violets will make

A

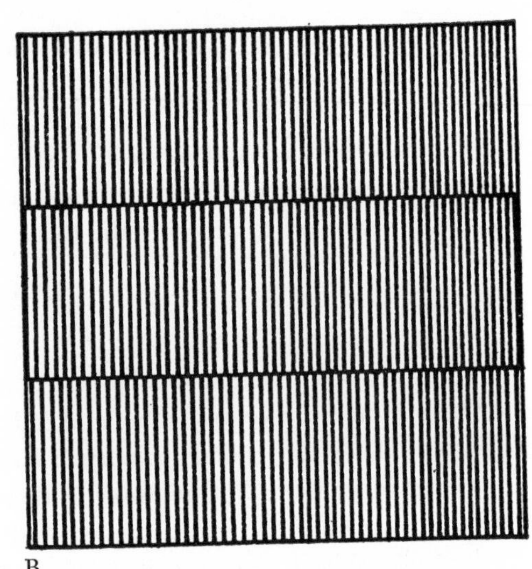
B

Opposites, whether they be black and white, or blue and orange, intensify each other when sizable areas of each are juxtaposed. If, however, the areas of each are very small, they tend to neutralize one another. (*George McLean*)

a room seem cooler, quieter, and larger. Miscellaneous furnishings will appear more related to one another against warm walls than against cool. Shapes, especially outlines of objects, are emphasized when object and background contrast in hue, an observation you can easily check by placing a blue vase against a blue or green background and then against one of yellow or orange. A sofa upholstered in red or yellow will usually seem larger than if upholstered in green or blue. In such ways, the size and character of a room can be markedly altered.

Effects of Hues on One Another: Harmony and Contrast

Relationships are as important with hues as with space and form. The effect of hues on one another depends on *which* hues are brought together and *how* they are combined.

Complementary hues when **placed** next to each other contrast vividly. Each color seems more intense and the effect is strong, bright, and sometimes harsh if the area of each hue is large enough to be perceived as a separate color. But if the areas of two complementary hues are very small, as in a textile woven of fine red and green yarns, the effect at normal distances is one of lively, luminous neutrality. And if opposites are **mixed** together, grayness results. Red mixed with a little green becomes grayer (or lower in intensity) while approximately equal amounts give a neutral brownish-gray.

Analogous hues—blue and green, for example—produce a more harmonious effect if placed next to each other. When actually mixed together, or when small spots of each are intermingled, they create another hue—blue-green.

Thus, with hues you can create an infinite number of effects, ranging from sharp contrasts through soft harmonies to neutrality. Place sizable amounts of bright orange against blue, red beside green, or yellow-green adjacent to red-violet and you have an immediate feeling of excitement, vibration, lively opposition, and also of full, well-rounded balance. A combination of blue, blue-green, and green tends to be more restful because these hues are both related and cool. Yellow, yellow-orange, and orange introduce no sharp conflict but their harmony is not so quieting as with the cooler hues.

Intermediate degrees of harmony and contrast come when hues neither adjacent to nor opposite each other on the Color Wheel are used. Yellow and blue-green, for instance, give an effect midway between harmony and contrast because blue-green is midway between yellow and its complementary hue, violet. Yellow and green, being closer together, bring a little more harmony. Yellow and blue, which are farther apart, produce more contrast. In summary, the effect of combined hues depends on their degree of harmony or contrast, on the size of the area allotted to each—and on their value and intensity, to which we now turn attention.

► VALUE

Lightness or darkness of colors affects us and our surroundings quite as forcefully as does hue. The same space can be made to seem dark and cosy (or cramped) with dark values or light and open with light values as illustrated below.

Dark wood, wallpaper, or paint *as well as* low levels of illumination reduce the apparent size of a room. Light walls and bright light do the opposite. (*Walter Zowajski*)

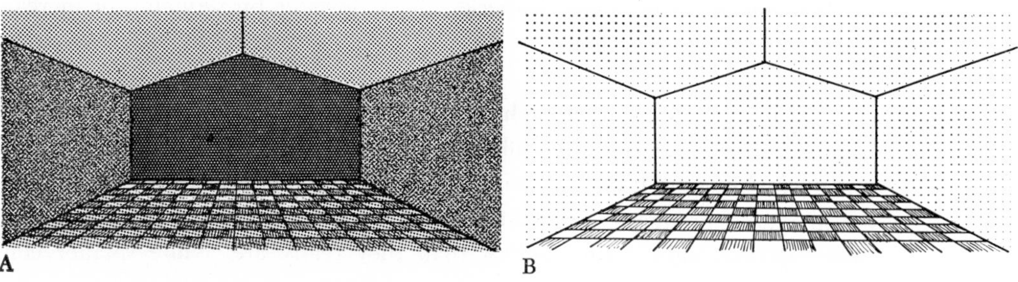

The handsome and purposeful organization of values in Figure 152A might be analyzed into three basic components. First are the areas of glass—the window wall, glass door, and the windows above the fireplace—which visually open the room to the outdoors. These are ever-changing elements. On bright days they are the lightest parts of the room, at night the darkest, and they make the marked seasonal changes of color an integral part of the room. The second component is the walnut walls, the gray floor, and the furniture all of which range around middle value. These large areas of harmoniously related, moderate values counterbalance and steady the fluctuations seen through the glass and give a comforting feeling of unchanging enclosure. The third includes the light-value elements, such as the ceiling, fireplace hood, and rug. These provide stimulating value contrast and reflect light pleasantly by day and night. In summary, the values in this room are balanced and moderate. Three other possibilities are shown in Figures 152B and 153A and B.

The steps between black and white, which define the lightness or darkness of colors, can be as numerous as you wish but seven is a convenient number; adding black at the bottom and white at the top gives a total of nine value steps. Values above the middle are called *light* or *high* (and often referred to as *tints*), those below the middle are called *dark* or *low* (and often noted as *shades*). The Value Scale facing page 146 shows the seven value steps for green, orange, and violet.

Study of the Color Wheel reveals that the hues differ in value. Yellow is at the *high-light* step, violet is *low-dark*, and the others are graded in between. These are called *spectral* or *normal values*—that is, the values that approximate the degree of lightness or darkness of each hue as seen in the spectrum. They are also the values at which each hue seems most characteristic.

How is the value of a color changed? Raising the value of a color makes it reflect more light. Lowering it reduces the reflected light. With paints, this is usually done by adding white, gray, or black. It can also be accomplished by altering the amount of light reaching a surface—that is, by closing or opening the draperies at windows or by reducing or increasing artificial illumination.

How do values affect each other? The story here is similar to that with hue—contrasts accentuate differences. Black looks blacker when seen against white than it does against gray, just as red looks redder against green than against orange. In brief, strong value contrasts make dark values seem even darker, light values lighter than they really are, while smaller contrasts tend to reveal values in their true character. Strong value contrasts also tend to separate objects; minimum contrasts unite them: in Figure 152A the fireplace hood stands out from the wall but the sofa is allied with it.

How do values affect our feelings? Light values (like warm hues) raise spirits and stimulate us to be active—unless they are all so monotonously light that they seem weak and pallid. A predominance of middle values is relaxing and comforting (Fig. 152A). Strong value contrasts are stimulating (Fig. 153A). Closely related values are quieting.

How do values affect the apparent size of an object? Usually, but not always, the lighter the value the larger the object or space seems to be. Painting the walls of a room in light values increases apparent spaciousness (Fig. 149B); white houses look larger than do those of dark brown. *But* the value contrast between an object and its background is important because contrast makes an object stand out, and anything that stands out seems to gain in bulk. Thus, against a white background a chair upholstered in dark fabric might look larger than it would if covered in material of lighter value.

What is the relation between value and apparent distance? Generally, objects high on the value scale and with no strong value contrasts seem farther away than do those that are darker. A white ceiling seems higher than does one of a dark color. Thus if you want an effect of spaciousness, predominantly light values are indicated. *But* some contrast is needed as a yardstick. A room entirely in white, for example, would probably not seem so large as if one wall or some of the furnishings were in grays with small accents of dark hues.

How do value contrasts affect the outlines of objects? Contrasts emphasize outlines, a point well illustrated in Figure 152A. Compare the sharpness of outline of the two sofas or the radio-phonograph cabinet with the fireplace hood. If you have a piece of furniture, a vase, or a lamp that has contours you wish people to notice, place it against a background of contrasting value. If you want to minimize its outline, place it against a wall of the same degree of luminosity.

Many rooms look spotty and disunited because there are many strong value contrasts scattered throughout. Frequently walls are light and furniture is dark. In consequence each piece seems to stand conspicuously alone. Making some of the furniture lighter or some of the walls darker often results in a more harmonious integrated whole. Other rooms are lifeless

The value pattern of a room creates its own atmosphere but needs balance and some contrast to be pleasantly effective.

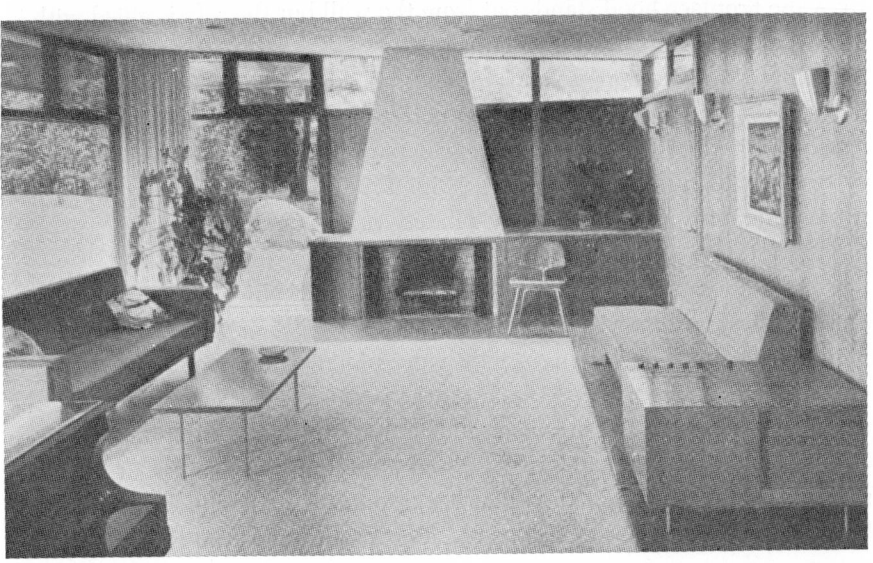

A

Above. A Connecticut living room in which the pattern of values is sensitively related to the architecture and the outdoors. Huson Jackson, architect; H. Seymour Howard, Jr., associate. (*Photograph by H. Jackson and H. Edelman*)

Below. A predominance of dark values makes the same room seem warm, enclosing, and smaller. (*Walter Zowajski*)

B

A

Above. Sharply contrasting but balanced light and dark values brings dramatic vitality. (*Walter Zowajski*)

Below. With all values high, the room is spacious and refreshing but tends toward monotony. (*Walter Zowajski*)

B

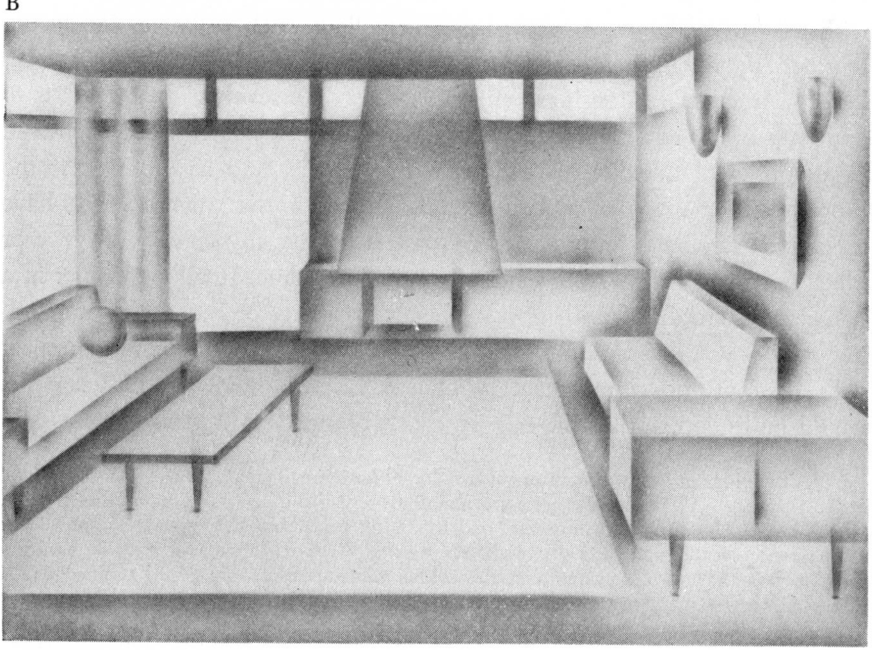

because the patterns of value are monotonous. Introducing contrasts at important places—white or light-value furnishings or accessories if the room is predominantly middle or dark in value, or dark ones if light values predominate—will enliven it.

► INTENSITY

Colors vary in purity or strength, the degree to which they differ from gray. Pink, for example, is always red in hue and light in value; but it can be *vivid,* almost *pure* pink or *dull, gray* pink. This is called *intensity.*

Scales of intensity can be as long or short as you wish, but for convenience we have illustrated one with two steps between full intensity and complete neutrality. This is shown in the Intensity Scale facing page 146 for the primary and secondary hues. The steps are described as *full intensity, two-thirds intensity, two-thirds neutral,* and *neutral.* Full intensities are often referred to as *high* or *strong,* the more neutralized as *low* or *weak.*

Full intensity is possible only at the normal value of each hue. Raising or lowering any hue from its normal value (in other words, adding varying amounts of white or black) reduces the intensity.

How is the actual intensity of a color changed? Intensities can be heightened by adding more of the dominant hue or by illumining the object with light of that hue. A wall of grayed yellow, such as beige, can be intensified by repainting it with a brighter yellow or by casting yellowish light on it. Actual intensities can be decreased in several ways. First is to add some of the complementary hue. In the Intensity Scale, yellow is grayed by adding violet, violet by yellow, red by green, and so on. This is the procedure of many painters because hues grayed in this way appear to have a complex liveliness and variety. Second is to mix any color with gray or black (or even white). They literally "gray" the hue. If all the colors in a home are neutralized with gray or black, harmony or monotony, depending on how you feel about it, is developed.* Third is to illuminate the object with light of the complementary hue. A bright blue wall, for example, would be dulled during the day by sheer, orange-tinted glass curtains and

* Changing any one dimension of a color almost inevitably changes the other two, at least slightly. Available pigments are almost never absolutely pure: grays, blacks, and whites tend to be either warm or cool and thus alter the hue with which they are mixed. It is possible to change intensity without altering value *if* you use a gray or complementary hue that absolutely matches the color's value, but this is seldom achieved. One of the dimensions can be modified much more than the other two, but it is extremely difficult to change one and hold the others constant.

at night by translucent lampshades of the same hue. Fourth is to lessen the intensity by lightly stippling or glazing a blue wall with orange, a device happily used in some paintings but usually much less successfully on the walls of homes.

Be warned, though, that none of these neat little formulas always works as anticipated. The third suggestion, in particular, might backfire. There is no question that illuminating a surface with light of a complementary hue will *actually* lower its intensity. But, as noted in the next section, placing complementary hues near each other tends to increase the *apparent* intensity of each. Thus, while lighting a blue wall with orange light will tone it down, seeing orange-tinted curtains or lampshades in relation to a blue wall makes each hue seem more saturated. *Generalizations about color relationships are worth knowing, but none of them always holds true.*

How can the apparent intensity of a hue be changed? It can be heightened in three ways: placing it next to its complementary hue of approximately the same intensity; adjacent to gray (or in some instances black or white); and next to a color of the same hue but of lower intensity. Suppose, for example, that you wish to make a faded green sofa look greener without reupholstering it. Put some cobweb gray or maroon pillows on it; place it in front of a gray wall, on a gray rug, or both; or use pillows, wall, or rug that are green but more neutral than the sofa.

If the sofa's color is too intense, it can be made to look grayer with bright green pillows on it or a brilliantly colored painting above it.

How do different intensities affect our feelings, apparent size and distances, and distinctiveness of outlines? Different hues of high intensity usually make one another look more vivid, especially if there are nearby neutral colors to give a point of reference. If all colors are equally pure, all may lose in apparent strength. Intense colors:

- Stimulate and exhilarate, compel the observer's attention.
- Increase the apparent size of an object.
- Decrease its apparent distance from the observer.
- May distract interest from an object's outline by diverting attention to the hue itself *or* call attention to its shape, depending on the background.

Colors of low intensity have different effects. Neutralized red is pleasantly warm and cheerful while pure red is exciting; grayed green is restful, pure green is actively refreshing. Low intensities make objects seem smaller, farther away, and less conspicuous.

Summary of Effects of Hue, Value, and Intensity *

	Hue	*Value*	*Intensity*
Feelings	Warm hues are stimulating, cool hues quieting.	Light values are cheering, dark values restful to depressing; contrasts are alerting.	High intensities are heartening and strong; low intensities are peaceful.
Attention	Warm hues attract more attention than cool.	Extreme values tend to attract the eye; but contrasts or surprises are even more effective.	High intensities attract attention.
Size	Warm hues increase apparent size of objects; but on walls they decrease apparent size of room.	Light values increase apparent size of objects; but strong contrast with background is equally effective.	High intensities increase apparent size of objects; used on walls, they decrease apparent size of room.
Distance	Warm hues bring objects forward; cool hues make them recede.	Light values increase distance, dark values advance. Sharp contrasts in values also bring objects forward.	High intensities decrease apparent distances.
Outline or Contour	Warm hues soften outlines slightly more than do cool hues; contrasting hues make outlines clearer than do related hues.	Value contrasts are most potent way of emphasizing contours.	Moderate intensities sharpen outlines more than either extremely high or low.

► TYPES OF COLOR SCHEMES

Planning a color scheme ranks high among the exhilarating aspects of home planning. You can assert your individuality and enjoy the freedom that comes from knowing that satisfying color costs no more than that without character or appeal.

In theory, countless color schemes are suited to homes. In practice, however, only a few can be classified, probably because these types just about exhaust the possibilities of orderly selection from the Color Wheel.

* All such generalizations assume that the other two dimensions of color, the background, etc., are held constant. For example, "artillery" red is normally more stimulating than "peppermint" green—both are of middle value and full intensity. But "peppermint" green is likely to attract more attention than "African brown," a color that is red in hue but low dark in value and two-thirds neutral.

In color, as in design, a sense of order has advantages. This does not imply that other color combinations are without merit, nor does it imply that standard color schemes should be unimaginatively followed. Standard schemes are nothing more than time-tested basic recipes or points of departure, as you wish. You can and should vary and individualize or feel perfectly free to disregard them.

Typical color schemes fall into two major categories and each has subtypes.

Related	*Contrasting*
Monochromatic	Complementary
Analogous	Double complementary
	Split complementary
	Triad

Related color schemes which are composed of one or several closely neighboring hues generally lead toward unity and harmony. Contrasting schemes, based on hues far apart on the Color Wheel, have greater variety as well as a balance of warm and cool hues. The two types are basically different, but neither is inherently better than the other.

A diagrammatic color wheel illustrates how three types of color schemes can be evolved. In this example, **complementary** schemes are shown as orange and blue, *or* red-orange and blue-green. A **double-complementary** scheme is produced by combining the two complementary schemes. A **split-complementary** scheme is illustrated by the lines connecting yellow, red-violet, and blue-violet. (*"Money Management," copyright by Household Finance Corporation*)

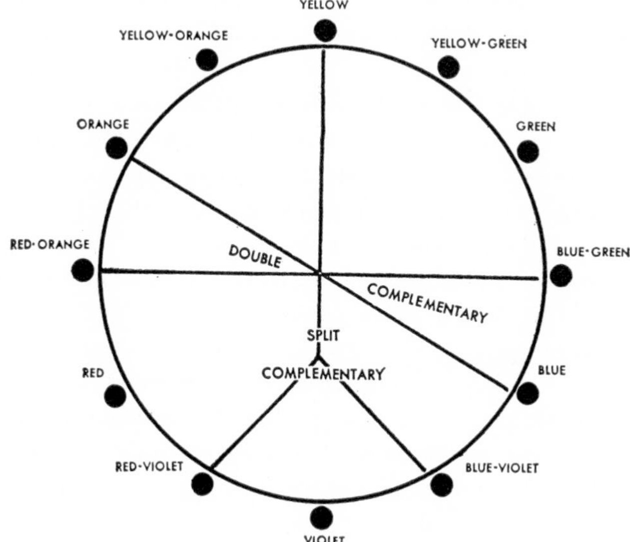

Monochromatic Color Schemes

Monochromatic (literally, one hue) color schemes are based on a single hue, although small amounts of other hues are generally used as accents. A room or even a whole house might have different values and intensities of orange or green. The advantages of monochromatic color are:

- Unity and harmony are firmly established.
- Spaciousness and continuity are emphasized.
- The effect is quiet and peaceful.
- Some degree of success is almost assured in advance.

The major danger is a possible monotony. This can be avoided by:

- Different values of the hue ranging, for example, from light tan to deep brown.
- Varied intensities possibly all the way from pure orange to almost gray.
- Diversified forms, textures, and spatial relationships.
- Use of white, gray and black.
- Accents of other hues.

The living room shown in Figure 152A, discussed earlier from the point of view of value relationships, has a monochromatic color scheme quietly subordinated to the view outside. Not only is there minimum contrast of hue, but except for small accents all colors are of low intensity. The basic hue is orange–brown walnut walls and teakwood furniture, natural linen curtains and wool rug. These are saved from monotony by the natural variations of wood color and grain as well as by the textural interest of rug and draperies. The gray terrazzo floor also has a lively visual texture. In contrast are the smooth white plaster fireplace hood and ceiling. When viewed closely, the Scotch linen upholstery falls outside the monochromatic scheme, for it is woven of red and green yarns, but from any distance it tells as a neutral color. The unobtrusive bluestone used on the tops of the cabinets near the fireplace brings a small subtle difference. Strong contrasts of hue are introduced by the comparatively small painting, plant, and sofa pillows. The largest and most important contrasts, though, are the colors of the landscape and the clothes of the people using the room. It is a restful, harmonious room but by no means dull. In similar fashion a room, possibly a bedroom, could be done in blues, greens, yellows, or pinks and reds, most of which would be quite neutral and any or all enlivened by textures and patterns, contrasting accents, and white, gray, or black.

Monochromatic color schemes are liked today because they let us see the room and the people in it. Also they are good foils for whatever can be seen through large windows, for distinctive furniture, or for individual collections of any kind.

Analogous Color Schemes

Analogous color schemes are based on three or more colors related by the fact that each of them contains some degree of one hue. In other words, the hues fall within any segment of the Color Wheel that is less than one half the way around. Thus, if the common hue is blue, the colors could be as closely related as blue-green, blue and blue-violet, or as separated as blue-green, blue-violet, and red-violet. The distinctively furnished room in Figure 160 is based on yellow, orange, and orange-red with green contrasts.

Analogous color schemes, although harmonious, have more variety of hue, and consequently more variety of warmth and coolness, than do monochromatic. Typically, though, they are predominantly warm or cool and hold together more strongly than do schemes based on contrast.

Contrasting color schemes give a pleasantly balanced opposition of warm and cool sensations, call attention to the different hues through contrast. They can be vividly brilliant if highly saturated hues, such as scarlet and emerald green, are brought together, but rose gray and sage green are comparatively quiet.

Complementary Color Schemes

Built on any two hues directly opposite each other on the Color Wheel, complementary schemes are exemplified by green and red, yellow and violet, or yellow-orange and blue-violet. They offer a great range of possibilities. Yellow and violet, for example, can be as startling as golden glow and fuchsia, as moderate as ivory and amethyst, or as somber as olive drab and gun metal.

Double Complementary Color Schemes

A development of the complementary scheme, double complementaries are simply two sets of complements. Yellow and orange with their respective complements, violet and blue, are an example. Worth noticing in this example is the fact that yellow and orange, as well as their complements, are near each other on the Color Wheel. This is usually the case because if the hues are widely separated, it is difficult to see the order on which this scheme is based. Double complementary schemes combine the harmonious aspects of analogous types with the contrast found in complementary combinations.

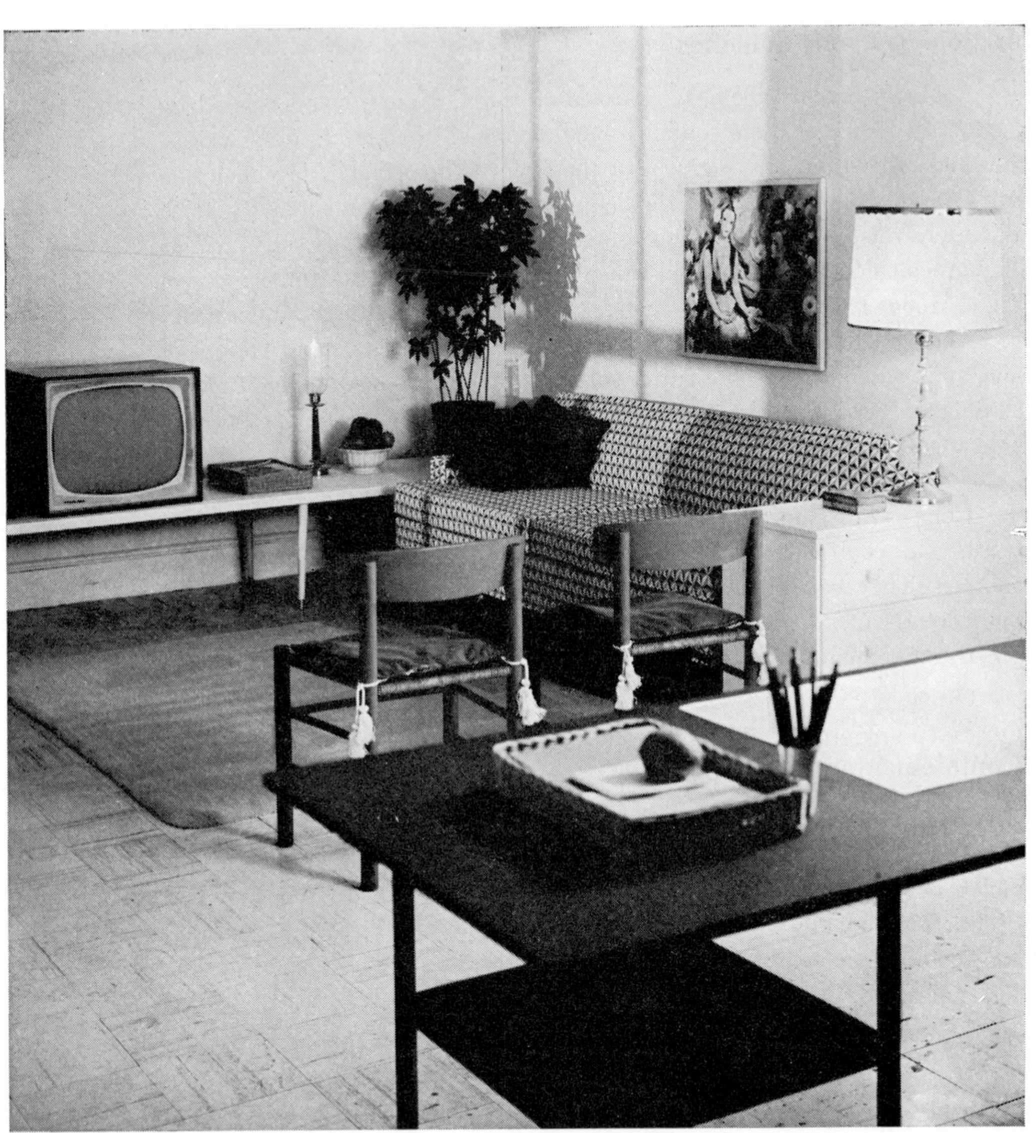

An analogous color scheme of yellow, orange, and orange-red brightens an unpretentious living room. Walls of a subtle grayed yellow and marbleized composition flooring of the same hue but higher in value establish a quiet background. Yellow and orange of greater intensity appear in the brass lamp and the painting. Light and dark orange are combined with white in the printed textile on the sofa, and the small rug is pumpkin color. Fairly intense orange-red occurs in the foreground table and one pillow. Contrasts are introduced by the dark green plant and emerald green pillows, the moss green frames of the chairs and the yellow green of the chairs' cushions. A white chest and lampshade plus one black pillow complete the color organization. (*Photograph by Louis Lemus. Courtesy of* LIVING for Young Homemakers)

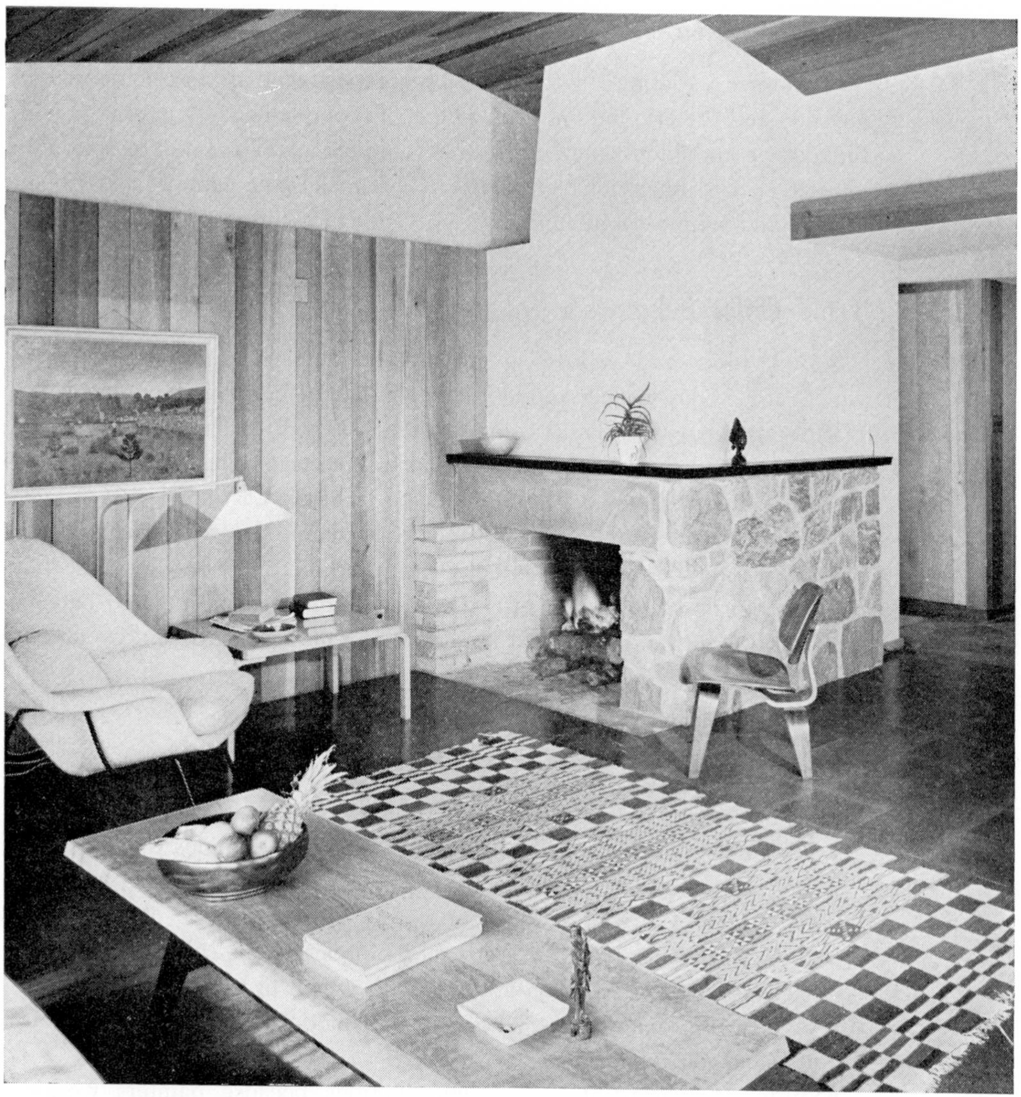

The materials in this New England living room might well be the basis for a complementary color scheme of blue and orange. Orange, in varying degrees of intensity and differing values, is the dominant hue of the dark brown cork floor, the lighter browns of the wood walls and ceiling, and the tans of the wood furniture. Slate-blue stone in the fireplace and the paved entrance hall provide the complement, a hue picked up in greater intensity in the rug. Color might well reach its greatest purity in cadmium-orange upholstery of the lounge chair. The large areas of white plastered walls and the smaller spots of light in the lampshade and rug vitalize this rather subdued scheme by their strong value contrast. The textures and color variations of the cork floor, the handwoven rug, the wood, and the stone add richness. Joseph Stein, architect. (*Photograph by Hans von Nes*)

Split Complementary Color Schemes

Another variation on the complementary theme is that composed of any hue and the two hues *at each side of* its complement, as in orange with blue-green and blue-violet. Blue, the complement of orange, is split into blue-green and blue-violet (Fig. 163). This makes the contrast less violent than in the simple complementary type and adds interest and variety.

Triad Color Schemes

Red, blue, and yellow; green, orange, and violet; blue-green, red-violet, and yellow-orange—any three hues equidistant apart on the Color Wheel—are known as Triad color schemes (Fig. 164). In case such combinations sound shocking, remember that full-intensity hues are seldom used in homes. Red, blue, and yellow might be translated as mahogany, French gray, and beige. Green, orange, and violet could be sage green, cocoa brown, and dove gray. Thus although triad schemes can be vigorous, they can also be subdued. In any case, the effect is one of well-rounded balance with variety held in check by a readily apparent, systematic unity.

► DECIDING ON A COLOR SCHEME

Of the many ways of starting to develop a color combination, the following have been found useful:

- Start a scrap book or clipping file of color combinations that you like. Include advertisements, magazine covers, reproductions of paintings, and so forth, as well as domestic architecture.
- Collect swatches of cloth, wallpaper samples, paint color cards, and a package of assorted colored paper with which to try out ideas.
- Visit furniture stores, art museums, and model homes and make notes of what you especially like or dislike.
- Study original paintings or reproductions because painters working freely with pigments to express their ideas are one source of stimulation.
- Study the colors in the nearby landscape and those more distant.
- Look carefully at the colors used in your home and those of your friends, paying attention to first as well as to the more important lasting impressions.
- Make a list of your favorite colors.
- Look at a list of color schemes, such as the one on pages 166 and 167, not as something to copy but to expand your horizons.

An urbane living-room corner, suggesting a small city apartment, could be enhanced by a split complementary color program. Orange, quite high in value but of low intensity, would brighten the plywood wall, the slat bench, and the table. The sides of the fireplace might well be blue-violet so dark as to seem almost black, the wall above it a light, neutralized blue-green. The sofa's cover could be either blue-violet, somewhat higher in value than the fireplace, or a rich blue-green. Brighter colors in the terra-cotta lamp base with its shade of yellow-orange banded with blue-green, a yellow flower bowl, and the multicolored books are sparkling accents. George Nelson, designer. (*Herman Miller Furniture Company*)

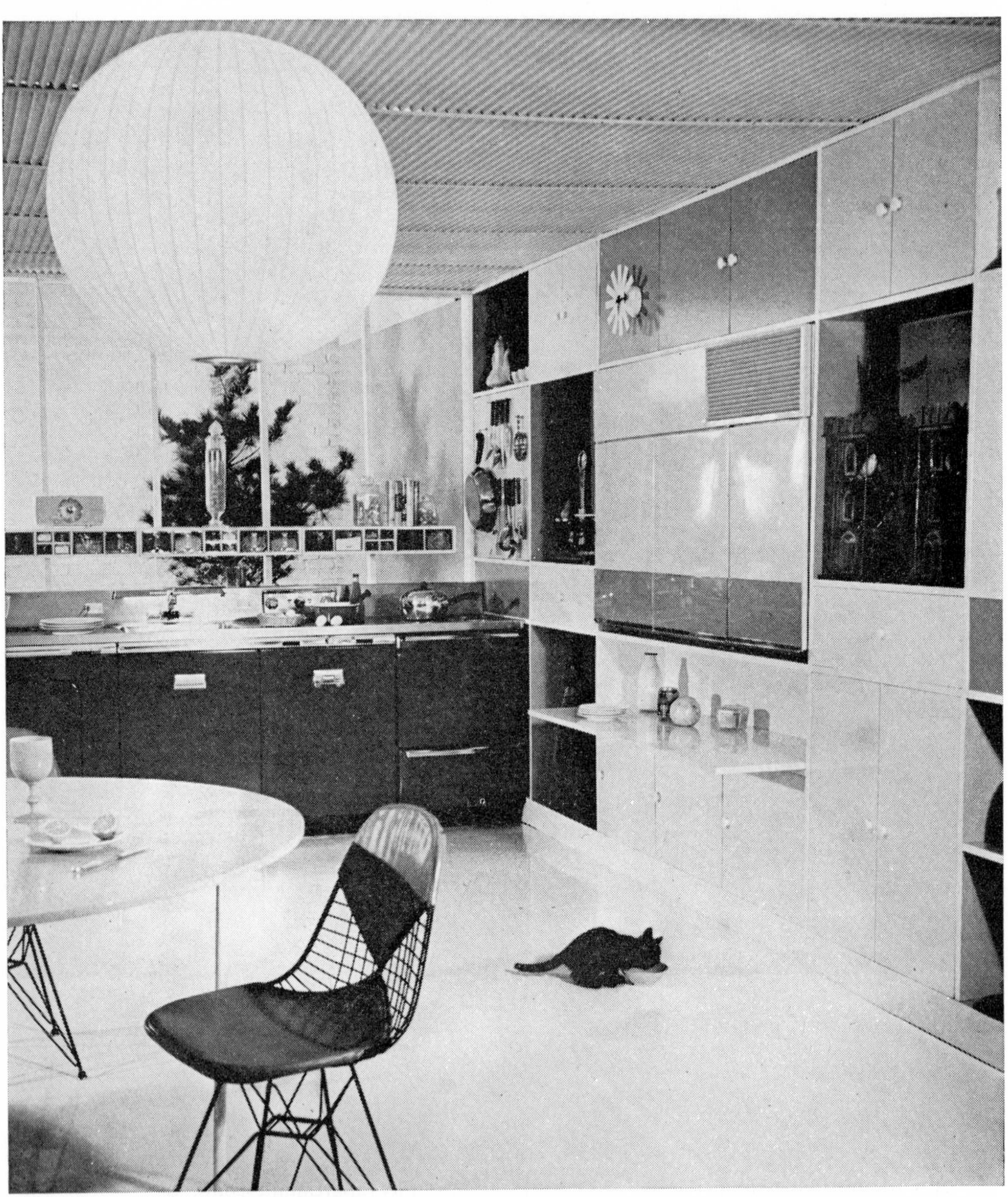

A triad color scheme of blue, red, and yellow interpreted in buff on the corrugated ceiling, royal blue on the long sink and laundry unit, and pink on the table top and some panels of the storage wall where the two other hues appear as turquoise and soft lemon yellow. Tangerine chair pads are a striking accent. White in the large bubble lamp and the vinyl floor underscores and unifies the room. These inspiriting colors in the newer impervious materials are not difficult to maintain. George Nelson, designer. (*Photograph by Nina Leen. Courtesy of Life Magazine © Time, Inc. 1954*)

When you are reasonably certain you know what you want, borrow large samples—a full length of drapery material, a piece of upholstery large enough to cover a good portion of a chair or sofa. It may save money in the long run to get a large piece of wallboard and paint it the color you think is best for your walls. Study these at different times of day or night because their effect will change with the kind of light. Large samples are important because:

- Increasing an area of color often changes its apparent hue, value, and intensity.
- Color combinations at small scale only hint at the full-scale effect.

Factors to Consider in Selecting Colors

Color combinations are generally best when thoughtfully related to you and your family, your possessions, your whole house and specific rooms, and the surrounding environment.

You and your family. The people using a home every day always come first in sensible interior design. For example:

- Active, vigorous families and young people often like strong contrasting colors.
- Quieter or older persons generally prefer somewhat cool, neutralized, harmonious schemes.

Your possessions. The furniture and accessories now owned as well as planned purchases both limit and suggest possible color schemes.

- A collection of antique furniture, good paintings, or individualized accessories might determine your colors.
- Miscellaneous furnishings can often be pulled together by a related scheme of warm, middle value, low intensity colors.
- If starting from scratch, your favorite color scheme might be the guide in selecting furnishings.

Your rooms. The walls of the rooms, including the windows and their treatment, the doors and fireplaces, are the largest color areas. Floors and ceilings come next in size, then furniture and accessories. Typical color relationships are as follows:

- Floors are moderately dark in value and low in intensity to give a firm, unobtrusive base and to simplify upkeep, and they are warm in hue because cold floors are seldom liked.

Room	Walls	Floors	Ceiling	Furniture and Upholstery
Entrance Hall	1 of autumn brown paneled wood; 3 of sage green; opens into a room paneled in blue spruce green.	Sage green shag rug.	Sage green.	Oak; no upholstery.
Living Room 1	1 of Empire blue; 3 of ecru.	Sand shaggy rug.	White.	Bamboo and reed, surf green upholstery.
Living Room 2	Redwood (burnt umber in color).	Sage green shaggy rug.	Sage green painted wood.	Oak built-ins, chairs with lacquer red seats and backs; mistletoe-green textured upholstery.
Dining Room 1	3 of Lincoln green; 1 of pearl gray brick.	Plywood squares stained mahogany.	Pearl gray.	Mahogany; upholstered in deep chrome green.
Dining Room 2	Lichen green.	Cinnamon, bottle green, and smoke brown Oriental rug on oak floor.	White.	Mahogany with chestnut; ivy-green and black needlepoint upholstery.
Kitchen 1	3 of ash-gray wood; 1 of salmon-pink plaster.	Reused brick and navy blue linoleum.	Terra cotta.	Terra-cotta cabinets, stainless steel tops, one black and white marble top, stainless steel range units, white refrigerator.
Kitchen 2	Peach bloom; Yale blue and white figured tile behind range.	Rose-gray jaspe linoleum blocks, black cove.	Cobweb gray acoustical tile.	White metal cabinets and appliances, dark cardinal-red linoleum and oak counter tops, black lacquered chairs, oak dining counter with pearl-gray top.
Bedroom 1	3 of plum; 1 of mist.	White shag rug.	Iris mauve.	Antiqued white wood and walnut, old-rose upholstery; robin's-egg-blue bedspread.
Bedroom 2	1 of emerald green: 2 of willow green; 1 of grass green.	Old ivory and black jaspe linoleum blocks and old ivory shag rug.	Willow green.	Black iron, wicker, and glass; chamois and emerald-green upholstery; deep chrome-yellow and old-ivory bedspread.
Bathroom	Upper walls bisque, lower walls French gray tile, molding of peach bloom tile.	Garnet linoleum with gun-metal border.	Bisque.	Peach-bloom cabinets with dove-gray counter tops, white fixtures, chrome fittings.

;OLOR SCHEMES

Draperies	Accessories	Comments
'one.	Oak driftwood, copper bowl, large-leaved plant.	Green and orange; welcoming and natural.
istachio green and white oliage print.	Black iron lamp base with chartreuse shade; peacock-blue glass ashtrays.	Analogous scheme (blue, green, and yellow); relies chiefly on impact of green against blue for interest.
traw-colored, rough-texured drapes.	Brass lamps with bronze shades; brass clock, plants, pewter vases; lacquer-red ashtrays and cigarette box.	Analogous scheme (green, yellow, and orange) as restful as a shady woodland.
earl-gray, black, and sage-reen geometric pattern.	Charcoal-gray stone sculpture, green plants.	3 basic colors are green (fairly high intensity), red (very low intensity), and gray; strong, rich contrasts.
astilian-red damask.	Silver chandelier and hollow ware, white porcelain bowl, gold-framed portraits.	Complementary scheme based on green and red; balanced, gracious, cheering.
ourmaline-blue, white, and lack printed linen.	Stainless steel and copper pans and bowls, white electrical appliances, clear glass jars.	Monochromatic red-orange relieved by grays; varied textures add much interest.
ale-blue plastic.	Dark cardinal-red and white canisters.	Triad (red, blue, and yellow) with much white; fresh, lively, and balanced.
obin's-egg blue.	White iron flower container, white lamps and shades, white pottery.	Analogous scheme of blue, violet, and red; white contrasts with harmonious hues.
Villow-green fishnet.	White pottery breakfast dishes, white picture frames, brass lamps with white shades, brass vases.	Greens and yellows, black and white; sparkling and invigorating.
arnet drapes and shower ırtain.	Garnet and white towels.	Monochromatic (red) with gray; pleasant relief from antiseptic or pallid colors.

- Walls are lighter in value than floors to provide a transition between them and the ceilings, quite neutral in intensity to keep them as backgrounds, and are more often warm than cool.
- Ceilings are very light in value and very low in intensity for a sense of spaciousness and efficient reflection of light; frequently they are white but may be tints of either warm or cool hues.

This standard approach resembles nature's pattern of colors and gives a satisfying up-and-down equilibrium. Although it has much to recommend it, you need not follow it unthinkingly. Light floors, for example, make a room luminous by minimizing heavy shadows and reflecting light upward. Dark walls give comforting enclosure, make rooms seem smaller, and unify miscellaneous dark furniture; intense colors are stimulating and refreshing deviations. Dark ceilings, lessening the apparent height of walls, make rooms seem more intimate.

Use of rooms is much less important today than it was when only certain colors were deemed appropriate for specific rooms.

- Entrance areas can be in any colors that welcome visitors and introduce them to the character of the house.
- Group living space we expect to be cheerful and hospitable. Because this space is used by many persons for various activities, it is seldom the best place for overwhelming, aggressively individualistic colors.
- Dining space, if a separate room and used only a few hours a day, provides opportunities to experiment with more dramatic schemes, although some people prefer quiet colors as a background for dining.
- Kitchens have no limitations other than the three or more large pieces of mechanical equipment (which no longer need to be white), the constant cleaning required, and the tendency to get overly warm. Aside from these, any colors the kitchen worker likes are suitable.
- Bathrooms are small and used only for short periods. They, too, are a good place to experiment.
- Bedrooms are the individual's refuge, and it is out of place to recommend colors for this sanctum.

Room use is a very general factor in color schemes, and specific guides are useless unless you want to repeat the stereotypes that make many houses dull.

Room size, shape, and character seem to change with different color treatments, a factor often underestimated. In planning a new house, you should consider color along with the other aspects of design. Older houses are most easily remodeled by an "architectural" use of color. A few examples are:

- Cool hues, light values, and low intensities make rooms look larger.
- Rooms too long and narrow can be visually shortened and widened by having one end wall warmer, darker, and more intense than the side walls.
- Rooms that are too square and boxy seem less awkward if one or two walls are treated differently from the others, or if one wall and the ceiling or the floor are similar in color.

Windows and orientation affect the character of rooms and have a bearing on color schemes.

- Rooms well lighted by large windows or good artificial illumination do not distort colors. Those less well lighted make colors seem darker and duller.
- Rooms facing south and west get more heat and more light (of a yellowish hue) than do those facing east or north. These differences can be minimized by using cool colors in south and west rooms, warm in east and north; they can be maximized by putting warm colors in warm rooms and cool in the others; or the differences can be left as they are by using the same colors in all rooms.

Regarding rooms of a home separately has grave dangers because a home is a unit, not a collection of rooms, especially with contemporary open plans. Unified color schemes recognize this and bring harmony and continuity; they increase visual spaciousness and make it possible to shift furnishings from one room to another without disturbing color schemes. This makes sense. But what about monotony? That is a matter of personal opinion—and the colors used.

If one total color scheme seems too limiting, give thought to having one color carry through all the floors, the walls, the ceilings, *or* the draperies. Or there can be a more complex carry-through, such as this: mellow grays, pinks, and greens of a patterned fabric in the living room are the basic colors and spread out into walls of gray, a ceiling of very pale pink, and a blue-gray carpet. The dining room has the same carpet and ceiling but one of the greens in the fabric becomes the wall color and the pink is modified into cedar for the draperies. The master bedroom has the same carpet, three walls of gray, and the fourth wall and ceiling of pink, a bedspread of green, and curtains of soft yellow. Such devices as these create a sense of consistent wholeness.

Architectural character of a sort positive enough to be a factor in color selection is regrettably uncommon. If, though, your home or even one room in a home has such quality, regard it as an asset and emphasize it with appropriate color.

Your environment, regional and local, is a subtle factor. How much attention should be given to it is a personal decision. Connecticut, Louisiana, New Mexico, and Oregon environments do not suggest identical color schemes but ones weighted by consideration of their differing climates and geography and the architecture these conditions produce. Specific location is also of consequence. An apartment or town house in the fog belt of San Francisco might not indicate the colors that would seem appropriate to a ranch house on California's rolling hills that are typically green in winter and spring, straw-yellow in summer and fall. Sensitive study of the environment helps in achieving a color scheme that does not seem completely foreign to its larger setting.

► ECONOMIES WITH COLOR

Color can more than earn its cost, in fact actually save money if wisely used.

- A coat of paint on one or more walls of a room will change the atmosphere more cheaply than any other single device.
- Old, battered, nondescript furniture takes on renewed vitality with new paint.
- Bands of color painted around windows are inexpensive substitutes for draperies; floors painted in suitable colors, possibly textured with spatterdash, lessen the need for rugs.
- A preponderance of light-value colors can cut your electric bills and probably let you see better.
- Warm colors in your home make you feel comfortable at lower, probably more healthful, temperatures.
- Cheering colors lessen the apparent need for vitamins and tonics.
- Colors that do not fade, or that fade gracefully, minimize replacement.
- Nature colors, especially if patterned, not only reduce daily and weekly maintenance but remain passably good looking longer than do most clear sharp colors.
- A unified color scheme throughout the house makes for economical interchangeability of furniture, draperies, and rugs.

Free-standing laminated wood arches support a roof hovering over walls of glazed brick and glass that enclose a house in Florida. Victor Lundy, architect. (*Photograph by Lisanti, Inc.*)

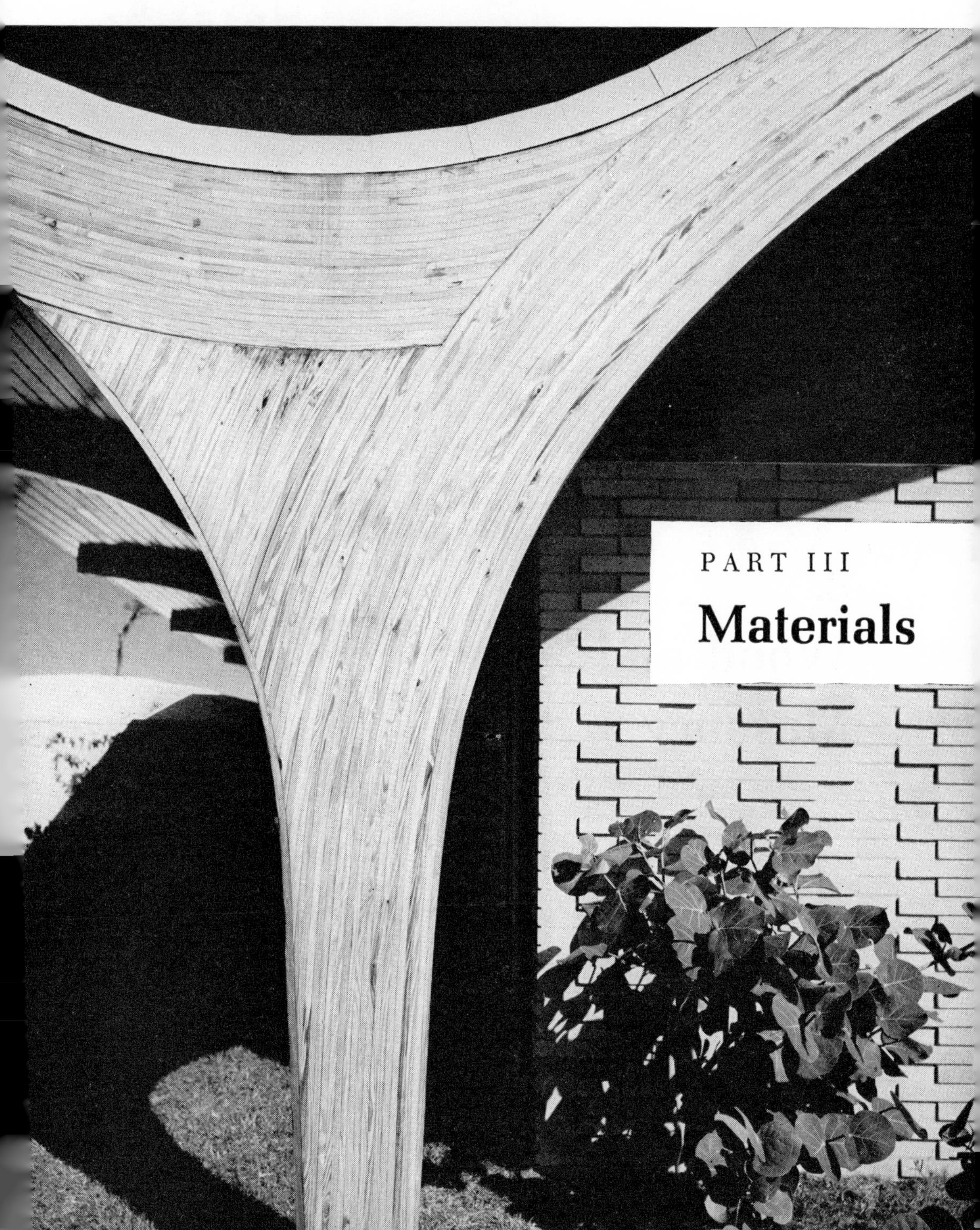

PART III

Materials

8. Wood and Masonry

Our homes are built of materials, each having special potentialities and limitations that indicate appropriate forms and uses. We cannot go far toward realizing a satisfying home without understanding the nature of the materials from which it is constructed and with which it is furnished. Together with planning and design, materials determine the usefulness, economy, beauty, and individuality of homes.

▸ WOOD

No material but wood could have given so naturally the inviting informal character of the deck terrace shown in Figure 174A or related it so well to its surroundings. Most immediately noticeable is the floor of redwood boards laid in checkerboard design, which introduces a handsome structural pattern of light and dark. Built-in seats and railings echo the clean-cut, simple de-

Above. Wood is fibrous, stone is granular. (*United States Plywood Corp.* and *Smithsonian Institution*) tails of the protecting roof and the structure of the wall. Although all forms are strictly geometrical with rectangles predominant, the effect is neither hard nor formal. There is, though, a strong sense of man-made order that contrasts happily with the free-growing trees in the background and in pots. Imaginatively and sensitively designed, frankly revealed, material and structure add up to a kind of beauty favored by many today and appreciated by the Japanese for centuries.

There were many reasons for selecting wood as the chief building material. One is its remarkable strength in relationship to its size and shape. Most notable is its *tensile* strength; it resists breakage when subjected to bending or pulling forces, as anyone who has handled a bomboo fishpole knows. Tensile strength permits wood to be used for spanning gaps, such as those above the sliding doors, in the railings, and in the built-in seats. Its tensile strength also suits wood to cantilever construction (defined as nonvertical members supported at only one end) as seen in the roof that projects freely beyond the house walls. Wood, further, has considerable strength in *compression* (retains its shape under pressure), which makes it useful for such uprights as the vertical posts supporting the house wall and the legs holding up the chairs and tables. In addition, wood is used because it makes floors and furniture seem slightly resilient. Also it does not get so hot or so cold as do metal and masonry, an important factor in outdoor living areas. Furthermore, it does not readily transmit heat or cold, which makes it a good insulator when used for walls or roofs.

Wood is comparatively inexpensive in original cost and in the labor needed to shape and fasten it together, and it can be economically maintained over long periods of time. Such weather-resistant woods as cedar, cypress, and redwood survive exposure to weather with little upkeep when used for exterior walls, roofs, terraces, and outdoor furniture. The original cost of interior walls of wood is greater than plaster walls, but if finished with varnish or wax require little to sustain them in good condition. At the end of ten years the total cost of wood and plaster is about the same, and from then on wood costs less in time, energy, or money. Hardwood furniture demands relatively little care because it seems to absorb those scratches and dents it cannot resist.

We would like wood for its beauty and individuality even were it not for its utility and economy. Wood grain and color show a perfect union of variety and unity: no two pieces are identical, even the two ends or sides of one piece are not exactly alike, and yet there is a powerful, organic unity in each piece and among many pieces (Fig. 184). The rhythms are as subtle and inevitable as those in waves or clouds and range from almost parallel linearity to an intricate complexity of curves. Some wood grains

A

B

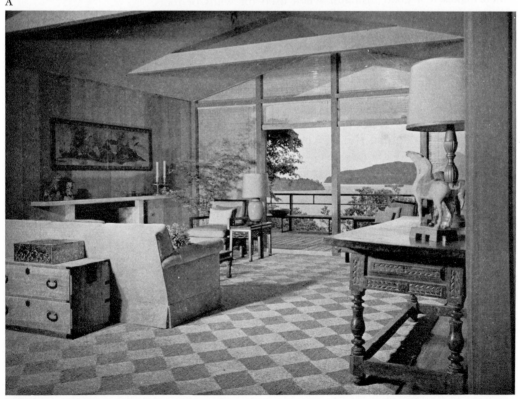

are emphatic, others quietly subordinate. Whatever the patterns, they always seem to be in equilibrium. Finally, wood is as pleasant to touch as to look at.

Wood's limitations are similar to those of other organic materials: it burns, rots, decays; it is attacked by insects; and it may swell, shrink, or warp with changes in moisture content. The first step in overcoming these limitations is the consideration of other materials more suitable for certain uses: masonry or metal where there is a fire hazard or masonry where there is excessive dampness. The second step is the selection of the best wood for specific conditions because woods vary greatly. Redwood and cedar, for example, resist rot and decay; mahogany and walnut have high shape and size stability. The third step is proper drying. This reduces the high moisture content of living wood to minimize rot and decay, shrinkage, and warpage. Woods, however, will always vary in moisture content and shrink or swell with variations in humidity, the soft woods more than the hard. The fourth step is designing objects of wood with sensitive regard for the nature of the material. The fifth step is applying an appropriate preservative or finish. Finally, comes sympathetic care and maintenance of the object as it is used.

Wood is handsomely used as the basic material in a hillside house overlooking San Francisco Bay. Campbell and Wong, architects.

Left above. Geometric yet informal, a spacious sheltered deck projects out over the hill.

Left below. The meticulously detailed interior is an unobtrusive background for beautiful furnishings and the spectacular view. (*Photographs by Morley Baer*)

Below. The deceptively simple plan of the living, dining room, and terrace is marked by a sensitively proportioned regularity.

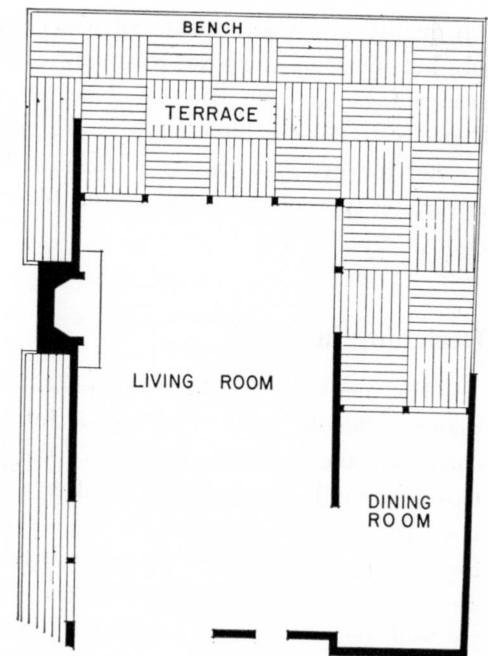

Selecting Woods

Wood comes from plants ranging from pencil-thin bamboos to Australian eucalyptuses that are nearly 400 feet in height and California redwoods as large as 100 feet in circumference. Differences in strength, hardness, durability, and the like are almost as great as is the diversity of appearance of trees.

Somewhat arbitrarily, wood is often classified as *hard* if it comes from broad-leaved trees that in colder climates drop their leaves in winter, such as maple, oak, or walnut; and as *soft* if it comes from those trees with needlelike leaves retained throughout the year, as typified by pine, cedar, and redwood. In general, wood from the second group is softer, coarser in grain, less attractively figured, and costs less. It is easier to work with conventional tools but does not lend itself readily to fine finishes or intricate shapes. There is, however, considerable overlapping between the two types. For example, southern yellow pine is harder than chestnut, gum, basswood, or poplar although the latter four are classified as *hard* because they come from broad-leaved, deciduous trees. Douglas fir and redwood, both from needle-leaved evergreens, are approximately as hard as chestnut or gum. On pages 177-180, the significant characteristics of woods often used in homes are tabulated so that you can see for yourself what the qualities of different woods are and make decisions wisely.

In selecting woods, keep in mind that every piece does not have to be top quality in every respect. All wood should be strong enough to do its job, but for some purposes relatively weak woods are adequate. Hardness is advantageous if the wood is subject to wear, of less importance otherwise. Capacity to take a high finish is desirable in furniture wood but is not needed for exterior siding or shingles. Beautiful grain and figure are a rewarding type of indoor ornament, but they are pretty much wasted outdoors.

Designing in Wood

The medieval fireplace wall (Fig. 182A) illustrates most of the basic shapes suited to wood. Flat boards form the wall panels, the seat of the chair, and the seat and supports of the bench. Chiefly because of wood's tensile strength, the board or plank is a typical, useful form seen not only in chairs, benches, and cabinets but in flooring and siding. A second typical form is the round pole, reminiscent of trunks and branches of trees. These are seen in the legs and arms of the three-legged chair. That wood can go well beyond simple planks and poles is evident in the beautifully

QUALITIES OF DIFFERENT WOODS

Name	Source	Color and Grain	Character	Uses
Alder (Red)	One of few native hardwoods in Pacific northwest	Pleasant light colors from white to pale pinks, browns. Close, uniform grain.	Lightweight, not very strong; resists denting, abrasion; shrinks little.	Chairs, other furniture.
Ash (White)	Central, eastern U. S.; Europe	Creamy white to light brown. Prominent grain resembling oak; pronounced elliptical figures in plain-sawed or rotary cut. Burls make decorative veneers.	Hard, strong, wears well; intermediate to difficult to work; intermediate in warping.	Furniture frames requiring strength; exposed parts of moderate-priced furniture; cheaper than most durable hardwoods.
Beech	Central, eastern N. America; Europe	White or slightly reddish. Inconspicuous figure and uniform texture similar to maple.	Strong, dense, hard; bends well; warps, shrinks, subject to dry rot; relatively hard to work, but good for turning; polishes well.	Middle-quality, country-style furniture; good for curved parts, rocker runners, interior parts requiring strength; also floors, utensil handles, woodenware food containers (no taste or odor). Often stained or painted; natural wood pleasant.
Birch	Temperate zones; many species, yellow birch most important	Sapwood, white; heartwood, light to dark reddish-brown. Irregular grain, not obtrusive; uniform surface texture; undulating grain called "curly."	Usually hard, heavy, strong; little shrinking, warping; moderately easy to work; beautiful natural finish; stains, enamels well.	Plywoods; structural, exposed parts furniture, usually naturally finished (esp. Scandinavian); can be stained to imitate mahogany, walnut.
Cedar	North Pacific coast, mountains	Reddish-brown to white. Close grained.	Rather soft, weak, lightweight; easily worked; little shrinkage; resists decay; holds paint. Red cedar repels moths, has many small knots.	Shingles; siding; porch, trellis columns; vertical grain plywood; cabinet work; interior paneling.
Chestnut	Eastern U. S.; Europe; Asia	Soft grayish-brown. Coarse, open grain much like oak.	Soft, light; splits easily; warps little; resists decay; easy to glue.	Core stock in plywood; cheaper furniture; interior of finer furniture.
Cypress (Southern)	Southeastern coast U. S.; southern Mississippi Valley	Slightly reddish, yellowish-brown, or almost black; weathers silvery gray if exposed. Open grain.	Moderately strong, light; resists decay; holds paint well.	Doors, sash, siding, shingles, porch materials; occasionally outdoor furniture.

QUALITIES OF DIFFERENT WOODS (Cont.)

Name	Source	Color and Grain	Character	Uses
Elm	Europe and U. S.	Light grayish-brown tinged with red to dark chocolate-brown; white sapwood. Porous open oaklike grain, delicate wavy figure, many unusual figures.	Hard, heavy; hard to work; shrinks; swells; bends well.	Somewhat sparingly in furniture; curved parts of Provincial types; extensively used now for decorative veneers.
Fir (Douglas)	Pacific coast U. S.	Yellow to red to brownish. Coarse grain, irregular wavy patterns, especially rotary-cut plywood, "busy."	Rather soft, quite strong, heavy; tends to check, split; does not finish well.	Plywood (some given striated surface or textural pattern) for interior walls, doors, cabinet work; interior, exterior trim, large timbers, flooring; low-cost furniture, especially interior parts.
Gum (Red or Sweet)	Eastern U. S. to Guatemala	Reddish-brown; often irregular pigment streaks make striking matched patterns. Close-grained figure much like Circassian walnut.	Moderately hard, heavy, strong; tends to shrink, swell, warp; susceptible to decay; easy to work; finishes well.	Most used wood for structural parts, with or imitating mahogany, walnut, also exposed as gumwood.
Mahogany	Central, South America; Africa	Heartwood pale to deep reddish-brown; darkens with exposure to light. Adjacent parts of surface reflect light differently, giving many effects, small-scale, interlocked, or woven grain, to ribbon, stripe, or distinctive figures.	Medium hard, strong; easy to work, carve; shrinks little; beautiful texture; takes high polish; always expensive.	Most favored wood for fine furniture in 18th century; much used in 19th century, today in expensive furniture finished naturally, bleached, stained dark.
Maple (Sugar, and Black, both called hard)	Central, eastern U. S.	Almost white to light brown; small, fine, dense pores. Straight-grained or figures (bird's-eye, curly, wavy).	Hard, heavy, strong; little shrinking, swelling; hard to work; has luster, takes good polish.	Early American furniture, but not stained unpleasantly hot red-brown used in imitation pieces today. Now used as solid wood for sturdy, durable, unpretentious, moderate-priced furniture. Good material for hardwood floors.

Name	Source	Color and Grain	Character	Uses
ak (many arieties, wo groups, Vhite and ed)	All temperate zones.	White oaks: pale grayish-brown, sometimes tinged red. Red oaks: more reddish. Quite large conspicuous open grain, fancy figures rare.	Hard, strong; workable, carves well; adaptable to many kinds of finishes.	Long popular for furniture, solid and veneer; standard wood in Gothic period, early Renaissance in northern Europe, continuously used in United States. Floors, wall panels, plywood, etc.
hilippine ahogany not a true ahogany ut resembles it)	Philippines	Straw to deep reddish-brown according to species; pales when exposed to light. Pronounced interlocking grain gives conspicuous ribbon figure.	About as strong as mahogany, less easy to work; greater shrinking, swelling, warping; less durable, harder to polish.	Extensively used for furniture past few decades; also plywood wall panels.
ine (many) arieties milar in haracter)	All temperate zones.	Almost white to yellow, red, brown. Close-grained.	Usually soft, light, relatively weak; easy to work; shrinks, swells, warps little; decays in contact with earth; takes oil finish especially well, also paint. Knotty pine originally covered with paint.	Throughout world for provincial, rustic furniture, notably by early American settlers. Early Georgian furniture for ease of carving, also paneled walls. Often all painted, or decorative patterns here and Europe. Now inexpensive cabinetwork, doors, window-sash frames, structural members; some furniture.
oplar	Eastern U. S.	White to yellowish-brown. Close-grained, relatively uniform texture.	Moderately soft, weak, lightweight; easy to work; finishes smoothly, holds paint well.	Siding; interior, exterior trim; inexpensive furniture, cabinetwork, especially when painted or enameled.
edwood	Pacific coast U. S.	Reddish-brown; lightens in strong sun; becomes gray or blackish if allowed to weather. Inconspicuous parallel grain in better cuts, contorted in others; highly decorative burls.	Moderately strong in large timbers, but soft and splinters easily; resists rot and decay.	Exterior siding, garden walls, outdoor furniture; some use for interior walls, cabinetwork.

QUALITIES OF DIFFERENT WOODS (Cont.)

Name	Source	Color and Grain	Character	Uses
Rosewood (several species, grouped because of fragrance)	India, Brazil	Great variation from light to deep reddish-brown. Irregular black, brown streaks in fanciful curves.	Hard, durable; takes high polish.	Extensively used in fin 18th-century furniture chiefly veneers, inlays 19th-century solid wood. Increasing us in furniture today.
Tupelo Gum	Southeastern U. S.	Pale brownish-gray heartwood merges gradually with white sapwood. Lask of luster makes interlocking grain inconspicuous; no figure of importance	Hard, heavy, strong; good stability; moderately easy to work; tendency to warp.	Same purposes as Re Gum, although it is somewhat weaker, softer.
Walnut (American or Black)	Central and eastern U. S.	Light to dark chocolate-brown, sometimes dark irregular streaks. Distinctive, unobtrusive figures of stripes, irregular curves; stumps, crotches, burls give intricate, beautiful figures.	Hard, heavy, strong; warps little, moderately easy to work, carve; natural luster; takes good finish.	In America from ear liest times for goo furniture, but especially in 19th century now in high-grade fur niture, paneling.
Walnut (Circassian) (also called English, Italian, European, Russian, etc.)	Balkans to Asia Minor, Burma, China, Japan. Planted Europe for wood, nuts.	Fawn-colored, many conspicuous irregular dark streaks give elaborate figures; butts, burls, crotches add to variety.	Strong, hard, durable; works, carves well; shrinks, warps little; takes fine polish.	A leading furniture wood since ancient times; Italian, French Spanish Renaissance; England, Queen Anne 1660-1720 called Ag of Walnut; importe for American furniture

carved panels and the handsomely turned (shaped on a lathe) supports of the chair. More intricate ornament is seen in the lacelike tracery at the top of the paneling and the carving on the bench.

Metal, stone, brick, and tile have been used with equal sensitivity but, expectedly, each shape is affected by its material and its function. The metal stand is an intricate design of slender, curved forms well-suited to metal but next to impossible in masonry or wood. Metal is also appropriately used in the andirons: not only is metal fireproof but strong enough to be thin and still hold burning logs in place. Although refined by carving, the stone supporting the fireplace hood has the sturdy solidity associated with masonry. Square tiles on the floor and rectangular bricks backing the fireplace make a design point of the fact that they were made in small pieces and fitted together. Thus, each material has been handled sympathetically in terms of its own special character and in terms of man's varied needs.

Many persons today are of the persuasion that the shapes given to wood, or any other material, should develop out of its special qualities. Wood normally grows in tapering, pole-shaped trunks and branches. Stripped of bark and cut into usable lengths, these poles have been used in most parts of the world as frameworks for tents covered with bark or skins, or for huts sheathed with bark or bunches of grass. Refined in shape, such poles are found in historic and contemporary homes as posts and pillars, legs of tables and chairs (Fig. 182A), lamp bases, and rolling pins. Tree trunks have been used, vertically or horizontally, as house walls in typically log-cabin fashion. Clearly, the pole is a basic wood shape, but further shaping is necessary before it can be used to any great extent.

Trunks and branches can be squared to make heavy or light beams or sawed into thin planks for siding or sheets for plywood and veneers (page 184). Rectangularity facilitates fastening them together as shown in Figures 174A and 183A. The timber can also be sawed into round blocks suitable for garden paving or turned into bowls and plates.

There are three more basic possibilities for handling wood. One is literally "unwrapping" the log by peeling it into very thin continuous sheets for veneers and plywood (Figs. 184D and E). The second is bending wood into the curved shapes often seen in chairs (Figs. 182B and 99). The third is grinding or splitting wood into small pieces that are then pressed together for wallboards; grinding, softening, and bleaching it to make paper; or dissolving it and transforming the result into synthetic fibers.

These possibilities demonstrate the great virtuosity of wood, the manifold shapes it will take. Not every kind of wood is equally suitable for all these shapes, but one or more is nearly perfect for each.

Solid Wood. Solid wood needs no explanation. Its advantages are:

- the satisfaction that comes from knowing that all of the wood is the same as the surface;
- the edges of table tops, chair seats, etc., do not expose the layer-cake construction of plywood;
- the wood can be turned or carved;
- the surface can be planed in case of damage, or thoroughly sanded for refinishing, without fear of going through to another wood;
- the surface cannot loosen or peel off (as it may in improperly constructed veneers).

Major disadvantages are high cost and a tendency to warp, shrink, or swell.

A

The wondrous potentialities of wood are almost unlimited.

Above. A section of a medieval room in which wood, masonry, and metal are each used and shaped appropriately. (*Courtesy of the Pennsylvania Museum of Art, Philadelphia*)

Left. Charles Eames' chair with seat and back of molded plywood and supports of bent laminated wood has become a contemporary classic. (*Herman Miller Furniture Company*)

B

A

Above. Wood is still used extensively for the skeletons of most houses. (*Stanford University*)

Right. A screen made of thin strips of bent wood makes a striking pattern against a wall of striated plywood. (*Thonet Industries*)

B

Wood structure is a complex organization of fibers and pores. Concentric *annual rings* that develop yearly increase the tree's girth; *vertical fibers* and *pores* run parallel to the trunk; and *medullary rays* radiate from the center at right angles to the vertical fibers and pores. The way in which wood is cut produces notably different results.

Left and below (left). *Quarter-sawed* lumber is cut parallel to the rays. It shrinks less in width and also twists less than does plain-sawed. The grain pattern usually shows predominantly longitudinal stripes.

Left and below (right). *Plain-sawed* lumber, cut at right angles to the rays, is usually cheaper. The grain pattern is usually irregular parabolas and ellipses.

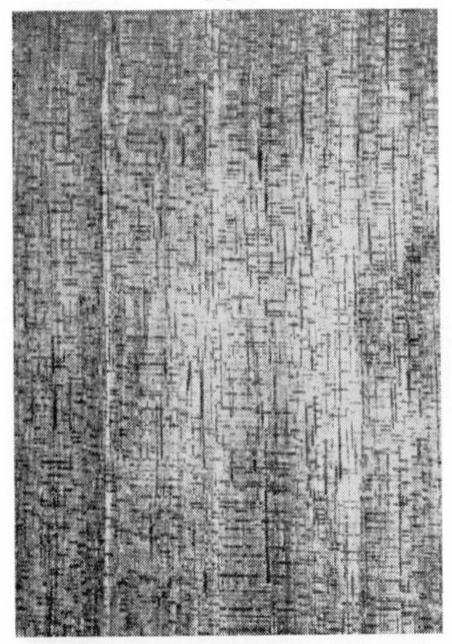

A

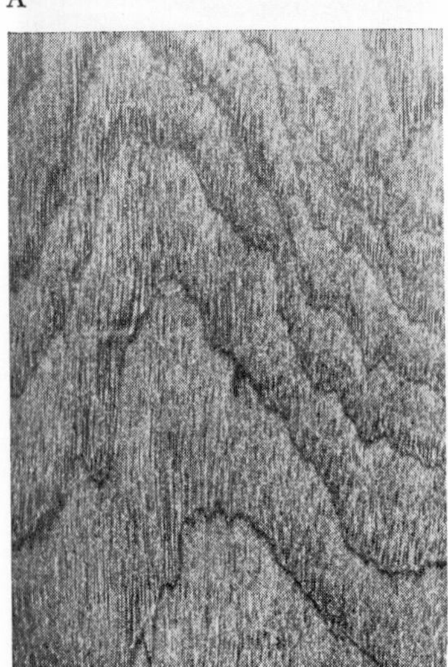

B

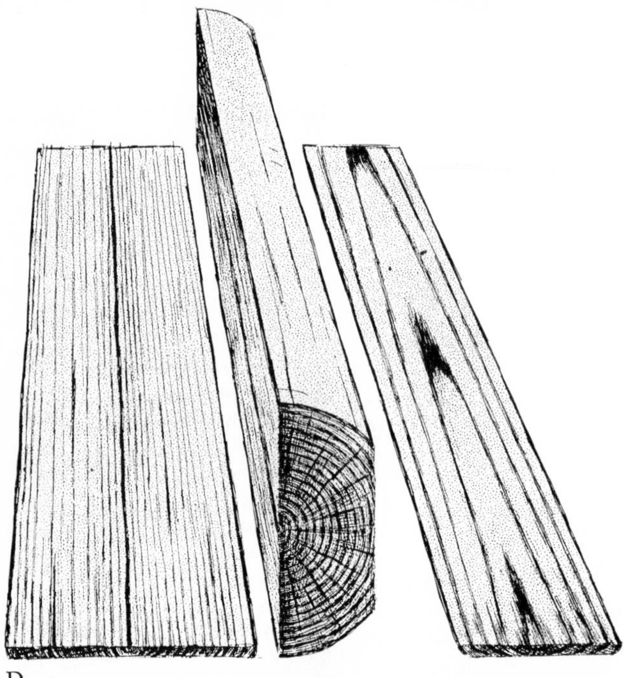

D

Left and below. Rotary-cut wood is unpeeled into thin, continuous sheets by holding a knife-edge cutter against a log rotating on a lathe—something like taking paper towels off a roll. Rotary-cut lumber shows a complex, often large-scale grain pattern.

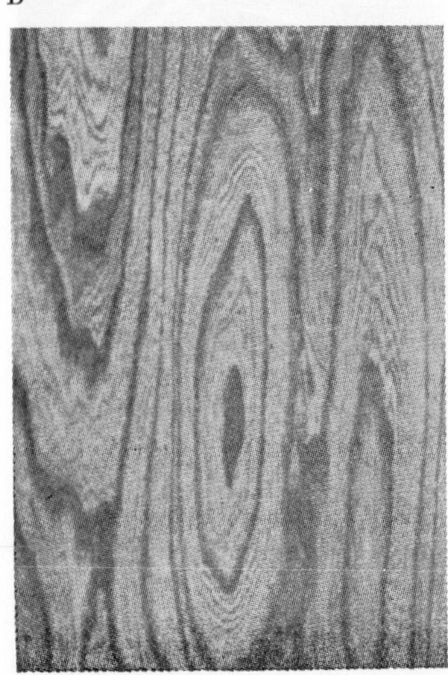

C

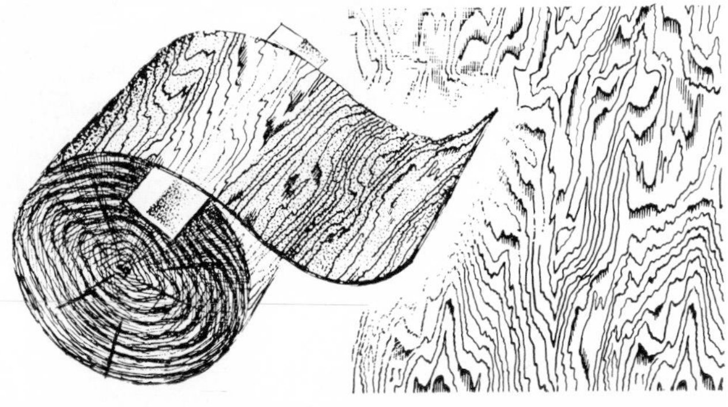

E

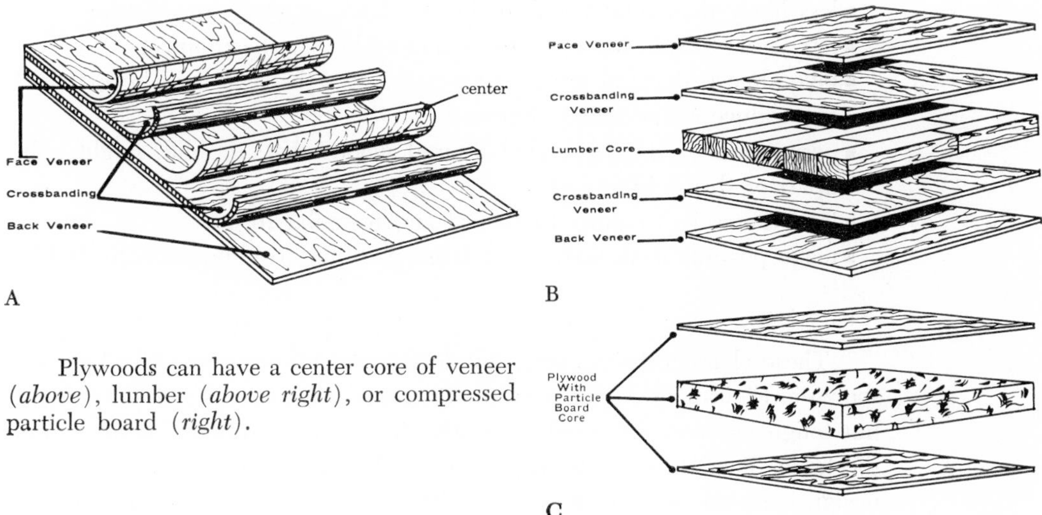

Plywoods can have a center core of veneer (*above*), lumber (*above right*), or compressed particle board (*right*).

Veneers, Plywood, and Laminated Wood. All these are layer constructions consisting of one or more sheets of thin wood, thicker boards, or paper.

Veneers are thin sheets of wood produced by slicing with a knife, sawing, or rotary-cutting. They may be glued to the top of thicker lumber to make what is referred to as "veneered wood," glued to paper for wall coverings, or glued to other veneers as in plywood and laminates. Often, though, the term is used to refer speoifically to the exterior surfaces which are usually of wood more expensive than that underneath.

Plywood is composed of an odd number of veneers glued together with the grain of adjacent sheets at right angles to each other.

Laminated Wood is a type of plywood in which the grain of successive layers goes in the same direction. It is frequently used for those parts of furniture, such as the legs of Charles Eames' chair, which are bent and in which the major stresses and strains are in one direction.

The popular notion that veneers and plywoods are cheap substitutes for the real thing is in part a misconception. To be sure, they are usually less expensive than solid wood, especially in the better grades of hardwood, because the expensive wood goes much further when used as a veneer. But they also have other advantages:

- readily available in much larger pieces (4′ x 8′ or 4′ x 12′) than is solid wood;
- greater strength in many respects than a single board of the same thickness and weight;

- less likely than solid wood to shrink, check, or warp excessively;
- less liable to splitting by nails or puncturing by sharp objects;
- give almost identical grain on several pieces that can then be matched to produce symmetrical figures;
- permit use of fragile, highly figured woods that, if solid, might split apart or shrink irregularly;
- lend themselves readily to curved and irregular forms;
- make possible flush surfaces of large size that are dimensionally stable.

These characteristics open new design possibilities, some of which are shown in Figures 187A and B. In the first, rotary-cut Douglas fir, low in cost but tough in wear, was used for walls, shelves, light trough, cabinets, and the table. The sturdy table was simply and inexpensively constructed in a design harmonious with its architectural setting. Between the kitchen and dining area, the wall was surfaced with similar plywood cut into smaller pieces with the grain running horizontally. This device visually lengthens the wall, reduces its scale, and adds interest through juxtaposition of varied grain patterns. For contrast, the built-in cabinet at the left is surfaced with larger pieces of plywood in which the grain runs vertically. In Charles Eames' conversation alcove, one sees beautifully matched veneered panels of three rare woods used as magnetic accents against many plain, but colorful, surfaces.

Known in ancient Greece and Rome, veneering was revived during the Renaissance, considerably improved in the nineteenth century, and greatly improved during the past few decades. The major drawback—the possibility of the veneers coming apart—has been almost eliminated by new adhesives. Plywood bonded with waterproof adhesives is practical even where moisture is a problem—exterior walls, kitchens and bathrooms, and boats.

Ornamentation in Wood

Wood comes with great diversity of built-in or structural ornament in its grain and figure. Not only does each species of wood have its own general type of pattern, but different aspects of these patterns can be brought to light by the way in which the woods are cut (Fig. 184). In addition to the beauty of typical grains, some woods show amazingly intricate deviations of figures that have long been cherished by furniture designers. *Stripes* and *broken stripes, mottles* and *blisters* of irregular, wavy shapes; *fiddle-back; rain-drop; curly;* and *bird's-eye* are but a few, to which must be added all the figures found in *stump* or *butt wood, crotches, burls,* and *knots.*

A

Plywood and veneer can unify a whole house or can be used sparingly as large accents.

Above. Inexpensive but durable, rotary-cut Douglas Fir plywood has many uses including walls, built-in and free-standing furniture. Willard Francis Hall, architect. (*Photograph by Julius Shulman*)

Below. In his own home, Charles Eames has used beautifully figured veneer on the end wall of a storage unit, more conservative patterns for doors and drawer fronts, very unobtrusive grain for the supports of the coffee table. (*Photographed by Julius Shulman*)

B

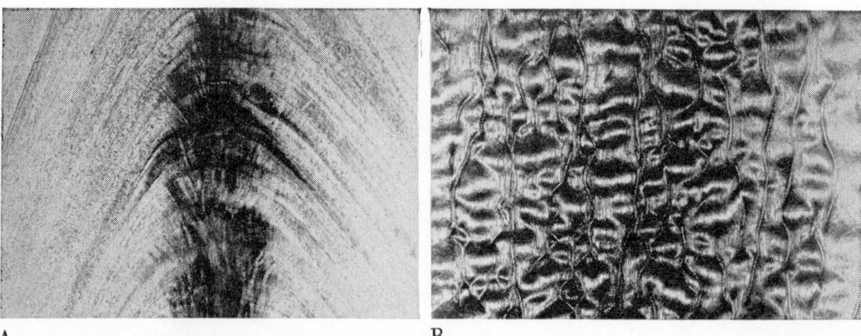

A B

Figures in wood can be rich and varied. Both these boards are mahogany, at left a crotch figure and at right a blister figure. (*U. S. Forest Products Laboratory*)

Texture of the surface is also a kind of ornament and largely determines the effectiveness of the grain. *Roughly sawn* wood, which has a rough, light-diffusing texture that minimizes the grain, is not pleasant to touch and is used for exterior work where a rustic character is wanted; *resawn* wood is considerably smoother, with a soft texture something like a very short-pile fabric, and reveals but does not emphasize the grain; *smoothly finished* wood reflects light, emphasizes the figure, and is good to touch. Two new surface treatments, *striated* and *etched* plywood, are illustrated in Chapter 11.

Joints. The way in which different pieces of wood are brought together creates structural patterns of considerable importance. Overlapping shingles and siding have long been appreciated not only for utilitarian reasons but because of their enlivening patterns of light and dark. A similar effect is produced when boards have beveled edges, as in the terrace shown in Figure 174A. Much smaller beveled edges, such as those in the end wall of Figure 187A, are less noticeable but still add interest.

Moldings. Long, narrow strips not flush with the surface are called moldings. Although they can be made from many materials, today they are usually of wood. And today they are much less favored than in the past because of our desire for simplicity and easy-to-clean homes. Moldings, though, can be labor-savers as in the base moldings and the old-fashioned chair rails that help keep furniture from rubbing against walls. They can also emphasize direction or set up a rhythmic pattern of their own, as they do in board-and-batten construction in which the narrow battens covering the joints between boards set up a vertical or horizontal movement (as illustrated in the split-level house in Chapter 18). In much historic work, the Port Royal parlor for example, they frame such elements as the painting and separate it from its background and they also form transitions between planes as in the elaborate moldings that relate wall and ceiling.

Carving and Turning. The nature of wood has suggested carving from earliest days in all parts of the world, and the great periods of furniture are known as much for their carving as for their more basic qualities of design. Out of the spirit of the age and the kind of wood used, Gothic carving in oak, Renaissance carving in walnut, and eighteenth-century carving in mahogany effectively enhanced form. Turning is also an old art, and ever since man invented the lathe he has enjoyed the diverse ways in which a rapidly rotating piece of wood can be shaped for furniture parts, balusters, and columns. Designers of almost every period produced turnings with distinctive profiles, such as the spirals of India and the European Baroque; the sixteenth-century melon bulbs; the seventeenth-century balls or sausages; and the spool, bead and ball, knob, vase, and so forth.

Elaborate turning and carving of high quality are rare in contemporary furniture (although coarse, insensitive, machine ornament is still with us). Good carving and turning take much time and skill to produce, and they increase household maintenance noticeably—but they can be very beautiful (Figs. 190A and B).

Inlay, Intarsia, Marquetry, and Parquetry. These are ways of combining different woods, metals, ivory, shell, and other materials so that the contrasting colors and textures make patterns in a plane surface (Fig. 190B). *Inlay* has come to be a somewhat general term covering them all; *intarsia* refers to that type in which the pieces are inlaid in solid wood; *marquetry* is used when the design, usually representational, is inlaid in veneer and then glued to a solid backing; and *parquetry* refers to geometric patterns, especially in floors.

In spite of today's paucity of such ornamentation in wood there is a marked trend away from extreme austerity. Some persons find delight in putting old furniture in contemporary settings (Fig. 190C) and some designers are exploring concentrated enrichment suited to our age, a few examples of which are illustrated in Chapter 14. The most marked trend, however, is toward sculptural forms in chairs, sofas, and tables. Designed to be pleasing when seen from any angle, the chairs by Charles Eames and Finn Juhl (Figs. 182B and 7B), to mention but two, combine honesty of purpose with sensuous delight and lyricism.

A

B

Carving and inlay are the two major types of man-made ornamentation in wood.

Above left. A seventeenth-century French armchair displays the Baroque love of richly carved surfaces. *Above right.* Delicate inlay and carving are characteristic of late eighteenth-century English furniture in the Adam style. (*Courtesy of the Metropolitan Museum of Art*)

Below. Boldly elaborated Victorian furniture contrasts handsomely with a contemporary setting. Campbell and Wong, architects. (*Photograph by Morley Baer*)

C

Wood Finishes

Anything done to a freshly sanded piece of wood takes away some of its pristine satiny beauty—but that beauty will soon disappear even if no finish is put on it. All but a few woods used in a few ways need some protective finish to keep the surface from absorbing dirt and stains; to give an easy-to-clean smoothness; to minimize excessive sudden changes in moisture content; to protect the wood from rot, decay, and insects; to keep it from drying out and to replace the lost oils; to minimize fading or darkening of color; to emphasize the grain with oil, change the color with stain, or hide both color and grain with opaque paint—in short, to protect and embellish.

Finishes can penetrate or stay on the surface; be transparent and colorless, transparent but colored, or semi-opaque or opaque; and they can vary from a dull mat to a high gloss. To say that any one of these finishes is better than the others, except for a specific purpose, would be to fly in the face of facts. Today, however, many people like to see wood changed as little as is compatible with its use and therefore prefer transparent, colorless, dull finishes. Few of us like the finish to be more noticeable than the material underneath, as it often is on heavily varnished, cheap furniture. And we can also say that, *generally speaking:*

- Opaque finishes hide the wood character, give a smooth uniformity, and offer great possibilities for color.
- Transparent finishes reveal the character of the wood and do not emphasize minor damage that comes with use.
- Penetrating finishes (except plastics which impregnate the wood and also give a surface coating) produce a soft surface through which stains may penetrate, but do not chip or crack.
- Glossy finishes reflect more light, are more durable because of their hard dense surface, are easier to clean, but show blemishes more than do dull finishes. Gloss can be reduced by adding more thinner to the paint, rubbing with sandpaper, steel wool, or pumice—it will also dull with age and use.
- Many thin coats of any finish, sanded or rubbed between coats, give a more durable, pleasant result than one or two coats applied thickly.

But since that is about as much as can be said on general matters, let us look at some of the ways in which wood can be treated, as summarized in the chart on pages 192-193.

WOOD FINISHES

Name	Composition	Application	Result	Use
Bleach	Various acids, chlorine compounds.	Brush (if bleaching agent is strong enough to affect wood, will also affect skin).	Lightens wood, neutralizes color, usually makes grain less conspicuous; not dependably permanent; wood loses some of luster.	Widely used few years ago to mak furniture pale, blonc bleached—reaction t dark stains popular with previous gene ation. Occasionally used on outdoor sic ing, furniture to giv weathered look.
Enamel	Varnish mixed with pigments to give color, opaqueness.	Brush or spray over undercoat since enamel has less body, covering power than most paints.	Generally hard, durable coat, like varnish; usually glossy, may be dull; rubbing with pumice, oil gives satiny surface. Wide range of colors.	Used chiefly on fu niture, cabinets, wal getting hard use an washing. Also on floors.
Lacquer	Cellulose derivatives, consists of resins, one or more gums, volatile solvents, a softener, and a pigment (if colored).	Regular lacquer best applied with spray as it dries rapidly (15 min.), brushing lacquers dry slowly, make brush application feasible.	Harder, tougher; more resistant to heat, acids, less elastic than paints, varnishes; costlier, but time saved, durability offset this. Not suitable for outdoor wood because of expansion, contraction. Usually glossy, may be rubbed to satiny finish; dull lacquers also available.	Transparent lacque much used on furn ture, walls; opaqu used on furniture.
Oil	Boiled linseed oil, or varied other oils; usually thinned with turpentine.	Brushed or wiped on, excess wiped off, allowed to dry, sanded or rubbed, between 5 and 30 coats, more the better. Hot oil sinks into wood, brings out grain emphatically.	Penetrating, very durable finish with soft luster; darkens and yellows wood somewhat at first, considerably in time. Protective, not conspicuous. Must be renewed.	Oil, often mixed wit beeswax, used in Eu rope from early time to 17th century, als in America in 17t century. Now use on informal indoo outdoor furniture, siding. Also on muc contemporary Scan dinavian furniture.
Paint	Pigments suspended in linseed oil or, more commonly now, varied synthetics that harden on exposure to air. Usually contain drier to hasten hardening. New types dry quickly with little odor, are easy to apply and have excellent covering power. Glossy to mat surfaces.	Brush, roll, or spray.	Opaque coating, varies from hard, durable gloss to softer dull finishes. Hides character of wood.	Long used to protec embellish wood ir doors, outdoors. Painted furniture popular in ancient Egypt, Orient, in Eu rope since Middle Ages; much Early American furniture painted. Widely use now on exterior, in terior.

WOOD FINISHES (Cont.)

Name	Composition	Application	Result	Use
Shellac	Resinous secretion of insect of southern Asia, dissolved in alcohol. Varies from lemon yellow to pale orange when pure; made white by bleaching with alkalies.	Brushed, rubbed, or sprayed; dries rapidly; many thin coats, each rubbed, gives best finish.	Changes character, color of wood very little, especially white type. Rubbed to soft satiny finish or high brittle gloss (French polish). Fragile finish, wears, badly affected by heat, moisture. Water spots. Good as filler or undercoat for varnish, wax.	Used today primarily as an easily applied, quick-drying undercoat.
Stain	Dye or pigment dissolved or suspended in oil or water.	Brushed, sprayed, or rubbed.	Changes color of wood without covering grain (often emphasizes grain or changes surface noticeably); usually darkens wood to make look richer.	Frequently used to alter color of furniture woods thought unattractive, or in imitation of expensive woods. Now decreased interest in dark wood. Used outdoors to compensate for weathering.
Varnish	Various gums, resins dissolved in drying oils (linseed, tung, or synthetic), usually combined with driers. Gums, resins make hard, lustrous; oils make elastic, durable. Dye or pigment makes varnish-stain.	Brush or spray, many thin coats best. Dries slowly or fast, depending on kind, amount of thinner used.	Thin, durable, brownish skin coating, little penetration; darkens wood, emphasizes grain. Ranges from dull mat to high gloss. Best when not thick, gummy.	Known by ancients, not used again until mid-18th century. Widely used today on furniture, floors, walls, chiefly interior.
Wax	Fatty acids from animal, vegetable, mineral sources combined with alcohols. Usually paste or liquid. Vary greatly in hardness, durability.	Brushed, sprayed, or wiped on, usually several coats. Often used over oil, shellac, varnish, but may be used alone.	Penetrates raw wood, especially liquid waxes. Darkens, enriches, brings out grain; gives soft to high luster depending on type and amount of polishing. Must be renewed often, surface wears, washes off; many show water spots, make floors slippery. Difficult to remove entirely, cannot use other finishes over wax.	Very old way of finishing wood. Generally used today as easily renewed surface over more durable undercoats; some liquid waxes used alone on walls, floors, furniture.

More than other material, wood ties the typical house together structurally and visually. It remains one of our most useful, beautiful materials and has more than held its own in spite of the great advances in plastics, glass, and metal. In fact, the newer materials, having relieved wood of some uses to which it was not completely suited, have allowed us to see more clearly how wonderful wood is. Much as we admire and respect other materials, few of them arouse the deep responses—love, if you will—that wood generates. It is the major structural material in most houses and often used for exterior or interior walls, roofs, and floors. For furniture, it has no peer, and it is well suited to such varied small household objects as bowls, salad forks and spoons, and lamp bases. Together with the much more expensive masonry, it is the standard material for garden walls and structures for outdoor living.

► MASONRY

Rocks in their natural shapes have been admired for centuries by Orientals and others as elements in landscape design. Rock gardens or walls that aim to re-create natural effects at small scale are typical examples. The sculptural qualities many boulders possess make them effective, no-maintenance garden features twelve months of the year. Thrown into contrast with geometric paving and garden walls, as well as with the softer and lighter forms of plants, the strong hard beauty of rocks can be forcefully accentuated as it is in Figure 195A.

Near the other end of masonry's range are the richly modeled, pierced concrete walls and the precisely shaped and laid stone, brick and block in Figures 195B, 199A and B, and 201A.

The materials of masonry are stone, brick and tile, concrete, plaster, and mortar—all of which come from mineral compounds found in the earth's crust. Their diversity is at least as great as that found in wood. Masonry substances, however, differ from wood in several ways significant to the home builder. They are of crystalline rather than fibrous structure and typically they are hard, dense, and heavy.

The excellences of masonry materials are numerous. They do not burn, rot, decay, or invite insects and rodents. Most of them are long-lasting and require little maintenance. Also they will retain their shape under great weight. Perhaps no other group of materials affords such widely varied colors and textures and they can be shaped in countless forms or laid in innumerable patterns.

A

Above. Naturally sculptured boulders arranged in a circle of sand create a garden focal point in a near-desert setting. The precise, manmade wood fence dramatizes the view. Lawrence Halprin, landscape architect. (*Photograph by Rondal Partridge*)

Below. Concrete can be modeled in diverse ways from the unimaginative mass of a plain, solid wall to the pierced, intricately convoluted designs of Erwin Hauer.

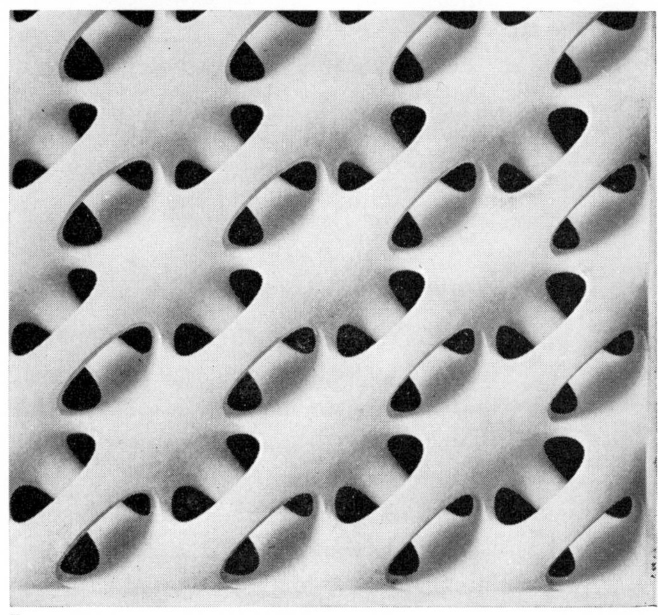

B

These qualities explain why most great historic architecture still in existence is of masonry. Generally, these are large public or religious buildings, but throughout the world are thousands of unpretentious houses and barns built of stone or brick. The essence of historic masonry construction (with the exception of Roman work in concrete) was piling blocks on top of one another and usually joining them with mortar. Because such walls must be thick and rest on very solid foundations, they are expensive. Furthermore, they do not lend themselves to large unobstructed openings unless they are arched, and they offer no space for the ducts, pipes, and wires now deemed essential. Thus, such construction is not used extensively today. Instead, masonry is reinforced with metal to decrease its weight and bulk without lessening its strength, or a masonry veneer is fastened to a structural frame. Often, masonry is confined to a few large simple expanses of wall in which there is a minimum of doors or windows; such other materials as wood or metal are used where openings are large or numerous as illustrated in Figures 198B and 199B. Varied kinds of masonry also serve us well in foundations, fireplaces and chimneys, and outdoor paving or interior floors that rest on the ground.

Masonry, though, has limitations other than high original cost. Although comparatively permanent, plaster and stucco crack, concrete blocks chip, and the softer stones disintegrate more rapidly than might be expected. All are difficult to repair. In comparison with wood or metal, masonry is not very strong in tension. Further, most masonry offers fairly poor insulation against cold and dampness and most of it reflects rather than absorbs noise.

Masonry can be divided into two major categories: the **block** materials—stone, bricks and tiles, concrete, or glass blocks—which are delivered to a building site in their finished form and put together on the job with mortar; and the **plastic** materials—concrete and plaster—which may be used at the building in a semiliquid state.

Stone

Stone, a concreted earthy mineral, has so many desirable qualities that it would undoubtedly be used more widely if it were not so costly. Resisting fire, stone seems naturally associated with walls and fireplaces. Belonging to the earth, it seems at home when used for floors subject to hard use and for outdoor paving. Promising permanence, it gives garden or house walls a uniquely assuring character. Wherever used, the crystalline structure, varied colors and textures, and differing degrees of opaqueness and translucency add up to a very special visual and tactile appeal.

Although there are innumerable kinds of stone that could be used in homes, four are most commonly seen today:

- **Limestone,** which includes varied sedimentary rocks, is relatively soft and easy to cut. Colors range from almost white to dark grays and tans. Its most common use is in exterior walls.
- **Marble,** a compact crystalline limestone, takes a beautiful polish, is often variegated, and comes in white, grays, pinks and reds, greens and black. Contemporary designers, searching for structurally ornamented materials, have found it a handsome substance for fireplaces, bathroom walls, and table tops.
- **Sandstone,** a natural concrete of sand grains, looks and feels sandy. Usually tan, it may also be reddish, greenish, or black. Exterior walls and paving are typical uses.
- **Slate** is a sedimentary rock that splits easily into thin sheets with smooth surfaces, makes good interior floors or outdoor paving. In addition to the typical bluish-gray, slate is available in green, red, or black.

Brick and Tile (Clay)

One of the oldest artificial building materials, bricks are still in favor because, in addition to the general assets of masonry, they are easily made by hand or machine from clays found almost everywhere. They weigh less than stone, which is important in shipping and laying them. Finally, they can be made in many sizes and shapes, colors and textures, and they can be laid in varied patterns. Their only drawback is cost. Figures 182A, 190B, and 199B show the precise rectangularity usually associated with brickwork and also illustrate that bricks are particularly effective when used in large, comparatively simple masses.

Cost usually precludes an entire new house of brick. But, being fireproof, bricks are frequently used for fireplaces and chimneys; for exterior or interior wall surfaces where they last long, are attractive, and require almost no upkeep; and for garden paving because their color and texture render them glareless and nonslip. Wherever seen, bricks introduce an orderly rhythmic pattern of a scale appropriate for homes.

Typical clay bricks are blocks of clay hardened by heat in a kiln. A standard size is 2¼″ x 4″ x 8¼″ but their dimensions may vary considerably. Although "brick red" is a common phrase, colors range from almost white, pale yellow, and pink through oranges and reds down to browns and purples. On the basis of texture as well as resistance to breakage, moisture, and fire, bricks are conventionally divided into several types.

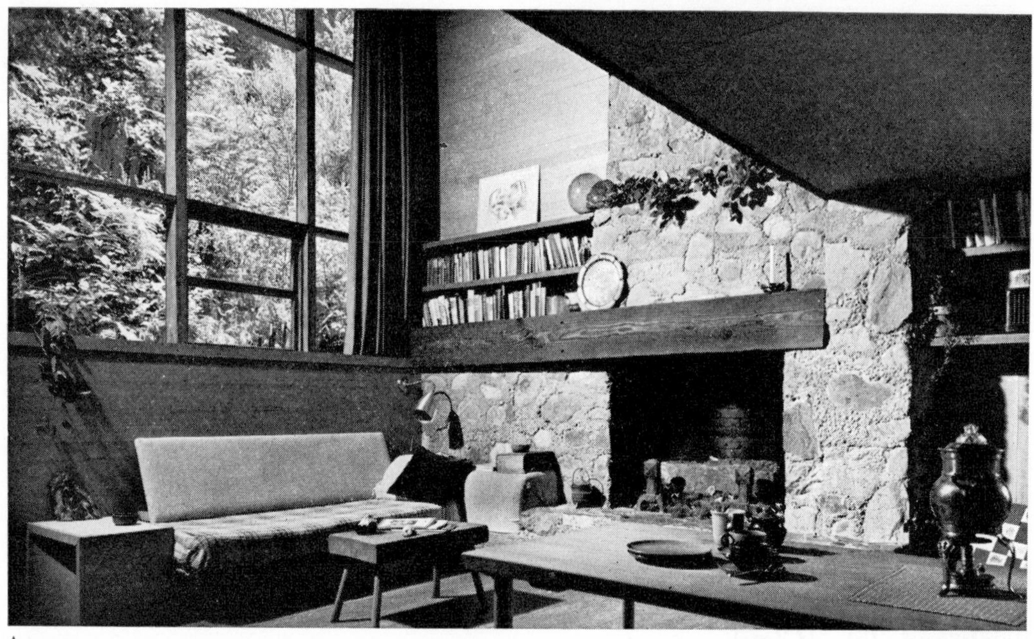

A

The kind of masonry and the manner in which it is used impart a distinctive spirit to domestic architecture.

Above. Rubble masonry, rugged and informal, is that type in which untrimmed or only slightly trimmed stones are laid irregularly. It is usually the least costly kind of stonework. Eral Leek, architect. (*Photograph by Charles R. Pearson. Courtesy of* SUNSET Magazine.)

Below. Random Ashlar is more disciplined but still rustic. The stones are more or less rectangular in shape but of varying sizes. Usually it gives a decided feeling of horizontality even though the joints are not continuous. Anshen and Allen, architects.

B

Right. Ashlar masonry has precisely cut stones, usually rectangular, laid in regular patterns. It is the most formal and most expensive type. The Palazzo Gondi, a Renaissance town house in Florence, Italy, is a handsome example. Giuliano da San Gallo, architect. (*Italian State Tourist Office*)

Below. The precise shape of brick makes sophisticated, elegant designs possible. In contrast to the illustrations on the opposite page, everything in this design is strictly rectangular. Thornton Ladd, architect. (*Photographed by Julius Shulman*)

A

B

- **Common** or **sand-struck bricks,** made in a mold coated with dry sand, have slightly rounded edges and are used for exposed side walls or as a base for better-quality brick.
- **Face bricks,** usually formed by forcing clay through a rectangular die and cutting with wire, have sharp edges and corners, are more uniform in color and texture, and more resistant to weather than are common bricks.
- **Paving** or **flooring bricks** are those made harder by firing at higher temperatures to withstand abrasion and to lessen absorption of moisture.
- **Fire bricks** are usually yellow, and are used for places subject to great heat, such as the backs of fireplaces.

A second type of brick, known as **adobe,** is made of clay that today is usually combined with a cement or asphalt stabilizer and is dried in the sun. Adobe bricks have been used in warm, dry parts of the world for centuries and have recently come back into favor in our own Southwest.

Like bricks, clay tiles are composed of heat-hardened clay but they are usually thin and glazed. They are discussed and illustrated in Chapters 9 and 11.

Concrete Blocks

Once an ugly duckling used apologetically for foundations, concrete blocks are now widely used for their decorative as well as utilitarian qualities.

They have many of the characteristics of clay bricks, but they are made with cement, are not fired (although drying may be hastened with low heat), are usually quite a bit larger than bricks so that a single thickness of blocks can be made into a sturdy wall, and are almost always hollow. Most popular today are the *lightweight-aggregate* blocks made with such lightweight, porous materials as cinders, pumice, or volcanic ash instead of sand and gravel. About half as heavy as the older type, they are less expensive to transport. Being larger than bricks (8″ x 8″ x 16″ and 4″ x 8″ x 16″ are typical sizes), they can be laid more rapidly. Their porosity provides some insulation against heat and cold and also absorbs noise. Finally, their colors are much pleasanter than the older, chilling gray. In mild climates, walls of these blocks need no treatment other than waterproofing although they can be painted or plastered. If left exposed inside and out, as in Figures 100A and 201A, the pleasantly rugged texture appeals to those who like to see that nothing is covered up, that the structure, the interior and exterior walls are one and the same thing frankly revealed.

A

Concrete blocks have broken out of the shackles that once confined them to foundations.

Above. Frank Lloyd Wright demonstrated their versatility in a house that coils up from the Arizona desert. (*Photograph by Maynard Parker. Courtesy of* House Beautiful)

Below. A small sample of the dozens of ways in which concrete blocks can be shaped and laid. (*National Concrete Masonry Association*)

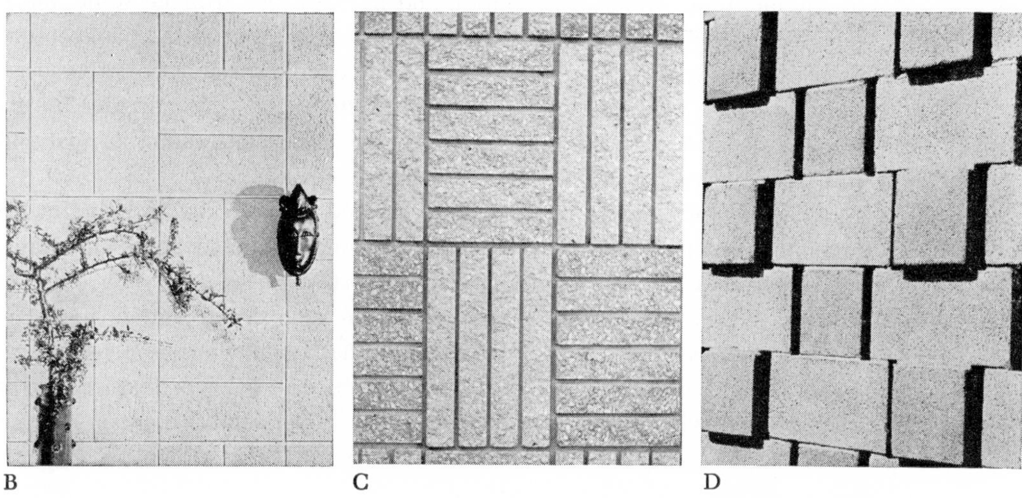

B C D

Glass Bricks

Hollow blocks of glass which can be set together in mortar come in many sizes and shapes. They also vary in the amount of light and heat they transmit. Some, for example, reflect the high summer sunlight but allow the winter sun's low rays to warm the interior. Glass bricks are one of the few materials that admit light but give varying degrees of privacy, provide reasonable insulation against heat and cold, and make a supporting wall of any strength. Further, the manner in which they diffuse light and create changing abstract patterns out of objects seen through them is highly decorative. They have been used to illumine entrance areas, bathrooms (Chapter 11), kitchens, and other rooms where natural light combined with privacy is wanted. They have not, however, been widely used in homes probably because their bright glitter seems "commercial" and their cost is fairly high.

These are the major block-masonry materials. We now turn to the two masonry materials—concrete and plaster—that are used on the job in a semiliquid state.

Concrete

Concrete is a kind of stone made by man from cement, sand, and gravel. One volume of cement to two of sand and four of gravel is the usual mix for concrete, which begins its existence as a thick slush, takes the form of any mold into which it is poured, and hardens into artificial stone. Since the Romans used it extensively, concrete is not new; but in the past century the variety of ways in which it has been employed, especially in large structures, makes it seem like something quite different. Its great virtues are its plasticity before it sets and its durability after it hardens. No other material combines these two qualities to the same degree.

Two factors have tended to limit poured concrete to such basic but unemphasized parts of the home as foundations, basement floors and walls, walks, terraces, and driveways. First, the cost of forms used only once on the site is very high for anything other than such crude, simple forms as for foundations or floors. As yet, this cost has not been completely overcome. Second, ordinary concrete is not attractive in color or texture, and it is associated with basements and sidewalks. Fortunately, there are many ways of getting around this second disadvantage.

A

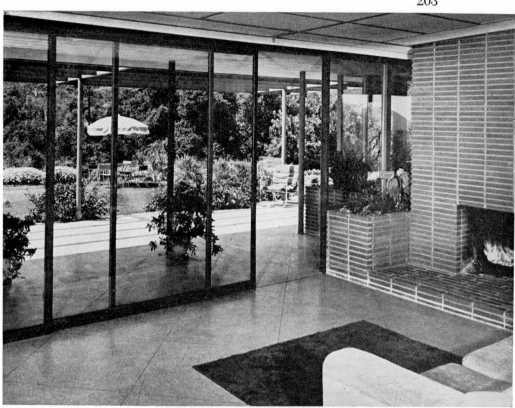

Above. Masonry and glass effectively bring indoors and outdoors together. The terrazzo floor continues from living room to terrace as does the brick planting box. (*Pittsburgh Plate Glass Company*)

Right. Emile Norman proves that a concrete wall can be something of great interest and lasting beauty. (*Photograph by Maynard Parker. Courtesy of* House Beautiful)

B

- Concrete can be prefabricated in blocks or slabs under efficient mass-production methods, using the same forms over and over.
- Concrete can be made from materials other than sand and gravel to improve its color and texture as well as its insulating qualities.
- The surface can be varied by adding colored pigments, troweling it smoothly, or giving it any number of possible textures.
- The gravel used in the concrete can be exposed in either of two ways—*terrazzo* is the term used for concrete made with stone chips and polished to reveal an irregular mosaiclike pattern; *broom-finished* describes the pebbly-surfaced concrete made with round pebbles from which the surface coating of concrete has been brushed off.
- Paints and dyes (of special types to withstand the strong alkaline reaction of concrete) can be applied to the surface, the paints usually being thick enough to smooth the surface while the dyes are transparent and penetrating.
- Plaster or stucco can be applied as a surface coating.
- Concrete can be carved and enriched with other materials (Fig. 203B).

Plaster and Stucco

Extensively used all over the world as a surface coating for walls, *plaster* is a pasty composition of lime and water to which sand is sometimes added. It is usually applied to lath, a term now used to describe thin strips of wood, sheets of expanded metal, or specially prepared gypsum boards, but it may also be applied directly to any masonry surface rough enough to hold it. For interior work, two coats are generally used—a rough sandy undercoat and a smooth white finish coat which can be left as it is or painted, papered, or covered with canvas or other fabric as embellishment and protection. *Stucco* refers to waterproof plaster used on exteriors.

Plaster has been popular for ages because it is not costly, can be applied without visible joints to surfaces of almost any shape, smoothly hides anything behind it, and is an excellent background for varied surface treatments. Its disadvantages are minor, but it does crack, is more costly and has less insulating value than many wallboards, is so commonly used that it escapes attention, and often chips when you hang a picture or fasten shelves or lamps to the wall. Stucco is an excellent exterior finish provided precautions are taken to prevent cracking and the air is clean enough so that it is not soon streaked with soot and other dirt.

Both plaster and stucco lend themselves to kinds of sculptural enrichment, as can be seen in the walls and ceilings of many historic homes. Today these materials await a creative approach.

Design in Masonry

Masonry forms that are usable and beautiful have a range as great as those suited to wood. An important difference, though, is that the appearance of the raw materials of masonry—clay, sand, cement, or stone—does not usually suggest shapes so specifically and clearly as does a growing tree or even a felled log. Until they have studied the inherent qualities of masonry materials, architects, designers, and home builders are provided with fewer guides and clues. The problem becomes one of deciding what is wanted, finding the most appropriate raw material, and changing it as necessary to achieve a specific goal.

Quite unlike the long, slender shapes appropriate to wood, blocky shapes both in the individual pieces and the whole design are typical of much masonry. Joined together with mortar, these blocks can give the irregular chunkiness of rubble masonry or the regularly repeated, clear-cut rectangular patterns of ashlar stonework and brickwork. These effects are not often seen in other materials. Stone can also be sliced into thin veneers for surfacing, but these are typically thicker than in wood. Almost always at least implied in masonry is thickness, density, and weight; but these can be emphasized or subordinated by moldings, turning, carving, or inlaid designs.

Another major type of masonry design is that possible with plaster or poured concrete. Holding any shape they are given by mold or mason's tools, these materials have the potential of forms that are curved or angular, simple or complex. Hardly touched as yet, the possibilities of fluidity of design await the talents of designers who can, as Erwin Hauer and Emile Norman have done, develop techniques that make evident the highly plastic qualities these materials possess.

Masonry has its own special appeal—a long-lasting, substantial security. Masonry is of the earth and *in today's homes* seems most effective when its solid, earthy character is revealed, when it is used in masses that are sizable and simple. That masonry holds other potentialities is evinced by the sensitively humanized forms in marble created by the Greeks, the soaring spires and lacelike tracery of the Gothic builders, the rich polychromy of Persian and Spanish tiles, or the miraculously thin shells that are reintroducing curved structural forms into contemporary architecture.

9. Ceramics, Glass, Metal, and Plastics

VARIED MATERIALS, IMAGINATIVELY COMBINED, distinguish the table setting reproduced in Figure 207A. The thin porcelain bowl enhanced with intricate geometric designs in gold stands on a plate with a vigorously free pattern. To the left, a thicker stoneware plate relies on form and textured glaze alone for its effect. The slender Venetian goblet whose shape is accented by swirling strands of colored glass rises gracefully above the small compact dark Mexican glass, the short tumbler whose thin transparency finds support in a richly modeled base, and the unfolding free-form cigarette holder. Ornate silverware, sparkling with small-scale detail, stands next to an unornamented spoon of black plastic. Marks of the silversmith's hammer enliven the ashtray's surface, restrained ornament emphasizes the smooth reflecting handle of the nearby knife.

Glass, metal, and plastics are equally eloquent in making the terrace in Figure 207B livable and

Above. A Japanese wine bottle, unmistakably wheel-thrown, relies solely on subtle form and deep-lustered brown glaze for its beauty. (*Stanford University Art Gallery, Mortimer C. Leventritt Collection*)

A

Varied materials can be successfully combined in the few square feet of table setting or the larger scale of a terrace.

Above. Wonderfully dissimilar materials and shapes have been brought together by Alexander Girard in a high-spirited table setting. (*Georg Jensen, Inc.*)

Below. The differences between glass and plastic, metal, stone, and bamboo have been resolved in a calm, precise unity. Henry Eggers, architect. (*Photograph by Maynard Parker*)

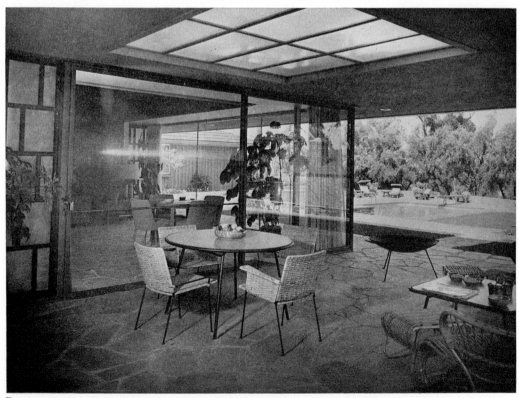

B

structurally secure. The large sliding panes of glass would not have been feasible without their metal frames and the hidden steel that supports the roof. No material yet discovered, other than metal, could have supported the chairs and tables with such slender forms. Figured glass visually lightens the table top, while translucent plastic in the skylight brings light without excessive heat or glare.

In a table setting or in an entire house, ceramics, glass, metal, and plastics are serviceable and beautiful. They have been grouped in one chapter because they have important characteristics in common. Since all are shaped while in a plastic, liquid, or malleable state, the diversity of appropriate shapes is tremendous. All are subjected to heat in processing. With the exception of some plastics, all are inorganic—which means that they will not burn, rot, decay, or appeal to insects and vermin. Each of these materials, nonetheless, has its own special potentialities and limitations that challenge sensitive designers and bring liveliness to our homes.

► CERAMICS

Long before early man began to write he fashioned useful and symbolic objects from clay. From then on, this material has been of continuing and conspicuous importance in homes. All of us are aware of the dishes used for eating, of ashtrays, vases, and lamp bases. But this field also includes many sculptural objects, bricks and tiles, chimney flues, and drain pipes. All these are *ceramics,* which is a short way of saying "objects made from clay and hardened by heat." Essential steps in the process are:

- finding a suitable clay or combining several clays;
- moistening the clay sufficiently to make it workable;
- shaping the clay by hand, on the potter's wheel, or in a mold;
- allowing the pieces to dry until they are "leather hard"; and
- firing the pieces to harden them permanently.

The process could stop at this point but usually involves:

- decorating the piece with carving or painting, and
- glazing it with a glasslike coating.

Ceramics differ in terms of **body** and **glaze, form** and **ornamentation.**

Body

The clays used for the body of ceramics affect the characteristics of the finished product. Some are white, others black, and between these extremes are many tans, grays, and reds. Textures range from coarse, irregular, and open to fine, even, and dense. Clays also have different melting points (the temperatures at which they lose their shape). Generally those clays that hold their shape at high temperatures make the stronger objects because the separate particles fuse together, or vitrify, into a dense, homogeneous, glasslike, waterproof mass. Almost always several clays are mixed together in varying proportions to produce the desired combination of qualities. For convenience, ceramic bodies can be grouped into four major types although each has a wide range of characteristics which may overlap those of other types.

- **Earthenware,** made from coarse clays and fired at comparatively low temperatures, is typically thick, porous, opaque and breaks quite easily. The Pennsylvania plate and the hollow tiles used as grilles (Figs. 210A and 213A) illustrate these qualities as do bricks, flower pots, and much Mexican pottery. The glazes are usually soft and show scratches. More refined earthenware, however, can be shaped and ornamented as sensitively as the vases in Figure 210B or as formally as Wedgwood dinnerware.
- **Stoneware** is made from finer clays and fired at higher temperatures. The clay particles are fused together and the body becomes waterproof, stronger, and more durable than earthenware, but, like it, opaque. Stoneware is favored for the better grades of decorative pottery and tableware. Some is used for oven-to-table ware. The medium soft glazes can be much more varied than can those suited to earthenware.
- **China** is a somewhat general term describing vitrified ware that is translucent if thin. Because its qualities place it between stoneware and porcelain, it might better be called "semiporcelain" but *china,* originally referring to the European ware imitating true Chinese porcelain, has persisted as the most used name.

  English china or *bone china* has a white, translucent body and a soft but brilliant glaze.

  American vitreous china has unusual resistance to breakage and chipping. Glazes and decorations resist scratching.
- **Porcelain** is reserved for high-grade, expensive dishes and ornamental wares. Fired at high temperatures, it is completely vitrified and often translucent. The body resists breakage and the glazes are very hard.

The purist would say, with some justification, that earthenware suggests simple, vigorous shapes and ornamentation, and that increasing precision and refinement should be expected as one goes from stoneware to china and porcelain. Not always, however, does this happen, for other factors affect ceramic design.

The relationship of ornamentation and glaze to form has fascinated potters for centuries.

Left. On an early nineteenth-century Pennsylvania earthenware plate, transparent glaze protects a vigorous sgraffito design. (*Courtesy of the Metropolitan Museum of Art*)

Left center. Katherine Chou, exploring new forms and techniques, has achieved a festive freedom. Glazes actively participate in the inventive outcome. (*Courtesy of Craft Horizons*)

Left below. Maija Grotell has allowed heavy brown and white glaze to triumph over a simple stoneware shape. (*Photograph by Harvey Croze*)

Below. A seventeenth-century Chinese porcelain vase, disciplined and serene in outline, has a smooth lustrous glaze that emphasizes without dominating the sensitive shape. (*Courtesy of the Metropolitan Museum of Art*)

A

B

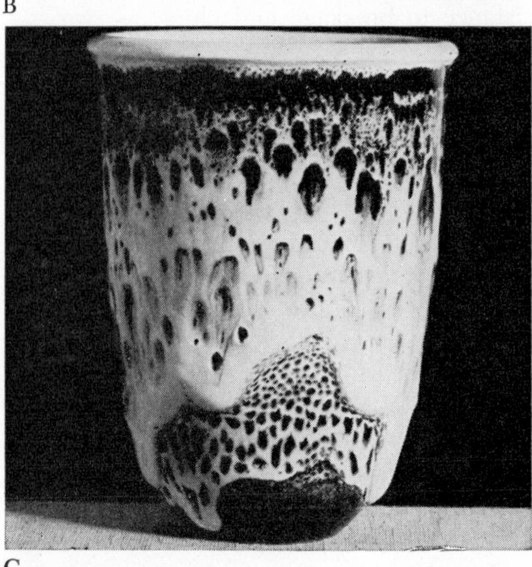

C

D

Form in Ceramics

The possibilities and limitations of the shape of any material are determined by its physical properties, the methods by which it is formed, the intended use of the object—and the skill and sensitivity of the designer. These are the physical properties of clay: before firing, it is composed of small powderlike or granular particles that can be mixed with a little water to make a plastic mass or with more water to make a creamy liquid called *slip;* but, after firing, clay is hard and brittle, has little tensile strength, and therefore breaks quite easily when hit or dropped. Thin edges or protruding parts are especially vulnerable.

While being shaped, clay is either plastic and therefore responds to any pressure, or it is liquid and will take the shape of any mold into which it is poured. Almost any shape is possible, as the history of ceramics proves, but most dishes and vases are round and relatively compact. Why? Because round forms come naturally from the potter's wheel and the mass-production jigger and jolley. They are easy to hold in our rounded hands, and they are a pleasant relief from the basic rectangularity of our homes. Important, too, is the fact that they have a minimum of edges to chip. In short, rounded forms, compact in outline, seem especially appropriate to ceramic dishes and ornamental pieces.

This does not rule out other possibilities. Angular shapes are basic in bricks and tiles; in household ceramics angular shapes can occasionally be useful as well as welcome surprises. Some extending forms, such as spouts on teapots or handles on cups, are worth the hazard of breakage. Then, fortunately, there is the creative urge to explore and experiment, to find forms that will reawaken our senses as do those created by Katherine Chou.

Glazes

Glazes are glassy coatings fused at high temperatures to the body of ceramics. They increase usefulness by making ceramics waterproof and easy to clean. Their textures and colors, an example of structural ornament, are primary sources of beauty. Limitless in variety, they enable each potter to express his convictions in finding a glaze he deems appropriate to the body, shape, and use of each piece.

Figure 206 and Figures 210A through D illustrate a few of the effects glazes can produce. The dark brown glaze with its subdued texture and soft luster serves to enhance the shape of the Japanese bottle. On the Pennsylvania plate a transparent glaze, almost as thin and clear as water, protects and intensifies the colors of the applied design. Glazes of earthy colors and varied textures applied in unexpected ways emphasize the sprightly, highly plastic character of Katherine Chou's vases. Thick, treacly, and emphatically textured, the glazes on Maija Grotell's jar intentionally dominate the uneventful, simple shape they encase. Not so with the Chinese porcelain on which the brilliant pure white glaze, as elegantly precise as the vase, is secondary to the form. For each of these pieces, the glazes were sensitively and purposefully chosen.

Glazes differ in the degree to which they join with and "fit" the body. A broken piece of glazed earthenware will show that the glassy coating forms a distinct layer on the porous body, but on most porcelains the glazes are so completely integrated with the clay that there is no sharp division between the two. If glaze and body do not have the same coefficient of expansion, the glazes will develop quickly or with use a series of cracks. In decorative pottery such effects may be planned for their ornamental value. On dishes used for food, these cracks are more likely to be the result of poor workmanship.

Ornament

Often the basic form plus such structural ornament as the potter's tool marks and glazes make applied ornamentation unnecessary, a point made clear by Figure 206. There is, however, an ever-present urge to enrich a plain surface, and ceramics have received at least their share of decoration. The medium seems to invite modeling, carving, and painting.

Modeling and carving, which give a three-dimensional play of light and shade, range from scarcely noticeably incised designs (Fig. 210B) through modeling in low relief on decorative pieces (Fig. 210D), to vigorous sculptural ornament on large urns. Sgraffito (literally *scratched*), a very ancient process, is illustrated in the linear designs on the Pennsylvania plate (Fig. 210A). It is done by putting on a thin coating of clay, different in color from that of the base, and then scratching through to reveal the color underneath.

Colored pigments can be applied with a brush, through a stencil, transferred from decalcomanias, or printed mechanically. This decoration can be underglaze or overglaze and the design possibilities are endless. *Underglaze* designs are applied before the final glazing which protects it from scratches and wear. *Overglaze* patterns are applied to the surface of glazed ware and fused with it at a low firing temperature. It is the cheapest and most common type of ceramic enrichment and when well done is moderately durable.

Ordinary tile takes on fresh meaning when used imaginatively in architecture.

Right. Humble earthenware drain tiles create a captivating pattern of light and shade in a contemporary Mexican house. Anshen and Allen, architects. (*Photograph by Maynard Parker. Courtesy of* House Beautiful)

Below. Mosaic tiles on exterior walls can be at one with the house shape yet add their own active, colorful enrichment. John Johansen, architect. (*Tile Council of America*)

A

B

With such possibilities, it is easy for inventiveness and technical skill to exceed taste and common sense. What, then, is suitable enrichment for ceramics? As discussed in Chapter 6, ornament is at its best when it is appropriate to functions, form, size, and material. As an example we can take plates used at the table. Their functions are to hold food and please the eye, but they must also be handled many times. They are shallow, usually circular dishes about 10 inches in diameter made of fired clay. Suitable enrichment emphasizes these qualities. That is why the decoration, if any, on most plates is circular in movement, rounded rather than angular, flat rather than heavily modeled, conventional or abstract rather than naturalistic, and small in scale. Because clay is either plastic or liquid when shaped, the most natural ornament has something of these qualities. Finally, ornament should be vital in itself. The decorated plate in Figure 207A illustrates all these attributes, and the plain plate demonstrates that applied ornament is not requisite.

Architectural Ceramics

Ceramics in homes go well beyond dishes and vases. Bricks and tiles belong both to ceramics and masonry, for they are clay hardened by heat and are set in mortar. That tile can be an important component of architecture is shown in Figures 213A and B as well as in the floor of the medieval room (Fig. 182A) and the tile bathroom (Fig. 275B). Durable, maintenance-free mosaic tiles energize with color and pattern what might have been commonplace walls in a Connecticut house. Small in scale, they throw into effective contrast the large areas of glass. With their sparkling juxtaposition of dark and light, they are a major factor in relating the building to the intricate play of light on foliage. Perhaps most significant, they bring an intimate, human scale to a house remarkable for its strict geometry. Equally effective are the hollow, unglazed earthenware tiles used to fill the gaps between stone piers in a home in Mexico. In this instance, ordinary drain tiles create a distinctive, ever-changing pattern of light and shadow. And they shelter from rain, excessive sun, and wind an outdoor living area. The revival of interest in tile that is decorative in itself and in ornamental uses of ordinary tile brings back an almost forgotten medium of expression for those interested in colorful, durable architectural enrichment. Contemporary designers have contributed a wide range of patterns, three of which are illustrated in Figures 280G, H, and I.

The distinctive qualities of brick speak for themselves when used for floors, walls, and fireplaces as illustrated in Figures 12, 39A, 119A, 140B, and 290, and the houses designed by Alden Dow in Figures 294B and 302A.

► GLASS

The development of glass from a semiprecious material available only in small pieces to one that can be bought anywhere and installed in large sheets has altered our homes as much as any single factor. Its history is fascinating. Glass-making appears to have developed from ceramic glazes, some of which have been dated as early as 12,000 B.C., but the oldest piece of pure glass was made around 7,000 B.C. The Romans made glass objects of such beauty that the best were valued higher than vessels of gold. The Romans also had sheets of glass for windows, but window glass was not common in small homes until the end of the eighteenth century. Today glass is an everyday, extraordinarily versatile material.

Glass is made by melting and fusing at very high temperatures sand and an alkali, such as potassium or sodium, as the basic ingredients. Other elements give special qualities. Crystal, the finest glass, contains lead. Color comes from minerals—red from gold and copper, blue from copper and cobalt, yellow from cadmium and uranium. Special effects, such as opacity, bubbles, or crystallization, and special forms, such as glass fibers and insulation, result from chemicals or the way in which glass is treated.

The general characteristics of glass are as follows:

- transparency unrivaled until recently by any other common material;
- capacity to refract light in a gemlike way;
- wide range of colors, degrees of transparency, and textures;
- plasticity, malleability, and ductility that permit a great variety of shapes from threadlike fibers to large thin sheets;
- unaffected by water and most alkalies and acids;
- does not burn (but will melt at high temperatures);
- moderately high resistance to scratching, but
- low resistance to breakage through impact, twisting or bending, and sudden temperature changes (except with special types).

Household Glass

Glass tumblers, bottles, and baking dishes are made by *blowing* or *molding*. In blowing glass by hand, the craftsman dips a hollow metal rod into molten glass, blows it into a bubble, and then shapes the hot, soft material into the desired shape. Because this is expensive, most household glass is molded. In this process, molten glass is blown or pressed by machinery into cast iron or wood molds. Molded glass can be shaped with Spartan simplicity or with great intricacy of shape and surface pattern.

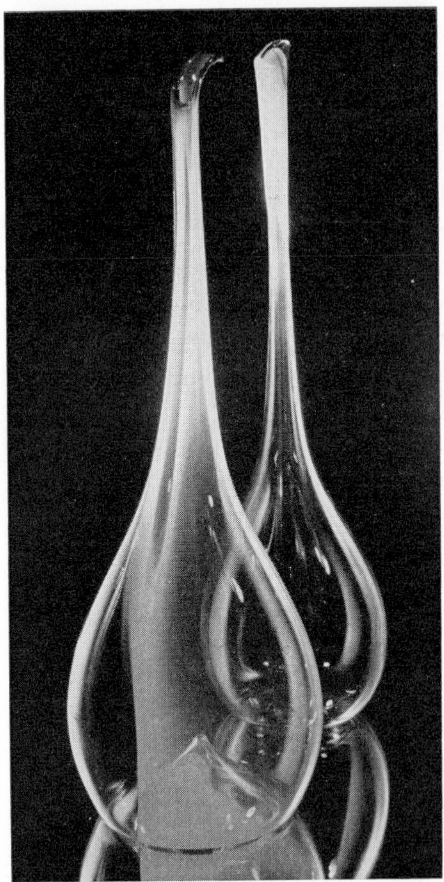

A

The bubble and related shapes are characteristic of blown glass. Transparency is a nearly unique attribute and flowing plasticity a cogent design inspiration.

Left. Two vases that look as though they might just have dropped from the glass-blower's rod. F. Meydam, designer. (*Royal Leerdam Glassworks*)

Below. The molten plasticity of crystal has been solidified into a light-modeling whirlpool bowl. (*Steuben Glass*)

B

Clear, colorless glass is the standard material from which to drink liquids because it:

- allows us to see what we are drinking and enjoy the crystal clarity of water, the color of lemonade or wine, and the pattern of bubbles in ginger ale or champagne;
- gives an exciting play of reflected and refracted light;
- is nonabsorptive, tasteless, and odorless;
- feels pleasantly cool and smooth to hands and lips;
- is not harmed by anything we can safely drink;
- is inexpensive.

Fragility is the only drawback, a small price to pay for its good qualities unless you have small children, eat outdoors or casually in various parts of the home. Then tumblers of anodized aluminum, stainless steel, or the more durable plastics are worth considering.

Glass is also used for other food receptacles with varying degrees of satisfaction. Glass salad bowls and plates are refreshing when filled but become less attractive than opaque wares as the meal nears completion. Glass cups can hold hot tea or coffee but seem less appropriate than ceramics for ordinary use. Glass cooking utensils have their special advantages but they are harder to clean and less durable than metal.

Glass, along with metal, is particularly suitable for candleholders because of the way in which it sparkles. It makes attractive flower containers if you have good-looking flowerholders, arrange the stems under water attractively, and keep the water very clear. It is the standard material for mirrors and is also used for table tops. Glass (especially colorless and transparent), though, loses most of its beauty if not kept polished. Finger and water marks or specks of dust are more conspicuous on clear shiny glass than on most other materials.

Form in Household Glass. What was said about form in ceramics might almost be repeated because, in both, form is given to an amorphous substance while it is plastic or liquid; the final product is hard, brittle, and breakable; and process, material, and use lead naturally, although not exclusively, to rounded forms. As the bowl is a natural shape for clay, the bubble is for glass (Fig. 216A). "Simple," "compact," and "rounded" are three key words describing the most expressive and useful shapes in glass. Sharp edges, angular forms, and extended parts can all be made, but these seem more in the nature of metal than of glass.

Two other characteristics deserve mention. The first is that glass, technically speaking, always remains a liquid, never changing its physical properties when passing from a liquid to a solid state. Therefore even when rigid, as it is at ordinary temperatures, it is actually an "undercooled liquid," a quality shown especially well in the whirlpool bowl (Fig. 216B). Second, with glass we can achieve an almost perfect union of form and space. We look less *at* a glass bowl or tumbler than *through* it to the space enclosed and the space beyond. Large windows give a similar effect. Contemporary designers and architects interested in relationships between form and space have a special feeling toward a material that so closely unites the two.

Ornament in Household Glass. It is not always easy to draw a sharp line between form and ornament in glass. Structural ornament can be introduced before glass is shaped by adding substances that give it color. Other ingredients make it cloudy or translucent; some are suspended as opaque particles or produce bubbles. Sometimes form is carried to such a degree of complexity that it becomes as highly decorative as the stems of the goblets in Figures 219A and B.

Hand-blown glass. A skilled glass blower can do many things to enrich a piece while it is still hot (and most can be reproduced by machine). He can, for example, "drop on" globs of molten glass (Figs. 216B and 219A) to produce highly plastic, almost liquid, ornament or such useful devices as handles. The whole piece can be fluted or ribbed, edges can be crimped. Bases and stems of goblets can be elaborated (Fig. 219B). Various colors can be combined to make mosaic, striped, or swirling patterns (Fig. 207A).

Molded and pressed glass. Highly ornamented as well as plain glass can be produced by these methods. Ornamentation is usually derived from hand-made types and may resemble cut or engraved ware. Most characteristic is that glassware in which the pattern is raised slightly above the surface and has slightly rounded edges, as in the well-known Sandwich glass.

Cut glass. Although glass was beautifully cut by the Romans, the technique was given new life about A.D. 1600 when a court jeweler in Prague applied gem-cutting techniques to glass. Rich effects come when the design is cut through an outer coating of colored glass to reveal colorless glass underneath. In colorless crystal, cutting gives many surfaces to catch and break up light in a diamondlike manner.

Engraved glass. As with cut glass, engraving is done with wheels and abrasives, but engraving produces a shallow intaglio that by optical illusion often seems to be in relief. Firmness of form, sharpness of edge, and easy flowing curves distinguish engraved glass from that which is pressed, cut, or etched.

Ornament in and on glass takes many guises, but almost all play up the material's sparkling transparency.

Right. Delicate gilding with touches of red enamel enhances the bowl of a seventeenth-century German goblet. Defying staid notions of harmony, vigorous "dropped-on" globular ornament strengthens the base. (*Courtesy of the Metropolitan Museum of Art*)

Below. Glass invites shaping, cutting, and engraving to bring out exhilarating patterns of light. (*Fostoria Glass Company*)

A

B

Etched glass. Either hydrofluoric acid or sandblasting are used to etch glass. The frosty etched surface may be left in that state or polished to smooth transparency. Etching is often used to imitate engraving but the designs are not so sharp or so subtly modeled. Usually shallow and delicate, etching can be 2 inches deep, as it is in some heavy French pieces.

Enameled and gilded glass. After looking at some of the cheap enameled or gilded glass frequently seen today, we are tempted to call these processes inventions of the devil. But in the past some very beautiful glass was made by burning colored enamels (Fig. 219A) or gold and silver into the surface. This type of ornamentation is at its best when glass, enameling, and gilding are of high quality, the design is precise and refined, and the workmanship skillful.

The most satisfying ornament in glass, no matter how achieved, is that which exploits what the material does with light. It can be as vigorous as that suitable for wood or ceramics but, since the pieces are usually small, heavy ornament is rare. The typically smooth surface and fine, nongranular composition make very delicate, refined, precise decoration highly effective. The transparency of glass makes possible ornament that is embedded in the material, a kind that was unique until the development of plastics.

Architectural Glass

Glass for windows is made by two processes. In *drawing,* the way in which most window glass is made, molten glass is drawn from furnaces in never-ending sheets, flattened between rollers, and cut into usable sizes. Although satisfactory for most purposes, drawn glass is usually not so strong or so thick and free from flaws as is plate glass. In *rolling,* the method by which plate glass is made, molten glass is poured onto an iron casting table, distributed and smoothed by rollers, then ground and polished. Today sheets of plate glass more than 50 feet long can be made.

Although glass for buildings is generally thought of as transparent, colorless, and smooth, it can be frosted or pebbly, ribbed or corrugated, or colored to control light, heat, and vision. Some architectural glass has a core of metal mesh, which reduces breakage hazard and is also decorative. In the past, you had to choose between opaque walls and transparent windows and then frequently cover the windows with curtains or blinds for protection. Now one permanent material can give you an entrance area or a bathroom illumined by natural light without sacrifice of privacy, a screen between rooms that divides without separating, or windows that diffuse glareless light.

Glass Textiles and Insulation

The great versatility of glass is indicated by special types used for draperies and heat-cold insulation. Spun glass had been used for centuries in a purely decorative way, but not until about 1893 were its utilitarian values appreciated. Then neckties and dresses of spun glass and silk were exhibited as curiosities: they were heavy, scratchy, and too stiff to fold. As discussed in Chapter 10, glass textiles have come a long way since 1893. Glass fibers today are also widely used for insulation against extreme temperatures and sound. Another development is foam glass, made by introducing a gas-producing agent into molten glass. Filled with so many tiny air bubbles that it will float on water, it has excellent insulating properties.

► METALS

Although man learned to reduce metal from ore around 5,000 B.C., its use in domestic architecture was unimportant until recently. Today the typical "wood house" uses about four tons of metal, double that used twenty years ago, and the amount is increasing each year. But only a few of these 8,000 pounds are visible. Such is not the case with the house illustrated in Figure 222A in which the unique structural qualities of metal, visibly exploited, make possible a new approach to house design. Four heavy steel frames, from which a 30′ by 85′ roof is suspended, are the only supports in the Illinois house. Under this sheltering, floating canopy, walls and windows have been placed wherever desired. The result is a boldly confident separation of structure and enclosing surfaces.

Metal, like masonry, ceramics, and glass, is inorganic and therefore does not burn, rot, or decay. But metal differs from these other inorganic substances in some important respects: it rusts or corrodes (with a few exceptions) when exposed to moisture and air, and it has great tensile strength. Metal's capacity to transmit heat, cold, and electricity is unequalled. The surface is usually shiny and nonabsorbent.

With the possible exception of plastics, no other material can be shaped in so many ways. It can be melted and cast in simple or intricate molds. In the solid state, it can be rolled, pressed, or turned on a lathe as well as hammered, bent, drilled, or cut with saws and torches. Separate pieces can be welded together or joined with bolts and rivets.

This unique complex of qualities—tensile strength; meltability, ductility, and malleability; conductivity; resistance to fire and decay; and potential beauty of color and surface—make a house built today without metals hard to imagine. A partial list would include such inconspicuous but essential

A

Daring frankness can be joined with classic poise in houses or tables constructed with glass and metal.

Above. Freely exposing the strength of metal, the frame of architect Jacques C. Brownson's house in Geneva, Illinois, becomes a potent design asset. Surrounding woodlands give the needed privacy.

Left. The acme of simplicity, plate glass rests in a slender but strong steel frame to form a small-scale coffee table that takes almost no visual space. William Armbruster, designer. (*Edgewood Furniture Company*)

B

uses as structural members and reinforcing in masonry; conductors of water, heat, and electricity; weatherproofing and foil insulation; and nails and screws. Metals are thinly concealed by protective coatings of enamel in stoves, refrigerators, and washing machines. They become noticeable in hinges, handles, and doorknobs; in faucets, radiators, or warm-air vents. They are conspicuous in metal tableware and furniture, cooking utensils and lighting fixtures. More frequent each day is their use for window frames, roofs, and exterior and interior walls. Generally, they are used thoughtfully because they are expensive in original cost.

Following is a brief description of those metals most important in homes.

Aluminum. Not until 1885 was it feasible to extract aluminum economically even though it occurs in most common clays. It is a whitish metal, light in weight and easily worked. It oxidizes to a soft gray but does not deteriorate indoors or out. Thus it is valuable for cooking utensils, tumblers, pitchers, trays, and easy-to-move outdoor furniture (Figs. 373B and C) that requires minimum maintenance. It is a carefree material for window frames and screens, siding and roofing, gutters and drainpipes. The surface can be highly polished or brushed to a silvery softness. *Anodizing* gives a long-lasting, satiny surface in a range of bright metallic hues.

Chromium. This blue-white metal that takes and keeps a high polish is widely used as a thin plating where durability, easy maintenance, and brilliant shine are wanted. It is frequently seen on faucets, toasters, and kitchen forks and spoons, lighting fixtures and metal furniture as well as the gewgaws on ranges and automobiles. Because it is hard and resists corrosion it takes little care, except that fingermarks or watermarks are conspicuous. Typically, it is cold, hard, and glittery; assertive rather than harmonious. It can, though, be domesticated with a brushed finish.

Copper. Polished copper is a beautiful orange color with a lustrous surface that quickly oxidizes to a dull greenish-brown or, sometimes, to a lively blue-green. Fortunately, oxidation causes no serious deterioration. It is soft and easily shaped but durable, which makes it excellent for pipes carrying water. Next to silver, it is the best conductor of electricity. It has a disagreeable taste and odor but conducts heat quickly and evenly, which explains its use on the *bottoms* of pots and pans. It is long-lived, beautiful, but expensive in first cost for eaves, troughs, and roofs. Inside the house, copper's color and luster have a warm friendliness that is unique.

Iron and Steel. A grayish metal known for thousands of years, iron is commonly used but almost never in its pure state. It is widely available and strong, relatively easy to work when cast in liquid form or wrought

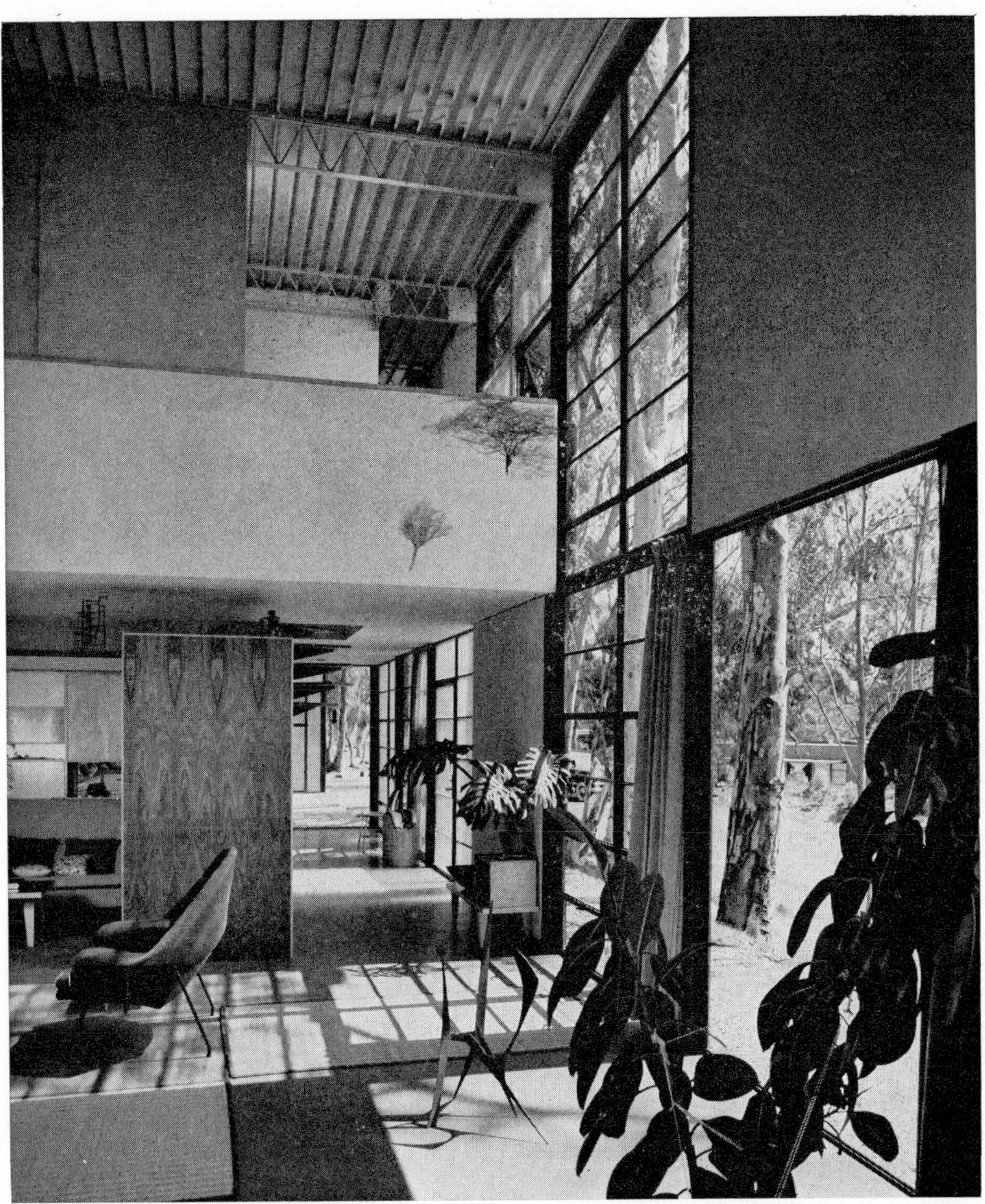

In Charles Eames' house near Los Angeles, a light steel framework not unlike a boy's Erector set provides a structural system that permits great freedom in locating walls and floors, in choosing the most suitable materials to enclose and subdivide space. It also has its own distinctive beauty when explicitly revealed as it is in the ceiling. (*Photograph by Julius Shulman*)

with tools. Its great disadvantage is the speed with which it rusts. It can be *galvanized* with a zinc coating, or painted to discourage rust.

Steel is iron made hard with chemically dissolved carbon. Its development has made possible not only skyscrapers and suspension bridges but the house discussed earlier. It is the structural material in kitchen equipment and furnaces and also in many metal window frames. Most so-called "iron" furniture is made of steel. Because steel rusts like iron, it is invariably painted or enameled. *Stainless steels* are another matter, for they have been made resistant to rust and staining by the addition of chromium. Hard, durable, and a pleasant blue-gray, stainless steels make the most durable and inexpensive (in the long run) of all cooking utensils as well as thoroughly satisfactory, nontarnishable knives, forks, and spoons.

Pewter. This term covers a wide range of alloys of tin, zinc, antimony, and copper. Old pewter, made of tin and lead, is a dull, soft, blue-gray metal. Many newer types resemble silver. In general, these are serviceable but rather soft alloys that resist tarnish and have a pleasant luster.

Silver. It is no whim or happenstance that silver has long been cherished as the most desirable of metals for flat and hollow metal tableware: it is the whitest of metals, reflects almost twice as much light as stainless steel and noticeably more than chromium, and takes a genuinely beautiful polish. Furthermore, it is a workable metal, so soft when pure that it must be hardened, usually with copper—sterling silver contains 7.5 percent copper. Its one great drawback is that it tarnishes rapidly and soon becomes blackish if the coating of silver sulfide is not removed; but this, unlike iron rust, causes no serious damage. Silver is frequently plated over an alloy base, and if the plating is heavy enough, it will last a long time but, of course, solid silver will remain in good condition indefinitely.

Form in Metal

Were it not that metal is heavy and expensive, you might say that almost any form that man can design is suitable for metal. It will take and hold any shape that can be given to wood, masonry, ceramics, or glass. Its most distinctive quality, though, is its great tensile strength that makes possible, as well as durable, shapes that are slender but strong. Good examples of this characteristic are the structural members of the two houses (Figs. 222A and 224), the slender handle of the pitcher (Fig. 226B) and the thin supports of the table (Fig. 222B). Sharp edges, as on knives, are more durable in metal than in any other material. Expressively used, metal contributes a precise thinness that distinguishes it from the comparatively heavy solidity of wood, masonry, and ceramics.

A

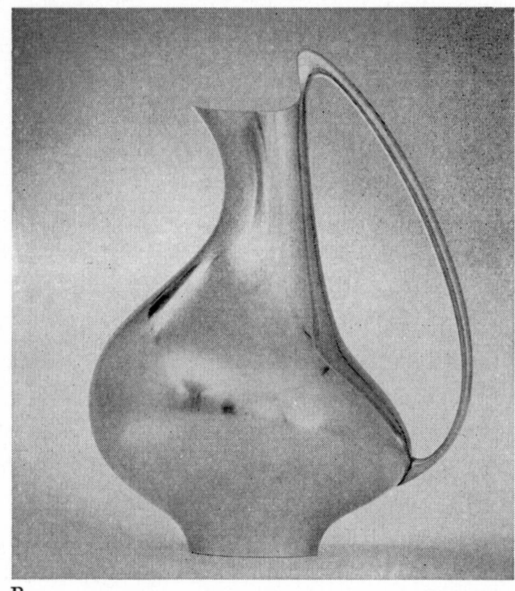

B

Metal can be given almost any form or surface texture.

Above left. A shiny stainless steel coffee pot designed by Sigvard Bernadotte and Acton Bjørn revitalizes a traditional form. (*Moderna Kök A.B.*)

Above right. A sterling silver water pitcher, designed by Henning Koppel, of unfettered shape and satiny surface. (*Georg Jensen, Inc.*)

C

D

Above left. A detail of a medieval jug shows amazingly fine-scale, vital ornamentation. (*Courtesy of the Metropolitan Museum of Art*)

Above right. Mechanically stamped patterns increase the strength of metal sheets, give a sparkling surface that obscures scratches. (*Rigidized Metals Corporation*)

Ornament in Metal

Highly polished metal, such as that of the Swedish coffee pot (Fig. 226A), gives mirror reflections, interestingly distorted on rounded surfaces; softly polished surfaces mellow and diffuse reflections, as on the silver pitcher (Fig. 226B). These together with color become distinctive types of structural ornamentation.

As with form, there are really no limitations for applied ornament. Because metal is strong, ornament can project boldly and be deeply undercut to produce brilliant highlights and cool dark shadows as seen in the sculptural handle of the ewer (Fig. 226C). Because the surface is grainless and reflective, very delicate engraving, modeling, or stamping is effective (Fig. 226D). Because molten metal can be cast and then becomes rigid when cool, ornament can appropriately be fluent or decisively static. This leads to several suggestions. The first is that ornament need not be compactly related to form. Second, small-scale intricate patterns show to good advantage. Third, decisively linear or angular decoration is more at ease with metal than with other materials. Fourth, relatively formal, controlled, and precise enrichment seems more felicitous than does the free spontaneity of designs on peasant pottery, for example, or the informality often attractive in printed textiles. Metal is an expensive, hard material that lasts too long for spur-of-the-moment ornament.

► PLASTICS

Chemistry is said to have begun with the medieval alchemists' unsuccessful attempts to transmute base metals into gold. Today's chemists transform wood, coal, milk, and many other substances into new compounds tailor-made for specific purposes. The essence of this miracle is as old as the universe. The wonder of plastics is that man is now able to produce, on an enormous scale, materials in many instances better suited to specific needs than those nature provides. At first, most plastics were cheap substitutes, commonplace in appearance, for more costly metals, ceramics, or glass. Objects were small and seldom durable.

All this has changed in the last few decades as the illustrations in this section prove. Nowadays, plastic dishes are lightweight and durable. Translucent panels for screens or room dividers have become works of art. The seats and backs of chairs can be molded in one piece, and the plastic house is a reality. These, and the many unmentioned plastics in homes, are changing the way we live.

Families of Plastics

Most plastic objects used in homes are made from the nine resins discussed in the following paragraphs. Each name refers to a family of plastics with basic common characteristics but with considerable diversity. The terms "plastic" and "synthetic" can be applied to the same material—for example, molded nylon is called a "plastic" but nylon threads are referred to as "synthetic."

Acrylics. The most glamorous and glasslike of the plastics, acrylics with their exceptional clarity, brilliant surface, and ability to "pipe" light can be made into extremely decorative panels (Fig. 232C). They are also favored for combs and the backs of hairbrushes. A remarkable combination of qualities—good light transmission, strength and stiffness, ability to withstand outdoor weathering and even sudden temperature extremes, lightness in weight—permit great architectural freedom in flat or domed skylights. For all these uses, acrylics can be colorless or tinted, patterned or plain. Although unaffected by most foods and household chemicals, they are rather easily scratched by grit of any sort. Lucite and Plexiglas are trade names.

Aminos (Melamines). The widespread use of these plastics for counter and table tops, as well as for dinnerware, is based on their exceptional durability. Hard and not easily scratched or chipped, they resist damage from water, food stains, and heat. When thin, as in the surfaces of such high-pressure laminates as Formica or Micarta, they transparently reveal whatever pattern or material is underneath. If thicker, as in such dinnerware as Melmac or Lifetime Ware, they become translucent or opaque. Colors, extensive in range, do not fade or lose brilliance. Surfaces can be high-gloss, satiny, or nonglare.

Cellulosics. Offering designers almost unlimited possibilities, cellulosic plastics come in a wide range of colors from clear transparent to opaque, including variegations and simulations of marble, wood grain, and mother-of-pearl. They retain a bright lustrous surface unless scratched by abrasives. Although resistant to most household chemicals, they may be stained by some medicines and foods. They withstand subzero temperatures and water up to 130°F. Their many uses include vacuum-cleaner parts and housings for radios and clocks; piano keys, soap dishes, and cutlery handles; flashlight cases and toys. Forticel, Lumarith, and Tenite are a few of the trade names.

Polyamides. "Nylon" is the generic term applied to this group. Transparent in very thin sections but usually opaque, nylon comes in many colors. Although resistant to abrasion, the hard glossy surface can be scratched. It has high tensile strength and is relatively rigid and hard. Most

A

B

Above left. Durable *Melmac,* molded with calculated refinements, produces a pleasant play of light and shadow on the slightly textured surface. (*M. J. Rosenfeld Company*)

Above right. Highly polished silver and black nylon combined in ware of luxurious refinement. (*Lunt Silversmiths*)

Below. Prefabricated roof-and-wall panels of tough plastic form a dome-shaped house that rests lightly on its site. Eliot Noyes, architect. (*General Electric Company*)

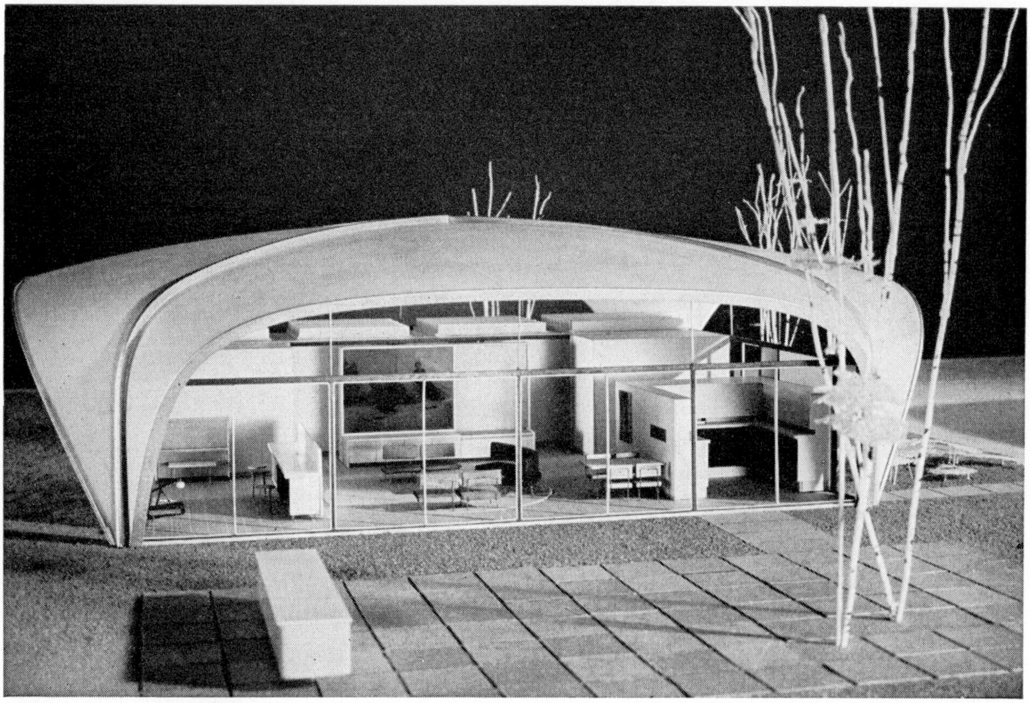

C

common chemicals do it no harm but coffee, tea, and colored foods leave stains. Neither freezing nor boiling temperatures affect it adversely. It is not, however, recommended for continuous outdoor exposure. These qualities make it useful for some tumblers and dinnerware, bristles and backs of brushes, combs and soap dishes. It is also made into long-wearing bearings and gears, quiet rollers for drawers, and textile fibers.

Phenolics. Opaque and tending to darken on exposure to light, phenolics are usually black, brown, or dark colored. Hard and rigid over a wide range of temperatures, they are resistant to mild acids, alcohol, oils, soaps, and detergents. Being a poor conductor of heat and electricity, they are widely used for handles on cooking utensils, electric irons and toasters as well as for radio and television cases and telephone sets. Newer uses are drawers and other parts of furniture. Roofs made of phenolic-impregnated paper and window frames of phenolics with wood fillers have been successfully produced. Trade names include Bakelite, Durite, and Resinox.

Polyesters. When reinforced, usually with glass fibers, polyesters can be formed into strong but thin translucent sheets that are widely used as translucent patio roofs, luminous ceilings, and light-transmitting walls and partitions. They can also be molded into lampshades and skylights, rowboats, or the seats and backs of chairs. They range from stiff to flexible and from hard to soft. The color range is good and they show high resistance to chemicals and weather. Among the trade names are Bakelite, Filon, Laminac, and Plaskon.

Polyethylenes (Polythenes). Easily recognizable by their flexible or semirigid character and waxy surface, polyethylenes have gained wide acceptance in squeezable bottles, nesting bowls and refrigerator dishes, pails and dishpans. Semitransparent to opaque depending on thickness, they come in many colors. They are light in weight, very resistant to breakage and chemicals. Polyethylene objects perform well at subzero temperatures and boiling water can be poured into them but they should not be boiled. Alathon, Dylan, and Tenite are three of the trade names.

Polystyrenes (Styrenes). The lustrous surface of these plastics, ranging from extreme smoothness to satin and many special finishes, is warm and pleasant to touch. Crystal clear types "pipe" light as do the acrylics, and there is a limitless range of translucent and opaque colors. They are relatively inexpensive, tasteless and odorless, and resistant to household chemicals and foods except cleaning fluids and citrus fruits. Food-freezing temperatures do not affect them. Most types are unharmed by hot foods for short periods but lose their shape if boiled. Hard and rigid, they stand up well under normal household use but not under bending or severe impact. The list of uses is long and varied; kitchenware, refrigerator parts and dishes, measuring spoons and combs; Venetian blinds and drawers; wall tiles and as a core for sandwich-type wall panels. Trade names include Catalin Styrene, Styron, and Lustrex.

Vinyls. This versatile family includes rigid and nonrigid types in any transparent, translucent, or opaque color. Varied surface effects are produced by embossing or printing. They are tough, strong, lightweight, and low in cost. Although they withstand foods, chemicals, and normal household use very well, they cut readily, stiffen in cold except for special types, and rigid vinyls are harmed by temperatures above 130°F. Among the diverse uses are shower, bathroom, and kitchen curtains; tablecloths, draperies, upholstery, and wall coverings; lamp shades and luminous ceilings; flooring and counter surfacing; and experimental kitchen sinks. Vinylite, Velon, and Ultron are three of the trade names.

Despite their variability, certain qualities taken together differentiate plastics from other materials. The range of color and texture, actual or simulated, seems limitless, and they come in all degrees of transparency to opacity. They feel warm and pleasant. Truly "plastic," they can be formed into almost any rigid or flexible shape. Typically, they are tough and durable in relation to weight and thickness. Absorbing little or no moisture, they neither rot nor mildew. Their resistance to chemicals is variable but generally good. Their strength and dimensions are with a few exceptions noticeably affected by extreme temperatures. In price, they vary greatly.

Forming and Fabricating Plastics

Plastic resins come to forming machines as powders or granules, compressed tablets or liquids, which under heat and pressure can be shaped as designers wish. Powders or tablets can be compressed in steel molds, liquids can be forced through dies to form continuous sheets, rods, filaments, tubes, or pipes. Some can be drawn into thin sheets or blown into molds. Others can be blown full of gas or air to make light but strong insulation.

Film and sheeting for shower curtains, upholstery, or laminates are made by spreading plastic solutions on wheels up to 25 feet in diameter, by extruding the compound through a wide die, or by calendering—passing it between several rollers to get the desired thickness and surface texture. Rollers are also used in giving other materials a plastic coating. In laminating such materials as Formica and Micarta, layers of cloth, paper, wood, or glass fibers are impregnated with uncured resin or alternated with uncured plastic film, then pressed into a single sheet.

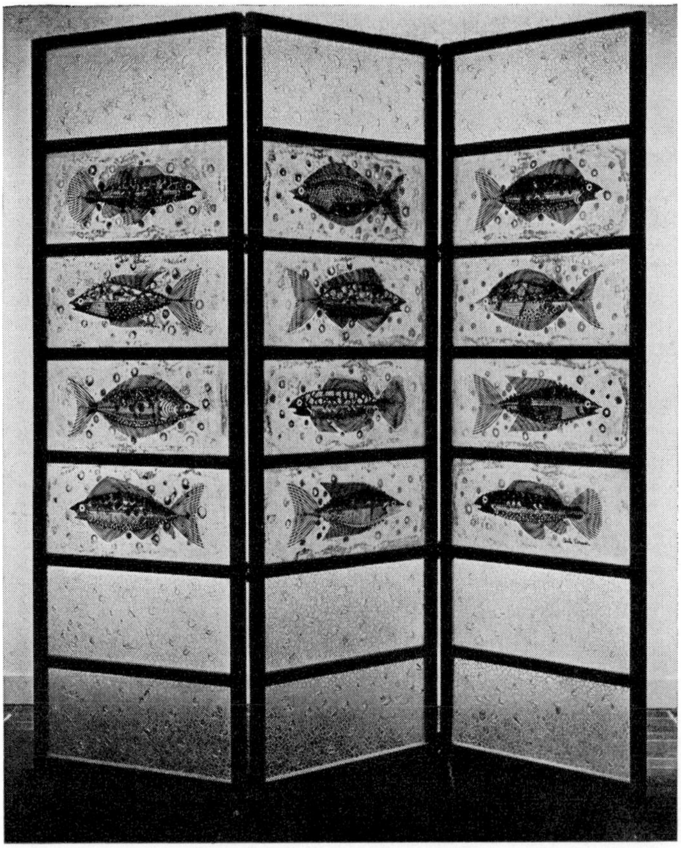

A

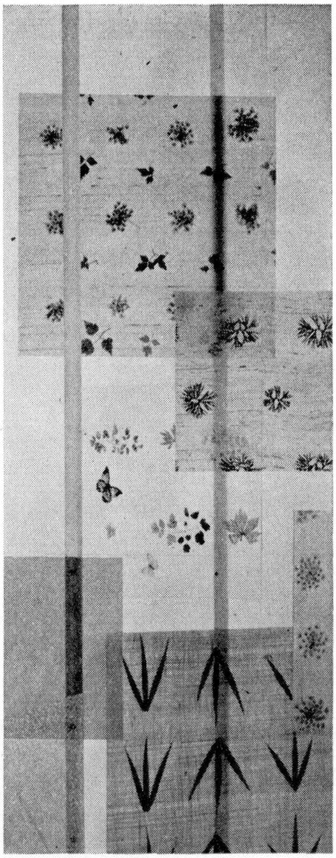

B

Plastics hold only partially explored decorative possibilities.

Above left. In a plastic screen by Emile Norman, fish designs of glass, brass, and bronze are encased in plastic.

Above right. Manufactured acrylic panels are available in many colors, textures, and patterns. (*Wasco Products*)

Below. Freda Koblick, interested in the forms obtained by hardening plastic at different rates, heightened the impetuous but surely patterned effect with embedded slices of rock.

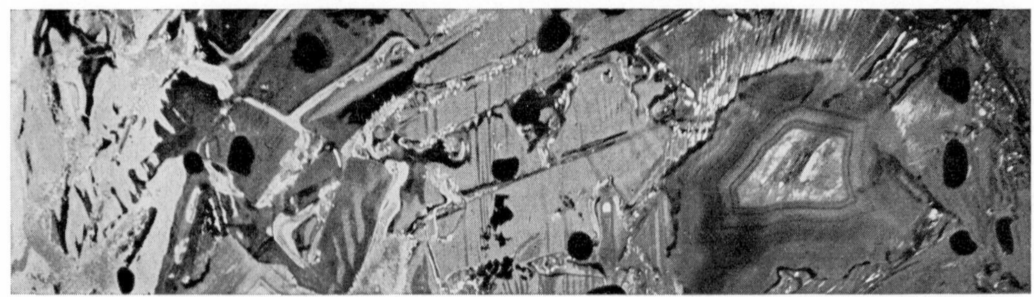

C

Design in Plastics

Plastics "are almost as nearly a chart of specifications as a group of materials." Unlike natural materials, the basic qualities of plastics are chemically and physically created by man. Thus instead of designing to suit a material, man can precisely design the material to meet a specific need. This brings new challenges and problems. It indicates close, continuing cooperation between chemist, manufacturer, and designer. And it gives the designer a characterless powder to mold. There is no age-old craft tradition in which to seek cumulated knowledge or inspiration.

In spite of plastics' potentiality for new forms, few have been developed. The shapes of plastic dishes closely resemble those made of clay because these have been found serviceable and pleasant. Handles of knives and forks, even though made of nylon, are fashioned to fit our hands and therefore do not differ markedly from handles of wood or metal. Polyethylene pails and dishpans weigh little, do not rust, dent, or scratch surfaces; but for utilitarian reasons the shapes are like those found in metal. But in furniture (Chapter 14), experimental houses, and decorative panels (Figs. 229C and 232C), distinctive "plastic" forms have been produced. Although plastics can be ornamented as easily as any other material, the majority of plastic objects are relatively simple. Those that are patterned, such as laminated sheets or floor coverings, often are made to look like older materials.

All this is understandable when you remember that the resins used in plastics have little if any distinctive character and seldom inspire distinctive shapes. Consumers and manufacturers, even many designers, conservatively prefer that which is at least partially familiar to anything completely new. Giving unfamiliar form and ornament to a new material is a tough design assignment and a business risk. Thus, in evaluating plastics, about all we can do is to ask such general questions as: Does the form and ornament suit the purpose? Is it pleasant to see and touch? And is the material attractive and well suited to the functions?

Even though plastics seldom as yet have been distinctively designed, they have had enormous impact on homes. Plastic cases for radio, phonograph, and television sets are cheaper than wood or metal. Plastic surfaces and drawers for furniture lighten housekeeping as do plastic curtains, upholstery, and lampshades. Floors and countertops surfaced with plastic reduce noise and breakage, and are easy to keep. Humble objects—dishpans and mop pails—are available in bright, cheerful colors. Plastic furniture of the present and plastic houses of the future may change many of our concepts of home planning and furnishing. Finally there is the whole realm, as yet hardly explored, of plastics as unexpected sources of visual delight.

10. Fabrics

VERY EARLY IN HISTORY, man, finding that animal skins, leaves, and bark were not always available in pieces of suitable size and weight, set about to improve on nature. He wanted something to protect his body, to make his living quarters more comfortable, and to satisfy his need for spiritual stimulation and satisfaction—and he produced fabrics. More than anything in the house, except the people, fabrics humanize our homes because of their pliant responsiveness to our needs. They are useful in controlling light coming through windows and in giving privacy without solid walls. They insulate against extreme heat and cold and they absorb noise. They provide easily removable and cleanable coverings for tables and beds and pleasant-to-touch upholstery for chairs and sofas. Beyond these service functions, fabrics bring beauty and individuality.

Several distinctive characteristics of fabrics are worth noting.

Above. A pre-Columbian textile from Peru. (*In the Brooklyn Museum Collection*)

- No other material comes in such width and breadth and can be readily used in those dimensions.
- Uniquely pliable and manipulatable, they can be folded, draped, pleated, or stretched; and they can be cut, sewn, or glued together with simple home equipment.
- They are one of the materials most frequently and easily replaced.
- They are noticed because they are used in quantity throughout the home, look and feel softer than other materials, and are often brightly colored or richly patterned.
- They link together people, furniture, and architecture in a way unequalled by anything else. Carpets and other fabrics fastened to floors and walls adhere strictly to the "architecture" of the house. Upholstery and table linens adapt themselves to the seating or tables on which they are used and at the same time relate those pieces to our clothes. Curtains and draperies can partake of the architectural quality of windows as well as relate openings to the enclosing structure and to the furniture in the room.

Thus, in addition to usefulness, fabrics have two important functions. First, they make their own very special visual and tactile contribution. Second, they can be strong unifying elements within a room and from one room to another. In this chapter, attention will be focused on fibers, the processes by which fibers are transformed into fabrics, and fabric design. In succeeding chapters, consideration will be given to fabrics' potential integration with walls, windows, floors and furniture. Thereby, while duly stressing the distinctive qualities of fabrics, we hope we have avoided discussing them as items separate from the whole house.

Fabric is a general term referring to anything manufactured by hand or machine, but it has come to be applied especially to **cloth. Textile** refers only to **woven fabrics.** In addition to weaving, fabrics can be made by knitting, felting, or lacing together natural or man-made fibers and also by fabricating plastics into sheets. Performance and appearance of fabrics is a product of several factors: the qualities of the basic material, the process by which it is fabricated, the finish, and the applied ornamentation.

► FIBERS

The term "fiber" is defined as a threadlike object or filament, but it has also come to mean that which gives substance or texture. Both meanings apply to textile fibers. Nature provides an abundance of fibers that in

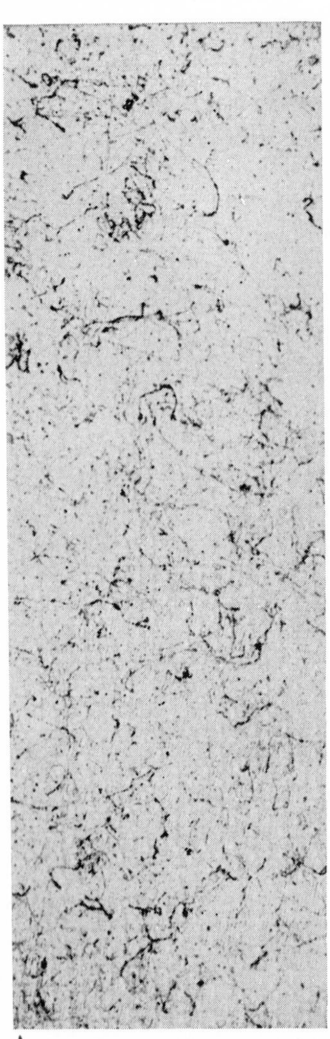

A

B

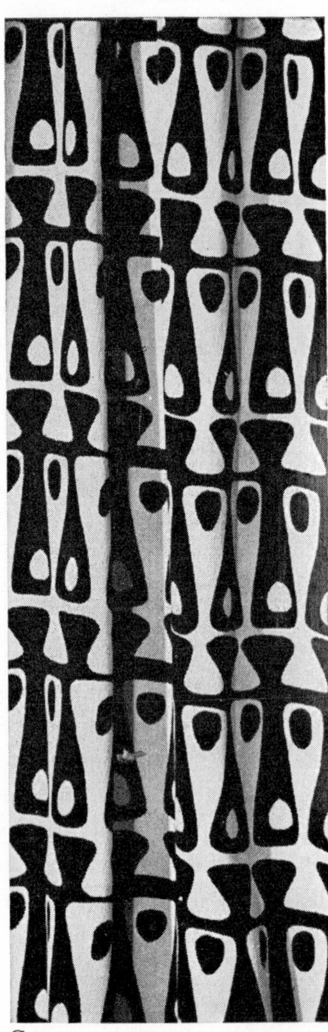

C

The scope of contemporary fabrics is increased each year.

Left. Durable wall fabric of color fused to the underside of a vinyl sheet, to which a suedelike backing is joined, can be cleaned with soap or fine steel wool. Lively dark lines add visual texture to a geometrically regular, embossed surface. Similar materials, but with an elastic, knitted cotton backing, make tough, form-fitting upholstery. (*U. S. Plywood Corp.*)

Center. Drapery material hand-woven by Margaret Coffin has horizontal stripes of blue, violet, and gray mercerized cotton alternating with narrower bands of jade green novelty yarn and thin lines of metallic filaments. Its beauty comes from the fibers and the structural patterns in which they are woven. (*Montclair Art Museum*)

Right. Matt Kahn's hand-screened print on linen is notable for its lively, accented rhythms. It would be tonic for a room with the miseries. (*Konweiser Fabrics*) their natural state suggest weaving. These include reeds and grasses, wool and hair of animals, fibers enclosing the seeds of some plants, and the filaments insects spin for cocoons. There are also many natural fibers that need only a little processing, such as some wood which splits easily into thin strips or the stems of such plants as flax and jute. To these, scientists have added many fibers of their own invention. The table on the following pages gives the significant facts about the qualities of the more important fibers and the uses for which they are most suitable. It shows that fibers differ from one another in many ways: strength and elasticity; resistance to abrasion, sun, moisture, mildew, and fire; and tactile and visual qualities. Each fiber has its strong and weak points; none is ideally suited to every purpose.

Man-made fibers share some highly desirable qualities: they are of unlimited length in contrast to the comparative shortness of wool and cotton; they tend to repel, rather than absorb, moisture and soil; and they offer little foothold to insects, mildew, or fungus. Some of the synthetics are better suited to a few specific conditions than are any natural ones. As yet, however, few if any artificial fibers can be used with full assurance for as many purposes as can wool or cotton—in part, at least, because the old fibers are better understood. Natural fibers, to be sure, have their weaknesses but these are rapidly being minimized by new ways of treating them. For example, they can be made resistant to soil and stains, shrinkage and moths, or crushing and wrinkling.

More and more, different fibers are being combined in textiles to increase beauty, utility, or both. The Nylo-Saran upholstery in Figure 237D is

Man-made fibers open wide the possibilities for new usefulness and beauty.

Left. Nylon and Saran yarns are combined to produce a soft yet long-wearing and virtually stain-proof upholstery. (*Virginia Fibre Corporation*)

Right. Fibers of nineteen vibrant metallic colors woven into a rug with thick and thin stripes, rough and smooth textures, demonstrate aluminum's versatility. Marianne Strengell, designer. (*Aluminum Company of America*)

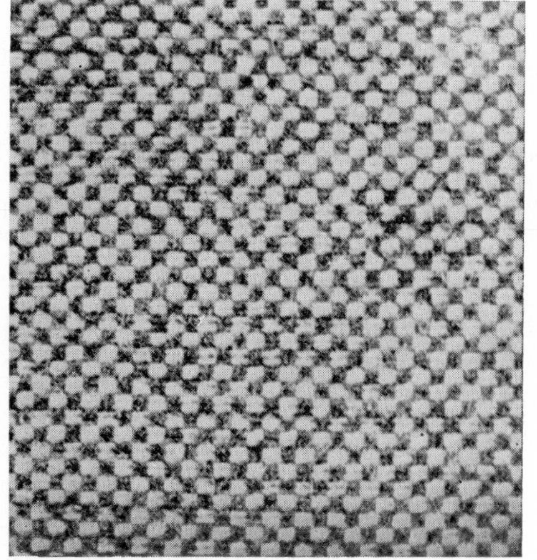

D

E

TEXTILE FIBERS

Fiber and Fiber Type	Appearance	Uses	Maintenance	Other Characteristics and Special Treatments
Acetate Cellulose Acetate Blends with most fibers	Pleasant hand and luster. Drapes well. Good color range.	Bedspreads Curtains Draperies Rugs Upholstery	Dry clean or wash, dries quickly. Iron with cool iron.	*Celaperm, Chromspun, Jetspun* result of new dye processes in which color is integral part of fiber, strongly resistant to sun, washing, dry cleaning. Retains heat-set pleats and creases
Acrilan Acrylic copolymer Blends with all fibers	Warm hand; bulky, wool-like touch. Wide color range.	Blankets Rugs	Slow to soil. Dry clean or wash, dries quickly. Little ironing. Discolors in dry heat.	Warmth without weight. Highly resilient. Retains heat-set pleats and creases. Subject to static electricity.
Arnel Cellulose triacetate Blends with most fibers	Pleasant hand and luster. Drapes well. Excellent color range.	Draperies	Slow to soil. Dry clean or wash, dries quickly. Little ironing.	Retains heat-set pleats and creases.
Cotton Cellulose Blends with most fibers Cotton-Dacron blend outstanding	Pleasant, soft, dull surface. Fair drape. Excellent color range.	Bed and table "linens" Bedspreads Curtains Draperies Rugs Towels Upholstery	Soils, stains, wrinkles easily unless treated. Dry clean or wash; can be boiled. Irons easily.	*Mercerizing* increases luster, softness, strength capacity to absorb dye. New processes can make remarkably water-repellent, soil- and wrinkle-resistant, quick drying little or no ironing.
Dacron Polyester Blends with cotton, wool, rayon, orlon, nylon, silk	Crisp or soft pleasant hand, depending on blend and fabric construction. Good drape. Fair color range.	Curtains Draperies Upholstery	Slow to soil. Dry clean or wash, dries quickly. Little ironing.	Bulk leads to lightweight, warm textiles. As strong wet as dry. Retains pleats and creases.
Fortisan Saponified acetate Not blended but combined with other fibers	Sheer. Drapes well. Fair color range.	Curtains Draperies	Dry clean, or wash—solid colors. Iron at temperature for most delicate combined fibers; otherwise like cotton.	Used in warp yarns in combination with other fibers. Fine and lightweight but exceptionally strong and stable. Curtain hems stay straight after cleaning.
Glass Fiberglas Silica, sand, and an alkali	Lustrous, silky, and heavy. Good drape. Fair color range in dyes, printed many hues.	Curtains Draperies	Slow to soil. Hand wash and hang with no ironing. Dries quickly.	May become brittle. Breaks if sharply creased. Embedded in plastic for lamp shades, wall panels, etc.
Linen Flax yarn Blends with cotton, rayon	Clean, fresh, lintless. Fair drape. Good color range.	Curtains Draperies Rugs Table linens Towels Upholstery	Soils and wrinkles easily. Washes and irons beautifully. Can be boiled.	Stronger when wet. Sanforized to reduce shrinking. Can be made wrinkle-resistant.

RESISTANCE to

Abrasion	Fading	Fire	Mildew	Insects	Felting Shrinking	Stretching	Sunlight	Wrinkling
Poor	Fair	Poor	Good	Fair	Fair	Fair	Loses strength gradually	Fair
Fair	Good	Good if closely woven *	Good	Excel-lent	Good	Good	Loses strength gradually	Good
Fair	Excel-lent	Excel-lent	Good	Excel-lent	Excellent	Good	Loses strength gradually	Very good; recovery excellent
Fair	Good	Poor	Poor	Poor	Poor unless San-forized or pre-shrunk	Good when Sanforized	Loses strength gradually	Poor unless treated or blended
Good	Good	Good	Excel-lent	Excel-lent	Good	Excellent	Loses strength gradually	Excellent
Good	Good	Poor	Fair	Fair	Excellent	Good	Very good	Fair
oor	Good	Excel-lent	Excel-lent	Excel-lent	Excellent	Excellent	Excellent	Excellent
air	Excel-lent	Poor	Good	Excel-lent	Poor un-les San-forized	Good	Loses strength gradually	Very poor unless treated or blended

* Burns with chemical ferocity if loosely woven. Rugs should be tested.

TEXTILE FIBERS (Cont.)

Fiber and Fiber Type	Appearance	Uses	Maintenance	Other Characteristics an Special Treatments
Nylon Polyamide Blends with acetate, wool, cotton, rayon, Dacron	Pleasing hand, natural luster. Good drape. Good color range.	Bedspreads Curtains Draperies Rugs Upholstery	Slow to soil. Dry clean or wash, dries quickly. Little ironing.	Outstanding strength and lightness. Can b heat-set to keep shap permanently. Subject t static electricity.
Orlon Acrylic polymer Blends with wool, rayon, cotton, silk, Dacron	Warm, soft hand, similar to wool. Good drape. Good color range.	Blankets Curtains Draperies	Slow to soil. Dry clean or wash, dries quickly. Little ironing.	Almost as strong wet a dry. Subject to stati electricity.
Saran Copolymer of vinylidene, chloride and vinyl chloride Blends with most fibers	High luster. Good drape. Excellent color range.	Curtains Rugs Upholstery Excellent for outdoor furniture.	Slow to soil. Wash, can be sponged between washings, dries quickly. Little ironing.	Tends to wrinkle an form folds. Subject t static electricity. Non absorbent, resists chem icals, stains.
Silk Silkworm cocoon-protein Blends with most fibers	Lustrous, smooth; unique crunchy softness. Drapes well. Excellent color range.	Curtains Draperies Rugs Upholstery	Dry clean or hand wash. Irons easily.	Greatest tensile strengt of any natural fiber. Very elastic, weaker when wet. Takes dye brilliantly. Poor conductor of electricity. *Weighted* to give heavier body, better drape.
Viscose Rayon Regenerated cellulose Blends with most fibers	Bright or dull luster, pleasing hand. Drapes well. Good color range.	Blankets Curtains Draperies Rugs Table "linens" Upholstery	Dry clean, or wash, iron like silk or cotton, depending on type and finish.	Absorbs moisture and swells when wet. Reduces static in blend Can be made to lo like cotton, wool, silk. New processes make r sistant to shrinkage, felting, and wrinkles.
Wool Sheep-protein Blends with most fibers	Soft, dry, warm hand. Drapes well. Good color range.	Blankets Draperies Rugs Upholstery	Dry clean or wash in cold water. Press over damp cloth.	*Worsted* yarns made long fibers laid paralle tightly twisted into smooth strong yarns di ferent from *woolen*. Wool-synthetic blend reduces shrinkage b has tendency to pillin New processes can mak wool even more resista to soil, water, stains, an wrinkles.

RESISTANCE to (Cont.)

Abrasion	Fading	Fire	Mildew	Insects	Felting Shrinking	Stretching	Sunlight	Wrinkling
Excel-lent	Good	Good	Excel-lent	Excel-lent	Excellent	Excellent	Loses strength gradually	Very good
Fair	Good	Good	Good	Excel-lent	Good	Good	Outstand-ing resist-ance to sun rot	Good
Good	Excel-lent	Excel-lent	Excel-lent	Excel-lent	Good	Good	Darkens slightly	Fair
Fair	Good	Poor	Good	Fair	Good	Good	Poor	Very good
Fair	Good	Poor	Poor	Fair	Poor unless treated	Fair. Poor when wet	Loses strength gradually, faster than acetate	Poor unless treated or blended
Fair	Good	Good	Fair	Poor unless treated	Poor unless treated or blended	Fair to poor	Loses strength gradually	Excellent

an example. Both fibers resist ordinary hazards but their list of assets is not identical. Nylon is the strongest of fibers but it gradually weakens in strong sunlight. It resists wrinkling better than does Saran and it also feels softer, but its colors are more limited and subject to some fading. By combining the two fibers, the drawbacks of each is limited. Sometimes two or more fibers are blended in one yarn; in other instances, two or more yarns of different fibers are woven together.

► YARNS

"Yarn" is the term used to describe fibers that have been twisted together to make them sufficiently strong and long for weaving or knitting. With natural fibers, yarn-making includes cleaning the fibers, drawing them out so that they are more or less even and parallel, and spinning or twisting them into yarn. Man-made fibers are clean, continuous, and parallel as soon as they become filaments so that the process is simply one of twisting them together. Yarns vary in the kinds of fibers used either alone or in combination, the type and tightness of twist, and the size of the finished product.

Long fibers laid parallel to each other and tightly twisted give yarns smoother and stronger than do short fibers somewhat randomly arranged and loosely twisted. Nature provides only one long continuous fiber—silk—while all synthetics have that characteristic. Any of them, however, can be cut into short pieces for different effects. Length of fiber and tightness of twist lead to the following types of yarns:

- **Cotton.** *Carded* yarns have only the very short fibers removed and the remaining ones somewhat straightened. *Combed* yarns are composed entirely of long fibers laid parallel before spinning which makes the yarn stronger and smoother. *Lisle* is tightly twisted from combed, mercerized fibers.
- **Silk.** Most high quality silk is made from long continuous filaments, but *spun* silk is made from the short fibers that cannot be unreeled from cocoons.
- **Synthetics.** These fibers originate as continuous, parallel, more or less smooth strands called *filaments,* which are usually twisted into ply yarns. They can, though, be cut into short lengths and blown apart, then brought together in a mass something like cleaned but uncombed cotton or wool, and these *staples* are twisted into soft yarns known as *spun* rayon, nylon, etc.

Twisting fibers tightly or loosely is only the beginning of possible variations. Fibers can be given a right- or left-hand twist and these can be put together in two-, three-, or four-ply yarns. There are many special twists, of which crepe, slub with thick and thin, nub, snarl, ratiné, and bouclé are only a few. Rubber cores can be covered with fibers to give elastic yarns, and fibers can be wrapped with metallic wires.

Size of yarns ranges from spider-web single filaments to silk yarns of 200 strands or to ropelike cords. Textiles can be made entirely of one size (Fig. 245C) or may combine several to many sizes (Fig. 244C) as need and desire indicate.

► FASTENING THE YARNS TOGETHER

There are four basic ways of making fabrics from yarns.

Felting, probably the first process discovered by man, is simply matting fibers together with heat, moisture, and pressure. With this treatment, wool and hair, cotton, and some spun synthetics bend and interlock to make a dense, somewhat fuzzy and resilient fabric of no great strength. Felts are used today chiefly as rug cushions.

Knitting, an old art perhaps first used by prehistoric man in making fishnets, is done by interlacing one yarn in a series of connecting loops with a blunt rod or needle. Patterns are produced by combining plain, rib, and purl stitches, plus many complex variations. Knitted fabrics usually have quite a bit of stretch which makes them more suitable for clothing than household use.

Twisting, the process by which laces are made, is the twisting together of yarns that run in two or more directions. Rightly or wrongly, lace curtains, bedspreads, and antimacassars have fallen from favor and about the only appearance of lace in today's home is in tablecloths or mats.

Weaving is the interlacing of yarns at right angles to each other to make textiles. Two definitions are important. *Warp* yarns run lengthwise on the loom and in the fabric. *Filling* (also called weft or woof) yarns run crosswise to fill and hold together the warp. Weaving is an ancient art with a rich history of accomplishment. Contemporary textiles by no means surpass the technical excellence or beauty of the best from the past.

The apparently enormous complexity of weaves can be reduced to four basic types plus Jacquard, which is a mechanized way of handling one or more types usually in intricate patterns. These are illustrated on pages 244, 245, and 246.

The very few **basic** weaves lead to innumerable modifications and innovations.

Plain weaving is simply one filling thread over one warp yarn and under the next (or groups of filling and warp yarns regarded as one). Variations are basket weaves, in which two or more warps are crossed by two or more filling yarns, as in monk's cloth; and rib weaves, such as rep and poplin, in which a single filling yarn passes over and under groups of warp, or several filling yarns pass over and under warp yarns in regular alternation.

A

The warp is alternating yarns of silk twist and novelty cellophane, the filling of blue leather strips and dyed reeds. Planned as a wall hanging, the pattern of this fabric is orderly and composed but enlivened by the yarns and the subtle mutations in the rhythms. Designed and woven by Hilda Dial. (*M. H. deYoung Memorial Museum*)

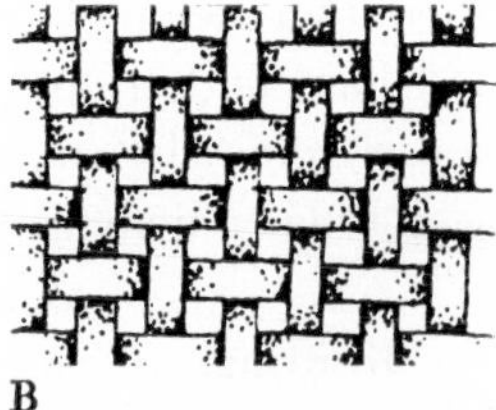

B

Floating-yarn weaves differ from plain weaves in that filling yarns "float" over or under several to many warp yarns; or the warp yarns may float over the filling. There are several well-known kinds of floating-yarn weaves. *Twill* is typified by diagonal lines; *satin* by long floats which, minimizing the over-and-under texture of most weaving, give marked smoothness of surface; *piqué* has pronounced ribs or cords resulting from exposed warp threads; *honeycomb* has square or rectangular designs on both sides. In addition, there are many individualized variations, and floating yarns can be combined with other weaves.

C

Blue cotton joined with bright copper and natural hemp yarns make a lively hand-woven drapery material through which some light and air can pass. Light-colored, thick yarns float over the orderly grid in lightly disciplined disobedience. Designed and woven by Marie Torman. (*M. H. deYoung Memorial Museum*)

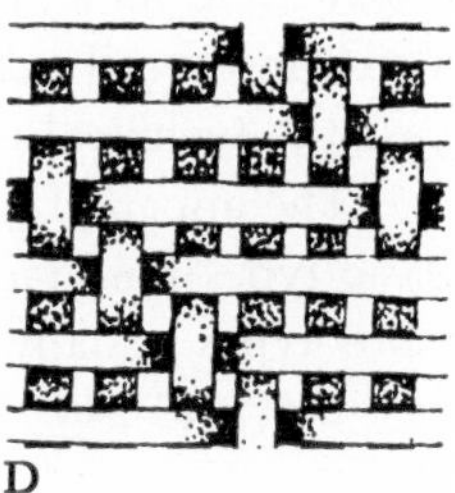

D

Pile weaves are distinguished by a set of yarns that stand up from the flat-lying warp and filling. If the loops are not cut, such textiles as *terry cloth* and *frieze* are produced. Cutting the loops results in *velvet, plush,* and the like. Patterns are formed if some loops are cut and some uncut, if some of the pile is higher than the rest, or if different colored yarns are used.

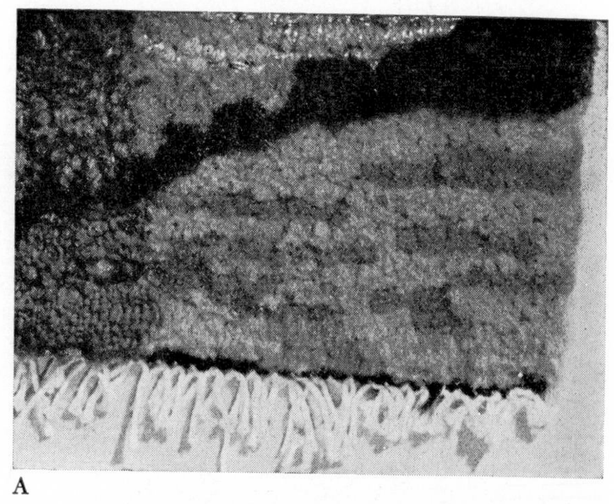

A

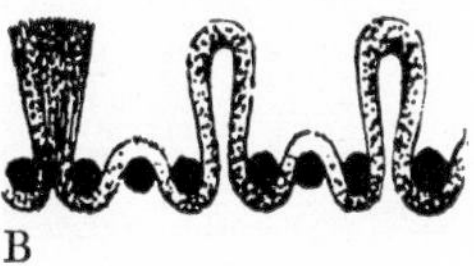

B

A rug sample, hand-woven by Bittan Valberg, combines metallic yarn with nylon in red, violet, black, orange, and pink for an eventful floor covering. Uncut pile accents large areas of high- and low-cut pile. (*Smithsonian Institution*)

Leno weaves give more-or-less open, lacy effects by locking warp and filling in figure eights. *Marquisette* and many other porous textiles are leno weaves. Usually, the weave is at such small scale that the design is hardly noticed, but coarser versions create handsome patterns.

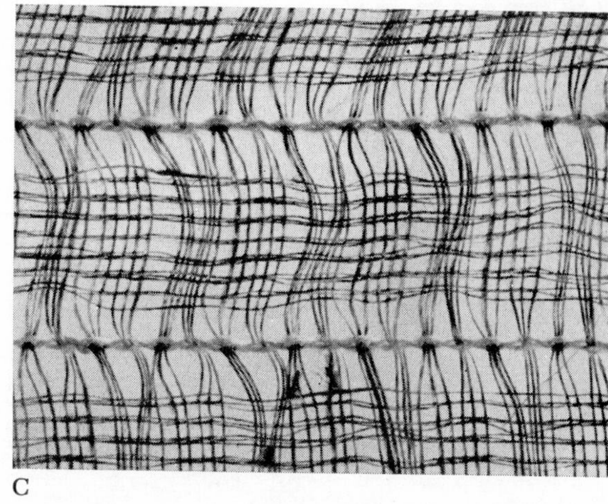

C

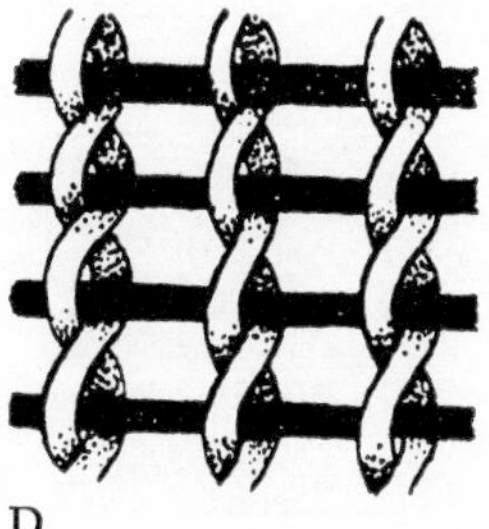

D

Linen warp with hemp and rayon filling in a leno-weave curtain material. Its fragile, almost frivolous appearance belies its actual strength. (*Kagan-Dreyfuss*)

Jacquard or **figure** weaves are not types of weave but a mechanized way of producing woven patterns that can be simple or of great intricacy. They include flat *damasks*, raised *brocades*, cut and uncut *velvet*, and many kinds of carpets.

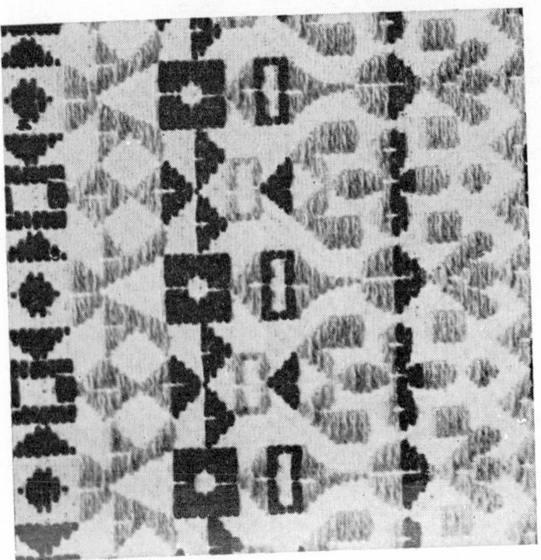

A

B

C

Above left. A contemporary brocade in cotton and spun rayon in which an unexpected blending of colors and juxtaposition of shapes beget an iridescence that is rare today. Coarse yarns floating over a plain weave create a figure that is equally good but different on the two sides of the textile. Alexander Girard, designer. (*Herman Miller Fabric Collection*)

Above right. Finely spun silk together with coarser tussah silk and Bemberg introduce minor textural variations in a brocade whose forms expand and contract with assured serenity. (*Boris Kroll Fabrics*)

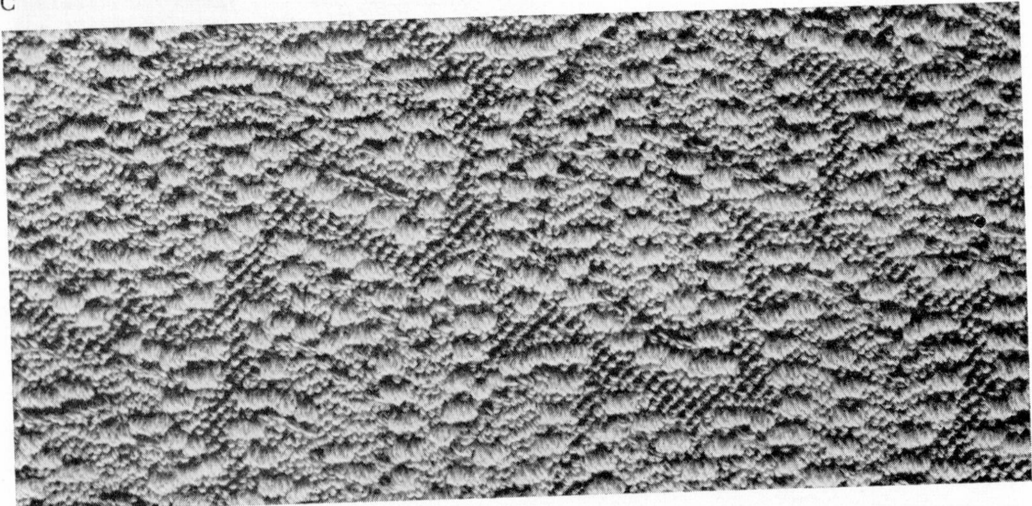

D

Uncut-loop yarns of wool are varied in height in this pile-weave carpet. The inexact repetition creates a pebbly surface interesting in design and durable in use. (*A. & M. Karagheusian*)

Weaves, like fibers, affect durability and maintenance.

- Loose weaves of any kind, but especially diagonal and those woven of different and inappropriately combined fibers, may pull out of shape.
- Loose weaves, such as monk's cloth, or satin weaves with long floated yarns on the surface are likely to catch and break if used on furniture.
- Ribbed or corded weaves often show wear, especially on the raised portions, more quickly than do flat or pile weaves.
- Loose weaves, unless specially treated, are highly susceptible to shrinkage.
- Napped textiles show wear and dirt quickly; pile textiles do not.
- Napped or pile textiles show spot cleaning less than do flat weaves.
- Smooth weaves show spots more readily than do rough.
- Soft, cut-pile textiles get mussed-looking quickly.

► FINISHING THE FABRIC

Fibers are found or made, spun into yarns, made into fabrics. But when most fabrics come from machine looms, they are far from ready for use. Various kinds of finishing give them their final appearance and qualities. *Beetling* or pounding with steel and wooden hammers gives cotton and linens luster. In *calendering,* fabrics are pressed between rollers to give smooth finishes and to tighten the weaves as well as to polish them to a highly glazed sheen or emboss them with moiré, crepe, or other patterns. *Crabbing* tightens and sets the weave in wool, and *fulling* shrinks and compacts the textile. *Gigging* and *napping* give such textures as are found in flannel and fleece. *Shearing* and *singeing* remove surface fibers, fuzz, and lint. *Shrinking* lessens the tendency of most fibers to contract when exposed to moisture. *Starching* makes cotton lustrous and stiffer; *weighting* compensates for gum lost by silk in the cleaning process. By such means, lifeless sleazy textiles are transformed into usable, attractive materials.

There are also some finishing processes that notably change the behavior of fiber and fabric. Textiles can be made:

- *Crease-resistant* by impregnating the fibers with resins. This gives textiles more firmness and better draping qualities as well as making them pleasanter to touch. Dyes become more permanent and shrinkage in spun rayons, light cottons and linens, and velvets is reduced.
- *Fireproof and flameproof* by chemical treatment. A worth-while safety precaution, this also makes textiles heavier, stiffer and longer lasting. It gives additional resistance to weathering and sometimes to insects and mildew.

- *Glazed* with resins that give a more or less permanent smooth, lustrous surface which resists soil and improves draping qualities. Glazing is usually limited to textiles used for curtains, draperies, and slip covers.
- *Mildew- and moth-resistant* in varying degrees of permanence.
- *Shrink-resistant* chiefly through carefully controlled shrinking. In some processes, chemicals supplement moisture, heat, pressure, and tension.
- *Soil-resistant* by coating or impregnating fibers or fabrics with chemicals that make them less absorbent.
- *Starched* permanently by coating the surface with cellulose chemicals that withstand washing. Starching keeps textiles crisp and firm, gives a smooth lintless surface and longer life.
- *Water-repellent* by coating or impregnating the fibers with wax, metals, or resins. Such treatment makes fabrics hold their shape better, as well as helping to keep dirt on the surface.

Dyeing the Fabric

Textiles can get their dye colors when they are unspun fibers, spun yarns, or woven textiles; and in some synthetics, such as Chromspun and Celaperm acetate, the dye is mixed with the liquid from which the fiber is made. Although generalizations about dyes are risky, the synthetics in which the dye is part of the fiber seem to be the most color-fast. Next come the fibers or yarns dyed before weaving, and last come the textiles dyed after weaving. Today, however, there is less difference between the latter two than in the past.

The kind of dye and also the hue affect color-fastness, but almost all will fade in varying degrees if exposed to sun or washed. Unless you want to protect fabrics from sun and use at the possible cost of happy family living, you will do well to get the most nearly fade-proof textiles available. Since all textiles change with time, it seems wise to select those that will mellow gracefully rather than those that will look tired and worn-out when they fade. The following characteristics mitigate the results of fading:

- **Color.** The colors most common in nature—grays, greens, browns, soft yellows, and oranges—retain a pleasing appearance longer than do colors of higher intensity. Mixtures, such as in tweeds, do not become as listless as faded solid colors. Dark colors may lose their richness and depth with even a little fading. Many blues lose their brilliance quickly.
- **Texture.** Definite textures with their play of light and shade compensate for loss of color.
- **Pattern.** Intricate or diffused designs lose less of their character than do those whose interest lies chiefly in brilliant contrasts, precision, or clarity.

Three textile designs inspired by natural forms are markedly different in character.

Upper. Naturalistic foliage, fruits and flowers interlaced in a manner reminiscent of seventeenth-century English design. The flat textile has been imprinted with three-dimensional forms. (*Arthur H. Lee & Sons*)

Center. Conventionalized interpretation in a contemporary print emphasizes inner structure rather than surface appearance. The crisp, informal design is open and spacious without recourse to perspective or light, shade, and shadow. (*D. N. & E. Walter Co.*)

Lower. An *abstract* interpretation is illustrated by a piece of sixteenth-century Persian cut velvet with woven design. The motifs have been transformed into formalized shapes and organized in a series of compressed parallel planes closely related to the two-dimensional surface. (*M. H. deYoung Memorial Museum*)

This is no condemnation of bright, solid, or dark colors or of decisive patterns—but you will probably more quickly feel the urge to replace them.

Printing the Fabric

The easiest, least expensive way to add applied design to fabrics is by printing, a process known for at least 5,000 years. Pigments mixed to the consistency of thick paste are applied to the finished fabric or to the yarns prior to weaving by one of three methods:

- **Roller printing** is by far the most commonly used method. Pigments are applied from copper rollers engraved with the design. One roller is made for each color, but an effect of more colors than rollers can be achieved by engraving different parts of a roller to different depths and by printing one color over others. In warp printing, the yarns are printed before weaving which gives a soft diffuse quality, such as in cretonnes.
- **Block printing** is done by hand from wood blocks often surfaced with metal or linoleum. Block-printed fabrics have the slight irregularities characteristic of most handcrafts and are expensive.
- **Screen printing,** done either by hand or semimechanically, is a type of stencil printing especially suitable for patterns produced in relatively small quantities.

► COATED FABRICS AND PLASTIC SHEETING

Barely hinting at their oilcloth ancestry, the new coated fabrics combine minimum maintenance with a full spectrum of color and texture possibilities. Made by fusing a vinyl surface onto a textile backing (Figs. 236A and 250), they are strong, flexible, and impervious. The better grades are as

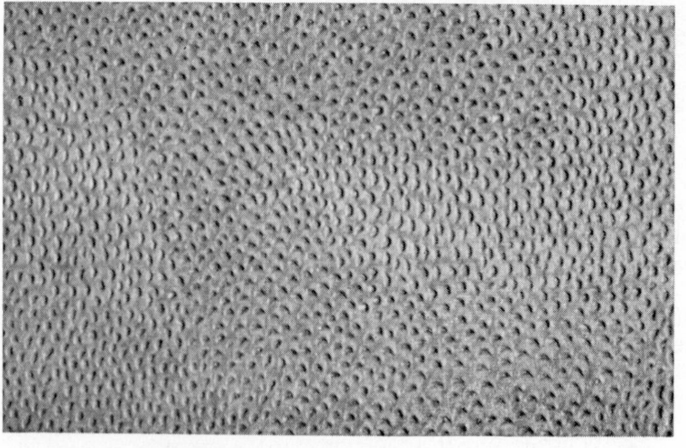

A small-scale nondirectional pattern for a vinyl plastic upholstery fabric designed by Russell Wright is visually altered with each change of light or angle of viewing. *(E. I. duPont de Nemours & Co.)*

nearly indestructible as is any material suitable for wall covering or upholstery. Resisting stain and soil, the surface can be cleaned with a damp cloth. Tough and resilient, they seldom crack, chip, peel, or scratch. Textures range from leatherlike smoothness to deeply molded, three-dimensional patterns. The fade-proof colors can be light or dark, brilliant or muted. Expectedly, many of the designs imitate leather or textiles but a few exploit the unique character of this new product. Although they do not have the friendly tactile qualities of textiles, they are ideal materials for kitchens and for family and children's rooms.

Vinyl plastic sheeting comes in varied thicknesses from thin films suitable for window and shower curtains to heavier weights for tablecloths and draperies. They take all colors, either integral with the material or printed on it. As with vinyl-coated fabrics, there is no limit on textural patterns and the surface can be glossy, dull, or made fuzzy like flannel or velvet. In sum, these durable and decorative fabrics greatly extend the home-furnishing repertory.

► FABRIC DESIGN

Nothing used in contemporary homes, except wallpaper, offers the freedom of design that comes naturally in fabrics. This is of special significance today when other materials are likely to be handled with restricted simplicity. The increasing urge for intricate ornamentation and emotional impact can be most readily and inexpensively satisfied with fabrics.

Looking at the fabrics illustrated in this chapter, you can see strict linear geometry brought to life by contrasting fibers in the leather-and-reed wall covering whose rectangularity is obedient to the loom on which it was woven and to the wall of which it is a part. The floating-yarn drapery, Nylo-Saran upholstery, and aluminum rug also have a sturdy regularity that is basic in most weaving—but the leno-weave curtain is fluent and carefree in rhythm. One of the brocades is crisply punctuated with staccato shapes, the other is more flowing. "Austrian Contemporary" (Fig. 252D) is boldly vigorous, "Catalano" (Fig. 252B) is delicately small in scale. The printed patterns on page 253 further exemplify the diversity of feelings and moods that textiles can bring into homes.

All that was said in Chapters 5, 6, and 7 is generally applicable to fabric design, which can be structurally part and parcel of fiber and weave, applied to the finished cloth, or a combination of the two. Yet fabrics have their unique characteristics that should be taken into account. Some of the more important qualities—**pliability, continuousness, flatness,** and **structure**—are discussed and illustrated on the following pages.

A

Fabrics have several qualities that affect their design.

Pliability suggests patterns that are supple and pliant, unless the fabric is intended only to be stretched flat on walls or floors. This does not rule out angularity but it makes extreme rigidity or hardness questionable.

Left. "Baradur" unifies diverse flexible, curvilinear motifs with occasional angular accents. (*F. Shumacher & Co.*)

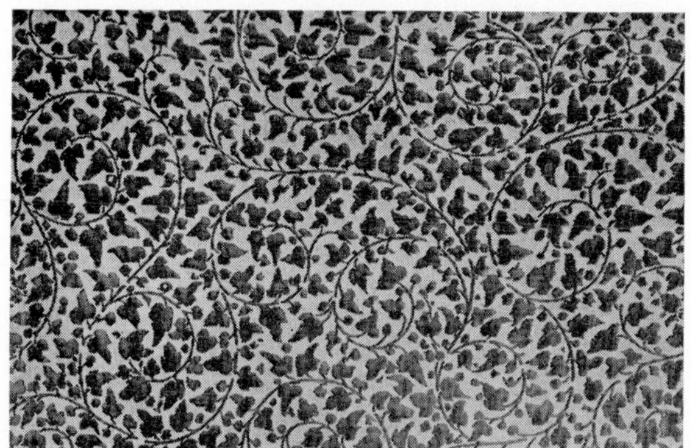
B

The **continuous, sheetlike** nature of fabrics provides one of the few opportunities for uninterrupted, endless patterns without definite beginning or conclusion. Designs that lead the eyes easily in all directions seem especially appropriate.

Left. "Catalano" has a mazelike meander of leaves organized on pliant, spiraling stems. Mario Fortuny, designer. (*Fortuny, Inc.*)

C

The **flatness** of fabrics suggests two-dimensional compositions. There are numerous exceptions to this statement and many of them are successful. In general, though, an illusion of great depth or of strongly modeled forms is open to doubt.

Left. "Venerable Sir" enlivens the surface of an Orlon casement textile with blocks of Chinese characters. Maggie Miklas, designer. (*Edwin Raphael Co.*)

D

The **structure** of warp and filling is apparent in most textiles. It may be of sufficient interest so that nothing more is needed. If applied ornament is desired, the weave and fiber are logical considerations. Delicate patterns are robbed of their delicacy by coarse textiles, bold designs often seem clumsy on fine cloths.

Left. The "Austrian Contemporary" series includes a crisp but varying triangle pattern on natural linen. Wavering lines are reminiscent of the yarns that make the textile. (*Greeff Fabrics, Inc.*)

A B C

Scale and implied activity are critical factors in selecting fabrics, as illustrated in three drapery materials with patterns markedly varied in size and rhythm.

Left. "Syncron" is small in scale, quiet in its balance of thin horizontal and thicker vertical stripes. Undemanding but not dull, it would be appropriate where there is no special reason for attracting attention toward windows. (*Edwin Raphael Co.*)

Center. "Fugitive Stripe" is larger in scale and more varied in rhythm but still placid in movement. (*Schiffer Prints*)

Right. "Suspension" is large in scale, active, and stimulating with its rising and falling forms. In almost any room it would be emphatic. (*Ruth Adler*)

► LIST OF FABRICS

The fabrics listed below are some of those most frequently used. They have been divided into five categories, based primarily on thickness, which is an important factor in determining their use. There is, however, quite a range within each category and some overlapping between categories. Most of the fabrics can be woven from a number of different fibers but a few such as *ninon* are made from only one. Fabric names are a strange miscellany being based on: the fiber, such as *linen,* which has come to mean a special kind of linen textile; the weave, such as *satin;* the early use, such as *monk's cloth;* or a trade name, such as *Indian Head.*

FABRICS

Very Thin

Almost transparent fabrics suitable for glass curtains; sometimes for summer bedspreads, dressing-table skirts, table coverings as well. Most of them can be made of cotton, silk, a synthetic, or even wool.

Bobbinet	Fine and sheer to coarse and open plain lace with hexagonal meshes. Soft yet with character; most effective when very full; coarser types best for straight folds; sheer well suited to tie-backs and ruffles. White, cream, ecru, pale colors.
Cheese-cloth	Cotton in loose plain weaves, very low thread count. Very inexpensive; short-lived; informal. Usually off-white.
Dimity	Fine, tightly twisted, usually combed cotton; plain weave with thin cord making vertical stripe or plaid; often mercerized. Fine, sheer, crisp; straight folds or tie-backs. Usually white; occasionally tints or printed patterns.
Filet	Square-mesh lace knotted at intersecting corners. Fine to coarse but usually giving a bold, heavy effect. White, cream, ecru, and plain colors.
Marquisette	Leno weave in many fibers. Sheer and open; soft or crisp; fine to coarse. Very serviceable; launders well. Usually white, cream, or pale colors; sometimes printed or woven patterns.
Ninon	Acetate in plain *voile*like or novelty weaves. Very thin; smooth, silky, pleasant sheen; replacing *silk gauze.* Best in straight folds. Plain colors, self-colored stripes, or shadowy figures.

Organdy — Cotton in plain weave; like sheer, crisp muslin, but crispness washes out unless specially treated; folds keep their place. Often used without draperies; frequently tied back. Many plain colors; also printed or embroidered designs.

Point d'esprit — Variation of *bobbinet* with dots that give it more body. White, cream, and pale colors.

Swiss Muslin (Dotted Swiss) — Cotton in plain weaves; usually embroidered or patterned in dots or figures. Fine, sheer, slightly crisp. Can be used alone, usually draped; effect generally informal. White and plain colors, usually light; figures may be colored.

Theatrical Gauze — Linen or cotton in a loose, open, crisp weave with a shimmering texture. Often used without draperies for colorful, informal effect. Wide range of plain colors, often two-toned.

Voile — Open, plain weave, sheer and smooth. Drapes softly; gives more privacy than marquisette. Various textures; many colors, usually pale; sometimes woven patterns.

Thin

Translucent fabrics suitable for glass curtains or for draperies, with sufficient body to be used alone and give a measure of privacy, although not at night. May also be used for dressing-table skirts, table coverings, and summer bedspreads.

Casement Cloth — Almost every known fiber in plain or small-figured weaves. Flat and lustrous. Usually ecru, but in a few other colors.

Fiberglas — Glass fibers in varied weaves and weights from sheer marquisette to heavy drapery fabrics. Translucent to opaque; can be washed and hung almost immediately without shrinking or stretching. Good range of colors; plain or printed.

Osnaburg — Cotton yarns, coarse and uneven, in an open, plain weave; similar to *crash*. Usually medium weight, natural color, but can be light or heavy weight, any color, printed patterns. Strong and long-lasting; rough textured; informal.

Muslin — Cotton in a soft, plain weave; light to heavy qualities. Bleached or unbleached; also dyed and printed. Inexpensive, durable, informal; often used alone at windows.

Pongee Wild silk in plain weave with broken crossbar texture caused by irregular yarns; also imitated in cotton and synthetics. Fairly heavy; often used without draperies; shrinks unless treated. Usually pale or dark ecru, but can be dyed.

Sheeting, Cotton Smooth, plain weave, medium to heavy weights. Inexpensive and informal. White, pale colors, or printed.

Sheeting, Plastic Smooth or textured, plain or printed, thin or thick. Used mostly for bath and kitchen curtains, shower curtains, table coverings. Waterproof, wipes clean.

Silk Gauze Plain weave with a slight irregularity in threads, making an interesting texture. Hangs well; is never slick. Wide range of colors.

Light Weight

Fabrics suitable for draperies, and for bedspreads, dressing-table skirts, pillows, screens, wall coverings, table coverings, and slip covers; sometimes for upholstery in the heavier grades. Many can be made of cotton, silk, or a synthetic; come in a wide color range, and can be washed.

Antique Satin Variation of smooth satin with a dull, uneven texture. Variety of weights but usually heavier than satin. Widely used for upholstery and draperies.

Broadcloth Cotton, synthetic, or silk in plain or twill weaves; spun rayon or wool in twill weaves. Varies greatly in terms of fiber and weave. Cotton and synthetic types used for draperies, bedspreads, tablecloths.

Bunting Cotton or wool in a loosely woven, thin, plain weave. Usually white or off-white, but can be dyed. Cotton bunting usually neither durable nor colorfast; wool used for draperies.

Calico Cotton in a plain weave, printed with small-figured pattern. Inexpensive and informal.

Challis Wool, synthetic or cotton in a soft, plain, firm weave. Usually printed with small floral designs but sometimes a plain color.

Chambray Cotton or linen in a smooth, close, plain weave. White frosted appearance on wide range of colors.

Chintz Cotton in a close, plain weave, usually with a printed design, and often glazed. Washing removes glaze in many types.

Drill	Cotton in diagonal twill weave. Firm, heavy, very durable textile. Typical color is gray but other colors available.
Faille	Plain weave with decided flat crosswise ribs. Difficult to launder but wears well if handled carefully. Varies from soft yet firm to quite stiff.
Gingham	Cotton in light to medium weight, plain weave; woven from colored yarns. Strong, launders well. Checked, striped, and plaid patterns.
Homespun	Irregular yarns woven in loose, plain weave. Texture is somewhat rough and irregular; informal character. Plain colors; dyed; or woven of mixed yarns.
India Print	Printed cotton cloth from India or Persia and with characteristic, intricate designs in clear or dull colors. Inexpensive and durable. Fades—but pleasantly.
Indian Head	Plain weave, firm and smooth. Trade name for a permanent-finish cotton, vat-dyed, colorfast, shrink-resistant. Inexpensive and durable.
Jaspé Cloth	Plain weaves; varied yarns give unobtrusive, irregular, blended stripes. Generally firm, hard, and durable. Can be in any color, but usually fairly neutral, medium dark, and monochromatic.
Linen	Flax in a plain firm weave. Cool touch, good body, launders well; wrinkles easily unless specially treated. Often has hand-blocked designs.
Moiré	Ribbed, plain weave with a watermarked appearance. Most moiré finishes can be steamed or washed out—more permanent on synthetic fibers.
Oxford Cloth	Plain basket or twill weave, light to rather heavy weights. Durable and launders well.
Piqué	Plain weave with narrow raised cords running in one direction, or at right angles to each other (waffle piqué). Durable; interesting texture.
Poplin	Plain weave with fine crosswise ribs. Firm and durable.
Rep	Plain weave with prominent rounded ribs running crosswise or lengthwise. Reversible.
Sateen	Cotton, usually mercerized, in a satin weave; flat and glossy, with a dull back. Durable, substantial, but with a tendency to roughen. Often used for lining curtains.
Satin	Satin weave, smooth, delicate fabric with very high sheen. Durable; somewhat slippery.
Seersucker	Plain weave with woven crinkly stripes. Durable, needs no ironing.

Shantung Plain weave with elongated irregularities. A heavy grade of *pongee,* but with wider color range.

Taffeta Close, plain weave, slightly crossribbed. Crisp; sometimes weighted with chemical salts; cracks in strong sunlight. *Antique taffeta* has unevenly spun threads.

Medium Weight

Fabrics suitable for heavy draperies and upholstery as well as for wall coverings and pillows, some also suitable for slip covers, bedspreads, screens, and table coverings. Made of heavier fibers of cotton, flax, hemp, jute, linen, silk, synthetic, or wool, they are available in a wide color range but few are washable.

Bark Cloth Cotton in a firm plain weave with irregular texture due to uneven yarns. Plain or printed. Durable.

Brocade Cotton warp yarns, silk, or a synthetic filling in a variety of weaves but with a raised design achieved by floating the filling yarns. Woven on Jacquard loom. Usually has a multicolored floral or conventional pattern.

Brocatelle Satin weave against a thinner twill background. Similar to *damask* but with much heavier design and thick padded figures. Usually self-toned or one additional color. Used mostly as upholstery on large sofas and chairs.

Burlap Loose basket weave. Heavy and coarse; interesting texture. Often fades quickly.

Canvas Cotton in a plain diagonal weave. Heavy, firm, and durable. Strong solid colors, as well as stripes or printed designs. Often used for awnings, outdoor curtains, and upholstery.

Crash Plain weave with a rough texture caused by uneven yarns. Often hand blocked or printed.

Cretonne Cotton in a firm, plain, rep or twill weave. Fairly heavy texture and bold design. Similar to chintz but heavier, never glazed, and patterns are usually more vigorous.

Damask Any combination of two of the three basic weaves; flat Jacquard patterns. Firm, lustrous, reversible. Similar to *brocade* but design is not in relief. May be referred to as *Figured Satin.* One or possibly two colors used.

Denim Cotton in a heavy close twill weave. Warp and filler often in contrasting colors; can have a small woven pattern. Inexpensive; washable; Sanforizing prevents shrinking; reasonably sunfast.

Duck Cotton in a close, plain, or ribbed weave. Durable; often given protective finishes against fire, water, mildew. Similar to *canvas.*

Hopsacking Loose, plain weave. Coarse and heavy. Inexpensive and durable.

Mohair Hair of Angora goats (or now often mixture of cotton and wool) in a plain, twill, or pile weave or with a woven or printed design. Resilient and durable. Novelty weaves from sheer to very heavy.

Monk's Cloth Jute, hemp, flax, usually mixed with cotton or all cotton in a loose, plain or basket weave. Coarse and heavy; *Friar's Cloth* and *Druid's Cloth* similar but coarser. Not easy to sew, tendency to sag. Usually comes in natural color.

Sail Cloth Plain weave. Heavy and strong. Similar to *canvas* or *duck.* Often used on summer furniture.

Serge Twill weave with a pronounced diagonal rib on both face and back. Clear, hard finish.

Terry Cloth Cotton or linen in a loose uncut pile weave; loops on one or both sides. Very absorbent; not always colorfast; may sag. Not suitable for upholstery but useful for draperies and bedspreads.

Ticking Cotton or linen in a satin or twill weave. Strong and closely woven. Durable; best known in white with colored stripes but may have simple designs. May not be colorfast but is washable.

Heavy

Fabrics suitable for upholstery because of heavy weight and durability; in lighter grades for draperies, pillows, bedspreads, slip covers, wall coverings, even table coverings. Most available in a variety of fibers in a wide color range; few are washable.

Bouclé Plain or twill weave. Flat, irregular surface, woven or knitted from specially twisted bouclé yarns; small spaced loops on surface.

Corduroy Cotton or a synthetic in a pile weave, raised in cords of various sizes giving pronounced lines. Durable, washable, inexpensive.

Frieze — (Also called *Frizé.*) Heavy-pile weave. Loops uncut or cut to form a pattern; sometimes yarns of different colors or with irregularities used. Usually has a heavy rib. Extremely durable.

Matelassé — Double-woven fabric with quilted or puckered surface effect caused by interweaving to form the pattern. Needs care in cleaning, but otherwise durable.

Needle Point — Originally handmade in great variety of patterns, colors, and degrees of fineness. Now imitated on Jacquard loom. At best, has pronounced character ranging from delicate to robust; at worst, looks like weak imitation.

Plastic — Wide variety of textures from smooth to embossed; used for upholstering and wall-covering. Resists soil, wipes clean. All-plastic not for use over deep springs; fabric-backed more pliable, easier to fit.

Plush — Cut-pile weave. Similar to velvet but with a longer pile. Sometimes pressed and brushed to give surface variations; sculptured by having design clipped or burnt out of pile leaving motif in relief; or made to imitate animal fur.

Tapestry — Weave with two sets of warps and wefts; woven on a Jacquard loom. Heavier and rougher than *damask* or *brocade.* Patterns usually pictorial and large, but not necessarily.

Tweed — Soft, irregularly textured plain weave. Yarns dyed before weaving; often several to many colors combined.

Velour — Short, heavy, stiff cut-pile weave. Slight luster, and indistinct horizontal lines. Durable.

Velvet — Pile weave with loops cut or uncut. Luxurious but often shows wear quickly. Lustrous or dull; light to heavy grades; plain, striped, or patterned.

Velveteen — Cotton or a synthetic woven with a short, close, sheared pile. Strong, durable, launders well.

Webbing — Cotton, jute, or plastic in narrow strips (1″-4″) of very firm, plain weave; plain, striped, or plaid design. Jute used to support springs; cotton or plastic interlaced for webbed seats and backs.

(*Dunbar Furniture Co. Edward Wormley, designer.*)

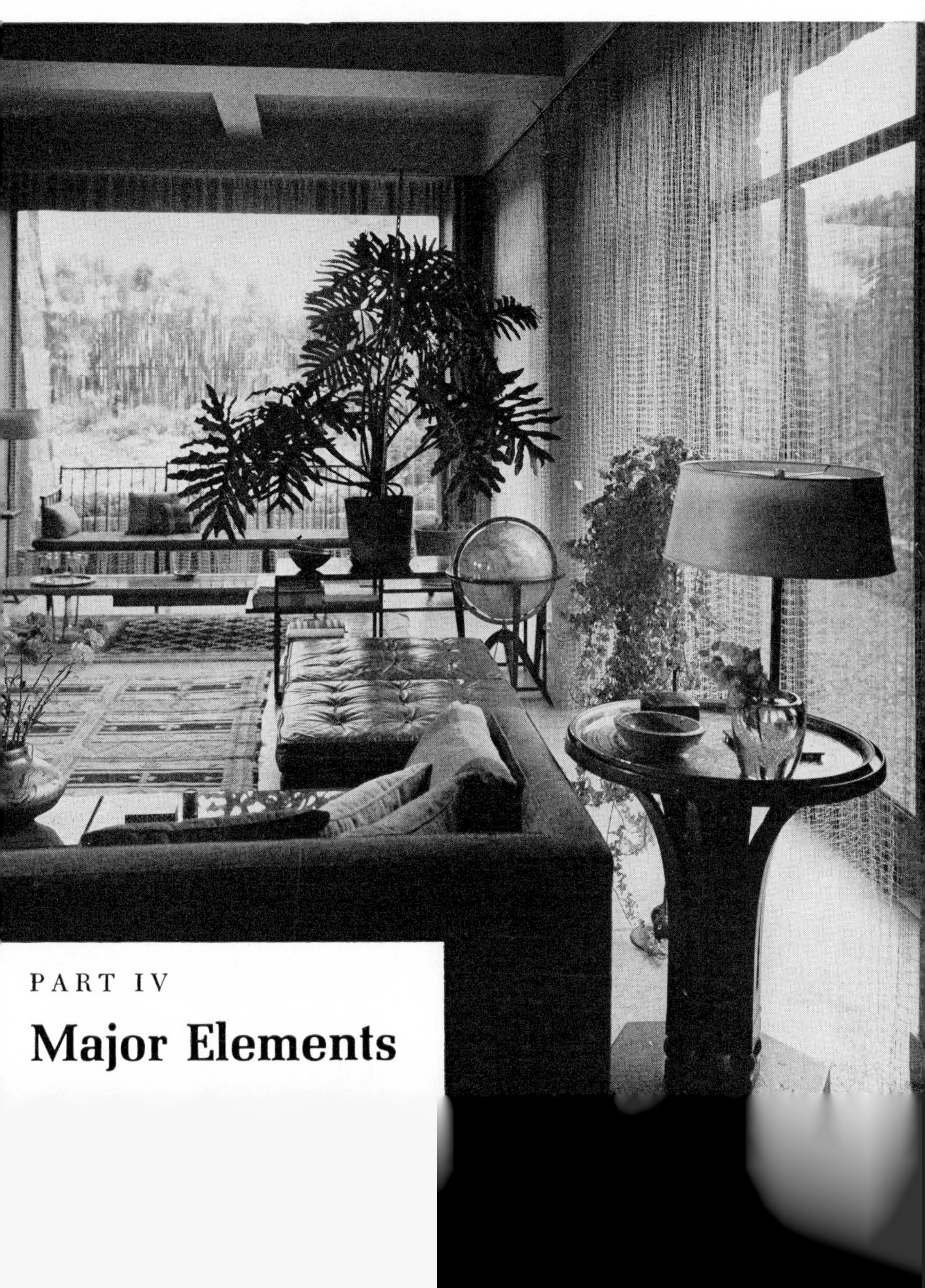

PART IV

Major Elements

11. Walls and Fireplaces

DETERMINING OUR MOVEMENTS and vistas, as well as giving protection and privacy, walls are perhaps the most strategic elements in our homes. They affect light, heat, and sound. They govern room shape, size, and character to become the enclosure against or with which we live. That walls can be far more than innocuous backdrops can be demonstrated by historic and contemporary examples. Well-proportioned walls are a continuing source of deep satisfaction. Appropriate colors, textures, and materials relate architecture to furniture in a positive manner. As houses become smaller, walls are increasingly "used" for built-in storage and furnishings that are attached to walls rather than standing on floors.

Walls, however, are seen and used in relation to the windows, doors, and fireplaces that are parts of them, to floors and ceilings that complete the enclosure, and to furniture, accessories, and people. All these should be considered as integral parts of the whole.

Above. Prefabricated metal fireplaces are inexpensive, come in many shapes. (*Kosmak*)

A

Above. The Daphne Room in the Raleigh Tavern, Williamsburg, Virginia, is a handsome room for formal eighteenth-century dining. (*Colonial Williamsburg*)

Below. A miniature reproduction of a typical Cape Cod living room shows that not all American Colonial rooms were formal. (*Thorne American Rooms in Miniature, The Art Institute of Chicago*)

B

► WALLS MAKE SPACE LIVABLE

Eighteenth-century Formal Elegance

Mastery of design, a distinguishing characteristic of eighteenth-century American homes, is quite as evident in walls and fireplaces as in the formal exteriors and graceful furniture of that period. The Daphne Room (Fig. 263A) is a case in point. In total concept and every detail, form is sensitively related to function: size and shape, door and window placement, furnishings and ornamentation fit the enclosed space to formal dining. Unified by strictly ordered rectangularity, the high-ceilinged room is complexly varied in detail. The quickly appreciated, basic equilibrium is elevated to importance by many subtleties. Large rectangles and small curves interplay rhythmically while each part has been assigned its due share of emphasis.

The walls hold much interest. Three horizontal bands bring into balance what might have been an excessive verticality. Each band is clearly differentiated from the other two in proportion and treatment yet the three form a harmonious entity. A dado (the lower, decorated part of a wall) surrounds and unifies the lower space and the furniture seen against it. Completely satisfying, it does not submit to any simple mathematical analysis or rigidly follow any rules. It is a little more than one quarter of the wall's total height, slightly lower than the top of the fireplace opening and the chair backs, and becomes the bottom of the window frames. Rectangular panels, mostly horizontal but adapted to the available area when necessary, rest on a baseboard and are topped by horizontal moldings. Of durable material, the dado covers the portion of the wall most subject to damage and dirt. Thus, it is a wall treatment that brings together usefulness and economy of maintenance, beauty and individuality.

Wallpaper covers the middle section, which is slightly more than two thirds of the wall height. Being at eye level, it is a logical place for a pattern of continuing but undemanding interest. It, too, is marked by unified contrasts. Double lines of beadlike forms suggest vertical panels; intricate arrangements of foliage and garlands have a precisely ordered rhythm and yet, paradoxically, look lively and free. The cornice (projecting moldings at the top of a wall) stops the vertical movement and relates the walls to the horizontal ceiling plane. But the cornice becomes more than a mere transitional element because of the stately, measured rhythm of the dentils (regularly spaced, rectangular blocks somewhat resembling teeth).

The fireplace is dominant because of its central position, large size, and decorative treatment. The firebox opening is a horizontal rectangle framed with marble and then with moldings like those of the doors, but sensitively reduced in size to put them in scale with the shape they outline. The overmantel treatment, basically a rectangular panel slightly wider than high, echoes the opening below. Interest is held by the diversity in the enclosing frame. It rests on, or begins with, scrolls and it concludes with a broken pediment that suggests an incomplete enclosure for the pineapple finial. Thus, the overmantel introduces three forms not found elsewhere in the architecture of the room though hinted at in the wallpaper and draperies: scrolls, the interrupted diagonals of the broken pediment, and the finial derived from nature.

All openings are symmetrically placed, rectangular, and strongly framed to establish them as important units worth looking at. Emphasized by projecting moldings, the doorways have markedly tall, slender proportions. Again what might have been an excessive verticality is checked by two devices: the moldings at top and bottom are extended to prepare the observer for the horizontal floor and door top; and the frame is capped by a full-bodied convex molding and a cornice. The doors have six panels, which are similar to but not dull repetitions of those on the dado. The windows, too, are vertical holes cut in the wall, but they are a little more nearly square than are the doors. Conventionalized floral patterns in the silk damask draperies echo the curves in wallpaper and furniture. The draperies are hung to emphasize, yet humanize, the architectural rectangularity of the windows and the whole room. Long, vertical folds restate window and door shape, while the curves brought by the tiebacks give a curtsylike gesture, and the swaglike valances relate the draperies to the clothes and manners of the people for whom the room was designed.

Worth noting is the fact that, although the doors provide access to other parts of the house and the windows give some contact with the outdoors, both do this in a guarded way. Their relatively small size and elaborate treatment offer ways to get out or look out of the room, but neither invites one to do so. Enclosure, not openness, is emphasized and a great deal has been done to make the room worth staying in.

Time-honored materials, all in general use today, surface the enclosing planes. The medium-dark, oak plank floor with a transparent, penetrating finish takes wear well and gives the room a substantial base. The plain plastered ceiling gives a light, unobtrusive top. The walls are wallpaper over plaster, combined with painted wood. Why is this wood painted? Because the smooth uniformity of opaque paint clearly reveals the delicately refined details that the free organic grain of wood might weaken.

What effect does this room produce? It seems formal and dignified yet gracious and hospitable, carefully reasoned but with touches of the fanciful, not austere but certainly not casual. Its complexity does not permit full appreciation at a glance because it is full of details and refinements that do not demand attention and yet are there when one wishes to enjoy them. It would hardly be proper to call these walls and fireplace, windows, and doors a "background" because in large part they make the room what it is—a beautifully appropriate enclosure for the sturdy yet graceful mahogany furniture created for gracious, upper-class eighteenth-century life. No wonder formal eighteenth-century design is appreciated today, but so often it is crudely imitated and inappropriate for the way all but a few live now.

American Colonial Semiformality

From about 1750 to 1850 many modest living rooms on or near Cape Cod resembled the one shown in Figure 263B. Thus, like the Daphne Room, it is part of our cultural heritage but it is much less formal. Similar materials are used on walls, floor, and ceiling but with less refinement. Braided and hooked rugs on random-width planks give the room an unassuming but interesting base. A slightly recessed fireplace wall, paneled in painted wood, enlivens the space. This paneling unifies the fireplace, stairway opening, and adjacent door in a clear geometric organization, basically similar to some contemporary designs. But the paneling also visually differentiates this section from the rest of the room. Again this is similar to today's predilection for treating one wall, or part of one wall, differently from the rest in the interests of dominance and subordination, variety in color and pattern.

The fireplace is made quietly dominant not only by size and position but by the moldings framing the opening, the shelf with its accessories, and the painting above them. Wallpaper, with a lively, but not aggressive, diagonal pattern that contrasts pleasantly with the painted wood, covers the other walls. On the stairway walls, however, the paper has an active curvilinear motif subtly suggesting the movements one makes in climbing stairs. Openings in this small room are placed where they function best with no arbitrary insistence on bilateral symmetry. Unpretending and unaffected, the room is heartwarming, natural, livable.

Twentieth-century Semiformality and Informality

A jump of almost two centuries and across the country to California brings us to the contemporary rooms illustrated in Figures 268A and B and 270A and B. These, too, are rectangular and rely chiefly on such age-old materials as wood, stone, plaster, and glass. But these rooms seem more open and active because almost every part of them leads to something else rather than holding attention at separated, ornamented spots.

Refinement of design and workmanship, reminiscent of eighteenth-century work but not imitating it, distinguish the remodeled living room. Without destroying the room's basic character, the architect transformed this space into an environment congenial to an active mid-century family and their collection of fine old furniture and works of art. For durability and beauty, the walls are covered with natural-finish oak plywood around the fireplace and oak boards elsewhere. Handsomely organized shelves and cupboards make large sections of the walls useful for storage and for display of plaques and vases. But the fireplace and adjacent wall are simply treated to become foils for painting, prints, and furniture.

The room is a spacious rectangle measuring 18′ x 30′ and is generally symmetrical. Entering the room through an opening in the middle of the west wall, you notice a fireplace centered at one end and balanced by symmetrical bookshelves at the other. Many design factors, though, keep this space from appearing to be just a symmetrical rectangle. The fireplace is flanked on one side by a shallow recess for an antique secretary, but on the left a passageway lined with storage units and unimpeded by doors leads your eyes on toward the dining room. Two other broad openings visually extend your attention beyond the confines of the walls. On the entrance side the living room opens into the lanai through a 9-foot "archway," which can be closed with sliding, translucent Japanese panels. Opposite this, but off-center, three sliding glass doors make half the wall a transparent invitation to enjoy the deck and landscape. The only windows as such are panes of fixed glass over bookshelves.

None of these openings, in fact no part of the room, is accentuated as a separate unit by enframing ornament. Quite the opposite effect, continuity and unity of part with whole, has been deliberately sought. Oak on all walls and the ceiling beams brings a consistency of color and texture. The beams carry rhythms set forth in the walls over and across the room. Built-in light troughs, which send light up or down and almost encircle the room, underscore the horizontal alignment of doorways and shelves in this room and in the dining room beyond. Although the room has overtones of geometric formality and unpretentious elegance, it adroitly avoids stiffness and prescription. Furniture arranged near solid walls brings enclosing security; freedom and openness come with the explicit emphasis on the continuity of this space with that which surrounds it.

A massive, floor-to-ceiling stone wall establishes the character of the living room in Figure 270A not only by its scale, texture, and color but by its placement. This wall, actually long enough to fill one end of the room, has been slid over so that it projects into the garden at the left and leaves the corner at the right free for windows. As in the diagram of contemporary

A

B

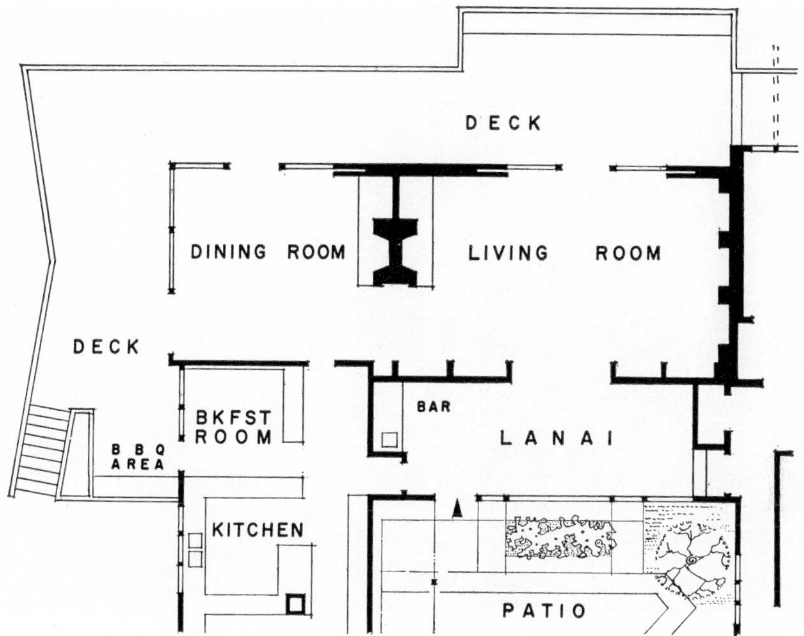

In this remodeled living room the original dignity has been heightened by a simplified treatment of its lofty spaciousness. Morgan Stedman, architect.

Left above. One end has furniture grouped around a fireplace. The vertical-grain wood and blunt-arrow shape carry upward to the high ceiling, accented but not weighted by beams.

Left below. The opposite end is a library with comfortable seating, shelves to hold books and accessories, and a broad counter with drawers and cupboards underneath. (*Photographs by Maynard Parker. Courtesy of* House Beautiful)

Above. The plan shows how living, dining, lanai, and deck areas open into one another without losing their identity.

spatial organization (Fig. 133), the "box has been opened" and space has been defined by planes that assert their independence. The firebox seems little more than a horizontal cavity echoing the proportions of the whole wall until you notice the projecting stone ledge at its left, the recessed wall at its right, and the three vertical stone blocks. This substantial horizontal wall meets the tall, narrow windows squarely and with no transition other than the three vertical blocks of stone. The decisively vertical windows carry around the corner to fill most of the adjacent wall and open the room to the landscape. Opposite the fireplace is a broad unadorned opening into the entrance hall, while the fourth wall is opaque except for the windows that in the photograph are letting sunlight into the room. The ceiling is plastered and the wood floor is covered with rush matting.

A

Above. A massive stone fireplace wall and band of floor-to-ceiling windows enclose and open a large living room while substantiating its informal dignity. The exterior of this home is shown in Figure 198B. Anshen and Allen, architects. (*Photograph by Stone and Steccati*)

Below. In a living room projecting into the tree tops, walls are compositions of panels of clear glass contrasting with white, off-white, and dark-brown plaster. Sometimes they are lightly veiled with sheer curtains or half obscured by shelves. Smith and Williams, architects. (*Photograph by Julius Shulman*)

B

This room seems serenely peaceful and relaxing because all the forms are simple and each material is in a large continuous area. It is enlivened by satisfying proportions, varied materials used so that the character of each can be appreciated, and the pleasant contrast of a stone wall holding you in and a glass wall letting you out. Rough textures and asymmetry bring their typical informality, and yet the room has a basic dignity, almost grandeur, that approaches formality.

In contrast to the warm enclosure of the preceding living room, the one in Figure 270B seems open and spacious. Cantilevered out over a wooded ravine, it is appropriately light and airy. The geometry of the exposed posts and beams is as pleasant visually as it is structurally efficient. Glass, bookshelves, and panels of plaster painted in light-reflecting colors contrast pleasantly with the naturally finished wood framing. The buoyant feeling is heightened by the light-colored composition floor and the canopy-like plywood ceiling. Set off-center in a wall of glass, the fireplace does not compete with the view. The total feeling is that of a pavilion, lighthearted and gay.

► MATERIALS MAKE WALLS

Although we take walls for granted, the building of vertical enclosures was a great achievement for early man. Since then, practically every known material has been tried in the search for efficiency and beauty.

Wall Construction

The technology of wall construction is beyond the scope of this book, but some knowledge of what walls are and how materials affect their characteristics can help you in choosing the walls most appropriate for homes.

Walls that are fixed, opaque, and of one material are the easiest to understand. Log cabins and structures of solid stone or brick are examples. Although historically important, they are rare today because they are usually expensive. Furthermore, they are comparatively poor insulators, leave no concealed space for pipes and wires, and are not amenable to the broad unobstructed openings now in favor. All-masonry walls, however, have great appeal with their comforting sense of permanence as well as their color and texture. Steel reinforcing increases their stability, and space can be left for insulation and utilities.

Today most walls are compounded of varied materials or of the same material used in different ways. Wood-frame walls are the most common. They are familiar to builders and not expensive. In addition to resilient stability, they allow space for insulation and utilities. Usually, but not necessarily, they support the roof. Surface treatment, inside and out, can be varied. They can be thought of as three-layer sandwiches, although they can have five or more layers:

- **Structural frame** of wood studs (closely spaced 2 x 4's or more widely spaced heavier posts) from floor to ceiling.
- **Exterior layers** of diagonal wood sheathing and insulation or sheets of strong insulating composition board. This is covered with weather-resistant surfaces of wood, asbestos, or metal siding, shingles or sheets; with lath and stucco; or with a veneer of brick or stone.
- **Interior layers** of lath and plaster, of plywood, wallboard, or wood paneling.

In 1955 one out of every twelve houses built in the United States was prefabricated. In 1959 about 140,000 new factory-made houses ready to be assembled in a few days were carried to their sites on trucks. Prices range from a few thousand dollars for vacation houses to $40,000 and over for luxury models. This may be news, but the principles of prefabrication are old. Prehistoric nomads in southeastern Asia developed wooden houses and our Plains Indians had tepees that could be quickly erected. Today prefabrication of walls has made great strides and promises many striking innovations. Panels of wood, metal, or synthetics, efficiently made in factories, can reduce construction costs without loss of individuality—one company alone produces wall panels that can be used in 1,200 different designs. Most of these panels are rectangular, ready to be fitted to wood or metal structural frames. But in experimental models (Fig. 229C), wall, roof, and even floor fabricated as one unit point toward completely new concepts of wall design.

Although walls are generally thought of as being fixed, vertical, opaque, and supporting the roof, they no longer need have any of these characteristics. The following types are rapidly becoming common:

- Walls that are independent of the structure, as in Figures 222A or 224.
- Transparent or translucent walls of glass or plastics, as in Figures 199B or 275A.
- Walls that are integrated with ceilings, as in Figure 229C or Alden Dow's house (Fig. 350).
- Movable walls that slide into pockets, fold like accordions, or are storage units on casters (Figs. 320, 40A).
- Walls less than ceiling height to give visual privacy without tight enclosure (Figs. 39A, 72).

Wall Materials and Surfacings

The materials from which walls are made or with which they are surfaced profoundly affect the character of our homes. The Chart of Wall Materials (pages 276-279) enables us to compare their many differences. Notice that:

- All exterior materials can be used for inside walls, a possibility highly regarded by contemporary architects and designers because it accentuates indoor-outdoor relationships and by housewives because it often reduces housework.
- Some materials usually thought of as flooring, such as linoleum or cork, bring to walls the same serviceability they give floors.
- Many new materials expand the range of possibilities.

None of this need concern those who are happy with plaster or wallboard painted white or buff. All of it should concern those who want qualities other than these have.

In each of the rooms illustrated so far, the walls contribute significantly to the room's personality. They indicate appropriate furnishings. More important they affect patterns of living.

The unique function of walls is the organization of space into livable units, but they perform many other tasks. In terms of **use,** they are primarily protective screens separating the house as a whole from the outdoors and partitioning the interior into spaces for home activities. They can insulate against heat, cold, and noise, and they reflect or absorb light and sound. Increasingly they are used for built-in storage, furniture, and lighting to save floor space. Typically, they hold up the roof. In terms of **economy,** good walls have low original cost, are long lasting, require minimum maintenance, keep fuel bills low, and take little space. Regrettably, it is nearly impossible to find a wall with these five characteristics. This forces you to decide what is most important in *each* wall and usually to make some compromises. Masonry walls, for example, last long with little care but they are thick and expensive. In terms of **beauty,** walls should be appropriate to the activities they shelter. Exterior walls shape the mass of the house and establish its relationship to the site. Interior walls shape the indoor space and establish its character. **Individuality** comes when walls genuinely express the family's needs and preferences, are appropriate to their particular functions.

Some of the ways in which plywood, wallboard, patterned glass, and mosaic tile can be used on walls are shown on pages 274 and 275. The characteristics of varied wall materials are tabulated on pages 276 through 279; a sampling of new and old products is illustrated on pages 280 and 281.

A

Left. Plywood, plaster, and tile are skillfully brought together in one end of a living room and a patio entrance. Vertical-grain plywood, cleanly detailed around an opening, has been carefully matched to sheathe a wall without noticeable joints. Painted walls in the patio entrance increase the sense of spaciousness through their color and texture contrast with the wood. Michael Goodman, architect.

Below. A boys' bedroom has space-saving bunks built into one end of the room and a porthole window that would intrigue most boys. Walls and ceilings are covered with tan wallboard of three shapes: squares tiles on the ceiling, rectangular pieces on one wall, and vertical strips on the other. The different sizes and shapes, together with slight color variations, set up rhythms that make the room lively and increase its apparent size. No apologies are needed for this inexpensive material when it is used imaginatively. It withstands abuse but can be refinished, absorbs noise, and serves as a bulletin board. Edward D. Stone, architect. (*Photograph by Frank Randt*)

B

Right. Patterned glass makes the walls and ceiling of a small entrance inviting. The glass is fitted into simple wood frames that are the structure of the house. Its translucency floods the space with natural or artificial light, creates a changing series of patterns, and affords privacy on a small lot. Another view of this house is shown on page 82. Gordon Drake, architect. (*Blue Ridge Glass Co. Photograph by Julius Shulman*)

A

B

Left. Clay tile and glass brick used with good sense and taste make this more than just another tiled bathroom. Both materials are waterproof and easily cleaned. On the walls the tile has been laid in an ingenious design, but on the floor, where less interest is needed, the pattern is simple. Glass bricks have been used thoughtfully. They provide ample light while giving privacy, and they insulate against heat and cold. Their shape harmonizes with the tile, and they fill areas sufficiently large and simple to avoid glare or spottiness. (*Mosaic Tile Co. Photographed by Hedrich-Blessing*)

WALL MATERIALS

Exterior and Interior

Material	Character	Use	Finishes	Advantages	Disadvantages
Asbestos (panels, shingles, siding). Cost: moderately low.	Noticeable textures and new colors make these interesting; may resemble wood from a distance.	Interior: occasionally where durability and easy upkeep are important. Exterior walls.	None needed, but can be painted.	Rare combination of low cost and upkeep; high resistance to fire, weather, and insects.	None except rather commonplace quality.
Brick (adobe). Cost: varies greatly from one locality to another.	Earthy solidity combined with handcraft informality. Large in scale. Noticeable pattern of blocks and joints unless smoothly plastered.	Interior-exterior walls, chiefly in mild climates.	Stucco, special paints, or transparent waterproofing.	Unique character. Resists fire and insects. Newer types made with special binders and stabilizers are stronger and more weather-resistant than older types.	Older types damaged by water. Walls must be very thick or specially reinforced. Sturdy foundations required. Comparatively poor insulation for weight and thickness.
Brick (fired clay). Cost: high but less than stone.	Substantial and solid; small-scale regularity. Many sizes, shapes, and colors. Can be laid in varied patterns.	Interior-exterior walls, exterior surfacing or garden walls. Interior: around fireplaces.	None unless waterproofing is necessary; interior walls can be waxed.	Satisfying texture and pattern, durable, easily maintained; fireproof.	None other than heat-cold conduction and noise reflection.
Concrete. Cost: moderately high.	Typically smooth and solid-looking but can be highly decorative.	Interior-exterior walls in mild climates. Exterior walls elsewhere.	Exterior: usually painted or stuccoed. Interior: painted, plastered, or surfaced with any material.	Permanent, durable, low maintenance. Can be cast in varied shapes and surface treated in many ways.	Comparatively poor insulator; requires sturdy foundations and costly forms.
Concrete blocks (light-weight aggregate). Cost: moderate.	Typically regular in shape, moderately textured, and bold in scale but many variations are possible.	Interior-exterior walls in mild climates. Exterior and garden walls anywhere.	Exterior waterproofing necessary; no interior finish needed but can be painted.	Moderately handsome, durable, easily maintained; fireproof; fair insulator.	None of any consequence.
Glass blocks. Cost: moderately high.	Somewhat hard, brittle, and bright; in decided contrast to most wall materials.	Interior: partitions. Interior-exterior walls in baths, kitchens, entrances, etc.	No finish needed.	Transmits light while giving privacy, insulation; not easily broken, needs only dusting and washing, resists fire and deterioration.	None other than cost.

patterned). Cost: moderately high.	terned glass transmits diffused light.	dow walls. Occasionally for garden walls on windy sites with views. Interior: patterned glass for translucent partitions.	curtaining for privacy and control of light, heat, and cold).	outdoor relationships. Patterned combines light and varying degrees of privacy.	heat-cold insulation; needs frequent cleaning.
Metal (panels, siding, shingles, and tiles). Cost: moderate.	Varies greatly depending on size, shape, and finish; often regarded as unhomelike.	Interior: sometimes used in kitchens and bathrooms. Exterior: house and garden walls.	Aluminum, available in many colors, needs no finish. Steel comes with baked-on enamel.	Lightweight in relation to strength. Resistant to fire, etc. Enameled and aluminum panels need minimum upkeep.	Although very durable, metal surfaces are difficult to repair if damaged.
Plaster (and stucco). Cost: moderately low.	Typically smooth and precise but can be varied in texture. The only surfacing material that shows no joints, breaks, etc. Excellent quiet background.	Interior: plaster in any room. Exterior: stucco for house or garden walls.	Exterior: special weather-resistant paints. Interior: paint, paper, or fabric.	Moderately durable if properly finished; suited to many easy-to-change treatments; fireproof; special types absorb sound.	Often cracks or chips.
Plastic (panels embedded with glass fibers). Cost: moderately high.	Extremely varied but usually translucent, textured, and colorful. Thin and flat or corrugated; thicker panels with cores of varied materials.	Interior: partitions. Interior-exterior walls. Garden walls.	None.	Similar to patterned glass except breaks less easily, lighter in weight, can be sawed and nailed.	Not thoroughly tested for longevity.
Stone. Cost: high.	Substantial, solid; impressive; natural colors and textures.	Interior: usually around fireplace. Exterior and garden walls.	None unless waterproofing is necessary.	Beauty and individuality; durability, ease of maintenance; fireproof; ages gracefully.	Poor insulator; reflects sound; not amenable to change.
Wood. Cost: moderate.	Natural beauty and individuality of grain and color.	Interior: one wall or entire house. Exterior walls and garden fences.	Needs protective finish to seal it against water, stains, dirt.	Fairly durable, easily maintained; good insulator; adaptable to many forms; ages well inside.	Few kinds are weather-resistant unless treated; burns; attacked by termites.

WALL MATERIALS
Interior Only

Material	Character	Use	Finishes	Advantages	Disadvantages
Cork. Cost: moderately high.	Sympathetic natural color and texture.	Interior: any room; only plastic-impregnated types suitable for baths and kitchens.	None needed but can be waxed.	Durable, easily kept, sound absorbent, good insulator.	Harmed by moisture, stains, etc., unless specially treated.
Glass (opaque tiles or panels). Cost: high.	Smooth, shiny surface; many colors.	Interior: bathroom or kitchen walls.	None.	Lasts long (unless broken), easy to clean (but spots show), unharmed by water, stains, etc.	None except noise reflection, brittle appearance, and possible breakage.
Linoleum. Cost: moderate.	Smooth, mat surface; great variety of colors and patterns.	Interior: hard-use rooms.	Needs no finish but can be waxed.	Durable, easily maintained, reduces noise somewhat.	None unless you do not like its character.
Plastic (thin, rigid tiles). Cost: relatively low.	Similar to clay tile except variety is sharply limited.	Interior: kitchens and bathrooms.	No finish needed.	Easy to keep and apparently durable; simple to install; light weight.	Similar to clay tile.
Plastic (Vinyl tiles or sheets). Cost: moderately high.	Similar to linoleum.	Interior: can be used where durable, resilient walls are wanted, such as in play space or above kitchen counters.	None needed but can be waxed.	Similar to linoleum but more resistant to cuts and stains.	Cost.
Rubber (tiles). Cost: moderately high.	Much like linoleum.	Interior: can be used where durable, resilient walls are indicated.	None needed.	Similar to linoleum but colors are brighter and clearer.	May be harmed by grease and stains.

Tile (clay). Cost: moderately high.	Repeated regularity sets up pattern; great variety in size, shape, ornamentation.	Interior: kitchens, bathrooms, and around fireplace. Exterior: occasional ornament.	No finish needed.	Can have great beauty and individuality; very durable, easily maintained; resistant to water, stains, fire.	Hard and cold to touch, reflects noise, can crack or break.
Wallboard (cane and fiber). Cost: low.	Soft, porous surface; no pronounced character in typical tan or gray but available in harder, textured surfaces.	Interior: any room.	If not factory-finished, needs paint or wallpaper.	Moderately durable, good heat-cold and sound insulator.	Absorbs moisture and dirt, shows wear.
Wallboard (Gypsum or plaster). Cost: moderately low.	Noncommittal. Joints show unless very well taped and painted.	Interior: any room.	Paint, wallpaper, or fabric.	Not easily cracked, fire-resistant, can be finished in many ways.	Visually uninteresting in itself; needs protective surface.
Wallboard (plastic laminates). Cost: high.	Shiny, mat, or textured surface; varied colors and patterns.	Interior: kitchens, bathrooms, or any hard-use wall.	None needed.	Very durable, unusually resistant to moisture, stains, dirt; cleaned with damp cloth.	Although wear-resistant, it can be irremediably scratched or chipped. Reflects noise.
Wallboard (pressed wood). Cost: moderate.	Smooth, mat surface with slight visual texture; also patterns imitating leather, tile, etc.	Interior: hard-wear rooms.	Needs no finish but can be stained, waxed, painted.	Tough surface is hard to damage.	None of any importance.
Wallcovering (plastic). Cost: moderately high.	Many patterns; pleasing textures; mat or glossy surfaces.	Interior: walls.	None needed.	Very durable; resists moisture, dirt, stains; cleans with damp cloth.	None of importance.
Wallpaper and fabrics. Cost: moderately low.	Tremendous variety of color and pattern.	Interior: any wall.	Usually none but can be protected with lacquer.	Inexpensive, can give decided character, some kinds very durable and easy to keep.	Must be chosen and used carefully.

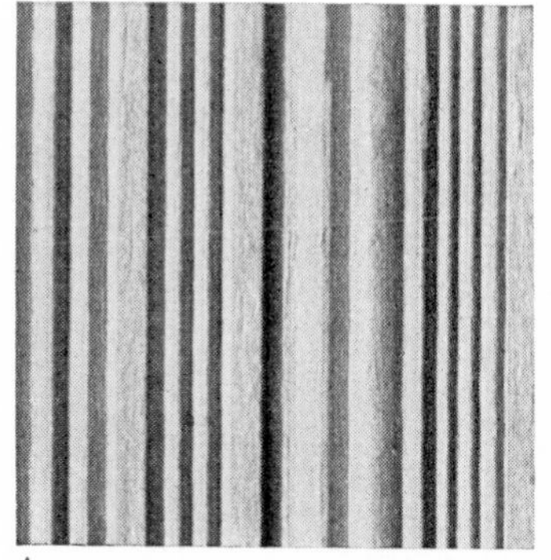
A

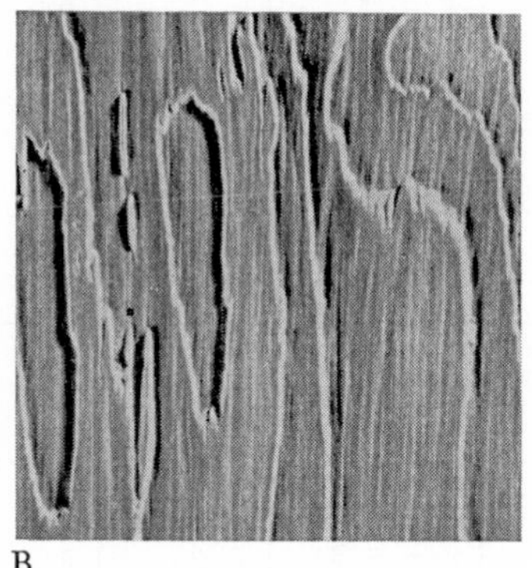
B

C

Left. In *striated* plywood, grooves minimize the grain and give a lively, directional rhythm. *Center.* Resembling weathered wood, *etched* plywood makes the grain conspicuously three-dimensional. *Right.* In this *particle board,* cedar flakes are bonded together in a lively visual texture. (*U. S. Plywood Corporation*)

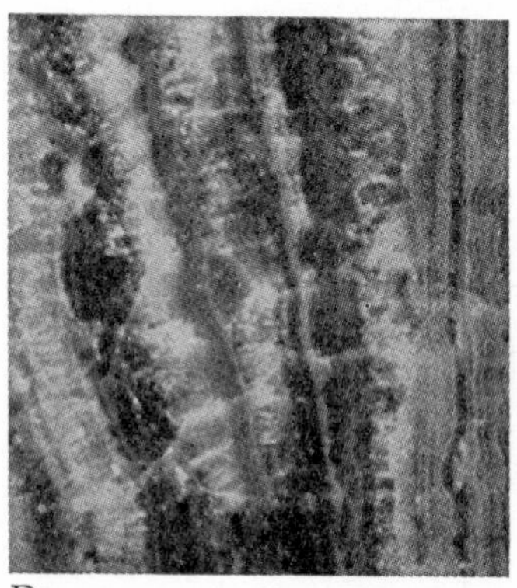
D

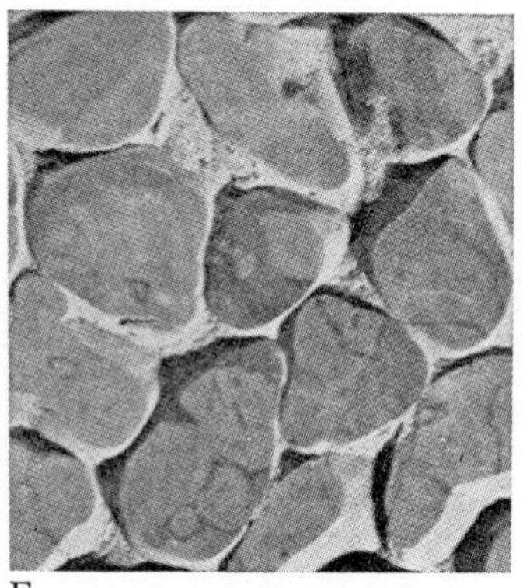
E

F

Left. Marble is beautiful and expensive. *Center* and *right.* Cement tiles from Italy are imbedded with many materials, including polished marble pebbles and mother-of-pearl shells. (*Marble Institute of America; Fred Dean Co.*)

G

H

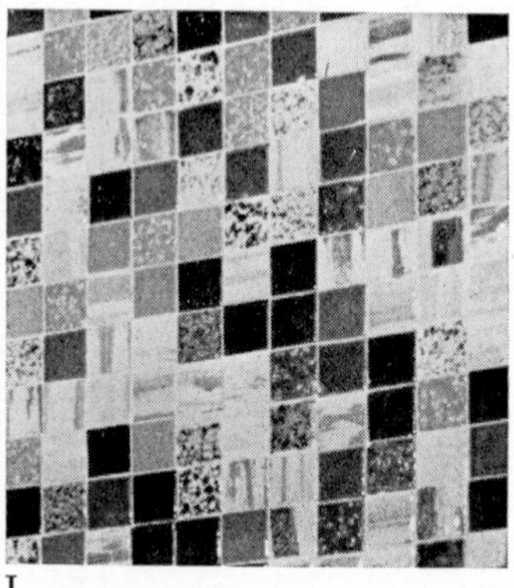
I

Left. Triangular tiles permit bold, active walls (*Gladding, McBean & Co.*). *Center.* Sculptured earthenware tiles elevate walls to importance (*Design-Technics*). *Right.* Mosaic tiles have endless diversity (*Murals, Inc.*).

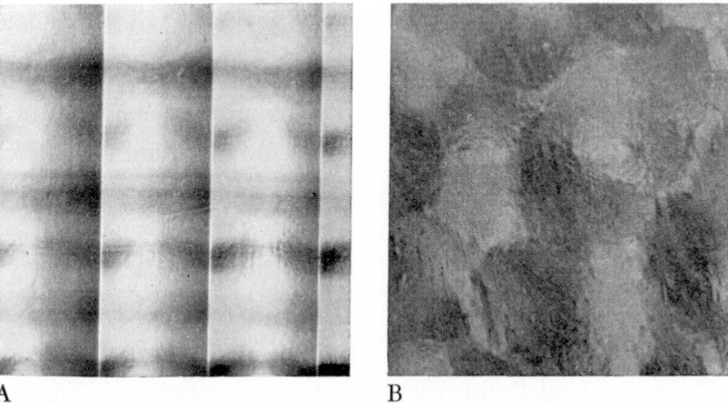

A B

Left. "Doublex" obscure glass transmits light but not sight through its disciplined pattern. *Right.* "Velvex" translucent glass is informally mottled. (*Blue Ridge Glass Co.*)

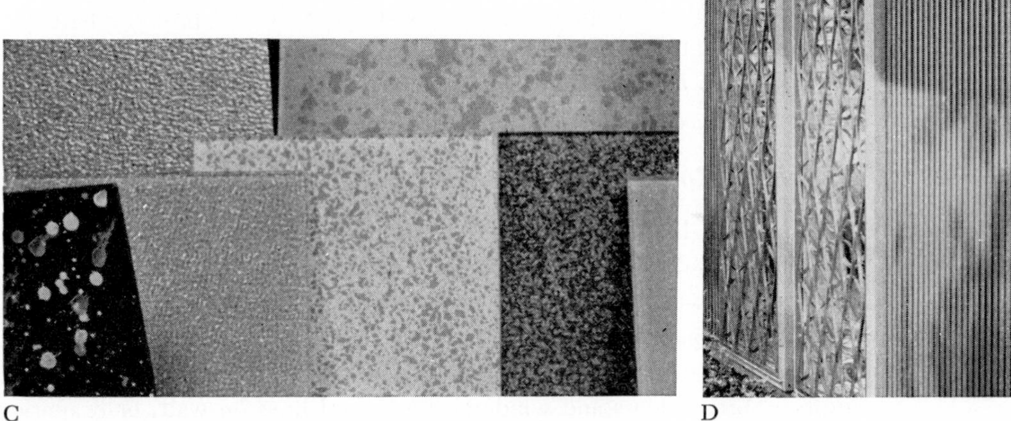

C D

Left. "Spandrelite" comes in unlimited colors and varied textures (*Blue Ridge Glass Co.*). *Right.* Vibrantly colored aluminum panels and grilles make weather-hardy, carefree walls (*Aluminum Company of America*).

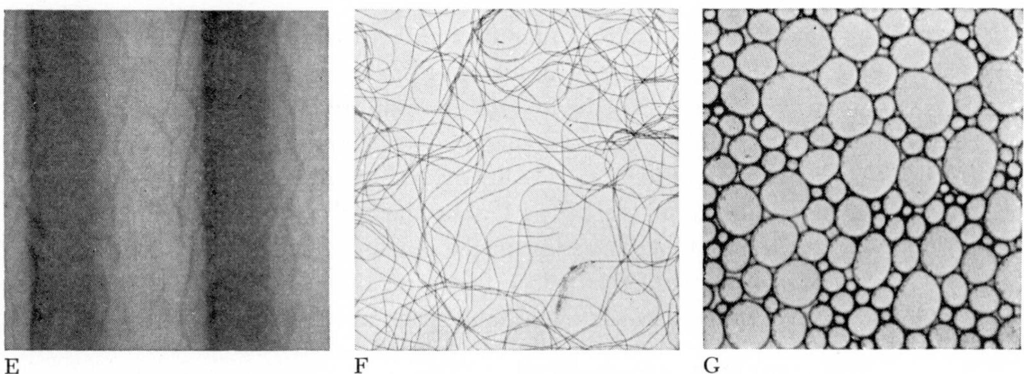

E F G

Left. Corrugated plastic makes luminous walls (*Alsynite Co.*). *Center.* Dark filaments add interest to flat plastic panels (*Polyplastex United, Inc.*). *Right.* Paper tubing is the core of new plastic panels. (*U. S. Rubber Co.*)

► DESIGN GIVES CHARACTER

A number of specific factors combine to give walls their character. Some pertain primarily to use; others to economy, beauty, or individuality. Walls can have any degree of any of these factors or any combination of them.

Degree of Formality and Informality

The Daphne Room, and the Gordons' living room in Figure 12, are more formal than the Cape Cod living room or those illustrated in Figures 270A, 274B, and 292B. Formality comes when a room makes you feel a strict, firmly established, unchanging order. Symmetrical balance and pronounced regularity are the fundamental means, but formality is increased when the forms seem stable and precise, surfaces are smooth, and proportions make you feel upright. Use almost never indicates symmetrically balanced walls, but such walls have their own kind of beauty.

Degree of Horizontality or Verticality

The high, light ceiling and the up-and-down movement of fireplace, doors, and windows give the Daphne Room a dominant verticality. The narrow floor-to-ceiling windows make the living-room window corner in the Davies' home (Fig. 270A) look tall, but this impression is strongly counterbalanced by the horizontal fireplace and furniture. Low ceilings and furniture, broad doors and windows, horizontal lines on walls or draperies stretch space out and usually seem informal.

Degree of Activity or Passivity

Walls become active to the degree that their design and their materials arouse interest, especially if they suggest movement. This is accentuated when they are integrated with built-in furniture. Typical smoothly plastered, uniformly painted walls are passive backgrounds. The wallboard in the boys' bedroom (Fig. 274B) is slightly activated by the pattern of joints and color variation, and the tile pattern on the bathroom walls (Fig. 275B) sets up a lively rhythm. The walls in the remodeled living room are active because they are *used* for built-in furniture; those in Figures 270B, 290, and 296B are active because they shape space unconventionally.

Degree of Smoothness or Roughness

Here the range is from glassy smoothness to stony roughness with countless intermediate steps provided by plaster and wallboard, tile and brick, wood and plastics. Smoothness is often associated with formality, roughness with informality. A dominant consistency of one kind of surface is desirable, but variety and contrast are usually needed.

Largeness or Smallness of Scale

Of tremendous importance is the scale of the walls in relation to the size of the space, character of furnishings, and personalities of the people. The scale of the walls is large in Figures 270A and 296B, moderate in Figures 268A and 292B, and small in Figures 263B and 296A. Large scale is produced by big, bold forms and textures. It reduces visual space but is impressive. Moderate-to-small-scale walls make rooms spacious and homelike.

Degree of Enclosure or Openness

The book-lined corner in Figure 268B is enclosing and protecting but the wide opening to the lanai extends the space into the patio. Translucent glass, as used in Figures 275A and B, suggests partial enclosure. Large areas of glass and light color make Figures 270B and 292A spaciously open. Enclosure is brought about by opaque, substantial-looking walls; by warm, dark colors and noticeable textures; also by small, separated, framed doors, and windows with small panes and protective draperies.

Openness comes with a maximum of transparent, translucent, or apparently thin unobtrusive walls and a minimum of walls that block view or movement. Receding colors and inconspicuous textures are also contributors. Of great importance is continuity of materials, forms, and colors not only within the room but with space in adjacent rooms and the landscape.

Degree of Light Absorption or Reflection

Color value is the most critical factor, white reflecting up to 89 percent of the light striking it and black as little as 2 percent. But surface texture must be considered because the smoother the surface the more light is reflected. In the past when windows were small and artificial illumination poor, very light walls were frequently needed to make rooms bright. Today, with larger windows and improved artificial lighting, many people find that darker, textured walls create a more sympathetic enclosure for themselves and their furnishings. Nevertheless, light-colored walls are refreshing, increase apparent size, and make rooms easier to illumine.

Degree of Sound Absorption or Reflection

Smaller houses and open plans, greater freedom for children, and labor-saving but noise-making devices, and the trend away from massive upholstered furniture and heavy draperies make many contemporary homes noisy. Ways of dealing with this problem are discussed in Chapter 15.

Durability and Maintenance

The amount of time and money taken by walls affects the satisfaction they give. Some materials—masonry, tile, and vinyl plastics—are durable and easily maintained anywhere. Some, such as fragile but colorfast wallpapers, last long with little care on walls that do not get hard use. Basic questions are: What kind of use will the wall get? How easily is the material damaged? How easily can it be cleaned or repaired?

Degree of Heat-Cold Insulation

In the interests of economy and comfort, this factor (discussed in Chapter 15) is consequential.

► APPLIED WALL FINISHES

When a wall surface is not completely satisfactory, various finishes can be applied in the interests of use, economy, beauty, and individuality. Paint, wallpaper, and wall fabrics are the most common types.

Paint

Today nearly all interior paints are made from various synthetic resins. They can be grouped in two basic categories:

- Water-thinned, or Latex, paints are extremely easy to apply. Since they are water soluble when wet, spots can be wiped up with damp cloths and paintbrushes cleaned with soap and water. They dry rapidly and have little odor. After a few weeks of "curing," they resist soiling and unlike calcimine, can be washed. Their velvety surface is surprisingly durable.
- Solvent-thinned paints include the old oil and the new synthetic paints. They are preferred for use on wood, especially furniture, and can be had in dull, semigloss, or gloss types.

Being the easiest of all finishes to apply, paint leads many people into doing their own wall finishing. Nothing so quickly and inexpensively changes the character of a room. Paint finds its place in the smallest apartment and the most elaborate mansion in good part because it is the only finish with which it is feasible to dictate the exact color. But although color is paint's most conspicuous quality, texture and durability should not be overlooked.

Next to color in importance is paint's ability to give a uniform surface to whatever it covers. Sometimes smooth paint will not cover all blemishes and sometimes you do not want smoothness. Then it can be **stippled** with a stiff brush to obliterate brush marks and give a soft mat finish, or it can be **spattered** with one or more colors to give some vibrancy and minimize spots or scratches. More pronounced textures are produced with special paints, by applying the paint with special rollers, or by going over the wet paint with sponges or whiskbrooms. These are easy and inexpensive ways to cover plaster cracks or wallboard joints, and they give walls varied surfaces.

Wallpaper

Long known in the Orient, wallpaper has been used in Europe for about five centuries and in this country since early days. "Poor man's tapestry" was a good name because wallpaper came into use in humble homes as an imitation of the expensive textiles used by the wealthy. Wallpaper's advantages are many and varied, because wallpaper:

- Can be used in any room in the home.
- Can be tested for its effect in advance by borrowing large samples.
- Is available in many colors, patterns, textures, and degrees of durability.
- Has the most positive character of any wall surfacing in its price class.
- Makes a room seem to shrink or swell, gain height or intimacy, become more active or subdued, more or less formal.
- Minimizes by illusion or camouflage architectural awkwardnesses.
- Hides disfigured walls.
- Makes rooms with little furniture seem furnished.
- Distracts attention from miscellaneous or commonplace furniture.

Wallpaper has no inherent disadvantages. Some persons may not like its "papery" look and many patterns are dull or ugly, but these are not faults of the material.

It is possible to find papers appropriate to almost any way of living, any kind of furnishings, any exposure or special factor. Wallpapers range

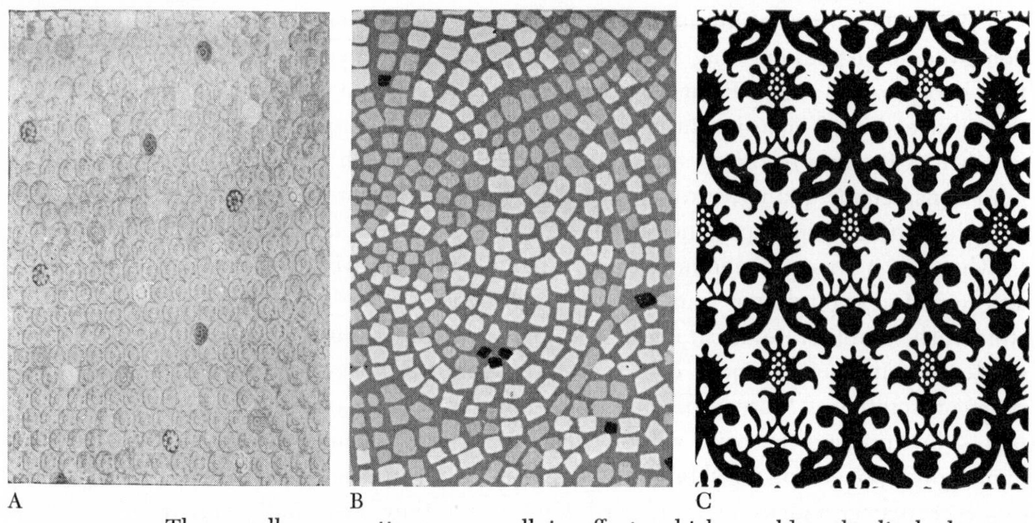

Three wallpaper patterns, over-all in effect, which would make lively but not aggressive backgrounds.

Left. "Damascus" is a decorative monochrome, crisp in detail but subtle in effect (*Stockwell*). *Center.* "Mosaic" is intriguingly complex at close range but at a distance becomes a softly vibrant curvilinear pattern (*Katzenbach and Warren*). *Right.* "Napoli," an intricate example of variety in unity, expresses the organic character of growing plants without imitating their actual appearance (*Piazza Prints*).

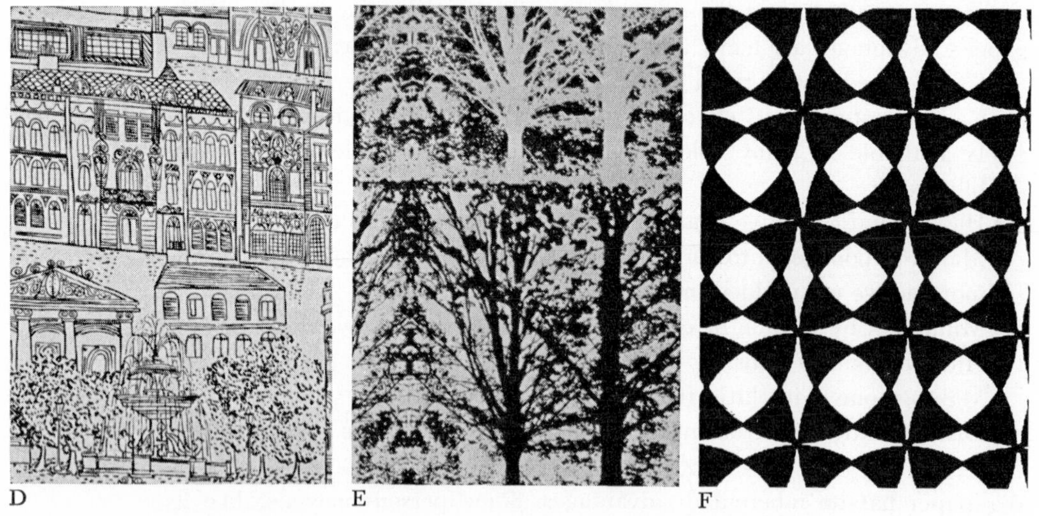

Architecture, trees, and abstract shapes can be transformed into distinctive wallpapers.

Left. "Paris Scene" is based on line-drawing notebook sketches, depicts buildings informally arranged in horizontal lines (*Ben-Ami Associates*). *Center.* "Forest" was reproduced from a photographic negative; re-creates the indefinite textural quality of a forest. Alternating closely set rows of positive and negative prints produces horizontal bands balanced by the vertical alignment of tree trunks (*Ben-Ami Associates*). *Right.* "Mirage" exemplifies some of the possibilities of geometric design. It seems to move and change as one looks at it (*Laverne*).

from solid colors through textured effects, small and large patterns, to mural or scenic designs. Most have a dull mat finish that may or may not be washable, but some are glossy. Then there are the less usual types. Flock papers with their raised, fuzzy nap look like textiles. Marbleized papers hint at the gloss and depth of marble, and metallic papers bring luster and can help a little in insulating rooms against heat and cold.

Selecting a pattern and color is not easy. Wall-length samples of several patterns can be brought home, fastened up, and observed at different times of day and night. Wallpaper is a kind of applied ornament that may noticeably affect the apparent size, shape, and character of rooms. Consider it in the light of the criteria for ornament discussed in Chapter 6, making these more specific by keeping in mind that the wall and paper are flat and continuous, like fabrics, and that in most instances the pattern will cover very large areas. In addition:

- Plain colors look much like paint but come in varied textures.
- Textural patterns are more active, more pronounced in character, and more effective in concealing minor damage than are plain colors.
- Abstract patterns do not go out of fashion quickly and seem especially suitable to walls.
- Stylized designs almost always seem more appropriate than do naturalistic representations.
- Scenic wallpapers are something like mural paintings.
- Bold conspicuous patterns reduce the visual importance of the space, furniture, and people.
- Conspicuous isolated motifs often make walls look spotty.

Wall Fabrics

Just about every textile known to man has at one time or another been draped over, stretched on, or pasted to walls. Today—if we think of fabrics untouched by plastics—we are likely to think of such durable stand-bys as canvas, burlap, or denim. Or we might consider grass cloth, as appropriate today as it was years ago, with its subtly textured woven grass glued to a tough paper backing of soft colors or dull metallic luster.

More likely, though, we will think of the host of new plastic-coated, plastic-impregnated, or just plastic fabrics. Most are embossed with textures or have printed designs. They are likely to be far more durable than typical wallpapers, resist stain and dirt, withstand repeated cleanings, and hide serious wall defects—even to holding cracked plaster in place. A number of them perform equally well as upholstery, thereby opening the way for close harmony between two parts of the interior.

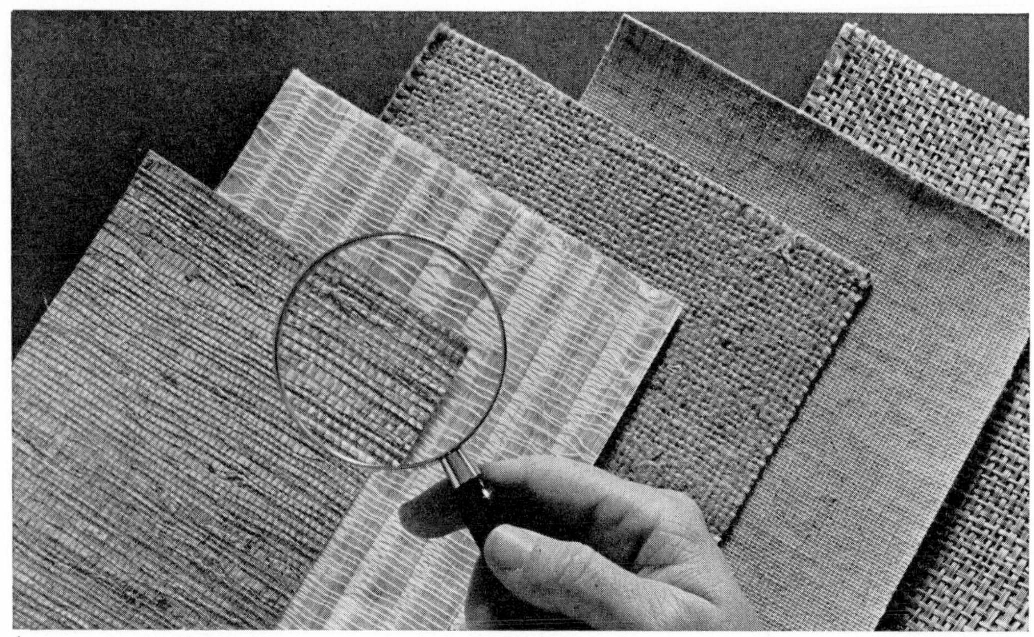

A

Wall fabrics woven of natural fibers last long, bring outdoor textures and colors inside the house. From left to right: *Grass cloth,* with its inimitable lustrous surface, combines elegance with informality and comes in many subtle colors. *Raffia grass cloth* has conspicuously coarser texture, more pronounced vertical lines. *Burlap,* as durable on walls as in gunny sacks, is available in many colors. *Hemp paper* is comparatively smooth and small in scale. *Abaca* is stiff and coarse-textured. (*Photograph by Clyde Childress. Courtesy of* SUNSET Magazine)

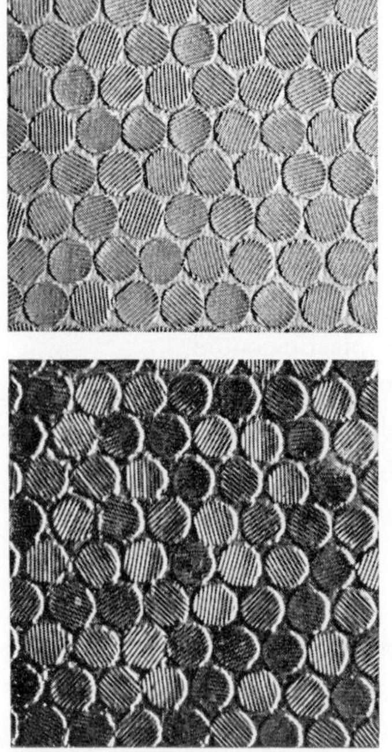

B

C

D

Plastic wall coverings minimize the old distinction between the useful and the ornamental.

Left. "Mirra Disc" in muted or sparkling metallic colors has coinlike dots (*L. E. Carpenter & Co.*). *Center.* "Shado Star" is precise and formal (*L. E. Carpenter & Co.*). *Right.* "Curvilinear" is a plastic wall covering with a richly modeled sinuous surface (*Laverne*).

Paint, wallpaper, and wall fabrics are wondrous means of enlivening and protecting walls. Their relatively low cost makes frequent change possible, and their general lack of permanence makes new applications probable. They do not have the substantial character of wood or masonry but they compensate with their challenging variety.

► FIREPLACES

Fireplaces and fires are *costly:* a fireplace may cost as much as a bathroom, and a good log fire in many places is about as expensive as a home-cooked meal for two. Further, storing fuel takes dry space, getting it into the firebox takes labor, and the after-fire cleanup is a chore. Most fireplaces are *used* for fires less than 1 percent of the time. When in use, they provide heat for people or cooking, and light and ventilation, all of a hard-to-control sort.

But open fires are *beautiful,* and fireplaces even without fires can be substantial centers of interest. A fire's warm, constantly changing, beautifully shaped and colored flames and embers produce a kind of lighting equalled only by sunrises and sunsets. Open fires are also associated with pleasurable outings and probably deeply buried feelings about the importance of fire to man. There is nothing that lifts the spirits on a cold, cheerless day or night like a fire, warming hands and hearts. Then, too, every fire has its own *individuality;* in fact every moment of a fire differs from every other, and fireplace design need follow no stereotypes. Thus, even though the most perfectly designed fireplace is hopelessly out-of-date in terms of use and economy, open fires are not outdated in terms of human satisfaction.

Purposes of Fireplaces

Light is a chief purpose of fireplaces today because the illumination they provide is unique. It is restfully soft and warm enough in color to make even pallid persons look sun-tanned. The concentrated, flickering light is almost hypnotically relaxing and draws people together like a magnet.

Heat from a fireplace on a cold day seems well worth its cost, even though it creates drafts on the floor and may throw thermostatically controlled furnaces off balance. Heat output can be increased and controlled by designing the firebox to throw heat into the room, having a damper to control the draft and a projecting hood to radiate heat (Fig. 292B). Prefabricated fireboxes and vents, like small warm-air furnaces, circulate heated air and are the most efficient.

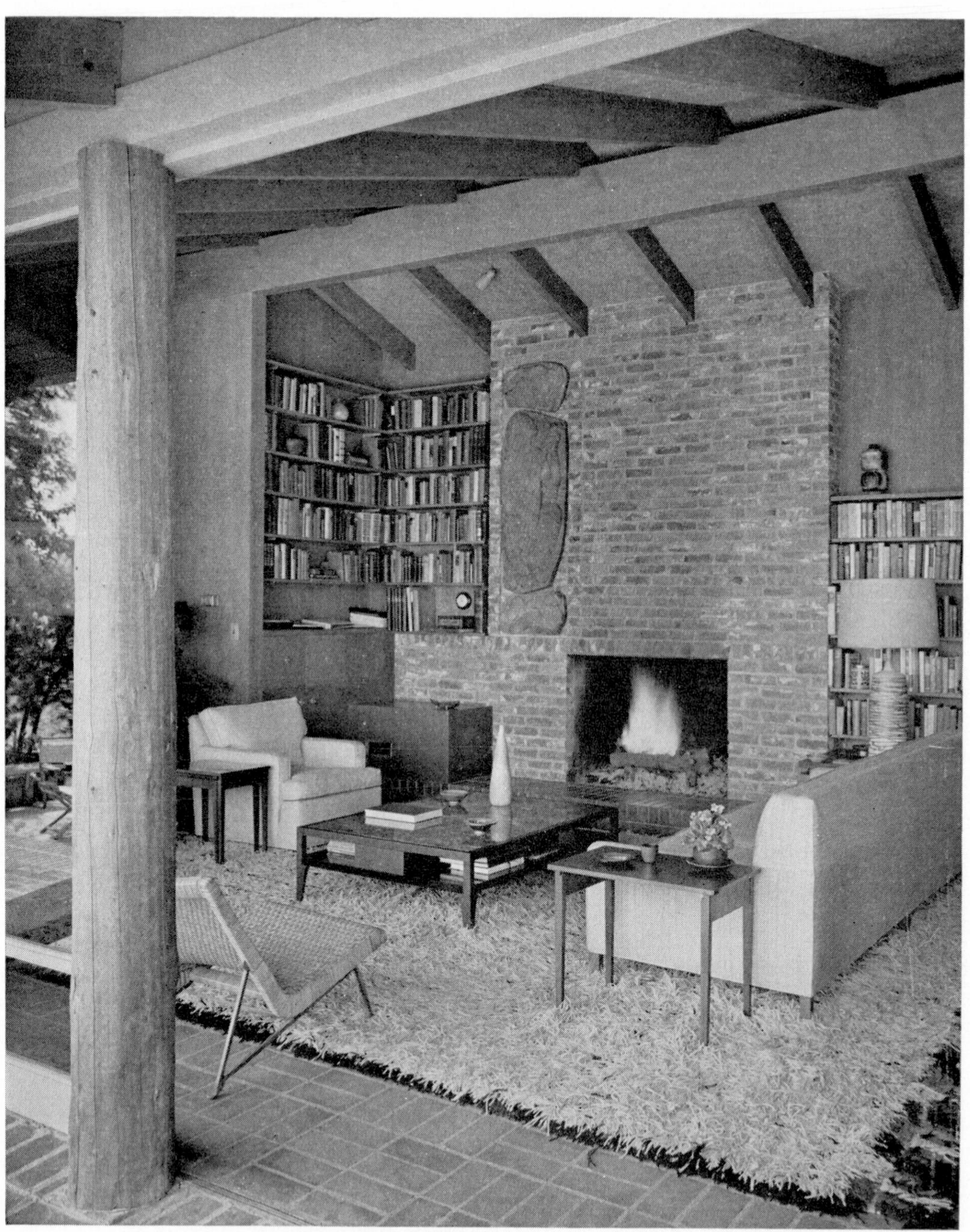

Distinctively regional in character, a Seattle fireplace has an unassuming naturalness. Its location near a corner together with the rug, furniture group, and bookcases suggests a sheltering haven. Roland Terry and Philip Moore, architects. (*Photograph by Dearborn-Massar. Courtesy of* SUNSET Magazine)

Cooking over an open fire is a pleasant way to make fun out of much work. It is informal and divides labor among host, hostess, children, and friends. If done often indoors or outside, some or much equipment is needed. Essentials are adjustable grilles, long-handled forks and pans, and a floor not harmed by sparks or grease. Work is lightened if a fireplace is in or near the kitchen, there is a special cupboard where equipment is permanently stored, or a wheeled cart is at hand. It sounds complicated but it is enjoyable, especially for those often-difficult occasions when adults and children are at the same party.

Ventilation is hardly a major function of fireplaces but fireplaces do ventilate rooms, rather violently when there is a good fire, moderately when the fireplace is cold and the damper open.

Symbolism of "hearth and home" continues to be important. Gathering around a fire for stories, popcorn, or whatever unifies persons of all ages and interests, makes them feel cheerfully warm and secure.

Finally, fireplaces provide busy householders with a somewhat dangerous place to burn trash and the hyperactive host or hostess with a harmless outlet for nervous energy.

Fireplace Design

Your first thought about fireplace design ought to be directed toward getting a fireplace that leads to a good fire because one that does not draw well or sends smoke into the room is worse than useless. This, however, is a technical matter best left to experts. Safety is equally important. The several hazards can be reduced by fireproof roofs and chimney tops that retard sparks; screens to keep sparks out of the room, andirons or baskets to keep fuel in place; and hearths high enough to keep babies at a safe distance. Then comes fireplace work, which can be lessened if indoor-outdoor fuel storage is near by, an ashpit permits outside ash removal, and the firepit is lowered a few inches to restrain the ashes.

Location. When fireplaces were used for heating, nearly every room had one. Today most houses have but one and this is in the living, dining, or family space. Sometimes the same chimney serves a social fireplace in the living room and a barbecue in the kitchen or family area. Occasionally, one or more additional fireplaces are put in seclusion rooms or master bedrooms. Outdoor fireplaces are usually near the group-living terrace, although they may be at some distance for short, inexpensive vacations away from the house.

Where should they be put in the room? There are no rules, but several factors should be kept in mind. Fireplaces are usually large, more or less

A

Left. Precise and smooth, a moderately small fireplace placed off center in a window accents the open airiness of the whole room, another view of which is shown in Figure 270B. Smith and Williams, architects. (*Photograph by Julius Shulman*)

Below. A pebble wall and raised hearth contrast strikingly with a smooth steel hood. Here, as in the rest of the room, the breadth of treatment is notable. Dorman and Morganelli, architects. (*Photograph by George de Gennaro*)

B

dominant elements. They demand considerable maintenance when burning and therefore should be accessible. They are natural centers for furniture arrangement and usually attract as many persons as space around them permits. They are frequently on outside walls where the chimney can be an exterior design factor.

The typical location is the center of a long wall, a safe, sane and perhaps too-familiar practice. This leads toward a static symmetry with emphasis in the middle of a long wall, but it tends to shorten the room visually (the Daphne Room is an example). It allows maximum visibility for large groups and suggests a symmetrical furniture arrangement. The center of one of the short walls is also safe and sane but somewhat less common. Again it is stable, but it makes the room seem longer and may suggest one furniture group near the fireplace with another at the other end (Figs. 268A and B and 269).

Fireplaces may also be in the end of a spur wall that acts as a room divider (Fig. 294A), or they can be free-standing structures that delineate continuous space into areas for different activities (Figs. 108B and 294B). Prefabricated fireplaces (Fig. 262) sometimes deliberately assert their independence of their surroundings and can be spotted wherever they can be connected to a chimney. Other locations include room corners, which emphasize the room's longest dimension and limit furniture groups to quarter circles.

Appearance. Although consistency with the whole house is a major consideration, fireplaces can have their own special beauty and individuality. The questions to be answered are much like those about walls.

- What degree of formality is wanted?
- Should horizontal or vertical lines predominate?
- How active and dominant should the fireplace be?
- What degree of roughness or smoothness seems best?
- Which materials are most appropriate?
- Should the fireplace be large, small, or intermediate in actual size and in scale?

Almost any combination of these qualities is feasible as can be seen in the illustrations in this chapter. For example, the fireplace in Figure 290 is informal and has a vigorous, balanced contrast of horizontals and verticals. Large in size, its dominance is augmented by the varying texture of used bricks, the sculptured plaques, and its studied relationship to the flanking shelves. The precise, smooth regularity of the fireplace in Figure 292A has overtones of formality. Comparatively small in size and scale, it is subordinate to the large areas of glass and the unusual ceiling design.

A

Fireplaces in spur walls or the center of a room can double as space-dividers.

Left. Informally rustic, a fireplace wall of used brick shields the kitchen from direct view. (*Photograph by Ernest Braun*)

Below. Clear-cut cubes of brick and plaster form a fireplace island separating living room activities. The trim geometry is repeated in the shelves and skylight. Alden Dow, architect. (*Photograph by Hedrich-Blessing*)

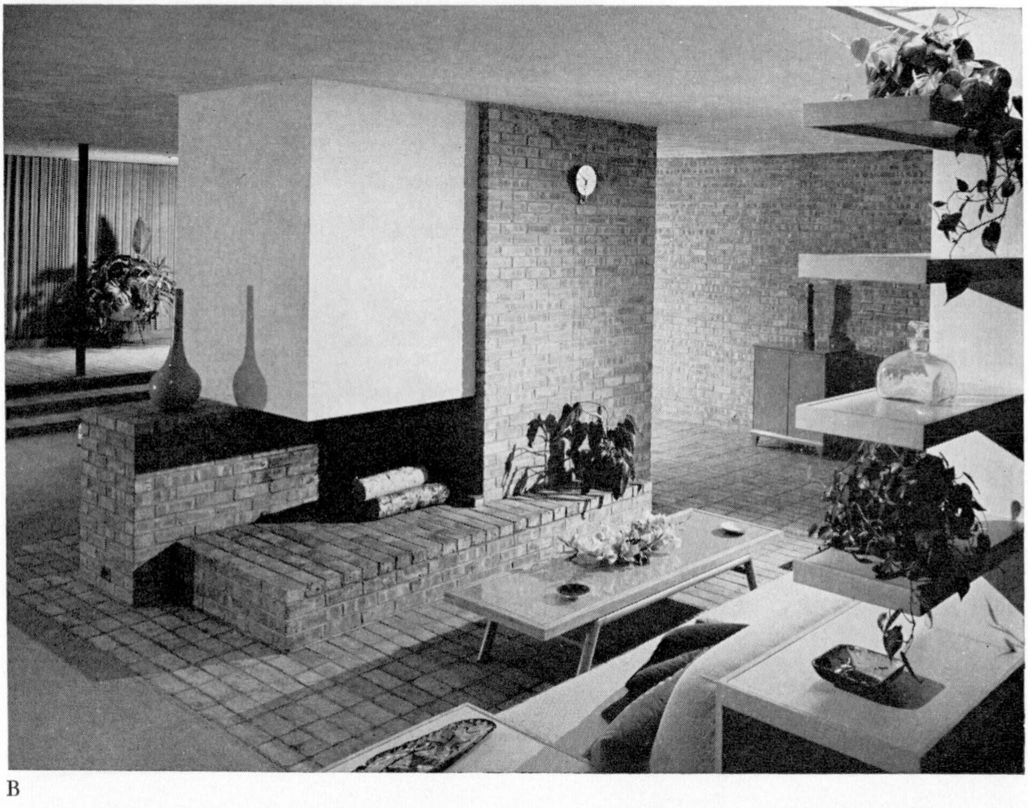

B

Size. Fireplaces can be of any size. Determining factors are: size and scale of the room and its furnishings, the effect the fireplace is intended to produce, the materials from which it is made, and the kind of fires wanted. Of all elements in the home, fireplaces lend themselves best to overscaling without seeming unpleasantly obtrusive. But very small fireplaces (Figs. 91B and 262) can have refreshing charm. It is easy to increase the importance and apparent size of fireplaces by enriching them with bands of contrasting materials (Fig. 268A), by integrating them with bookshelves or built-in furniture (Fig. 290), or by making them an integral part of large areas of masonry (Figs. 270A, 292B, and 296B). Also, fireplaces seem larger on small walls than on big ones.

Relationship to Walls, Floors, and Ceilings. The way in which a fireplace is related to the planes enclosing the room profoundly affects its character. Fireplaces can be simply holes, perhaps framed unobtrusively, in an unbroken wall, and this is the least noticeable treatment (Fig. 268A). They can project from the wall a few inches or several feet, and this increases their impact. When they leave the wall entirely, in a free-standing block of masonry or as an independent unit in metal (Figs. 262 and 294B), they become still more conspicuous. Going in the other direction, fireplaces can be recessed slightly or in an alcove deep enough for furniture that makes them invitingly sheltering.

The fireplace unit may extend to the ceiling, which accentuates its verticality. If it terminates a little or well below the room's top, as in Figure 292A, it can lead to a horizontal or blocky effect. The bottom of the firepit may be at the floor level, or it can be at seat height, in which case the hearth is usually extended to give sitting space (Figs. 292B and 294B). Raised fires are more comfortably seen and enjoyed, become more a part of the room, than those at floor level. The firepit can also be lower than the floor. If the depressed space is large enough for furniture, it tends to draw people into a convivial huddle and subdivide a room without partitions.

Materials. Materials turn our thoughts at once to masonry and metal since neither is damaged by fire. Brick and stone look substantial and permanent, tile can be plain or decorated, and metal can be shaped in many ways and transmits heat into the room (Figs. 292B and 297). These materials come in numberless textures: smooth tile and polished marble, shining copper and dull iron, brick and stone in all gradations of roughness. And there is no end to the color possibilities.

The fireplace in Figure 296B is a virile, substantial statement. Walls, fireplace, windows, floor, and ceiling are as handsomely unified as they were in the Daphne Room—but here the similarity ends. Stone, wood, and glass are the materials, each used in large areas and each fully revealing its

A

B

Some fireplaces are integral with the walls of the house, others are added embellishments.

Left. This carved marble fireplace is as formal as the chair and accessories. Intricately ornamented fireplace equipment provides interest even without a fire. (*Photograph by John H. Lohman*)

Below. A fireplace as "built in" as the upper one is "set in" and as vigorous as the other is refined. Roger Lee, architect. (*Photograph by Roger Sturtevant*)

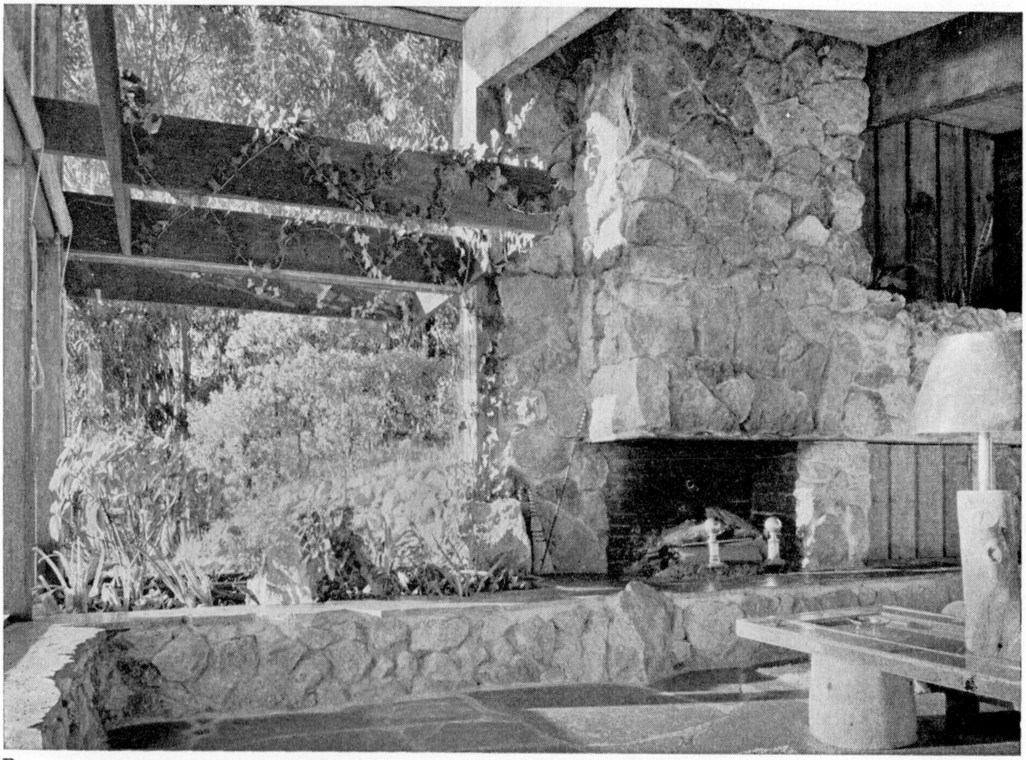

own inherent individuality. The massive stones are rough on the vertical planes but smooth on the ledge and floor. Heavy beams support plank ceiling, lighter beams form the indoor-outdoor trellis, and foot-wide boards and narrow battens sheath the wall at the right. Large sheets of glass unite the room with the landscape.

These materials are organized in a powerful angular, continuing design. A seat-high ledge encircles two sides of the room, forms a planting box inside and out, and then becomes the hearth. The firebox, a simple cavity open on two sides, is part of a wall as decisively vertical as the ledge is horizontal. At one side of the fireplace, glass opens the room over the planting box and through the trellis to the wooded hillside. Then the glass continues across the adjacent wall to open the room to a dramatic view of San Francisco bay. Thus one part of the room is as sheltering as a cave, the other as open as protection from weather permits.

In conclusion, fireplaces are a delightful extravagance, a natural focal point for living and furniture arrangements, and most effective when they are clearly part of the architecture, not a decorative afterthought. Today most fireplaces are as simple and sturdy as those in seventeenth-century American houses and are greatly appreciated in part because they are so seldom used.

In contrast to the sleekly simple fireplace on page 262, Victorian prefabricated ones are delightfully intricate in design. (*Photograph by Ernest Braun*)

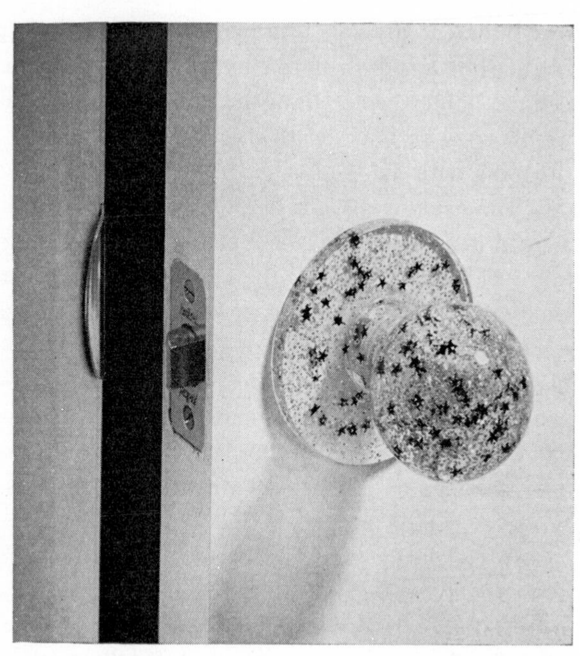

12. Windows, Curtains, and Doors

WINDOWS AND DOORS visually and physically relate one space to another. The "wind's-eye" of old was a narrow opening to let out some of the fire's smoke and to let in a little fresh air, to help light the room, and to permit peephole glimpses of what was going on outside. These are the three functions of windows—*ventilation, light,* and *view* —but only the last is unique. Ventilation can often be handled better through louvered and shuttered openings, air-conditioning, exhaust fans, and the like. Light can be produced and precisely controlled electrically at lower total cost than natural light can be brought through windows that, all factors considered, are expensive. But only through transparent windows, doors, and walls can we enjoy the outdoors from protected enclosures. The way in which windows, doors, and walls can open up or shut in space is dramatically shown in Figures 299A and B.

Above. Plastic doorknobs make doors decorative as well as useful. (*E. I. duPont de Nemours & Co.*)

A

Opening the end of an apartment living room transforms a formerly dreary space.

Above. A window wall with a sliding glass door floods a small room with light and allows enjoyment of a spectacular cityscape. Sheer glass curtains diffuse glare when necessary, ceiling-hung draw curtains provide privacy and insulation. Campbell and Wong, architects.

Right. Before remodeling, the small window and mismatched door did little to enhance the space. (*Photographs by Morley Baer*)

B

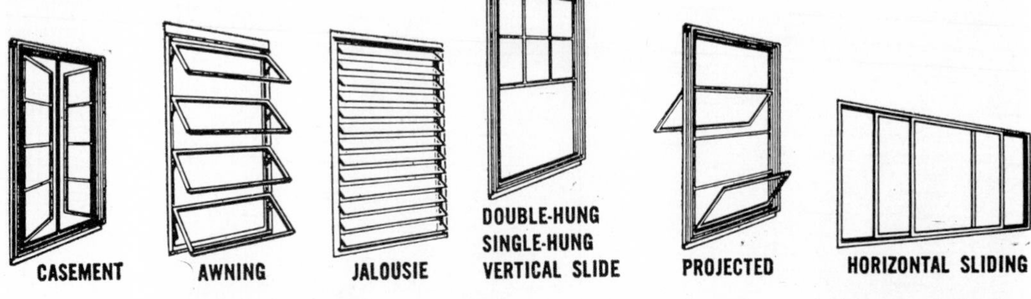

Prefabricated window units allow great freedom of choice. (*Aluminum Window Manufacturers Assn.*)

► TYPES OF WINDOWS

The major types of movable windows used today are illustrated above. They can *slide*, as in the double-hung or horizontally sliding designs, or *swing*, as in casement or awning types.

Double-hung windows usually have two sashes (the frame, usually movable, in which panes of glass are set) that slide up and down. Weights, springs, or friction hold them in place when open. Usually they are higher than wide and the sashes are of the same size and shape. Their advantages are numerous. They are easy and inexpensive to install and seldom warp or sag. Hardware is simple, weatherproofing is effective. They can be opened top or bottom, and they do not project to get in the way of people and curtains inside or people and plants outside. The major drawbacks are these. Not more than half the area can be opened and when open there is no protection from rain. They are difficult to clean from inside unless the sash can be removed or pivoted and inconvenient to operate when furniture is under them. In addition, some persons find the horizontal cross-bar that cuts the window in half visually annoying.

Horizontally sliding windows are like double-hung windows placed on their sides, and their advantages and disadvantages are similar. Usually, though, they have the horizontal proportions popular today and are often combined with fixed glass that gets rid of the bar in the middle.

Casement windows, hinged at one side and swinging in or out, were in common use long before sliding types. Their major assets are that the whole area can be opened, and they can be adjusted to direct breezes into the room or to reduce cold drafts. Equipped with crank-operated hardware, they are easy to operate even when over furniture. In the better types, both sides of the glass can be washed from inside. Casement windows also have drawbacks. In-swinging casements are seldom used because they interfere with furnishings, and those that swing out over terraces or walks are serious hazards. They offer no protection from rain and are not easy to weatherproof tightly. Typically they are tall and narrow, and the cross bars needed for strength break up the outlook and complicate washing.

Awning and **projected windows** are like casements but hinged at the top or occasionally the bottom. Disadvantages are similar to those of casements: small panes of glass, sashes that take space when open, difficulty of getting a tight seal. In addition, they collect dust when open. But they have the notable advantage of giving precise, draft-free control of ventilation while admitting little if any rain or snow.

Jalousie windows are awning-type but with very narrow strips of glass. With all of the advantages of the awning type, they are also favored because they take little space and odd shapes are not costly. Difficult to clean and to weatherproof, the many small panes of glass also interfere with views. But for precise control of ventilation, they excel all other types.

In addition to these window types, transparent or translucent materials can be used in other ways. **Fixed glass** or **plastic** can be used in very large single pieces and is inexpensive to install because no hardware or screens are needed. Fixed glass is often combined with doors or windows that open or with louvered ventilators to provide fresh air (Figs. 299A, 304, and 309).

Skylights and **clerestories,** windows in the ceiling or high in a wall between two roof levels (Figs. 301, 302A and B), light and ventilate a house with no loss of privacy or interference with furniture arrangement. Perhaps more significant, they can bring daylight or moonlight into the center of the

Abundant light coming through glass wall at left is balanced by light from high clerestory windows, which are also efficient ventilators. (*Victor Thompson*)

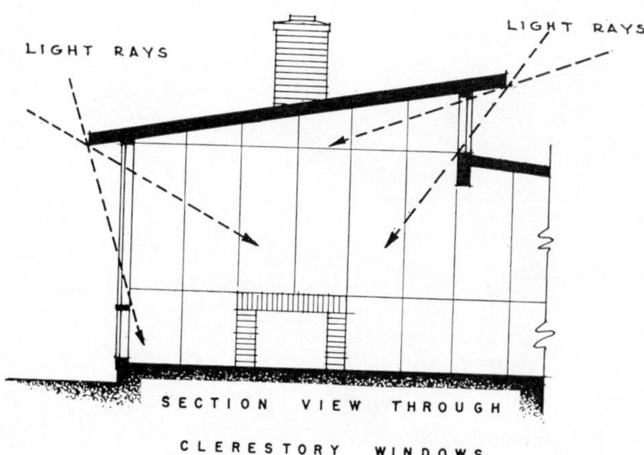

A

B

Left. Sunlight from a vigorously patterned, peaked skylight floods a "windowless" interior garden room in Midland, Michigan. Alden Dow, architect. (*Photograph by Bill Hedrich. Hedrich-Blessing*)

Below. In Libertyville, Illinois, soft light from a narrow clerestory illumines a room and accents ceiling and wall textures. Frank Lloyd Wright, architect. (*Photograph by Maynard Parker. Courtesy of* House Beautiful)

house. Light coming from above can reveal hitherto unnoticed qualities of furniture, sculpture, and plants; can give new dimensions to form and space. With them, it is unnecessary to stretch the plan out for light in all rooms: economically compact plans can have kitchen, laundry, and bathrooms grouped far from "windows" yet be well lighted and ventilated.

Wood and metal are the materials typically used to hold the panes of glass in windows and walls. Metal is stronger (which makes thinner strips possible), does not shrink or swell noticeably, and has a uniform texture harmonious with glass. With the exception of aluminum and stainless steel, metals used in windows must be protected by paint; and, because all metals conduct heat and cold readily, moisture may condense on the inside of metal sashes in cold weather. Wood shrinks, swells, and has to be given a protective finish, but it does not encourage condensation.

► DESIGN AND LOCATION OF WINDOWS

Views and privacy, light and ventilation, heat and cold, and furniture arrangement are among the major factors determining window design and location. Cleaning and curtaining follow closely. Interwoven with these is the larger matter of architectural composition, the relationship of windows to the mass and space of the whole house and landscape.

Views and Privacy

Normally, the larger windows face the best outlook, whether it be a view of a city, a lake, or one's own private patio (Figs. 299A, 304, and 310A). Those necessarily facing the street or nearby neighbors are smaller, higher in the wall, or of translucent material. Most of us nowadays like windows that encourage those inside to look out but not neighbors or passers-by to look in. This is achieved by placing large windows toward the rear of the property, by building fences or planting hedges, and much less well by resorting to view-blocking curtains.

Light

Natural light is cheerful, and for eyes and spirit it is almost impossible to have rooms with too much daylight. But it is unfortunately easy to design rooms that seem unpleasantly bright because strong contrasts of light and dark lead to glare. This comes from *too little light* and in the *wrong places. More light means less glare if the windows are well planned.* Until recently

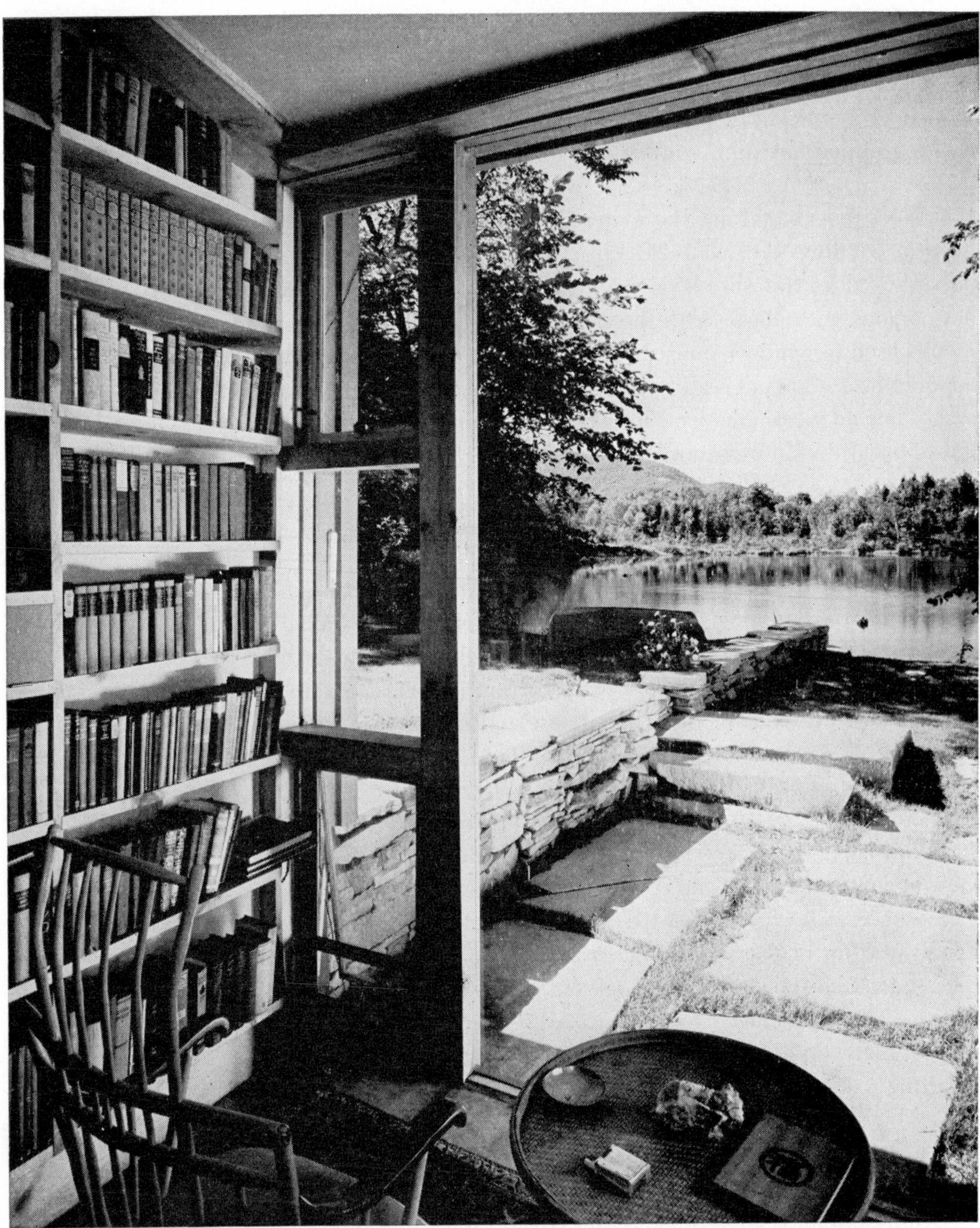

The full delight of a Vermont lake is enjoyed through a window wall that combines fixed glass with sliding glass doors and awning-type windows for controlled ventilation. Carl Koch and Associates, architects. (*Photograph by Ezra Stoller*)

most windows were holes cut out of the wall, and the first thoughts were of getting curtains to "soften" the light. Large areas of glass in the best contemporary design, however, seldom seem too bright. Here are some of the factors:

- Light coming from more than one direction minimizes heavy shadows and makes you feel enveloped by light rather than having it shot at you.
- Light entering the top of a room illumines the ceiling and spreads through the room more than does light entering at lower levels.
- No part of a room ought to be more than about 1½ times the ceiling height from a wall with adequate windows or from skylights.
- Overhangs projecting beyond windows reduce the glare of the sky and mellow the light entering the room (Fig. 310B).
- Windows to the floor are best when the surfacing material outside does not reflect a glaringly bright light. Light-absorbing materials or the shade from trees or trellises are indicated.

No thinking about the light from windows is complete without remembering that windows, the lightest elements in a room by day, are very dark at night unless they are lighted or curtained inside or the immediate view outside is illumined.

Ventilation

The most comfortable ventilation unnoticeably lets stale air out from near the room's top and draftless fresh air in from near the floor. High windows or louvered openings above windows (Fig. 309), skylights, and exhaust fans accomplish the first while low windows or ventilators do the second. There are times, though, when you want to feel a breeze sweeping through your home from wide-open doors and windows. Rooms are most quickly aired if the openings are on opposite sides, one of which faces the prevailing winds.

Heat and Cold

To date, most colorless, transparent materials are poor insulators. Hence extreme temperatures are important factors in window design and placement. Double glass, by reducing fuel consumption, usually pays for itself in about three years in cold climates and also keeps houses markedly cooler in summer, particularly when *the sun does not strike the glass.* More important is to get windows in their best places. Glass facing south brings welcome winter sun, but with a properly designed overhang excludes summer sun because

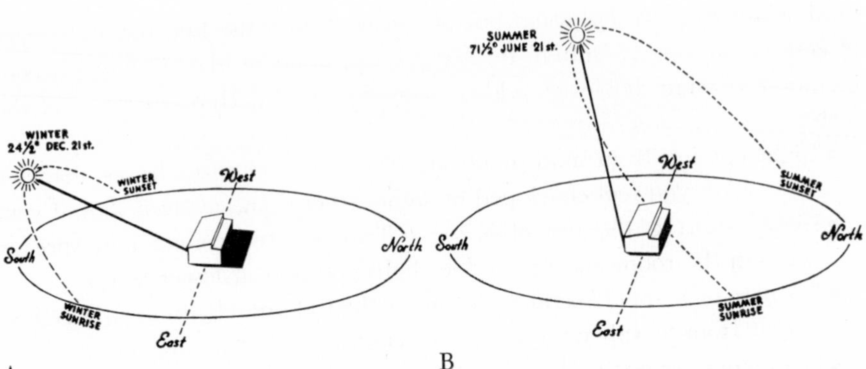

A B

Winter and summer sun position at noon in Chicago. In winter the sun is low and stays well south of due east and west. In summer it is high and its arc is well to the north. (*Libbey-Owens-Ford Glass Co.*)

then the sun is high in the sky (Figs. 306A and B). Glass facing east brings the morning sun, cheering in winter and seldom too hot in summer. Glass on the west, however, brings hot afternoon heat deep into the house. Then, because curtains help only a little, you are forced to rely on something outside, such as nearby shade trees, vine-covered arbors, very wide overhanging roofs or awnings. Thus in terms of heat and cold in most parts of our country, glass on the south is best, followed by that on the east. On the north, glass brings winter cold, and on the west summer heat.

Properly designed overhanging roofs let desirable winter sun in through *south* windows but keep hot summer sun off the glass. (*Libbey-Owens-Ford Glass Co.*)

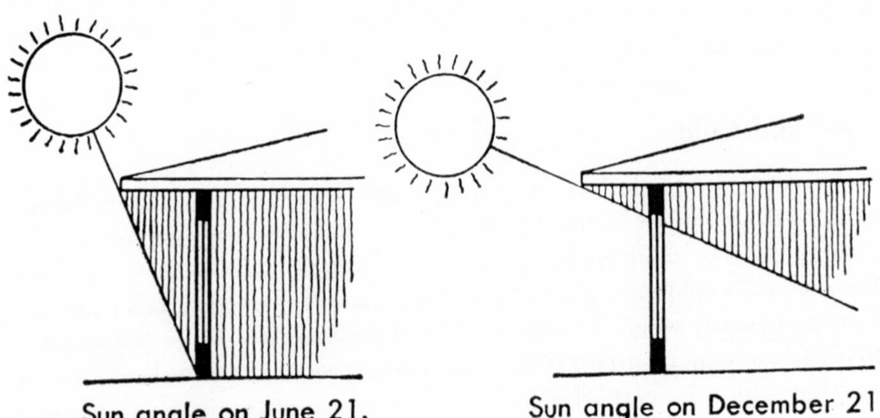

Practical window-sill heights vary with room use and furniture arrangement. Three heights meet most needs, help unify interior and exterior design. (*Courtesy of* House and Home © *June 1955*)

Furniture Arrangement

The location and design of windows and doors determines in large part how furniture can be arranged. In general, the more openings in walls, the harder it is to arrange furniture. This situation is aggravated if the openings are separated one from another and if windows come below the ordinary table heights of 27 to 30 inches. Windows grouped in bands high enough to allow placing tables or sofas beneath them facilitate furniture arrangement; clerestories and skylights raise no problems. Windows to the floor make indoor and outdoor space seem continuous but lose most of their value if much furniture, or any heavy pieces, are put next to them. Thus, although they increase *visual* space they often reduce *usable* space, as is evident in Figure 310A.

Cleaning

All glass benefits from frequent cleaning, especially in dusty or sooty locations or when it can be reached by small children. It is easiest to clean when the panes are large, can be reached without excessive stooping or climbing, and is easy to get at, outside as well as inside. Clerestories and skylights bring special cleaning problems, often lessened with translucent glass or plastics.

Curtaining

Although curtains and draperies have much in their favor, they are not without cost. An economical first step is to plan so that as few windows as possible absolutely demand curtaining—wisely oriented high windows or window walls facing screened gardens or protected views are examples.

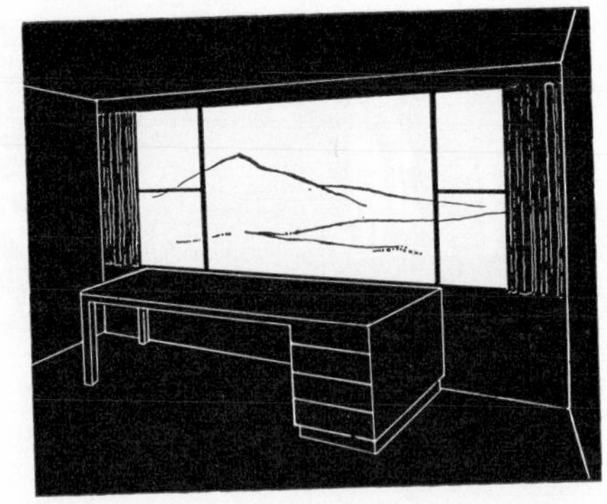

Separated windows with small panes of glass framed by draperies give an effect quite different from that produced by a band of glass with pulled-back draw curtains and a minimum of bars. (*Matt Kahn*)

Curtaining problems are simplest when windows are grouped, vary little in size, shape, and distance from floor and ceiling.

Architectural Composition

So far windows have been discussed in terms of what they can do to make home life more comfortable, but stopping at this point might lead to a hodge-podge design. Openings today as in the past are a vital factor in architectural design, but no single aspect of home planning shows greater change. The same aims and principles of design operate as general guides, but the specific patterns are notably different from anything known heretofore. Contemporary trends can be summarized as follows:

- Windows and doors are designed as integral parts of the architectural shell rather than as isolated, ornamented, cutout holes.
- Windows are typically grouped in bands, usually horizontal, and when feasible windows and doors are combined in harmonious units.
- Large areas of glass are placed where they serve best; small windows are strategically located for balanced lighting and ventilation plus privacy.
- Unity and simplicity of effect is emphasized by using as few shapes, sizes, and types as possible and by aligning tops of windows and doors.

The design of openings is at least as important, from an architectural point of view, as the design of opaque portions of the home. Windows are conspicuous day and night, inside and outside. Their thin, smooth, light-transmitting material contrasts strikingly with what is around it. By day, windows are usually the brightest element inside the house and the darkest outside. At night, if the interior is illumined, windows are dark from the inside and light from the outside. Beyond these physical characteristics the fact that enclosed and unenclosed space interpenetrate each other through windows and doors endows them with a unique psychological importance.

Window Walls

Audaciously opening the house to its surroundings is in some respects as significant as man's long struggle to secure his dwelling against the environment. Box-tight enclosure has never been completely satisfying to man, and the urge toward the paradoxical union of security and openness has a long, varied history. Walled gardens allowed Egyptians, Greeks, and Romans to open part of their homes to the outdoors. In the later medieval period, areas of glass quite large enough to be called "window walls" were not uncommon. Many houses built fifty or more years ago had sizable "picture windows." Thus seemingly revolutionary, contemporary window walls are an evolutionary step.

Grouped windows of fixed glass fit into the pattern of structural framing and plywood panels. Ventilating louvers above and below windows provide ventilation and conceal insect screens. John Yeon, architect. (*Douglas Fir Plywood Association*)

A

B

Although window walls are now standard features even in many tract houses, they are not unmixed blessings chiefly because they are incompletely understood. They should not be thought of as merely bigger windows but as a different way of planning the house and garden. They flood rooms with light; and, when poorly designed, with glare, heat, or cold. In visually uniting house and yard, they affect furniture arrangements and color schemes as well as the design of the landscape. Some of the major problems they raise, and ways of avoiding or solving them are listed below.

Problems	*Solutions*
Loss of privacy	Face window wall toward private part of property; build fences or plant hedges; use curtains and draperies.
Glare of light	Balance light with windows in other walls or skylights; have overhanging roof or trellis; plant suitable shade trees near by.
Excessive heat or cold	Orient toward south or southeast; use insulating glass; provide overhead protection or trees; have insulating draperies that can be drawn when necessary.
More glass to clean	No easy solution. Use professional window-washer's techniques.
Greater quantity of curtaining	Place window wall so that curtains are not essential.
Furniture arrangement	Plan room so that major furniture group is related both to window wall and other dominant units, such as fireplaces.
Color schemes	Take account of relationship between colors inside and those seen through the glass.

Left above. In architect Eliot Noyes' own home, the interior shows how light is balanced by the two window walls and how closely united are living room, covered passage, and the simply landscaped inner court with only a glass screen between.

Left below. Deep roof overhangs and projecting fieldstone walls protect the recessed glass walls with their sliding doors. The parklike Connecticut setting is easily maintained. (*Photographs by Ezra Stoller*)

Right. The plan of the Noyes' house illustrates the use of a central court to separate group-living from private-living wings.

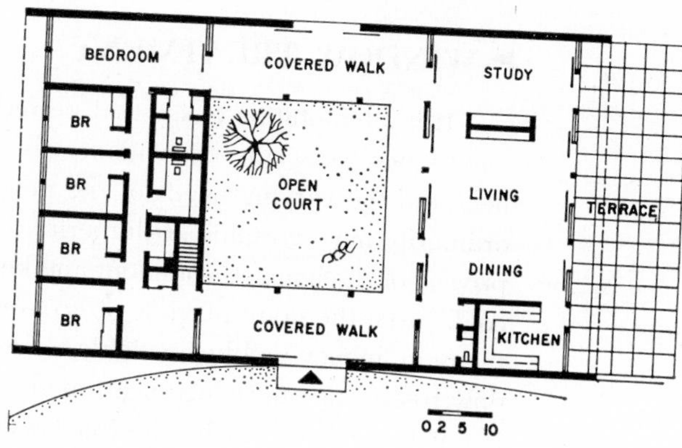

Problems	*Solutions*
Fading of colors	Choose colors that do not fade or that fade pleasantly; exclude sun with projecting roof, planting, or curtains.
Black and cold at night	Illumine window with lighting trough above it; light terrace or garden outside; draperies.
Design and maintenance of landscape	Plan at least the immediate landscape architecturally to harmonize with interior; use paving, fixed outdoor furniture, sculpture, and plants that remain attractive all year with little care.

There are innumerable ways of designing window walls. When they fill an entire wall from floor to ceiling (Fig. 310A), there is minimum break between indoors and out. If they begin above the floor, there is room for furniture. They can follow a gable to its peak (Figs. 11 and 43A). There may be a minimum of divisions as in the Noyes' house, or a strong pattern of verticals or horizontals (Fig. 299A). They can, as we have seen, join a room with an extensive view or focus attention on a small enclosed court. Although typically associated with living or dining areas, window walls can make kitchens or halls expansive (Figs. 75A and 328A). If well planned, they are quite feasible in bedrooms or even bathrooms. Properly designed, they can be used in the East as well as in the West, in the North or the South.

Windows are costly. Glass is expensive to buy and replace, difficult to make weather-tight around the edges, must be cleaned often, is likely to run up heating and cooling bills. If the glass is movable, screens and window hardware are needed. Almost all windows bring the added expense of curtains, draperies, or blinds. But sensibly large, well-placed windows are well worth their cost.

► WINDOW TREATMENT

It is a temptation to say that perfectly planned windows need no "treatment," but we would then ignore the great changes in outdoor light and heat and the varying needs of the people inside. Thus, in terms of *use*, we ordinarily have curtains or draperies, blinds or shades inside to control the privacy of the home, the amount and kind of light that enters it, and heat and cold. From the point of view of *economy* the less you put at your windows the more money will be available for other purposes, although efficient window treatment can reduce heating and cooling bills. Furthermore, whatever is put there ought to be durable; resist the ravages of sun, moisture, and moths; and be easily maintained. *Beauty* comes from the inherent attractiveness of the fabrics chosen and from the way in which they relate the windows to the whole room. *Individuality,* here as elsewhere, is less a matter of being "different" than of solving your own problems well.

Window treatments can be separated into those inside the house and those outside. *Exterior window treatments,* often overlooked, are out of the way of furniture and take no wall space inside the room.

- **Awnings** of duck can be adjusted as the weather varies to protect windows from sun, rain, and dirt. Available in many designs and colors, they give a soft pleasant light inside and out. They are, however, short-lived, subject to fading and soiling as well as to flapping in the wind. Metal awnings, usually aluminum, can be stationary or roll up. Higher in first cost, they pay for themselves over the years. Although they can be designed as part of the structure, they often look like stuck-on afterthoughts.
- **Shutters** are seldom used today except for the dummy ones employed to make small windows look larger on pseudo-colonial houses, and for securing vacation houses against marauders or windows against violent storms, but they can effectively temper light, heat, and cold.
- **Grilles** and **fences** of masonry, wood, plastic, or aluminum placed close to windows or some feet away control privacy, sun, and wind in any degree desired depending on their design and location.
- **Overhanging roofs** and **trellises** are the most permanent exterior shading devices but bring no privacy. They can be solid and opaque, of translucent plastic or glass, or merely a framework for vines. In addition to protecting windows, they can be large enough to shelter outdoor living areas. When well designed, they visually relate the house to its site and contribute greatly to exterior design (Figs. 119A, 141A, and 310B).
- **Trees, tall shrubs,** and **vines** give cool, ventilated shade but not until they are of some size.

Interior window treatments, in addition to curtains and draperies, include shades, blinds, and shutters. These can move sideways or up and down, the latter having the definite advantage of being completely out of the way when not wanted.

- **Fabric roller shades** are inexpensive and can cover part, all, or none of the glass. They reduce light and give privacy in relationship to their thickness and opaqueness. The newer ones are easy to clean and come in many colors, textures, and patterns. Their several drawbacks include the fact that when pulled down they cut the light from the top of the window first—and that is the best light. They block the breeze or whip around noisily, and they have neither the architectural quality of blinds or shutters nor the softness of draperies.

- **Bamboo** and **split-wood shades** perform much like those made of fabrics. They differ in that they let some light through, give some or much notion of what is outside, and have pleasantly natural textures and colors (Figs. 317A and C).
- **Venetian blinds,** much used in Colonial days (Fig. 263A), now come in metal and plastic. Their special advantages are almost complete light and air control—straight into the room, down toward the floor, or up toward the ceiling—and complete disappearance behind a valance. They are durable but not expensive, and their horizontal lines are pleasing. They do, however, collect dust and dirt that are not easy to remove.
- **Vertical blinds** of metal, plastic, or fabrics (Fig. 315B) can easily be shaped to fit and unify odd-sized openings. They control light from side to side, rather than up or down, and emphasize the height rather than the breadth of windows and walls. Of importance to housekeepers, they collect less dust than Venetian blinds.
- **Grilles** or **screens** of wood or other materials deserve consideration, especially when windows are not well designed, when there is no view, and when privacy is requisite. Figure 315C shows how one wall of a small city apartment has been unified with Japanese grilles, called Shoji panels, of intricate pattern and how another free-standing panel separates the living room from the entrance.
- **Shutters** of the old-fashioned inside type have recently staged a comeback. They can become a unified part of the wall (Fig. 52B) and for many have pleasant associations with the past. Although they last almost indefinitely, their first cost is rather high.

The above might be called "hard" window treatments. Since none of them does much toward humanizing windows, they are often combined with draperies.

► CURTAINS AND DRAPERIES

In addition to controlling privacy, light, and heat, curtains and draperies soak up noise in proportion to the area they cover, the thickness of the fabric, and the depth of the folds. They make rooms homelike and effectively cover up the bareness of those not completely furnished—a point worth remembering when you do not get all your furniture at once. With them, you can change the apparent size, shape, and character of a room or conceal architectural awkwardnesses. Small rooms look larger if curtains and dra-

"Hard" window treatments are usually architectural in effect.

A

B

Above left. Green, yellow, and white Venetian blinds in narrow widths are combined in a spirited window treatment. Melanie Kahane, interior designer. (*Bridgeport Brass Co.*)

Above right. Vertical blinds can be easily adapted to sloping ceilings and windows of varied heights. (*Stiller, Rouse, Berggren & Hunt*)

Below. Japanese wood grilles, called Shoji panels, backed with rice paper mask unattractive, viewless windows but allow light and air to enter. They can also be used as doors. A similar panel, but without paper backing, makes an airy space-divider. Campbell and Wong, architects. (*Photograph by Ernest Braun*)

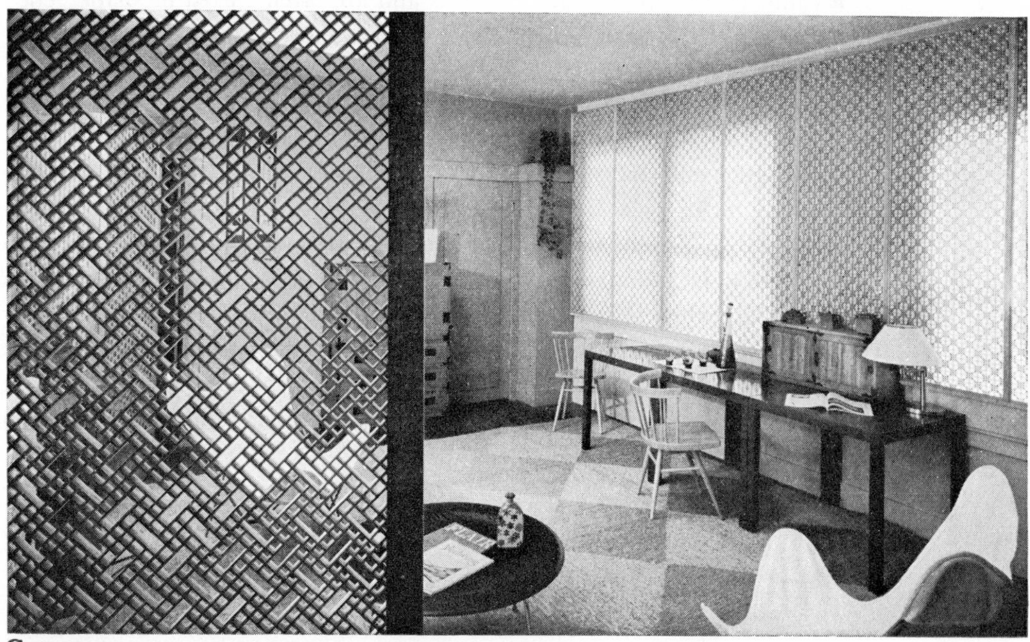
C

peries blend with the walls; low rooms look higher if draperies go from ceiling to floor. Gloomy rooms seem brighter if gay colors or invigorating patterns are used near windows. Walls chopped-up with windows or jogs can be unified by generous glass curtains and draperies, and some eyesores can be completely concealed.

You can direct almost any degree of attention toward windows by the fabrics you select and the way you hang them. Unpatterned materials similar to the wall color, acting as inconspicuous transitions between opaque walls and clear glass, encourage us to look *through windows.* Moderate color contrasts and patterns direct attention *toward windows.* Bold or unusual colors and designs usually cause us *to look at the draperies* rather than the windows.

A few definitions are now in order.

- **Glass curtains** are of thin materials and hung next to the glass.
- **Sash curtains** are a type of glass curtain hung on the window sash. They can be stretched taut between rods on the top and bottom of window sashes or hung in loose folds.
- **Draw curtains,** usually of translucent or opaque fabrics, are mounted on traverse rods. In the past, they came between glass curtains and draperies. Nowadays they are more often used alone.
- **Draperies** are any loosely hung (not stretched) fabric. Thus, the term really includes all curtains. Generally, though, draperies are thought of as heavy fabrics that can be drawn or stand idly at the sides of windows purely for decoration.
- **Cornices** are horizontal bands several inches wide placed at the window top (or the ceiling) to conceal curtain tops and the rods from which they hang. They can also function more positively in relating the whole window treatment to walls and ceiling.
- **Valances** are simply wide cornices and are often varied in shape. They can be of hard materials or fabrics, such as those in the Daphne Room.

Glass Curtains

Softening and diffusing light, glass curtains (Figs. 317B and C) also temper the glitter of glass and relate it to the rest of the room, give partial privacy, and decrease the necessity of keeping windows spotless. They make a room seem light and airy, especially when used without draperies. They are needed most when the outlook is unattractive or there is constant need for some privacy. Glass curtains (along with lamp shades and translucent plastic or glass panels) can make one unique visual contribution: they bring light into the room *through* color and pattern a little as stained glass does in Gothic cathedrals and in Victorian homes.

"Soft" window treatments relate windows to upholstered furniture, woven floor coverings, and clothing.

A

B

Above left. Bamboo blinds and draperies bring textural variation in a room where subtle textures are important. (*Photograph by Morley Baer*)

Above right. Coarse net, hung from ceiling to floor in simple folds, diffuses the light while unifying wall and window in a New York City apartment. Edward Wormley, designer. (*Dunbar*)

Right. A bamboo drapery partially screens a dining space, glass curtains give some privacy, and draw curtains with a printed design consonant with the wood walls and linoleum floor can be drawn when desired. (*Congoleum-Nairn*)

C

A wall with two separated windows is a typical curtaining problem that can be solved in a number of ways with different effects. At the *left,* curtains aligned with the windows cover the wall space and produce a horizontal band. In the *center,* café or tier curtains hung from two rods can give a checkerboard effect, but they could be slid along the rods to cover either the windows or the walls. At the *right,* curtains from window tops to floor make the wall and windows seem tall and narrow. (*Matt Kahn*)

Materials. A great variety of simple materials have taken the place of our great-grandmother's beautifully rich curtains, some of which are listed as "Very Thin" fabrics on pages 254-255. Any fabric that hangs well and withstands sun, washing, or cleaning is suitable.

Color and Pattern. Color is especially important because the light filtering through glass curtains takes on their color, giving the whole room that color cast, and also because glass curtains are conspicuous from the outside. Therefore, they are usually a neutral light color and, for exterior harmony, identical or very similar in all rooms. They can, however, be pink or yellow to warm a cool room or pale green, blue, or lavender to cool a hot one. Although customarily plain, suitable fabrics are available with woven or printed patterns, which are useful in rooms that need interest at the windows without adding draw curtains or draperies.

Tailoring and Hanging. Simplicity is the best guide: a neat heading that fits its space and is shirred or pinch-pleated on a simple rod, a double hem at the bottom for weight, and a minimum width of at least twice that of the window for ample fullness.

If combined with draperies, glass curtains usually hang inside the window frame, close to it and the glass, and are long enough to clear the sill without leaving a noticeable gap. Used alone, they can be hung outside the frame and cover two or more grouped windows with a unifying film. Sometimes two or more sets of glass curtains are hung in the *café* or *tier* manner (Fig. 318) to emphasize horizontality or give privacy without always reducing light from the window tops.

It is difficult to believe that the windows at the *left* and in the *center* have the same size, shape, and position in the wall. Two factors account for the different effects: size and shape of panes of glass and design of curtains. The window at left is an integral part of the wall composition and looks large and unified; that in the center looks like an isolated hole in the wall, chiefly because curtains are at variance with window and wall shape. At the *right* a window wall is effectively treated with thin glass curtains and heavier draperies. (*Matt Kahn*)

Draw Curtains

Flexible control of light, heat and cold, and privacy is the primary useful purpose of draperies that slide on rods. Often, though, they are used alone, and then they take over all the esthetic functions of window treatment.

Materials. Fabrics used for draw curtains need sufficient strength, durability, and flexibility to withstand being pulled back and forth and to hang gracefully when stretched or pulled together. Thus, many thin glass-curtain materials and some heavy upholstery fabrics are suitable. Between these two extremes is a challenging array in the drapery, bedding, dress, and suiting sections of almost any store. Coarse or fine *nets* soften without obscuring windows. *Organdy, pongee,* and *silk gauze* are relatively smooth and rich looking. Such textiles as *monk's cloth, Osnaburg,* and *tweed* are thicker, rougher, and more casual. *Denim* is sturdy and durable; *Indian Head* is clean and crisp; *chambray* has a smooth, slightly silky texture; *gingham* is informal. *Glazed chintz* has a crisp shiny surface that intensifies its colors and patterns. *Satin* hangs in soft folds, is dressy when woven of smooth silk, informal when made of heavier, loosely twisted threads. *Damasks, brocades,* and *brocatelles* have woven, often formal, patterns.

To this list can be added *bamboo* and *wood* textiles, substantial and informal, plus many plastic fabrics.

Color and Pattern. Appropriateness to the home and its occupants is the only defensible generalization. Draw curtains are least noticeable when related to the walls. They become more conspicuous if they repeat or echo the color and character of such large units as furniture or floor. They become emphatic when they contrast strongly with the rest of the room.

Color, chiefly color value, is typically the most noticeable factor—very dark curtains against a light wall, or vice versa, stand out sharply. Scale and character come next—large-scale patterns with vivid contrasts or those that differ from other large areas in the room become dominant. It is a matter of deciding what degree of dominance or subordination, harmony or contrast, is most appropriate. A sampling of the myriad possibilities is shown in Chapter 10.

Tailoring and Hanging. Draw curtains are almost invariably most effective and useful when they hang in straight folds, which at least cover all the window frame and begin and stop at sensible points. They fit their setting best when they begin either slightly above the top of the frame or at the ceiling, and when they end slightly below the bottom of the frame or near the floor. Usually the longer the better unless there is good reason for stopping them short. Also the fuller the better (from 1½ to 2½ times the width of the space they cover). When pulled back, it seems more sensible to have them cover frame and wall rather than window. French, box, or pinch pleats take care of fullness at the top and a generous bottom hem helps them hang well.

Draperies

Draperies began their life in the textiles that warmed physically and visually the cold walls of early homes and migrated from the walls to beds and windows. Today they are most often found at windows, sometimes at large doorways or separating parts of a room. Occasionally they are used as wall hangings. They differ from draw curtains only in that they are sometimes heavier and that they do not necessarily pull across the opening they guard.

Windows are an expensive, valuable asset. Their primary functions of outlook, light, and air should not be unnecessarily interfered with by window "treatment." The thoughtful design—location, size, shape, and type—of windows is a distinguishing trait of the better contemporary architecture. This is supplemented by due regard for overhanging roofs, trellises, and planting as necessary. Although interior curtains and blinds are still important, they are becoming increasingly less critical. This is another instance of the trend toward thinking about all factors in advance of building and of solving as many problems as possible architecturally. Exterior, interior, and landscape architecture are approaching a functional integration.

► DOORS

Doorways allow us and our vision, as well as light, sounds, smells, breezes, warmth, and cold to travel in and out of the house and from one room to another. Doors control these in varying degrees depending on their location, design, and material. Contemporary doors run the gamut from stout, opaque doors of wood or metal, which shut everything in or out, through those of translucent glass or plastics to sheets of glass narrowly banded with metal (Fig. 310B). Folding doors of wood or bamboo slats or covered with fabrics are additional possibilities. Further, doors can be designed so that only part of them opens, such as Dutch or barn doors in which the top can be open but the bottom closed.

In rented quarters or in a home already built you can do less about the doors than about the windows, but the following are possibilities:

- Remove unneeded doors to create greater openness.
- Seal up or cover with a wall hanging doors that are unnecessary for traffic.
- Refinish doors and their frames so that they blend with the walls.
- Paint some or all doors in contrasting colors or decorate them so that they become dominant features.

If you plan to buy a house, it pays to look carefully at the location and design of doors. And if you are planning to build your own home, it pays to consider very carefully how doors, and openings without doors, can serve best.

Types of Doors

As with windows, doors can swing or slide and they can also fold.

Swinging doors, by far the most common type, like casement windows are hinged at one side. They are widely used because they are easy to operate, have simple hardware, can be made to close automatically with closing devices, and can be effectively weather- and sound-proofed. Their major disadvantage is that the arc through which they swing must be left free of furniture.

Sliding doors need not take otherwise usable room or wall space when opened, can disappear completely to give a great sense of openness. They do, of course, have to go some place and can vanish into a wall. Or they can slide in front of a wall, often done when door and wall are glass (Fig. 310A). Although sliding doors can be suspended entirely from overhead tracks, they usually perform better if they also slide along tracks or grooves in the floor (which are hard-to-clean dirt catchers). On the debit side, the movements required to open and close them are not so easy to make as for swinging doors, and there is no inexpensive way to make a sliding door, especially a screen door, close itself. Often they do not glide so quietly and smoothly as one would wish; and the backs of sliding doors cannot have narrow shelves or hooks, which are especially convenient on closet doors. They can be very much wider than swinging doors which emphasizes horizontality and spaciousness.

Folding doors slide along tracks, usually at the top, and fold like an accordion. They take little space when collapsed and come in diverse colors and textures. In general, they are not so soundproof as other types and sometimes tend to stick, but they are excellent for those situations in which you want to be able to open or close a large opening inexpensively (Fig. 323A).

Location of Doors

Because doors and windows have so many points in common, almost everything said about locating windows applies to doors, but there are two important differences. Doors govern traffic paths and they are often opaque.

Traffic paths, like highways, are usually best when short and direct and when they disturb as little as possible areas for work or quiet relaxation.

Furniture arrangement is largely controlled by door location because you ought to leave a traffic path between every set of doors in a room and allow space for those that swing. From this point of view, have as few as feasible and keep the necessary ones close together if other factors permit.

Views and privacy are controlled by door location and material. In a bedroom, for example, a well-placed door, even when open, does not bring bed or dressing area into full view. Doors between cooking and dining areas are best when they do not direct attention toward the major kitchen work areas. Opaque materials are typically used where there is no view and privacy is always needed. Translucent materials function well where there is neither view nor the need for absolute privacy. Transparent materials allow two-way vision.

Light can come through doors as well as windows, and transparent doors are frequently combined with windows (Figs. 310A and 325) as a means to architectural unity. Glass doors give a special pleasure in that they permit one both to look and to go out.

A

Above. Oak folding doors that match the walls open almost completely to reveal as much of a buffet counter and storage area as desired. When pushed back, they take almost no space. Lawrence Schwall, architect. (*Pella Wood Folding Doors*)

Right. An unpretentious, inviting entrance is recessed under a projecting roof. Patterned glass suggests without disclosing what is beyond. L. R. Davidson, architect. (*Blue Ridge Glass Co.*)

B

Ventilation can be quickly accomplished by opening doors, especially in opposite walls, during hot weather. There is nothing like opening doors to "air out the house," but ordinary doors are not suited to gentle, controlled venting.

Heat and cold coming through light-transmitting doors is the same as that coming through windows and the same comments apply. Opaque doors stand somewhere between windows and walls: they do an adequate job if well weather-proofed and concentrated on the side away from winter winds.

Cleaning a glass door is like cleaning a window except that finger marks are more frequent and it is easier to get at both sides. Opaque doors, too, get their full share of finger marks particularly around the knobs—metal or plastic plates help a little but are seldom very attractive.

Curtaining is usually accomplished with draw curtains that can cover, or expose, the entire area of glass (Fig. 319). The best solution is to locate glass doors where they need never be curtained, but that is not always easy. In older houses, "sash" curtains are sometimes used on glass doors.

Door frames and trim today are usually reduced to a minimum. Door trims, however, are useful. They put a durable, easily cleaned, and replaceable-if-necessary band at a part of the wall getting above-average abuse. They also inexpensively mask the joining of two materials if walls and doors are not the same.

Design of Doors

In historic houses the design of doors gave architects and craftsmen opportunity to display their inventiveness and thereby to enrich interior and exterior design. Even the crudest doors of vertical planks held interest through their structure, material, and typically decorative nails and hardware. Panel doors, in which the spaces between the necessarily heavy framework were filled with thinner wood, set the stage for exercises in proportion and design of moldings (Fig. 263A).

Today the majority of doors are of the completely plain, flush-panel type in which plywood sheathes a strong but light core. They are easy to clean, as beautiful as the wood (or other covering) used, and as inconspicuous and noncommittal as can be. Hinges can hardly be seen and the knob is typically a simple little ball projecting on a simple shaft from a small circular disk. These are popular today because they are inexpensive and emphasize continuity and movement. There are, however, doors and doorknobs (Fig. 298) that satisfy the increasing urge toward positive, enriching pattern.

Design and location of windows and doors are fundamentals in home planning. The most conspicuous and the most used parts of walls, they deserve far more thought than they often get. Two common errors result from failing to balance all factors. The first is putting doors and windows of diverse character wherever they seem to be needed, a practice that leads to architectural chowchow. The second is insistence on certain kinds of doors and windows organized arbitrarily in what may be a visually satisfying pattern but which does not meet utilitarian needs. These are extremes to avoid. The openings in our homes can be beautiful and practical —if both aims are kept in mind.

A simple but audacious two-story grid of windows and a door projects a hillside living room into a breath-taking panorama of trees, water, and mountains. Joseph Esherick, architect. (*Photograph by Rondal Partridge*)

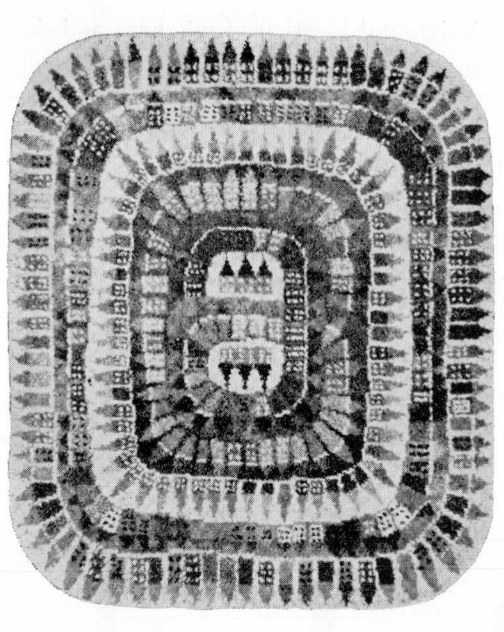

13. Floors, Floor Coverings, and Ceilings

FRANK LLOYD WRIGHT ONCE SAID that "A house is more a home for being a work of art," a philosophy he applied as creatively to floors and ceilings as to other aspects of home design. In the Prices' home (Fig. 328), floors and ceilings are integrated with walls and windows to shape space and give it character. The wide passageway, rhythmically divided into bays, has a plain light horizontal ceiling that unobtrusively broadens this space, subtly directs attention on and out. The floor is prominent, and this is one appropriate way to design a circulation area. Dark, polished concrete is a handsome foil for the rugs, designed by Mr. Wright, in which squares, rectangles, and lines are inventively diversified. They accent the length of the hall while acknowledging its varying widths. Their strict geometry is as consonant with the architecture of the house as with the loom on which they were woven.

Both floor and ceiling are appropriately dif-

Above. A pile rug, handwoven by Ingrid Dessau, which is an abstract representation of a town. (*Photograph by Conrad Brown*) ferent in the living room. This is primarily a space for sitting and relaxing, not for walking through. The large plain rug has no leading lines or directional patterns, but the ceiling is worth looking at. Following the lines of the hip roof, the central section rises in proportion to the size of the room and this ascendancy is underlined by wood battens. The lower horizontal portion establishes a plane, which continues throughout the house, at human scale. It binds together the horizontal floor and sloping ceiling, gives a sheltering effect, and also provides a place for direct and indirect lighting.

Floors and ceilings, together with walls and windows, are the big enclosing surfaces that keep us warm, dry, and safe. Depending on their design and material, they can raise, depress, or do nothing for our spirits. They can be commonplace or individualized, costly or inexpensive, easy or difficult to maintain. Appropriateness and relationships are of uppermost importance in these big, permanent architectural elements. One can play around to his heart's content with flower arrangements and table settings, pictures on the wall, or different furniture arrangements which cost only one's time. Not so with the major architectural elements where changes are usually troublesome and expensive. New concepts of space, new materials and colors have lifted the design of floors and ceilings well out of the routine-necessary category into the realm of positive, contributing elements.

► FLOORS

Floors are flat, horizontal surfaces meant to be walked on, less often to be run, jumped, or danced on. They take a limited amount of wheel traffic, such as vacuum cleaners, service carts, and children's toys. They support us and our furniture and provide insulation against the earth's cold dampness. As we all know, but sometimes forget, floors get the greatest wear and most dirt of any part of the house. But floor design and materials are not so completely mundane as these factors imply. In fully developed architecture, they contribute to the expressive character of the whole house. They can define and separate areas without benefit of walls, suggest traffic patterns, and be as dominant or subordinate as one wishes.

In houses with basements, floors are typically of two sorts. Basement floors are concrete slabs poured directly on the earthen subgrade or a foundation of crushed rock. Those above grade usually consist of supporting floor joists, a rough floor of inexpensive wood laid diagonally for strength, heavy paper to retard the passage of air and moisture, and a finish flooring of hard wood. Or sheets of plywood or composition board can be used

A

Floors and ceilings in the Harold C. Price, Jr., residence in Bartlesville, Oklahoma, express as well as fulfill their functions. Frank Lloyd Wright, architect.

Above. In the passageway, a dominant rug calls attention to the floor. Definite and directional, the design suggests movement. The subordinate ceiling has rhythmically placed lighting fixtures.

Below. In the living room, a large plain rug is a subdued but unifying base for furniture, walls, and ceiling. Accented with wood battens, the ceiling contributes to the room's spaciousness. (*Photographs by Maynard Parker. Courtesy of* House Beautiful)

B

instead of the finish flooring, and these can be covered with such hard floorings as linoleum or vinyl tiles, or with carpets.

The growing popularity of one-story, ground-hugging, basementless houses has changed these procedures. In such houses, floors are often concrete slabs basically like those in basements but with important differences. They are reinforced with metal to minimize cracking and the surface is hardened, integrally colored, and carefully smoothed. Heating masonry floors has greatly lessened one former disadvantage—cold, tired feet—for it appears that combined coldness and hardness rather than hardness alone brings foot fatigue. In summer, however, with the heat turned off the coolness of such floors is welcome. Concrete slab floors reduce construction and maintenance costs. They also make practicable a low house intimately related to outdoor areas, as in Figure 328A.

The matter of suitable floors and floor coverings deserves early and careful planning, especially in view of possibilities hardly dreamed of a generation ago. Some of the important factors are these:

- **Durability** usually comes first because floors take severe punishment, chiefly from the abrasion of feet but also from the weight of furniture, especially when moved. Durable floors have a surface sufficiently tough to prevent wearing through to another material. They do not crack, splinter, or disintegrate, nor do they get permanently indented or otherwise make noticeable the hard use they get.
- **Economy of upkeep** is of great importance, and the generalizations in Chapter 4 about easily maintained surfaces pertain to floors. Upkeep is lessened when floor materials resist stains and bleaches, do not absorb liquids or dirt. Neutralized colors near middle in value and camouflage patterns reduce labor, regardless of material or surface texture. Floor areas without jogs or crevices are easier to sweep, vacuum, or mop than those of complicated shape. And somewhat surprisingly, certain tests indicate that carpeted floors take less labor to maintain than do those with hard surfaces.
- **Resilience** cushions impact, thereby reducing foot fatigue, breakage of things dropped, and the noise produced when we move around.
- **Warmth,** actual and apparent, is welcome in all but excessively hot climates. There are three ways to make floors actually warm: put the heating elements in the floor, have the heat in the ceiling so that the floor will be warmed by radiation, and insulate the floor. There are also three ways of making floors look warm: warm hues, middle to dark values, and soft textures.

A

B

Floor treatment holds manifold possibilities for visual design.

Above. Wide bands exaggerate a room's length, call attention to the end walls. The same rubber tile laid in alternating squares seems to make the room larger, directs more attention to the floor if the color contrast is great. (*Courtesy of* LIVING for Young Homemakers)

Below. Jaspé striped linoleum in two colors, laid with the stripes at right angles to each other, visually differentiates two areas. Also worth noting are the lighting fixture, bulletin board, and toy storage. (*Congoleum-Nairn*)

C

- **Light reflection** is usually associated with ceilings and walls, but much light hits floors day and night. The more floors reflect the brighter your home will be and the lower the utility bills. Notice how much more light is reflected by the rugs in the Prices' hall than by the dark concrete floor.
- **Sound absorption** is not the same as the noise reduction resulting from resilience. Rough, porous materials lessen noise already made, an observation that is as true of floors as of ceilings, walls, and furnishings. Pile rugs rate high on this quality.
- **Appearance** brings us again to that everyman's land of likes and dislikes and to appropriateness to specific situations. Few question the importance of use and cost. Many overlook the strategic potential of floors as sources of personalized esthetic expression and satisfaction. We have seen that they can be keyed up, as in the Prices' hall, or subordinated as in their living room. They can alter the apparent size, shape, and character of a room or suggest division of space without walls (Figs. 330A and B). Many illustrations in previous chapters are worth looking at again specifically for the design and treatment of floors.

Obviously these are broad generalizations to which there are many exceptions. For example, durability and economy of upkeep are vastly more critical in kitchens and family rooms than in studies where appearance might be more significant. These factors also set up conflicts, for there is as yet no one flooring material that is perfect in every respect. Thus, once again, it is sensible to decide what is most important and to make such compromises as are necessary. In part, at least, this explains the widespread practice of covering the permanent floor, partly or completely, with removable fabrics. It is logical to distinguish between the *hard* flooring materials that are more or less permanent and either part of the structure or securely fastened to it, and the *soft* rugs or carpets that are relatively easy to remove.

Hard-surface Flooring Materials

The rock floors of caves or ground beaten down by use were probably the first hard-surface floors used by man. Stone smoothed and set in place, brick and tile and wood followed. Until a century or so ago these were the sum total of possibilities. Today many new materials supplement the older materials. The chart on pages 334 to 337 briefly summarizes the characteristics of those frequently used now. In comparison with rugs, almost all are durable, cool and not very resilient, more or less stain-resistant, and can be cleaned with a mop. But these general similarities should not obscure

Hard flooring materials are diversified. The visual effect comes from the inherent qualities of the material, its size and shape, color and pattern, and the way in which it is laid.

A

B

Stone and ceramic tile are durable indoors and out, easily maintained.

Above left. The beauty of flagstone lies in its subtle variations in color and texture. When sizable pieces are laid in irregular patterns, the effect is ruggedly informal and bold in scale. (*Libbey-Owens-Ford Glass Company*)

Above right. Eight-inch squares of dark red, unglazed tile are orderly yet not formal, moderately large in scale. Small mosaic tile, glazed in many colors has a quite different character, as shown in Figures 280I and 275B. (*Leslie I. Nichols*)

Wood has visual warmth, infinitely varied grain, and some resilience.

Below left. Random width, wood-pegged planks have a homespun appearance, especially when the grain is pronounced. They accentuate one dimension of a room. (*E. L. Bruce Company*)

Below right. Small, mosaic blocks of different woods have a nonrepetitive, checkerboard pattern. (*Miller Brothers Company*)

C

D

Composition flooring is available in many sizes and shapes, literally hundreds of colors and textural effects. It offers the least expensive way of individualizing floors. Much depends on the way in which the pieces are laid.

A

B

Above left. Long, narrow asphalt tiles in four harmonizing colors are laid so that the short ends do not align. Home owners can derive much pleasure from organizing such patterns to suit their rooms and their personal preferences. (*Flintkote Company*)

Above right. Asterisk-shaped inserts suggest the most frequently used path in a combination laundry and bathroom. Many other designs are on the market, and you can plan and cut your own. (*Armstrong Cork Company*)

Many of the newer products have genuine intrinsic beauty, satisfying from a distance and rewarding when studied closely.

Below left. Large, irregular chunks of cork have a fascinating organic beauty. Vinyl, fused to the cork under heat and pressure, resists stains, moisture, and wear. (*Armstrong Cork Company*)

Below right. Translucent vinyl chips bound together with transparent vinyl has a slightly embossed surface that, together with the intricate pattern, camouflages scratches. (*Armstrong Cork Company*)

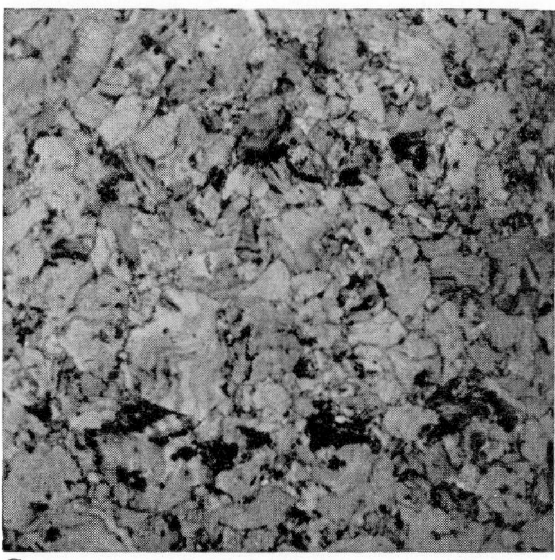

C

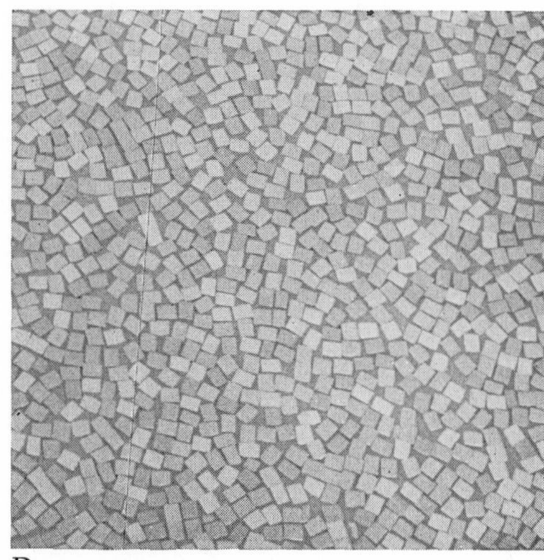

D

Material	Source or Composition	Use	Size and Shape	Patterns
Asphalt Tile	Natural asphalt, asbestos, or mineral fibers, pigments.	Recommended for laying over concrete directly on ground. Especially suitable in much-used areas.	Standard is 9″ x 9″ but others available.	Tiles are plain marbleized; laying creates typical ti patterns.
Concrete	Cement, sand, aggregates, and water.	Can be left uncovered indoors or out; also the standard base for clay tile, brick, and stone; can be covered with wood, resilient flooring, or rugs.	Usually poured in slabs but tiles are available. Sometimes marked off in rectangles by wooden or metal screeds.	Can be given surfa interest by exposi aggregates. Terraz has mosaiclike p terns from marble chips.
Cork	Cork shavings and granules compressed and baked to liquefy natural resins.	Floors not subject to hard wear, water, grease, stains, or tracked-in dirt.	Squares 9″ by 9″ or 12″ by 12″; also rectangles 6″ by 12″, 12″ by 24″, etc.	Chunks of cork different color g fine to coarse t tural patterns.
Cork (vinyl)	Same as cork but with vinyl added as a protective sealer.	Any floor where heavy-duty durability is not important.	Same as cork.	Same as cork.
Linoleum	Wood flour, ground cork, gums, linseed oil, and pigments pressed onto burlap foundation.	Floor of any room but especially kitchens, bathrooms, children's rooms, activity spaces, and the like; also suitable for tops of counters, desks.	Standard tiles are 9″ x 9″; in rolls 6′ to 15′ wide.	Practically unlimit ease of inlaying p mits individual signs.
Rubber Tile	About 25% rubber and 75% minerals and cotton fibers.	Similar to linoleum except that it can be laid directly over on-grade concrete floors.	9″ by 9″ to 18″ by 36″.	Usually plain or marbleized.
Stone	Slate, flagstone, marble, etc.	Chiefly entrances, outdoor paving, and near fireplaces, but can be used in any room except kitchen.	Usually not more than 2′ square; rectangular or irregular.	Natural veining, shapes of stones, a patterns in wh they are laid.
Tile and Brick (clay)	Heat-hardened clay. Tile is usually glazed, brick only occasionally.	Areas getting hard wear, moisture, and dirt—entrances, hallways, bathrooms, activity space, or any place except kitchen where effect is wanted.	Tiles are ½″ to 12″ square; or rectangular, hexagonal, etc. Standard bricks are approximately 2″ x 4″ x 8″.	Typical patterns come from arrange ments of single combined colors. Tile, however, w varied designs.

LOORING MATERIALS

Colors	Durability	Maintenance	Comments
ıll range of hues but lors are neutralized; coming available in hter, clearer colors.	Excellent but can be cracked by impact and dented by furniture. Some types not grease-proof.	Easy—mopping and usually waxing.	Least expensive composition flooring; eight times as hard as rubber tile; noisy; and slippery when waxed.
mited range of low-ensity colors, but can painted, waxed with lored wax, etc.	Very high except that it often cracks and can be chipped. Serious damage difficult to repair.	Markedly easy if sealed against stains and grease. Waxing deepens color and gives lustrous surface but is not necessary.	Least expensive since it can be both base and finish flooring. Hard and noisy. Cold (welcome in summer) unless radiantly heated.
ght to dark brown.	Comparable to linoleum. Dented by furniture, etc.	Not easy. Porous surface absorbs dirt, etc., which is hard to dislodge. Sweep, wash, and wax.	Luxurious in appearance; resilient and quiet.
me as cork.	Same as cork, but more resistant to denting, dirt, grease.	Very easy. Sweep, wash, and wax as needed.	Vinyl makes colors richer; less resilient and quiet than cork.
actically unlimited. ew types come in light, ear colors as well as rk and neutral.	Moderately high in better grades. Resists denting better than asphalt but not so well as rubber and vinyl flooring.	Moderately easy—wash and wax, do not use varnish or shellac.	Attractive, flexible, quiet, moderate in cost. No real disadvantages, except need for frequent waxing.
nlimited range; often ighter and clearer an in linoleum or phalt.	Similar to linoleum but more resistant to denting. Some types damaged by grease.	Average—washing with soap and water; wax or rubber polish.	Very similar to linoleum, but twice as resilient and twice as expensive.
sually grays and tans ith variation in each ece and from one ece to another. Marble mes in wide range of lors.	Very high but chipping and cracking difficult to repair.	Easy—minimum sweeping and mopping.	Solid, permanent, earthy in appearance. Usually bold in scale. Hard and noisy. Cold if floor is not heated.
icks usually red. lazed tiles in all colors.	Generally high but depends on hardness of body and glaze. May chip or crack but fairly easy to replace. Appearance of brick and unglazed tile usually improves with wear.	Easy—dusting and washing. Unglazed types can be waxed. Porous types absorb grease and stains.	Satisfyingly permanent and architectural in appearance. Can relate indoor to outdoor areas. Noisy, expensive, and cold.

Material	Source or Composition	Use	Size and Shape	Patterns
Vinyl	Vinyl resins. Best grades are 100% vinyl. (Less expensive and durable have only vinyl surface.)	Any indoor floor. Special types available for basement floors.	Usually 9″ by 9″ tiles. Also by the roll.	Great variety w new designs com to market frequen Trend away from patterns imitating other materials t ward those developed from the material and its u
Vinyl-asbestos	Durable vinyl combined with moisture-resistant asbestos.	Any indoor floor including on-grade and below-grade concrete floors.	9″ by 9″ tiles are typical.	Mottled, spattere striated, and cork are most frequen seen.
Wood (Hard)	Oak, birch, beech, maple, pecan.	Any room in house except kitchen and bathroom; usually most of it is covered by rugs.	Strips 1½″ to 3½″ wide; planks 2″ to 8″; parquet blocks 9″ x 9″, etc.	Color and grain wood. Usually laid parallel strips; a comes in blocks varied parquetry p terns.

the equally important differences among them. Brick, stone, and clay tile are costly but last for generations, indoors or out, while cheap enamelled linoleum wears out in a few years. Cork and rubber are much more resilient than asphalt or concrete. Inlaid linoleum, available in dozens of patterns usually with a mat surface and somewhat neutralized colors, is not expensive. Vinyl comes in many diversified patterns and the colors can be fresh and bright. It resists stains notably, and often has a naturally glossy surface, but it is not cheap. These floorings have become as respectable in living rooms as they are serviceable in kitchens.

Colors	Durability	Maintenance	Comments
Wide range including refreshing light, bright colors. In some, translucency gives depth of color rivaling marble.	Promises to give very long surface. Cuts tend to be self-sealing. Resists almost everything including household acids, alkalies, or grease; denting, chipping, etc.	Very easy. Built-in luster lasts long; imperviousness keeps foreign matter on surface.	Pleasant satiny surface at home in any room. Quiet and resilient. Moderately expensive—but the nearest approach to an attractive, durable, easily maintained floor.
Fairly wide range but usually muted.	High general durability, resistant to grease, alkali, and moisture. Can be dented by furniture, etc.	Among the easiest. Resilient underlay retards imbedding of dirt.	As hard and noisy as asphalt and not so durable but more easily kept in good condition. Cost is about halfway between asphalt and all-vinyl.
Light red, yellow, tan, or brown.	High but shows wear.	Medium high; must be sealed, then usually waxed and polished.	Natural beauty, warmth; fairly permanent, moderately easy to refinish; but fairly hard, noisy, moderately difficult to keep looking well, especially in traffic areas. Moderately expensive.

► RUGS AND CARPETS

Soft floor coverings add warmth, visual softness, and texture, resilience and quietness, and a friendly intimacy to floors. As with wallpaper, soft floor coverings give rooms a "furnished" look even with little furniture. They explicitly relate the floor to upholstered furniture, curtained windows, and clothed occupants. With their color, texture, and pattern, they contribute markedly to the character of homes, and they, like hard materials, can alter the apparent size and shape of rooms. Technical advances together with new concepts of taste and housekeeping have added countless new possibilities for individual expression.

A few definitions are in order. **Rugs** are made or cut to standard sizes and are usually not fastened to the floor. **Carpeting** is a type of rug that comes by the yard in widths from 27 inches to 18 feet or more, is cut and pieced (if necessary) to cover all the floor, and is fastened down. **Broadloom** refers to floor textiles woven on looms more than 36 inches wide—the term does not describe the weave, fiber, color, pattern, or any quality other than width.

A

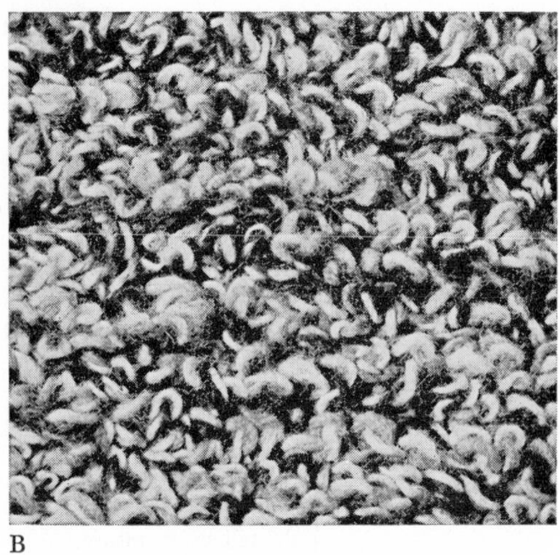

B

Pile rugs are liked for their softness, quietness, and durability. Except for very light or very dark solid colors, they mask a little dust and minor damage. Wool and cotton are the most used natural fibers; synthetics include rayon, nylon, and Acrilan. They are availabe in countless colors, textures, and patterns.

Textures range from velvety smoothness to woolly roughness and show marked differences in character and scale.

Above left. Cut pile in solid colors is uniformly smooth and soft, complacently harmonious with almost everything. This example is tuft-woven Acrilan. (*Firth Industries, Inc.*)

Above right. Rugged and informal, coarsely looped carpet rayon in four colors would not show crushing. (*Bigelow Rugs and Carpets*)

High and low, looped and cut pile can be combined in many patterns.

Below left. Identical in fiber and colors to the plain carpet directly above, this "Companion" design could be used for visual separation of areas without loss of continuity. The pattern, inspired by a Spanish tile, is carried out in knotted, twisted, and cut pile. (*Firth Industries, Inc.*)

Below right. Twelve-inch squares with parallel lines in high and low cut wool pile are architectural in character. Insets of different colors make personalized designs possible (*Waite Carpet Company*)

C

D

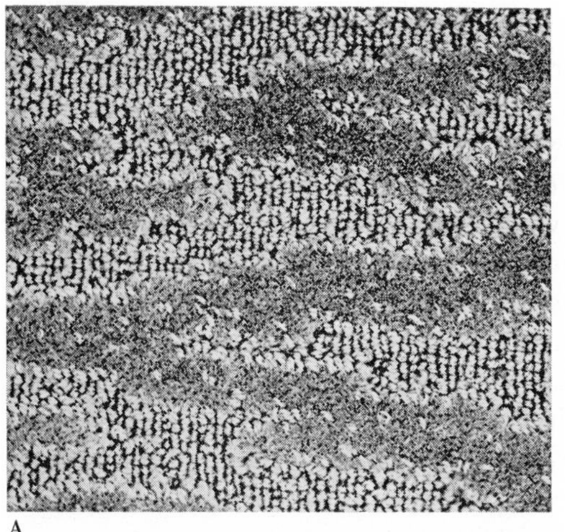
A

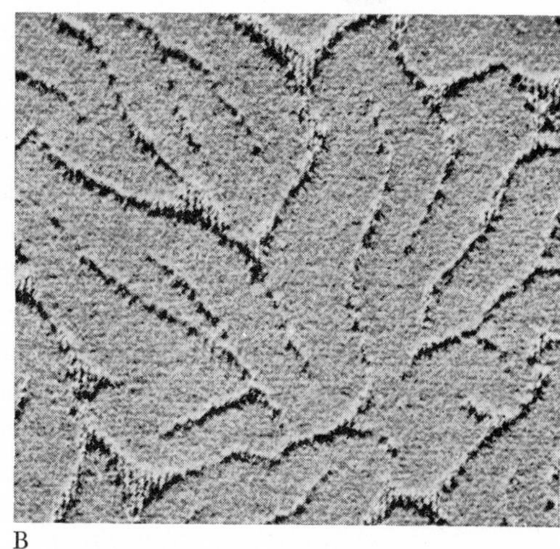
B

Natural forms continue to inspire carpet designers.

Above left. Blending the easy movement of a quiet surf with the sturdiness of Acrilan fibers, "Harbor View" is designed for minimal care and casual living. The design results from high-cut pile, shadowed with paler loops against a low-looped background. (*Magee Carpet Company*)

Above right. A strongly conventionalized leaf design has precisely delineated, varied rhythmic lines. (*Mohawk Carpets*)

Hand-woven rugs allow householders to have one-of-a-kind coverings on their floors.

Below left. Even a detail of a seventeenth-century Caucasian rug reminds us of the lasting beauty and practicality of these floor coverings, as handsome in modern as in traditional homes. (*Philadelphia Museum of Art*)

Below right. Jan Van Daalen interweaves brown, black, white, blue, and yellow nylon in an imaginative design. (*Smithsonian Institution*)

C

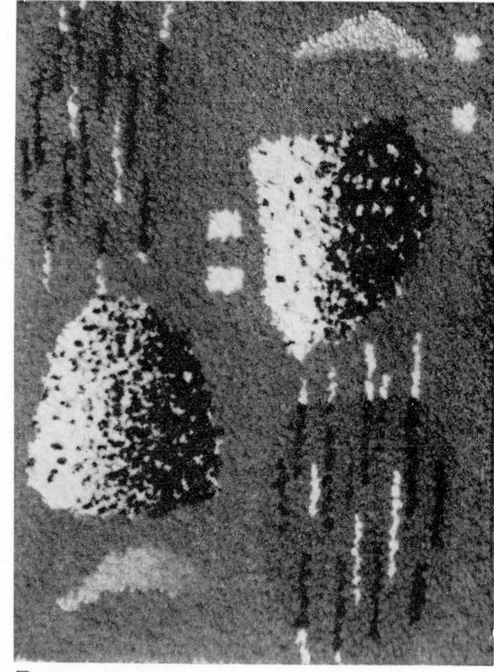
D

Most rugs used in homes today are textiles woven by machine. In the past few years there has been great increase in the use of synthetic fibers for the reasons cited in Chapter 10. Fibers affect cost, cleaning time, and appearance. Recall that wool is wiry, resilient, and long lasting, while cotton is soft and crushable, harder to keep clean but the colors can be brighter and the cost is lower. Carpet rayon is fairly strong and dirt resistant, the colors can be fresh and clear. More resilient than cotton, it is still crushable: both fibers perform best when the tufts are densely packed together and, in cotton, uncut pile is more serviceable than cut. Acrilan, nylon, and Saran are all durable and dirt-resistant, come in almost any color and an increasing diversity of textures. Acrilan has exceptional resilience but may be a fire hazard; nylon is amazingly long-wearing; and Saran scorns spills and stains.

A few more than half of the common types of rugs are pile weaves that are either *woven* or *tufted* (pp. 338-339). The remainder are various types of flat weaves illustrated on pages 342-343.

Durability of Rugs

The wearing quality of rugs is the product of several factors.

- Fibers vary conspicuously in the wear they will take, as noted earlier in this chapter and detailed on pages 238-241.

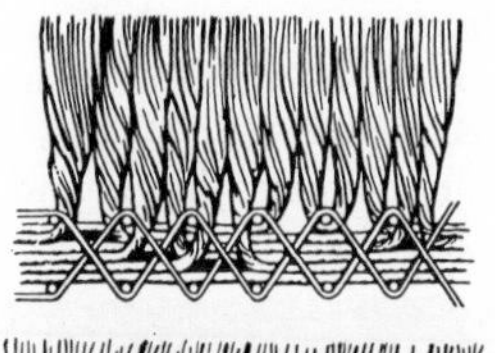

Woven carpeting is made on looms with pile and backing produced in one operation. There are four standard weaving processes.

Wilton comes in many patterns, solid or combined colors, and varied textures. The pile is cut or looped.

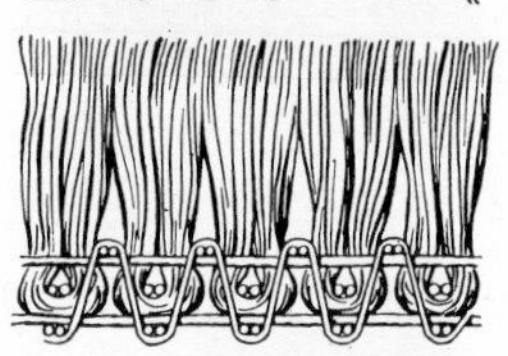

Axminster permits the greatest diversity of pattern because each tuft of pile is individually set by machine. The pile is usually cut.

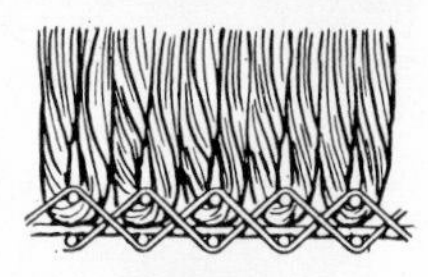

Velvet is generally monochromatic, but many textures can be created with high and low, or cut and uncut, pile.

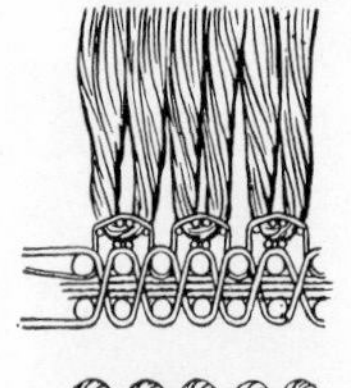

Chenille is thick, soft, and luxurious; can be woven in any pattern, combination of colors, or size and shape to 30 feet wide. (*Carpet Institute, Inc.*)

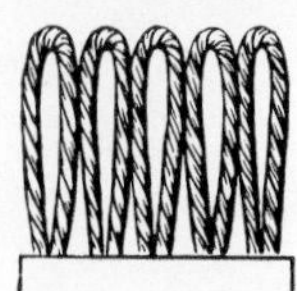

Tufted rugs have pile yarns sewn onto a fabric and usually secured with latex.

- In pile-weave rugs, density of pile is of great importance: the more tufts per square inch, the more durability. Length of pile is less important, although high pile often indicates good quality and may make the rug last longer. The backing, though, should be strong and flexible, tightly woven, and with the tufts held securely. In flat-weave rugs, tightness of yarn and weave prolong usefulness.
- Cushions can add years to a rug's life as well as making it more pleasant to walk on. Under small rugs, they should be skid-proof.
- Rugs that can be turned to equalize wear, or reversed, save money. Covering heavily used portions with small, replaceable rugs can be an economy, especially with wall-to-wall carpeting.
- Good care is essential. Embedded dirt is harmful, as are many stains and spots. Moths and mildew destroy or weaken many fibers.

Not a few rugs are replaced before completely worn out because they have faded, become permanently stained, or grown tiresome. With today's large windows it pays to get permanent colors or those that fade pleasantly. Stain-resistant fibers or soil-retarding treatments are good investments but no more so than floor coverings that will please one as long as they last.

Size of Rugs

Personal preferences, the way of living and character of the home, and cost largely determine the amount of soft floor covering in a home. Rugs, carpeting, or a combination of both can be appropriate.

Wall-to-wall carpeting makes rooms look luxurious and comfortable. If the pattern is quiet and the color muted, it makes rooms seem spacious. It is one of the best means of unifying a room or relating several adjacent spaces. Because it fits the room exactly and is fastened to the floor, carpeting gives a sense of security and permanence. Covering a larger area than a typical rug, it is more expensive. It cannot easily be sent to the cleaners, moved to another room or house, or turned to equalize wear. In general, carpeting seems more appropriate for living rooms, master bedrooms, and studies than for family rooms, children's bedrooms, entrances, and halls.

Rugs are adaptable. They can be had in any size or shape. If they cover the entire floor, or almost all of it as in the Prices' living room, the effect is similar to that of carpeting. They can also be small accents calling attention to a special part of the home or, when larger, can hold together a group of furniture. In homes with open plans, they can define areas without enclosing walls. With rugs, you can economize on size rather than quality and select those that make a specific impact on one part of a home.

Flat-weave rugs are comparatively inexpensive. They combine resilience with a cool, clean-cut appearance. All can be cleaned quickly with a broom or vacuum. Many can be easily washed. Nearly all can be reversed for twice the wear and half the cleaning. Kraft fibers, linen, hemp, rush, and sisal are the most common materials, but they can be woven or braided from almost any yarn. They are especially useful where pile might interfere with activities or the moving of furniture. Although not so diversified as pile weaves, flat-weave rugs come in many patterns and textures.

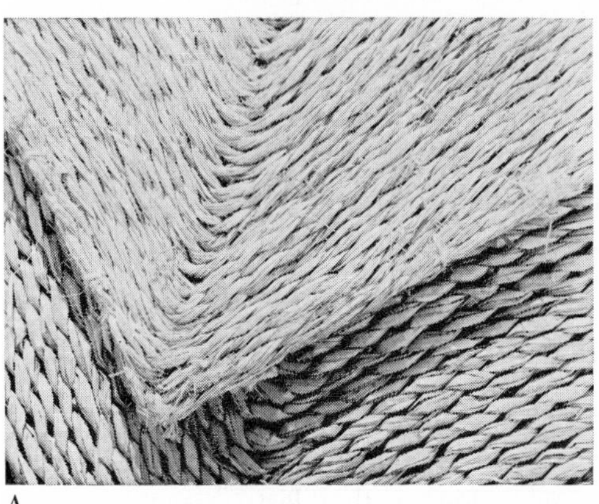

A

B

Hemp, rush, and sisal rugs, once relegated to porches, bring natural informality inside the house. Costing about as much as cotton rugs, they often stand up better under wear and cleaning.

Left. Hemp (*upper*) and rush (*lower*) are available in 1′ to 3′ squares that can be sewn together into rugs of any size or shape. (*Photograph by Ernest Braun. Courtesy of* Sunset)

Right. Heavy sisal, woven in a diagonal pattern, has a natural silky sheen. (*Continental Importing*)

C

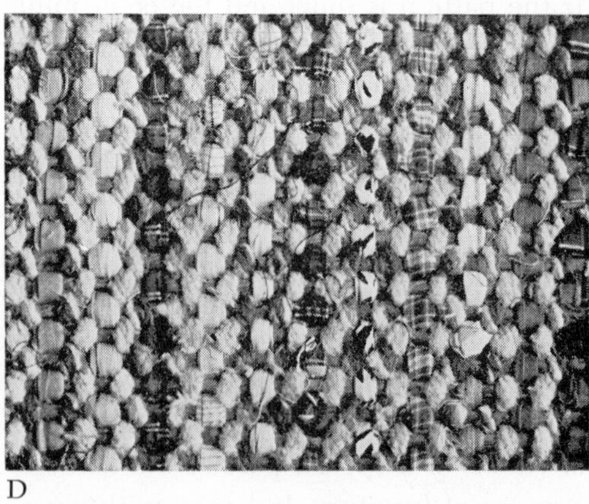

D

Linen and rayon come in many weaves and colors.

Left. Linen has long been noted for its handsome texture and durability. (*National Automotive Fibres*)

Right. Stripes of bright, many-colored textiles interwoven with rayon in a "hit-and-miss" design look contemporary yet recall the past. (*Waite Carpet Co.*)

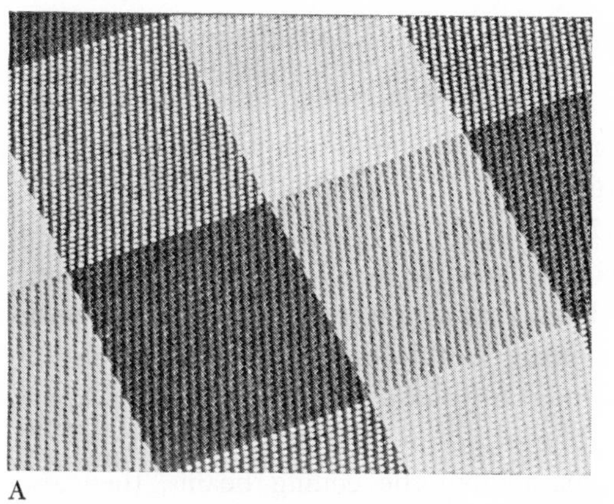
A

B

Kraft fibers are usually woven in plaid or tweedy patterns.

Left. Plaids have a long-established appeal. In rugs, bold plaids call attention to one part of the floor, emphasize length or breadth. (*Waite Carpet Co.*)

Right. Kraft combined with soft rayon fibers give a soft yet durable surface. (*Waite Carpet Co.*)

Below. Rugs hand woven of wool by the Southwest Indians are worth what they cost in terms of durability, beauty, and individuality. Their abstract designs, although regular and geometric, seem informal. (*Photograph by Milton Snow for Navajo Service*)

C

► BEAUTY AND INDIVIDUALITY IN FLOORS

In the living rooms shown on page 345, the floors were thoughtfully planned as integral elements appropriate to the whole design. Openness, continuity, and informality were sought and achieved in the suburban house by open planning, large windows, a strongly directional ceiling, and also by the floor treatment. Asphalt tile, neutral in color and with a scarcely noticeable striated pattern, coordinates all the major rooms in the house. It is quietly subordinate without being merely dull. An area rug, also of muted but of more varied colors, marks a pause in the big smooth expansiveness as a conversation center. The stripes in the rug are like a keyed-up version of the tile pattern; and, paralleling the ceiling beams, they also direct attention outward.

The rug in the city apartment is a focal point. Bold in its contrast of black and yellow, the rug keynotes the room's color scheme. With its opulent curves firmly organized around the intricate double medallion, the rug also holds attention in the center of this space from which there is no view. Rubber tiles, marbleized in black and white, differ from the rug in almost every specific detail yet their rich deep luster and color are consonant with the formal elegance of the room's rug, furnishings, and accessories. This leads to a positive, lively harmony quite different in character from the harmony resulting merely from repetition.

Applying the aims and principles of design to floors brings to mind both general and specific points. The expressive character and beauty of the material itself, its effect in the specific space for which it is being considered, and the relationship of all the floors in a home to one another and to the whole house deserve careful thought.

Form follows function suggests that color, texture, and pattern look as though they belonged on floors and were meant to be walked on. Thus many designs suited to draperies, upholstery, or wallpaper are not at home on floors.

Variety in unity applies to the material itself as well as to its relationship to the room and the whole home. Except for rugs definitely planned as accents, it is usually desirable to pay special heed to singleness of effect.

Balance, according to many, dictates that the floor should be darker than walls, furnishings, or ceiling. Exceptions, as numerous as they are delightful, prove that here as elsewhere there are no laws. It is, though, gratifying to have rooms in equilibrium and the relationship of floors, especially in color value, to other parts of the home is consequential.

Hard-surface, composition tiles and area rugs contribute to the markedly different character of two living rooms.

Right. Floor and ceiling emphasize spacious informality, direct attention through the window wall in a surburban house near Washington, D.C. Keyes, Smith, Satterlee, and Lethbridge, architects. (*Photograph by Robert C. Lautman. Courtesy of Luria Brothers*)

Below. Enclosing and somewhat formal, the conversation area in a city apartment is visually centered on an elaborately patterned rug. (*Photograph by Hans van Ness. Courtesy of* Good Housekeeping)

A

B

Rhythm of a type suggesting easy walking seems generally logical. Although only children as a rule dare express in their physical movements the rhythms indicated by strong lines, checkerboards, and sweeping curves (Figs. 330A and 345B), such marked rhythmic patterns unquestionably affect the feelings of adults.

Emphasis is a matter of giving each part of the home the degree of importance deemed most appropriate. Plain floorings and neutral colors emphasize spaciousness and free our eyes for other things. Patterns range from those that almost escape notice to those that are compelling climaxes.

Selection of Flooring Materials

Getting suitable floors takes time but the dividends from wise planning are large. Money can be saved and long-term enjoyment increased if you give more than a passing glance to every floor you see, not only in homes but in shops, restaurants, and public buildings. Visiting stores that sell floor coverings or looking at mail-order catalogs inform you of what is generally available. Periodicals on interior design, especially those written for professional architects and decorators, report new developments. When this information is related to an analysis of a specific situation, such questions as the following can be answered.

How much and what kind of use will the floor get?

- How heavy will the traffic be?
- Will it bring mud and grit?
- Will traffic be concentrated in spots or paths or evenly distributed?

How much will the floor cost?

- How much money should be spent on the "first cost" of floors?
- How much time or upkeep money is available?

What kind of beauty is indicated?

- Informal or formal? Delicate or rugged? Passive or active?
- What kind of visual relationship between one room and others, between indoors and outdoors, is wanted?

How individualized ought the floors to be?

- How can the floors best contribute to the character of the home?
- What degree and what kind of personalization is wanted?

Whatever the answers to such questions, you will do well to study large samples in the places they will go. Floors are too big, expensive, and heavily used to be taken lightly.

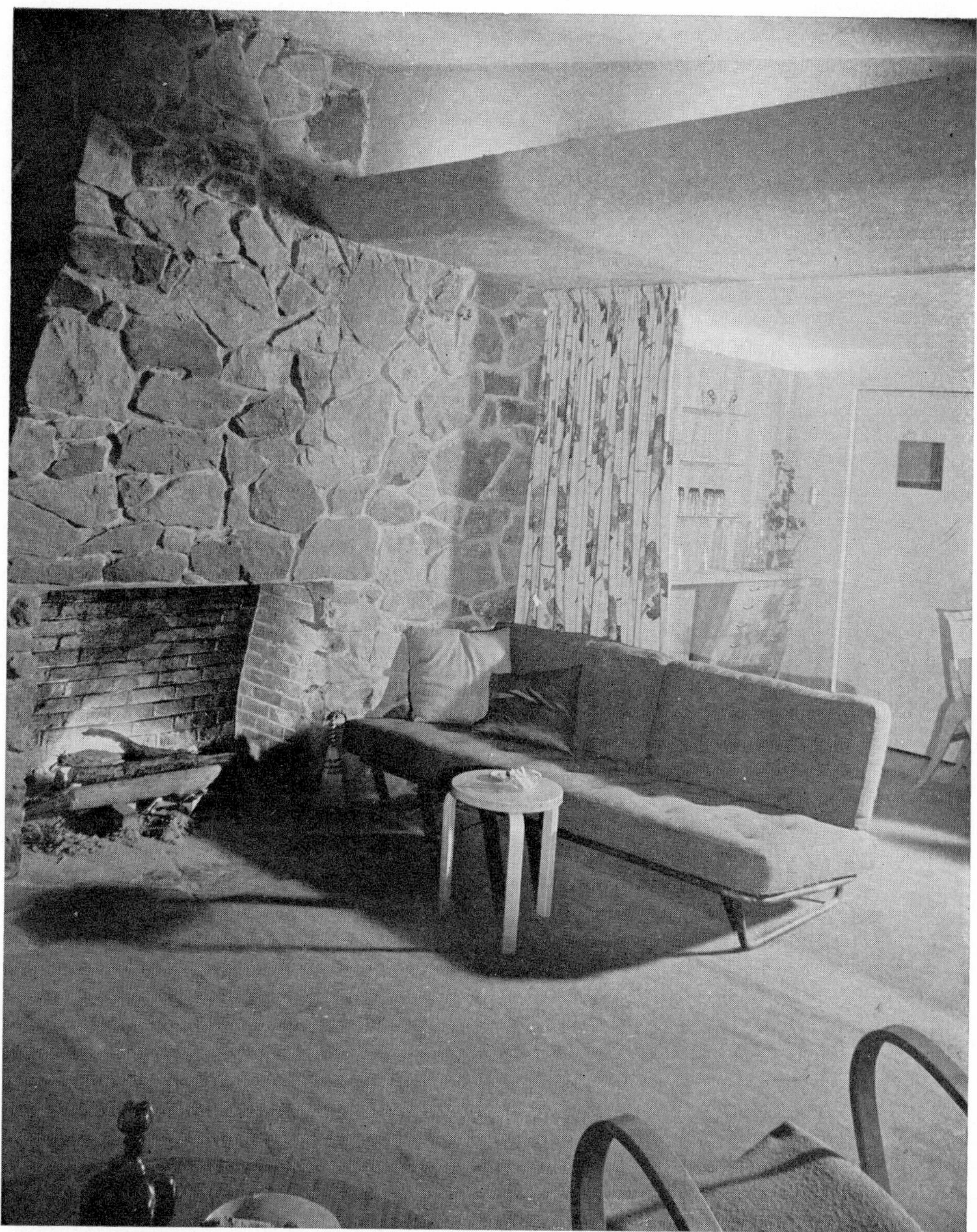

A sloping plaster ceiling in a Massachusetts home reaches its high point at the fireplace. The lowered section, which continues into the dining space, makes the sofa corner more intimate, provides indirect lighting, and improves acoustics. Carl Koch, architect. (*Photograph by Ezra Stoller*)

► CEILINGS

Although not *used* as are the other parts of the house, ceilings protect us and they affect illumination, acoustics, heating, and cooling. Typical ceilings are the same size and shape as the floors they parallel, are surfaced with plaster or composition board, and are painted white or some very pale hue. There are several reasons for this stereotype. It literally designs itself and is inexpensive to build and maintain. It gives unobtrusive spaciousness and it reflects light well. In most cases, we notice ceilings little and do correspondingly little about them. Perhaps it is just as well in a busy world to have one large undecorated surface in every room. But ceilings can be otherwise as we shall see in discussing their height, shape or direction, material, color and texture, and ornamentation.

Height

Ceiling heights are determined by resolving our needs for head room, air to breathe, and economy with our desires for space pleasantly proportioned and in character with our living. Minimum humane heights are 7′0″ for basements, 8′6″ for the first floor, and 8′0″ for the second. Heights beyond these may well be justified and lesser heights, especially in a part of a room, may seem cosy and sheltering.

There are notable and varied differences between the consequences of low and high ceilings. Low ceilings are enclosing, intimate, and typically informal. They reduce winter heating costs (except with radiant heat in floors) but make rooms warmer in summer. High ceilings often seem formal and dignified, as in Figures 12 and 263A, but without losing dignity they can express informality, as in Figures 86B and 349B. Unless seriously out of scale with a room's length and breadth, high ceilings are likely to make rooms seem airy and expansive.

Ceilings can also energize space and differentiate one area from another, as shown in Figure 347. Dining rooms can be set apart by lowering the floor as well as the ceiling (Fig. 32A). Hallways can be distinguished from living and dining rooms by low trellises, and quiet conversation areas can be demarcated by ceilings appropriately lower than those in the rest of the group-living space (Figs. 39A, 224, and 350). A desk corner in the living room can be anchored by a supplementary ceiling, low and horizontal (Fig. 59A). Much more than flat lids on the tops of boxes, ceilings can join with floors, walls, and furniture in an exciting complex of interpenetrating planes, as illustrated in Figures 43A, 86B, 140B and 141A, 352A and B.

A

Materials, shape, and color determine the character of ceilings.

Above. Double-pitched ceilings add interest and spaciousness, especially when the structure is exposed. In this example, the slope is comparatively gentle, and both wood beams and plaster have been painted the same color in keeping with the room's semiformal refinement. (*Gump's*)

Below. Rippling metal roof decking accented by louvered skylights, used both indoors and out, helps integrate an all-steel house with its gardens. A. Quincy Jones, architect. (*Photograph by Julius Shulman*)

B

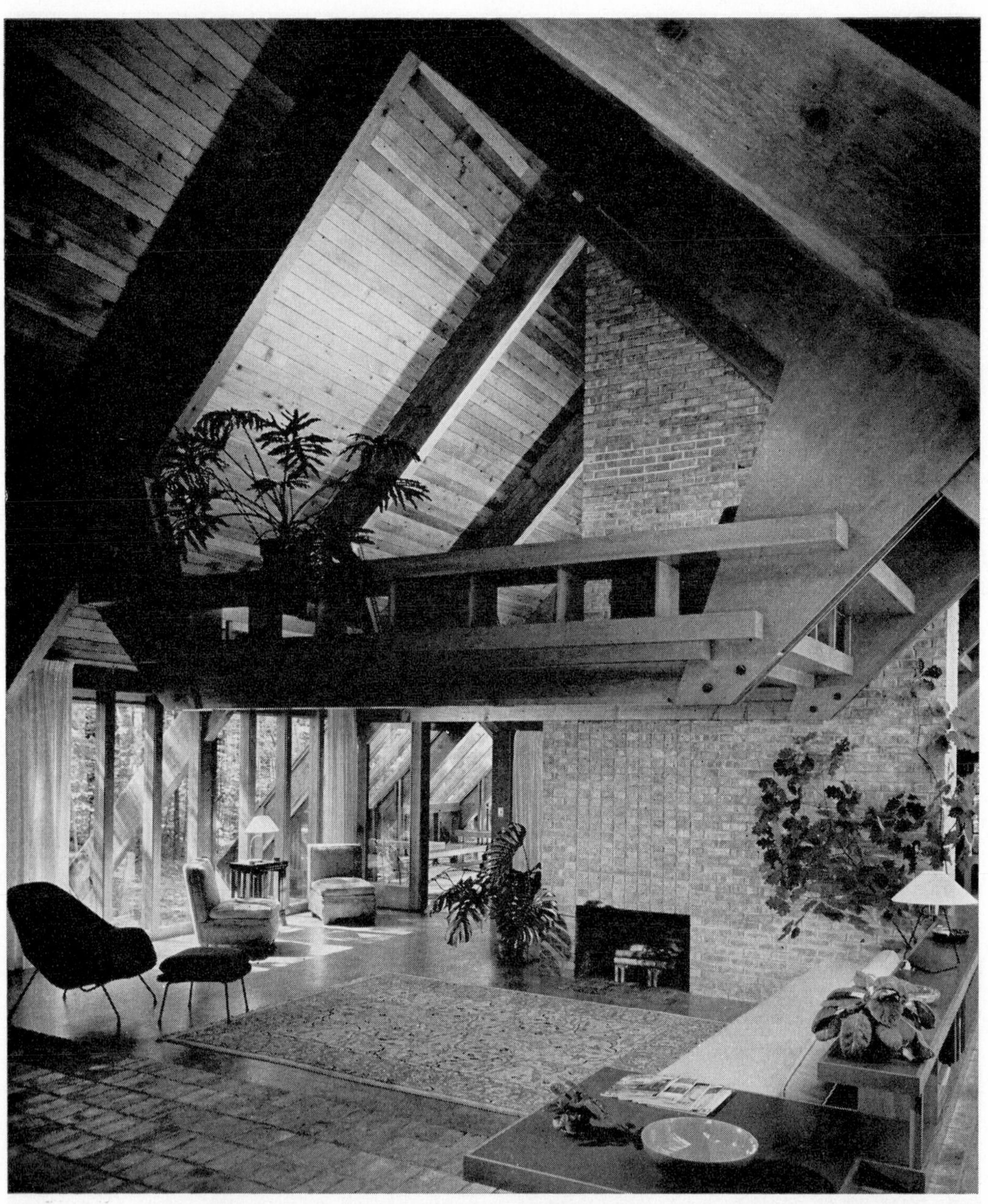

Ceilings take precedence over walls in a house in Midland, Michigan. Heavy timbers, which support the ceiling of matched cedar boards, rise from ground to ridge pole to give dramatic triangularity. In the living space, areas for different uses are indicated by brick or concrete floors, accented with a handsome Oriental rug. Alden B. Dow, architect. (*Photograph by Bill Hedrich. Hedrich-Blessing*)

Shape and Direction

It is easy and customary to have ceilings echo floors, but some of the deviations hold more interest.

Coved ceilings, in which walls and ceiling join in a curve rather than at right angles, make the space somewhat more plastic and flexible with a little of the spaciousness of the curved, continuing sky. If carried to their logical conclusions, ceilings become vaults or semispheres or free-form curves, wonderful shapes that may well become inexpensive possibilities with rapid developments in laminated wood, metal, thin-shell concrete, and plastic structures (Figs. 171, 229C, and Chapter 19).

Gabled, or double-pitched ceilings, follow the lines of the roof. Familiar in barns and many old English homes, they also let you look up in an increasing number of contemporary homes. They lead the eye along the line where the two halves meet and emphasize a room's dimensions and dominant directions (Figs. 117A, 268A, and 350).

Lean-to, single-slope, or shed ceilings also follow the roof. Informal and spacious, they handle sound well and call attention to the highest part of the room (Figs. 25A, 43A, and 347).

Materials

Plaster is the common ceiling material because it gives an uninterrupted surface that can join plastered walls without joints, thereby passively unifying the sides and top of a room. It can be smooth or textured, left plain, painted, or papered. Wallboard is much like plaster except that it leaves joints which can be concealed with tape and paint or emphasized with wood battens. Wood in stripes, planks, or plywood is both handsome and homelike. Acoustical tiles in many sizes and patterns bring texture and noise reduction. Metal has been used sparingly to date in homes but its possibilities are illustrated in Figures 224 and 349B.

Not all ceilings are opaque. There are skylights of clear or translucent glass or plastic, and there are luminous ceilings that fill rooms with diffused artificial light.

Color and Texture

Heaviness overhead is usually not pleasant unless the weight is clearly supported. That together with the advantages of having ceilings which reflect light explains the frequency of light colors and fine textures. Special effects of considerable impact, however, can be achieved with ceilings

A

B

painted or papered in strong colors or made of some of the darker woods. It is well to remember that ceilings, especially at night if much light is directed toward them, bathe everything below with their reflected color. A yellow ceiling, for example, would enliven yellows, oranges, or yellow-greens below it but would dull any blues or violets.

In conclusion, ceilings are the easiest part of the house to forget. If you do next to nothing with them, hardly one person in a hundred will notice. Moreover, a large plain foil has its merits whether people are conscious of it or not. On the other hand, the esthetic potentialities of ceilings—and floors—ought to be jealously husbanded, not neglected. Two houses that explore these potentialities are shown in Figures 352A and B. In the first, the roof is a dominant, urgent force suspended over a walled court, part of which has been enclosed with glass to form the house proper. Floors and walls have purposely been kept simple to intensify the excitement of the roof form. In the second, the floor is the compelling element, following as it does the stepped-down terracing of a hillside. Planting beds and floating steps mark and divide the levels, a redwood-scored concrete-aggregate patio becomes the dining room floor, and the rough texture of the living room rug repeats the pebbled concrete but with a softened touch. Conversely, the ceiling is smooth and undemanding, a gentle foil for the activity underfoot. In both houses, the architects have looked at floors and roofs creatively, not as mere protection but as motivating forces in their designs.

Structural advances are leading to new form-space concepts about floors, ceilings, and roofs.

Left above. In North Carolina, roof and ceiling of laminated wood, measuring 62 feet on each side, projects daringly over terraces and an enclosed space 38 feet square. Defined as a hyperbolic paraboloid, the shape has a continuously changing double curvature. Eduardo F. Catalano, architect. (*Photograph by Ezra Stoller*)

Left. In a house on sloping ground, the floors are a series of terraces connected by cantilevered steps. The ceiling is a light cover over this three-dimensional expression of the site. Boyd E. Georgi, architect. (*Photograph by Julius Shulman*)

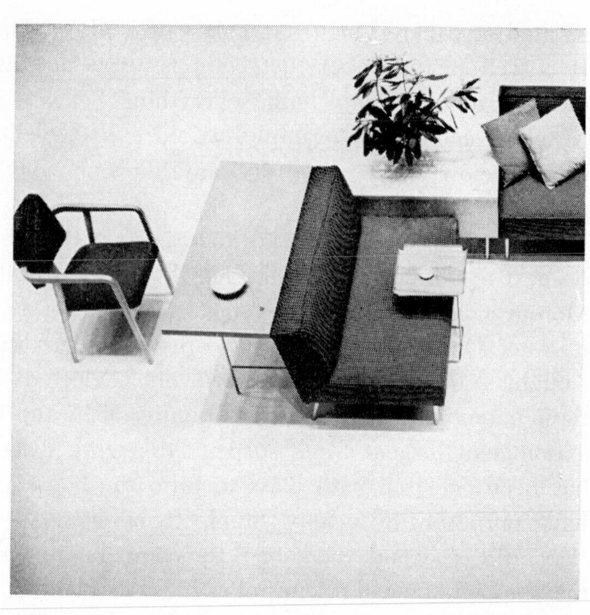

14. Furniture Selection and Arrangement

Furniture is the major transition between architecture and people. It enables us to impress our personal tastes on our living quarters even when they are architecturally the same as those of our neighbors and when most furniture is mass-produced. Proof of this can be found in Figures 356A and 357A. Although dissimilar in total effect, these two rooms have several general points in common. The unfurnished spaces were identical, and the furnishings for each were selected with a desired character and an arrangement in mind. In both, the furniture is organized into three groups, traffic paths are left open, and separation of living from dining space is suggested. Beyond these basic similarities are many specific differences.

The Merrys wanted and got a somewhat formal effect with emphasis on broad continuing forms unified by their similarity. Strict rectangularity of furniture and its arrangement leads to an architectural, almost built-in effect. This is particularly evident in the major conversation group.

Above. Unit furniture fits together compactly. (*Herman Miller Furniture Co.*)

Two sofas butting against a corner table fit one corner of the room compactly. A convenient L-shaped coffee table stresses the relation of this furniture group to the whole L-shaped space. Diagonally opposite is a secondary group consisting of an easy chair, small table, and radio-phonograph, all aligned with the walls. Living and dining areas are differentiated by a substantial storage cabinet projecting into the room. Dining chairs and table fit their space as precisely as do the storage units against the long wall. Unpatterned draperies and carpeting contribute to the over-all integration of architecture and furnishings.

Most immediately noticeable in the Dunns' room is variety and spontaneity, a feeling of openness and freedom to move pieces of furniture easily. The major conversation center, in the same logical corner as the Merrys', is a lively combination of straight-lined and curved pieces. A simple rectangular sofa, right angled to a wall-length bench, acts as an anchor. The reed chair supported by thin metal legs has slightly curved arms, the rectangular plywood coffee table has turned up edges and curved legs, the capacious encompassing lounge chair of molded plywood is made resilient with foam rubber and soft upholstery fabric. The lounge chair, placed diagonally near a three-legged round table, leads up to a sprightly room divider—two wood poles holding a painting in mid-air. Casually but not carelessly arranged, the other corner has a cabinet against the stairway wall, a chair at a congenial angle, and a floor lamp. Dining furniture faces the window. The entire long wall, given some prominence by its dark color, is unified with continuous benches flexibly used for seating, table space, and the base for interchangeable cabinets. A group of six family photographs are a focus of interest subtly related but subordinate to the larger portrait. This is a visually active room in which our eyes jump in staccato fashion from one intrinsically interesting object to another. Some pieces, the sculptural plywood chairs for example, assert their independence from the rectilinear space; others, such as the benches and storage units, obediently follow the lines of the room. Without rigid correspondence, there is agreeable relationship of forms to one another.

Equally practical and pleasing, these two rooms show how families with differing needs and attitudes can individualize their homes with the vast array of furniture available today.

Furniture has been discussed and illustrated on many preceding pages of this book. In Chapters 2, 3, and 4 we considered it as a factor in group and private living and in keeping house. In Chapters 5, 6, and 7 we focused attention on design quality and in Chapters 8, 9, and 10 we thought about materials. Keeping these previous discussions in mind, we are ready to think specifically about choosing furniture that has lasting values.

A

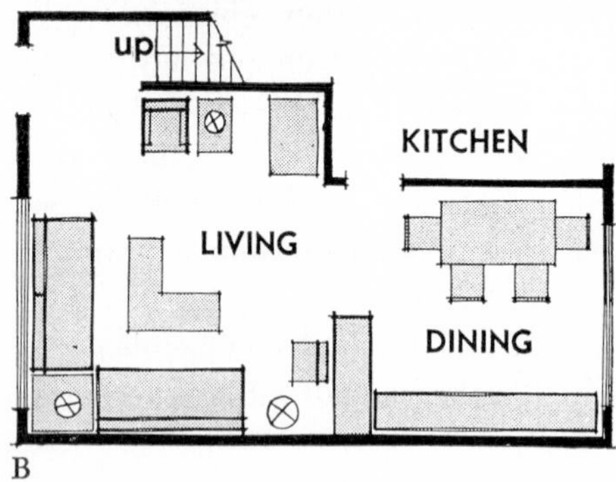

B

These two living-dining rooms in Minneapolis were exactly the same until they were furnished by families with differing ideas. Both are equally "good."

The O. W. Merry family sought regularity. In design and placement, the furniture corresponds with the lines and character of the room. (*Photograph by Reynolds, Infinity, Inc. Courtesy of* Better Homes and Gardens)

A

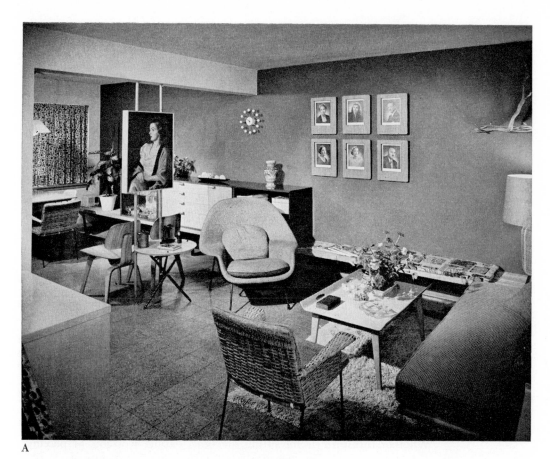

Less uniform in design and less regular in arrangement, the furniture in the O. W. Dunn home is a counterpoint of lively curves against rectangularity. (*Photograph by Reynolds, Infinity, Inc. Courtesy of* Better Homes and Gardens)

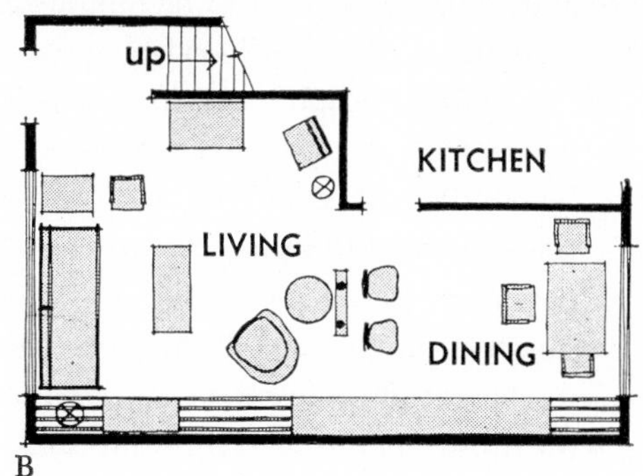

B

► SELECTING FURNITURE

Developing critical ability in the choosing of furniture depends not only on knowledge but on consciously sharpening your native aptitude for seeing and evaluating differences. "Practice buying" rather than random window-shopping is a profitable investment of time. In stores, catalogs, magazines, and books you can see many kinds of chairs, tables, and cabinets. Compare and contrast one with the others, noting carefully the excellences and weaknesses of each piece. Very few are totally good or totally bad. Some chairs and sofas look neat and trim, nicely scaled for typical rooms, but they may not be as comfortable as they look and the price may be high. Others may be very comfortable, durably constructed and upholstered, moderately priced, but big and bulbous. As you continue to look, think, and compare, you become able to size up *all aspects* of a piece of furniture and evaluate it as a whole. So that no factor will be overlooked, it pays to take a checklist along on paper or in your mind.

You also will build a sensible but personal scale of values. For some persons, comfort—or beauty—may transcend all other considerations although most of us seek a balance. Good as a general scale of values is, none can be applied rigidly to every specific situation. Living-room furniture, for example, seldom needs to be as easily maintainable as that in family rooms.

Use and Economy

Whether furniture be for sitting, sleeping, eating, working, or playing, use and economy are not to be minimized. Convenience, comfort, flexibility, space required, length of service, and cost of maintenance are major factors.

- **Convenience** applies chiefly to efficient storage facilities and to the ease with which often-moved furniture, such as dining and pull-up chairs, can be handled (Fig. 367B). All furniture, however, is moved from time to time and should be no heavier than necessary for use, strength, and appearance. Large pieces should be on glides or casters.
- **Comfort** applies chiefly to pieces on which we sit or sleep but also to the height of tables and desks and to leg room under them.
- **Flexibility** pertains to furniture that can be used in more than one room or for more than one purpose (page 359). Until recently most furniture was designed for one room and one use. Typical dining-room sets had a table, china cabinet, and buffet appropriate only in an ample, separate dining room. Only the chairs could be used elsewhere but no matter where placed they had a "dining room" character. Now many pieces are multipurpose. There are unit cabinets and chests suitable for any room

Multipurpose and unit furniture saves space and money.

A

Right. With little effort, this comfortable sofa converts into a single or double bed. Designed by George Nelson. (*Herman Miller Furniture Company*)

B

Below. Cases with drawers and doors, part of a coordinated line of unit furniture, are of amber mahogany and supported on aluminum legs. The doors are "textiles" woven of thin wood and aluminum rods. Designed by Edward Wormley. (*Dunbar Furniture Manufacturing Co.*)

C

and in many combinations, chairs usable anywhere. Tables are *easily* expanded or contracted, chairs or sofas convert to beds (Figs. 367A and 57A). This saves money and space, unifies homes with open plans.

- **Space required** becomes increasingly important as homes become smaller. Accordingly, contemporary designers have:

  Eliminated protruding moldings and curved legs on cabinets so that they can be fitted tightly together.
  Brought storage units to the floor or hung them on walls.
  Designed cupboards and drawers to fit their contents.
  Used materials—metal, plywood, foam rubber—that reduce size.
  Developed folding, stacking, and nesting tables and chairs.
  Reduced both size and scale to a minimum.

  These developments have been so gradual that they escape attention until one sees an inherited antique in a new little home.
- **Length of service** depends on physical and psychological durability. Physical durability is determined by materials, construction, and finish. Psychological longevity is equally critical, but harder to appraise. For continued satisfaction choose well-proportioned furniture in which the materials are honestly and suitably used, which is flexible and seems right for you. Avoid revivals, for they seldom last long. At the expense of seeming timid, do not jump for the latest novelty or fad. Good sense and moderation are safe guides.
- **Cost of maintenance** includes cleaning, repairing, refinishing, and re-upholstering. Cleaning burdens can be lightened as discussed in Chapter 4. Strong materials and firm construction lessen repairing. Durability of finish and ease of refinishing are important: painted furniture, whether wood or metal, may need new paint every few years; transparent finish on wood, supplemented by wax or polish, lasts a long time; and such materials as aluminum and chromium may last indefinitely without being refinished. Upholstery fabrics may serve from two to twenty years or more depending on the material and the use it gets. The cost of reupholstering is determined by the price of the fabric, the amount needed—and the labor involved. It would be low for the chairs shown in Figures 365B and 382C but substantial for the lounge chair in Figure 365A.

► FURNITURE TYPES

Furniture can be classified in terms of its primary use: beds, sofas, and chairs; tables and desks; and storage units.

Beds

Reducing physical strain to a minimum is the purpose of beds. Individuals vary in their specific ideas about sleeping comfort, and about the only way to find out whether a bed is right for you is to try it.

Most beds now have a springy foundation and a resilient mattress. The typical foundation is either the inexpensive, lightweight, moderately comfortable flat springs or the more bulky, expensive, and comfortable coil springs. Mattresses have been filled with just about everything from straw to hair—and just air. Today the least expensive are filled with cotton. The better grades have inner springs covered with padding or are of foam rubber. Foam rubber has several advantages: it is lightweight, easy to keep clean, harbors no insects or allergy-producers. It seldom needs to be turned, lasts long, and has about one half million air cells in each cubic inch for resilience.

Even if funds are low, buy good mattresses and springs and support them on simple wood legs or the more convenient metal frames on casters. Add the useful but not essential headboards, footboards, night tables, and other paraphernalia later. In small quarters or for occasional guest use, a studio couch or davenport that becomes a bed is a sensible economy (Figs. 103B and 359A and B).

Bedspreads are usually the most conspicuous part of a bed. Serviceable bedspreads do not wrinkle excessively when taken off the bed or when you nap on them. They are heavy enough to stay in place or they are carefully fitted, and they can be laundered or cleaned easily. Strong colors or vigorous patterns on bedspreads make the bed loom large; unobtrusive colors or designs make the room seem larger. Bedspreads, curtains and draperies, and rugs with a family resemblance bring unity: spread and draperies can be obviously matched or more subtly related with harmonious color, texture, or pattern.

Sofas

Chesterfield, couch, settee, settle, davenport, divan, lounge, or sofa—which do you call the seat for two or more people?

Chesterfield is an overstuffed sofa with upholstered ends.

Couch is a sofa with a low back and one raised end.

Davenport is used in the United States to describe an upholstered sofa often convertible into a bed, but originally the word meant a small writing desk, named after its maker.

Divan is a Turkish term used for large, low couches without arms or backs that developed from piles of rugs for reclining.

The design of sofas offers much greater opportunity for individuality than those usually seen might lead you to think.

A

Left. Sensitive shape and proportion can minimize the bulkiness typical of most sofas. Folke Ohlsson, designer. (*Dux, Inc.*)

Below. A beautifully shaped frame of beech and teak, panels of cane, and foam rubber cushions compose an unusually small-scale love seat. (*John Stuart, Inc.*)

B

Lounge is a type of couch often with one high end for reclining.

Love seat is a small sofa or "double chair" for two persons.

Settee is a long, light seat with a back and sometimes arms; it is often upholstered.

Settle is an all-wood settee.

Sofa comes from an Arabic term and is used to describe any long upholstered seat for more than one person.

Being American, we will use *davenport* and *sofa* interchangeably to describe that piece of furniture which seats two or more. The variety is legion: straight, curved, or angled to fit your room; with or without arms but more comfortable with them; in one piece or sectional, the latter permitting different arrangements; long enough for a six-footer to stretch out on or not quite, but better if they are; heavy and massive, delicate and graceful, or light and simple but sturdy. Here are suggestions:

- No more bulk than needed for comfort and strength.
- Long enough to stretch out on.
- Low and deep enough for relaxation but high and firm enough so that a person can get up under his own power.
- Arms for comfort.
- Convertible into a bed if you need extra sleeping space.
- Sectional if you like to change your arrangements and can keep the sections tightly together.
- Upholstery that combines beauty and durability.

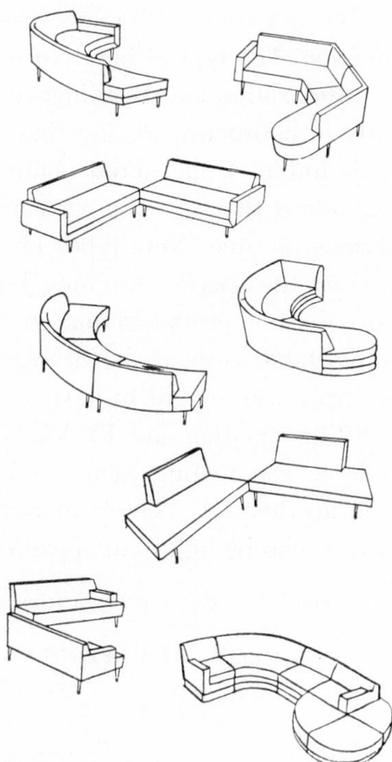

Sofas in one piece or in separate units come in many sizes and shapes. Separate units facilitate change, enable you to fit furniture to space. (*Modern Designs*)

Chairs

Logie * writes that sitting has become the most universal occupation of man because we work, study, relax, eat, and travel while seated. Leading such a sedentary life, we should be expert sitters, but we are not because until very recently no serious studies of sitting were made. We now know that comfort results when weight and pressure are spread and tension is eased by having:

- The height of the seat somewhat less than the length of the sitter's lower legs, so that the feet rest on the floor and the legs can be relaxed.
- The depth of the seat somewhat less than the length of the upper leg so that there is no pressure point under the knee.
- The width of the seat ample to permit some movement.
- The seat shaped as in a Windsor chair or an Eames' chair (Fig. 182B) or resilient so that pressure is not concentrated on the small weight-bearing edge of the pelvis.
- Both seat and back tilted backward to buttress the weight.
- The angle between seat and back of 95° or more.
- The chair back support the small of the sitter's back.
- The position of the seat and back adjustable for different persons (as in typists' chairs) or for different ways of relaxing (as in the old-fashioned Morris chairs and the new reclining chairs).

Comfort is further increased if the chair offers a place to rest the head and relax the neck and has arms to support our arms.

Chairs are used for several purposes and their form should follow their function. The typical family needs chairs for each of the following:

Relaxation and Reading. In the group living space, in studies, and possibly in bedrooms, seating that allows each member of the family to relax is desirable. Upholstered chairs and davenports are about the only kind that adjust themselves to varying individuals and are comfortable over long periods of time. New types of springs and foam rubber have greatly decreased the space-consuming bulkiness typical of all really relaxing furniture of a few years ago and enable us to get pieces as light, trim, neat, and comfortable as those shown in Figures 362A and 382B. Even so, such pieces are heavy and ought to have permanent positions in the room.

Conversation and TV Viewing. Although these activities are quite possible in the seating mentioned above, "pull-up" chairs that support you well are helpful. These can have shaped seats of wood, metal, or plastic; or they can be lightly upholstered, webbed, canvas-covered, or, the unbeat-

* Gordon Logie, *Furniture from Machines.* Allen and Unwin. 1947.

A

Several kinds of chairs are needed for comfort and efficiency and many distinctive designs are on the market.

Above. A Swedish lounge chair and ottoman, designed for relaxation, look strong yet soft and resilient. The desk chair holds the sitter in a good position for work. Folke Ohlsson, designer. (*Dux, Inc.*)

Right. Sloping seats of stretched fabric and adjustable backs provide comfort in Orient-inspired chairs of rattan joined with rawhide. (*The McGuire Company*)

B

able in terms of price, Chinese split cane chairs (Fig. 80B). Whatever the material, pull-up chairs should be easy to get hold of, light to lift, and strong enough to stand frequent moving.

Eating, Working, and Games. For these activities you need sturdy, easily moved chairs with a relatively upright back to keep the sitter alert, a seat and back shaped or lightly padded to lessen pressure, and upholstery that resists abrasion and dirt. The most frequently used family eating place ought to have enough chairs or built-in seats always ready to seat the family, but it is sensible to have more of the same kind of chairs elsewhere to bring out for large groups. Chairs of this sort can be seen in many illustrations throughout the book.

Tables

The essence of table design is the supporting of a flat slab off the floor; this is reduced to its lowest common denominator when a home craftsman supports a piece of plywood or a flush door on four pipe legs—which, by the way, is an inexpensive way to get a good table. There are problems, however, in all table design and these include getting:

- Necessary strength and stability;
- Supports out of the way of feet and legs;
- Right height, size, and shape for its use;
- Durable materials.

The typical family needs a variety of tables differing in use and therefore in size, shape, height, and materials.

Dining Tables. Sit-down meals require a table that is stable enough to be unjarred by the unpredictable movements of children or of a man carving meat; has a top large enough to give each person two feet of elbow room; is high enough to give leg room between chair and the lower surface; has supports out of the way of sitters' feet and knees; and can be extended in size. Since tablecloths and underpads have become more rare in daily living, it pays also to look closely at the durability, ease of maintenance, and beauty of the top surface. Most dining tables are rectangular because they are harmonious with rectangular rooms, can be pushed snugly against a wall or into a corner, and are slightly less costly to make. In the right place, however, a round or oval table will give an inimitable friendly group feeling. Check dining chairs and tables together because often their legs interfere with each other, the heights of the two are not coordinated, or the space between chair and table is insufficient for the sitters' comfort.

Gate-leg dining tables can be round, oval, or rectangular. Of teak wood with natural finish, this example expands from 18″ to 64″ in width. Hvidt and Nielsen, designers. (*John Stuart, Inc.*)

A

Chromium-plated steel frames, plastic table top, and plastic upholstery bring economy and attractiveness together. (*Daystrom*)

B

Below. Elegant, sculptural slenderness is among the possibilities of cast aluminum. D. Lee DuSell, designer.

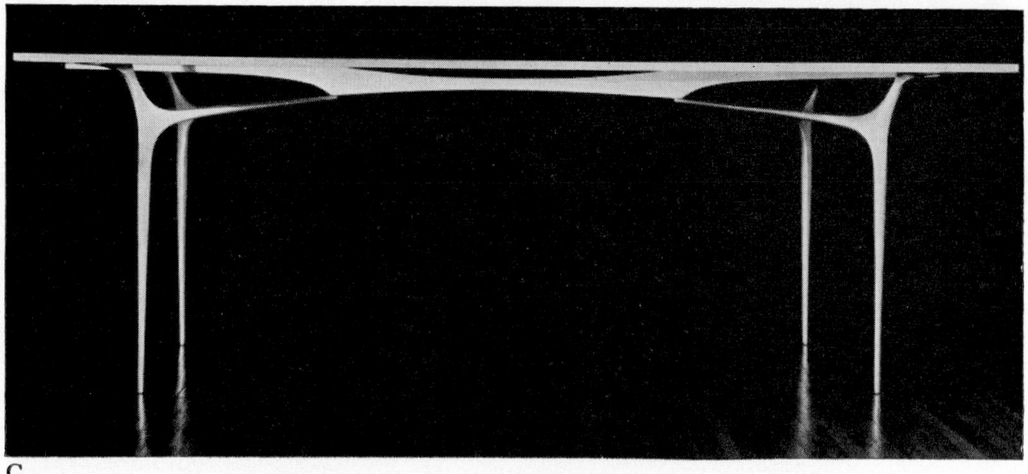

C

Drop-leaf tables (Fig. 367A), in use since Elizabethan days, can be quickly and easily expanded or contracted. Add-a-leaf dining tables can be expanded to large size but they cannot be changed quickly or easily and the leaves require storage space. Some contemporary folding tables can be compacted to 9 inches or stretched to 110 inches (which provides space for 14 people).

Coffee Tables. We have come to think that no davenport is complete unless faced with a long low table on which ashtrays, books, magazines, newspapers, accessories, plants, flowers, and snacks abound. This is a modern invention somewhat taking the place of the older, higher living-room table. Most coffee tables, though, seem to have been designed only for the "long, low, open" look—they have no storage space for the little things needed in that part of the room; they are too low to be reached comfortably from the sofa and to give foot room; and if in scale with the sofa, they usually block traffic. Really functional coffee tables are about 20 inches high and have some storage space. Their tops are durable and their supports strong but slender. Contemporary designs include many variations on new and familiar themes.

End Tables. It might be said that the old living-room table disintegrated into many little tables, because convenience now seems to demand a table however small within easy reach of every chair. Thus you usually find a table at each end of the davenport and probably for each group of chairs. Unlike coffee tables, these end tables seldom interfere with feet and often provide shelves or drawers for supplementary storage. They look better if of the same height as the arms of upholstered davenports and chairs but are more convenient and less a spill-hazard if somewhat lower or higher. Often these tables are used for lamps, although a lamp table, strictly speaking, is a little higher. Nests of tables, the top one acting as an end or coffee table, simplify entertaining greatly.

Card and Game Tables. Seldom handsome, the folding card table is a wonderful gadget. Cards and other games are best at tables several inches lower than those for eating, and collapsible card tables are ideal for occasional games, bridge luncheons, or buffet suppers, and supplementary serving at festive dinners. Space permitting, a permanent card table with at least two chairs always there is a handy set of equipment for any family liking games, doing homework, or enjoying varied eating spots.

Kitchen Tables. Once banished in the drive for compact efficiency, tables in kitchens or adjacent alcoves are again found to be as useful as our grandmothers knew them to be. Since they often serve for eating and food preparation, they differ from dining tables only in having greater strength and durability. Not all of them are glaring white and chrome; in fact some

Small tables are important in today's living, come in many sizes, shapes, and materials.

Right. Sewing tables are dual-purpose. This Danish import has a teak top and oak frame both finished with natural oil and wax. N. Chr. Staer, designer. (*R. L. Sines and Associates*)

A

B

Left. A substantial carved wood base supporting a marble top in a notably decorative table. (*Weiman Heirloom Furniture*)

C

Above. Wood and chromium-plated steel in a design which has a drawer and lower shelf for storage. Ico Parisi, designer. (*Singer Cabinet Shops, Inc.*)

D

Left. Metal triangular tables can be combined in many ways or stacked for storage. D. R. Bates and Jackson Gregory, Jr., designers. (*Vista Furniture Co.*)

have become so friendly that few mind seeing them from the living room (Fig. 367B).

Desks. The essentials of desks are a suitable surface for writing and convenient and accessible storage for writing materials and papers. That every household needs at least one good writing place is obvious. How large and complex the unit and where it is placed depends on the family's habits. A desk can be a table with only one drawer, a compartment in an arrangement of unit furniture (Fig. 365A), or a piece of furniture designed for serious desk work. Space-saving devices include writing surfaces that fold down and out or slide in and out. A vertical file drawer or two is the most sensible way to store all the pieces of paper related to household operation compactly, conveniently, and accessibly. The file can be part of a desk or purchased separately in units of one to four drawers.

Storage

Storage is a major problem today. Living quarters are smaller and attics, "spare" rooms, basements, barns, and sheds have all but disappeared. More people have more things to put away and apparently have less time in which to do it. Yet we favor the "uncluttered look" in our homes. An intelligent program is needed.

- Discard things neither used nor enjoyed.
- Cut down on purchases of unnecessary articles, especially bulky ones.
- Plan active storage in terms of the criteria listed on page 66 of Chapter 4.
- Provide as much dead storage space as needed for seasonal objects of all sizes and shapes. Typical families can use space equivalent to a one-car garage (10′ x 20′), but it is more convenient if distributed where needed rather than concentrated in one spot.

Making these dreams come to life means giving at least as much thought to storage in all parts of homes as is typically given to kitchens. Convenience, visibility, accessibility, flexibility, and maintenance are quite pertinent in living and bedrooms. Phonograph records near the player, books convenient to reading chairs, toys where children are supposed to play are but a few examples.

This goes beyond what most of us call furniture and that is precisely what was intended because efficient storage is part of total home design. The least that one should expect is *empty space* for cupboards and chests, and for trunks, baby carriages, bicycles and outdoor furniture, and the like. It is far better if these facilities are *built into* the house (Fig. 371C). We

Good desks and storage facilities save time and energy.

Right. A child's desk of unusual design has a deep drawer and stool which can be swung out of the way. (*Fleetwood Furniture*)

A

B

Above. A simple desk and modified Windsor chair, ample built-in storage units, and a couch on casters give the study in the Danish home of architect Eric Stengade unpretentious, individualized charm. (*Photograph by Andresen*)

Right. Shelves and drawers, pegboard wall, and racks on the backs of closet doors encourage a young lady to keep her possessions conveniently accessible in the bedroom already seen in Figure 50B. Morgan Stedman, architect. (*Photograph by Maynard Parker. Courtesy of* House Beautiful)

C

store things by standing them on floors or shelves; hanging them on walls or the backs of doors, or from ceilings; or putting them in drawers or chests. Which is best depends on the use, size, shape, fragility, and value of the object, but it is provident to take advantage of every inch of available space.

Bookcases. These are the simplest pieces of furniture because even though books come in some eighty different sizes, more than half are about 5″ x 7½″ and few exceed 7½″ x 10″. The shelves should be adjustable but seldom need to be more than 8″ or 9″ deep. Books on open shelves are handsome and also absorb noise, but without protection they are not easy to keep clean.

Some book and magazine storage can well be used in every room. In kitchens, a single shelf may hold all of your cookbooks. A few shelves on living-room walls or under tables will conveniently hold currently used volumes, but you may find more space is necessary. Low bookcases double as tables and if sufficiently long and well planned, unify a wall; or they can reach to the ceiling to become forceful architectural elements (Fig. 371B). They can frame and relate doors and windows or they can be free-standing, partial or complete dividers between two rooms or parts of one room.

Chests of drawers. These are best when they have strongly joined, dust-proof drawers that slide easily and handles that you can grasp easily. Shallow drawers at the top are a great convenience. Relatively small units that fit together increase flexibility of placement. Drawers either in chests or combined with cupboards are typically used for table linens and silver: shallow drawers with flexible dividers are worth their cost. Although we take sliding drawers for granted, they were not widely used until the seventeenth century.

Cabinets. Although found infrequently outside kitchens, dining space, and bathrooms, cabinets with doors and adjustable shelves or vertical dividers are welcome in every room. Doors on cabinets beget the same problems as do doors between rooms. Swinging doors work easily and allow narrow storage racks on the back, but they get in the way when open. Sliding doors open only part of the cabinet at a time and give no door-back shelves. Where space in front of cabinets is at a premium or people move around when doors are open, sliding doors are a good solution, but in other places swinging doors have distinct advantages.

Radio, phonograph, and television cabinets are furniture for which there is no historical precedent. The early ones seemed intent on making themselves conspicuous. Nowadays, they usually take their place as units integrated with other cabinets and bookshelves or are built into the wall (Figs. 25B and 41A).

A

Outdoor living becomes pleasurable with appropriate furniture.

Above. Chairs, benches, and a table of weather-resistant redwood furnish a protected patio. Henry Hill, architect. (*Photograph by Morley Baer*)

Below left. Synthetic webbing and aluminum frames make lightweight, durable, inexpensive chairs. (*Martin Fabrics Corp.*)

Below right. From Italy comes a modern "gondola" chair of unusual refinement. Seat and back are of woven cellophane, the frame of anodized aluminum. It folds compactly for convenient storage. (*Interiors' Import Co.*)

B

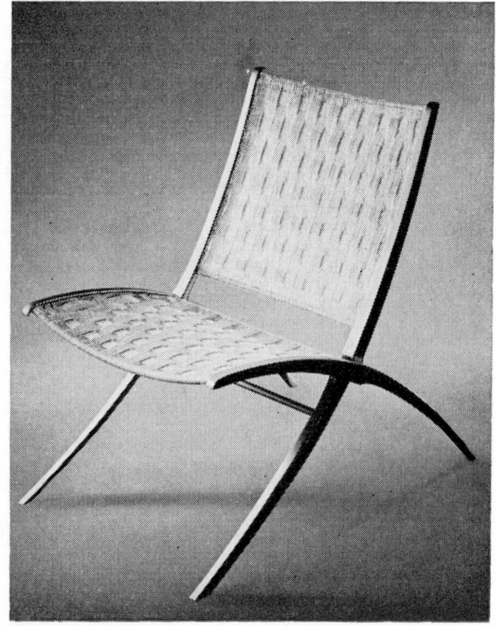

C

Screens

With a venerable history as ornamental space dividers, screens are especially welcome in open-plan houses or multipurpose rooms (Fig. 396A). They can be moved or adjusted to divide areas into comfortable units without completely shutting out what is beyond. And they can be folded inconspicuously against walls. There are no limits to materials: sheer silk and rice paper; clear or translucent glass and plastics (Fig. 232A); tapestry, brocades, and leather; shutters and bamboo poles; curved or flat plywood (Fig. 183B); humble wallboard that can be painted or covered with wallpaper or fabrics. The latter are wonderfully useful for such seasonal or topical displays as Christmas cards, maps, or children's paintings. With these possibilities, screens can be almost as heavy and substantial as walls, actually sliding or folding walls, or they can be light and free-standing. They can be plain or ornamented, the same or different on both sides, harmonious or contrasting with their surroundings.

Outdoor Furniture

Interest in outdoor living has led to many kinds of weather-resistant furniture. There are many good structural materials. Redwood (Fig. 373A), cedar and cypress last long. Aluminum never rusts, stays cool in the sun, and is light in weight. Copper weathers handsomely and chromium-plated steel is durable. Tables present no special problems. Nor do the frames of chairs and chaises, but making them both weatherproof and resilient is not easy. Few if any springs, cushions, and pads are unharmed by water. The seating most nearly approaching care-free comfort has metal frames with synthetic webbing seats and backs (Figs. 373B and C). Then come the wood or metal chairs and lounges with cushions that should not be left out in the rain. With these, it is advisable to have a rain-free outdoor living area (Fig. 27B and Chapter 20) or weather-tight storage nearby.

► BUILT-IN FURNITURE

The first built-in furniture may have been a natural rock ledge found in a protected spot and used for sitting or sleeping. It was not, however, until a few centuries ago that furniture integrated with the architectural shell was much used. Even clothes closets were unknown, clothes being stored in bulky wardrobes or chests. In the nineteenth century, home designers began to use walls more intensively. We may no longer care for the elaborate Victorian fireplace mantels loaded with bric-a-brac, but we cannot help admiring the dish cupboards with doors opening into both kitchen and

A

Built-in cabinets or seating unify architecture and furniture.

Above. Storage cabinets are adroitly fitted into a geometrically paneled dining room wall in Mt. Pleasant, Philadelphia, 1761. (*Courtesy of the Pennsylvania Museum of Art, Philadelphia*)

Below. Luxuriously deep and long, a built-in sofa is shaped in friendly angles as is the custom-made coffee table. Welton Beckett, architect. (*Photograph by Maynard Parker. Courtesy of* House Beautiful)

B

dining room. Early in his career Frank Lloyd Wright began thinking of the house as one unified whole and built storage, seating, and tables as an integral part of the architecture (Fig. 86B).

Built-in furniture, surprisingly, more often than not promotes flexible living because such furniture takes less space than movable pieces, thereby leaving maximum free space in the centers of rooms as illustrated in Figures 25A, 28B, 39A, 50A, 52A and B, 57B, 59A, 72B, 82, 108B, 140B, and 187A and B. It also can minimize dust-catching crevices, give a feeling of permanence and security, and break up the boxiness of rooms. At the same time it reduces the visual clutter brought by many isolated pieces of furniture, which have an irritating tendency to get out of their best position. Coming into the modern home through kitchen cabinets, medicine chests, linen closets, and bookcases, built-in furniture is rapidly spreading and could well be used in every room.

► MATERIALS AND CONSTRUCTION

Grandfather used to say that he could quickly estimate the quality of a man's suit by the way the buttons were sewed on, but there is no quick and easy way to size up furniture materials and construction. Much time and disappointment would be saved if clear and specific labels appeared on each piece or if the manufacturer's specifications were available for each line. Lacking such, you will do well to look at every piece literally from every angle, get all possible information from the salesman, and try to purchase from stores that stand behind their merchandise. Furniture is no better than the materials from which it is made, the methods by which it is joined, and the ways in which it is finished. Here are some preliminary tests:

- Does the piece stand firmly on the floor and resist staunchly your efforts to make it wobble? This is particularly important in tables, especially if expandable, and in desks and chairs.
- Do all movable parts—drawers, drop leaves, and the like—operate easily and steadily?
- Are all joints tightly and smoothly fitted together?
- Is the finish durable, smooth, and evenly applied? Is it composed of many coats properly dried and rubbed, or one or two coats that look thick and gummy in any crevice or indentation?

Then look at the places of greatest wear.

Tops of tables, desks, counters, bookcases, cabinets, and chests. Ideally, these should resist scratching, denting, breaking, staining, and wetting.

Properly finished hard woods are satisfactory if kept reasonably free from liquids; plastic laminates are remarkably durable but noisy and shiny; linoleum is quiet but the lighter colors show stains; vinyl tiles or sheets have all the advantages of linoleum (except low price) plus greater resistance to stains and cuts; vinyl cork is good to look at and touch, resilient and stain resistant; glass is light and airy, a breakage hazard, and needs constant cleaning; and marble is rich, heavy, noisy, and can break and stain.

Edges of tables, doors, and drawers. These are the surfaces most easily nicked and marred and all but the most durable materials show wear. Hard wood or replaceable metal or plastic strips help.

Runners of drawers. Hard wood or noncorrosive metals are needed here. Often-used large and heavy drawers should be suspended on rollers and tracks.

Handles, knobs, and hinges. The soil that collects on and around handles and knobs is ample evidence of the use they get. Hard woods and dull metals are still the most serviceable, but plastics are entering the field (Fig. 298). Hinges ought to be of the best possible quality and securely fastened into wood hard enough to hold screws under strain.

Lower part of legs and bases. To be kicked by feet, caressed by mops and brooms, and nuzzled by vacuum cleaners is the preordained fate of this part of furniture. Reduce to a minimum parts that touch the floor and then make the necessary ones simple, of medium dark wood or of metal, with finishes that do not scratch or chip readily.

Seating surfaces, stuffing, and springs are discussed below.

We now look in more detail at wood, metal, and upholstered furniture.

Wood

Wood, the standard furniture material, should be thoroughly dry and of a variety that is stable in size and shape to minimize shrinking, swelling, and warping. Each wood has its own qualities and the knowing craftsman may combine several kinds in one piece. Structural parts are best when of strong wood, such as ash or birch, but need not take a good finish or be beautiful unless visible. Exposed surfaces ought to wear well, be hard enough to resist scratching and denting, have a pleasant finish, and be beautiful in themselves. Mahogany, walnut, oak, maple, and birch have these qualities. Redwood, on the other hand, has a pleasant color and stands weather, but it is soft and splintery. The advantages of plywood have been stated, and some hard-pressed composition boards have proved their value for table tops, backs of chests, and parts of drawers.

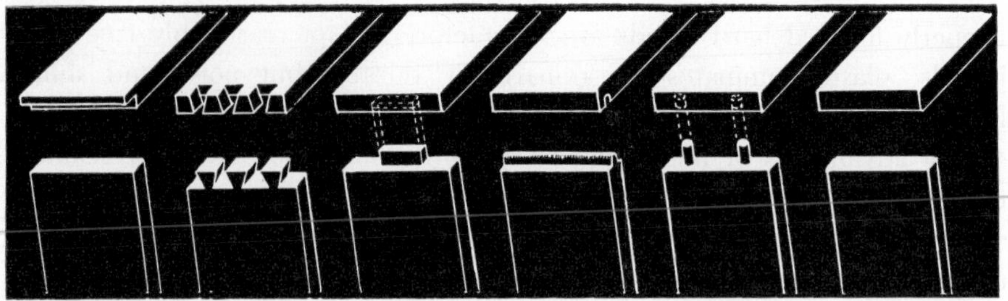

The way in which wood is joined critically affects the durability and appearance of furniture. Typical joints include *rebated, dovetailed, mortise-and-tenon, tongue-and-groove, doweled,* and *butt.* (*Matt Kahn*)

Wood in furniture can be joined in a number of ways (Fig. 378):

- **Rebated** or rabbeted joints have a groove cut from the edge of one piece to receive the other member.
- **Dovetailed** joints have flaring tenons (or tongues) on one piece and mortises (or grooves) on the other. They are used in most good drawers.
- **Mortise-and-tenon** joints have a mortise (a hole or cavity) in one piece of wood into which a tenon (projecting piece) cut in the end of the other fits securely. They are usually stronger than doweled joints.
- **Tongue-and-groove** joints are much like mortise-and-tenon except that the tongue and groove extend the width of the boards.
- **Doweled** joints have wooden pegs (or dowels) inserted into holes in the two pieces of wood to be joined.
- **Butt** joints are the simplest and weakest and have no place in furniture unless reinforced with corner blocks.

All joints need glue, and synthetic resins are very much stronger than vegetable or casein glues. Frames of chairs, sofas, and case goods also need triangular wood or metal corner blocks tightly screwed and glued in place for reinforcing. Screws strengthen joints much more than do nails.

Metal

Used since antiquity, metal for furniture is enjoying a new popularity. Mass production has greatly lowered the cost, and designers have found metal uniquely suitable for furniture that is strong and durable but not bulky. Steel with a baked enamel finish is well known in kitchens and bathroom cabinets and, more recently, in indoor-outdoor chairs and tables. It comes in many colors, is easy to wash, and maintains its good appearance if not kicked or banged. Steel is also widely used for legs and frames of chairs, tables, and storage units. The typical rods and tubes or right-angle

A

B

Metal and plastics lead to new sculptural furniture shapes.

Above left. Great sophistication marks George Nelson's plastic shell chair poised on slender steel legs. (*Herman Miller Company*)

Above right. One-piece drawers and slide-panels of durable plastic minimize dirt-catching crevices, can be faced with wood. (*Robert A. Schless & Co.*)

Below. In the family room of a North Carolina home, Harry Bertoia's wire-mesh chairs complement the room's rectangularity. Carl Koch, architect. (*Photograph by Alderman Studios*)

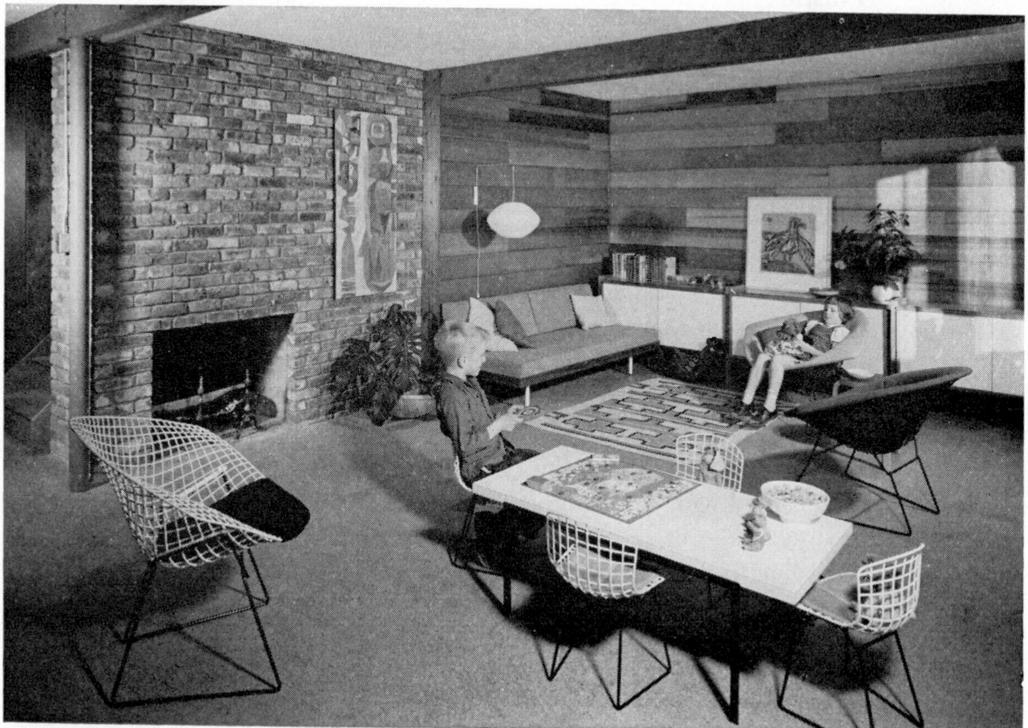

C

strips can be handsomely efficient (Figs. 373A and C), or they can be merely "blacksmith modern." Rusting quickly, they need a protective surface treatment and the usual black paint gives many pieces a spidery or "anopheles" look. They can, though, be coated with any color and some metallic enamels have a soft but rich glow. Chromium plating gives lasting protection and surfaces that range, visually, from glittering hardness to pewterlike mellowness.

Notably different from the "pipe and angle-iron" designs are those based on the sculptural potentialities of metal. In the hands of Harry Bertoia, sculptor and designer, steel wire mesh (Fig. 379C) becomes a responsive medium for free-form chairs that are both graceful and comfortable. Aluminum, lightweight and nonrusting, has also led designers to explore forms that have no associations with plumbing shops or forges. Some of the tapering, sculptured pieces (Figs. 367C and 373C) are elegant far beyond their cost. Aluminum's natural color is pleasantly sympathetic but it can be permanently treated with wondrously varied hues.

Metal can be joined by welding, riveting, or bolting. Welding gives smooth, strong joints, but bolts and rivets are satisfactory if you do not mind seeing what holds the pieces together. Most metal furniture is so much stronger than normal household use demands that construction is generally less a problem for the consumer than it is in furniture made of wood. *But* repairs are much more difficult.

Plastics

These materials have affected furniture design and maintenance in two markedly different ways. Most common are the durable surfaces—vinyl tiles and laminated melamine sheets for table and counter tops, vinyl upholstery for chairs and sofas—which have greatly extended the range of easily kept colors. More striking are the molded chairs and drawers (Figs. 379A and B). Thin and lightweight, amazingly strong yet slightly resilient, polyester reinforced with Fiberglas can also be molded so that seat, back, and arms of a chair are one continuous piece. The plastic shell, much warmer and pleasanter to touch than metal, can be left as it is, coated with vinyl, or upholstered with foam rubber and fabric. The drawers, molded of high-impact Styrene, eliminate the costly inner frame and center-slide case construction of ordinary storage units. Both chairs and drawers have a minimum of dust-catching joints. Exciting as these developments are, they are still to be regarded with some caution. There is the possibility of eventual dulling or discoloring, of pitting or scratching, or of breakage. As yet, repair or refinishing runs the short gamut from difficult to impossible.

Upholstered Furniture

The stuffing and covering put on chairs and sofas to make them conform to our contours can be of several degrees of comfort.

Fabric Stretched Over Frame. Until the Renaissance, upholstery was chiefly textiles, rushes, or leather stretched over frames and often supplemented by loose cushions. It is still used for lightweight, inexpensive resilience (Figs. 365B and 373B). The frame ought to be attractive as well as strong, the upholstery durable and securely fastened to the frame but easily removable.

Simple Padding. Figure 367B illustrates the next step, which consists of thin layers of resilient materials covered with a fabric and secured to the frame. Since the seventeenth century, this has been the standard way of making frequently moved chairs comfortable. Until recently, long curled hair was the best and the most costly padding, but today rubberized hair and foam are also good. Down, kapok, moss, and cotton are moderately satisfactory.

Stuffing and Springs. Although springs were placed under the stuffing during the eighteenth century, it was not until around 1914 that massively overstuffed pieces came into prominence to raise comfort to a new high and drop beauty to a new low. This complicated process includes:

Frame of strong wood well joined or of metal or plastic.

Webbing woven in a simple basket weave and tacked to the frame.

Springs, if coiled, tied to the webbing and frame. Springs should be close enough to prevent sagging but not so close that they rub. Newer approaches reduce bulk and weight with little if any loss in comfort.

Burlap covers the springs, protects the padding.

Padding or *stuffing,* similar to *simple padding,* comes next.

Felt padding gives back and arms smooth, soft contours.

Muslin covers the padding on the better chairs and sofas.

Final fabric hides all.

Much simpler but not less expensive is foam rubber on a plywood base or, more comfortably, on webbing or firm but thin springs (Figs. 382B and C). The last word in complexity—and presumably in comfort—is provided by some "contour chairs" shaped to relax all muscles and equipped with built-in heating, cooling, and vibrating mechanisms.

A

B

Upholstery affects the appearance, comfort, and economy of chairs and sofas.

Above left. Both of these brocatelles are suitable for this chair, but the one at the left makes it quiet and formal while the one at the right is more dynamic and dominant. (*Lehman-Connor*)

Above right. Resilient webbing attached to a wood frame supports contoured foam rubber that is covered by a textile. (*Fabry Associates*)

Below. A strong wood frame of comfortable size and angles supplemented with removable foam-rubber cushions and fabric makes an easy-to-maintain chair. (*Jens Risom Design*)

C

D

Upholstery Fabrics

Because fabrics become an integral part, usually the most conspicuous, of the furniture to which they are fastened and because they are what we most often touch, they deserve attention as *furniture* as well as *fabrics.* The least we might expect is that they look comfortable to sit on, feel good to hands and arms, and resist abrasion and soil. Visual relationship to the shape they cover and the setting in which they are placed lifts them above the merely useful. Beyond that are fabrics with their own distinctiveness or those used with originality.

Seeing identical pieces of furniture covered with varied fabrics alerts us to the forcefulness of color and design in altering the apparent shape, size, and character of any form (Fig. 382A). In rooms with several or many pieces of upholstered furniture, the whole effect can be changed with different furniture covers. All that we know about the psychological effects of hue and value, emphasis and scale can be put to use in selecting upholstery. Also our knowledge of fibers, yarns, and weaves is strategic. For upholstery, how does wool compare with cotton, silk, or nylon? In textiles, it pays to look for long fibers and tightly twisted yarns, for weaves that are tight, because loosely woven textiles snag easily. How do pile weaves compare with flat weaves? Which textiles and patterns contribute to serviceability? Do not overlook materials that are not textiles. Leather has long since earned its place because of its durability and ease of maintenance, its surface pleasant to touch and to see. Today it is challenged by plastic fabrics that are markedly serviceable in hard-wear situations and available in a vast array of colors and textures.

► PLANNED BUYING

Without a plan (and by *plan* we mean something that grows and develops, not a static blueprint) acquiring furniture can become as frantic and disordered as Christmas shopping often is. It can be even worse than Christmas shopping because much more money will be spent and you have to live with your own purchases. Buying the large essential pieces first, then filling in with the smaller, less costly items is a sensible approach. Over the first two years, it might work out in this way:

First Year	Second Year
Living Room	
Sofa or studio couch	1 or 2 chairs
1 easy and 1 pull-up chair or 2 of either type	End tables
Coffee table	Desk
Rug and curtains	Draperies if needed
2 lamps	Accessories
Dining Space	
Table	2 more chairs
4 chairs	Additional storage units if needed
Unit chest and cabinet for dishes, linen, and silver	Draperies if needed
Rug and curtains	Accessories
Bedroom(s)	
Springs and mattresses on legs or frames	Dressing table
Chest of drawers for each person	Room-sized rug
Mirror	Accessories
1 chair	Draperies if needed
Lamps	
Scatter rugs	
Curtains	

Depending on budgets and personalities, it may or may not be wise to purchase in the first year a few really good pieces to have and enjoy, even if that means going without some of the furnishings your friends have. By the third year, things start accumulating as they will continue to for many years. It is often wise to put most of the furnishings money away this year and perhaps the next so that about the fifth year a few of the good things that you know you need and want can be afforded.

When buying furniture, keep these points in mind:

- Take your time and watch your budget.
- Buy only what you know you need.
- Keep in mind the total pattern of your furnishings, but also buy only furniture that is good in its own right.
- Express yourself rather than trying to impress your friends.

► ARRANGING FURNITURE

Furniture arrangement is a matter of coordinating furnishings with both family and architecture.

Group Living Space

The *major conversation center* is typically the dominant furniture group in the home. In those homes without family rooms, it may also have to be used for music and television, reading and buffet suppers, although segregating the noisier activities is a boon. This furniture grouping is best when people face each other; and the furniture is stabilized in a corner, around a window wall or fireplace, or is built up with eventful furniture and wall treatments. Possibilities for seating arrangements, some of which are illustrated in Figures 386A and B and 387A and B include:

- Chairs and sofa arranged in a circle around a table.
- Sofa with a chair or two at each side, all facing a coffee table.
- Two sofas facing or one sofa facing two chairs, often at right angles to a fireplace in large rooms.
- Two sofas at right angles to each other or one sofa at right angles to two chairs, often in a corner although one unit may project into the room.

A *secondary conversation* or *reading center* often supplements the major group in larger rooms (Figs. 386C and D). It is usually planned for two to four persons and is placed in a minor position.

- Two chairs, and the necessary table, at right angles to each other.
- Two, three, or four chairs (or a love seat or two) facing each other over a table and usually near a window.
- Three chairs near a small round table.
- Four chairs at the sides of a game or card table.

Television cabinets are conspicuous and often not very attractive, but have to be placed so as to be easily seen by a number of people.

- Relating a television set to the total design of a fireplace wall often gives an unobstructed view from the major seating group while minimizing the set's bulkiness.
- A set on casters can be moved into position for viewing, out of sight when not in use.
- Sets on swivel mounts can be placed in walls or cabinets between two rooms where they will serve both.

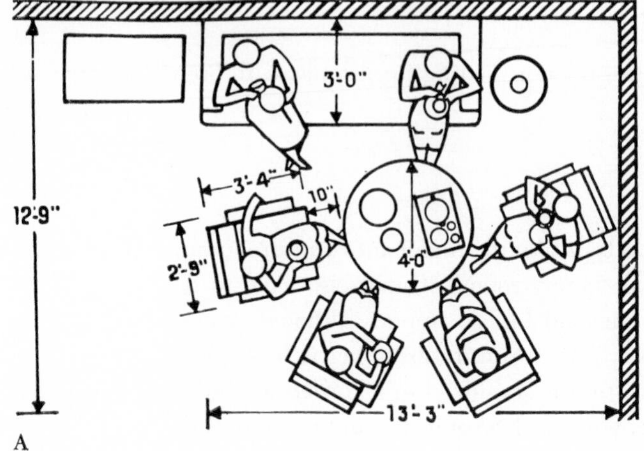

Left. Major conversation groups are most satisfactory when they are more or less circular in shape and when the maximum distance between people is 8 to 10 feet. Large upholstered chairs are comfortable but space-consuming. Pull-up chairs and sofas take less space. (*From* ARCHITECTURAL FORUM. *© 1937 Time, Inc.*)

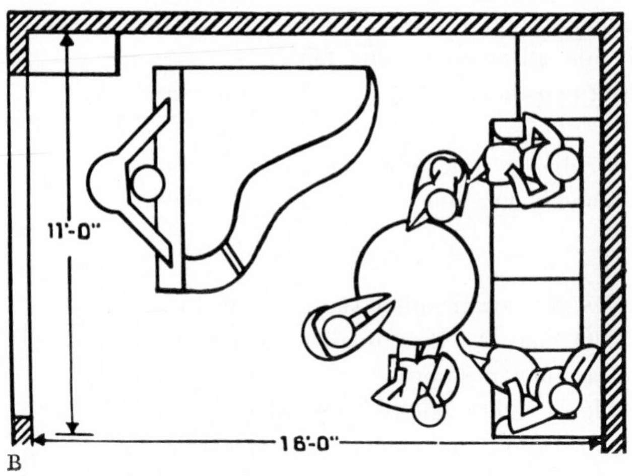

Below. Secondary conversation or reading groups and a table for games or snacks are useful additions. (*From* ARCHITECTURAL FORUM. *© 1937 Time, Inc.*)

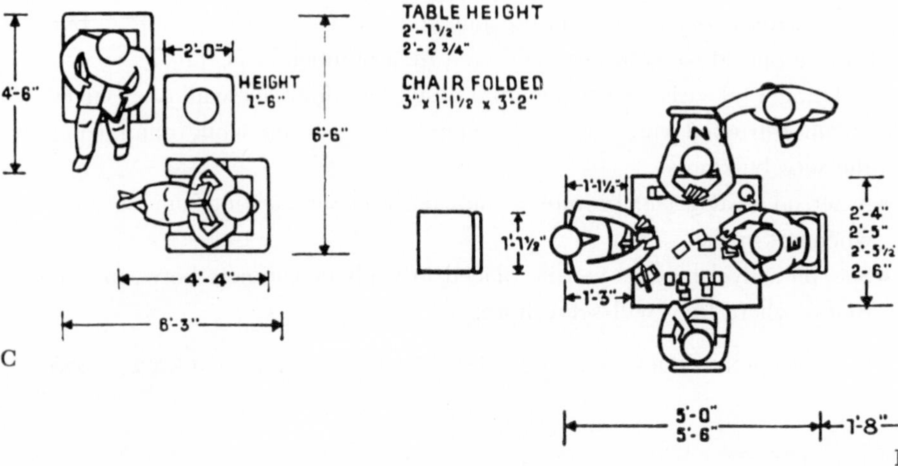

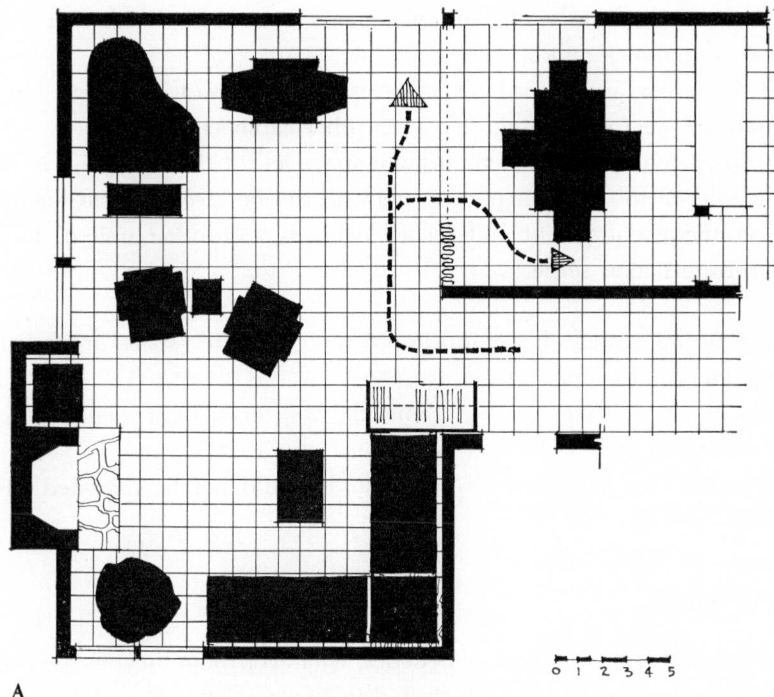

A

Above. An L-shaped living-dining space well planned for group living. Two sofas and three chairs make a congenial conversation group around the fireplace and the radio or television at its right. The piano and card table are appropriately located. The dining space can be opened or closed with a curtain. The excellent circulation pattern enables people to come into the room from the entrance area and proceed to the conversation center, piano, card table, dining space, or terrace without going through any furniture group. Each square represents one foot. (*Victor Thompson*)

Below. A long, narrow, symmetrical room with two doors presents problems and potentialities. The most serious problem is that of arranging a major conversation group that is relatively free from traffic. Potentialities include zoning the ends for different activities, in this case a music center and an area for quiet reading or desk work. (*Victor Thompson*)

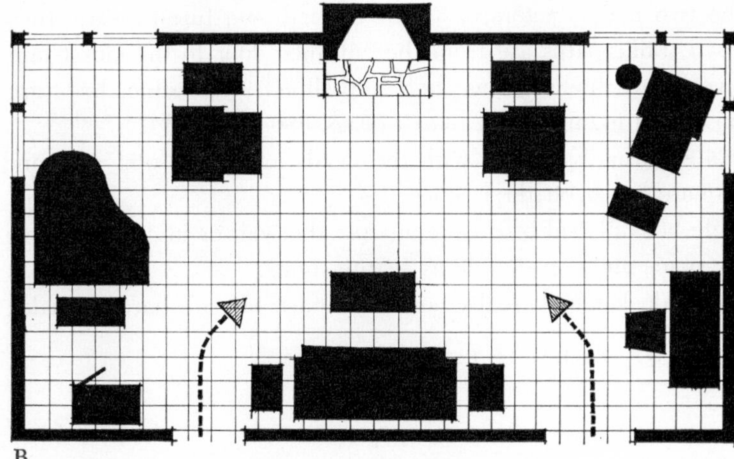

B

Radio and phonograph equipment vary tremendously in their importance to different families.

- Small radios and record players can be put almost anywhere but are more satisfactory if integrated with other cabinets.
- Records require convenient storage space and if the collection is large, a corner of the room or part of one wall can be given over to them.
- Combining equipment and record cabinets with other unit or built-in furniture makes sense.

Pianos are visually large and impressive, need free space around them for acoustics and people.

- Upright models can be flat against the wall or at right angles to partition a room (Fig. 398).
- Grand pianos are physically large and should not be crowded (Figs. 387A and B).

Dining Space

Dining tables and chairs or benches, whatever room they are placed in, can be arranged in the ways illustrated in Figures 389A, B, and C.

- Rectangular or round table in the center of a dining room or large kitchen or at one end of the living room increases the importance of meals and simplifies serving.
- Table with one end against a wall takes less floor space and fits into the room.
- Table and seating, especially built-in, in an alcove take minimum space and stay in place, but somewhat complicate getting in and out and also serving the meal.

Bedrooms

The two major factors in arranging bedroom furniture are these: the most used traffic paths are from the entrance door to the closet and chest of drawers and should be as short and direct as possible; beds are large and can be put in only a few places (Figs. 390A, B, and C).

- Beds are usually placed with the heads against a solid wall and with adequate space on three sides.
- Single beds placed broadside against the wall or in a corner give more free space and can double as seating units.
- Double-decker beds really conserve space but are hard to make.

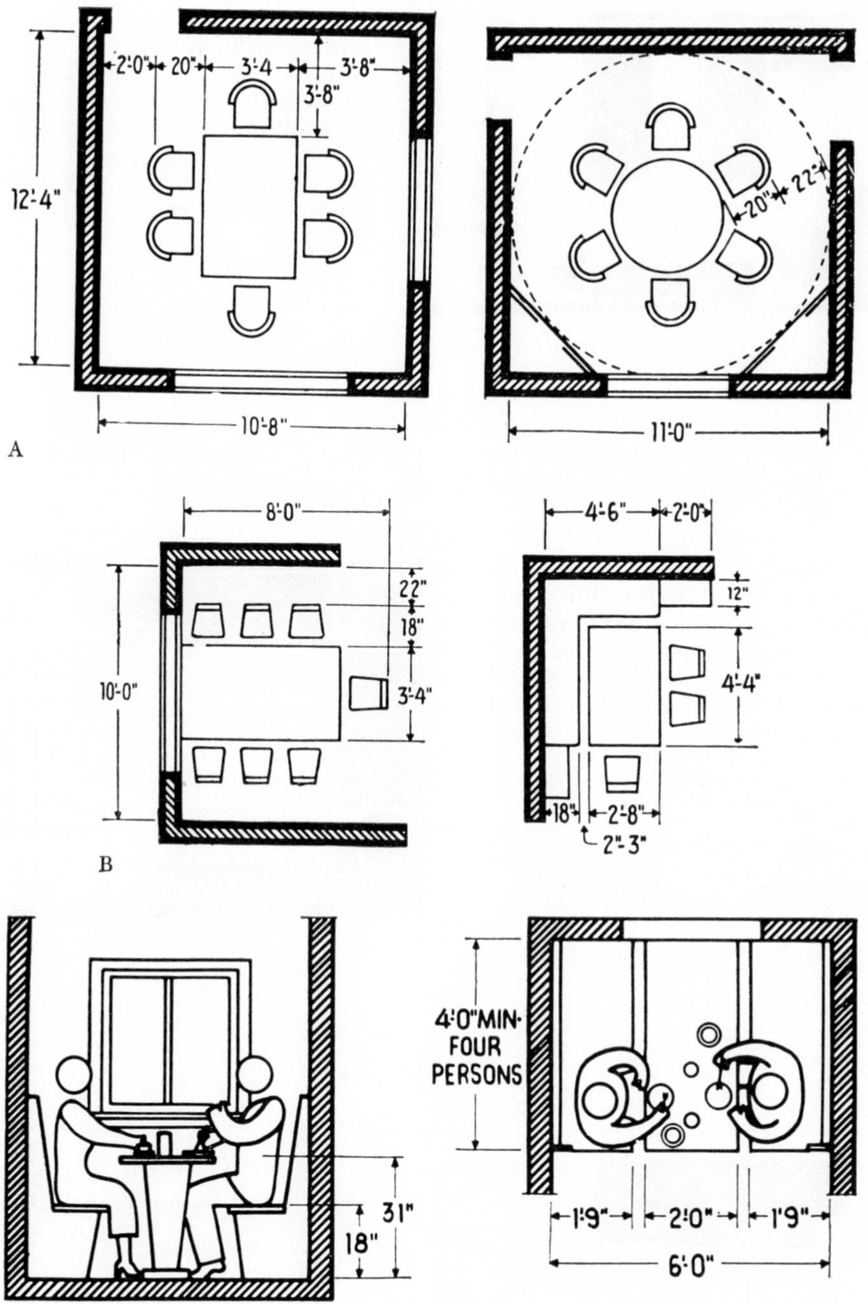

Dining tables can be in the center of the room, in alcoves or corners, or at one end. Space is saved when they are against the wall and seating is built-in, but this complicates getting in and out as well as serving meals. (*From ARCHITECTURAL FORUM*. © *1937 Time, Inc.*)

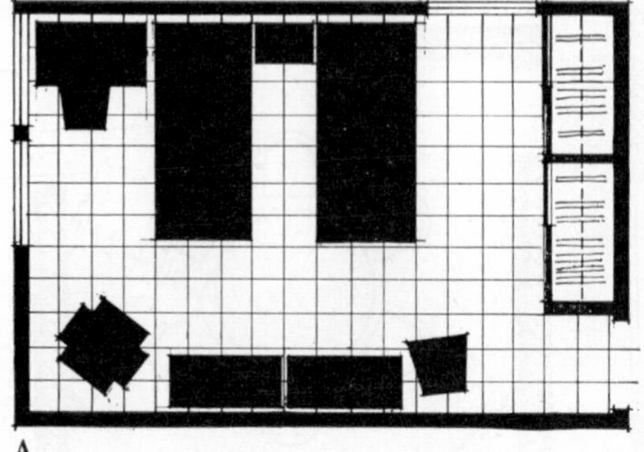
A

Left. Twin or double beds are conventionally placed with heads against a solid wall. In this plan, the beds do not interfere with the frequent trips from the bedroom door to closets or chests, but they wisely segregate the desk and lounge chair. (*Victor Thompson*)

Right. Twin beds placed broadside against the walls and in a corner make a bedroom seem larger and offer nicely sequestered space for two desks. This arrangement, however, complicates making the beds. (*Victor Thompson*)

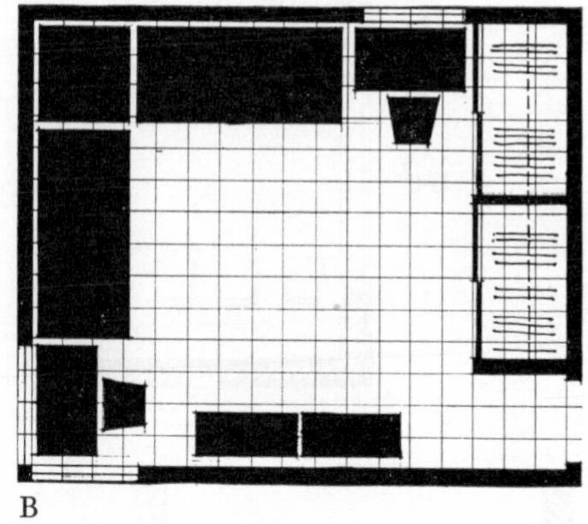
B

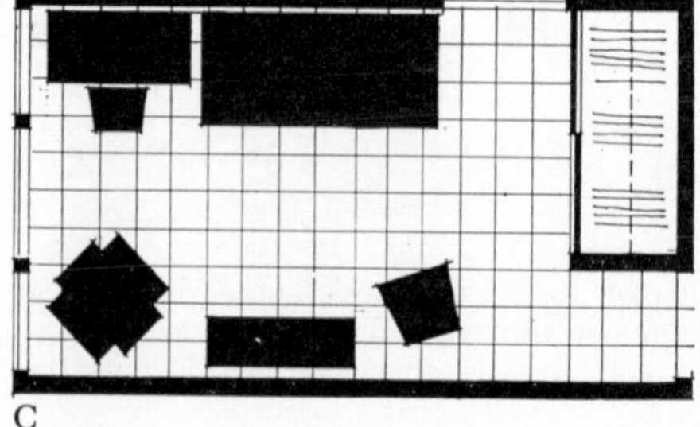
C

Left. A small bedroom planned and furnished so that it also functions as an individual's retreat. (*Victor Thompson*)

- Chests of drawers are best next to or in closets and/or near windows if they have mirrors above. Two chests side by side or one double chest save space as well as visually balance the bulk of the bed.
- Drawers combined with cabinets, a dressing table, and possibly a desk will also conserve space (Fig. 52A).
- A dressing table is best placed at right angles to or in front of a window so that adequate light will fall on the face. A dressing table will often fit into the space between two closets (Fig. 52B).
- A chair placed adjacent to the closet and chest of drawers will complete the dressing center.
- An easy chair, lamp and small table placed near a window form a pleasant reading spot in a bedroom (Fig. 60).

Sizes and Shapes of Furniture

Little progress can be made in arranging furniture without knowledge of the size and shape of specific pieces and also of the all-important clearances between pieces of furniture or furniture and walls for foot room, circulation, and the like. Figure 395 shows typical furniture pieces drawn at a scale of ¼″ equaling 1′0″. The range of sizes and shapes is indicated in the following table.

Furniture Sizes and Clearance Spaces

LIVING ROOM	*Small* DEPTH	WIDTH		*Large* DEPTH	WIDTH
Sofa	2′6″	x 6′	to	3′	x 9′
Love seat	2′6″	x 4′	to	3′	x 5′
Easy chair	2′6″	x 2′4″	to	3′4″	x 3′3″
Pull-up chair	1′6″	x 1′6″	to	2′	x 2′
Coffee table, oblong	1′6″	x 3′	to	3′	x 5′
Coffee table, round	2′ diam.		to	4′ diam.	
Coffee table, square	2′	x 2′	to	4′	x 4′
End table	1′6″	x 10″	to	3′	x 1′8″
Bridge table	2′6″	x 2′6″	to	3′	x 3′
Flat top desk	1′6″	x 2′8″	to	3′	x 6′
Secretary	1′6″	x 2′8″	to	2′	x 3′6″
Upright piano	2′	x 4′9″	to	2′2″	x 5′10″
Grand piano	5′10″	x 4′10″	to	9′	x 5′2″
Bookcase	10″	x 2′6″	to	1′	x –

Furniture Sizes and Clearance Spaces (Cont.)

Clearances

Traffic path, major	4′ to 6′
Traffic path, minor	1′4″ to 4′
Foot room between sofa or chair and edge of coffee table top	1′
Floor space in front of chair or sofa for feet and legs	1′6″ to 2′6″
Chair or bench space in front of desk or piano	3′

DINING ROOM	*Small* DEPTH WIDTH		*Large* DEPTH WIDTH
Table, square	2′6″ x 2′6″	to	5′ x 5′
Table, rectangle	3′ x 5′	to	4′ x 8′
Table, round	2′7″ diam.	to	6′4″ diam.
Chairs, straight	1′4″ x 1′4″	to	1′8″ x 1′8″
Chairs, arm	1′10″ x 1′10″	to	2′ x 2′
Buffet	1′8″ x 4′	to	2′ x 6′
Serving table	1′6″ x 3′	to	2′ x 4′
China cabinet	1′6″ x 3′	to	1′8″ x 4′

Clearances

Space for occupied chairs	1′6″ to 1′10″
Space to get into chairs	1′10″ to 3′
Traffic path around table and occupied chairs for serving	1′6″ to 2′

BEDROOM	*Small* DEPTH WIDTH		*Large* DEPTH WIDTH
Bed, twin, Hollywood	6′2″ x 3′3″	to	6′8″ x 3′8″
Bed, full, Hollywood	6′2″ x 4′6″	to	6′8″ x 5′
Bed, twin, head and footboards	6′10″ x 3′3″	to	7′2″ x 3′8″
Bed, full, head and footboards	6′10″ x 4′6″	to	7′2″ x 5′
Bed, youth	5′9″ x 3′		
Crib	2′ x 4′	to	2′6″ x 4′6″
Night table	1′0″ x 1′3″	to	2′ x 2′
Dresser	1′6″ x 2′6″	to	1′9″ x 5′
Chest	1′4″ x 2′6″	to	1′7″ x 3′2″
Dressing table	1′6″ x 3′4″	to	1′8″ x 4′
Bench	1′3″ x 1′10″	to	1′6″ x 2′
Wardrobe	1′6″ x 3′2″	to	1′9″ x 4′
Chair, easy	2′4″ x 2′4″	to	2′8″ x 2′8″
Chair, pull-up	1′3″ x 1′6″	to	1′6″ x 1′9″
Chaise longue	2′ x 4′	to	2′4″ x 5′6″

Furniture Sizes and Clearance Spaces (Cont.)

Clearances

Space for making bed	1′6″ to 2′
Space between twin beds	1′6″ to 2′4″
Space in front of chest of drawers	3′
Space for dressing	3′ to 4′ (in both directions)

KITCHEN	*Small* DEPTH WIDTH		*Large* DEPTH WIDTH
Range	1′9″ x 1′8″	to	2′2″ x 3′4″
Refrigerator	2′1″ x 2′	to	2′6″ x 3′
Sink	1′8″ x 2′	to	2′1″ x 5′6″
Automatic washer	2′1″ x 2′1″	to	2′7″ x 3′8″
Automatic dryer	2′1″ x 2′1″	to	2′7″ x 3′8″
Ironing board	3′8″ x 11″	to	4′6″ x 1′3″
Ironer	1′3″ x 2′2″	to	1′5″ x 2′11″
Cabinets, base	2′1″ deep; 15″, 18″, 21″, 24″, 30″ wide; 2′6″ to 3′ high		
Cabinets, wall	6″ to 13″ deep; 15″, 18″, 21″, 24″, 30″ wide; 12″, 18″, 30″ high		

Clearances

Working space in front of cabinets and counters	2′ to 6′
Counter space between equipment	3′ to 5′
Attachment or ventilation for some washers, dryers, stoves, etc.	3″ to 5″ (at back)

BATHROOM	*Small* DEPTH WIDTH		*Large* DEPTH WIDTH
Bathtubs	2′6″ x 4′	to	3′ x 5′
Lavatory	1′3″ x 1′6″	to	2′ x 2′
Toilet	2′ x 1′10″	to	2′6″ x 2′
Shower	2′6″ x 2′6″	to	3′6″ x 3′6″
Bathinette	1′9″ x 2′11″	to	2′ x 3′

Clearances

Space between front of tub and opposite wall	2′6″ to 3′6″
Space in front of toilet	1′6″ to 2′
Space at sides of toilet	1′ to 1′6″
Space between fronts of fixtures	2′ to 3′

Arranging Furniture on Paper

To save time and money as well as to avoid disappointments, it is wise to know what you want and how it will fit into your space before buying or attempting to place furniture in the rooms. Planning on paper is worth many times the small effort it takes.

1. List all activities you want to provide for, the furnishings and equipment each requires.
2. Make accurate drawings of the plan of each room so that ½ or ¼ inch represents 1 foot. Cross-section paper helps greatly. First measure total length and breadth of the rooms and draw the major outlines on paper. Then locate doors, windows, fireplaces, radiators or heating vents, jogs, and any built-in features.
3. Make cardboard cut-outs of your furniture, similar to those in Figure 395 but at the same scale as the drawings of your room. Label each one.
4. Put the cut-outs on the plan, placing large pieces first and working down in size to accessories. Move them until the arrangement seems best to you. Then check circulation paths by drawing them on the plan.
5. Review the arrangement a day or so later and revise if necessary.

► GENERAL PRINCIPLES OF FURNITURE ARRANGEMENT

In a New York City brownstone house remodeled for his family, interior architect Joseph Aronson brilliantly demonstrates originality without affectation. The space available for living and dining is long and narrow, lighted only at one end by two windows and with a fireplace almost centered on one wall. In Figure 396A we can see seventeen pieces of furniture and many accessories ingeniously organized. Immediately apparent is the clear division of this space, by furniture and floor covering alone, into three distinct yet coherent areas. Each was planned in terms of use and beauty with all needed furniture and equipment conveniently and pleasantly placed.

The room is entered (lower left in photograph) from a foyer, which also gives access to the kitchen. A simple dining table, space-savingly set against the wall and with four chairs ready for use, is located in the corner. Diagonally opposite is a fifth chair. A triple-purpose cabinet that provides storage space for dining paraphernalia and a table surface for the sofa unobtrusively separates the entrance-dining area from the conversation

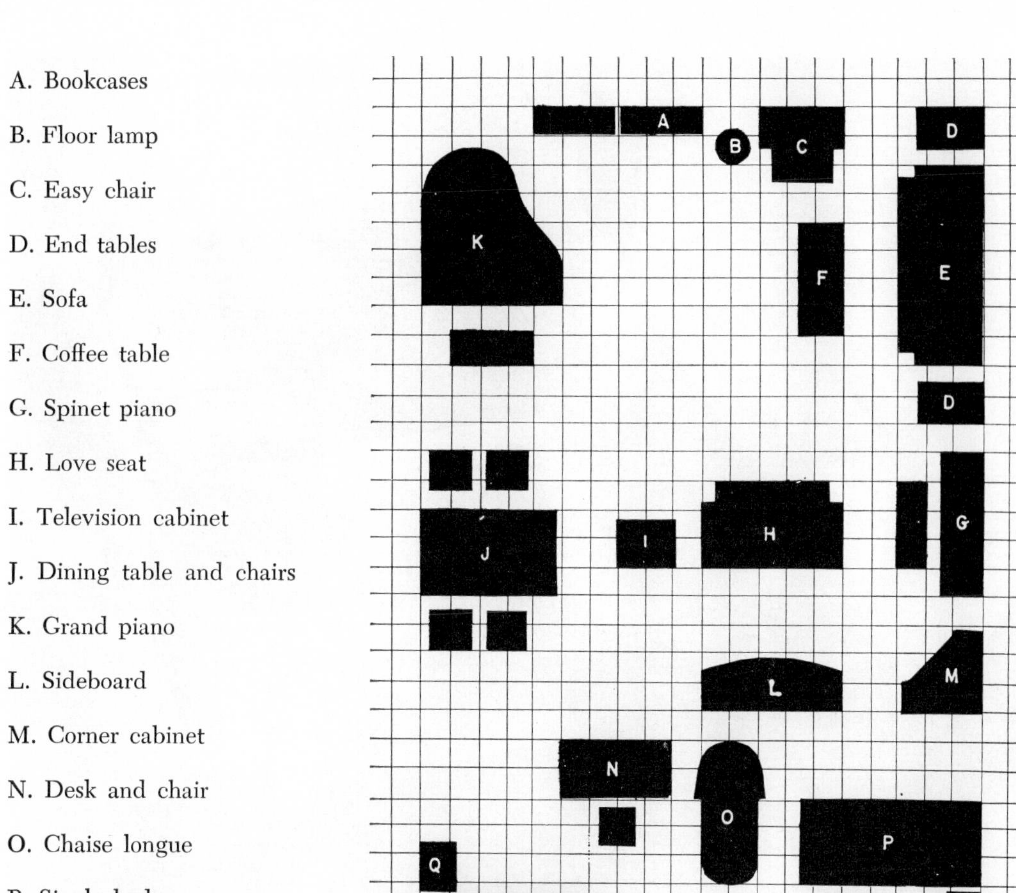

Becoming familiar with furniture sizes and shapes is an important early step in planning arrangements. Each square on this drawing represents one foot. (*Victor Thompson*)

A

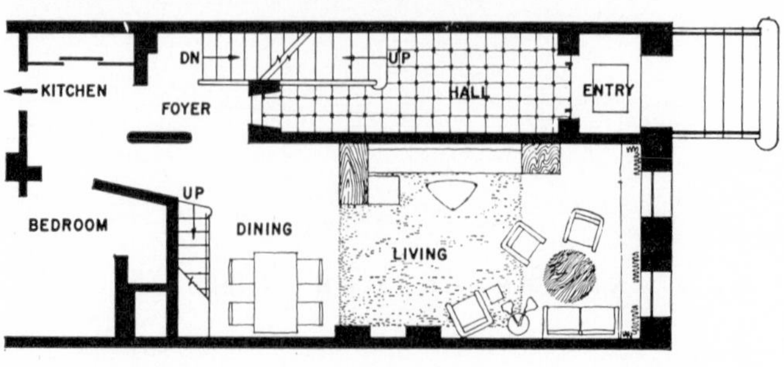

B

Above. In furnishing the living-dining space of his own house, interior architect Joseph Aronson skillfully solved every problem including the placement of paintings and decorative objects. (*Photograph by F. S. Lincoln*)

Left. The plan of Joseph Aronson's apartment shows how sensibly the space has been zoned with furnishings.

center. In the room's center is the dominant conversation group composed of a sofa firmly placed against a solid wall facing the fireplace, an easily moved ottoman, a coffee table, and a lounge chair at a sociable angle. Tables and lamps are convenient to each place where people sit. Beyond is the third group, a subordinate area for conversation or games.

Studying this room as a whole, we notice three fundamentals. Space and energy are conserved by placing major pieces in strict relationship to the walls and fitting them as compactly together as their shape and use permits: they are so rightly placed that moving them is seldom if ever necessary. Everything needed for each activity is available and conveniently placed, but there are no unnecessary items. Ample circulation paths are clearly suggested. In short, use and economy were not overlooked.

Nor were beauty and individuality. Singleness of effect amid variety, but no devitalized harmony, is evident. The major pieces of furniture are consonant but not blandly matched, and the arrangement corresponds to their semiformal character. Rectangularity of room and most of the furniture is frankly recognized. Moreover, arrangement carries beyond furniture: the rug aligns both with the sofa and the projecting wall near the fireplace; furniture near the window is appropriately light in character; and within each group the size and scale of furniture, lamps, and accessories is consistent. Variety, needed to keep even the best of ideas from becoming stale, strengthens the unity. Although the large pieces are similar in character, notice that the four small tables and the three lamps are decidedly unlike. Dining table and chest, related in use and shape, are at right angles to the wall while the two sofas are parallel. Sofa and ottoman are covered in glowing red, the lounge chair in copper-orange. Paintings, sculpture, and accessories show the family's wide range of interests.

Without being static, the whole room is firmly composed. Not even the painting over the fireplace is exactly symmetrical; everywhere, asymmetrical balance implies motion. Parallelism and rectangular shapes, restated many times but with differences, establish the dominant continuity, but when dullness threatens, circles and diagonals come to the rescue with an interplay of contrasts. The conversation group dominates. It is centrally located and defined by the contrasting floor covering. Here is the largest piece of furniture, the sofa, and the most entertaining, the coffee table with its free-curve glass top showing the sculptural wood supports. Here also is the fireplace which is the most richly ornamented spot, and the lounge chair, which is the most conspicuous diagonal. As further reinforcement, color intensity and contrast reach their height in this area. But the rest of the room is no monotonous background, for every part has varying degrees of assertion and reticence, minor climaxes and releases, movements and halts.

This is a room in which furnishings have been chosen and arranged to promote the kind of living this family enjoys. It neither overwhelms with an aggressive effort to be different nor does it follow worn-out formulas. It does not flaunt an "application" of any aims or principles of design, yet it shows a deep personalized understanding of forms expressing their purposes, the coherence of tamed differences, stability teamed with motion, concentration and relaxation of interest. Above all, it conciliates freedom and order.

Another view of Eric Stengade's home (Fig. 371B) shows how an upright piano at right angles to the wall, a lowered ceiling, and different wall treatment can suggest a segregated dining, game, or study space in a simple rectangular room. The large wall map is decorative and instructive. (*Photograph by Andresen*)

15. Lighting, Heating, Ventilation, and Acoustics

CONTROL of illumination, temperature, air movements, and sounds within an architectural shell makes that space comfortably habitable. Only recently have these aspects of the home been given the thought they deserve. Of the four, lighting is the one householders can do most about.

► LIGHTING

Light was discussed as a plastic element in Chapter 7 and as a factor in window design in Chapter 12. Now we consider illuminating our homes when daylight is inadequate. Good artificial illumination can:

- Enable us to see quickly and easily.
- Prevent accidents, especially at such hazards as stairways.
- Protect our health by minimizing eyestrain and by disclosing potentially harmful dirt.
- Contribute to the attractiveness of our homes.

Above. Festively shaped plastic light "puffs" diffuse light in all directions. Sesto Chiarello, designer. (*Damron Kaufmann, Inc.*)

At night, much of a room's character is determined by its illumination. With light, perhaps even more than with color, we can make rooms seem to shrink or swell, become intimate or formal. Important objects can be spotlighted, those of lesser interest de-emphasized. And with the equipment available today all this can be instantly changed by flicking switches or turning dimmers.

Three types of fixtures permit the Ronald Reagans to illumine their living room as the occasion suggests (Fig. 401A). Two of these are built-in. Fluorescent bulbs behind valances spread light down over walls and draperies on three sides of the room from which it is softly reflected. Glareless fixtures, recessed in the ceiling and planned in relationship to furniture arrangement, create pools of light over each chair and each sofa cushion. Portable lamps are the third type and these, treated as decorative accents, are the only conspicuous fixtures. With separate rheostatic dimmers, numberless effects can be produced. When all lights are on, as in the illustration, the room seems brilliantly luminous. The ceiling lights used alone allow people to talk or read and to enjoy the magnificent view of the city below with no reflections in the windows. Not only can interest be focused where wanted but the degree of emphasis can be exactly controlled. A predominance of light-reflecting colors contribute to this flexibility. Ceilings are off-white, walls and draperies light gray, the carpet a darker gray. Upholstery is pale beige. Subtle and sharp accents bring the contrasts needed. Lamp shades and picture frames are white and the wood of the furniture is satiny black. Bright reds, greens, yellows, and blues are distributed in the sofa pillows, lamp bases, paintings, flowers, and magazine covers. Planned in relation to architecture and furnishings, lighting can be the most versatile aspect of homes.

In another house (Fig. 401B) all artificial light in the living-dining space and the terrace comes from "eyeball" fixtures in the ceiling. Taking no floor or table space, they were carefully located to cast light on conversation centers and the painting. For variety, each fixture can be rotated, brightness controlled by dimmers. As in the Reagans' home, walls, floors, and furnishings were planned with lighting in mind. With all light coming from above, the effect might have been monotonous, unbalanced, or harsh were it not for the judicious disposition of color-value and texture contrasts throughout the space. Especially noteworthy are the way in which lighting unites living room and terrace at night and the ease with which good antique furnishings join with those of today in a modern home.

In lighting our homes, we have much to learn from theaters, aquariums, museums, stores and factories, and restaurants. Theaters have long exploited

A

Above. Inconspicuously recessed ceiling fixtures, cove lighting on the walls, and table lamps balance the light in Ronald Reagan's living room. William R. Stephenson, architect. (*General Electric*)

Below. Adjustable "eyeball" fixtures in the ceiling dramatize antique furniture and an old painting; flooding the terrace with light brings indoors and outdoors together in a contemporary home. Carl Koch, architect. (*Photograph by Ernest Silva. Courtesy of* LIVING for Young Homemakers)

B

lighting as a vital part of dramatic production. House lights lower, footlights come on as curtains part, and from then on lights of all colors, brightnesses, degrees of sharpness and diffusion focus attention where wanted and underscore the mood of the play. In aquariums, light is concentrated on the fish while the spectators have just enough light to let them see around, a practice sometimes followed in museums to rivet attention on a few things. At the opposite extreme are the factories, laboratories, and offices flooded with bright illumination everywhere to step up production. Restaurants range from flood- and spot-lighted lunch rooms to caverns of apparently deep purple with a candle on each table and gypsy music to reassure or unnerve you, according to your mood.

Types of Lighting

In terms of purpose, effect, and fixtures, there are two major types of lighting to which a third is sometimes added.

General lighting illumines the room more or less uniformly as the sun illumines the earth. It lets you see all the room in a reassuring way and brings to equal attention the design and color of the whole space. At best, it minimizes the bulkiness of furniture, the darkness of shadows, and the often harsh contrasts of local lighting. It is most often produced with ceiling fixtures or with lamps having reflector bowls and translucent shades (Figs. 403B and C and 411B). It is more truly general when lights concealed in coves evenly illuminate the ceiling or when lighting troughs "wash" large wall areas or curtained windows with light (Fig. 401A). Finally, the entire ceiling or large sections of it can bring light through translucent plastics or glass (Figs. 403A and 418A), and for the future there is promise of a "phosphor-and-glass sandwich" window that is transparent by day and a source of artificial illumination at night.

General lighting can be either *direct*—the light shines directly on objects you want illuminated—or *indirect*—the light is thrown against a surface, usually the ceiling, from which some of it is reflected. Indirect light is usually more pleasantly soft for general illumination than is direct light, but it costs more to operate and may make the reflecting ceilings or walls more dominant than you wish. General lighting is monotonously even in effect and seldom bright enough for reading or work. Therefore, it is usually combined with local lighting.

Local lighting provides the kind and amount of illumination needed at specific places for such activities as reading, cooking or sewing, or enjoying paintings (Figs. 401A and B and 414B). The light source can be high or low, but eye comfort suggests that it be shielded. Except in kitchens

That lighting is a potent design factor is shown by two rooms (on this page and the following), each of which is illumined in three ways.

Right. Direct general lighting from a luminous ceiling *alone* provides diffused but uneventful over-all illumination, accented a little by reflector bulbs over the fireplace. It seems better suited to entrances, hallways, and bathrooms than to living rooms.

A

B

Left. Semirecessed swivel spotlights can direct light straight down or diagonally against walls or draperies from which it is reflected. Reflector bulbs and concealed fluorescent tubes direct some attention to the framed drawings and cabinets.

Right. Suspended fixtures can give both direct and indirect light. Supplementing them with accent lights over the fireplace and cove lighting over cabinets and draperies leads to balance and diversity. (*Photographs by General Electric*)

C

A

Left. Indirect lighting, used alone, is often monotonously flat, especially when the brightness level is low. The white ceiling is efficient but obtrusive; contrasts and accents are clearly needed.

Right. Ceiling spotlights beamed directly down give dramatically sharp but harsh value contrasts. Shadows are black and heavy, would not flatter people. As in a room with windows on only one side, glare and gloom result. Comparison with Figures 401B and 403B demonstrates that other effects can be generated by adjustable ceiling floodlights.

B

C

Left. Direct and indirect general lighting gives balance as well as variety and unity. Illuminating the garden extends the room and eliminates the blackness of uncurtained windows. (*Photographs by General Electric*) and bathrooms, local lighting fixtures are most often movable floor or table lamps, but fixtures attached to the wall, ceiling, or major pieces of furniture are far less nuisance. A major design factor, this type of lighting enables you to create moods, to emphasize important objects, and to bring the visual delights of variety and rhythm.

Play of brilliants is usually seen only on Christmas trees or in fireworks, now that crystal chandeliers and candelabra are rare. It can, though, be produced by candles, by fixtures with many small bulbs or those in which some of the light comes through many small holes in metal shades or wood grilles (Fig. 418A). A similar effect is produced by focusing a bright light on accessories, wall surfaces, or lamp bases of reflecting materials, especially if they are richly ornamented. Of value only to the spirit, its effect is instantly appreciated when you enter a room with much sparkling light.

Specific Factors in Lighting

Planned lighting demands attention to brightness, location and size of light sources and direction of light, the color of light and its effect on colors, and the amount of light reflected by colors on ceilings, walls, and floors.

Brightness of Light. Our eyes are like fantastically miniature cameras that automatically adjust to different brightnesses. Perhaps their greatest defect is that they do not warn us quickly when they are being strained by too little light. Experiments have shown that most people will select as the best the middle of almost any range of brightness they see. If the range is from 10 to 30 footcandles, 20 is most likely to be chosen. When without the observers' knowledge the range is stepped up to from 30 to 100 footcandles, the middle will again be chosen. There is a great difference betwen 20 and 65 footcandles but over short periods of time our eyes do not tell us which is better. Many experts, however, agree that the following footcandles are needed for the activities listed and for general illumination of rooms.

For Activity	*Footcandles*
Reading—small type for prolonged periods	20-50
—casual	20-30
Sewing—fine needlework on dark goods	75-150
—prolonged average sewing	50-100
Writing	20-50
Card-playing	10-20
Children's study table	20-50
Kitchen work counter and sink	20-50
Make-up table or bathroom mirror	20-50
Workbench	20-100
Ironing	20-50

For General Illumination

Entrance halls and stairways	2-5
Living rooms	5-10
Dining rooms	5-10
Kitchens	10-20
Bedrooms	5-10
Bathrooms	5-10
Laundry	10-20
Libraries	5-10
Recreation rooms	5-10

Note that these are footcandles, "the direct illumination on a surface one foot from one international candle." The wattages necessary to obtain the desired footcandles of light vary with the distance between light source and surface, the design of the lighting equipment, and the amount of reflection from ceiling, walls, floors, and furnishings.

Keep the following in mind, too, when considering quantity of light.

- Bright light is stimulating, calls forth energy, and makes us feel as though we should be up and doing.
- Low levels of brightness may seem relaxing and restful, romantic, dingy and depressing, or even frightening, depending on the context.
- Moderately bright light brings no pronounced feeling other than general well-being.
- More wattage is needed in rooms of low color value than in those of light colors.
- Balance, rhythm, and emphasis come from appropriate distribution of quantities of light.

Glare is to be avoided. It comes from exposed, bright sources of light; incorrectly designed fixtures; too much light, especially from one direction; and excessive contrasts. The contrasting glare and gloom, frequently encountered in night driving and too often in homes, is an eye-fatiguing combination. For close work, the working area should not be more than 5 times as bright as the darkest part of the room, and a ratio greater than 1 to 10 is undesirable any place. But it is also fatiguing, both to the muscles of the eyes and the spirits of the occupants, to have every part of a room equally bright. Moderation in quantity and contrast of light is a sensible solution.

With rheostatic dimmers, brightness of light from almost any fixture can be instantly and smoothly adjusted from a candlelike glow to full brightness. The small cost of these dimmers could, in many instances, be more than made up for by reducing the number of separate fixtures which without rheostats are needed for varied levels of brightness.

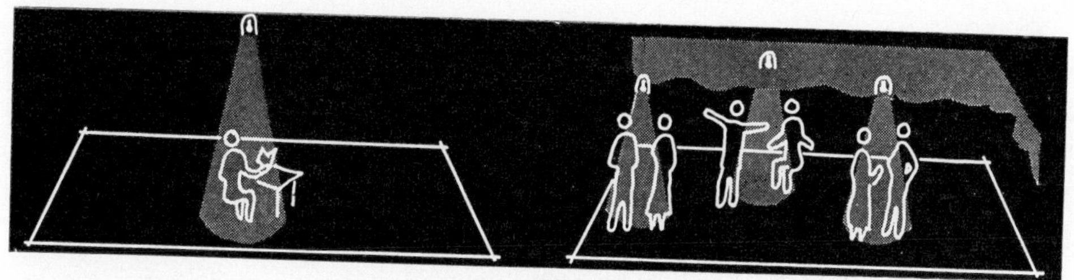

A small pool of bright light creates an intimate mood, separates an area from the rest of the room. Many pools of light plus illumination on walls and ceilings seem social and festive. (*Reproduced by permission from "An Investigation of the Small House," School of Architecture, Pratt Institute*)

Two facts are worth remembering. The *kind* of light is as important as the *amount*. The *Law of Inverse Squares*—"The illumination of a surface varies directly with the candle power of the source and inversely as the square of the perpendicular distance between the source and the surface"—always operates.

Location and Direction. Lighting from above seems normal, accustomed as we are to the sun more or less overhead, while lighting from other places is less expected. Here are some observations:

- Location of both the light source and the surface from which the light is reflected are important in the total effect.
- Light high in the room seems formal, makes us think of standing up and staying on our best behavior.
- Light sources exactly at eye level are seldom wanted.
- Light below eye level seems friendly and draws people together. It is also useful while watching television.
- Light from near the floor flatters people as do theater footlights, is a good safety device near steps and in halls, and is a refreshing surprise.
- Light from a number of sources, or well-diffused light, makes a room seem luminous rather than merely lighted, tends to spread interest throughout the room, and is comfortably undemanding (Figs. 401A and 403C).
- Strongly directed light, such as comes from one or two spotlights, is dramatic, emphatic, and often harsh. Our attention tends to follow its path—up, down, sideways, or diagonally—much as it does a solid form (Fig. 407).
- Light for working should illumine the task without shadows and should not shine in the worker's eyes.

Size of Light Source. Much depends on the size of the light source. Compare the luminous vault of the sky by day with its myriad play of brilliants at night.

- Broad sources of light—the sky, a skylight or an illuminated ceiling, and a window wall—give flat, glareless, uneventful light excellent for seeing, health, and safety because they minimize contrasts and shadows. Decoratively, though, they can be monotonous.
- Smaller light sources that diffuse light broadly through lenses, translucent shades, or reflectors approximate this effect.
- Very small light sources, especially if bright, have high accent value, emphasize parts of rooms, and make silver and glass sparkle, but they can be visually fatiguing and unless carefully used cause spottiness.

Color of Light. We have always been timid about using colored illumination in our homes, perhaps quite rightly because it is difficult and expensive. The color of light is determined by three factors: the light source, the diffusing or reflecting shade, and the room surfaces.

- White light shows colors as they are and has no pronounced emotional effect.
- Warm light flatters people, dispels the chill associated with darkness, and brightens warm color schemes but deadens blues and purples.
- Cool light makes rooms more spacious, separates objects one from another—and may make people look cadaverous.
- Warm and cool light are difficult to combine in the same room.

Effect of Colors on Amount of Light Reflected. No surface in the home reflects or absorbs all the light that hits it, but high-value colors reflect a high percentage and low-value colors reflect little. Listed below are the percentages of light reflected by some of the common colors.

Color	*Percentage of Light Reflected*	*Color*	*Percentage of Light Reflected*
White	89	Buff	63
Ivory	87	Pale Green	59
Canary yellow	77	Shell pink	55
Cream	77	Bright sage	52
Caen stone	76	Silver gray	46
Orchid	67	Olive tan	43
Cream gray	66	Forest green	22
Ivory tan	66	Coconut brown	16
Sky blue	65	Black	2

Clearly, white gives the most light for the money paid to the electric company and black gives the least.

Flames, Incandescence, and Luminescence

For untold ages man depended on the flames of fireplaces, candles, or lamps to illumine homes at night. Nowadays we seldom depend on flame light except occasionally from candles and fireplaces indoors, barbecues and Hawaiian torches outdoors. Although extremely inefficient, all give a warm, flickering, flattering light that seems hospitable, even festive. Electricity, though, is our major concern, and it produces light in two ways.

- **Incandescent** light is produced by heating any material, but usually metal, to a temperature at which it glows. Typical incandescent bulbs have a tungsten filament in a sealed glass container. A visit to an electric store will show that these bulbs come in many, many types.
- **Luminescence** or "cold" light is not produced by heat. *Fluorescence* is the only luminescent light source commonly used in homes. A glass tube with an inside coating of fluorescent powder is filled with vaporized mercury and argon, then the ends are sealed with two cathodes. When electric current activates the gases, invisible ultraviolet rays cause the fluorescent coating to produce visible light. Although fluorescent tubes vary less in size and shape than incandescent, they have a considerable diversity.

Incandescent and fluorescent bulbs have these desirable qualities:

Incandescent

Fixtures and bulbs cost less.
Light is sympathetically warm and "full" in color.
Textures and forms are emphasized because the light comes from a relatively small source.
Light comes the minute you push the switch.
There is no flicker or hum and less likelihood of radio interference.

Fluorescent

Bulbs last about 7 times as long as do incandescent.
Produce about 2½ times as much light for current used.
Light source is considerably larger, which spreads the light more and produces less glare.
Almost no heat is produced.

► LIGHTING FIXTURES

Ideal fixtures give us the kind and amount of light where it is wanted (use); balance original cost with the electricity they use, the ease with which they are cleaned and bulbs are replaced, and the space they take (economy); contribute to the esthetic qualities of our homes (beauty); and underline the distinctive character that we seek (individuality). Almost inevitably they contrast with other furnishings because they are quite different in purpose: this suggests that *some of them* be purposefully chosen as accents. In general, though, it is sensible to have most of them appropriate in size, scale, and character to the rooms and other furnishings. As with fabrics, lighting fixtures can set up their own pattern of design running through the entire home.

Fixtures today come in bewildering diversity, but the light sources fall into three basic shapes. They can be lines, as in fluorescent tubes or in long lighting troughs (Figs. 401A and 404A), which lead the eyes in a strongly directional movement. They can also be spots. If large, these are like little suns (Figs. 399 and 404B); if small, as in candles, like sparks or stars. Whatever the size, fixtures tend to become more or less static centers of attention. And there are broad planes that, like pieces of the sky, light large areas evenly.

Architectural and Built-in Lighting

As with built-in furniture, built-in lighting assures you that lighting was not an afterthought. It contributes to the home's total unity and can produce unique effects. The large ceiling panels in Figures 25A and 403A illustrate a trend toward illumination from large surfaces of low brightness. These together with the light troughs mentioned in the preceding paragraph are important parts of the whole architectural concept of the house. A few of the many other possibilities are shown in Figures 418A and B. Closely allied to truly architectural lighting are the many mass-produced fixtures that are set into or attached to ceilings and walls.

Ceiling fixtures, once banished from consideration, have staged a healthy comeback through vastly improved design (Figs. 411A, B, and C). Their possible relation to the ceiling plane is similar to that of fireplaces to walls. Some are inconspicuously recessed in the ceiling (Fig. 401A), others are flush with it (Fig. 328A), and the light can be softened with louvers or diffused with lenses. Shallow glass or plastic bowls, dropped a few inches, reflect light from the ceiling and diffuse light through the bowl. They can also direct a pool of light downward, making them inexpensive, three-in-one ways to light space for eating, hobbies, or homework. Others are dropped well below the ceiling as illustrated in Figures 403C, 411B, and 418B. Those adjustable in height and also in position (Fig. 411C) give welcome flexibility and facilitate maintenance. Adjustable spot and floodlights, now available with shades in many sizes, shapes, and materials, can be turned for direct

Ceiling fixtures can be handsome and efficient.

A

Above. Thin slices of shells from the South Seas held together with pewter bands glow opalescently, are delightful enrichment. (*Decorative Imports*)

Left. The top and middle fixtures have opaque shades that reflect light from bulbs placed below them. The others diffuse light through translucent shades and also direct light downwards, or sometimes upwards, through openings in the shades. (*Ledlin Lighting Co.*)

Below. One light meets many needs when it travels on a track and can be raised or lowered. (*Lightolier*)

B

C

light on work areas or visual centers of interest or on walls or ceilings for reflected light.

Wall fixtures, with a few exceptions, closely resemble ceiling and portable lights. As with ceiling fixtures, wall units were once popular, fell from favor, and are now back. It is true that once in a while they interfere with hanging pictures or with changes in furniture arrangement, unless they are of the pin-up kind, but these are small prices to pay for the fact that they are out of the way and free table and desk surfaces for other things.

Portable Lamps

Floor and table lamps can be moved when and where you need them, and they can be lively decorative accessories. In many instances, those that are unornamented and inconspicuous seem best—but genuinely handsome, decorative lamps can greatly enrich a room at the same time they provide light. A beautiful piece of ceramic or glass, a richly modeled work of metal, profits from light above it. So does some sculpture, such as the table lamp in Figure 22B, provided the sculpture is worth lighting and is appropriate to its setting. Unfortunately, good lamps of these kinds are expensive and hard to find. The plethora of "cute" little lamps and large "decorative" concoctions (see Fig. 404B) seen in many stores and, worse, in front of large windows are typically as ugly as inefficient.

Base and shade, although different in function and usually in material, are parts of one visual unit. This suggests a fundamental agreement between the two, some qualities in common but seldom exact repetition. Pages 415 and 416 illustrate a few of the ways in which variety in unity can be achieved.

Shapes of lamps ought to grow from their functions: the base supports the bulbs and shade; the shade shields our eyes from glare, directs and diffuses the light. But materials also play a determining role. The simplest base is a cylinder with a footing large enough for stability—breadth is more important than weight in keeping a lamp upright. If the support is of metal or wood, it can be more slender than if of clay or glass. All can be plain for simplicity of effect and maintenance or ornamented for concentrated interest.

Shades are usually truncated cones to spread the light downward, and these can be tall and steep for concentration or low and wide for dispersion. Shades can, or course, be rectangular or triangular, but rounded forms seem more congenial to light and we welcome the few curves we can sensibly get in our homes.

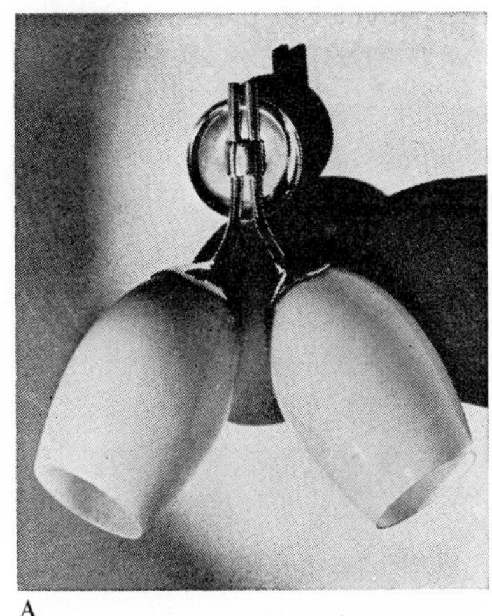

A

B

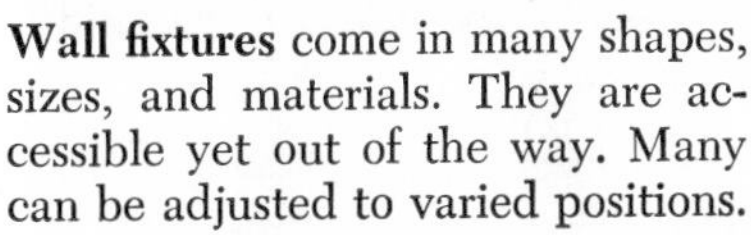

Wall fixtures come in many shapes, sizes, and materials. They are accessible yet out of the way. Many can be adjusted to varied positions.

Above left. Beautifully shaped translucent glass bowls on a brass base are enriching accents whether lighted or not. Paavo Tynell, designer. (*Finnish-American Trading Corp.*)

Above right. Sensitive proportions and elimination of all but essentials distinguish a swinging lamp with a linen shade. (*Hansen Lamps*)

Right. Handmade Venetian glass shades in brilliant colors make wall lamps eventful. Paolo Venini, designer. (*Altamira*)

Below right. A pantograph bracket allows this lamp to be moved in or out, up or down, and around in a 180° arc. (*Lightolier*)

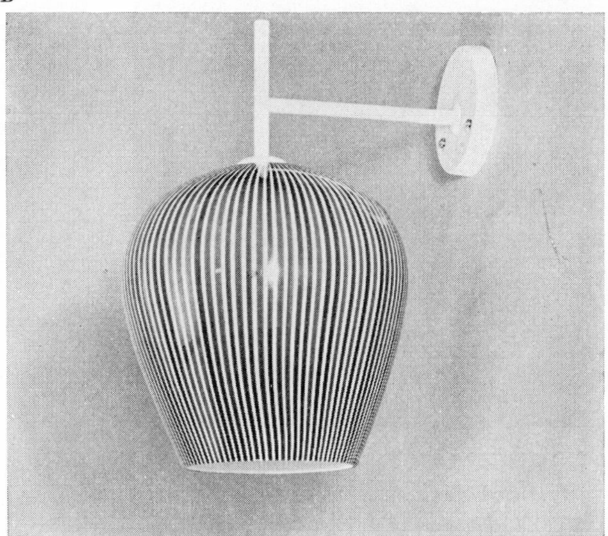

C

D

Floor lamps are portable yet put light high in the room.

Left. Similar in design to the wall lamp shown in Figure 413B, this floor lamp has unusual flexibility. (*Hosmer Lamps*)

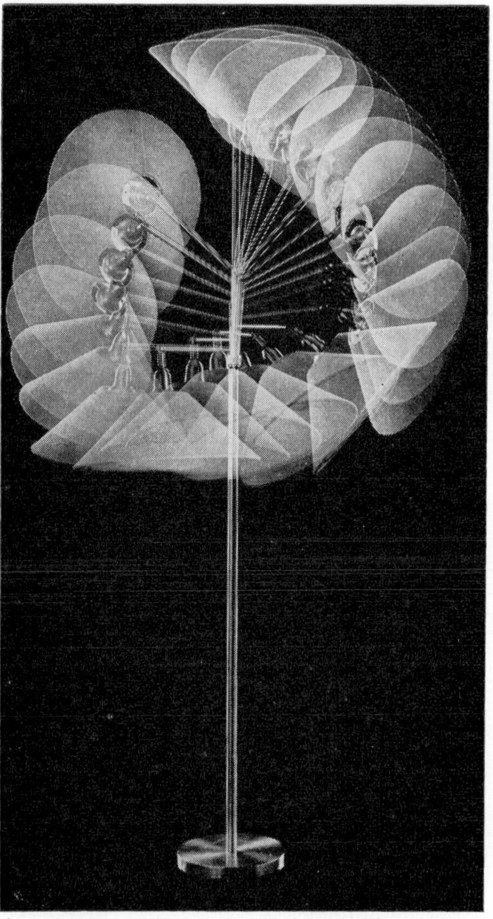

A

Right. Pole lamps, wedged tightly between floor and ceiling wherever one wishes them, are versatile. The top reflector floods the ceiling; the second illumines the paintings; the third diffuses light for reading; and the bottom one washes the wall with light. (*Courtesy of* Better Homes and Gardens)

B

A

B

Table lamps can be handsome ornaments.

Above left. A sensitively shaped wood base and a plastic shade that spreads the light from a lamp of unobtrusive distinction. (*Kurt Versen*)

Above right. A gleaming brass "spool" base with a shade of hand-woven brown and orange matchstick bamboo combines historic and contemporary forms. (*Frederick Cooper*)

Below left. A pear-shaped china base mounted on walnut is amiably related in shape and texture to a rayon shade, expresses formal refinement. (*Paul Hansen*)

Below right. Paper bubbles, variously shaped and suspended on thin wire legs, are festive and buoyant. Isamu Noguchi, designer. (*Bonniers*)

C

D

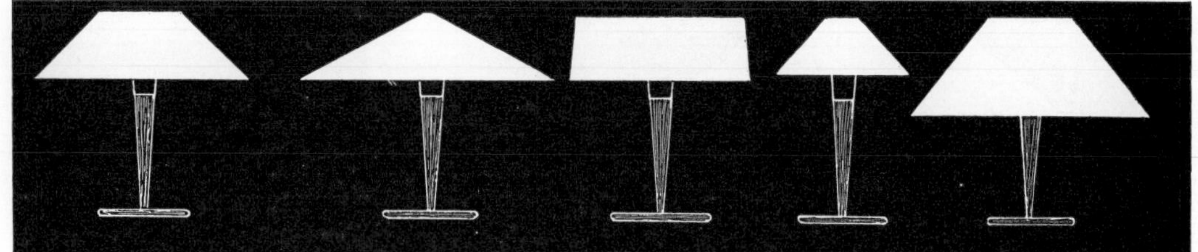

At the far left is a lamp in which shade and base are pleasantly compatible. A slightly broader, pointed cone gives a more energetic effect. A rectangular shade results in a more blocky appearance, satisfactory if this character is wanted. A shade that is too small makes the lamp look pinheaded, while one that is too large produces a droopy, top-heavy feeling. (*Matt Kahn*)

Size is determined by illumination requirements together with the size of the room and its furnishings. High lamps with large spreading shades illumine large areas and are in scale with large furniture, "overscaled" lamps can be dramatic focal points but unless sensitively used seem to crowd small space. The more lamps in a room the smaller each can be, but too many small lamps are cluttering.

Color is important, especially in translucent shades but also in the whole ensemble, because lamps when lighted are very conspicuous. Liking warm artificial light, most of us rule out blue, green, or violet shades of translucent materials, but in some rooms these colors may be desirable in opaque materials. Bases can be in any color needed in the room.

Lighting for Activities

Effective lighting has these characteristics:

- Sufficient, glareless light where needed for close work.
- Adequate, pleasant general illumination to reduce fatiguing contrasts.
- Good illumination at danger points.
- An over-all pattern that is rhythmic and balanced, that shows to advantage what is considered important.

In designing a home or revising the furnishings of a room, you will find that it pays to draw a plan with furniture arrangements. Next indicate where local illumination is needed. Then think about what kinds of general and accent lighting are wanted in relationship to the character of the room, the colors, and the textures of all surfaces.

Entrance areas benefit from friendly, welcoming illumination as a transition from the dark outside to the brightness of the living room, to let guests and hosts see each other in a pleasant light as an introduction to the home. Diffused light from ceiling or wall fixtures, perhaps supplemented by more concentrated, sparkling light on some object of interest makes a balanced effect.

Living and **family rooms** need general illumination, preferably both direct and indirect, to bring walls and furniture, floors and ceilings into soft visibility. Flexibly controlled, direct light is requisite where people read or sew, play games, or do homework. And some scintillating light adds animation.

Dining spaces deserve primary emphasis on what is most important—the table and the people around it. If some light is directed downward, silver and glass, dishes and food sparkle. Indirectly diffused light lessens glare and unbecoming shadows. That there are no rigid rules is shown in Figures 418A and B.

Kitchens need good light directed onto work centers and eating table plus a fairly high level of general illumination. Ceiling lights are almost indispensable, plus bands of light at strategic points (Fig. 70B). Kitchens are usually the best illuminated rooms in the house: much thought has been given to them, and we are likely to think in straightforward terms about this room.

Bathrooms need lights near the mirror to give shadowless illumination to a person's face. This is best achieved by bands of light on all sides of the mirror, next by lights on two sides or above and below. General illumination from a ceiling fixture or two is needed to light the rest of the room.

Bedrooms merit light for dressing, reading in bed, and such activities as desk work, reading, or sewing. Direct-indirect lights over the bed, reading chair and work surface and direct lights near mirrors may be all that is needed, but some general lighting is usually advisable.

Halls require only over-all lighting of low brightness. They can be adequately lighted from ceiling fixtures or glareless wall lights. The fixtures can also be almost at the floor as in theaters—the floor is what you want to see most and it is fun for a change to have light low in the room.

Stairways are hazardous. Accidents are lessened if the light clearly differentiates the treads from the risers. Ceiling or wall fixtures that send even, glare-free light downward do this well. Over-all lighting is unsatisfactory; spotty or distracting lighting is dangerous.

Exterior lighting is typically slighted. The minimum—seldom met—is illuminating the entrance so that it can be recognized and the house number so that it can be read from the street. It is better when both visitor and host can see each other in a good light.

A

B

Illuminating dining space is a problem to which there are many solutions.

Above. In an open-plan house emphasizing large simple planes of varied materials, a wood grille is appropriate in scale and character. Faceted into many small spots, the light would make silver and glass scintillate. Alden Dow, architect. (*Photograph by Hedrich-Blessing*)

Left. In an old remodeled farmhouse, dramatic illumination from an adjustable ceiling fixture is supplemented and balanced by concealed lighting in the cabinet and at the window. Eugene and Olive Stephenson, designers. (*Photograph by Lisanti. Courtesy of* Better Homes and Gardens)

Terraces, patios, and gardens can be enjoyed at night if they are lighted. This has become especially important with window walls and with landscape design that is integrated with the house (Figs. 401B and 404C). Seen from inside, lighted outdoor areas greatly increase the apparent size of the interior, lighten the windows and bring a little illumination into the house. Typical solutions are weatherproof fixtures mounted on exterior walls or overhanging roofs. More elaborate installations have spot and flood-lights concealed in the landscape.

Switches and Outlets

Every room in the house needs a light switch beside any door by which you enter or leave it. Stairs need switches at top and bottom, halls at both ends. Moreover, the switches ought to turn on the lights usually needed in that room. Outlets for lamps and appliances should be in every wall space 3 or more feet wide that is separated from other walls by doors or floor-length windows. On long walls, two or more outlets are often needed to lessen the hazards of long cords.

- Switches controlling bed lamps should be within *easy* reach of a person lying on the bed.
- Switches for outdoor lighting are most convenient if inside the house.
- Some outlets are more convenient if they are at about table height: near ironing boards for electric irons; near dining tables for toasters, coffee pots, etc.; along the back of kitchen counter space for appliances used there; near sewing centers for sewing machines; and in back of electric dryers and washers. Men appreciate outlets conveniently placed for electric shavers and, in workshops, for electric tools.

Many people find outdoor outlets desirable for electrically operated barbecues, portable lighting, or Christmas decorations.

It is relatively easy to get sufficient light on work surfaces to avoid eyestrain and to get some kind of general illumination. To achieve completely satisfying illumination in the whole house takes thoughtful planning, but our eyes and spirit deserve artificial illumination that is efficient and delightful.

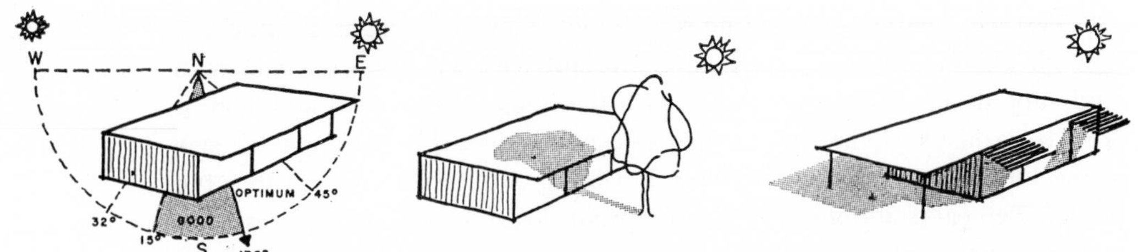

Comfortable temperatures are the result of house orientation and design as well as of mechanical equipment. *Left:* This is the ideal orientation for typical sites in the northeastern United States. *Center:* In summer, all surfaces possible should be shaded by trees. *Right:* Shielding glass by overhanging roofs and sunshades reduces heat gain 70 percent. (*Reproduced by permission from "An Investigation of the Small House," School of Architecture, Pratt Institute*)

► HEATING AND COOLING

Our great-grandparents would be astonished at our assumption that central heating will be built into most homes, for they typically depended on stoves and fireplaces for warmth. Our grandchildren may, in turn, wonder why we paid so little heed to the proved fact that all-year comfort is a matter of house orientation and design, of materials and construction as well as of mechanical equipment.

Artificial Heating

Heating and cooling systems are complicated mechanically. Even more complex is getting the best system for a specific house. Only experts should be trusted with its planning, but a householder benefits from knowing a few basic facts and principles.

- Artificial heat for homes is produced in three ways:
  - Heating air in a warm-air furnace;
  - Heating water in a boiler;
  - Sending electricity through a resistant conductor, as in toasters.
- Heat is brought to our living space through:
  - Registers emitting warmed air;
  - Radiators that are comparatively small, high-temperature units;
  - Radiant panels that are large, low-temperature surfaces.
- Heat then affects us and our homes by:
  - *Conduction* through solid matter, either continuous or in close contact, as when our feet are warmed by a warm floor.
  - *Convection,* or moving currents of air, as when the warm air blown from a register decreases the heat loss of our bodies.

Radiation when heat jumps from one solid to another without appreciably affecting the temperature of the space between, as in infrared heating lamps.

Artificial Heating Systems

Only a few years ago we could have written that there were two types of central heating: warm air, and hot water or steam, produced in a basement furnace and kept in circulation by gravity. A major improvement came with fans or blowers to force warm air into rooms and cold air out, and pumps to push steam or hot water through radiators. With these mechanical substitutes for gravity, furnaces no longer had to be in basements—and the centrally heated, basementless house became practical. Such a house also gave better circulation of heat. At about the same time, oil, gas, and electricity began to take the place of wood and coal, and thermostats were introduced to keep the temperature about where we wanted it. Then an old concept of heating large surfaces of rooms to relatively low temperatures was revived in the reintroduction of radiant-panel heating.

The general characteristics of different systems can best be understood if they are grouped in terms of the way heat is brought into our rooms.

Registers. Those systems that convect air warmed in a furnace into rooms through registers give quick heat and are moderately low in initial cost. The moving air, which can be cleaned and humidified or dehumidified, dispels stuffiness and tempers moisture content. Since the same ducts and

Warm-air registers, hot-water or steam radiators, or radiant panels heat our homes artificially. (*Reproduced by permission from "An Investigation of the Small House," School of Architecture, Pratt Institute*)

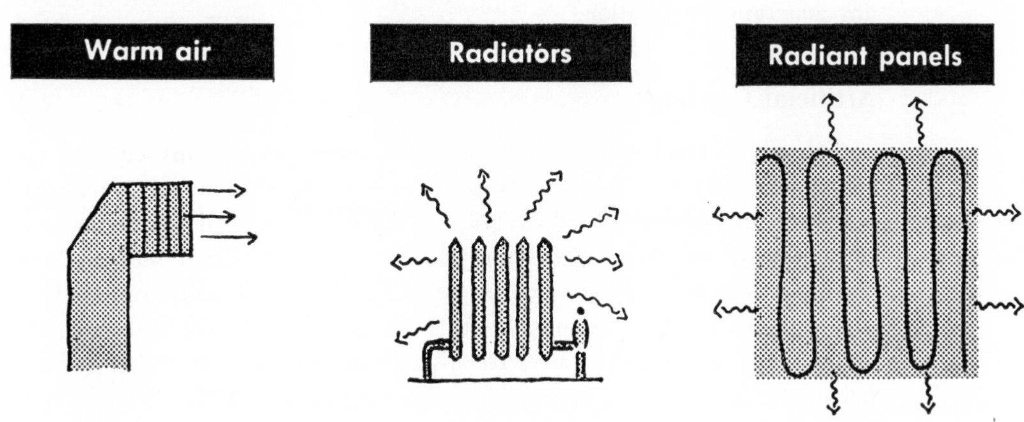

registers can be used for cooling, the cost of air-conditioning is lowered. The registers, though, may interfere with furniture arrangement and, except in the best installations, temperatures may fluctuate noticeably and the air may seem uncomfortably hot. Registers can be of the conventional type set in floors or walls, or they can be long, low baseboard units. The latter, usually along exterior walls, keep temperatures quite uniform.

Radiators. Hot water circulated through radiators give relatively uniform temperatures, although rooms cannot be so quickly heated or cooled as with registers. Usually more expensive to install, they give no control of the air other than temperature. Radiators unobtrusively fitted into baseboards have gained favor over the old, unsightly, space-consuming type.

Radiant Panels. Water or air heated in a furnace, or wires that transform electricity into heat, can bring floors, ceilings, or walls to low temperatures, which, in turn, radiate heat to us and our furniture. They keep us, the architectural shell, and our furnishings pleasantly and uniformly warm while the air stays relatively cool. The complete absence of registers or radiators is a blessing. Radiant panels are rather expensive to install but not to operate, and they require good insulation (which you ought to have anyway). Some types, notably hot-water pipes in concrete floors, do not respond so quickly to temperature changes outside as do those using warm air or electricity.

The preceding are the typical "single" systems, but there is a definite trend toward combinations. For example, warm air circulated under the floor and then into the room through registers gives quick responsiveness and uniformity. Hot water can also heat the floor as well as radiators located at normally cold spots. Then, too, there are the small units, individually heated by gas or electricity and usually placed in walls, which may be all that is needed in mild climates and can effectively supplement central systems in any geographical location.

Artificial Cooling

Home air-conditioning has come to be regarded in many parts of the country as almost a necessity because excessively high temperatures and humidity are enervating. Operating on the same principle as mechanical refrigerators, air-conditioners take heat and moisture from the air, keep clean air in motion, reduce housecleaning, and tend to keep families happily at home. Central cooling systems (often combined with heating) have many points of superiority over room-size units. It is reported that average homes can have cooling systems installed for about half the cost of a new car, and that the cost of operating them for an hour is equivalent to that of driving an automobile one and one-half miles. As with heating, this is a field in which amateurs can make costly mistakes.

Natural Heating and Cooling

Egyptians and Romans, Eskimos and South Sea Islanders adapted their homes to their climates with an efficiency that should make many of us blush with shame. Even the best engineered heating and cooling systems cannot be expected to give economical comfort in houses designed *against* their physical environment. Windows come to mind first and, as mentioned in Chapter 12, well-oriented glass areas reduce fuel bills. In a Minneapolis house with glass concentrated toward the south, these facts were observed one sunny winter Sunday. Outside temperature hovered around zero; directly inside the south window wall it was nearly 100, while the rest of the house stayed at 70 with no help from the furnace until the sun set. Heat loss at night and gain during the day were minimized with double-glazing and

Peter Lee's prize-winning solar house design for an Arizona site separates group living from private living with a breezeway. Exterior walls are decorative insulating masonry. The three terraces are roofed with louvers that shade them in summer and collect heat in winter. (*Courtesy of Association for Applied Solar Energy*)

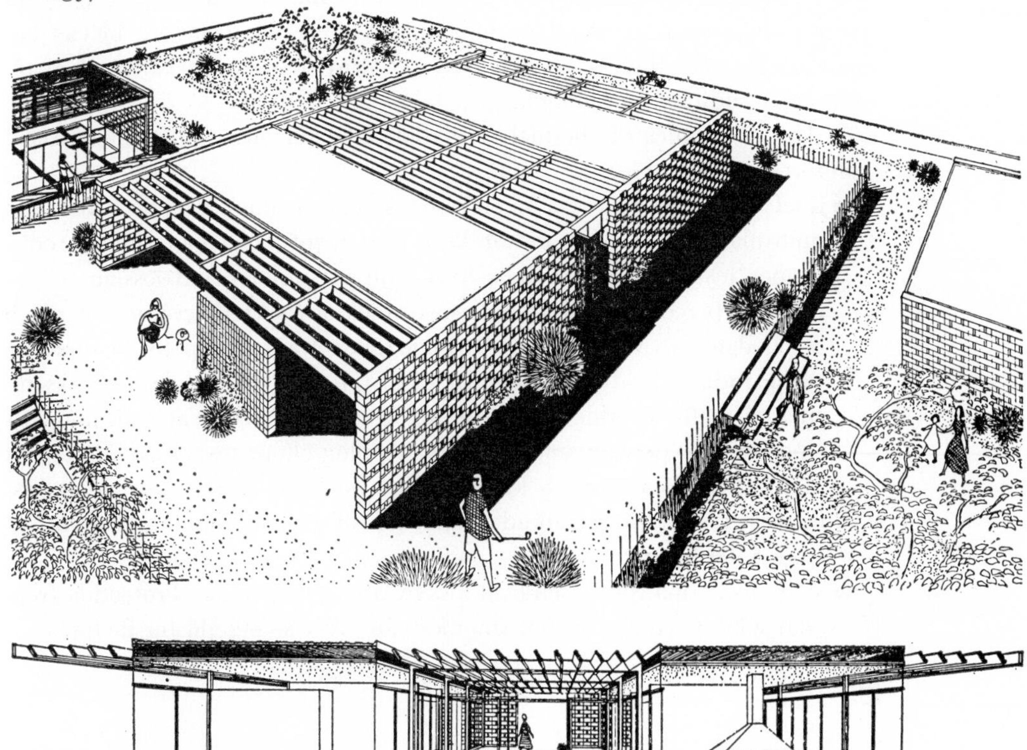

insulated walls and roof. Precisely designed overhangs kept summer sun off the glass.

Climate designing varies from one section of the country to another, and it can even vary on sites only a few hundred feet apart because of differences in elevation, the presence of trees or bodies of water. In some areas, summer cooling is the big problem, in others it is winter heating. Sometimes it is both, while in a few areas neither heat nor cold are extreme. Although there are a few fairly safe rules of thumb—keep large areas of glass on the south is one—the wise architect studies the general and local climate as carefully as he does the family who will live in the house. Perhaps he should give the climate more thought, for the house is less likely to move than the family.

Putting the sun to work, scientifically, has led to quite new concepts of over-all house design, not merely of placing windows where they perform best. Some of the results are quite startling, not at all because the designers sought to be "different" but because this aspect of architecture concentrates on different design factors.

Insulation

The materials in the house shell, and the way they are put together, are basic factors in insulation. Generally speaking, dense and uniform materials, such as metal and glass, conduct heat and cold readily, while such porous substances as wood or lightweight-aggregate concrete blocks are poor conductors—that is, good insulators. Most houses, regardless of material, need additional insulation.

The economies of thermal insulation are startling, and the increased comfort is remarkable.

- Roofs get up to twice as much radiant heat in summer as do walls, and uninsulated flat roofs transmit 25 to 50 percent more than pitched roofs. Proper insulation can reduce heat gain in summer and loss in winter up to 90 percent. Shade from trees can lower roof temperatures as much as 60 degrees. Windows with single glass transmit up to 35 times as much radiant heat in summer, and 10 times as much in winter, as insulated walls. Double-glazing is reported to reduce heat gain and loss from 45 to 60 percent, and weather-stripping eliminates about 70 percent of the heat loss through leakage. One hundred feet of unshaded east or west glass requires an additional ton of air-conditioning at a cost of from $300 to $800.
- Wall insulation can lessen heat loss by about 60 percent. Protection from cold winter winds and hot summer sun are also significant factors.

Most heat-cold insulating materials, from sawdust to spun glass, are porous, and it is the air imprisoned in small spaces that makes them effective. Another type is a thin coating of shiny, heat-reflecting metal mounted on heavy paper.

In planning for year-round thermal comfort, you should center your attention on three interrelated phases of house design: orientation of the house, especially major rooms and large areas of glass; materials and construction plus insulation; and mechanical equipment. Because the whole matter is full of pitfalls for the laymen, get acquainted with the fundamentals but leave the technicalities to trustworthy experts.

Some factors we can deal with, however, are those related to color, texture, and form. Recollect that color can, by looking warm or cool, noticeably affect our sensations of physical temperature. The amount of furniture and the textures of materials influence us in much the same way. A crowded room looks warm, a sparsely furnished one cool. Smooth materials seem cold, fuzzy ones hot. Compare the effect of the rooms illustrated in Figures 270B and 290. A lounge chair upholstered in wool looks warmer, and actually is, than an open chair of rattan and stretched fabric or one of metal and plastic (Figs. 365A and B, 373B and C). Draperies and blinds insulate against night coldness, somewhat less against daytime heat, transmitted through window glass. Rugs warm a cold floor and screens can shut off drafts in an otherwise comfortable room.

Double-glazed windows pay big dividends in extreme climates. Moisture condensation on the window at the right comes from warm air hitting cold glass. Two panes of glass in the other window keep cold out, warmth in, and the window free from moisture. (*Pittsburgh Plate Glass Co.*)

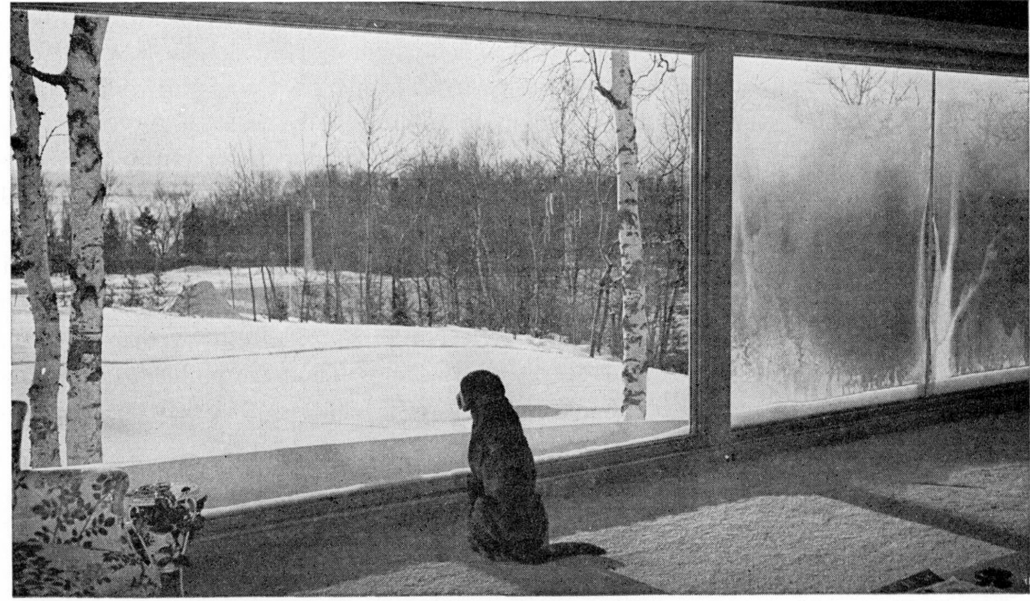

► VENTILATION

Good ventilation gets the hot stale air out of the tops of rooms, brings fresh air in, keeps the air in gentle motion, and accomplishes all this without uncomfortable drafts. Major devices are openable doors and windows, ventilating grilles, exhaust fans, warm-air furnaces with blowers, air-conditioning units, and portable fans.

The hot high air can be removed with windows, grilles, or exhaust fans placed high in the room or with ventilating skylights. Forced-draft warm-air furnaces, with the heat on or off, circulate the air as does most cooling equipment. Without one or more of these, a layer of practically motionless air is likely to stick near the ceiling. If stale air is taken out, fresher air is bound to come in. Usually it comes through windows or doors, but ventilators strategically placed in the walls are sometimes preferable (Fig. 309). These usually have horizontal louvers on the outside to ward off rain or snow, fixed insect screens, and hinged or sliding panels on the inside to control the flow of air. Their good points are numerous: being unobtrusive they can be more varied in size, shape, and location than can windows; affording privacy, they can be placed where windows are unsuitable; and having screens, permanently fixed and inconspicuous, they lessen the need for visually distracting insect barriers at windows.

Of all rooms, kitchens need the best ventilation and usually get it with exhaust fans supplementing windows and doors. Bathrooms come next but seldom fare as well. Windows or grilles high in the wall (Fig. 54A) can be opened much or little, or controllable ceiling ventilators, combine privacy with fresh air. Living and dining space also needs good air circulation, but this is ordinarily fairly well handled. The rooms are typically large and have windows on two or more sides. In contemporary planning, air flows through this space and to the outside as easily as people do. Doors plus windows and grilles, some high and others low and on different walls, is a good typical solution. Bedrooms benefit from fresh air without drafts. Again high windows or ventilators on two walls, supplemented by windows at normal height and doors, allow flexible control.

Form and color have a psychological effect on ventilation needs just as they do on every other aspect of our behavior. Warm, dark colors and heavy forms make it seem a little harder to find fresh air than do cool, light colors and small-scale, airy furnishings. Thus, the problem is not only to get adequate ventilation but to furnish homes so that they seem appropriately ventilated.

► ACOUSTICS

Noise, noise, noise! Television and Hi-Fi radio-phonographs, vacuum cleaners and electric washers, automobiles and aircraft—and children—all bring noises unknown in the house a generation or two ago. Yes, there were always children, but psychologists have made it clear that repressing the natural, noisy activities of children can be harmful. Coupled with an actual increase of noise are four factors that make it more noticeable. Houses have fewer and smaller rooms. Typical walls are not so soundproof as those thick, expensive walls of many older houses. Open planning has reduced the number of floor-to-ceiling partitions. Furnishings are not so bulky and noise absorbing as they used to be.

Sound travels through air and through solids. When air-borne sound strikes a solid, some sound is absorbed, part is reflected, and the remainder is transmitted to other parts of the home. Porous materials, such as acoustical ceiling tiles or soft wallboards, absorb most sound if thick but transmit noticeable amounts if thin. Dense materials tend to reflect sound back into the room. Noise is readily transmitted through even small cracks around doors or windows.

The first principle for a quiet home is: Find a quiet location away from factories and stores, heavily traveled roads, and major aircraft lanes. Trees and tall shrubbery absorb much unwanted sound originating outside the house.

The second principle is: Keep noisy spots together and segregate them from quiet zones, as in Figure 4B. This applies to the location of the rooms in relationship to the site as well as to one another. Fortunately, this usually dovetails with other desirable outcomes. Thus, for reasons of acoustics as well as use, it is logical to have the garage near the street where it can help shield the house from traffic noise and yet be convenient to kitchen, laundry, and home workshop. These, together with indoor and outdoor play space, make a logical unit. Then there can be a progression through the semi-noisy dining and living space to the quiet bedrooms and study or seclusion room. The spot where this principle applies least well is the bathroom, which is noisy but should be near the bedrooms. To take care of this and other situations we need three more principles.

The third principle is: Reduce unwanted sounds at their sources. In the kitchen, this indicates the use of resilient materials on as many as possible of the surfaces on which pans, dishes, and leather-heeled shoes are likely to clatter or bang. Counters covered with linoleum or vinyl cause less noise than do those surfaced with stainless steel, clay tile, or laminated plastics. Resilient floors are quieter than nonresilient. Important, too, is the selection of appliances that operate quietly. The kitchen has been singled out, but this principle applies to every part of the house.

Absorb sounds already made is the fourth principle. This can be accomplished by sound-absorbing materials and sound-diffusing forms. Think of the poorest materials and shapes—a precisely rectangular empty room with walls, floor, and ceiling of smooth metal or glass. Every noise would bounce back and forth until all energy was spent. The acoustics would not be improved much if a few pieces of rectangular smooth metal or plastic furniture were placed parallel to the walls. At the opposite extreme would be a room in which at least two of the walls are not parallel to each other and the ceiling is not parallel to the floor. The walls are broken with a projecting or recessed fireplace and storage cabinets, and the ceiling plane is interrupted by beams. Walls are surfaced with cork, the floor with carpet, and the ceiling with acoustical tile or plaster. The room is furnished with upholstered chairs and sofa, many books on open shelves, large plants on the floor or tables, and thick draperies at the windows. In brief, sound-absorbing materials are soft and porous; sound-diffusing shapes are almost anything other than uninterrupted, smooth parallel planes.

Fifth: Use sound barriers to keep noise out of quiet areas. Properly designed closets retard the passage of sound between bedrooms and bathrooms, halls, or other bedrooms. Bookcases, storage walls, and thick fireplace walls help keep group-living sounds from invading private areas.

Lighting, heating, ventilating, and acoustics make our homes physically comfortable or not. With the notable exception of lighting, they have little to do with beauty or individuality but they have much to do with human happiness. Planning for them should begin with the selection of the site and should be considered in every facet of home planning and furnishing.

Wall materials can absorb, transmit, or reflect sound. *Left:* A dense insulating wall, such as masonry, lessens sound transmission from one room to another but causes sound to reverberate in the room where it originates. *Center:* Absorptive materials, such as porous wallboard, soak up some reverberation but if thin allow sound to travel through the wall. *Right:* Absorptive material lessens sound reflection in the noisy room; insulating material reduces sound transmission to the next room. (*Courtesy of* Sunset Magazine)

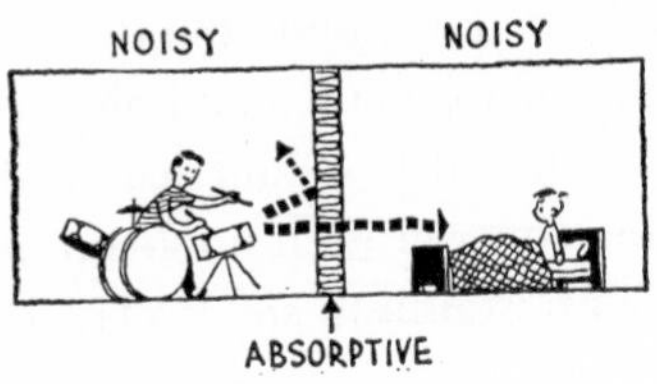

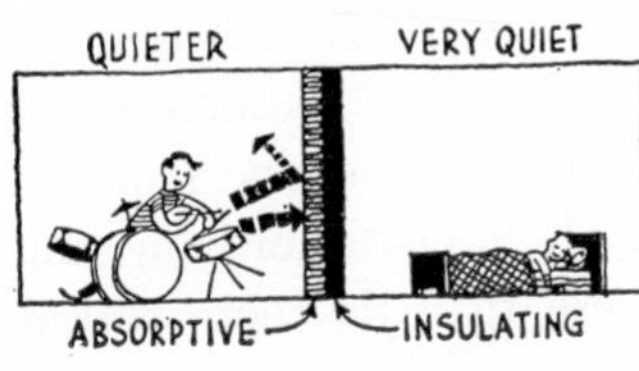

16. Setting the Table

SEVERAL TIMES A DAY homemakers provide food for their families. We could eat as some peoples do, each person dipping into the stewpot whenever hungry, but we no longer take food merely to keep alive. Eating has come to be a sociable occasion. Numerous experiments, as well as our own personal experiences, indicate that the environment in which we eat can affect our health and happiness.

Thus we "set tables" in order to eat together with comfort and pleasure. Comfort means good chairs and tables well arranged in sufficient space, with suitable light and ventilation, minimum noise, and appropriate tableware and table coverings. Pleasure comes not only from our companions and the food but from the spirit, beauty, and distinctiveness with which the table and the dining space are planned. Frequently, discussions of table settings overemphasize the "settings," as though, like paintings, they were ends in themselves, and "company meals." Day-to-day meals, though, are significant in family life and deserve more than routine treatment. In few other phases of home life is change so easily and economically possible.

Above. Handmade candleholders and a low bowl would greatly enhance a dinner table. (*Steuben Glass*)

► TABLE SETTINGS

Eating can be varied as was discussed in Chapter 2 and is illustrated on the following pages. The kinds of meals enjoyed most often and most thoroughly can well be the chief guide in selecting dishes and glassware, silverware, table coverings, and accessories. Books on etiquette usually divide table settings into formal and informal categories. With the first we need have no concern because it is needed by and appropriate to very few. But within the bounds of today's informal living, there is no dearth of imaginative possibilities.

Two Dinner Tables

The setting shown in Figure 431A is about as close as most families come to formality, but it is correctly described as informal. The tablecloth and napkins of rich but soft red linen unify and show to full advantage the dishes, silver, and glass. A strong feeling of order permeates this basically simple arrangement in which varied shapes and patterns are harmoniously combined. The many pieces of silver handsomely exemplify variety in unity and form follows function. The cigarette holder is plain as befits its subordinate role. Bread and butter plates and the efficient covered vegetable dishes have "gadroon" borders similar but not identical to those on the ashtrays and candleholders. Knives, forks, and spoons have rich ornamentation of a kind highly appropriate to silver and to the eyes and hands of those who use them. This progression from simple to complex reaches its climax in the candleholders. China and glassware are companionable with the silver. The intricate small-scale decoration on the plates emphasizes their shape and relates them to the knives and forks. The stemware is as sturdily shaped as the vegetable dishes, but the deeply cut pattern brings sparkle and makes it easier to hold. Chrysanthemums in a centered silver bowl bring the color harmony to its fullest intensity, but they are low enough to allow easy conversation across the table.

This is a setting that would attract favorable attention when guests enter the room and would reward closer study as they sat at the table. You would expect the room and its furnishings to be somewhat dignified, the guests to wear semiformal clothes, and the meal to live up to its setting.

Quite different in character, the second dinner table is distinguished by its playfulness. The amusing centerpiece sets the keynote. Its height deliberately suggests that conversation be with the persons at either side rather than across the table. Four red roses, each in its own porcelain vase,

A

Dinner tables can be conservatively correct or whimsical.

Above. A handsome dinner table in which the pieces are correlated although they do not match. (*Reed and Barton*)

Below. Spirited departures from the expected are enjoyed by those with courage and imagination. Alexander Girard, designer. (*Georg Jensen*)

B

can be enjoyed as individual flowers rather than as parts of an arrangement. White is the dominant, unifying color and it is liberally used in the plastic-laminate table top, the bleached straw place mats, the plates, and the translucent glass tumblers. Contrast and variety come with the natural wood of the centerpiece and the handles of the stainless steel tableware, the grayed pink napkins, the bright red and green of roses and leaves, and the prismatic colors of the dinnerware's pattern. This table, set for lively conversation and out-of-the-ordinary food, would be at home in a room that is lighthearted and gay.

A Luncheon Table

Lunch, served on the table shown in Figure 433A, would be informal and refreshing. The table could be set in a window-walled dining area, or it could bring an airy, outdoor atmosphere to even the most drab of apartment dining spaces. The beautiful grain of the table shows between the pale yellow mats, and this "nature" motif is emphasized by the branch angling asymmetrically down the table, the green-white grapes and red geraniums that give the centerpiece weight and interest, and the leaf-shaped napkin holders. White china, silver, and clear glassware—all plain but beautifully proportioned—complement the intricate design of the napkin holders and centerpiece.

A Buffet Table

Tables for buffet meals are seen at close range only for short periods of time while you walk around them to get food. Their appearance changes drastically as tableware and food are carried away by guests and family who may return for second helpings. Basic to their success is placing everything in a functional sequence, as has been done in Figure 433B. Starting near the right end of the table, you can pick up a plate, then advance to the meat platter, vegetable dish, and salad bowl after which you pick up silverware, napkin, and coffee. The next step—and this is a matter of furniture selection and arrangement—is finding a place to sit near a table, small or large, because very few people are at ease while trying to balance a plate and cup in mid-air or on knees.

Seen briefly while you are standing or walking, table settings for buffets can be bold and the centerpieces high, as in the one illustrated. Against a plain dark-brown tablecloth, white dishes with harvest designs and colors are conspicuous even in candlelight. The centerpiece overflows with an abundance of autumn vegetables and flowers above which the tall brown

Table settings gain from an appropriate idea coherently carried out.

Right. The informality of nature is the theme for this luncheon table. Dishes, glassware, and silver are plain; only the napkin holders are ornamented. (*Lord & Taylor*)

Below. A buffet table, efficiently arranged, is unified by the harvest theme of the centerpiece and decoration on the dishes. (*B. J. Brock and Company*)

A

B

candles rise. Whereas centerpieces as dominant as this and color contrasts as forceful as white plates on a very dark cloth might be overpowering at a sit-down meal, they are appropriate for a table enjoyed from across the room and, briefly, while standing near by.

► SELECTING TABLEWARE

In the table settings just described, it is apparent that success comes as much from the appropriateness of dishes, silver and glass, linens and accessories as from their arrangement. This is especially evident in the conventional expectedness of the first dinner table and the independence of taste in the second. But before tables can be actually set, the equipment must be in hand—chosen with its probable uses in mind.

Selecting tableware differs from most other aspects of home planning and furnishing in several important respects because of the ways in which it is typically accumulated and used. The pieces are acquired not only through planned (and occasional impulse) buying but by unpredictable gifts and inheritance. They can be variously combined and arranged with no cost other than imagination and a little time. The several kinds of tableware usually arrive in sets, and quick replacements may be indicated because of breakage, damage, or loss. Nothing else except cooking utensils is handled, moved from place to place, and washed as frequently. Finally, most families have everyday and company tableware and linens, a distinction seldom made elsewhere in the home. Putting these factors together raises unique problems and, more significantly, great possibilities for personalizing your home.

Although any piece of tableware can and ought to have its own intrinsic beauty, it is seldom seen in isolation. Ideally, each piece should be related through any considered degree of harmony or contrast to all else on the table, to the furnishings, and to the architecture of the room in which it is used. But how can that be done when all but a few persons get their tableware long before their permanent dining furniture and space? Do you select or design your *dining room and furniture* in relationship to dishes and silver? No, except in unusual circumstances. How, then, is the dilemma to be solved? One sensible procedure is to keep use, economy, beauty, and individuality firmly in mind, perhaps weighting beauty and individuality somewhat more heavily than in choosing a chair or bed. Liberated from confining stereotypes, we think in terms of our families' personalities and ways of living, of preferences for shapes and materials, colors and ornamentation. The home as a whole, present or planned, is important with special reference to eating, dining, and storage space and furnishings. The

A

Harmony and contrast can be happily joined in table settings.

Above. Related neutral colors and simple shapes call attention to the varied textures of different materials. (*Heath Ceramics*)

Below. The harmony of smooth textures and refined shapes is vitalized by strong value contrasts. (*Lunt Silversmiths*)

B

kinds of foods, and the manner of serving them, most enjoyed by family and friends are signposts. And the many facets of economy, well beyond first costs, include money for replacements and the day-to-day time and energy expended in getting tableware out and on the table, washing it, and getting it securely out of harm's way. In short, this is an individual problem satisfactorily solved only in a personal way, but there is a corpus of experience not sensibly overlooked.

Selecting Dishes

Dinnerware is usually the most conspicuous part of the permanent table equipment and therefore tends to set the character of table settings more forcefully than does silver or glass.

Use and Economy

- Size and shape are significant. Each dish should be large and deep enough to hold an adequate amount of food without spilling. Plates with rims permit easy grasping and provide a resting place for silverware but do not hold so much food as rimless ones. Cups should have finger-fitting handles, rims that fit the lips. Dishes that can be stored easily save time and storage space.
- Replacement as well as original costs merit consideration. "Open stock" patterns permit adding to a set as needed but are no longer a guarantee of availability for a long time. Read guarantees and suggestions for maintenance carefully. Vitreous ceramics and the better plastics resist chipping and breakage. Hard glazes reduce unsightly and unsanitary scratches; underglaze decorations are more durable than overglaze. Compact shapes lessen breakage. Raised ornament increases cleaning time, is more subject to chipping and scratching.
- Dishes that double as cooking and serving containers save time and assure hot food.
- Overly aggressive colors and patterns may become tiresome.

Beauty and Individuality

- Dinnerware comes in great variety, opening the path to many colors and patterns that will be yours *for a long time*. Relationship to other table appointments, furniture, and the like is at least as important as the beauty of pieces seen by themselves.
- Originality, in a mass-production age, is less likely to come from finding one-of-a-kind pieces than from choosing those that seem compatible with your preferences and are adaptable to varied settings. Personalization comes with the ways in which they are combined and arranged.

Shape and ornament give dinnerware its character.

Left. Sturdy simplicity is exemplified in the dinnerware designed by Russel Wright for easy housekeeping. (*Justin Tharaud & Sons, Inc.*)

A

Below. Sculptural ornament is intriguingly decorative but increases housework. (*Josiah Wedgwood & Sons*)

B

Above. A lively pattern of triangles in two colors reinforces the crisp thinness of china. (*Iroquois China Co.*)

Below. Colorful floral patterns are beautifully fitted to the rim and bowl of a dinner plate. (*Spode*)

C

D

A B

Glassware ranges from sturdy to fragile, plain to ornamented (as illustrated in Chapter 9).

Left. Glassware with nonchip rims, designed by Freda Diamond, is available in varied but compatible shapes. (*Libbey Glass Co.*)
Right. Goblets whose serene and impeccable contours are a beautiful statement of the nature of glass. Josef Hoffman and Oswald Haerdtl, designers. (*The Museum of Modern Art, New York*)

Selecting Glassware

Since almost everything said about dinnerware applies to glassware, only a few specific points are worth emphasizing.

- "Glassware" for everyday use can also be of unbreakable aluminum or stainless steel or of durable plastic.
- Colored glassware enlivens a table—but the color cannot be changed for different occasions and it alters, sometimes unattractively, the color of the liquid.
- Raised or lowered ornamentation sparkles handsomely but demands careful washing and polishing.
- Stemware has a buoyant, bubblelike quality that gives a "lift" to the table; but it is hard to wash, easily broken, and takes much storage space.

Selecting Flatware

Flatware may well be used by your grandchildren since it is seldom broken or seriously damaged. Therefore, it is provident to select it with regard for its potential permanence.

Use

- Flatware, like dinnerware, is much handled and it ought to handle pleasantly—be easy to pick up and hold firmly, balance well in the hand or on the plate, and have no irritatingly sharp edges.
- Use does not harm sterling silver or stainless steel but, with ordinary care, improves them by mellowing the surface.
- Pieces that cannot be put in a dishwasher may raise problems.
- Place settings, the units in which silverware is usually acquired, vary in the number and kind of pieces they include. Choose those that have the pieces you need or buy from open stock rather than yielding to the dictates of fashion.

Economy

- Sterling silver is originally expensive but does not wear out.
- Silver-plated ware costs less but the plating wears off rather quickly unless it is double or triple plated and reinforced at points of greatest wear.
- Stainless steel is durable, non-tarnishable, and seldom discolors. The price varies by weight and design.
- Dirylite is hard and durable, in the medium price range, but its gold color restricts its adaptability.
- The extra cleaning time which heavily ornamented patterns take may or may not be compensated for by their rich beauty.

Beauty and Individuality

- Flatware adds elongated forms and soft sparkle to table settings, but its real beauty is quite as much a matter of how it feels in the hands as of how it looks.
- Plain ware has a simple dignity and can be used in any context. But silver is an ideal material for intricate ornament.
- It is conventional to think in terms of harmony, but flatware, because of its small size and distinctive qualities, offers unusual opportunities to bring contrast and variety peaceably into the home.
- Its cost and long life, however, place flatware (and hollowware, too) at the bottom of the list of objects with which you can sensibly afford to experiment with faddish, possibly transitory tastes.

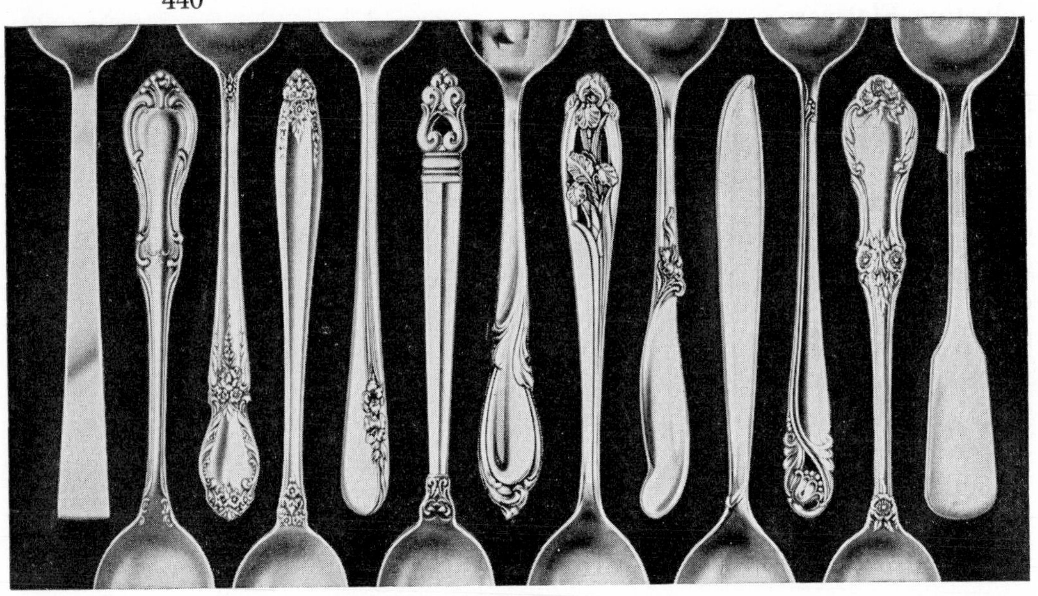

A

There is no excuse for not finding silverware appropriate to your way of living.

Above. Naturalistic, conventionalized, and abstract ornament, symmetrical and asymmetrical designs, small and large scale make an impressive array of differences. (*International Silver Company*)

Below left. Closely spaced, parallel grooves enrich the handles of an easy-to-hold stainless steel pattern. (*Dansk Designs*)

Below right. Full-bodied robustness of form distinguishes the stainless steelware designed by Italian designer Gio Ponti. (*Fraser*)

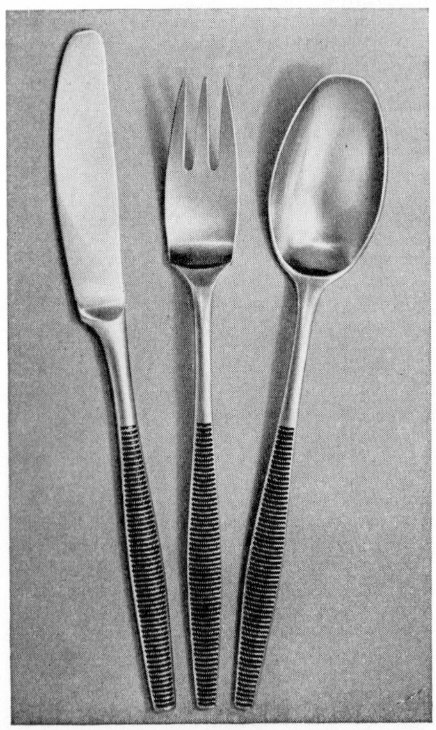

B

C

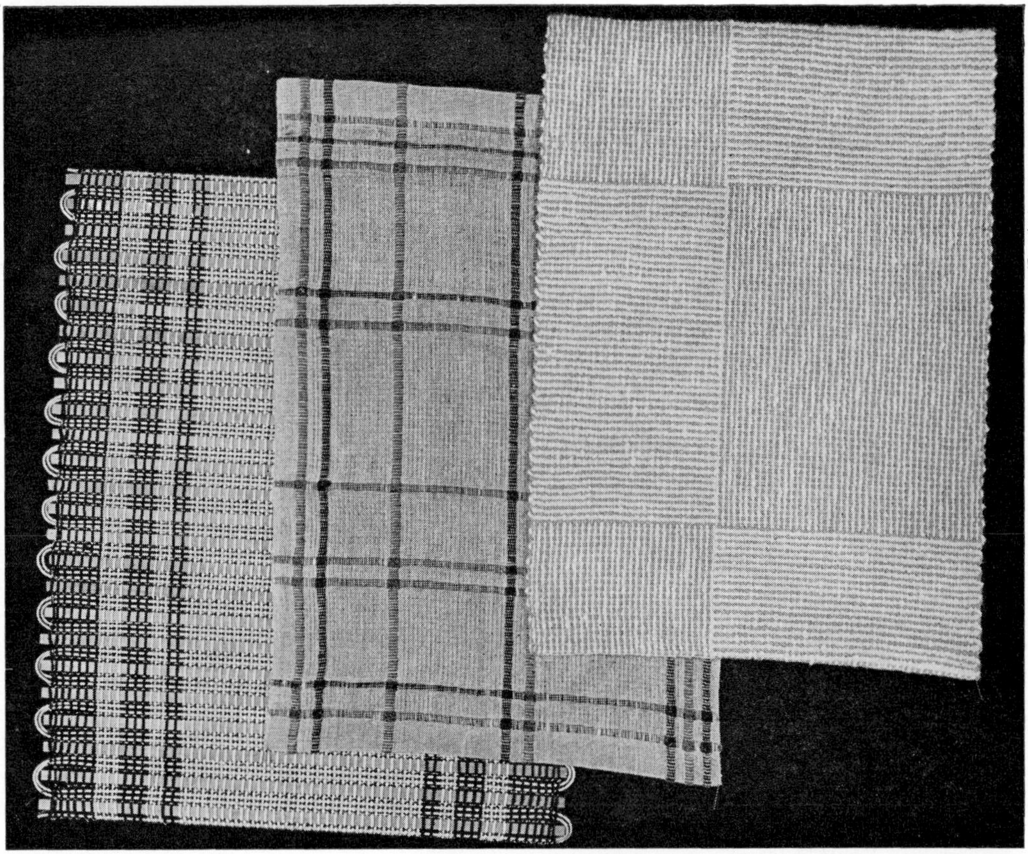

A

Above. Cotton, linen, and rayon combined with reed, jute, and metallic threads are some of the materials used in mats hand woven by Anna Person, Clara J. Chapman, Merdeces Hensley. (*Courtesy of Henry Gallery, University of Washington*)

Right. A tablecloth with bands of different colors and varied widths brings out the floral pattern on the plate and the pistol handled knife. (*Josiah Wedgwood & Sons*)

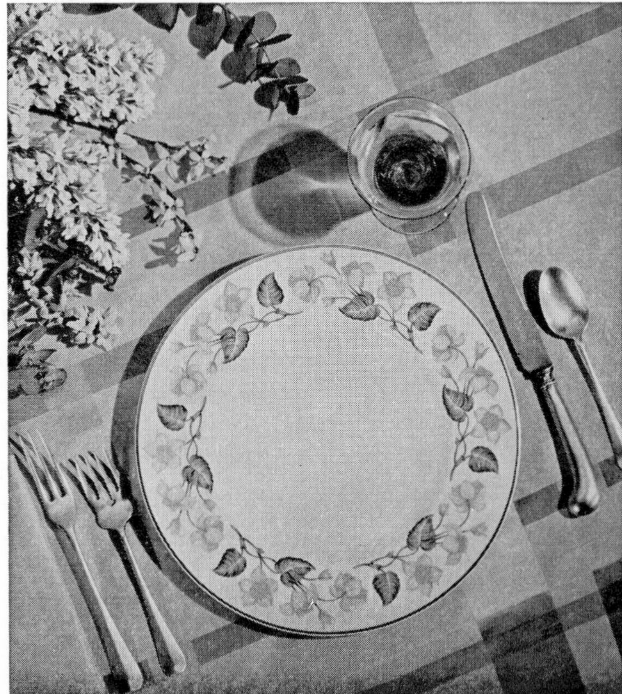

B

Selecting Table Coverings

Comparatively inexpensive and easily stored, table coverings permit variety and change. Easily cleaned plastics, new fibers and weaves, strong or subtle colors are a challenge to those with self-reliant discrimination.

Use and Economy

- Protecting table surfaces and lessening noise are major functions.
- Original cost is typically low to moderate. More important is maintenance time and energy.
- Tablecloths are harder to wash, iron, and store than are table mats.
- Resistance to stains and wrinkles is a significant factor.

Beauty and Individuality

- Typically regarded as backgrounds to dinnerware and food, table coverings are often plain or subtly patterned, but conspicuous patterns can be refreshing.
- Tablecloths can be decisive unifying factors.
- The soft textures of most table coverings supplement the typically hard smoothness of dishes, silver, and glass.
- Table coverings can make long-familiar dinnerware seem new.
- Indulge your personal urges on them—and on accessories.

Selecting Table Accessories

Table accessories are one small but vital part of the home's total enrichment, a subject discussed in the next chapter. Those used on the table are similar to, often the same pieces as, those used elsewhere at other times. Sometimes they are solely decorative; sometimes, as shown in Figures 443A and B, they are handsome ornaments in addition to being utilitarian. Flowers and leaves, fruits and vegetables are standard items that have inexhaustible diversity as do rocks and shells. Often it is the accessories, the most variable element of the setting, that most strongly underscore the table's theme.

Thinking about accessories naturally turns attention to centerpieces, for they usually are the table's dominant enrichment. We have come to expect that centerpieces be interesting but not conspicuously distracting. Their relationship to the rest of the setting as well as to the size of the table and the room is important. If people sit or walk around them, they should be attractive from all angles. Almost always it is desirable that they be low enough to permit across-the-table conviviality.

A
Handmade serving dishes personalize table settings.

Above. Sgraffito and painted decorations enrich the sensitive shapes of a stoneware casserole and soup tureen by Ernie Kim. (*Courtesy of M. H. deYoung Memorial Museum*)

Below. The soft luster of silver is allowed to speak for itself in the work of the French craftsman Tuiforcat. (*Photograph by Christof Studio*)

B

► PLANNING TABLE SETTINGS

The tables illustrated at the beginning of this chapter and those that follow touch only a few of the possibilities for setting attractive tables. Only one characteristic is common to pleasant settings: *an appropriate idea consistently and sensitively carried to its conclusion.*

Appropriateness is fundamental because good meals (and table settings are only part of them) are suited to: the persons who eat the meal; the dishes, glass, silver, and table coverings as well as to the dining space and furniture; the food served; or the occasion. It does not mean submission to any single factor or to any rules. How dull, for example, to think that a Christmas dinner with a white damask tablecloth, inherited china, and silver candelabra would be inappropriate in an informal modern house! We would not expect many meals of this character in such a setting, but the fact that they are exceptional makes them a lively event.

Ideas are legion. Many are firmly rooted in our traditions. Christmas bells and holly, Valentine hearts, cherries and an ax, Irish shamrock, the pumpkins and corn of autumn are not too obvious as a beginning. They are, rather, inspiring points of departure for seasonal tables. There are many times, though, when nothing specific is suggested. Then you look around the house, especially in the cupboards, for objects collected as a hobby or received as gifts that might be an inspiration. Magazines and shops also suggest a wealth of materials and ideas from which to choose.

Consistency means that the basic idea or theme is emphasized sufficiently to give the setting some degree of unity. Otherwise, it is likely to seem piecemeal, a random assemblage rather than an organized entity. It does not imply stereotyped conformity or obedience to rules but a sensitivity to what is effective.

Although table settings can be in strong contrast to the furniture and architecture of which they are a part, you have a special sense of rightness when they are at one with their surroundings. Three examples are illustrated in Figures 445A and B and 447.

A city apartment is suggested by the first table: it is urbane, somewhat formal and dignified in keeping with the furniture. The porcelain plates, slender stemware, and stainless steel flatware are notable for their precisely refined shapes. Almost the same color value as the table top, slightly textured linen mats bring restrained contrast with their grayed-blue hue. The seemingly artless centerpiece performs its job exceptionally well. In their texture and crisply defined form, the gladioli relate themselves to the plates, but whereas the plates are geometrically identical, each of the

Right. Handsome materials used in uncluttered rectangular and circular shapes bring tableware, furniture, and lighting fixture into complete unison. The effect is one of informal refinement. George Nelson, designer. (*Herman Miller Furniture Company*)

A

Below. A real sense of outdoor scale is shown in a buffet table arranged by Virginia Stanton. Strong shapes and colors, bold contrasts and textures are the keynotes. (*Photograph by Maynard Parker. Courtesy of* House Beautiful)

B

blossoms is organically different from the others. Laying them flat, a refreshing departure from the usual vertical arrangement, allows full enjoyment of the flowers without interference with conversation.

Set for an outdoor buffet, the second table is suitably bold and vigorous with its thick earthenware plates, raffia covered bottles, and provincial red-and-white tablecloth. Everything stands up well in strong sunlight against a background of rugged masonry. No centerpiece or accessories are needed. Colorful food, sensitively planned and arranged in varied but compatible dishes, and the lively cloth give all the visual interest required.

Frank Lloyd Wright has said that "arranging the table for dining is a great artistic opportunity," and he demonstrated this point handsomely in his Wisconsin home. Dining table and chairs take their place at one end of a large living space where they are part of a total design, not an eye-compelling protuberance. The furniture and tableware recapitulate at small scale the room's interplay of horizontals, verticals, and diagonals. Gradually ascending verticals draw attention upward to the sloping ceiling. The low-backed chairs begin the ascent, the tall goblets and the higher chairs continue it. On the dining table the low flower arrangement curves diagonally into the dramatic upright spray that, seeming to rise of its own accord up the stone pier, carries attention to the lofty ceiling. Our eyes then can move diagonally across the room until they are brought down by the Oriental sculpture, along a perpendicular light source to another table and the floor.

Appropriately, the table setting is fairly simple but an admirable example of harmony and diversity. The rich brown tablecloth ties in with the color of the wood and provides a unifying background. White Oriental plates are ornamented with figures in blue, brown, and green asymmetrically placed. They are a midway point between the plain cloth and the intricacy of the white flowers and green leaves, and they echo the Far Eastern screen on the wall behind the table. Dirylite flatware and slender goblets, simple but graceful in outline, bring a lightness and sparkle in keeping with the star-shaped flowers. Although ingratiatingly unaffected, this setting is an assured exercise in design—in itself and in relationship to the surrounding space.

Setting tables, and selecting the many things used on them, can be daily experiments in three-dimensional design. They are miniature versions of planning a house or selecting and arranging furniture, differing from these chiefly in their specific purpose and temporary nature. While enjoying great freedom in expressing personal urges, even whims, you can profitably think about and apply many of the facts and principles cited

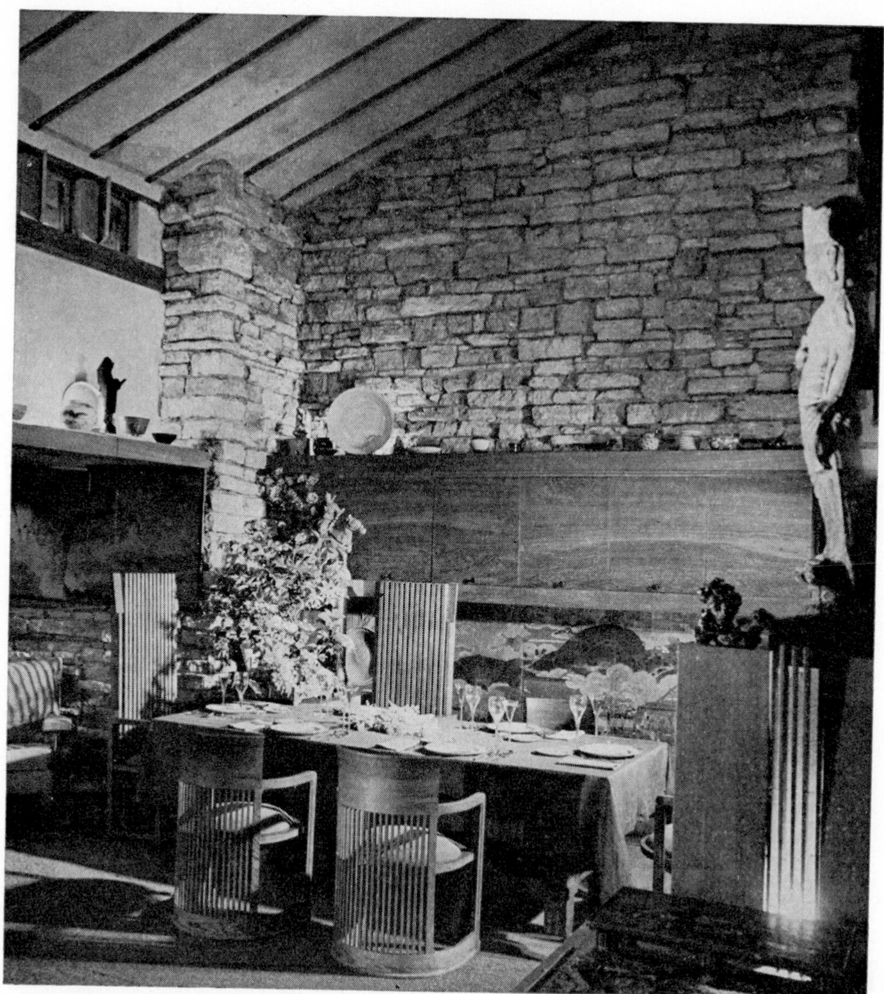

Genuine dignity and grandeur without a trace of pretentious formality are goals Frank Lloyd Wright achieved in a setting for a dinner. (*Photograph by Maynard Parker. Courtesy of* House Beautiful)

earlier in this book. The six steps listed in Chapter 1 may help you get started and lessen mistakes. The larger aspects of dining and food preparation, discussed in Chapters 2 and 4, are closely related to the ways in which tables are set. Design with light and color, form and space, and texture is one fundamental; another is the nature of materials. These are among the many situations in which you are faced with the challenge of responsible choices, perhaps of making the common seem uncommon, certainly of bringing together the serviceable and the beautiful.

17. Enrichment

"To add to the endowments of" and "to impart richer quality to" are dictionary definitions of *enrichment.* It is usually thought of as decorative accessories, plants and flower arrangements, and "art" and, in this chapter, these will be emphasized. There are, however, other important sources of enrichment, which include:

- People in the home with their different personalities, changing moods, activities, and clothes.
- Materials from which the house and its furnishings are made.
- Form and space, color and texture enjoyed by themselves and in relationship to one another.
- Patterns in draperies and upholstery, floor coverings and wall treatments, ornament on furniture and lighting fixtures.
- Books and magazines, table settings, and personal collections.
- Views through windows no matter how limited they are.

Above. In "Gopher," Nora Herz has transformed a pesky rodent into a sprightly ceramic sculpture. (*Courtesy of Montclair Art Museum*)

The logical first step in planning the enrichment of a home is to take inventory of such assets as you have and then to make certain that they are used to full advantage. The next step is to add whatever is needed for greater intensity or deeper impact; for a change of pace, an accent or emphasis through size or shape, color or texture, or intricacy. A few cherished accessories, pictures, or plants can quickly transform bleak, impersonal rooms into space that looks like home.

More than in almost any other phase of home planning, freedom of taste is appropriate in selecting the enrichment for your home. Embellishment without personal significance to those who live with it has little validity. There are, however, other considerations. One of these is intrinsic beauty or character. Appropriateness to the setting is another. And usefulness, in the many objects that serve us physically as well as psychologically, is not to be ignored.

Freedom of taste allows you to choose and combine what you like most, an approach refreshingly shown in Figures 450A and B. Family heirlooms or simply the things you grew up with, gifts from a dear friend, or those things made by yourself or someone close can bring a warm happiness each time they are seen. Too many such objects, esthetically unrelated, can make a room visually cluttered or disquietingly intimate to others, but if used with discretion they are a prime source of individuality.

Lasting appeal, however, depends on more than sentimental associations. It is only reasonable to expect that most accessories, prints, or paintings will be of interest to others. Excellence of design, beauty of material and workmanship are of special consequence if objects are "to add to the endowments of" a home. They need not be rare or expensive, but they add little if they are both commonplace and arranged unimaginatively.

Ideas on "appropriateness to the setting" have changed considerably since the days when "good taste" demanded that everything match. Harmony and unity are still important but so are surprise and variety. Noncommittal quarters and nondescript furniture, unfortunate conditions with which most of us have to put up at one time or another, cry out for enrichment with impact and individuality. They suggest a few important accessories with strong personalities: a large Oriental tray, colorful Mexican baskets, an India print covering a studio couch, a sizable ceramic bowl made by a local potter, grandmother's soup tureen or her patchwork quilt—almost anything that adds a few strong notes consonant with the occupant's preferences. Reproductions of paintings, original but inexpensive prints, even bright travel posters plus a plant or two can compensate for the mechanized, impersonal character of far too many rooms.

A

Above. In an old New Orleans house, inexpensive modern furniture, a carved antique screen, contemporary paintings, and bookcases that hold accessories as well as reading materials add up to a highly personalized interior. Jack Lamantia, architect.

Below. Complete freedom of taste in furniture, prints, and accessories—all of which have personal significance to their owner—make this modern San Francisco bedroom unique. Henry Hill, architect. (*Photograph by Roger Sturtevant*)

B

You may, of course, take up habitation in quarters of decisive character —a fine old Colonial or a profusely decorated Victorian house, or one that suggests English or Spanish parentage. Then the problem is different. A first impulse might be to search for objects from the period but good ones are hard to come by. A logical alternative is to think carefully about the size and shape of the rooms and get appropriate enrichment, regardless of period. Or you may find a contemporary house, simple yet with character, which provides a congenial setting for contemporary or historic, mass-produced or handcrafted arts and crafts.

Enrichment falls into three major categories: accessories, a wondrous group of strange bedfellows; flowers and plants; and paintings, prints, and sculpture.

► ACCESSORIES

The old saying that "one man's trash is another man's treasure" applies aptly to accessories. Some work for us, others are like the lilies of the field. Some are trivial and temporary, others significant and permanent. They can be made at home or in school, found on the beach, in the fields and woods. They are frequently purchased in gift and curio shops, often on trips, or discovered in second-hand stores and at rummage sales. Although we are seldom conscious of buying many accessories, they accumulate rather rapidly, causing us to wonder if they multiply in cupboards.

Some of the most common types deserve mention either because their use suggests limitations or their character demands special consideration.

- **Bowls and vases** of ceramics, glass, metal, plastics, or wood may work full time, part time, or not at all. If they are workers, check their efficiency as well as appearance. Make certain that a bowl used for snacks is easy to pass, that a vase for flowers is stable and holds enough water.
- **Candleholders** ought to hold candles firmly upright and catch the inevitable drip. If for dining tables, they are best when either high or low to keep the light away from eye level. If they are to be left out but seldom used, they should be worth looking at repeatedly.
- **Natural objects,** such as driftwood or branches of unusual structure, rocks or shells, are in line with the trend toward naturalism. They have much in their favor: little or no expense and long life, natural beauty, and individuality because no two pieces are identical.
- **Mirrors** can be primarily decorative or useful, small accents or wall size. They have the paradoxical qualities of allying themselves with what is opposite them by reflection and of dissociating themselves from the immediate background because of their striking dissimilarity to

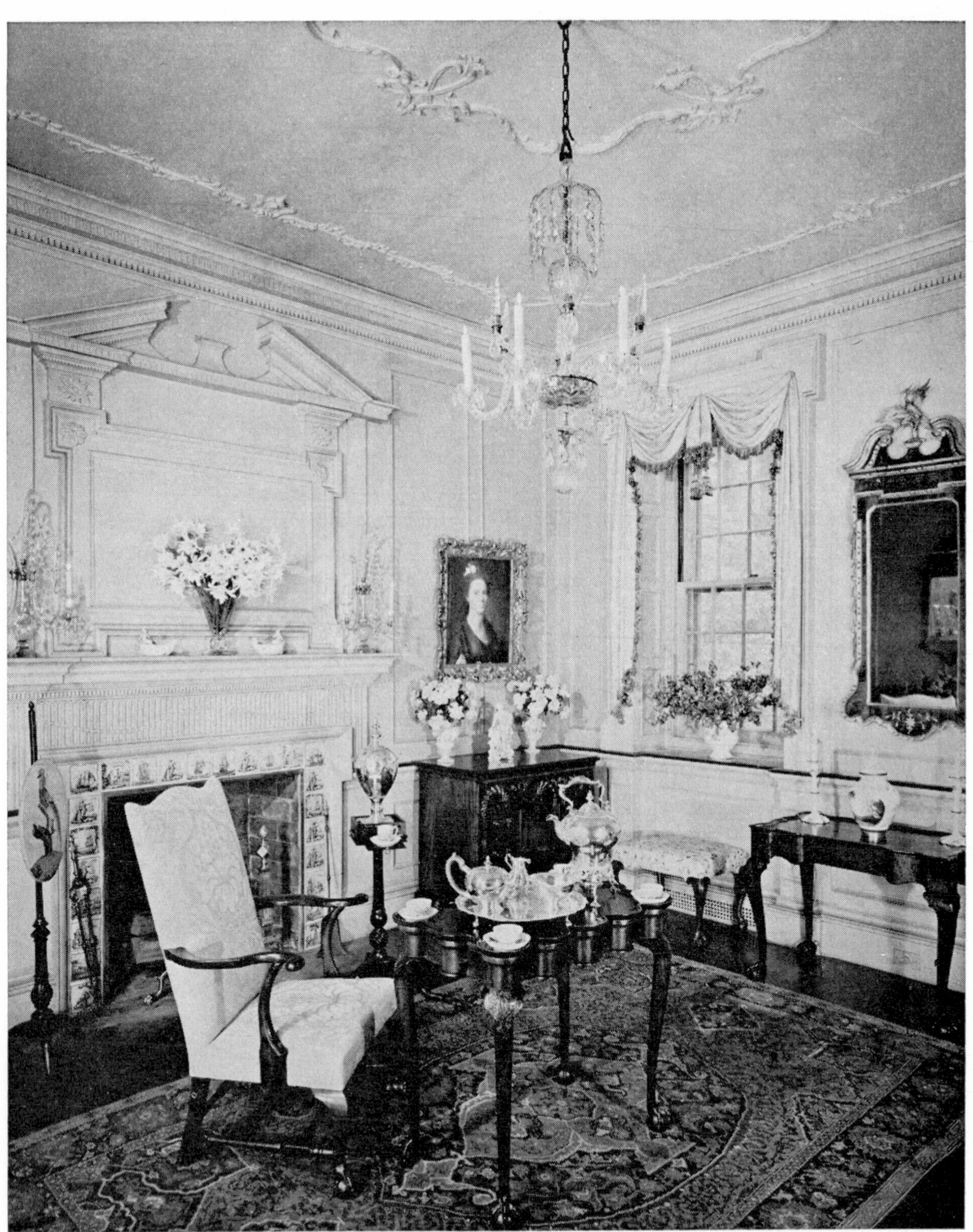

An abundance of formally arranged, exquisitely wrought accessories of silver, glass, and ceramics join with flowers, a painting, and a mirror to add sparkling richness to an eighteenth-century American parlor. (*Courtesy of Henry Francis du Pont Winterthur Museum. Photograph by Gilbert Ask*)

A

Accessories can quickly change the appearance of a coffee table, as is demonstrated in the Julius Shulmans' home, or even a whole room.

Above. A few circular objects differing in size and rhythmically spaced allow appreciation of each object and the wood of the table top.

Below. What could have been a miscellany is brought together by a dominant floral arrangement and sensitive placement of low rectangular cigarette box and books near the corners, higher rounded pieces near the flowers. (*Photographs by Julius Shulman*)

B

most wall surfaces. Their brightness adds sparkle to a room, their reflections increase apparent spaciousness. In entrances they provide a first or last opportunity to check your appearance. In living and dining rooms they are primarily ornamental and can be hung much like paintings, fill the space between windows to simulate a window wall, or cover an entire wall. In halls they can add apparent width or lighten a dark end.

These are only a few of the many objects that can have decorative value no matter what their major function is. Table mats and magazines, books and book ends, ashtrays and bowls of nuts, sofa pillows and lamps are others in this most numerous, if not most important, phase of enrichment. The diversity of size and shape, color and material is tremendous. This calls for special attention to selecting and arranging those objects that are to be seen together.

Variety in unity is of first-rank importance. Groups of accessories are usually most enjoyable when something is pre-eminent. This "something" can be one large, intricate or unusual piece, either standing alone or reinforced with smaller objects. Or it can be a dominance of rounded or angular forms, a sensitive study of related textures or colors. Then, a few calculated tensions will heighten the unity. Balance, from all angles, stabilizes the composition, repetition or progression brings rhythmic movement. When well done, the whole effect is many times greater than the sum of the parts.

► PLANTS

Figures 455A and B and 473B handsomely exemplify ways in which plants can humanize interiors. Relatively inexpensive, plants last much longer than cut flowers and with reasonable care get bigger. They provide interiors with needed diversity of form and color and give the gardener an indoor hobby.

Fashions change. The Victorians favored large and durable palms, Boston ferns weeping over the sides of tall stands, and maybe a fancy-leaved begonia or two. The "modernistically" inclined person of the 1920's and 1930's found the spiky, yellow-banded sansivieria (sometimes called "Mother-in-law's tongue") suitably hard, sharp, and unyielding. Today we have come to accept philodendrons and their relatives (Fig. 455A) for their bold, intricate patterns but also choose freely from the countless other species to get the effect we want. And another change has taken place in that plants are regarded as part of the whole furnishing scheme.

Right. Furniture of Chinese inspiration is in harmony with the Oriental sculpture and bowl. Diversity comes with the modern painting and philodendron. The painting is hung low enough to join forces with the statue and chest; the plant is near enough to be an integral part of the composition. Morris Sands, decorator. (*Courtesy of San Francisco Museum of Art*)

Below. Five prints, decoratively matted and framed, show to advantage on a painted brick wall. Two bowls and some books on a low table give a substantial base; a floor lamp strengthens the vertical movement. Growing plants and bare branches frame the composition. (*Murals, Inc.*)

A

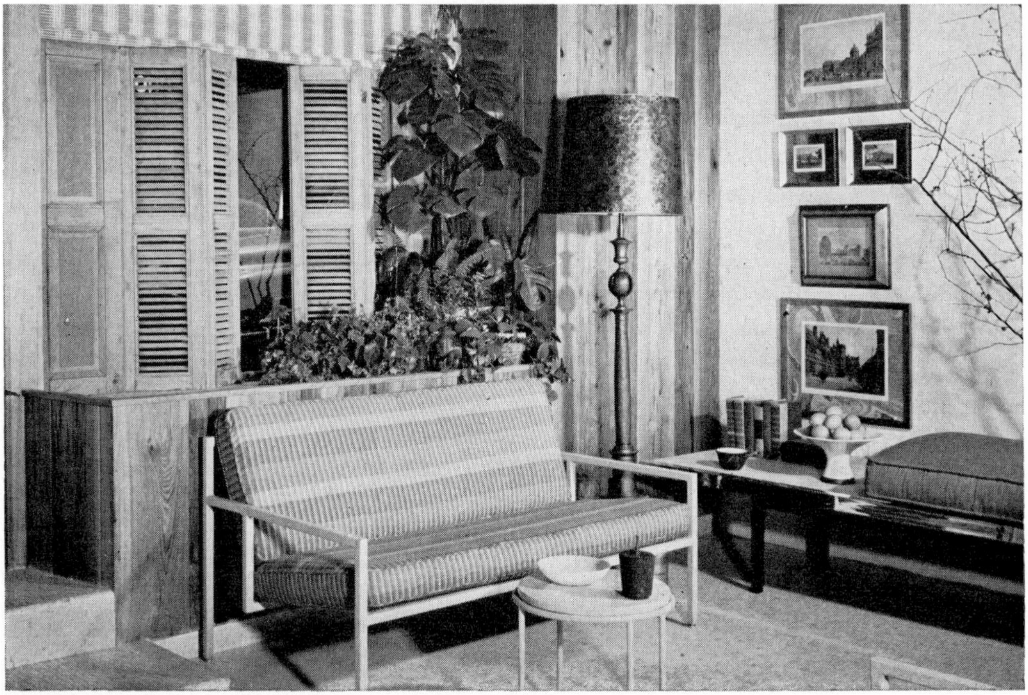

B

Each type of plant has its own requirements of light and heat, soil, water, and humidity for best growth. Almost none likes dark, hot, poorly ventilated rooms any more than do most of us, but a few will survive even under such unfavorable conditions. For hot, sunny windows, *cactus* and other *succulents* are logical choices. For moderately cool east or north windows, there are many to select from—*begonias,* which range from a few inches to several feet tall; *African violets; coleus* with gay foliage in reds, yellows, greens, and white; *ivy,* either plain or variegated, which can be trained around a window or up a wall; and all the *philodendrons.* For parts of rooms not near windows, such foliage plants as *philodendrons, rubber trees,* and *ferns* are indicated.

The containers in which plants are kept have much to do with their health and ornamental value. A little scouting will turn up much that is unexpected—sensitive and subtle pieces from Japan, bold wares from Mexico and Italy, Victorian jardinieres of brass, and an inspiring diversity from contemporary potters. Usually the container plays second fiddle to the plant it holds, but no lasting harm results from the opposite.

Plants are at their best when treated as any other type of enrichment, selected and placed where they will be real ornaments. Big, bold plants are good for major effects or to fill a space where furniture does not fit. At the opposite extreme are the small ones whose interesting foliage merits close study. Vary the size in terms of the space and purpose. On a coffee or end table, or on a narrow window ledge, a few or many small plants bring a pleasant feeling of small scale. Plants a foot or two high may be needed on a large table or cabinet. On the floor or a low stand, those from three to six feet high make their presence felt. And within the limits of whatever degree of unity is wanted, the kinds can be varied. Plants, like everything else, seem most at home when several of one type are grouped or distributed in an enjoyable pattern, but a few contrasts enliven the effect.

► FLOWER ARRANGEMENTS

Raised to the level of an eloquent art by the nature-loving Japanese and assiduously practiced by many in this country, flower arrangement runs the gamut from stuffing some blossoms into a vase to a fascinating hobby. In general, it can be solved just as any other home design problem:

- Decide what effect is wanted.
- Obtain suitable flowers, foliage, containers, holders, and ornaments.
- Arrange these, giving due regard to the aims and principles of design and to the setting.

Effect: Character and Basic Movement

Any attempt to categorize floral arrangements into arbitrary types can be a serious oversimplification. Accepting the risk, we suggest the following as a framework to guide first efforts.

Character

- Formal: symmetrical and precise
- Semiformal: more or less symmetrical in outline but not in details of arrangement
- Informal: asymmetrical and free

Basic Movement

- Vertical to slightly spreading
- Outward spreading
- Horizontal
- Downward

How do you decide? By considering the effect wanted in the specific setting and sizing up what is available. Harmony is always a safe first thought. The precise symmetry of very formal rooms suggests formal arrangements just as informal homes suggest those that are less strict. Quite as often as not, however, variety and contrast are needed. The solid stability of symmetrically arranged flowers at some point in an unassuming house has an impact similar to that of spirited freedom in formal interiors. Vertical arrangements come to mind for tall, narrow spaces—but low spreading ones might be more stimulating. This approach is somewhat idealistic and not always suited to the practical conditions under which most of us work. Usually, you do not have unlimited choice of materials, and then it is a matter of studying what is available and letting the effect grow out of the material.

Materials and Containers

The flowers and leaves at your command play a decisive role in determining possible effects because each plant has its own character and habit of growth. Arrangements which emphasize these distinctive personalities are likely to be most successful. Flowers will cooperate up to a point, but little is gained by pushing them beyond it.

The relationship between flowers and their containers is important but not dictated by rules. In the illustrations on the following pages, a black dish contrasts strongly in shape and color with daffodils. A copper vase harmonizes in shape and in color with sunflowers. Any degree of similarity

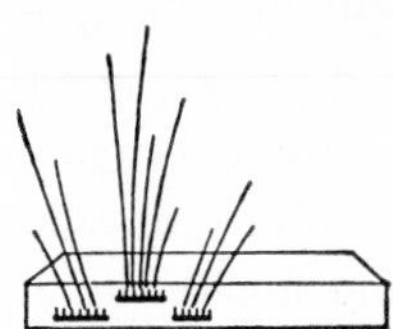

A rhythmic, asymmetric arrangement of daffodils displays the flowers to good advantage in a strongly contrasting low container. Laura Lee Burroughs, designer. (*Coca-Cola Company*)

or dissimilarity between the two can be effective. Usually, though, the container is subordinate to its contents, and simple glass, ceramic, or metal bowls or vases will happily hold varied flowers. Sometimes, though, a distinctive urn, cornucopia, or vase is almost as important as what it holds—there is no law saying that it cannot be more important—but common sense and the principle of dominance suggest that they should not be exactly equal. Those who enjoy arranging flowers appreciate having varied containers because it is stimulating to have a vase or bowl just right in size, shape, color, and texture for its contents and for its position in the home.

Arranging Flowers

If, for example, you have the florist's dozen of roses, carnations, or daffodils, you begin with one type of flower and all stems the same length —plenty of unity but little variety. The simplest solution is to put them in a moderately tall vase, spreading them a little but having them all about the same height. In short, much as they grew. This gives a spot of color, interesting only to the degree that the flowers themselves are. Another way

Sunflowers are large and vigorous, characteristics well exploited in a dramatic arrangement. The copper container echoes the color and character of the flowers. Laura Lee Burroughs, designer. (*Coca-Cola Company*)

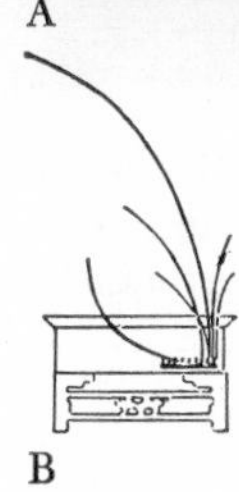

A decorated Oriental ceramic dish on a wood base holds a graceful organization of four Oriental poppies and two sprays of bush honeysuckle happily related to the painting on the wall. Laura Lee Burroughs, designer. (*Coca-Cola Company*)

A

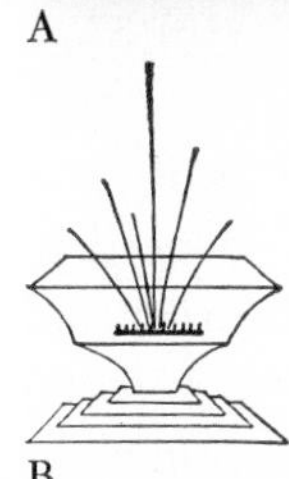

B

A formal arrangement of Lady Washington geraniums takes full advantage of their compact, symmetrical clusters. Two figurines, striped wallpaper, and a circular mirror complete the design. Laura Lee Burroughs, designer. (*Coca-Cola Company*)

might be to put them in a low circular bowl, shortening some of the stems to give a hemispherical mound. It would be symmetrical and orderly, good from all sides, suitable for a centerpiece—but a little obvious.

If, however, a low, rectangular, dark-colored dish is used, welcome contrast of shape, height, and color is introduced. Then, using three holders—and saving one flower for some other place—the blossoms can be arranged in three groups. A tall central group of five, almost but not exactly half, is dominant. A secondary group of three a little further from the center (the seesaw principle of balance) and at a greater angle, completes the composition (Fig. 458). This gives a lively, rhythmic radiation from the base, the asymmetrical equilibrium common in nature with gradually increasing weight toward the bottom. Unity is established by one kind of flower, variety by the varied heights and angles, placement and number in each group. With only five or six flowers, the central group alone would be pleasant.

Three other arrangements are illustrated in Figures 459, 460, and 461. The sunflowers form a bold downward curve. In shape, this curve resembles that of the container. Notice that the diagonal sweep is stabilized by the concentration of six blossoms standing upright in the center from which the three flowers on either side reach out. The effect is massive and expanding, as both flowers and container suggest, and in harmony with the rich abundance of late summer.

The third example hints at the Oriental approach of sensitively choosing a few flowers and then placing them with great subtlety. Asymmetric but far from casual, the blossoms and branches acknowledge their container and the painting that completes the composition (see also Fig. 473A).

The preceding arrangements are informal and asymmetric, but the Lady Washington geraniums have been symmetrically, almost primly arranged, in an old iron stove top. The dominant movement of the flowers is vertical in agreement with the French porcelain figures. The leaves, however, suggest the horizontality of the container. Other formal flower compositions are to be seen in Figure 452.

Dry Arrangements

These can be divided into the "semi-dry" arrangements of fruits and vegetables that last from a few days to several months and the "bone dry" of everlasting flowers and seedpods, leaves and bare branches, driftwood and rocks that last for years. They cost little or nothing and require no care other than the somewhat tedious job of removing dust. The principles are the same as those from which pleasing arrangements of fresh flowers develop.

In summary, these points are worth keeping in mind:

- Start with an idea or develop one as you go along. In most instances, avoid treating flowers as a disorganized blur of form and color.
- Accentuate the character of the flowers and leaves, their habit of growth.
- Select an appropriate container and one that will hold sufficient water and not tip over.
- Begin with the largest flowers or leaves and work down to the smallest.
- Keep in mind that variety in unity, balance, rhythm, and emphasis are important.
- Build the arrangement for the space it will occupy.
- Give the arrangement adequate light and a pleasant background.
- Rejoice in the fact that flower arrangements are one of the best, least costly means of experiment with individualized designs.

The expressive and decorative range of dry arrangements is without limits.

Right. A few dry palm leaves, a shallow bowl, and some pebbles—plus imagination and skill—make a strikingly decorative effect. Jack Daniels, designer. (*Photograph by Camera Center Studio*)

A

Below. One piece of weathered wood and three shells arranged horizontally on a Far Eastern mat have beauty and individuality many times their small cost. (*Photograph by Ernest Braun*)

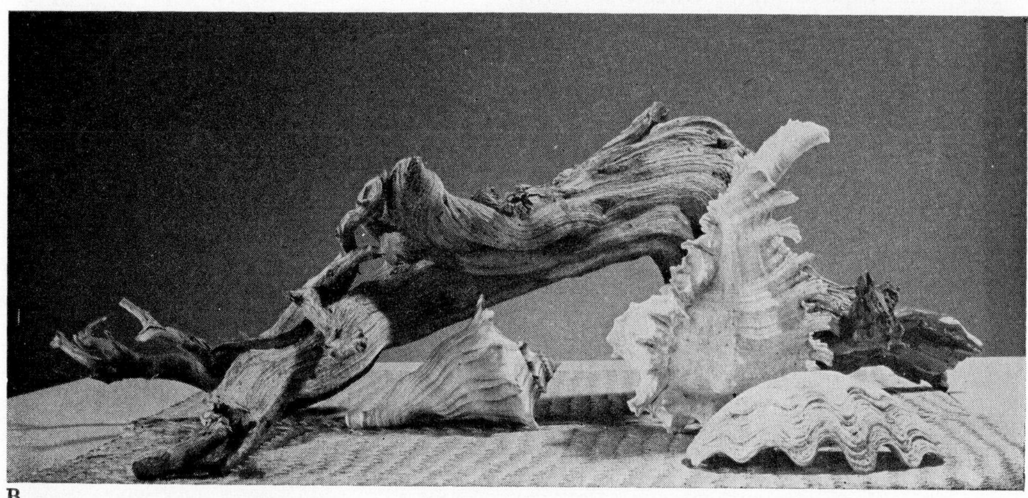

B

► PAINTINGS AND PRINTS

Artists creating in these fields aim to awaken and arouse, sharpen and deepen our ways of seeing, enlarge our spiritual experience and understanding. Designers, too, hold these aims but not to the same degree of intensity because their major problem is to enrich the forms and surfaces of utilitarian objects. In comparison with designs on plates or carpets, the fine arts are typically more richly complex and intense—greater variety of form and color, more intricate handling of space and texture, and, most important, a more profound penetration of significant human concerns. If they are worthy of being called fine art, paintings are not made to be repeated many times on a large surface or primarily to fit into their setting.

This is only part of the story because the fine and applied arts do have common characteristics. Both are produced for man's needs, have expressive qualities, are integrations of the plastic elements. Some work is midway between painting and pattern, or sculpture and ornament. It is about as effective when used once as when repeated many times. But in such instances, neither use is likely to be completely satisfying: the work is too thin to stand by itself and too rich to be repeated.

Thus, paintings and patterns should not be used in the same way because there are consequential differences between them. A few basic points about subject matter and content, medium and style are in order.

Subject matter is the "matter presented for consideration," the objects, if any, that the work of art re-presents. Typical categories include landscapes and seascapes, still lifes, and flowers, people and animals. Much contemporary painting, however, is abstract or nonobjective (Fig. 455A). It bears no more relationship to the visual world than does a symphony by Beethoven to the sounds of everyday existence. Such work has no subject matter—but it can have a wide range of emotional content.

Content is the idea or message, feeling or mood expressed. Art can express joy or tragedy, delicacy or vigor, restraint or exuberance, or any other human reaction. It is what the artist emphasizes in his subject matter, if any, and what he draws out of himself. The same general subject matter can have markedly different content—seascapes can be peaceful and serene, exhilarating, humorous, or ominous.

Medium refers to the materials used in the work of art. Typical painting media are watercolor and oil. Watercolors are usually done on paper with pigments made fluid with water, and the characteristic effects are fluid, transparent, and spontaneous, although they can be heavy and opaque or slowly and carefully worked. Oils, usually on canvas, are done with pigments mixed with oil. We tend to think of oil paints as heavier, more solid and opaque, and painted over longer periods of time than are watercolors. But oil paint can be used almost as thinly as can watercolor and the painting can be dashed off almost as quickly.

Style is the distinctive or characteristic manner in which works of art are conceived and executed. The word is used to describe the characteristics of a period, such as the Renaissance or Victorian, and of the individuality that a painter, such as Michelangelo or van Gogh, brings to his work.

Selecting Paintings

Are there any valid guides for selecting paintings for your home? Yes. Select those that give you lasting pleasure, that contribute to the character of your home, and that have some measure of esthetic value.

On *subject matter,* it is nonsense to say that landscapes and flower pieces are best for the living room, still lifes with fruits and vegetables for the dining space, and soporific subjects for the bedrooms. Paintings of any merit are too important in themselves to be put into categories of subjects suitable for certain rooms. If your family has special interest in boating and swimming, you can have a predominance of pictures that arouse such associations. If they are bird lovers, collect pictures of birds and hang them wherever they are effective. If they do not want to be tied down to specific associations, let them stretch their imaginations on abstractions.

On *content,* the same guides apply. Few persons want to wake each morning facing a deeply tragic painting, but it does not follow that all paintings have to be gay and lighthearted. Most persons enjoy paintings with varied content so that they can look at what they want at different times. It is wise, though, to stay clear of the innocuous, superficial pictures commonly found in hotel bedrooms or most in evidence in ordinary picture shops.

On *medium,* it is worth getting to know even a little about the many ways in which materials can be handled. You may develop specific likes and dislikes or come to enjoy diversity.

Style is no longer a matter of regulations. To be sure there is a deep consistency among works of art from one period, and in an eighteenth-century home with furniture from that period, eighteenth-century paintings would be most strictly appropriate just as contemporary paintings fit into modern interiors. Today, however, we assume that all art history is our heritage and that there should be no insistence on paintings that *match* furniture or walls. If your tastes are conventional, choose a conventional painting by someone living or a reproduction of something everyone has long since assured you is safe to admire. If your tastes are not stereotyped, find a good lively modern, a primitive, or something by a less known historic painter.

Color is near the heart of painting, yet choosing a painting primarily because the colors are pleasant in the room is about on the level of buying books because you like the color of the binding. Regard color, along with all the other attributes, as one important factor in the enjoyment of paintings in their setting. Feel as free to explore passive harmonies with the backgrounds against which the paintings are to be hung as to indulge in exhilarating contrasts.

Size is important because there is a tendency to hang paintings too small for the wall space and furniture with which they ought to be in scale. This is especially true of paintings over fireplaces or sofas, for even in the average living room the space above furniture profits from paintings that hold their own (p. 468). The character of paintings, almost as much as their physical dimensions, determines apparent size and visual weight. Thus, a misty painting in pale colors seems "lighter" than one with solid forms clearly defined in intense colors. Grouping a number of small paintings gives an effect somewhat like one larger picture (Fig. 455B).

Frames, Mats, and Glass

Frames visually enclose paintings and contribute to their importance and effectiveness. Also, they form a boundary or transition between the free, intense expressiveness of paintings and the typically more quiet architectural backgrounds. Lastly, they safeguard the edges, may hold protective glass, and facilitate moving and hanging. Their first duty is to enhance the pictures; their second is to establish some kind of relationship with the setting. Generally, this means that frames should either supplement the size, scale, character, and color of what they enclose—or simply be unobtrusive bands. Occasionally, marked contrast can accentuate the qualities of a painting. Only exceptionally should the frame dominate the picture. The wide, heavily carved and gilded frames of the past or any that project at the outer edges, "set off" paintings. Those of moderate width and simple design, harmonious in color with the walls and either flat or stepped back, relate paintings to walls.

Mats and *glass* are typical accompaniments of watercolors and prints. Mats enlarge these usually small pictures and surround them with rest space as a foil, especially important if the picture is delicate or if the background is competitive. In color, mats are usually white or pale-hued paper because these concentrate attention on the picture while harmonizing with typical walls. For special effects, mats can be of pronounced color and of textiles or patterned paper, cork, or metal. Effective if well done, the result may seem affected rather than appropriate after the novelty has worn thin. But they are not to be dismissed because of this risk.

In size, mats vary with the size and character of the picture as well as with the frame and the location. Heavy frames lessen the need for generous mats while large or important locations increase it. To correct optical illusions and give satisfying up-and-down equilibrium, the width of the top, sides, and bottoms of mats is usually different but not so varied that it is conspicuous. On horizontal compositions, the top is narrowest, the bottom widest, and the sides in between. With an 18″ x 24″ horizontal watercolor of moderate strength and narrow frame, the top margin might be from 3½″ to 4½″, the side margins ½″ wider, and the bottom about 1″ to 1½″ more than the top. For vertical pictures, the bottom is still widest but the sides are often wider than the top.

Glass is a necessary evil for pictures that cannot be protected by varnish. It protects them from surface dirt and abrasion and it also seems to intensify colors, but it invariably produces annoying reflections. Mats and glass usually go together on watercolors, graphic prints, pastels, and sometimes photographs. Oil paintings seldom have either.

Hanging Pictures

Locating paintings and prints so that they interact happily with their setting is an art. Since pictures help relate furniture to walls, they are often placed over something—sofas or groups of chairs, desks, tables, or bookcases. Centering them in a wall space or over a piece of furniture gives stable symmetry, while having them off-center creates more movement (p. 468). Keeping them at about eye level lets you see them comfortably, relates them to furnishings, and emphasizes the room's horizontality. From time to time, though, it is refreshing to have a painting stand for what it is worth on an otherwise blank wall. Useful guides to hanging are:

- Choose locations where enrichment of this special kind will be appreciated and the illumination is appropriate.
- Select paintings of appropriate size and strength for each location.
- Relate each painting to nearby furniture or its wall space.
- Group small pictures to avoid spottiness.
- Think about alignment of the major pictures in each room, for lining up the bottoms, tops, or centers brings order.
- Hang pictures flat against the wall with no wires or hooks showing.

A

Selecting and locating paintings ought to start, but not always end, with personal preferences.

Above. A formalized Chinese painting, symmetrically placed, as are the lamps and bookcases, becomes a focal center of attention. (*Gump's*)

Below. An abstract painting "opens" a living room wall. The asymmetry of the painting and its slightly off-center position stretch the space, bring a feeling of movement. (*Dunbar Furniture Company*)

B

Reproductions and Originals

Reproductions almost never give the full impact of original works. Typically they lack the full range and brilliance of color and also the textural interest. Sometimes the color bears little relationship to the original and reproductions are often at reduced sizes. It begins to sound as though reproductions should be avoided, but this is true only of those of poor quality. Some reproductions of watercolors can hardly be distinguished from the originals, and good prints of oil paintings are available at museums and art shops for little money. Here is one of the few cases where quality and cost are only slightly related because a print of a significant painting costs little if any more than a facsimile of something inconsequential. Since reproductions are inexpensive, you can afford to experiment with your taste. Frames with removable backs are inducements to change.

On the other hand, it is deeply satisfying to have the real thing. One of the all-too-few, one-of-a-kind objects in homes, original works of art have qualities that cannot be completely reproduced. Selecting an original is akin to creating one and, when purchased, it is yours alone. Original paintings or sculpture can often be purchased for the price of a lounge chair, and those of considerable quality may cost less than a Hi-Fi set. Many galleries and museums now rent original works of art for low fees, which can be applied to the purchase price. This is a good way to see how much pleasure various kinds of art give the family and how they look in the home.

► GRAPHIC PRINTS

Graphic prints fall into the rare category of quantity-produced originals because a number of "originals" can be printed from each plate and sold at moderate cost. All the typical kinds can be in black and white or in color (Fig. 455B).

Woodcuts and **Linoleum Cuts** are made by cutting blocks of wood or pieces of linoleum. Often they are in color, an art raised high by the Japanese.

Etchings typically resemble small, delicate pen-and-ink drawings, but contemporary printmakers have experimented with many effects of texture and mass far beyond the potentialities of an ink-dipped pen. Etchings are made by scratching through a waxy coating on a metal plate, then eating out (or "etching") the exposed metal with acid.

Drypoints are made by scratching directly into the surface of a metal plate with a sharp point and, except to the expert, are almost indistinguishable from etchings.

Lithographs are produced by drawing with a greasy crayon or ink on a block of stone or a sheet of metal. They are noted for their rich blacks and silvery grays.

Silk-screen Prints are made with a stencil through which thick ink is forced. This medium is particularly well suited to broad, simple masses of color, although textures and details are well within the range of possibilities.

Until recently, graphic prints differed from paintings in several ways important to the home decorator—smaller in size, more delicate and with less carrying power, and most of them in black and white. Thus, the typical print is not a dominant element and is best enjoyed from a short distance, such as above a desk or along a hall. Also, prints enjoy each other's company and are often hung in groups. Those of different size and shape can be brought into harmony by frames identical in molding and size with the necessary adjustments being made in the mats. Nowadays, though, many prints are large, boldly designed and colored. These can stand by themselves as important centers of attention.

► SCULPTURE

Bringing into three dimensions the intensity and expressiveness of painting, sculpture deserves far more consideration than it usually receives. There are many possibilities. Figurines, small sculptures of people or animals, abound in gift and variety stores, and the better ones are useful as adjuncts to flower arrangements (Fig. 461) or for variety in groups of accessories. The typical ones, however, are syrupy sweet and smooth, pastel-colored, and of very limited interest. But from time to time those with real character are available.

Sculpture of larger size and more expressive character is worth the time it takes to find, for it can make a unique contribution (Figs. 22A and 455A). Working in clay, stone, wood, metal, and plastics, contemporary sculptors are creating a diversity of pieces suited to homes. Second-hand stores and those featuring Oriental or Mexican arts are good sources. Museums and mail-order houses offer reproductions of serene Egyptian cats, spirited Greek horses, richly modeled Renaissance figures, forceful African or Mayan figures as well as contemporary work. As with paintings, reproductions of sculpture are not the equal of originals, but they can enrich

A

B

Sculpture—original, reproduced, or created naturally—deserves more consideration as home enrichment than it usually receives.

Above left. Carleton Ball's porcelain vase in the shape of a bird is an example of the one-of-a-kind pieces that are not expensive. (*Courtesy of Wichita Art Association Galleries*)

Above right. A reproduction of an Italian wall plaque depicting Saint George and the Dragon is one of many widely available replicas. (*Museum Pieces*)

Below. Quartz crystals are naturally sculptured in an amazing interplay of thrusts and facets. (*Courtesy of the American Museum of Natural History.*)

C

homes. All can be used in much the same places that you would put a good vase, flower arrangement, or plant. In addition, there is wall sculpture that relieves the dull flatness of most walls without taking otherwise usable space, and there are mobiles that hang from the ceiling and create constantly changing patterns.

► LOCATION AND BACKGROUND OF ENRICHMENT

There are two logical types of locations for enrichment: first, those places where persons normally look; and second, those places where you want them to look with interest and pleasure.

People normally tend to look more or less straight ahead; through doors, windows, or wherever distance invites exploration; and at anything that is large, different, or well illumined. Thus, you are sensible to think about putting some enrichment opposite the entrance door, somewhere in the first view of the living room, more or less opposite seating for conversation and eating, on the wall opposite a bed, in the space above a desk, and at the end of a hall. Outdoors, think about the major views from inside the house or from the terrace as well as the ends or turning points of garden paths. In each of these locations, the size and character of any enrichment deserves serious thought.

Entrance areas are introductions to the home. Usually they are small, which suggests something best seen at close range in a short period of time. A good table or chest with flowers, plants, or small sculpture below a mirror is one possibility if space permits. Or the enrichment can be on the wall—a distinctive lighting fixture or mirror, an uncomplicated painting or print, or a pleasing textile.

The first view into the living room is another matter, for the opposite wall or window is some distance away. In many modern homes this first view carries attention through the room out into the garden, which then becomes the place for interesting planting or fences, decorative urns or sculpture. In other houses, the fireplace wall is the first thing seen, and it may or may not need more than the architect has given in its design and materials. If the fireplace is small and simple, the wall above may have a painting or textile, large and strong enough to balance the opening below and to make itself understood from across the room—and also with sufficient interest to be worth looking at over long periods of time. In still other quarters the initial view may end in a blank wall that, typically, has a group of furniture and accessories. Whatever the specific situation, remember that it is gratifying to have something of interest greet the eyes. There are, however, instances in which the major point of interest is on a wall seen

A
Amount and kind of enrichment is a matter of individual preferences.

Above. The Japanese traditionally favor a very few exquisite objects sensitively arranged in simple, but not vapid, settings. (*Japanese Government Railways*)

Below. Chosen and placed with discerning taste, a profusion of diverse plants and accessories makes designer Alexander Girard's Detroit living room a collector's paradise, a delightful place to enjoy life. The old Moroccan brass table is a dominant element, the plain wall a quiet foil. (*Photograph by Charles Eames*)

B

only after you are in the room. Or it could be the floor enhanced with distinctively beautiful rugs.

Then there are the spots in most homes where you have to entice attention, such as uninteresting corners or small wall spaces that must be used. The writers have found in their efforts to arrange furniture in group living space for both large and small gatherings that it is helpful to suggest, not vocally but visually, that a few guests might be happier in a small separate furniture group than all overcrowding the major seating arrangement. Often this can be accomplished by reinforcing comfortable furniture with congenial illumination; prints, paintings, or textiles on the wall; and interesting objects on the table. Then, what was an unused corner becomes inhabited space, chiefly through appropriate furniture but also to a surprising degree through distinctive enrichment.

The effectiveness of any enrichment can be increased or decreased markedly by its setting. Should contrast or harmony be emphasized? A simple white vase would hardly be noticed against a white wall, moderately so against gray, but would stand out sharply from black. This raises two more questions. How much attention do you want to attract to that spot? How beautiful is the vase? Contrasting backgrounds are often recommended to "show up" accessories or paintings, but this is not the only way. Large, significant objects can proclaim their presence by being put in important positions, given a background against which they can be readily seen, and built up with smaller objects. At the other extreme some enrichment can take its place unobtrusively, a little murmur in a harmonious setting. Thus you achieve varying degrees of emphasis and subordination.

In summary:

- Select enrichment that is meaningful to you, contributes to your home, and has intrinsic interest.
- Think first in terms of a few large and important objects in scale with your rooms and furniture. Supplement these with others of varied sizes.
- Concentrate enrichment at important points related to the architecture and other furnishings.
- Study the design of arrangements as an artist studies the composition of a painting.
- Change accessories for variety, the seasons and holidays, and other special occasions.
- Plan convenient storage for those objects not always used.
- Consider breakage hazards if you move often or have small children.
- Weed out and upgrade the collection from time to time.
- Have courage to try something different, to express your own ideas.

A low-cost house by Roger Lee.
(*Photograph by Ernest Braun*)

PART V

The Whole House

18. Plan

Of all aspects of home planning and furnishings, the plan is probably the most important. It indicates the position of walls and openings; the location, size, and shape of space for living; and the ways in which furnishings can be arranged. In large part, the plan determines the family's living patterns and establishes the basic character of the structure. Many specific aspects of planning have been considered in preceding chapters. Planning is a summation and integration of the varied components into a unified whole. In this chapter we will concentrate on plan but, especially in the discussion of the first house, we will notice the relationship of plan to interior design and furnishings and to exterior design and landscaping, because all these belong together.

Above. A model by landscape architects Osmundson and Staley demonstrates how indoor and outdoor space can be related in a small house on limited land. (*Photograph by Theodore Osmundson*)

▶ THREE PRIZE-WINNING SMALL HOUSES

The houses illustrated in Figures 478, 485, and 488 deserve more than ordinary study because they were judged the best of 2,727 designs submitted in a national competition. The program stated that the houses should meet the requirements and resources of typical families. This meant that the enclosed area should not exceed 1,000 square feet because this is about as much as many families can afford, *not* because it is all the space a typical family needs. There were to be three bedrooms, and the houses were to fit on lots 60 by 100 feet. The success of these houses is indicated by the fact that within four weeks after the winners had been announced, twenty-two builders from coast to coast were negotiating with the designers for the privilege of building from their plans.

The First-prize Winner

Let us look at Bruce Walker's design in the light of what was said in earlier chapters about the requirements for group, private, and work activities, about design and color, materials, and the major elements of homes.

Living with Others. Four integrated areas give space for group living in Walker's plan: indoors, the all-purpose space and conversation alcove; outdoors, the terrace and screened porch. Moderately quiet, small-group *conversation* or *reading* is provided for in the end of the living space. It is an alcove about 8 by 10 feet, a good size and shape for from two to five persons, with a sofa and end tables against a solid wall, storage built in under the windows, two movable chairs, and a fireplace (backed up against the heater room so that only one chimney is needed). South light comes from a row of windows high enough above the floor to give usable wall space underneath and a feeling of enclosure, but low enough so that a seated person can see outdoors. Although no walls separate the conversation area from the all-purpose space, it is differentiated by being a dead-end alcove narrower than the rest of the room, by windows that are higher than those overlooking the terrace, by the different floor treatment, and by the ceiling, which changes direction along the line demarking the two areas. It is a retreat that gives a feeling of permanence and enclosure without becoming a cooped-up little box, and it can also become the stabilizing element of a much larger furniture group when more persons want to join.

Although the conversation area is only a few steps from the front door, kitchen, and terrace, it maintains its identity in plan alone, but its separateness could be underscored by furnishings. This is the logical place for the "best" furniture: a comfortable, handsome sofa and chair; a soft

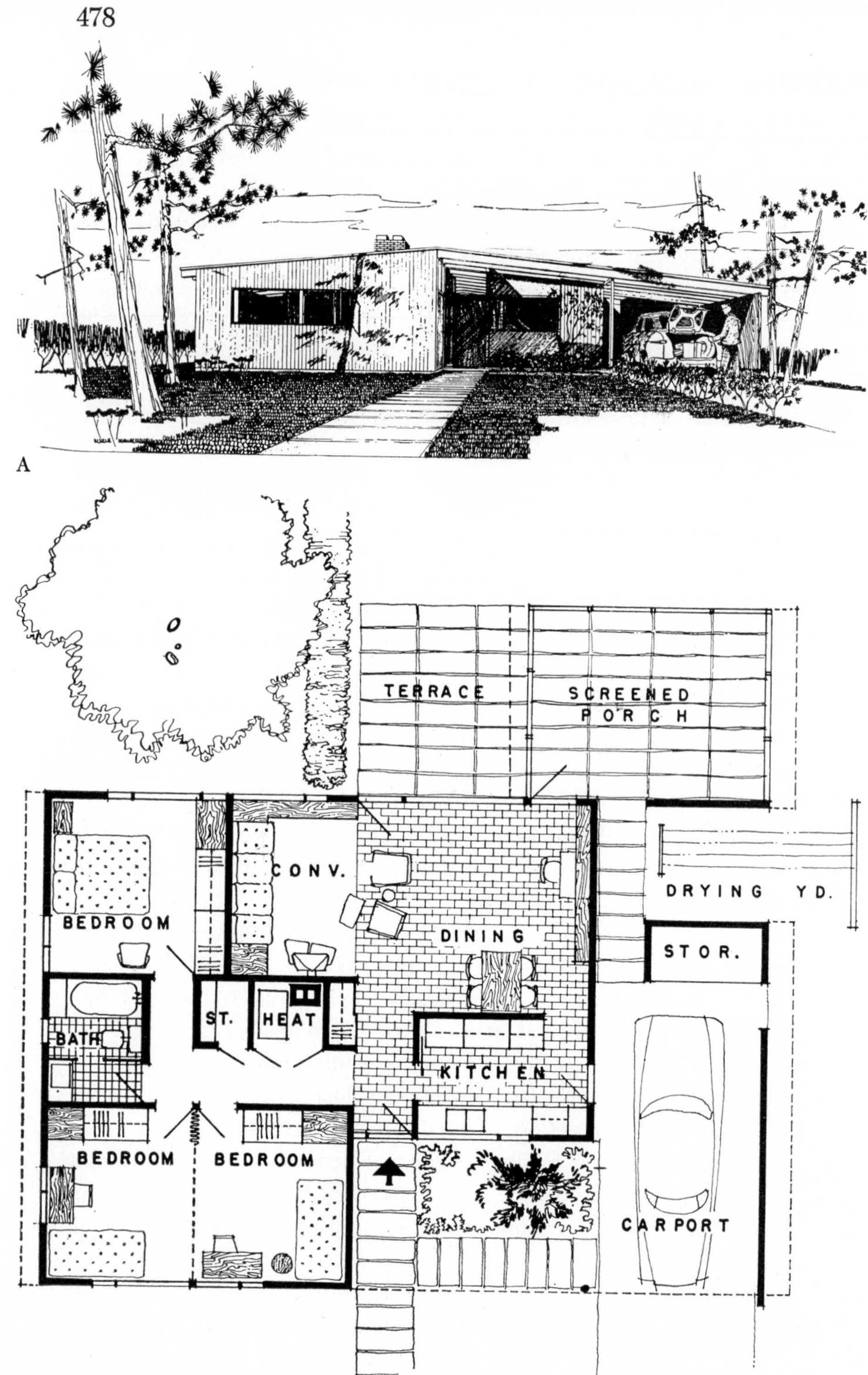

An efficient, beautiful plan based on a genuine understanding of a family's needs. The exterior is a logical outgrowth of the plan and the interior design. Bruce Walker, architect. (The Magazine of Building)

rug; and paintings or prints, wall sculpture or fabrics of special interest to the family. Especially in a small house, you are wise to use colors that carry through from one space to the others but these need not be monotonously repetitious. Warmer hues, stronger intensities, and lower values enlivened with sparkling contrasts would emphasize the enclosure and importance of this alcove.

Music could be centered in either or both of two locations. The cabinets under the windows in the conversation area could house a radio-phonograph, and the long wall in the all-purpose space could accommodate a radio, phonograph, television, or a piano. The sloping ceiling and the complex shape of this whole space would give good acoustics. *Games* of a quiet sort could be played at the dining table or on a card table placed where wanted.

Eating would normally and most conveniently take place at the table near the kitchen where there is adequate space for service and also for extending the table for celebrations. For variety, it would be easy to move the table over to the windows; television suppers might be enjoyed in the conversation area in chairs grouped around the receiver. The screened porch, terrace, and lawn, all easy of access, provide more comfortable and varied outdoor eating spots than in many houses twice this size but less well planned.

At this point, a few thoughts about the materials and furnishings of the all-purpose area are in order because they, along with the room's size and shape, affect its pleasantness and maintenance. Notice that the architect has indicated a tile floor that could be of such durable, easily kept materials as vinyl, linoleum, or asphalt. Using the same flooring in the entrance and kitchen unifies the three areas, makes them seem larger. Walls, too, should withstand use. Wood comes to mind although hard-surfaced wallboards or tough and washable wallpaper or fabric would be suitable. The two fixed units of furniture, built-in or assembled from interchangeable units but tight against the wall, could include cupboard, drawer and shelf space, desk and television, or whatever the family wanted.

Beyond that, furniture that is durable, easy to move, and light in design and color would preserve the room's openness and usability.

Small children's activities have good space in the two bedrooms, which can be joined by pushing back the folding wall, but they would also be enjoyed in the all-purpose space, terrace, porch, and yard.

In summary, varied kinds of indoor and outdoor group living spaces have been integrated to give usable and visual space far beyond that found in most houses this small. Large groups could spread from the all-purpose space to the terrace, porch, or lawn because all are interconnected and uncluttered. Terrace and porch more than double space for living in good weather. Moreover, these areas have been handsomely related to space for work and for private living.

Private Living. Bedrooms and bath are well segregated in a unit away from the noisy group areas with a sound barrier of coat closet, heater room, linen storage, and bedroom closets. Although not large, each bedroom has a good place for the bed, adequate space for dressing, and sufficient closet space. Notice that chests of drawers are beside each closet, which in turn is near the door. Each bedroom gets light and air from two directions through windows that are high enough above the floor to allow furniture beneath them and afford some privacy yet low enough to give an outlook. Draperies or blinds give flexible control. The bathroom is exceptionally well located and planned. While not much larger than the minimum, it is subdivided into one unit with the basin and another with tub and toilet which greatly increases its efficiency.

This plan solves well the problem of getting space adequate in size, suitable in shape, and efficiently zoned. But this is only the beginning.

Housework and Maintenance. With one exception, this phase of home life has been very well handled. *Getting meals* and *laundering* have been simplified in a kitchen measuring 7′6″ x 11′0″, which is small enough to save steps without being cramped. It is strategically located near the dining table, carport, and front door, and it is not far from screened porch and terrace and the bedrooms. It is in direct line of vision with the bathroom, where small children often need supervision. The plan is of the "opposite walls" type, putting work centers close together and not in this case inviting much through traffic because of easy alternative routes. *Straightening up* and *cleaning* are lightened by having some basic furniture built into each room: storage and table units in the conversation alcove; storage, desk, and music in the multipurpose space; and chests of drawers in each bedroom. There is at least one good, permanent place for such big furniture as sofa, dining table, beds, and desks. A walk-in linen cupboard is convenient to bedrooms and bath. Its size and central location make it a logical place to store household and cleaning equipment. Housework would be expedited by having bedroom and bathroom walls and floors smooth, durable and slightly patterned.

The one moderately serious weakness is insufficient general storage space, a matter that could be taken care of by trebling the carport storage space and designing it as well as that in Figure 481.

Well-designed storage in garage or carport is inexpensive in terms of its contribution to a well-ordered household. J. and C. Roberto, architects. (*Douglas Fir Plywood Assn.*)

Circulation. This plan is a model of "short, straight, desirable routes from here to there." The carport is beside the kitchen door and only a few steps from the front door, an ideal arrangement possible only when these two outside doors are near each other. Its nearness to the service yard and porch saves many trips through the house. From the front door, paths spread like the fingers of a hand to give direct routes to kitchen, coat closet, multipurpose space and conversation area, heater room and linen storage, any of the bedrooms, and the bath—without going through any other room. Yet the area devoted only to halls is small. The paths from front door to terrace and porch are also direct and cause minimum interference with furniture arrangement.

Orientation. Putting the sun, wind, and outlook in the right place has been simplified by designing this house for the ideally oriented lot with the street to the north. Then the important rooms can get winter sun and be related to private outdoor living areas. The kitchen faces north, good for the house's hottest room. Each bedroom has cross ventilation and light. Planned for a typical flat city lot, the house is as near the street as most city ordinances allow. This shortens the driveway and gives maximum space in the private backyard.

Beauty. The preceding analysis has shown how this house has been designed for use, but function, as we use the term, includes more than the utilitarian. Inside and outside, this house promises happy living. The carefully studied but unpretentious plan sets the stage for informal home life, while the handsome, friendly exterior gives a feeling of shelter and relationship to the site. It would not jostle its neighbors. Although the design takes advantage of new developments, notably in the windows, it is domestic in character and would never be mistaken for anything other than what it is—a small house for a typical American family living in the middle of the twentieth century. In brief, *its form follows its function.*

Can a house plan be beautiful? It not only can but it should be! Bruce Walker's plan is strictly rectangular in whole and in part with a number of interlocking L-shapes that establish a pervasive *unity.* There are three major L's—the whole enclosed area, the group living and work space, and the zone of private living. Notice that private and group portions interlock with the conversation area, a nice refinement because it is the quietest part of the group living zone. The L-shaped motif can also be seen in the layout of the functionally related multipurpose space, terrace, and porch; in the furniture against two walls of the conversation center; and in the walk from carport to front door. *Variety* comes because no two of the rectangles or L's are identical: each varies from the others in size and shape but all grow from the central idea.

The plan has a pleasant asymmetrical *balance,* for the visual weight of the slightly narrower but more solid-looking projecting bedroom wing is compensated for by the greater spread and visual interest of the wing on the right. The front entrance is almost exactly in the center although it appears to be much less formally placed. The major *emphasis* is found in the amount of space given to group living, logical in terms of use and effect. *Rhythm* is achieved by the consistent rectangles and L-shapes, and especially by the way major lines continue through the house. A strong central axis begins at the right corner of the bedroom wing, is carried through the plan by the floor treatment, and emerges at the rear in the edge of the terrace.

Here is an important point in integrated architecture: not only is this line dominant in plan but it parallels the high point of the roof seen from outside and the ceiling from the inside. Many other lines add their share to continuity: the front line of the bedroom wing is carried through by roof and paving to the carport's far edge; the carport kitchen door is in a straight line with the opposite kitchen door and the bedroom hall; the south wall of the house continues in the wall shielding the screened porch from the drying yard; the south edge of terrace and porch is one line as is the east edge of porch and carport. You might ask if this is "T-square and triangle" design, rigidly and coldly geometrical. We think not. Many lines do not carry through; but the major lines, continuing decisively through the plan, give satisfying order, clarity, and discipline too seldom found in house plans.

Now let us start erecting the enclosing walls and roof, as the builder would after laying the foundations, and see what happens. Do they give desirable privacy as well as light, air, and views where wanted? What is the effect of the whole and the parts?

From the street, the house presents a low informal composition, thoroughly satisfying at first glance and quite remarkable as its subtleties are investigated. The predominantly horizontal lines of the whole mass, the bands of windows, and the gently sloping roof relate it to the ground. But the absence of overhanging eaves (little needed on the north), the narrow vertical siding, and the opening in the roof near the entrance give an upward movement to balance the dominant horizontality. Had it not been for such devices, the house might have looked squatty and pushed into the ground rather than standing on and rising from it. The street side is not flat, like the side of a barn, but invites you into a recessed entrance court. This movement is repeated by the carport, the back of which recedes another 10 feet or so. These setbacks give a play of light and shade, a three-dimensional quality of space, time, and movement. And they divide the composition into three units varied in size and treatment to express the interior divisions but bound together by the simple roof line.

A beautifully organized sequence of form-space relationships are experienced as you start into the house. Walking toward the protectingly opaque door, you come into the hospitable shelter of the semienclosed entrance court as the first transitional step between outdoor and indoor scale. The width is the same as that of the multipurpose space, and the roof introduces you to the height and slope of the ceiling inside; but an opening above the planting bed gives a last glimpse of the sky as well as bringing light and air into kitchen, entrance hall, and bedroom windows. Small but not cramped, the entrance hall is the second transitional step, and while in it you notice that the lines of the floor and the ceiling ridge, carried through from outside, lead naturally into the living areas. Pausing while being relieved of coat and hat, you would almost automatically look toward the largest expanse of glass in the house. This is the most emphatic part of the interior, and it is not a confining center of interest, such as the typical fireplace, but an invitation to explore beyond. Fortunately, this is made physically possible by two doors leading to the outside. This general-purpose space is not large but the knowledge that it is a section of a continuing pattern, the glass reaching to the sloping ceiling, the potential of outdoor living, and then the contrast of the small secure conversation alcove all give it a big feeling.

Why was a sloping roof chosen in preference to a flat one? The designer did submit an alternate version with a flat roof and, consequently, horizontal ceilings of uniform height. They would not, however, appear as lively or satisfying as do the sloping roof and ceiling that rise buoyantly. The sloping roof introduces the only diagonals in the house, and the rhythmic building up and down gives variety, emphasis, and movement. From outside it fits commonly held ideas of what a roof should look like and from inside gives a refreshing change from parallel surfaces.

What kind of furniture and what colors? To us, this house calls for simple, unpretentious but sensitively designed furniture. In a house of this size, usefulness and beauty would be increased if most pieces were small in size and scale and harmonious in color, and if they were not individually "eye-catching" pieces.

Because the house is designed to harmonize with nature, natural colors and textures are indicated. Grays, tans, and browns or combinations of earthy colors for the large floor areas might be sparked with a few rugs in brighter colors. The same colors plus muted blues, greens, yellows, and oranges could be used for upholstery or draperies or on some of the walls. A few accents of jeweled-toned scarlet, cerise, magenta, violet, or strong acid green would complete the scheme. The exterior might well be naturally finished or stained lightly with gray or brown. You could, of course, paint the exterior white, yellow, or some other bright color, and the interior could be dazzling with clear strong hues or Spartan-pure with black and white. Certainly, though, these would go against the grain of the idea from which the house grew.

The Second-prize Winner

The design illustrated in Figure 485 differs from the first-prize winner in several significant ways, but before discussing them let us read part of what the architect, Ralph Rapson, had to say:

> The design of this small house for a warm climate was predicated on three basic concepts: 1) that "close" living, necessitated by a house of this size, makes it mandatory that the active living be separated from the passive, with the "heart" of the living—the kitchen—in direct control-contact with each; 2) that all major plan elements have through-ventilation; and 3) that these elements be enclosed in a basically simple shape for ease and economy of construction.
>
> The plan evolved from these basic factors provides two distinct though closely interlocking areas. One is a multipurpose area for active living; for children and adult rumpus and play; for sewing, ironing and clothes drying on bad days; where the family might take most of their meals and which the mother would not need to worry about keeping

spick and span, since guests would normally be entertained in the second area—the space for the more conventional type of living. The utility core, of which the food center is part, is placed between these elements for ease of access and direct control of both.

This has led to a plan divided into four front-to-back zones: going from right to left, we find a quiet living-dining zone 12′3″ wide, an entrance and utility zone 10′8″ wide, a multipurpose space of the same width, and then a line of bedrooms exactly as wide as the living-dining space.

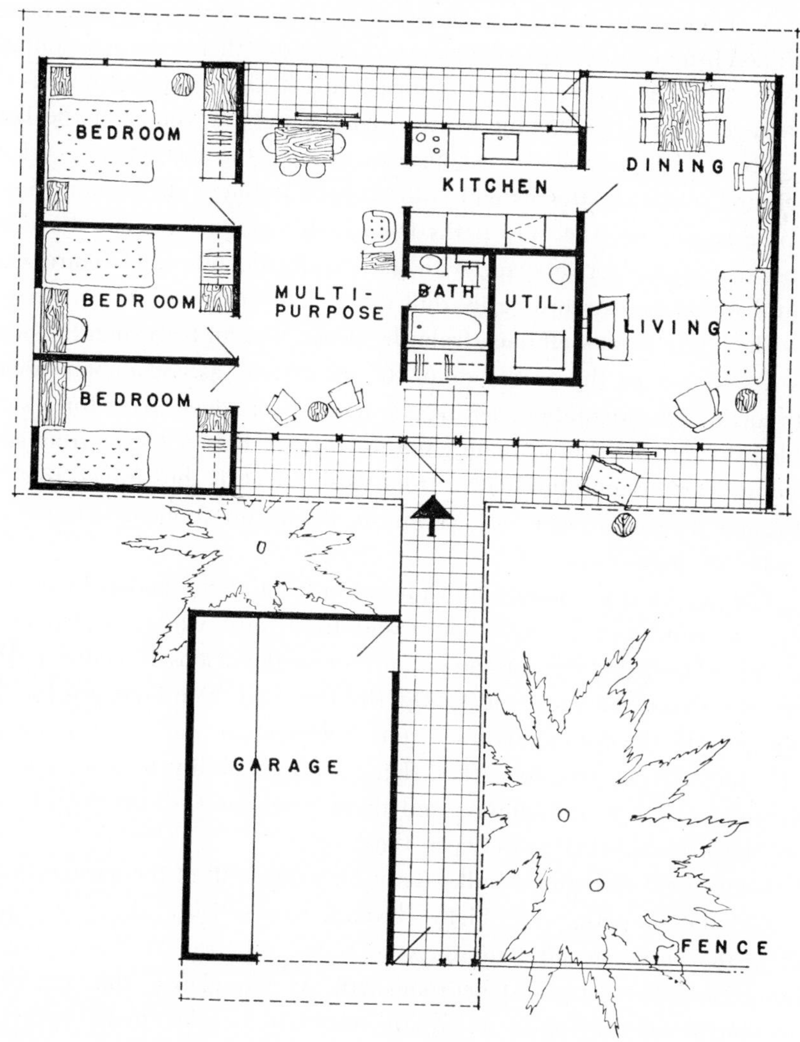

A plan distinguished by a compact, economical utility core that separates two areas for group living. Ralph Rapson, architect. (The Magazine of Building)

Let us study this plan by concentrating on the ways in which it differs from Walker's design.

Group living space is sharply divided into two separate units. As Rapson points out, this has notable advantages. It also raises problems. Both are long, narrow rectangles and these proportions are accentuated by window walls at each end. The two cannot be combined for large groups, and the division of group living space in a house this small cramps everything.

Kitchen, bath, and utilities form a compact central "utility core." This puts the kitchen in direct contact-control of both living spaces and the rear yard; and bringing the expensive, noisy utilities together reduces installation costs. Sensible as this sounds, it is offset in this plan by three serious disadvantages. First, this opaque central block closes the center of the house and robs it of its potential spaciousness. Second, the theoretically private, quiet, and related bedrooms and bath all open publicly off the noisy multipurpose space, and the only paths from bedrooms to bath are diagonally across this highly active space with glass walls at both ends. Third, noise control would be extraordinarily difficult to achieve.

The house is set well back from the street. The lot for which this house was designed is on the north side of the street; and, as is common practice with lots of this orientation, setting the house back gives space for a sunny outdoor-living area. Unfortunately in this case, the only entrance from street to house goes through the fenced front yard, which is thus forced to act as guest and family entrance, service entrance, and questionably private outdoor-living space.

The garage is a separate unit placed in front of the house. Placing the garage forward shields both house and front yard while shortening the driveway. Designing the garage as an independent, loosely connected appendage extends the house pleasantly. *But* this separation increases building costs because the garage requires four independent walls and a separate roof. More critical over the years, there is no possibility of a service yard adjacent to kitchen and garage, and there is no short, direct path for the many package-laden trips between these units.

Convenient storage for bulky items lines one wall of the garage. Amen.

Circulation paths are chiefly through rooms. Only about 30 square feet in the entry are *allotted* solely to traffic, whereas Walker's plan has around 75 in the entry and bedroom hall. At first glance, this appears to be a worth-while saving of 45 square feet; but it makes many paths that interfere with furniture arrangement in rooms and, as mentioned above, precludes a private bedroom-bathroom zone.

Orientation is well handled for a mild-climate house to be built on many sites. The window walls at both ends of both group living areas permits facing the house north or south, and with protection from afternoon sun it could face east or west.

The design is clean-cut, rational, and possibly a trifle rigid with its four front-to-back zones. Related in widths, these give an easily appreciated order, a systematic rhythm with some variety but do not produce a satisfying emphasis and forceful unity.

Our analysis has purposely emphasized the weaknesses of this plan to stimulate your critical ability, to get you to look at the parts by themselves and in relationship to the whole. In case we have gone too far, let us remind you that this house is superior to most built today and that it has these good points:

- Two separated living and eating spaces;
- Economical concentration of utilities;
- Abundant light and ventilation in the group areas (but not in the bedrooms);
- Use of the typically wasted front yard;
- Basic logic and adaptability of the plan.

What furnishings and color does this plan suggest? The plan's clean-cut, precise order might well be underlined so that the house would affirm its man-made character and assert its independence of nature as houses around the Mediterranean always have and as our Colonial houses certainly did. Lightweight, "functional" metal furniture with plastic upholstery would harmonize with the spirit of the plan. Pronounced contrasting colors could emphasize the planes and space. Thus, as the writers see it, this house would differ from the first-prize winner as strikingly in colors and furnishings as it differs in plan.

The Third-prize Winner

Wallace Steele's design was done with the Midwest in mind. His plan is an uninterrupted rectangle with the "front" entrance in the middle of the west side. The door opens into an entrance area 5 by 7 feet. Straight ahead is an ample clothes closet (which could be improved with wide sliding doors instead of the traffic-blocking swinging door), to the right a 5′ opening into the living room gives a view through large windows; to the left is an inconspicuous door to the kitchen. Space flows around this small block, through living room and dining space into the open kitchen. Were

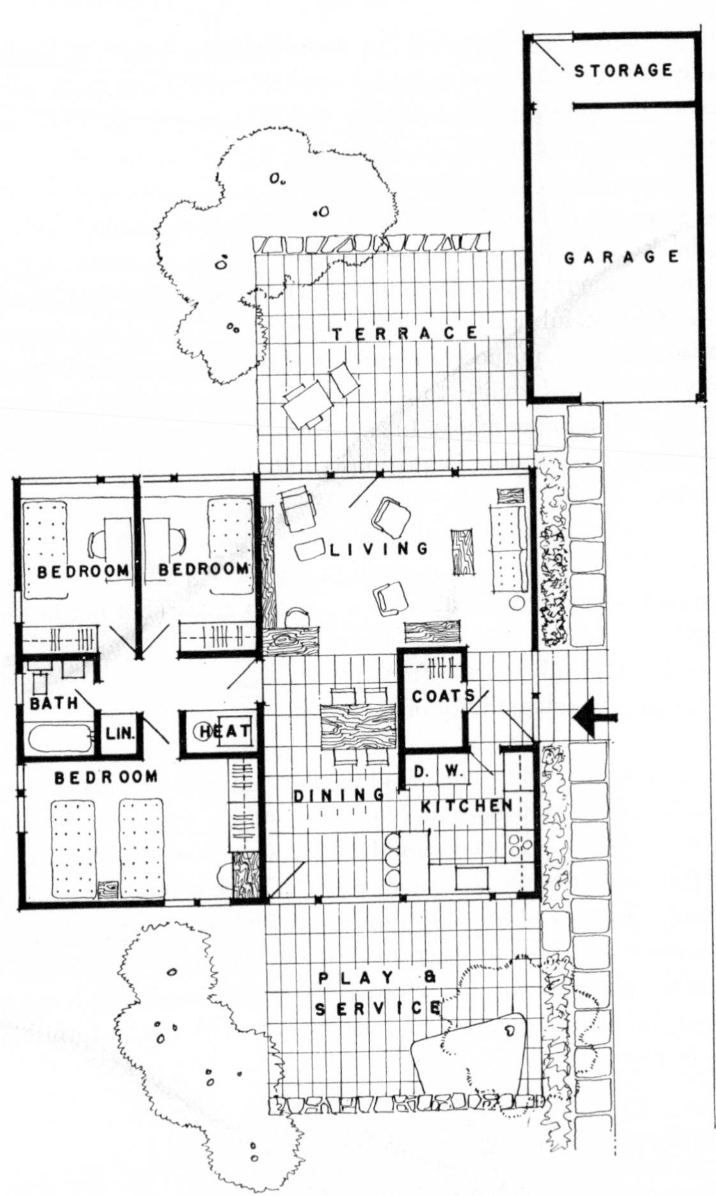

In this plan, the group-living space is L-shaped and can be used as one unit or separated into two rooms by curtains, screens, or folding doors. Wallace S. Steele, architect. (The Magazine of Building)

this the major family entrance, an undesirable amount of traffic would interfere with living room and kitchen activities—but the door into the dining-play space is more convenient for the many ins-and-outs of children, mother, and father.

The 11′2″ x 18′3″ living room has a south wall of glass and joins forces with the 15′9″ x 9′3″ dining area and with the kitchen beyond an eating counter. Thus the living room gains visual space through its window wall and wide openings into entrance and multipurpose space, but in giving over one long wall to glass and all but 4 feet of the opposite wall to openings, furniture arrangement is made difficult. As compensation, this open L-arrangement permits using these two rooms as one or separating them with screens or draperies, a possibility not found in Walker's or Rapson's plans. The 9′ x 9′ kitchen has work centers organized in an L-shape, but with the counter it becomes almost a U-plan. The only through-traffic path is short and comes desirably between food and laundry centers.

Bedrooms and bath are compactly fitted into a rectangle. The 9′3″ x 16′4″ master bedroom is of good shape and size, while the children's rooms are small but knowingly planned. The bathroom is a typical minimum installation.

The plan leads naturally to the three basic divisions of a yard—entrance, outdoor living, and service-play—each of which is segregated from the others but joined with related interior areas. The major criticism of this plan is the lack of architectural and functional relationship between garage and house, a matter of critical importance in Minnesota winters and one that could have been remedied easily by bringing the garage forward. Aside from that and the hard-to-furnish living space, this plan is good, economical to build and live in, quite flexible and not dull.

The three plans we have analyzed are economically small and compact, one story, and deviate little if at all from simple rectangles. Excellent as they are for low-cost shelter, all would be more comfortable if they were from 200 to 600 square feet larger to ease the tightness of small rooms. There are, however, many other types of plans.

► THE SHAPE OF HOUSE PLANS

Merely listing a few effects of the shape of a house plan—first and long-term costs, zoning and circulation, natural light and ventilation as well as heat and cold, exterior design, relationship to the site and outdoor living—indicates its critical significance. Each basic shape has its inherent qualities, as discussed in Chapter 6, and these qualities are at least as important in the layout of houses as they are in the design of textiles or the composition of paintings. And each basic shape can be varied imaginatively. After considering basic plan shapes, we will look at central-court houses and those with more than one level.

Square Plans

Of all typical plan shapes, the square encloses the most space with the least foundation, exterior walls, and roof: construction, exterior maintenance, and heating costs are low. In two-story houses, the square can lead to efficient room layout; in one-story designs, zoning and circulation are usually problems. If large, the center of the house may be dark and poorly ventilated unless skylights, clerestories, or central courts (Fig. 497C) are features of the design. Exteriors are likely to be boxy, especially if two stories, and hard to integrate with most sites.

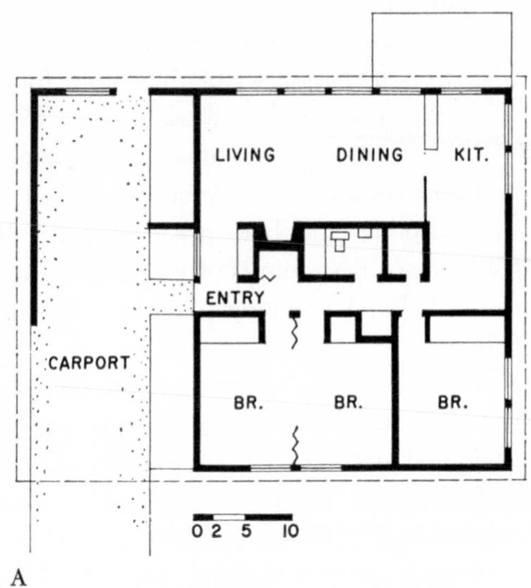

A

A carport extends the one-story Michigan house (*above*) designed by Richard Pollman and thereby greatly improves the exterior. Bedrooms are private and utilities are concentrated. Zoning and circulation are better than average for houses of this size and shape, even though the kitchen is on the side of the house away from the carport.

SECOND FLOOR

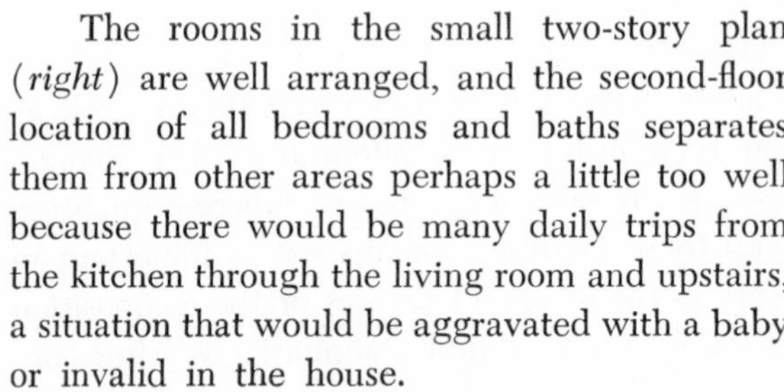

The rooms in the small two-story plan (*right*) are well arranged, and the second-floor location of all bedrooms and baths separates them from other areas perhaps a little too well because there would be many daily trips from the kitchen through the living room and upstairs, a situation that would be aggravated with a baby or invalid in the house.

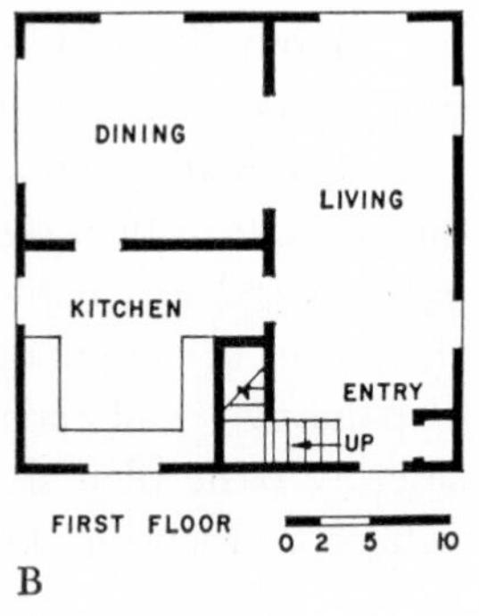

FIRST FLOOR

B

Rectangular Plans

Almost as economical to build as squares, rectangular plans can be flexibly varied. If the long dimension faces the street, houses look large and give privacy to the rear yard. Turned the other way, they fit deep narrow lots. Longer exterior walls give more area for windows and outside doors, sometimes an advantage in solar heating and summer cooling. In one-story houses, zoning and circulation are easier to handle. In two-story houses, many rooms can have through ventilation. In both, exteriors can be more pleasantly proportioned.

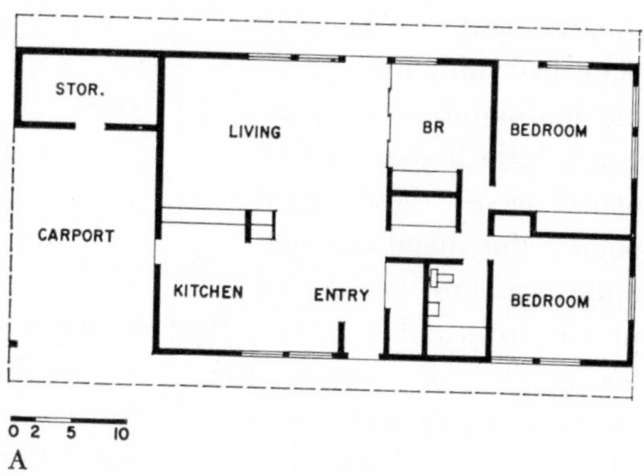

A

William Nathan's plan for a one-story house (*above*) is admirably designed. Sensible zoning keeps related areas together, and the efficient circulation takes minimum square footage yet interferes little with other activities. Separating one bedroom from the living room with sliding doors gives desirable flexibility in use of space.

Stretching a two-story plan into a rectangle (*right*) gives freedom to place windows where they function best. The large kitchen could accommodate family meals and the dining room could be a family activity space. The circulation pattern is good although, as in the square plan, the route from kitchen to bedrooms and bath is not short.

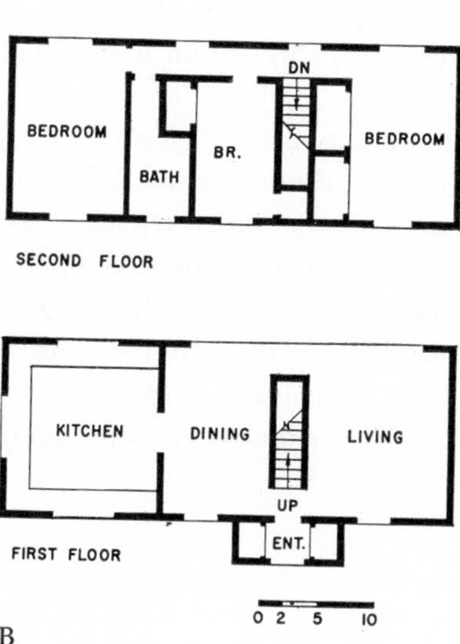

B

L-shaped Plans

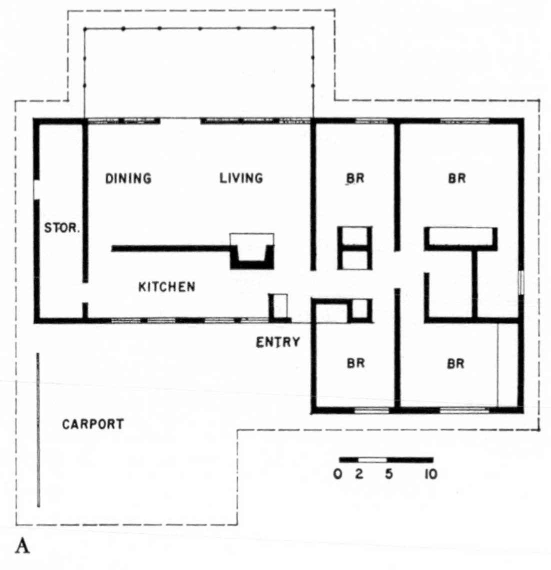

A

Spreading the plan out means more foundation, roof, and exterior wall—and usually more land. A large-scale builder has said that every time a plan turns a corner it costs $500. L-plans have six corners, square and rectangular plans have only four. Heating and plumbing costs are also a little higher. But L-plans have these good points: the shape can naturally separate group and private areas and permit excellent circulation, lead to pleasing exterior design, and provide an outdoor area sheltered on two sides. There can be more well-placed windows and better advantage can be taken of cooling breezes.

An ample carport makes a sheltered, convenient entrance to Ernest Kump's single-level house (*above*). Kitchen, dining, and living space are in one wing, bedrooms in the other. Circulation is excellent.

The two-story plan (*right*) shows a living and dining space only partially separated by the stairway, and three well-ventilated bedrooms on the upper floor. The spacious openness of the first floor, however, affords those entering the house or going upstairs no privacy, and an unduly long and twisted corridor is encountered on the upper story.

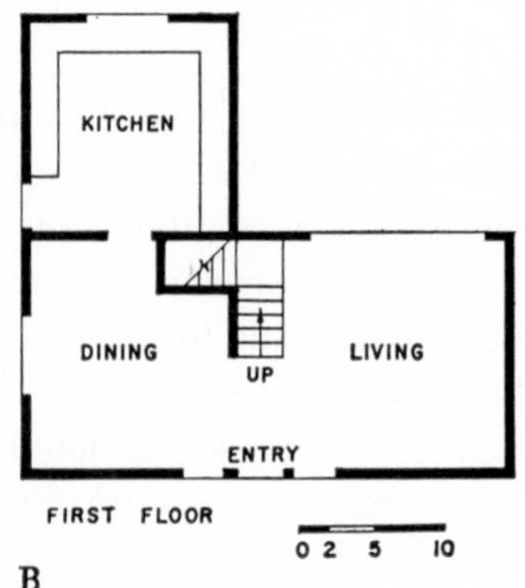

B

T-shaped Plans

With no more exterior walls but with two more corners than L-shaped plans, T-shaped plans have somewhat similar advantages and disadvantages. Construction costs are higher, but quiet and noisy areas can be separated.

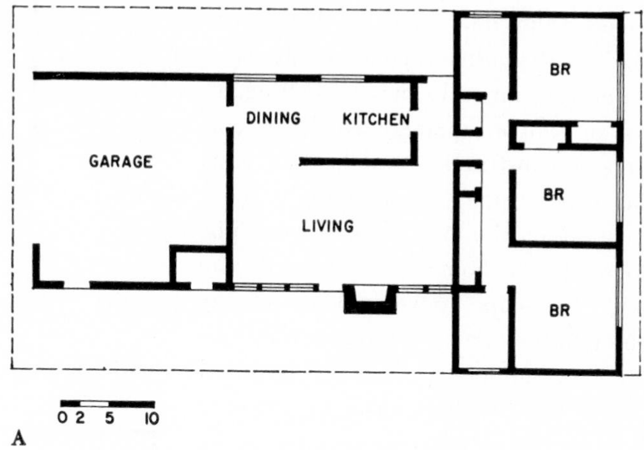

A

This shape also permits good orientation for all rooms. Two semienclosed, easily roofed areas on opposite sides of the house give a choice of sun or shade for outdoor activities. These terraces are a starting point for landscape design and usually make the exterior more ingratiating.

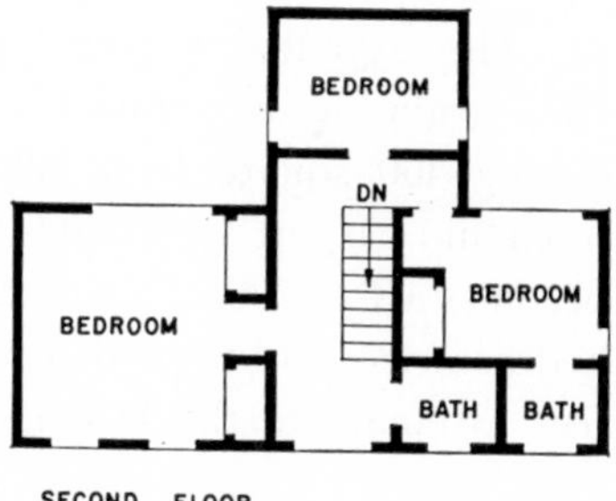

SECOND FLOOR

Anshen and Allen's plan for a one-story tract house (*above*), designed for a narrow lot, faces the garage toward the street. House and terraces are sheltered and unified by a simple roof.

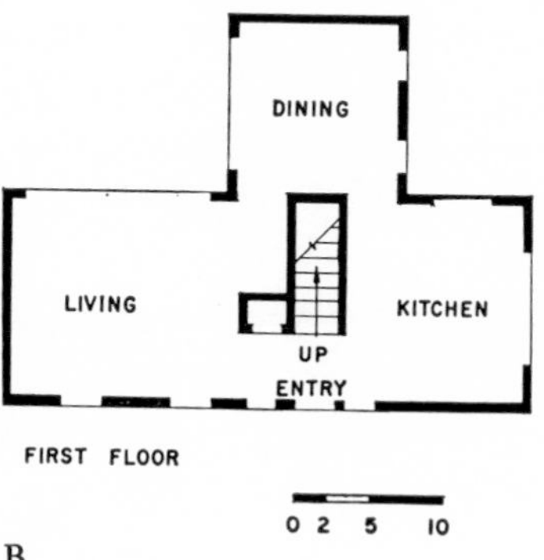

FIRST FLOOR

0 2 5 10

B

The two-story plan (*right*) separates kitchen, living room, and dining space and allows windows in each room on any of the exposures deemed best. A terrace for adults could fit into the corner formed by the living and dining rooms, one for children in that by dining room and kitchen.

U- and H-shaped Plans

Seldom used in modest two-story houses or in very small ones with a single story, these extended shapes can really separate several zones from one another. Abundant natural light and ventilation can easily be had because exterior walls may be half again as long as on simple squares, which, of course, increases construction and heating costs. Cooling expense may or may not be reduced depending on the local climate. Such plans tend to relate the house strongly to its site and landscape development, chiefly through the one or two patios they create. Sizable lots are usually required unless the house is close to property lines and large windows face the patio, as illustrated in Fig. 497B.

A

The expandable plan by Samuel Paul begins as a compact square enclosing 400 square feet. When living room and carport are added, the shape becomes a T of 706 square feet. A three-bedroom wing adds another 670 square feet to complete the H-shaped house.

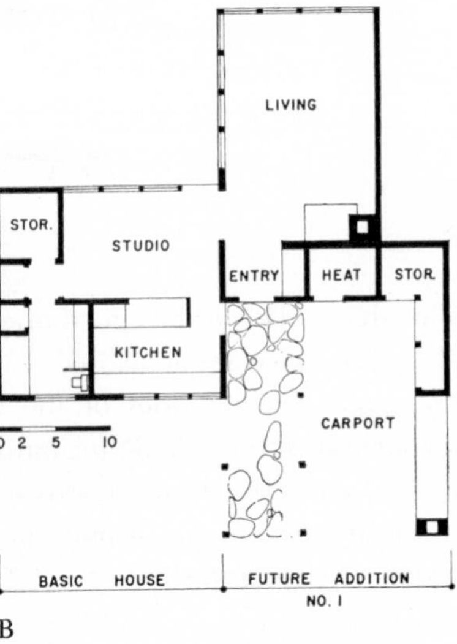

B

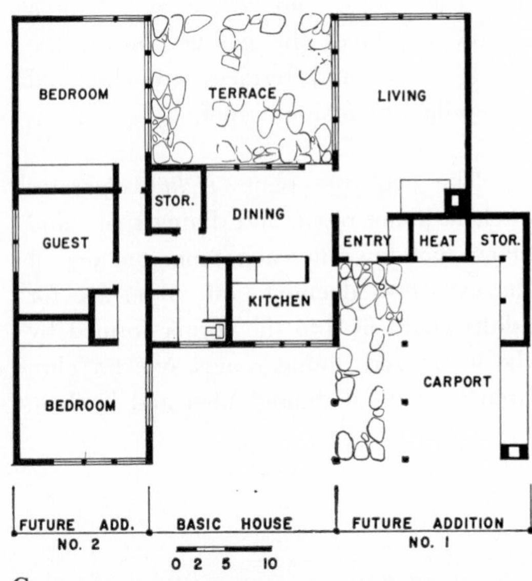

C

Diagonal and Curved Plans

Diagonals and curves, refreshing alternatives to boxy shapes, make lively and distinctive plans. Diagonals shape space dynamically, open unexpected vistas, and visually stretch rooms beyond their actual dimensions. Motivated by a promontorylike site overlooking Los Angeles, Rodney Walker's plan projects the living and dining space into the view by turning them at a 45° angle. The unconventional shape is echoed by redwood strips in the polished concrete floor and by the beams of the ceiling, which rises to a high point over the room's center.

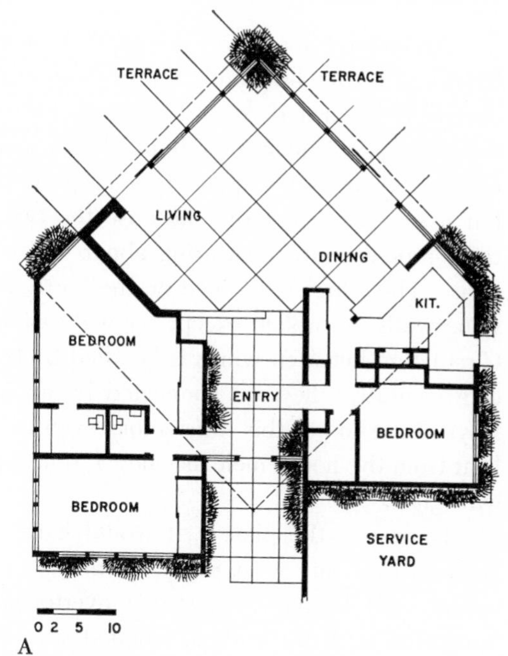

A

Rooms with curved walls have a quality that sets them apart from all other shapes. George Frank Ligar's circular house pivots around a freestanding fireplace in the center. Bedrooms built into the hillside contrast sharply with the living room that opens onto the terrace through ten glass doors. A conical roof with concentric rings of concrete shading bands of glass brings glareless light and good ventilation to living and bedrooms. Cantilevered benches and tables of concrete penetrate the glass wall.

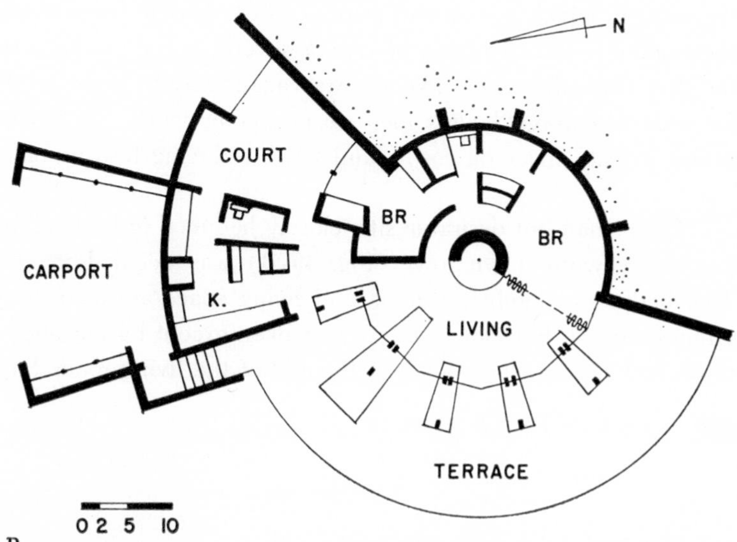

B

Court or Patio Houses

Architect Eliot Noyes designed the house in Connecticut (Figs. 497A, 310A and B) for his family with two concepts in mind: a central court and decisively separated zones for group and private life. The result has been described as a "square doughnut." It is a sizable house—the living-room wing encloses about 1,100 square feet of space, the bedroom wing about 1,500—but it seems much larger because the two wings are separated by a partially roofed court, measuring about 40 by 54 feet and surrounded by the house. The wings are joined on the north and south by 90-foot long rugged stone walls, unbroken except for wide sliding doors in the center of each. Circulation between wings is handled by two covered passages open to the court; aurally, they are connected by an intercommunication system. The Noyes have found this satisfactory even in New England winters (sun and heat from the house melt the snow), but the passageways could be enclosed with glass.

Daring as the plan is, it would hardly be worth reporting had it not been carried out with many subtleties. The plan is strictly rectangular, urbane and formal with strong overtones of symmetry, yet handsomely integrated with the rolling, wooded site. The stone walls harmonize with the natural landscape while solidly defining the house. Fifty-foot long walls of glass boldly open the living wing to a sweeping view on one side, to the secluded court on the other. This is not a house for everyone on any site, but it demonstrates how one family solved its problems of shelter with real ingenuity.

As builders around the Mediterranean, in the Far East, and in Mexico have long known, turning houses inside out gives maximum seclusion and climate control for outdoor living. This approach to house design is adaptable to all climates and to city, suburb, or open country. There are no limits to the ways in which houses and courts can be shaped (even though most are rectangular), and there can be one or several private living spaces open to the sky. This might seem like an extravagant way to build, which it can be, for such spread-out houses increase perimeter walls. Yet it can give more *usable* private space on costly land while reducing heating or cooling bills.

On a small but desirable site, closely hemmed in by neighbors, a house practically without windows (Fig. 497B) was deemed the best solution. Two bedrooms, kitchen, dining, and living space are compactly organized around a court. Exterior walls are unbroken except for entrance and kitchen doors and sliding glass panels at the end of the living room. Supplementing

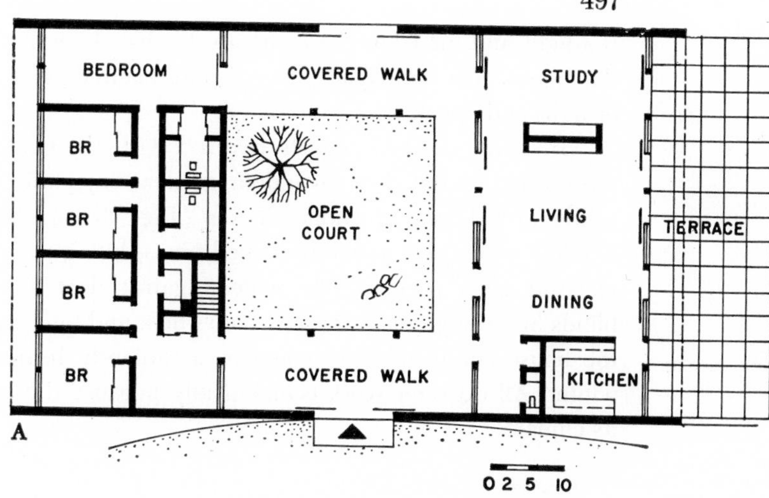

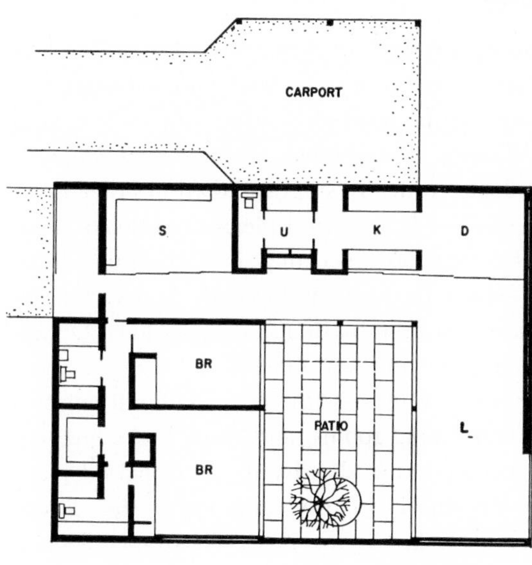

Court or Patio houses afford privacy for outdoor living and for interiors with window walls, make living comfortable in extreme climates.

Above. A central patio, reminiscent of Pompeian atriums, opens the core of a Connecticut house to the sky.

Left. A court with three walls of glass doors gives light and spaciousness coupled with privacy to a small New Orleans house. Sliding panels can open or close the study, kitchen, and dining space to the rest of the house. Laurence, Saunders and Calongne, architects.

Below. The wind, dust, and weather of Dallas, Texas, were mitigated by centering this house around a skylighted patio. Sealed fixed windows on the exterior balance the skylight, Enslie O. Oglesby, Jr., architect.

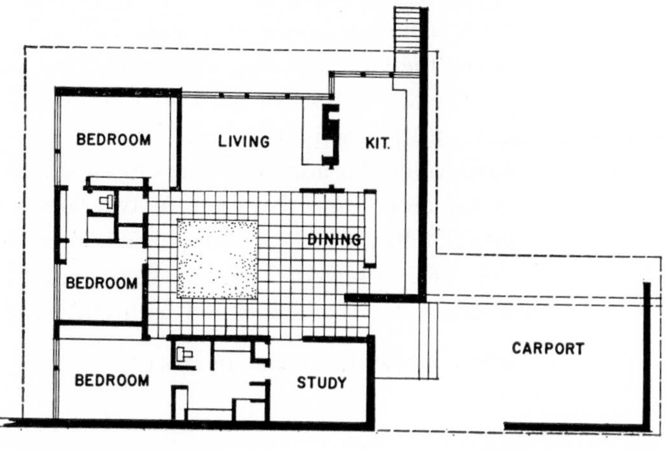

the light and air from the court are twelve skylights near the periphery of the house. The courtyard, paved and planted, gives a surprising feeling of light and space.

In some climates, courts covered with skylights function better than those open to the sky. An indoor garden, enjoyable night and day, is the center of a house in Dallas, Texas (Fig. 497C). Although windows and window walls give views from bedrooms, living room, and kitchen, all are of fixed glass permanently sealed against dust and weather. Aluminum blinds in the skylight control the sun's heat and light. A cooling system keeps the house comfortable in summer, a radiantly heated ceiling warms it in winter. All do their work economically because the house was planned for its climate.

► MULTILEVEL HOUSES

Houses with more than one story have impressive advantages. They are cheaper to build (less foundation and roof), to heat and sometimes to cool (less exterior surface). They can be built on smaller lots—or free more land for outdoor enterprises. Zoning is simplified. Typical practice is to group bedrooms on the upper floor, vertically segregated from other areas, where they have more privacy, summer breeze, and pleasant outlooks. Some special conditions, such as hillside lots, however, may indicate group living areas on the upper floor from which the view is typically better. But not everything is in their favor. Stairs can be fatiguing and hazardous. Designing exteriors that avoid clumsy high boxiness is difficult.

Typical of many two-story plans, Figure 499A has a centered entrance and stairway, separated living and dining rooms, and three bedrooms with cross ventilation. It has the advantages and disadvantages of closed plans.

A hillside site overlooking a ravine in Pennsylvania led to the efficient plan for a family with small children in Figure 499B. The upper floor, at ground level on the entrance side, has a formal living room and separate dining room sensibly shielded from the informal family room by the kitchen. Each room has access to a deck. Below are four bedrooms with windows facing the view; utilities, storage, and two bathrooms are built into the hill.

No law states that the stories of a multilevel house must coincide. Built as a vacation house on a small lot in Carmel, California, the plan in Figure 499C could be adapted to many situations. The gently sloping site suggested an entrance between the two floors. The L-shaped lower floor has a good kitchen, which can be opened into, or closed from, the ample living-dining space; a secluded parents' bedroom and bath; and a handsome terrace. Upstairs, two bedrooms and bath align with kitchen and bedroom below.

Right. Many houses built from plans basically similar to this one by architects Jameson and Harrison have proved livable and economical but a little commonplace.

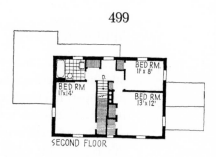

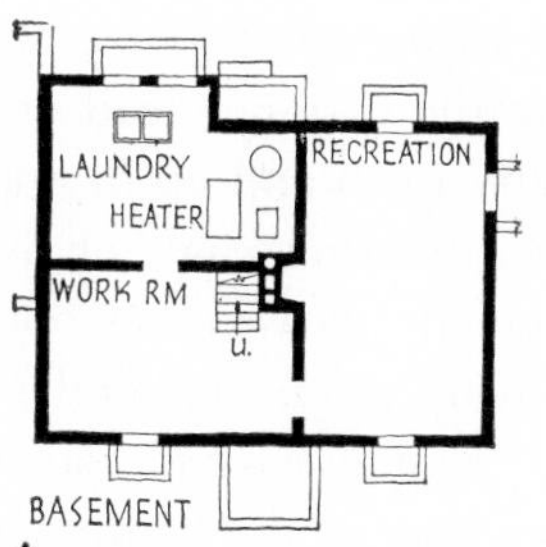

A

Below. Special conditions sometimes make it advisable to have bedrooms on the lower floor. John Perkuhn, architect.

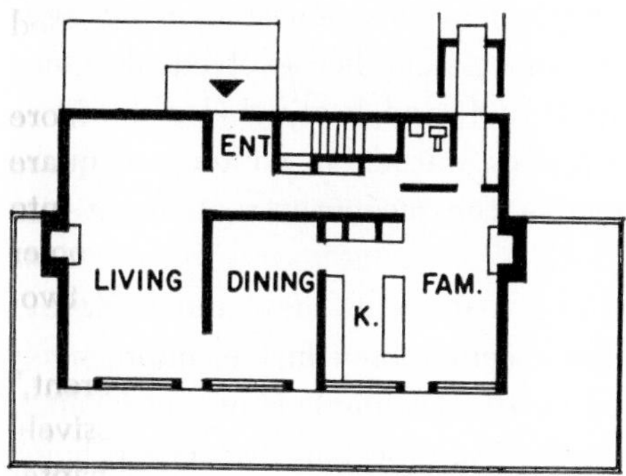

B

Below. Only about half of this house has two stories. Wurster, Bernardi and Emmons, architects.

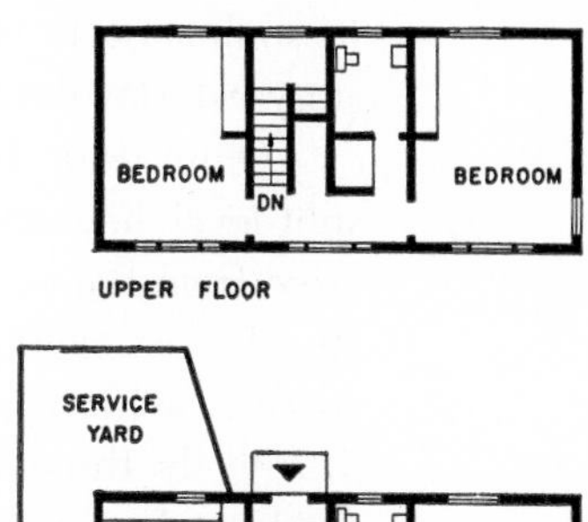

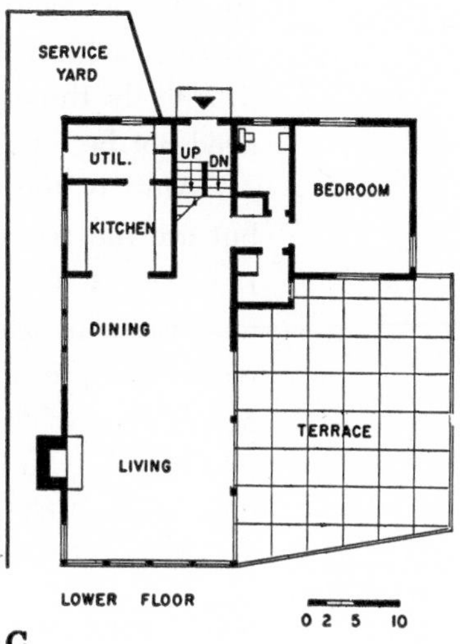

C

Split-level Houses

Although far from new, split-level houses have suddenly surged to attention. These are houses with three or more floors approximately one-half level apart in elevation. They have also been described as "a one-story ranch house and two-story Cape Codder locked in mortal combat."

The tri-level house on the opposite page is one of the better designs of this type. On a lot sloping gently down from the street, the house has its carport, entrance, and living room at the intermediate street level. Short stairways convenient to the entrance lead down to the dining (or family) room, kitchen, and utility room and up to a gallery serving three bedrooms and a bath. Thus, three differing kinds of living are vertically segregated. Noteworthy features include pleasant relationship of each level to outdoor space: a door at the living room's far end leads to a terrace; doors from dining and utility space give access to a paved area at the lower level; and a balcony runs along in front of the bedrooms. From the lofty living room, you can look up into the gallery (at some loss of privacy to those traversing it) and, through sliding panels, down in the dining space. The calm, unified exterior is exceptionally pleasant.

Good sense is evident in many aspects of this house. Leaving more land for outdoor activities than would a one-story house of equal square footage, the house saves on foundations, roof, and heating (building into the hillside is an old way of keeping houses warmer in winter and cooler in summer). It also avoids the aggressive conspicuousness of many two-story exterior designs.

Quite aside from the lure of anything that seems "new and different," split-level houses are liked because they seem roomy inside, impressively large from the outside as demonstrated by the Techbuilt House in Chapter 19. The segregation of three kinds of activities, especially two group living spaces, each on a separate floor minimizes family conflicts, and it can lead to a lively three-dimensional spatial experience. Stair runs are short, halls need not be long, and land is saved for other purposes.

Most of the serious problems of split-level houses are not inherent in, but are the result of unfamiliarity with, this approach to house planning. It is easiest to design "splits" for rolling terrain, but they can be adapted to hillsides or flat land with sensitive planning and grading. Awkward exteriors are prevalent. Although they cover less of the land than one-story homes, they seldom look comfortable on minimum lots. Most experts believe that it is next to impossible to design a wholly satisfactory "split" with less than about 1,600 square feet plus garage. Not all architects and builders have learned how to build them cheaply and heat them comfortably. Some

A

Located in Prairie Village, Missouri, this split-level house is one real estate developer's solution to the problems of contemporary planning. David B. Runnells, architect.

Above. The exterior is an unusually handsome statement of the tri-dimensional space inside. Boxiness is avoided by the projecting carport and balcony and by the double-pitched, overhanging roof. Equally noteworthy is the way in which bricks, vertical board-and-batten siding, and the slats of the balcony railing give scale and directional interest to each plane. (*Photograph by Hedrich-Blessing*)

Below. Drawings make evident the clear-cut, economical separation of quiet, semiquiet, and noisy zones. (*From ARCHITECTURAL FORUM. © 1950, Time, Inc.*)

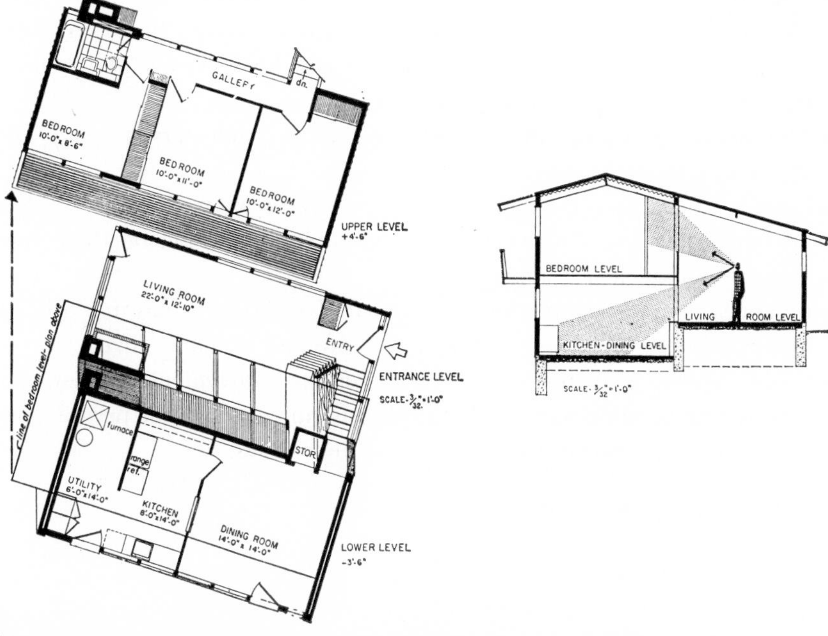

B

people just don't like the multilevel interiors, an attitude expressed by the person who said, "I'm always halfway up or halfway down but never anywhere in particular." But in many sections the good points of split-level houses have made them popular.

► SELECTING A HOUSE PLAN

How to achieve the house with the plan best for you takes careful thinking about many specific factors. In the following section we will concentrate attention on plans while remembering that, except for purposes of analytical study, the house plan should never be thought of as separated from interior, exterior, and landscape design.

Some Factors to Consider

Is the total amount of enclosed space, plus the usable outdoor space, suited to your needs? Many of us think that we want as much space as possible until we see a large old house for sale or rent. Then we begin wondering about cleaning, maintaining, and heating it, and how we and our furnishings would fit into rooms planned for another way of life. This leads to the conclusion that amount of space is not the only consideration, even though there is no complete substitute for adequate square footage. Living cramped by too many persons in too few square feet is probably worse than living in an inconvenient, hard-to-maintain, but big house—but not so bad as living in a house bigger than you can afford. Major factors are family size and ages, personalities and way of living, and finances.

- The house as a whole should give each person at least 200 square feet; 250 are better; 300 or more give comfortable living. Bruce Walker's plan would give four persons 250 feet each. Eliot Noyes' allows more than 500 for each of five persons.
- The larger the family the less square footage each person needs (or, at least, is likely to get).
- Families heterogeneous in ages and interests as well as those that are gregarious and extroverted need more space per person than those that are homogeneous and quieter.
- Finances—annual income and accumulated reserves to pay for original and continuing costs—are a major determinant of house size.
- Usable space is increased by good zoning, convenient relationships among rooms, minimum traffic through rooms, rooms that permit good furniture arrangements, and livable outdoor areas.

- Apparent space can be increased by large, grouped windows; generous openings between rooms; and strong relationship to outdoor areas—as well as the other space-giving devices discussed in Chapter 6.

Worth noting: extending the perimeter of a house a few feet adds surprisingly inexpensive space, averaging only about a third of the square-foot cost of the rest of the structure. It adds nothing for land and grading, windows and doors, and only a little for utilities.

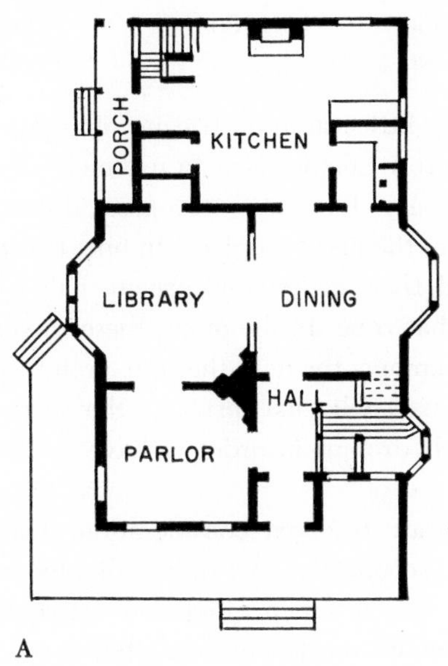

A

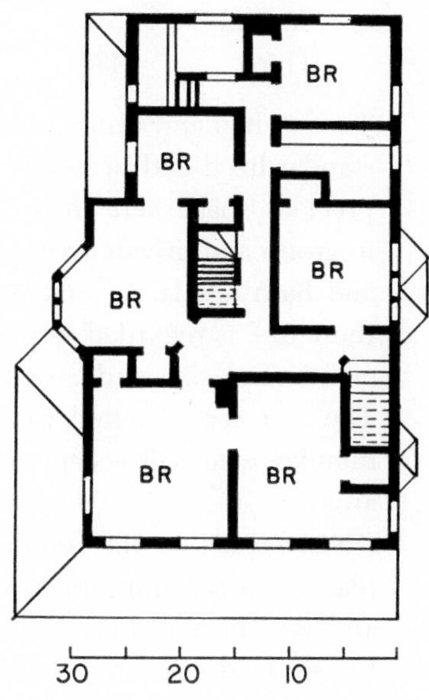

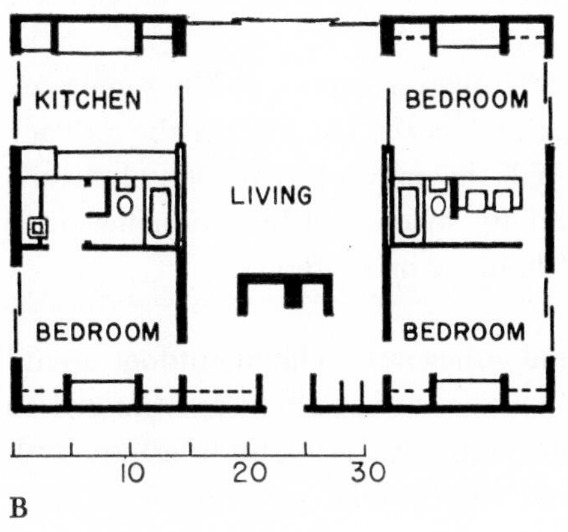

B

Comparing an ample Victorian house (*above*) with a compact modern example (*left*) by Edward D. Stone alerts us to the fact that few of today's houses are as capacious as those of our great-grandparent's generation. This reduction of size has determined many aspects of contemporary planning.

Is the space appropriately allocated for your needs? All the factors noted in the preceding paragraph affect the general divisions of indoor (and outdoor) space.

- The proportion of space allotted to group, private, and work activities can vary markedly even in houses of the same size. In the three prize-winning houses (Figs. 478, 485, and 488), the square footages (which can be translated into percentages by dropping the last zero) are approximately as follows:

	Group	*Private*	*Work*	*Total*
First	370	530	100	1,000
Second	550	350	100	1,000
Third	430	480	90	1,000

The kitchen and utility areas show little variation because equipment is standardized and in small houses few people want to use more of their precious space here than is necessary. But notice the great differences in group and private living areas in the first two plans. In one, bedrooms and bath are larger and open off their completely private hall which, therefore, is regarded as part of that zone. In the other, these rooms are of minimal size and circulation among them is through group space. The first seems suited to individuals who like privacy, the second to families who will accept cubicle bedrooms in order to have two social areas.

- Divisions within the *group space* are the next consideration. The first plan has minimum separation, the second has two rigidly divided areas, and the third distinctly draws a line between quiet and active living but without a fixed wall. Which would meet your needs best?
- Within the *work space* of small houses, divisions are usually minimal, consisting of nothing more than separating the furnace from the combined kitchen-laundry. In larger houses some segregation of cooking and laundry may be desirable.
- Divisions in *private areas* vary greatly even in houses of the same size, chiefly in the number of bedrooms and baths but also in the privacy given these rooms by a bedroom hall, by movable partitions between bedrooms or between them and activity space, and by the inclusion or exclusion of a room for individual hobbies or solitude.

Is the enclosed space well zoned and adjacent to related outdoor areas? Cities are zoned by designating certain areas for specific uses arranged so that related activities are together and those that might interfere with each other are separated. Homes benefit from similar planning.

- The minimum essential is segregating the quiet from the noisy areas. Plans can be quickly checked by coloring noisy areas red, quiet areas green, and then studying the pattern made.
- It is desirable to have well-defined zones for group activities, private living, and work and to have these zones extend into the landscape, as illustrated and discussed in Chapter 20.
- Two-story houses with bedrooms on one floor are, almost automatically, at least fairly well zoned.
- Typical zoning errors in one-story houses are often in indoor-outdoor relationships—separating the kitchen from the garage, thereby precluding a single convenient service yard (Fig. 485); facing the living room toward the street, which makes it difficult to unite with a protected terrace or lawn.
- Circulation paths logically come between zones, not through them.

Is the pattern of circulation satisfactory? Short, desirable routes from here to there simplify housekeeping and make home life pleasant but are hard to achieve. Little serious thought was given to good circulation, even in palaces, until the eighteenth century. Many people still forget that traffic through rooms greatly reduces their usable space.

Time, energy, space, and maintenance of floors can be saved with an efficient pattern of circulation. *Right* is the plan used for some years by a manufacturer of prefabricated houses. *Below* is the improvement made by architect Henry Hill. (*From* House and Home – *copyright Nov. 1952*)

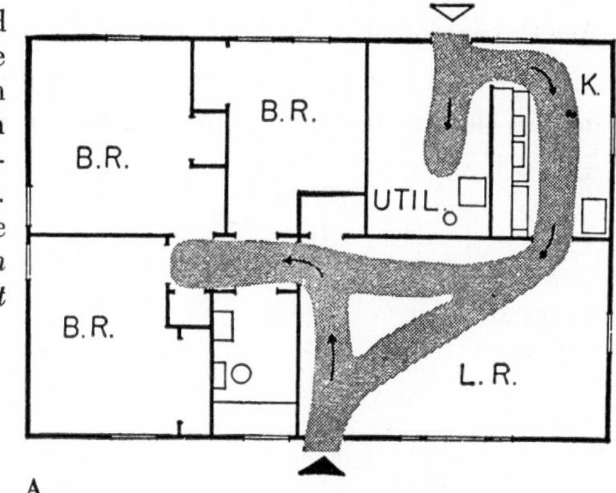

A

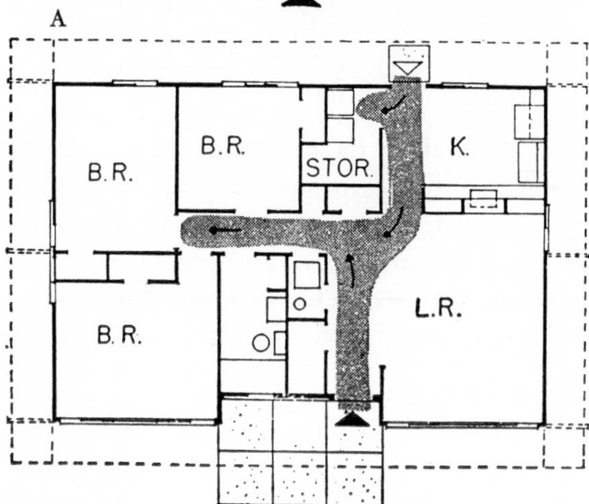

B

- Routes from garage to "front" and "back" doors should be short and offer protection in bad weather. Locating these doors near each other is a first step (Figs. 478 and 499B).
- Ideally, you should be able to get from outdoors to any room in the house, and inside from each room to any other, without going through another room except a multipurpose space.
- Keeping doors close together and near the corners of rooms shortens traffic paths and promotes good furniture arrangement. This applies to entrance doors and to doors into rooms and closets.
- Living rooms should not invite through traffic as they do in many "ranch houses," where the living room is the only link between the kitchen and bedroom wing.
- Important differences between new and old planning include:
  Incorporating the garage as part of the house (Fig. 478).
  More outside doors, especially from group living space, but also from bedrooms to terraces (Fig. 503C); having the "back" door open into a multipurpose area instead of smack into the kitchen (Fig. 488).
  Having a guest entrance area even in small houses (Fig. 490A).
  Widening what would formerly have been a narrow hall into a usable activity space or lining it with cupboards (Figs. 28A and 268A).

Are the rooms of suitable size? What was said about the total size of the house applies to room size because in general—but not always—house size is the chief determinant of room size. Below are typical square footages:

	Entrance Area	*Living Space*	*Dining Space*	*Dining Alcove*
SMALL	25-30	150-200	100-130	25-40
MEDIUM	35-40	220-280	150-180	50-70
LARGE	45-	300-	200-	80-

	Kitchen	*Bedrooms*	*Bathrooms*	*Heater Room*
SMALL	75-90	80-130	33-35	12-15
MEDIUM	100-140	140-190	40-45	18-25
LARGE	160-	200-	50-	30-

In thinking about these sizes, keep the following in mind:

- Actual square footages are the basic factor, but shape, location and size of openings; relationship to other rooms and the landscape; treatment of walls, floors, and ceiling affect usable and apparent size.
- Some families prefer, or need, many rooms even though each is small. Others prefer fewer and larger separated areas.

Will the rooms take needed furniture gracefully and efficiently? Are the shapes useful and pleasant? Furniture arrangement is a primary concern in planning, buying, or renting a home.

- First consideration is sufficient floor area for furniture and traffic.
- Second is suitable wall space, especially for such large items as beds and sofas.
- Third is the problem of getting the furniture into satisfactory groups, sequestered from and not hampering necessary circulation.

Generalizing about room shapes is hazardous because their use, size, and character qualify everything said below.

- Square rooms are hard to furnish. An exception is the separate dining room with a round table.
- Rectangles are the normal shapes. They usually work best when their proportions range from around 1:1.2 (approximately 10′ x 12′, 12′ x 15′, or 16′ x 20′) up to 1:1.7 (approximately 5′ x 8′, 10′ x 12′, or 12′ x 18′). If more nearly square than the first proportions, rooms lose their rectangularity without gaining the stability of the square. If their proportions closely approach 1:2, as they do in the living and activity rooms in Figure 485, rooms become corridorlike unless clearly differentiated by furniture into two or more areas (see Fig. 396B).
- L-shapes are happy solutions for dual-purpose rooms, such as living rooms with alcoves for conversation, music, or dining and kitchens with a semiseparated laundry. Bedrooms in which either the beds, a desk and chair, or closets and chests are put in their own nooks are remarkably pleasant.
- All the other wonderful shapes—circles, ellipses, and free curves, hexagons and octagons, nonrigid combinations of straight lines—bring variety and excitement as illustrated in Figures 495 and 509.

Does the house lend itself to desirable or necessary change? It is impossible to predict specifically what the future will bring, but knowing that life and change go together suggests planning for flexibility.

- Family patterns change as children are born, develop, and leave home. The newborn sleeps near his parents and for several years needs supervision; the child in elementary school begins to assert the independence that marks adolescence; and after high school a child usually lives at home only during vacations.
- Limited finances coupled with inability to predict family size suggest beginning with a small house carefully planned to permit adding more space as needed.

- Business opportunities, health, or the desire for change can make it necessary to sell or rent your home.
- All these indicate the advisability of:

  Selecting a plan that fits, or can easily be adapted to, the needs of others, possibly with the loss of some highly individualized features.

  Making certain that additional space can be economically added, unless you start with a sizable home.

  Keeping to a minimum hard-to-move interior partitions by substituting movable storage walls, sliding or folding doors, and the like.

This may sound as though you should plan for others or for a way of living other than your own present pattern. That is not intended. But the future is well worth thinking about when spending the amount of money a home costs.

Is—or can—the plan be effectively oriented on the site? *Orientation* is best defined as relationship to the environment. This includes the sun, wind, and outlook; the size, shape, and slope of the lot and its relationship to the street; and existing trees, rocks, water, and so forth. Orientation affects the directions in which different rooms face, the location of windows and ventilators, and the placement of the house on the lot. Here are some points to remember:

- The sun brings heat, light, and cheer chiefly from the south.
- Summer breezes usually come from the west and winter winds from the north, but they vary greatly from region to region, even from lot to nearby lot.
- Views follow no pattern—except that on typical city lots the best outlook is into your own private yard.

There is general agreement *for typical situations* on the following:

- Group living space deserves the best view, the privacy needed for living behind the house's largest windows, and winter sun. South to southeast is preferred.
- Kitchens also deserve a pleasant vista outdoors and ample daylight, preferably with morning sun. Northeast is desirable.
- Bedrooms need privacy. Southern exposures are most agreeable—but usually there is little choice.
- Bathrooms should be located where most convenient. Privacy can be assured by high windows and there is no great need for outlook or sun.
- Utility rooms can be anywhere because they need few if any windows.
- Garages need only be convenient to street and house entrances.

Placement of house on lot depends on the size and shape of each, the location of the street, any natural features and community restrictions. In general, though, the following is good practice:

- Maximum usable private yard and minimum driveway usually come when the long dimension of the house parallels the street and the house is as near the street as feasible.
- One usable side yard can often be had by placing the house nearer one side of the lot than the other.
- On lots facing south, the house is often pushed back and some of the front yard made private, as in Figure 485.

It is clear that no single house plan will fit every lot nor is a standardized location on all lots sensible. While there is no excuse for thoughtless orientation, many devices can alleviate difficult situations as noted in Chapters 12 and 20.

Is the plan beautiful? Once a house is built, the plan is not seen as a whole—but it is certainly experienced as you live with it. A plan without beauty and character is no more defensible than a fireplace or chair lacking these qualities. The plans in Figures 478 and 503B are unpretentious and informal yet carefully ordered. Eliot Noyes' home is based on a plan of crystalline precision. Those in Figures 495A and B are inventive and dynamic. Frank Lloyd Wright's plans liberate man's spirit.

Frank Lloyd Wright created plans which enrich the lives of those fortunate enough to live with them. (*Courtesy of* House Beautiful)

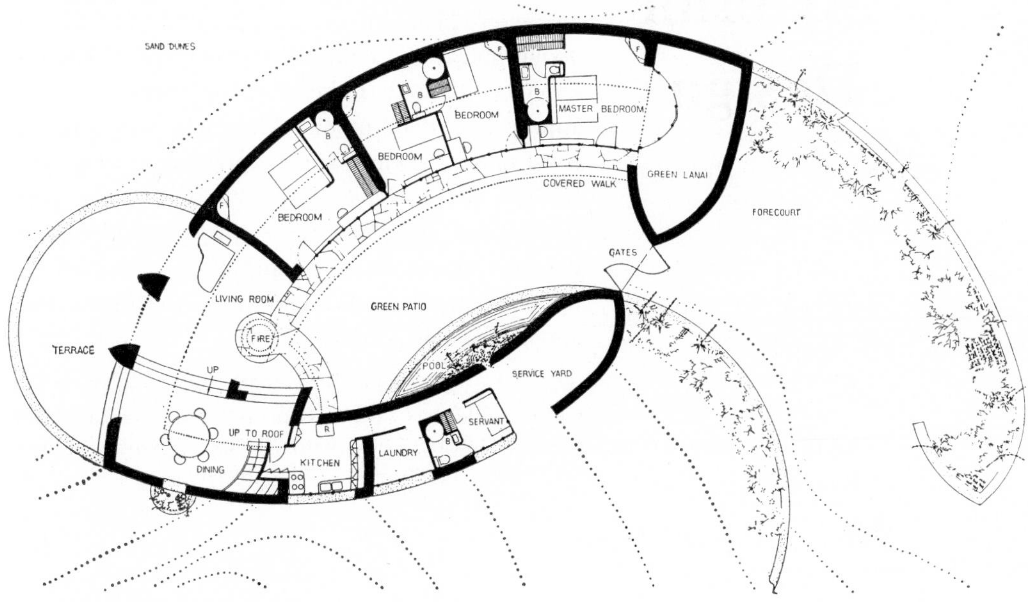

19. Exterior Design

WHEN HOMES ARE DESIGNED from "the inside out," exterior design becomes the outer expression of an inner plan for living. Relationship to the geographical and cultural environment and to the specific site may indicate some forms as more appropriate than others. Materials and ways of construction always affect appearance and cost. Individualized concepts of beauty are vital considerations. Bringing these factors into happy balance, giving each its appropriate emphasis in terms of specific conditions leads to designs that are honest and varied.

Above. In 1850 this Cottage-Villa exterior in the Rural Gothic style was said to express "a man or family of domestic tastes, but with strong aspirations after something higher than social pleasure." (*From A. J. Downing's* Country Houses)

► WAY OF LIVING AND ENVIRONMENT

In the few centuries of our history, New England has produced more than its share of good houses. We will look at two, each of which grew out of a family's needs conditioned by the time and place of living, and then at two houses specifically designed for atypical environments in California and Florida.

An Eighteenth-century House in Salem, Massachusetts

When built in the 1720's, the house shown in Figure 512 was contemporary. Now known as the Ropes Memorial, it is preserved as a document. Salem was then a prosperous seaport in close cultural contact with the mother country. And Colonial architecture, as Talbot Hamlin has written, is compounded of memories and the need for reassurance, homesickness for the old and desire for new national pride. During the seventeenth century, English architecture had shifted rather suddenly from medieval to classical forms. Architectural handbooks not only brought the news but explicit drawings of the latest style.

This posed problems for colonial builders who wanted to keep up with the times. Their climate was harsher, and they had neither the skills nor money for the precise masonry of English Georgian architecture. But Yankee ingenuity was available. In the seventeenth century, New Englanders had developed overlapping wood siding to weatherproof the half-timber structures built from old memories. In the eighteenth century, they used their wood-working skills to adapt so completely the new English designs that a distinctive style was born unintentionally.

The Ropes Memorial has the well-proportioned formality and sensitive detailing admired then—and now. The dominant doorway, slightly recessed and enriched with Ionic columns in 1807, leads into a central hall that gives access to the four rectangular rooms on the first and second floors. Identical windows with small rectangular panes in double-hung sashes, each at rest in its own allotted space, march regularly across the façade in two ranks. The once-utilitarian shutters stretch the windows out to suggest two horizontal bands. A cornice tight above the second-floor windows conciliates the vertical wall with the sloping roof. Three dormer windows, each under a small roof, help light what was once the "children's dormitory." A simple balustrade obscures the roof's peak. The two symmetrical chimneys mark the location of fireplaces on each of the three floors. In 1894, when the house was moved back from the street and put on higher foundations, the handsome fence (based on late eighteenth-century design) was erected to carry

The Ropes Memorial in Salem, Massachusetts, illustrates the impressive formality of eighteenth-century New England exterior design. (*Essex Institute*)

the spirit of the house out to the sidewalk and to separate the front lawn from the street.

In some respects, designing such houses was easy because they were based on patterns that permitted only minor liberties. Few questions were raised about formality versus informality, choice of materials or type of construction, location of entrance door and windows, or orientation. Sensitivity to scale and proportion, though, was important and some inventiveness could be applied to details. Although no two houses were identical, marked similarities led to harmonious towns. There is much to learn from such homes, especially about refinement of proportion and judicious use of ornament, even though our ways of living and consequently of building have changed considerably from those of eighteenth-century New Englanders.

Even this historic house has responded to the impact of changing conditions. In addition to the modifications mentioned above, large archways were cut in 1807 to open the parlor into the dining room, and in 1894 a wing for kitchens, bathrooms, and servants' quarters was built at the rear.

A Contemporary City House in Cambridge, Massachusetts

The house architect Carleton R. Richmond, Jr., built recently for his family is not many miles from the Ropes Memorial but more than two centuries of drastic changes in American life separate the two. The site is a well-located city lot, narrow but with a deep backyard facing south—and a six-story apartment building. The family wanted a flexible interior warmed by winter sun and functionally related to livable outdoor space.

Superficially, the street side of the house bears little relationship to the Ropes Memorial. Both house and lot are much smaller. The roof is flat, the glass is concentrated in two large areas, and there is no applied ornament. The balance is asymmetrical, the rhythm is dynamic, and there is no center of interest. Yet it, too, has a strict, geometric order. Opaque and transparent areas are aligned, horizontally and vertically, and strong lines lead our eyes quickly from side to side, top to bottom. A detailed analysis would reveal such interesting relationships as the progression of unequal vertical divisions and the diagonal relationships of wood and glass areas. These panels carry to the exterior important subdivisions of the interior space. Moreover, they convey the feeling of dynamic rectangularity found inside.

The façade is penetrated on the right by the garage, which gives quick access to all rooms. On the left, a short straight walk takes us into a sheltered recess and then into the entry flooded with light yet made private by translucent glass. Passing the study and the stairs to the upper floor, we descend five steps, reflecting a slight ground slope, into a two-story living zone. Sliding and folding doors unite or separate the living room from dining and study areas. A glass wall, floor to roof, dramatically extends this space.

What about views and privacy, sun and ventilation? The front is close to the street, which made figured glass advisable on the ground floor. Directly above the entry is a ventilating grille lined up with the bedroom windows. An unbroken brick wall gives privacy and thermal insulation toward the northeast. The opposite side has windows lighting and ventilating garage, kitchen, and master bedroom. It is the garden side, though, that is most noteworthy. By extending the side walls and roof and by designing a trellis, partly open and partly roofed, the architect made it possible to enjoy views of the garden and sky, the warmth of winter sun, and the pleasures of outdoor living without being looked at by neighbors. These practical devices, indicated by the site, also provide delight for the eyes.

The Richmonds had many choices to make—materials, character, and shape of house and roof; size and shape and location of windows. They

A

B

Left above. For his own home in Cambridge, Massachusetts, architect Carleton R. Richmond, Jr., designed a façade geometrically precise yet asymmetrical.

Left below. At the rear, the house is extended by a trellis that protects outdoor living space and large windows from summer sun and neighbors' views. (*Photographs by Joseph W. Molitor*)

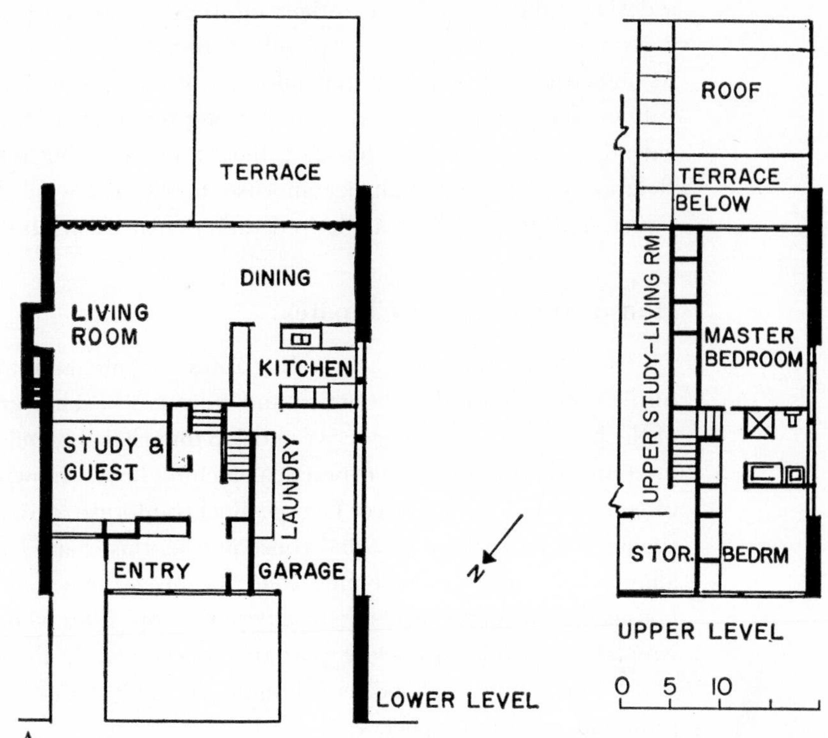

A

Above. Like the façade, the compact plan has a disciplined geometric order.

Below. A section through the house shows how summer sun and observation from without were excluded while permitting the occupants to enjoy an all-year view of the garden and the warmth of winter sun. (*Courtesy of F. W. Dodge Corporation,* Architectural Record Houses of 1954)

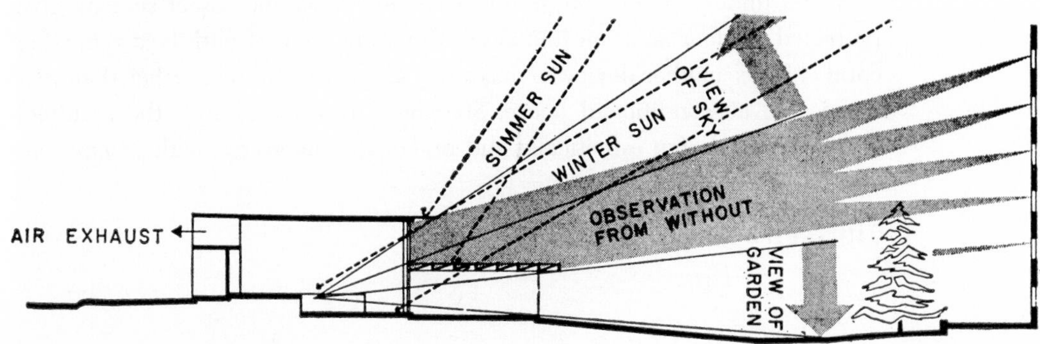

B

had no rules but neither did they start in a vacuum since they were familiar with and influenced by other modern houses. They decided to have a home that is distinctly urban, appropriate to a setting in which man-made streets, sidewalks, and buildings dominate, not evasive about belonging to a machine-age. Although concerned with beauty of form, they wanted a design intimately related to their informal living and to their lot. Several ways in which contemporary planning affects exterior design are evident. Asymmetric plans, efficient and informal, lead to asymmetric interiors. Private outdoor living suggests locating living rooms away from the street and extending the house with terraces, fences, overhanging roofs, and trellises. Relating windows to room size and use, to sun and wind, leads to shaping, sizing, and placing them as desired rather than by arbitrary rule.

Houses for Extreme Climates

By comparison with New England's climate and topography, California's Sierra Nevada mountains and Florida's beaches are extreme. Each of the houses shown on pages 517 and 518 unmistakably reflects the lay of the land and the weather. Two practical factors, heavy snowfall and economy of construction, led architect George Rockrise to use a triangular, A-shaped timber frame. Perhaps of equal consequence, this shape has a strong visual affinity for mountains and pine trees. Primitive man long ago found that houses in which roof meets floor on two or more sides were simple to build. Now it is feasible to enclose partially or completely the gable ends with glass. This aspiring shape, encouraging us to look up and then out, has profound spiritual impact.

Humidity and hot sun, hurricane winds and high tides, and insects can make most semitropical areas less than paradisiacal unless dwellings take these facts of nature into account. Lifting houses off the ground is an old way of letting cooling breezes or surging water go under the house. Doing this with concrete, the material used in the house in Figure 518A, discourages insects. Extending the house over its site allows moderate winds to go through the rooms, especially as in this example when the center is a genuine breezeway. Sliding doors control storm winds, which go harmlessly over and under this low house. Overhanging roofs and insect screens give protected outdoor areas on four sides. Covering the roof with heat-reflecting coral chips is another device to make this an architecturally, rather than mechanically, air-conditioned house. Starting with these factors, the architect ended with a design esthetically and practically integrated with its environment.

A

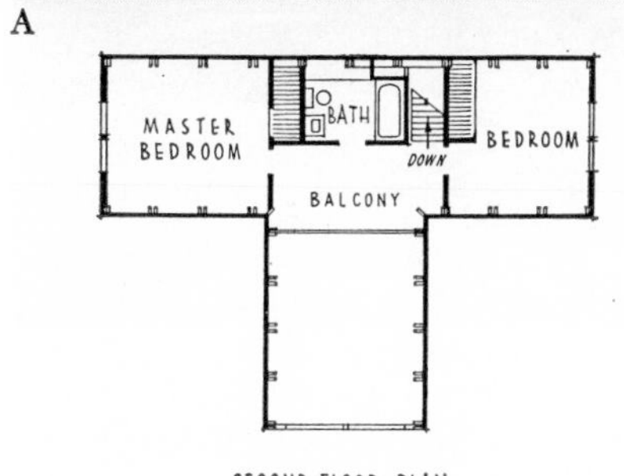

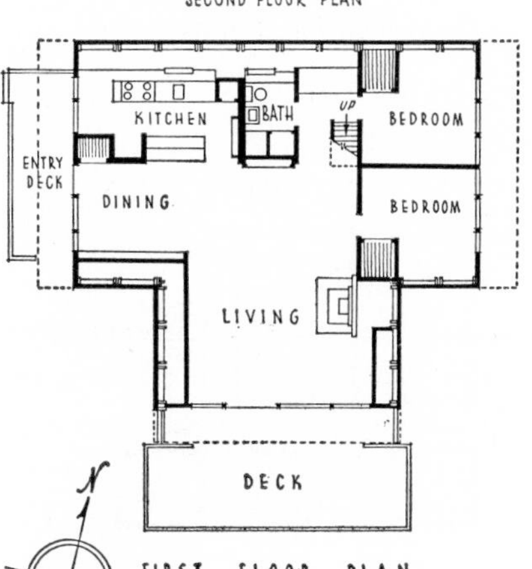

B

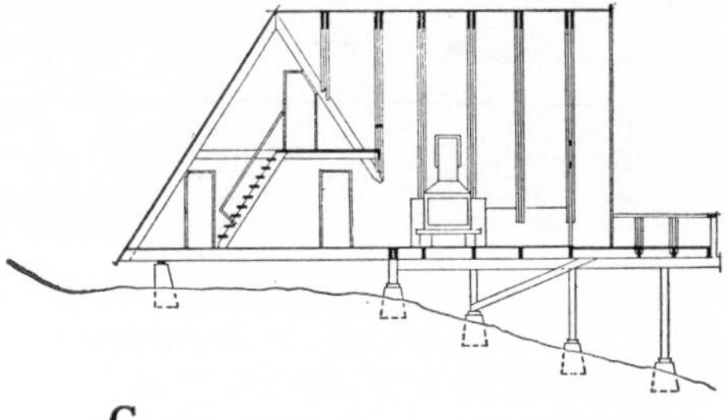

C

Sharply pitched roofs with eaves coming down to the floor shed the weight of heavy snow, visually relate exterior and interior to a mountainous setting. George Rockrise, architect. (*Photograph by Ernest Braun. Courtesy of* Sunset Magazine)

In 1,425 square feet of floor space, there are four bedrooms and two baths, kitchen and dining space, and a large living room with walls sloping up to the roof's peak.

A

A house designed by Robert B. Browne is stretched out over and elevated above its flat Miami site in deference to tropical winds, rains, and temperatures. (*Photograph © Ezra Stoller*)

Cooling breezes flow through and between the two enclosed units of the house.

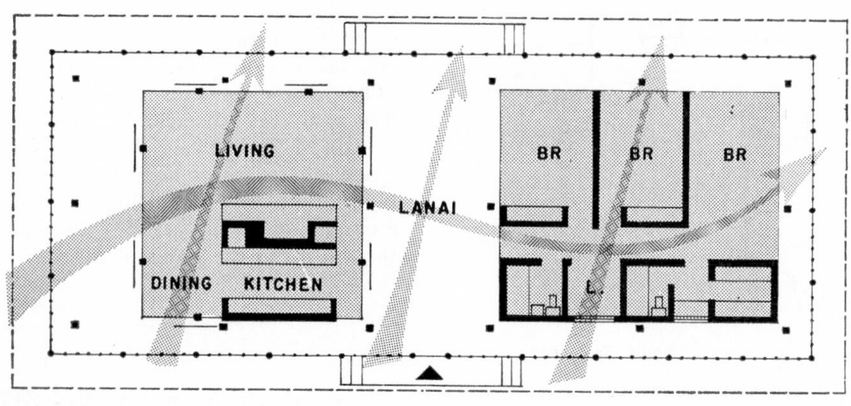

0 2 5 10

B

These four houses were all influenced by their surroundings. Where the climate is extreme, as in Florida and the mountains, recognition of this influence seems particularly important. But how significant is it generally? In certain respects, many "primitive" people have built homes better suited to their environments than have we. Indian pueblos and the raised breezy grass huts of the South Pacific are just about perfect examples of meeting the climate and landscape on its own terms with local materials. But each of these was built by people of a homogeneous culture, similar in their living patterns and restricted in their materials and building techniques. Such people almost inevitably built in a certain style because they had little choice, and over the centuries an efficient, consummate model was produced. Our culture is different. Within the same community are many dissimilar modes of life, and two families living on opposite sides of the continent may be more alike than near neighbors. Local materials are often more expensive than those efficiently processed elsewhere, while local craft traditions have just about died out. It is true that those houses with distinctly local or regional flavor are often deeply satisfying, as is the work of Frank Lloyd Wright. His house for the Arizona desert belongs to that colorful, arid scene as much as his Wisconsin home belongs to its lushly green hilltop (Figs. 201A and 553B). But an overwhelming proportion of building sites have no character other than that given by street layout and nearby houses, and modern heating and cooling methods can combat almost any weather. Then the more subtle hints of specific site orientation and individual domestic patterns can be used to give form to a house, aided by the character of the materials from which it is built.

► MATERIALS AFFECT HOUSE DESIGN

The cost and character of a house, the maintenance it requires, and the kind of living it suggests are in part determined by the materials from which it was built. This applies quite as much to structure, which can be visible or hidden, as to the surfaces. The character of materials, their beauty, strengths, and weaknesses, are as important to architects as to potters or weavers—more so, perhaps, because architects work with many more kinds of materials.

A House Built of Wood

In itself a house built of wood is hardly worth comment since most houses in this country are built of that material. But the one illustrated on the following pages is exceptional. It was designed by the same architects

A

B

who did the masonry house, illustrated on pages 108 and 213, for a rocky, mountainous site in Mexico. This house stands on an acre of land in rolling, semiwooded hills a few miles north of San Francisco. Although commissioned by a merchant builder with a pre-set cost, it has marked individuality and was sold before finished. The architects took full advantage of a lot with the street to the north. The pleasant U-shaped plan, three times as large as the three prize-winning houses in Chapter 18, links secluded rooms with a spacious loggia and terrace.

The essence of the design is an age-old system of wood construction—widely spaced *posts* support *beams* that hold up ceilings of *planks.* Not much of this is seen from the street, where the need for privacy indicated a simple façade of redwood siding, but the posts show as structural divisions in a band of windows. A brick chimney directs attention toward a recessed entrance court. On entering the house, however, you experience the sturdy architectural rhythm and unity of the revealed structure. From the south side, you can enjoy the way in which the structure visually binds interior and exterior to one another. The plan, as well as the photographs, show that this orderly framework permits great flexibility because the spaces between posts and beams can be treated as desired.

The structure can be as frankly and vitally the main force in house design as it is in Gothic cathedrals, a point ably demonstrated by Anshen and Allen's house in San Rafael, California.

Left above. The pervasive rhythm of posts and beams energizes the whole house with implicit motion.

Left below. Space flowing in many directions is given coherence by the flexible framework. (*Photographs by Rondal Partridge and Roger Sturtevant*)

Below. A spacious loggia allied with a terrace connects bedrooms with dining, kitchen, and family space.

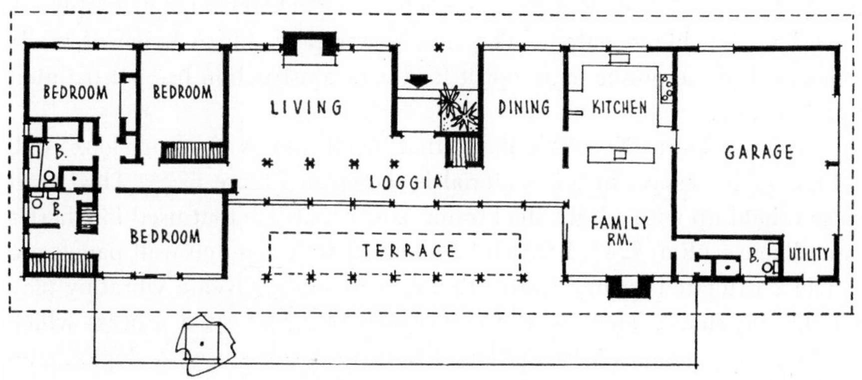

The colonnade of posts demarcating loggia from living room stands free from the floor to the 13′ ridge, except for the coat closet enclosed only to the necessary height. The spaces between the posts that separate the loggia from the terrace are filled with glass, but there is nothing but air and space between those on the terrace. Plank-and-beam ceilings allow similar flexibility in the ceiling and roof. Over the entrance court, an open panel brings daylight to this area. On the south, where sun control is important, a solid roof covers the recessed terrace and shades the window wall except for the space between seven posts where a skylight brightens the interior.

All structure and surfaces, except for some of the floors, are of handsomely detailed wood. Redwood siding with closely spaced vertical grooves, which produce a small-scale rhythmic play of light and shadow, was used for all exterior and many interior walls. Thick cedar shingles make a vigorously textured roof. The slender redwood pillars are refined out of the fence-post category by vertical grooves in the corners. The planks and the beams of the gabled ceiling are of tough fir. For contrast, some interior walls are surfaced with smooth, straight-grain Philippine mahogany plywood.

In the best architecture, the lines between inwards and outwards, or among materials, construction, and "design," are mighty thin. In this house, the regularity of the structural system gives coherence to the exterior, interior, and plan. Every part of the house, though, demonstrates that it is not a strait jacket. It would be difficult to live badly with such a carefree yet sensible plan. But it is the free-standing colonnades, outside and inside, that give this year-round home the sheer delight expected of vacation living.

A House Built of Steel

Developed centuries ago, steel has been a hard material to domesticate. Unlike wood, it seldom seems homelike. We acknowledge its usefulness in washing machines, automobiles, and skyscrapers. But a home of steel? Reluctance of the public to accept it for home construction has not daunted experimenters.

Designer Pierre Koenig believes that metal houses need not look cold, and one of his essays in this material is shown in Figure 523A. This small house is held up with a light steel frame, somewhat like that used in Charles Eames' house (Fig. 224). Roof and ceilings as well as some wall panels are of steel, corrugated for more strength but incidentally given a vibrating play of light and shade. They were prefabricated in a factory, a process which could effect economies if carried on at large scale. Because no single mate-

A

Houses of metal supported by slender, widely spaced posts permit great freedom of planning. Pierre Koenig, designer.

Above. The exterior brilliantly shows how steel can give sheltered openness, a lightness of form all its own.

Below. A steel frame holds the house together, but wood and plastic, brick, stone, and asphalt tile contribute to the bold counterpoint of lines and planes. (*Photographs by Julius Shulman*)

B

rial is equally functional for every part of a home, plastics and wood and masonry are used here where they perform better. Even so, it is a steel house.

Remember that steel is very strong, even when posts and beams are slender or panels thin. With it, architects can span wide gaps with a rigid structure. Open plans and window walls come naturally with steel as do lightweight opaque panels. Another attribute of steel is its amenability to precise machining, a quality of great importance when the components of a house are factory-made but assembled on the site. Although metals in themselves give minimum clues to appropriate forms, we have come to accept *structural* metal as being distinctly geometric, usually rectilinear. (That metal can be shaped otherwise is a potentiality for the future.) Accepting present trends in steel fabrication, Koenig has created a home with gratifying variations on a theme of rectangularity. Space is opened and closed, interrupted and continued with controlled vitality. It is delicate, light, livable geometry. But light steel construction is not the only way in which metal can affect exterior, and interior, design. For proof, look again at the *heavy* steel frame in Figure 222A from which a glass-walled house in Illinois is suspended.

There are some who have confidence that metal, seeming to defy gravity when rightly used, will open the way to freer living. To them, there is no need to bury this splendid substance in other materials. Quite aside from its uniquely important structural characteristics, its surface can be almost infinitely varied—galvanized or coated with baked-on enamel, painted or embossed with seemingly limitless colors and textures. Others more conservatively say that as yet the wearisome problems of keeping steel from rusting, of eliminating moisture condensation on surfaces that speedily conduct cold, have not been licked. They suggest using steel where it is necessary—but usually covering it up. Should metal assert its special individuality in homes, should it be "softened" to fit with arbitrary, perhaps outdated, concepts of "hearth and home," or should it be hidden? Such issues are not susceptible to true-false questions with a single right answer. We must ask: Why is metal used for this part of the home? How well is it handled? For whom is it intended?

Houses of Masonry and Plastics

As discussed in Chapters 8 and 9, masonry and plastics have their own extensive range of individuality. Looking back through earlier illustrations proves how varied masonry can be without losing its identity. The boldly dramatic, cantilevered roofs in the Robie house (Fig. 119A) are anchored by great masses of brick. In Chapter 8, several exemplary uses

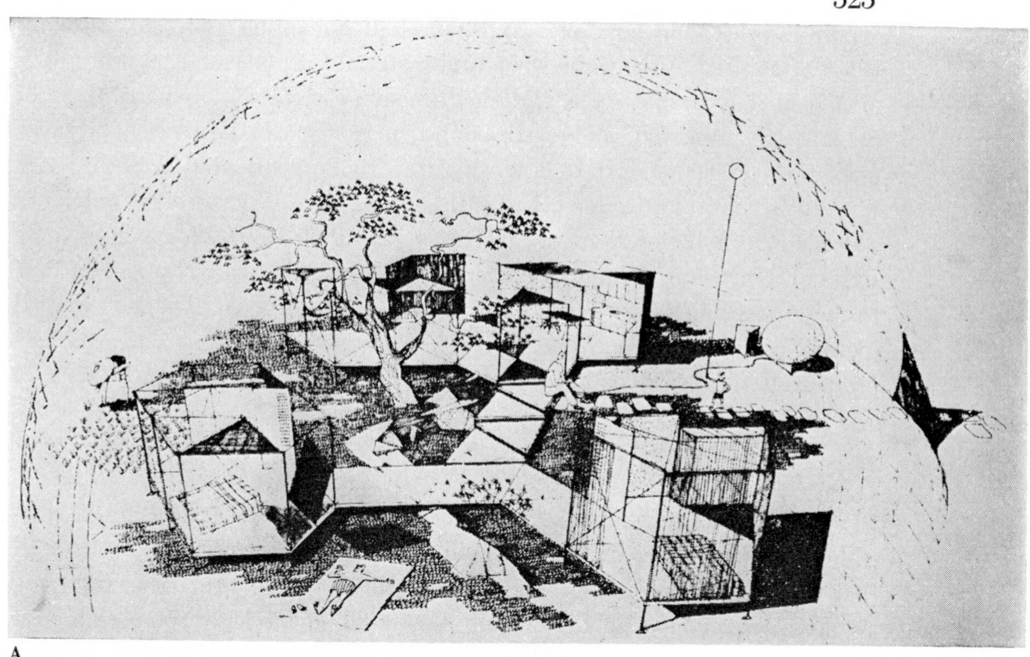

A

Plastics lead to wonderfully varied forms, quite unexpected in domestic architecture.

Above. A plastic-covered "geodesic" dome of thin metal rods could carry indoor-outdoor living far beyond its present limitations. Cabañalike units for different family activities could be freely dispersed. (*Society of Plastics Industry*)

Below. An experimental house, designed by Marvin Goody, is based on U-shaped molded plastic units measuring 8′ x 16′ that form ceilings, walls, and floors. (*Monsanto Chemical Company*)

B

of stone, brick, and concrete are illustrated. Excepting concrete, masonry is not often used as the basic structural material for homes but in a fireplace or a wall it is frequently a vigorous accent (Fig. 527B). Usually thought of as heavy, massive, and earth-bound, masonry can also be light, airy, and spirited as demonstrated by Figures 195B, 203B, and 213B.

At present, plastics have had little impact on exterior design, but there seems to be a better than even chance that they can add a wholly new series of dimensions. Figures 229C and 310B show that Eliot Noyes is as alert to these possibilities as to the established qualities of stone. Giant U-shaped molded plastic panels have been tried; plastic enclosed domes can weatherproof house and gardens to be partitioned at will (Figs. 525A and B).

► BEAUTY AND INDIVIDUALITY

If the preceding sections seem to indicate that exterior design is slavishly bound to efficient living, environment, and materials, rest assured that this was not intended. These materialistic factors are basic, but they are not constricting. All the houses illustrated so far have some claims to beauty, and their significant differences show that individualism is perhaps more alive today than in any earlier period.

To reinforce this point, let us look at two houses in Chicago suburbs (p. 527). Differences in house size and lot character, or the fact that one was remodeled and the other new, fall short of explaining fully why these houses are dissimilar. The owners knew and got what they wanted. Needing more and better space inside, the Lecats drastically changed the exterior. The original house had a sizable front porch that heavy street traffic had made useless. The old hip roof, broken on four sides by small dormers, made the upstairs dark and airless, the exterior cluttery. The roof was simplified into a two-slope gable. The front was unified by concentrating windows in a dominant vertical element, visually strengthened by unbroken panels of vertical siding.

The architects and owners of the second house decided on a disciplined rectangularity clearly defined by structure and materials. The exterior is not evasive about the cubical spaces it envelops or the structural grid of horizontal beams and vertical posts. On the side facing the best view rather than the street, the location of the living room and the multi-use room below are made evident by the two-story window wall with its strong horizontal between floors. On the left where the house goes into the hill, the panel of brick is highly appropriate, especially when the chimney indicates that fireplace and furnace are in this corner of the house. At the right, wood ventilating grilles are as handsome as they are serviceable. Compari-

A

Above. An old house in Wilmette, Illinois, was remodeled to replace a cut-up exterior with a simplified façade with windows integrated as the dominant feature.

Below. Panels of brick and ventilating grilles frame window walls in a house with a central court located in Flossmoor, Illinois. Schweikher and Elting, architects. (*Photographs by Hedrich-Blessing. Courtesy of* Better Homes and Gardens)

B

son with the Richmonds' house (Fig. 514A) and with Koenig's steel house (Fig. 523A) show how one basic idea—flat roof and rectangular panels in this instance—can be treated with individuality.

On the following pages other ways of capturing those qualities that can make exterior design more than a cover for "machines for living in" are illustrated.

► CONTEMPORARY EXTERIOR DESIGN

Growing out of a new way of living, a new technology of building and new materials, and tremendous increase in construction costs, exterior design today expectedly is not like that of the past. Except for large sheets of glass and slender steel supports, no single aspect differentiates it sharply from all past work. Flat roofs, for example, have a very long history. Continuous bands of windows (with very small panes of glass) occurred in England as early as the fifteenth century. Starkly simple exteriors were common in our Southwest. The Greeks and Romans integrated indoor and outdoor living handsomely. Nevertheless, contemporary houses differ notably from anything in history. Even though individualism leads to specific differences, most exteriors share these general characteristics:

- The character tends toward the unpretentious and informal, aims to *express* the way its occupants really live rather than to *impress* others.
- The house is designed for its climate, integrated with its site and landscaping.
- Exterior and interior are harmoniously related through large openings, repetition of shapes and materials, and forms that carry the eyes strongly from one to the other.
- Interest and variety come from sensitive design of basic space and form, frank revelation of structure and of the nature of materials.
- Horizontal forms relate the house to the ground, suggest comfort and rest, and make the house appear large.
- Unity predominates over variety, consistency over differences, perhaps to compensate for the complex diversity of contemporary life.
- Balance is asymmetric because it more flexibly coincides with utilitarian requirements, increases apparent size, seems natural for our concept of family life.
- Rhythms are fast moving with only a few interruptions or pauses, carry continuously around and through the composition.
- Emphasis is spread over the whole, not densely concentrated in spots.
- Simplicity, but not austerity, is a goal.

A

Roof shape is a decisive factor in the character of a house.

Above. A gently sloping, double-pitch roof unifies house, breezeway, and carport in a house in Pine Springs, Virginia. Keyes, Smith, Satterlee and Lethbridge, architects. (*Photograph by Robert C. Lautman. Lauria Brothers*)

Below. In Rye, New York, steel made it possible to roof 2,665 square feet with only eight columns as support. Interior space is opened and expanded into the landscape by the two diamond-shaped cantilevered roof units. Ulrich Franzen, architect. (*Photograph © Ezra Stoller*)

B

► JUDGING EXTERIOR DESIGN

Exteriors have the basic utilitarian function of sheltering the occupants and their possessions, but few persons are willing to stop at this point. Along with simple statements of fact, expressions of aspirations are needed. In ways appropriate to each specific situation, usefulness and economy ought to be considered in relation to beauty and individuality. Again, a series of questions are listed as one way of stimulating you to think through the various aspects of exterior design for yourself, hoping that you will become clearer on what you want for your own home.

What kind of living does the character of the exterior express? In this and earlier chapters we have seen some houses marked by dignified formality, others by a natural freedom and ease. A few are boldly adventurous with exciting new forms and materials, and there are those more closely related to the past. Compare the roofs. Steep and gently sloping, inconspicuously flat, interlocking diagonals, and repeated arcs—each of these has its own character that affects, variously, those seeing it or living under it.

Which of the exteriors suits you best? Perhaps none. Then you can enjoy the excitement of searching for one that does.

Is the exterior appropriate to its environment? Environment is physical and cultural, general and specific. It is economical to design a house suited to its climate, satisfying to shape it in the spirit of the landscape, sensible to adapt it to its specific site. Culture, traditions, and nearby neighbors ought not be ignored.

Falling complacently in line with what others have done is paralyzing, but undisciplined individuality can shatter community feeling. There is no single, easy, and sure solution. It is rather a sensitive recognition of and responding to what was there first, while remembering that architecture is always changing, you have your own preferences, and it is the second half of the twentieth century.

Is the exterior consonant with the plan? This is another puzzler. The plan, presumably reflecting the family's space needs, determines wall location and width of openings. Should it do more? We think it should, but how much latitude is there? It hardly seems fair to formalize externally an informal plan or to build with steel a plan intended for stone. The economies of building many tract houses from one or a few plans is fact. Having the exteriors identical is monotonous, but "treating" exteriors differently with slip-cover devices convinces almost no one. If the two-dimensional plan has no life of its own, then it matters little how it becomes three-dimensional space and form. What do you think?

Are the materials and construction suitable? Suitable for what? Climate, appearance, owners' personalities? First cost in relation to maintenance? Eager for ready-made certainty as we are, it is overly optimistic to expect it. With understanding of materials, we have to analyze our wants in order of importance and our bank accounts.

Is the exterior visually satisfying? Comparable to the rules of grammar, the aims and principles of design help us avoid that which is patently awkward but not the commonplace. We can ask the by-now-familiar questions about form and purpose, communality encompassing divergence, visual stability, constancy and movement, and degrees of primacy. These are time-tested, perhaps time-worn, basics that are about as useful to the creative architect or home-builder as arithmetic was to Einstein. They are foundations on which to build.

► A PREFABRICATED HOUSE

As a conclusion for the discussion of both Plan and Exterior Design, a truly remarkable house has been chosen. Underlying every aspect of the Techbuilt house (Figs. 532, 533, 535) is the desire to give ample, flexible space at moderate cost. Possessing an inner purposeful strength, the exterior grew out of a way of planning, a method of constructing, and unusual sensitivity to visual design. The shape is simple, the profile low. Broad overhangs contribute to a strong sense of shelter. Windows and exterior doors are organized in four units, one in the center of each wall. The symmetrical balance is assured but far removed from passivity by the dynamic ground-to-roof areas of glass and wood. A compelling rhythmic beat is set in motion by the 4′ module on which the house was developed, but monotony is dispelled by unifying the four center spaces with glass. This also produces an unmistakable dominance and subordination.

The structure is post-and-beam, the enclosing surfaces are panels. Four heavy wood beams, supported by steel posts, continue through the entire length of the house. Factory-built panels make the walls, second floor, and roof. All on a 4′ module, the opaque panels are plywood sheets bonded to wood frames. Those containing doors and windows can be fitted in as desired. Making these panels in factories saves little money but putting them in place does. Brought to the site in a single truck, they can be bolted to the frame by four men with no special tools or training in two days. Not a few handy-man owners, with a little help, have done it themselves. From then on, electricians, plumbers, and so forth can work regardless of weather.

The planning took into account our needs for change. Simply *enclosing* space is not expensive. "*Finishing*" it, up to our standards of living, is.

A

B

The fact that houses efficiently mass-produced by machines need not look mechanistic is proved by Techbuilt Houses developed by Carl Koch and Associates.

Left above. Without sentimental or costly compromise, age-old traditions of exterior designs are carried into contemporary terms.

Left below. The stalwart dignity and strong sense of shelter of the exterior also distinguish the interior. (*Courtesy of the Architects*)

Right. The shell of the house, delivered by one truck, looks like this when unloaded.

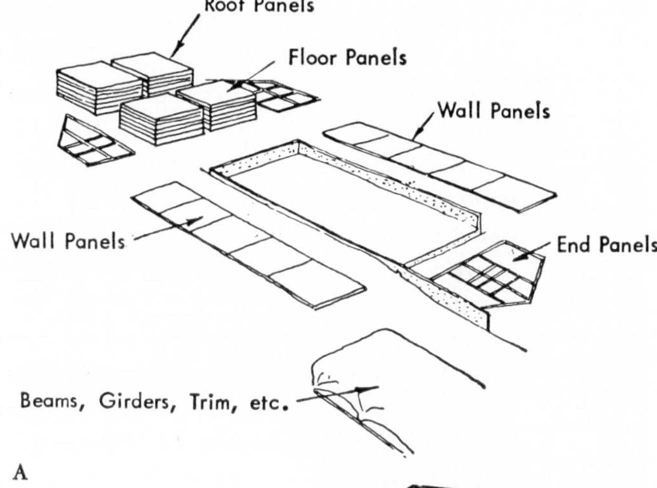

A

Right. Four men working two days can set up the shell.

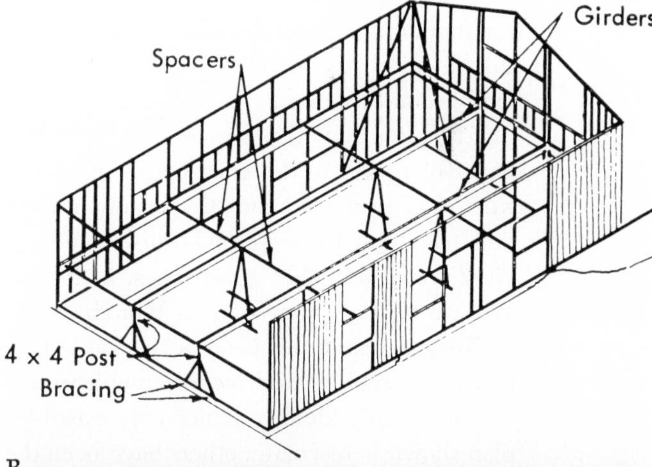

B

Right. Roof, floor, and solid wall panels can be surfaced with varied materials, window sections placed where wanted, to meet individual needs.

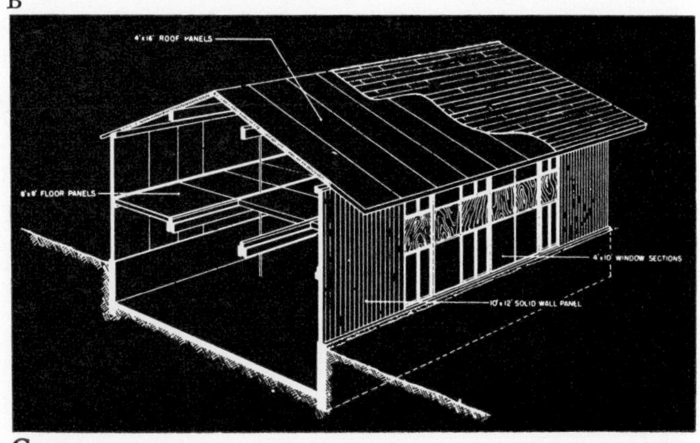

C

Adding more space can be nightmarishly costly. Koch's solution was this: weatherproof as much space in the original as will be eventually needed, finish it when necessary, and make it easy to rearrange. Observe that all hard-to-move units—entrance and stairway, fireplace, kitchen, laundry, and baths—are concentrated in the middle third of the plan. Passageways through this core connect the ends—two thirds of the house—which can be partitioned as desired, easily changed with movable storage walls, folding doors, and the like. Thus, the central utility-circulation core produces four other zones, segregated yet interconnecting, suitable in size and shape for many activities.

Koch faced the dilemma of two-story houses being economical but unpopular, attics and basements being cheap but seldom comfortable. In essence what he did was to make a whole house out of an attic directly above a basement. By dropping the lower floor only 3 feet 6 inches into the ground, most of which is needed for foundations anyway, he took advantage of the earth's costless temperature control for a pleasant ground floor. By raising the eaves just a little, he gained a useful "attic." And he avoided the high boxiness of most two-story exteriors. Obviously, the typical plans fit sloping lots best: there are a good many hillside lots and they have often led to awkward designs. On flat lots, the earth excavated for foundations must be carted away or used: if houses are designed with this in mind, the excess earth can be economically used to sculpture the land around a house.

Relationship to occupants and specific site? Without sinking into the tarpit of trying to design a house that would please everybody anywhere, Koch has produced one that, quite unbelievably, appeals to "advanced" architects and to people who just want a good home. Perhaps he has devised something that approaches, in its own modest way, the "universal." We are writing, however, as though all Techbuilt houses were identical. As Koch has said, this is not a "package" but a system of converging components that builder and owner complete at their discretion.

Thus individuality is not only possible but nourished. First, the basic plan shown here (many others have been developed) offers sixteen different room arrangements. Second, the plan can be flipped side for side or end for end or the two halves offset or at right angles. Finally, exterior and interior surface materials are chosen by the person who builds or buys the house. The potential permutations lead well up into higher statistics. In an age comforted by conformity yet striving for individuality, this approach to economical mass-produced homes, to the writers' knowledge, has no equal.

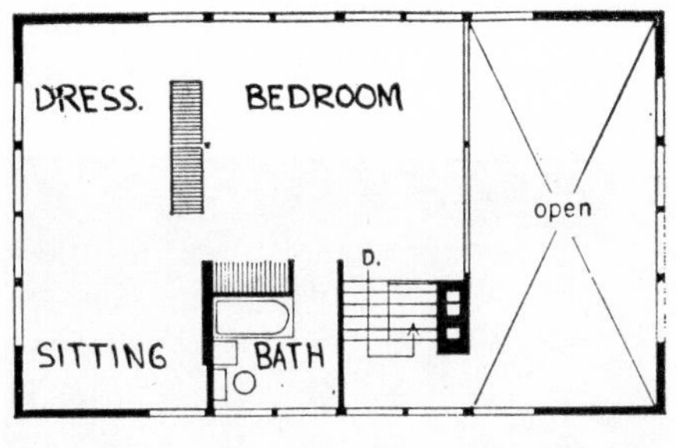

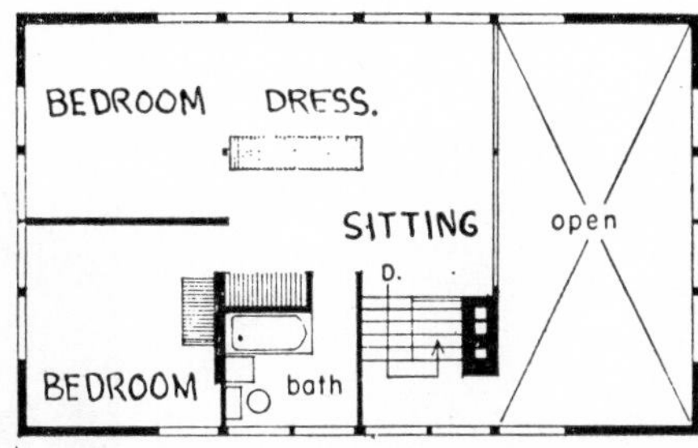

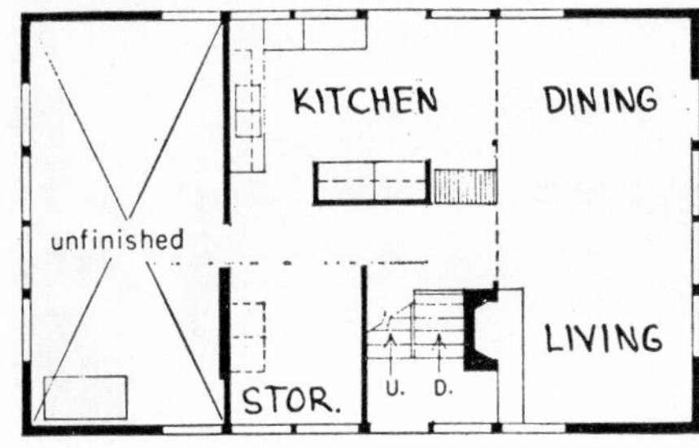

A

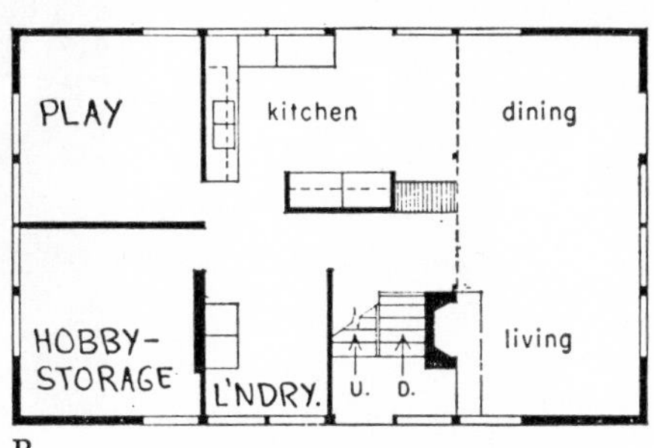

B

The Techbuilt House plan can be inexpensively modified as family patterns change. (*Courtesy of Carl Koch. All plans copyrighted 1953 by Techbuilt, Inc.*)

Above left. A young couple can leave part of the first floor unfinished and enjoy a two-story, living-dining space.

Above right. The arrival of a child indicates a second bedroom with play and hobby space below.

Below left. More children need and get more bedrooms.

Below right. Later the house can be easily converted into two apartments.

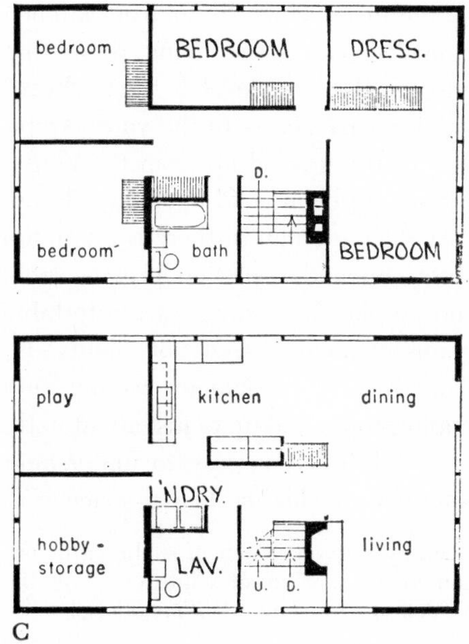

C

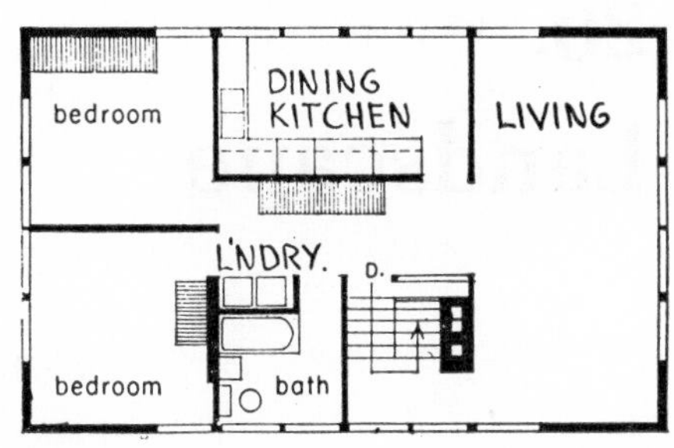

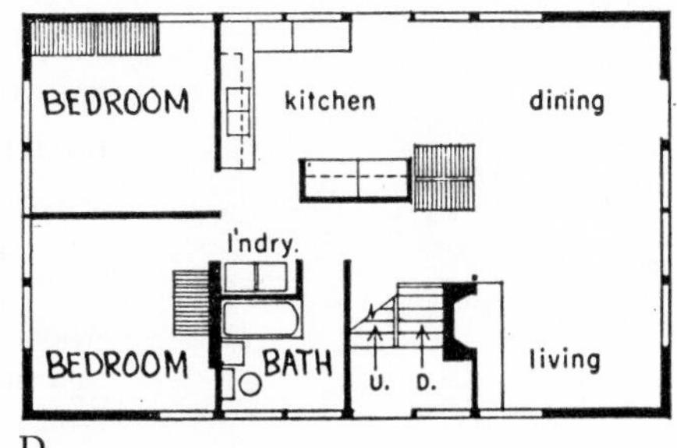

D

20. Landscape

"WHAT SHALL I DO WITH IT?" might well be the question that the man in Figure 538A is asking about his backyard, for it is a common one among homeowners. Most of the conditions are typical—a two-story house of little distinction, a narrow city lot with neighbors near by, a backyard 40′ x 50′, and a garage inconveniently far from kitchen and street. Less typical is the living room that overlooks and is on the same level as the backyard with a door giving easy access to the yard. Atypical is the slope of the ground up from the house, which both raises problems and opens up design possibilities. As the yard stands, there is minimum protection from sun and wind, no privacy from neighbors, and no place that suggests comfortable sitting. The miscellaneous tangle of plants, indecisively shaped lawn, inadequate paving, and picayune steppingstones add up to just about nothing—except possibilities. It is easy to understand why this potentially valuable living space was

Above. A gracefully curved bench of eighteenth-century inspiration invites one to sit while enjoying the landscape. (*Courtesy of Colonial Williamsburg*)

little used or enjoyed. Figures 538B, 539A and B show what landscape architects Osmundson and Staley accomplished.

Organized the space into outdoor rooms. Much as architects plan rooms inside the house, landscape architects design the land around the house. In this plan, there are three areas. A *service yard* near the kitchen provides space, courteously screened from the neighbors, for drying clothes and the like. A *patio* carries the living room outdoors. A *lawn* at the rear becomes a quiet retreat in this plan, but it could have been a children's play space or a gardener's hobby area. Although each area is differentiated from the others, none is completely separated—"open planning" was developed in landscape design long before architects took it over.

Made the ground surface usable. Sloping ground is attractive in large expanses, but it is not suited to intensive use. With limited outdoor space, the designers wisely made each area level. Further, they paved the most-used parts to provide hard, dry footing for people and furniture. Paving is easily maintained, can be used soon after a rain, warms quickly even in winter if exposed to the sun, and carries the feeling and function of interior floors into the landscape. Its only disadvantages are initial expense and the hard, hot glare that comes when the surface is too smooth and bright and there is insufficient shade. In this patio, raised planting beds, trees, and pergola reduce glare with their shadows. To give visual interest and minimize cracking, the concrete has been separated into squares with redwood strips.

Provided protection from wind, sun, and neighbors. A *fence* of redwood stakes around the rear of the property was a first step in increasing privacy and reducing wind, while serving as another transition between house and garden. The small scale of the narrow stakes increases the apparent size of the whole yard, and the spaces between them permit some circulation of air.

The *trellis* across the end of the living room makes part of the patio shady. In addition, it improves the appearance of the house by reducing its apparent height, and seems to increase the extent of the patio by bringing attention down from the top of the house—or the sky—to a more human level. As the paving was an underfoot link, the trellis is an overhead transition between architecture and landscape.

Several *trees* also control wind, sun, and views from outside while contributing their own unique beauty.

Separated levels with retaining walls. Economy suggested keeping an existing concrete wall that retained the upper level. Otherwise, a wall of more interesting material would have been placed so that the rear yard would not be divided into two equal strips. The new free-curve brick wall, supporting a flower bed at an intermediate level, brings welcome contrast of shape, texture, and color. In other places, walls are of redwood planks.

A

Above. Before it was landscaped, this backyard was an uninviting parcel of ground.

Below. Paving and a trellis, walls, plants, and furniture—all parts of a unified design, transformed the yard into useful and pleasant living space. Osmundson and Staley, landscape architects. (*Photographs by Theodore Osmundson*)

B

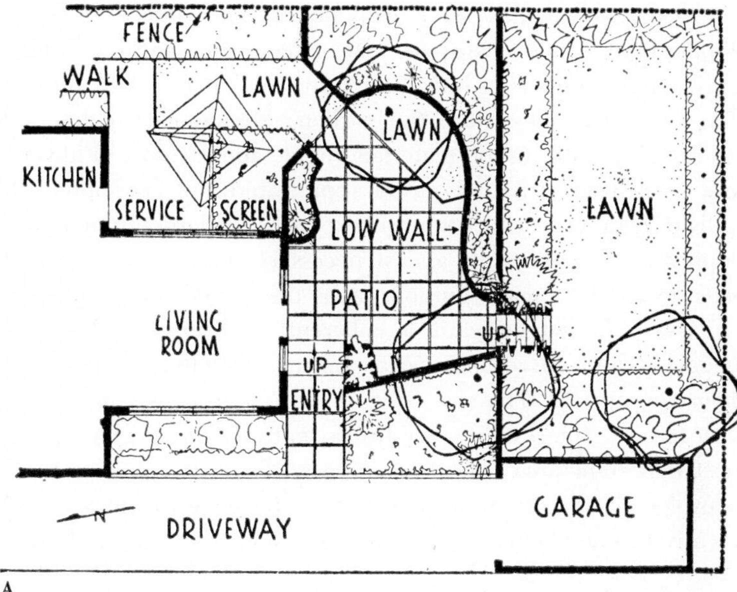

A

Above. The plan shows how the area was organized into three outdoor rooms: a patio, a secluded lawn, and a service yard.

Below. A free-curve brick wall visually expands the patio, raises plants to a height at which they can be easily enjoyed and maintained. (*Photograph by Theodore Osmundson*)

B

Low walls such as these have many points of excellence. In comparison with sloping banks, they save space and upkeep time, and they unify house and garden by bringing architectural forms and plants into intimate relationships. All year they state the garden's design clearly and create three-dimensional patterns of materials, light, and shadow. Flowers are raised to a level where they are easily appreciated and maintained. Finally, low walls provide good short-time sitting space for large groups. In this garden, sloping land made walls almost necessary; but even on a flat site, raised beds do much to make outdoor areas useful and interesting.

Gave the whole yard a coherent and sensible design. Rectangles, diagonals, and curves have each been used where their character makes them appropriate. The service yard has a logical rectangularity in keeping with its use. Interest is sensibly concentrated in the patio, for this is the most important area. The free-curve wall and the diagonals invite people to explore its shape. As a quiet foil for the diversity in the patio, the rear lawn is an unembellished rectangle, echoing the right angles of the service area.

Several of the many other approaches to small-garden design are illustrated on pages 541, 546, 547, 553, and 562. The first garden is for people who want maximum usable space and minimum garden work. Although a small trellis tempers light and heat in one area, it is an outdoor room for those who love the sun or live where overcast skies are frequent. The owners need never apologize that the floral display is not at its height because the ingenious pattern of pavement holds all-year interest from ground level and second-story windows.

Quite the opposite is the dooryard garden in which a front yard, measuring only 20′ x 30′ but screened from the street, has been transformed into a miniature woodland scene. Taking clues from the Japanese, the owners made everything small in size and scale. Although informal in effect, much thought was given to the composition. Pruning and shaping the plants, necessary to preserve the restrained character and small scale, would give the garden lover many hours of pleasurable work.

The garden in Figure 546 balances living space and garden work by progressing from a paved terrace, through a curved lawn that will need to be mowed and a flower bed for seasonal color, to the massed planting of easy-care shrubs. Figure 553 is actually an outdoor living room (needing only sweeping and a change of potted plants) placed in a natural woodland setting; while in Figure 562 shrubs and ground covers surround a pleasant brick and concrete terrace and a shade tree, all of which require minimum maintenance.

With the exception of size and consistency of design, these two gardens have little in common.

Right. A paved garden, softened by surrounding and accenting plants can be intensively used and easily maintained. Eckbo, Royston and Williams. (*Photograph by Ernest Braun*)

Below. Plants, water, and rocks informally arranged by the owners create a garden full of small-scale interest. (*Photograph by Morley Baer. Courtesy of* Sunset Magazine)

A

B

► PLANNING THE LANDSCAPE

Developing the yard is so much like other aspects of home planning that almost everything said in the preceding chapters is applicable. Here, too, we are concerned with modifying and controlling the environment for our physical and spiritual welfare. Integration of the practical and esthetic stands as the goal, and the basic approach outlined in Chapter 1 is valid.

Plan the landscape to promote the outdoor activities you prefer. Select the most appropriate land available and then modify it as necessary. Landscape design is essentially a matter of strengthening the relationship of your land to you and to your house. The crucial question is: What do you want from the land not covered by the house? Possibilities include:

- A pleasant setting that relates the building to the ground;
- Attractive "garden pictures" from windows or terraces;
- Space for outdoor relaxation, eating, and entertaining;
- Provision for active outdoor games, especially for children; and
- Room for the garden enthusiast to grow flowers, fruits, or vegetables.

On small plots, it is not easy to have all these. Then you decide on the relative importance of each. Even on a city lot, however, it is surprising how much you can achieve, as demonstrated in Figures 546A and B and 547.

Units of the Home Landscape

As houses are zoned into units for differing activities, so the home landscape is typically organized into *foreground, private living space,* and *service. Play space* and *"gardening" areas* may or may not be separate zones.

Foreground, the land between house and street, gives the building a setting and establishes landscape relationships with the community. Appropriateness to the size and character of the lot, the house, and community is desirable. But this need not mean unthinking duplication of what everyone else has done.

- The foreground can open the house boldly to the street with the typical expanse of shrub-bordered lawn, exposed entrance walk, foundation planting, and trees to frame the house.
- Among the other alternatives are secluding it with fences or planting (Fig. 546A) or treating it as a garden area (Fig. 551A).
- If not secluded, this area is often of little use to those living in the house and therefore tends to be smaller than it was some years ago.

Living space is the most important unit, unless special interests dictate otherwise, and therefore is usually the largest.

- Privacy from street and neighbors is desirable, suggesting a location at the rear of the property unless such factors as lot orientation or view require another solution.
- Typically, this unit commands the best outlook, even if that is only a controlled view of your own garden.
- Close relationship to living, dining, and cooking space increases usefulness.
- Livability is furthered by protection from wind, hot sun, rain, and snow.
- Firm pavement and suitable furniture are essentials.
- Attractiveness in all seasons deserves thought.

Service space, suitably designed and located, can relieve the house and yard of needless clutter, for it is here that you hang clothes, keep trash cans, and put temporarily an untidy miscellany of things.

- The most efficient location is near kitchen and garage, play space, and the gardener's plot (Figs. 478 and 547).
- Seldom attractive, it is best when screened from view.
- Size depends on specific conditions but few are large enough.
- Firm ground surface is needed, some protection from rain or snow almost a necessity.

Growing space for vegetables, fruits, and cut flowers is ideally in a separated plot where the total visual effect is of minor consequence but where soil and drainage are good. Full sun and protection from wind are recommended as is convenient garden storage. On small lots or when gardening interests are minor, growing space can be joined with living space—but then everyday appearance is a factor.

Play space for children is most efficient when readily accessible from children's rooms and easily supervised from the kitchen (Figs. 488 and 553B). If visually screened from other areas, adult standards of neatness need not be enforced. Play space merits as much area as can be allowed and some protection from inclement weather.

Although not a unit of landscape design, **foundation planting** merits comment because it often marks the beginning and too frequently the end of planning the yard. Consisting of planting close to the house, especially toward the street, it aims to tie the house to its setting and often to conceal the foundation. The stereotype is medium-high shrubs at the corners, accent planting near the door, and lower shrubs between. Frequently it is a miscellany of nursery stock that quickly gets out of scale with the building.

Today the trend is toward simplicity and restraint. Many modern houses, set low on the ground and with terraces on one or more sides, need little camouflaging (Figs. 514A, 518A, and 553A). A few choice plants may be welcome at such strategic points as the entrance, a wall with few or no windows, or at one or two corners. A wide band of ground cover from which a few shrubs or small trees rise but do not crowd up against the house has much to recommend it. Shrubs and trees can also be put in planting beds surrounded by brick, flagstone, gravel, or concrete. In brief, houses do not have to be engulfed in greenery.

Making the Plan

Figures 546-547 show how landscape zones can be organized. Placing the house toward the front of the lot gives maximum space for private outdoor living at the rear, and placing it crosswise on the lot opens it broadside to the garden. Economically, the garage is near the street to minimize the driveway area (driveways are expensive and wasteful of land). Also it efficiently opens into the kitchen and is near the service yard, moderately near the front door. This leaves a small foreground that has been secluded with a fence and planting. Privacy for the front yard and uncurtained windows facing the street are the gains.

An ample terrace leads people out into the private outdoor living area. The terrace is joined with the service area, yet screened from the less sightly parts. What might have been two cramped areas are openly planned to give a sense of expansiveness. Beyond the terrace a lawn performs its usual multiple functions of being useful to walk, sit, or lie on in good weather and of pleasing the eyes. It is a quiet foreground for the bed of flowers which, in turn, is enhanced by a background of fence and planting. Trees are placed to give shade where wanted, adding the high forms gardens need and making a pleasing pattern in themselves. A path invites you to stroll around and enjoy the landscape from varying angles.

Although this plan provides no specific place for children's play and limited space for hobby gardening, such activities are not ruled out. Service area, terrace, and lawn could accommodate a number of children, and the path encircling the grounds is a potential running track. The upper left portion could become a horticulturist's corner. Not ideal, this overlapping of uses illustrates the compromises most of us have to make.

Curves dominate this design, giving a big over-all unity. Sweeping around from front to back, they suggest pleasant visual and physical movement. They are neither rigidly geometrical nor are they nervous wiggles. They came, as the sketches show, from creative thinking, but this thinking was guided by the size and shape of the lot, the location of the house, and the needs and preferences of the owners. Close study shows that they are adroitly diversified. The fence across the front starts at the driveway close to the house, swings back to open the front lawn, straightens along the property line, again becomes a curve terminating in the screen planting. It affords privacy without boxed-in confinement. The path echoes without repeating the shapes of both fence and lawn. Beginning as a circular extension of the front porch, it then parallels the fence for a while before going beyond, in a sweep reminiscent of the front lawn, to join the terrace. The flower bed, intentionally simple so as not to compete with its contents, follows without exactly paralleling the path. Then comes the lawn, which is a variation of the flower-bed shape. The terrace carries this progression to its final step. It has the basic character of the lawn and flower bed, but the curve is more pronounced, the small planting beds subdivide it into more intricate shapes than those used elsewhere, and straight lines are introduced. Throughout this plan there is diversity growing out of a single idea, a rhythmic progression of shapes, intensification of interest near the house, and a gradual simplification as the boundaries are approached.

For those who are starting from scratch:

1. Select land that can give you what you need.
2. Design the house and landscape together.

For those who have a lot or a completed house and wish to try designing the landscape themselves:

1. Make a measured plan at a scale of 1 inch to 8 or 10 feet. Indicate property lines, house and garage, driveway and walks, existing trees and shrubs, the slope of the land. A 50-foot tape, cross-section paper, a drawing board, a ruler, and pencil are the tools.
2. List in order of importance the favored outdoor activities. Decide on the general character you want. Read about landscape design and visit every example you can. List ways of achieving your goal while keeping in mind what it will cost.
3. Then put the plan on a drawing board, and with plenty of tracing paper and soft pencils begin to design.

   Rough in the major units in a very general way. Try several locations and shapes for each on separate sheets of tracing paper. Review them critically.

A

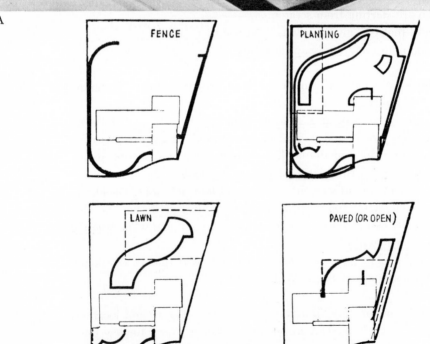

FENCE

PLANTING

LAWN

PAVED (OR OPEN)

B

Begin to refine the shapes, thinking of the best size and shape for each part and the unity of the whole design. A basic idea—formality or informality, curves or right angles—brings consistency, and carrying lines through from one unit to the others is a major unifying device.

Then start thinking about details—kinds of enclosure, types of ground surfacing, location and character of trees and shrubs—that will forcibly carry out the basic idea.

Check the plan carefully as a whole and in every detail to insure that it provides for all desired outdoor activities and that it has the spirit most congenial to you.

Set up a five-year development plan if you cannot afford all at once. It is sensible to get the ground surfacing nearest your house and the absolutely necessary enclosure first. Major trees, permanent background planting, and lawn also have high priority. You can wait, though, for highly desirable but expensive plants, fences, and overhead protection that are wanted but are not crucial. You can also delay for a while the development of the land farthest from the center of living.

Left above. Models of gardens are excellent ways to visualize designs before investing money and work. Unifying curves are the basis of this design. Douglas Baylis, landscape architect.

Left below. Sketches show the basic shapes of fence, planting, lawn, and paving. They are noteworthy examples of variety in unity.

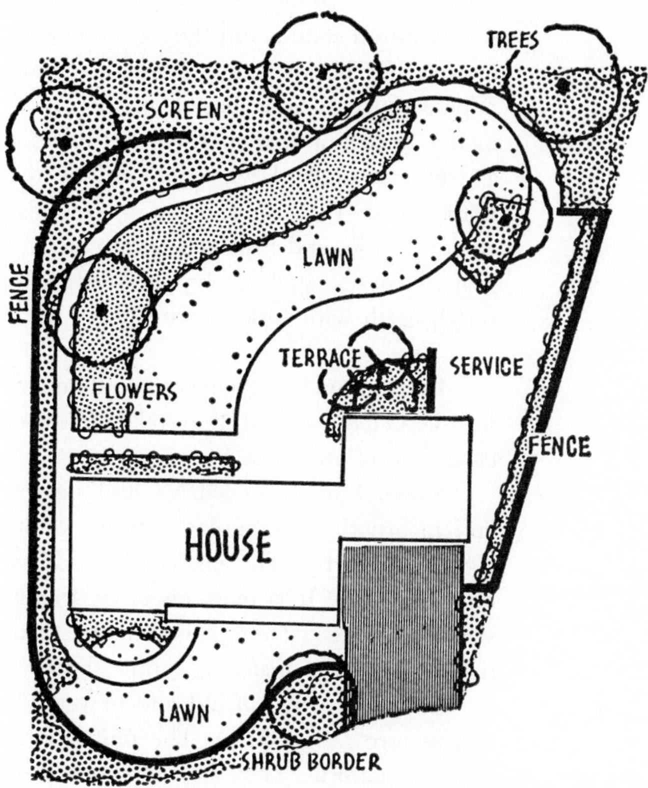

Right. Strong and simple, the plan makes the most of a medium-size lot. ("*Sunset Ideas for Landscaping Your Home*")

This is not the only way to develop a home landscape. Employing a landscape architect and a landscape contractor to carry out the design is the surest and quickest procedure. Or you can let the landscaping go along leisurely without a rigidly definite plan, a satisfactory way for the patient, sensitive lover of plants but one that entails the risk of never achieving a consequential unity.

► MATERIALS OF LANDSCAPE DESIGN

Before and while planning is under way, you need to garner some knowledge of materials, for they affect the result quite as much as they do in the house or its furnishings.

Ground Surfacings

Like floor coverings, ground surfacings can be divided into *hard* and *soft*, but lawns are about the only soft surfacing that can be walked on very much. So common are lawns in many temperate climates that it is a surprise to learn of their rarity in such drier regions as Italy, Spain, or our southwestern states. And they are uncommon in the Orient, not for climatic reasons but because they have no great appeal for these peoples. Their popularity with us is based on the low cost of getting them started and moderate cost of upkeep, their usefulness, and their quiet beauty. Physically as well as visually, lawns cool gardens in summer. Often-overlooked limitations include their unusability in wet weather, conspicuous wear with concentrated use, and insistently continuous need for maintenance. Other soft ground covers, such as ivy, wild strawberry, and trailing junipers cover rough earth with little maintenance, but they will not stand traffic.

Hard ground surfacings more than any other single factor make gardens livable. Once installed, they take almost no work, keep the garden's design clear, and relate house to land.

Stone. Usually expensive and nearly always beautiful, stone can be laid in orderly rectangular patterns or in informal random shapes (Figs. 198B and 199B). The choice depends on the character wanted and the funds at hand. It is most effective, though, when the individual slabs are sizable, not excessively jagged or irregular, and when they are laid in relatively large areas of strong, simple shape (Fig. 551B).

Brick. Effective in old and new gardens, brick is sympathetic in color and texture (Fig. 551A). The units, pleasantly small in scale, can be laid in many patterns. They are not slippery when wet or glaring in sun.

Right. A louvered redwood fence is an effective background for shrubs of diverse character. The pierced ceramic tiles enrich the fence and echo the intricacy of the foilage patterns.

Below. Concrete paving blocks that can be made by amateurs individualize paved areas. (*Photographs by Ernest Braun. Courtesy of* Sunset Magazine)

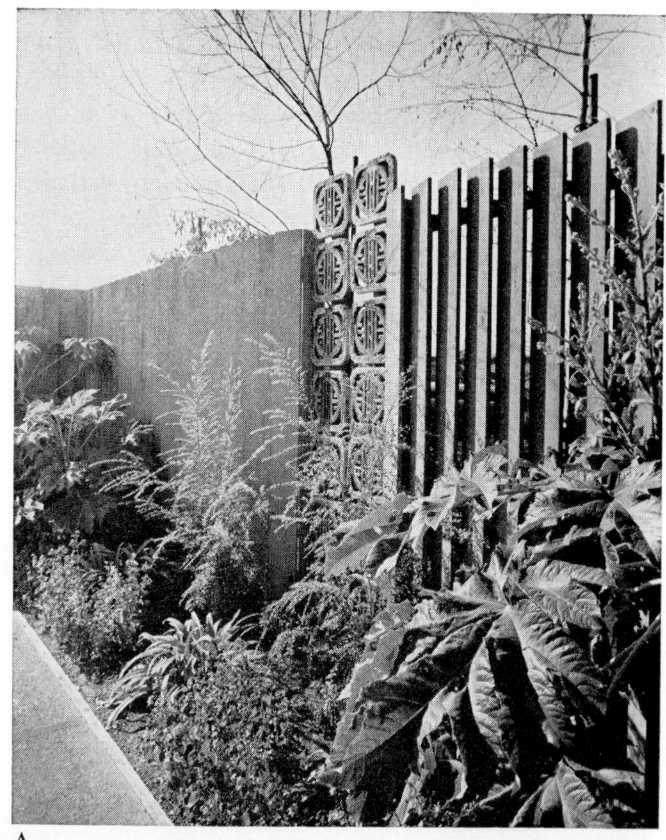

A

B

Concrete. Although not a material that wins the heart, concrete is widely used for its durability, moderate cost, and suitability to straight or curved shapes. New developments in color and texture permit innumerable variations (Figs. 541A and 549B). Radiant heating embedded in concrete can warm outdoor areas in cool weather.

Tar and gravel. Not a surfacing of great beauty, black-top or macadam as used for roads is unobtrusively satisfactory and inexpensive. With interest supplied elsewhere, it takes its place as a neutral floor but it can be enlivened with color or embedded with coarsely crushed rock.

Gravel. Crushed gravel, spread, watered, and rolled, is the least expensive hard surface. It provides dry, quite firm footing and color-texture variations harmonious with plants. As with brick, the cost can be greatly reduced if the owners do the work.

Fences, Walls, and Hedges

Comparable to the walls of a room, fences, walls, and hedges give privacy, lessen wind, and provide a background for plants and people. Architecturally, they delineate the three-dimensional space of the landscape.

Fences and walls, unlike hedges or other screen planting, take almost no space or maintenance and give immediate effect. Their variety is legion: they can be high or low; straight, angled, or curved; have open spaces or be solid; emphasize horizontals or verticals, or balance both; and have any degree of ruggedness or refinement. The range of materials, formerly limited to wood, brick, and stone, has been extended by concrete blocks, corrugated plastic or metal, plastic-impregnated screen, and clear or colored glass. Although walls and fences are typically similar in character to the house, they are often somewhat more rugged and less precise, partly for economy and partly to tie in with the planting.

Hedges of one variety of plant, clipped or allowed to grow freely, or of several types of shrubs provide good green enclosure—if space permits and if you are willing to wait a few years for the full effect and then work to keep it that way. A high degree of unity is achieved if only one kind is used; variety comes with many. The latter is seldom satisfying unless the selection is limited to about five kinds with at least three or more plants of each type massed together. Deliberately planned exclamation points are, of course, an exception.

A

The character of a landscape is determined by the materials selected and the way in which they are used.

Above. Beds of spring flowers, birch trees, and brick paths give a foreground garden a quaint, small-scale charm in keeping with the house. (*Photograph by Berton Crandall*)

Below. Flagstone paving and bold masses of planting relate Frank Lloyd Wright's home to its extensive site on a Wisconsin hillside. (*Photograph by Maynard Parker. Courtesy of* House Beautiful)

B

Overhead Protection

The sky is a magnificent, but undependable, ceiling. From it we get light and heat on many days but often too much of both for comfortable outdoor relaxation. On clear, cool nights it takes heat from the earth's surface. The most important function of overhead protection is tempering the climate. Not only does it lessen light, heat, cold, and wind but if waterproof, protects us, our furniture, and play equipment from rain and snow. A second function is giving the "not altogether unenclosed" sense of protection and security that comes with having something between us and the sky. The third function is to bring part of the above-head landscape down to human scale. Many persons have found that putting a sunshade over part of a terrace made the terrace look much larger because it was then not judged in relation to the vastness of the sky.

A thorough exploration of a weather-conditioned landscape development (Figs. 553A and B) shows how sheltering roofs and terraces, along with paving and walls, can make the outdoors comfortable in many kinds of weather. A roofed terrace at the living room's west end, protected by a solid storage wall at the north, is a real outdoor room. Defined by a low brick wall, the sun terrace faces south and west. The shade terrace is shielded by a 15′ x 30′ arbor of thin wooden slats and plastic panels. Near the kitchen is a small sheltered terrace, while the plans for additional children's rooms include a roofed play terrace secluded to the south and east. Integral with the design of the house, these terraces and walls, roofs and arbor make the house look and live way beyond its actual dimensions.

Encompassing almost as many variants as fences, overhead protection can be completely weatherproof and lightproof roofs of the same material used to cover the house. If of plastic or glass, rain and snow but not light are excluded. Canvas securely fastened to a framework performs much the same way but is relatively short-lived. Sunshades of wood, much like stationary horizontal Venetian blinds, reduce heat and glare while allowing air to circulate. Arbors and trellises (Figs. 538B and 541A) with vines bring nature and architecture together happily, but offer limited protection.

Nature's great overhead shelters, trees, are the primary ones for most of us and will be discussed in the following sections.

Plants

Plants are the materials that most sharply differentiate landscape design from architecture. Varying markedly from one part of the country to another, they exert strong regional influences. It is quite possible to develop

A

Designing house and landscape as one unit promotes livability. Architect Gordon Drake and landscape architect Douglas Baylis collaborated from outset to finish.

Above. Usability is greatly increased when the design offers sun and shade, enjoyment of breezes, and protection from wind. (*Photograph by Julius Shulman*)
Below. Both house and landscape are planned for future expansion.

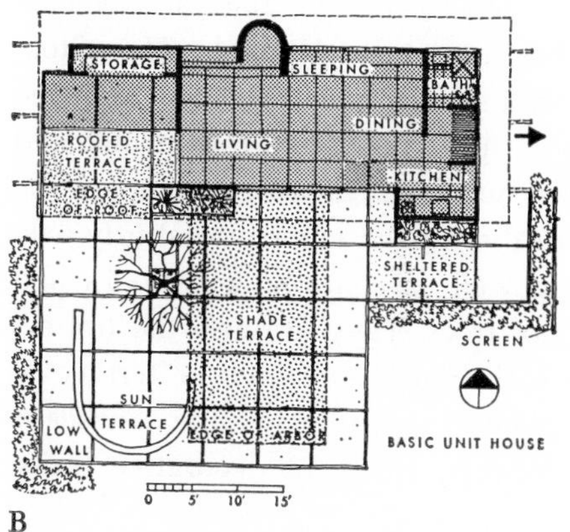

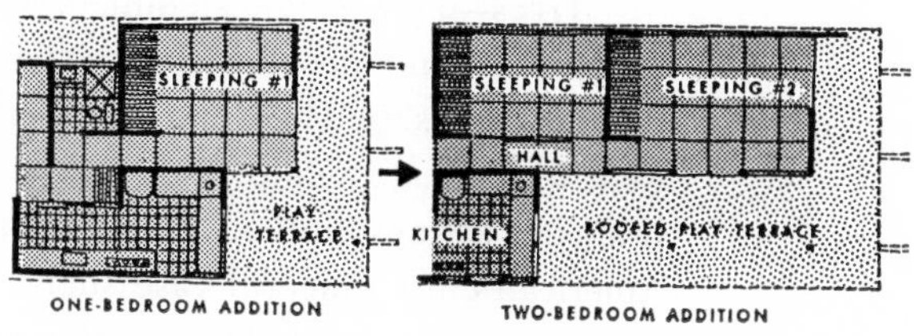

B

a landscape with plants alone, one that can be very beautiful in some seasons and enjoyable on the best of days and nights. With rare exceptions, though, it will fall short of being a "landscape for living."

The variety of plants is endless. Each has its own habit of growth (height, width, shape, and pattern of branching), its own growing needs (kind of soil, amount of water, degree of sun or shade, and temperature range), and its special type of leaves, flowers, and fruits. In no other phase of art can designers select from such diverse materials. Even within one genus and species, there are as many individual differences as in man.

Plants can be categorized in terms of growth and landscape uses.

Ground Covers are spreading plants, usually a foot or less in height, such as trailing junipers, vinca, and ivy. They are useful as low, permanent foregrounds or under trees or shrubs. Most are unobtrusive but some have conspicuous foliage or flowers.

Shrubs. Low- to moderate-height woody plants with several stems are used for background or screen plantings and also as decisive accents. Selecting the most appropriate shrubs is a game of deciding what effect is wanted and then finding the shrubs that will grow well in the specific location. For example, there are junipers with low, spreading branches densely clothed with blue-green needles. Their hardly noticeable flowers and fruits and their retention of leaves make them almost as constant in appearance 365 days a year as a brick wall. Bridal Wreath Spiraea, in contrast, sends many stems up from the ground to arch over in a vase shape. In spring, tender green leaves appear and then for a short period are all but hidden in a burst of white flowers. In summer, they are graceful green mounds, and in winter the branches are bare. Rhododendrons retain their big, leathery leaves the year round and in spring exclaim with their massive heads of flowers. These merely hint at the possibilities and limitations of shrubs.

Trees—high, single-stemmed, woody plants—are the biggest elements in gardens and deserve the respect that large size demands. Here, too, there is diversity. The difference between a slender, small-leaved birch tree with its delicate white bark and a stately pine with its strong trunk and branches always clothed with dark-green needles is great. Or compare the American elm's graceful vase shape with the rugged vigor of a sturdy oak. Tempering the light, heat, and wind as well as controlling outlooks and inlooks are the important contributions of trees. They are also the tall accents, the last step in the progression of heights from lawn or terrace to the sky, and as such are often focal points toward which the landscape builds up. Some of them have showy flowers, edible or decorative fruits, and bright autumn colors.

Flowers, somewhat comparable to the enriching accessories of interiors, come on all types of plants. Although we usually think of flowers as low annuals and perennials, the many shrubs and trees that have worth-while blossoms in addition to giving shade or enclosure are economical of time and space. Flowers show to best advantage against an appropriate background. The sky serves well for flowering trees, but lower ones are best appreciated when given a setting of shrubbery or fences. With the exception of deliberately planned accents, large masses of the same kind and color are most effective. The purpose should indicate the varieties chosen and the way they are used. Bold displays can be had with such herbaceous plants as marigolds, petunias, and geraniums; such shrubs as lilacs, floribunda roses, or azaleas; and the flowering cherries, crab apples, plums, and peaches. At the opposite end of the scale, lilies-of-the-valley and violets never compel attention but are rewarding when looked at closely.

Fruits, ornamental or edible, are almost as enriching as flowers. Most fruit trees have highly decorative flowers, and those with larger fruits, notably apples, are almost as gay when the fruit is ripe. In warm climates, oranges and lemons have flowers or fruits for many months. Many shrubs—barberry, cotoneaster, and firethorn—add color to the fall and winter landscape with their berries. It is wise, though, to avoid planting trees or shrubs with squashy fruits or hard pits near terraces, walks, and lawns.

Water

Quiet pools with or without water lilies are refreshingly cool and reflect the sky or plants above them in ever-changing patterns. Moving water, in fountains or streams, is a joy. There are, however, practical limitations. In all but a few instances, water in the garden has quite high initial cost and takes considerable maintenance. Pools of any depth are a hazard for small children and have an irresistible attraction for some breeds of dogs.

Man-made Enrichment

Similar to that used inside homes, but larger in scale and more durable, man-made enrichment is a handsome way of getting permanent interest in the landscape. Sculpture, be it a marble statue or a horse from an old merry-go-round, is a sturdy note of emphasis. Mobiles provide constantly changing patterns. Some artists have created paintings for outdoor use, others have covered sections of fences with pieces of scrap materials organized much like nonobjective paintings. Ceramic tile and pebble mosaics (Figs. 549A and B), ornamental pots and urns give year-round pleasure.

► LOCATION FOR LIVING

Selecting the Community

You seldom have free choice to live in the part of the country you like best, but everywhere you have a considerable range from which to select. For those who enjoy city life, a hotel, an apartment, or a house on a small lot may be the answers. At the other extreme is the farm. In between are intermediate possibilities, each with its complex of advantages and disadvantages.

In the long run, the community is perhaps more important than the individual lot, and your first searching may well be directed toward finding a section in which you feel at home. This usually means an area in which the families have similar socio-economic status and interests to your own. Community assets are good schools and recreational facilities, churches, shopping areas, and public transportation plus fire and police protection. Nuisances include traffic thoroughfares, railroads, and airports as well as noisy or fume-producing factories. Light industry—quiet, clean, and attractive—can be advantageous because of employment opportunities.

The original subdivision plans A and B are cut up into too many small, often badly shaped and placed lots. The revised plan is a simple, orderly arrangement that follows the land's contours. It has fewer but better lots. Length of streets was reduced by 3,400 feet, entrances to the subdivision cut from six and seven to two. (*From ARCHITECTURAL FORUM.* © *1946, Time, Inc.*)

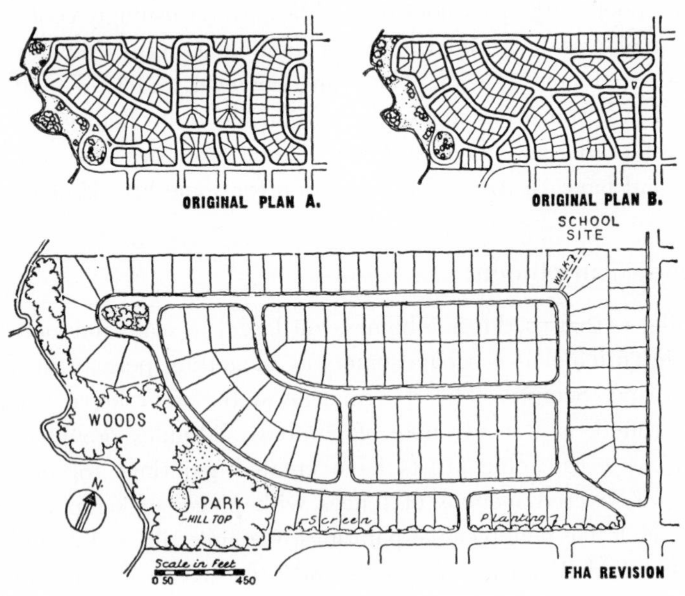

Selecting the Lot

So many, often conflicting, factors crowd together that you seldom find the perfect lot, but the following are factors to consider:

- **Convenience:** Near, preferably within walking distance of, schools, churches, and shopping—but not adjacent to them because of noise and traffic. Distance from the wage-earner's work is important, too.
- **Streets and Traffic:** A basic concern for most of us is finding a lot facing a quiet street. Other factors are the ease and safety of frequently traveled routes and the visual pleasantness of the total street pattern (Fig. 556).
- **Elevation:** Lots that are neither at the bottom of a valley nor on the top of a hill are conservative choices. Hilltops afford fine views but they may be cold and windy, are often expensive to build on. Low lots may be poorly drained, damp, and cold in winter and hot in summer. To some, they are also depressing.
- **Size:** The right size for your family and house are the only guides. Small to moderate lots, from 60′ to 75′ x 100′, bring proximity to neighbors and usually to needed facilities. They are not excessively costly to buy, develop, and maintain. If wisely planned, such lots often give more usable outdoor space than a large one you cannot afford to make livable. Larger lots have the luxury of space and seclusion, opportunity for large and more varied outdoor areas—but they are usually expensive, remote, or both. Lot size is also closely allied to house size and shape. Large houses require more ground than small ones, and sprawling one-story homes take more space than do compact two-story designs.
- **Shape:** A rectangle with the narrow side toward the street is the norm, but other shapes may lead to more personalized homes and gardens.
- **Orientation:** With the street toward the north, the house can be opened on the south overlooking the private area. Other orientations take more ingenious planning to enjoy the advantages of privacy and sun.
- **Slope:** Flat land is the easiest to develop—and the least inspiring. Hillside lots bring interest and individuality at a price.
- **Natural features:** Even one tree is an asset and several expedite landscaping. Outcroppings of rock, streams, and lakes may or may not be equally valued by lot-buyers and lot-sellers.

Selecting your location for living is a matter of balancing all factors in order of their desirability to you. One or more acres of wooded rolling land in a section where other properties are large gives the spaciousness and inconvenience of country living. A small house on a small lot, or an apartment, can be most economical in terms of your time.

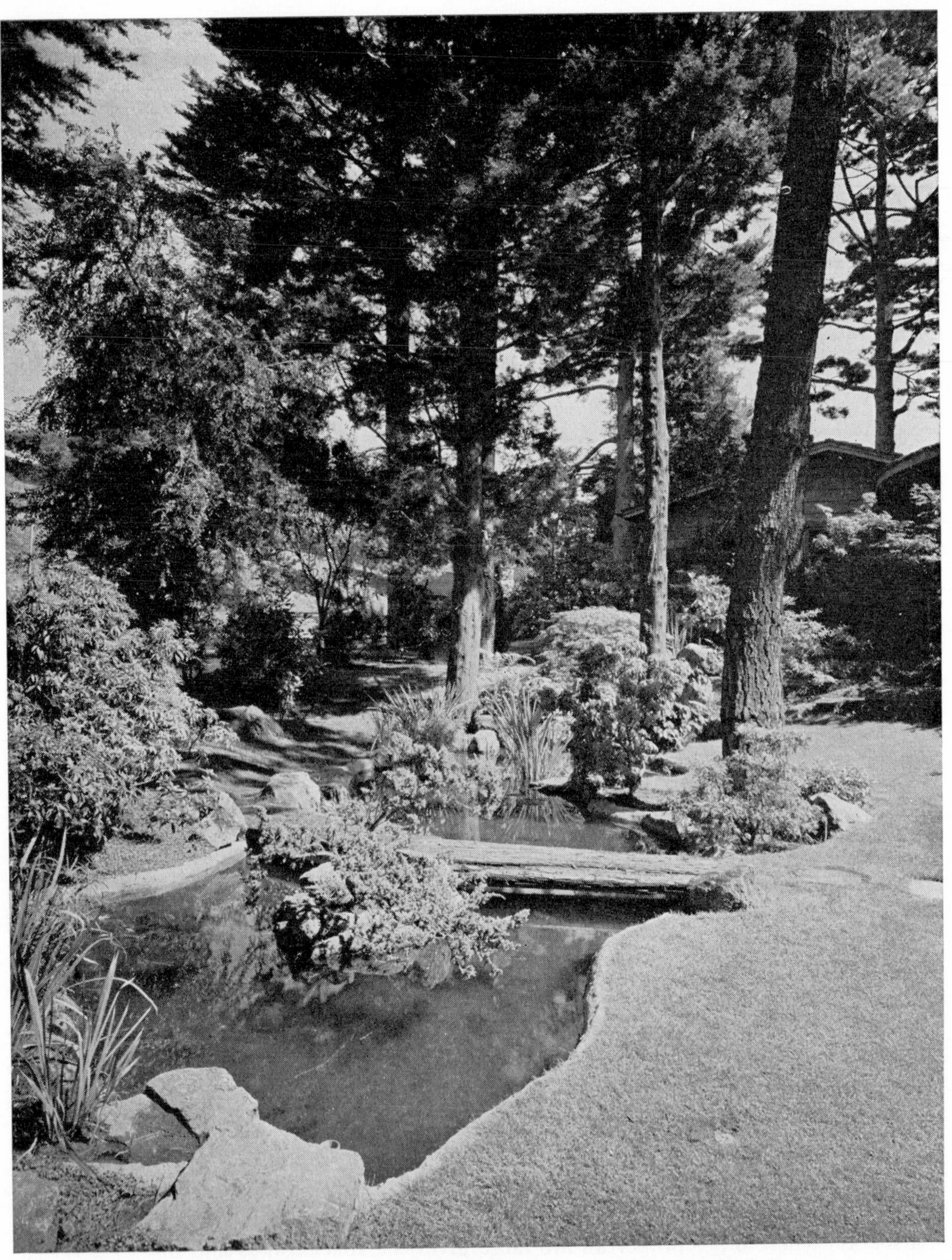

A rock-bordered pool and some noble pine trees make a relaxing sylvan retreat. (*Photograph by Morley Baer. Courtesy of* Sunset Magazine)

House and Landscape Design

Potential space for living extends to the property's boundaries, and the landscape deserves to be an integral part of the whole home development. No longer are hard and fast lines drawn between house and garden because, at best, they have much in common. Nevertheless, they are not identical and some of the major differences are worth consideration.

Gardens are used less intensively than are houses. In part this is because of the way in which landscapes are planned. The livability of a garden is closely related to its similarity to architecture—a protected patio is used much more than is an open lawn.

Landscapes are usually larger than are houses and, therefore, are appropriately larger in scale. A single-family dwelling seldom covers more than one fifth of the lot, leaving four fifths free for development. Further, the infinitely high sky, not an 8- or 10-foot ceiling, is the top of most landscaped areas. Thus, major landscape features must be decisively strong and large in scale or they will seem trivial.

Growing plants are the distinctive landscape materials. Plants are organisms with decisive but changing personalities. They change far more rapidly than do the comparatively static materials of houses. This inevitable transformation suggests that you be familiar with the life cycle of each plant, be prepared to modify the growth by pruning or replacing the plant when necessary. Better yet, design the landscape so that the changes become assets.

Landscape design is the modification of the land at our disposal for use and pleasure. For many years it was among the least sensibly handled phases of home design. Had contemporary trends made no other contribution than making us aware of how valuable our yards can become, it would have earned our respect.

21. Costs and Budgets

DISCUSSIONS OF COSTS AND BUDGETS are difficult and risky. Costs often vary from one part of the country to another, from one town to its neighbor, and from store to store in the same community. They go up and down with national and regional economic conditions and with new developments in each field. And they vary greatly on objects used for the same purpose, as for example on dining chairs, which can be had for as little as six dollars each and for as much as a hundred dollars or more.

There is only one way to be certain of the prices of furnishings when you are ready to buy—

- Visit your local stores, read the advertisements in your newspapers and in home magazines, and spend some time with mail-order catalogues.

And only one way to get a budget suited to you—

- Study your own situation, your needs, and preferences in terms of your income.

Above. Auguste Rodin's *The Thinker.* (*Gift of Adolph B. Spreckels, California Palace of the Legion of Honor, San Francisco.*)

► HOUSE AND LOT

The average cost of new houses increased more than 50 percent in the last decade, and many experts believe that the upward trend will continue. Generally higher prices account for part of this, but higher incomes have led to larger houses, better materials, more bathrooms, and much more and better mechanical equipment. Surveys show that enclosed-space cost ranges from around $9 to $20 or more per square foot.

Among the many factors that account for the variations in cost are the section of the country, and the type, quality, and size of the house. The kind and amount of mechanical equipment affects cost as does the inclusion or exclusion of such items as garages and basements, steel kitchen cabinets and tiled bathrooms, paved terraces and landscaping. In general, the cost per square foot decreases a little as house size increases, and "builders' houses" constructed in large numbers at one time are less costly than custom-designed, individually built homes.

Land costs vary quite as much as do those for buildings. There is a great difference between the value of unimproved farm land and well-situated lots with paved streets and sidewalks, water, electricity, and gas. Lot value is directly proportional to the desirability of the location and the size of the parcel. Because desirable land is getting scarcer, the cost of a lot in many regions now ranges around 18 percent of the total cost of a home, whereas a few years ago it was about 10 percent.

It is encouraging, though, to note that an occasional custom house, skillfully designed, is built for around $9 per square foot, and that typical houses of today tend to compensate for their higher cost with better planing, better materials, and better equipment. Despite costs, houses are being built at about the rate of one million per year.

► LANDSCAPING

The cost range of landscape development is even greater than that of house and land. With good soil, a lawn costs only the few dollars spent for seed and fertilizer. Small trees and divisions of shrubs given by friends complete the project. Expenditure of money, but not of time, is negligible. Thus, landscaping costs for small homes often are not even considered in the budget.

If, however, you develop a livable yard with paved terraces and suitable furniture, enclosing fences and overhead protection, and appropriate planting, costs can mount rapidly.

Here are a few average figures:

Ground Surfacings	*Cost Per Square Foot*
Lawn	2¢ to 25¢ (depending on soil, whether or not a sprinkling system is installed, and amount of work done by owners)
Asphalt paving	25¢ to 30¢
Concrete paving	50¢ to 80¢
Brick on concrete base	\$1.00 to \$1.75 (about the cost of a medium-price rug)
Enclosure (about 6′ high)	*Cost Per Running Foot*
Fence (wire)	\$2.50 to \$6.00
Fence (wood)	3.00 to 7.00
Hedge	.75 to 2.00
Wall (masonry)	8.00 to 15.00
Shrubs and Trees	*Cost Per Plant*
Shrubs	75¢ to \$15.00 (depending on size and variety)
Trees	\$1.50 to \$250.00 (depending chiefly on size)
Outdoor Furniture	*Cost*
Redwood table and benches for 6	\$18.00 to \$50.00
Metal or wood chairs	5.00 to 30.00
Suntan cots or chaises with mattresses	12.00 to 50.00

With a landscape design by Lawrence Halprin the owners did all of the labor and spent only \$250 for materials. (*Photograph by Ernest Braun*)

► COSTS OF FURNISHINGS

As with landscaping, the range of furnishing costs is more impressive and realistic than an average figure. In many instances top prices could be multiplied several times over for the very high-quality or individualized pieces, and a good sale may put costs below the lower figure.

Price tags on home furnishings are determined by many factors—materials and construction, excellence and individuality of design, supply and demand, and durability. Here are some examples. Silk is invariably more expensive than cotton, silver than stainless steel. Handmade objects and those with superior workmanship are usually high in price. Good design quality need not necessarily increase costs but it frequently does. Unusual or individualized objects are likely to be more expensive than are those turned out by the thousands. When demand exceeds supply, prices are raised. Durable items are often more costly than those with a shorter life, but price alone is not a certain guide to longevity. For instance, wool upholstery usually wears better than cotton, but an expensive silk damask would probably not withstand as much hard usage as would firm heavy cotton. When shopping, give thought to what percentage of your money is being spent for each of the several factors that affect cost.

FLOOR COVERINGS: HARD	*Cost Per Square Yard*
(9″ x 9″ tiles)	
Asphalt tile	$1.00 to $ 2.00
Cork tile	4.50 to 7.00
Linoleum tile	1.50 to 2.50
Rubber tile	2.50 to 6.00
Vinyl tile	2.25 to 6.00

A 10′ x 15′ floor area can be covered with vinyl-asbestos tile (*left*) for about $40 if the family does the work. For the same area pure vinyl (*right*) in a distinctive pattern costs about $375 installed. (*Armstrong Cork Company*)

A 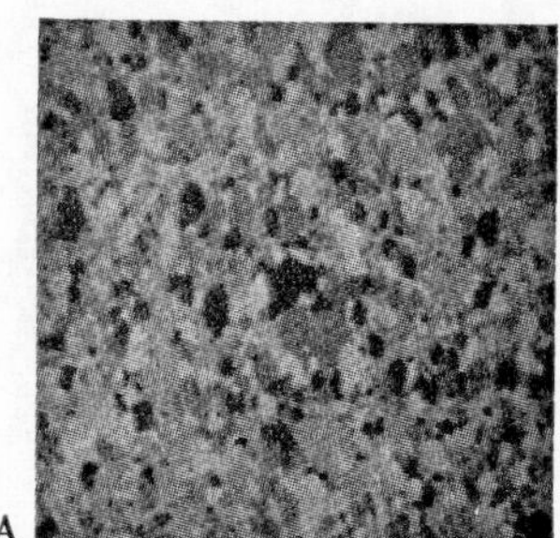

B 

Floor Coverings: Soft	Cost Per Square Yard	Cost of 9′ x 12′ Rug
Flat Weaves		
Kraft fiber (often combined with cotton, nylon, rayon)	$2.20 to $ 4.00	$ 16.00 to $100.00
Linen	7.00 to 12.50	90.00 to 150.00
Matting (rush, sisal)	2.50 to 5.00	30.00 to 100.00
Pile Weaves		
Cotton	3.75 to 10.00	22.00 to 150.00
Nylon	8.75 to 30.00	100.00 to 360.00
Rayon	3.50 to 15.00	40.00 to 180.00
Wool	8.00 to 30.00	55.00 to 360.00

Rug Cushions or Pads	Cost Per Square Yard	Cost of 9′ x 12′ Pad
Hair and jute	$ .95 to $ 2.00	$ 12.00 to $ 20.00
Rubber	1.80 to 4.00	19.00 to 50.00

Wall Surfacings (Materials only)	Cost Per Square Yard
Grass cloth	$3.50 to $ 4.50
Paint	.04 to .20
Plastic wall coverings	.75 to 5.00
Wallpaper	.04 to 2.00

The price per single roll of these wallpapers is 85¢ for the embossed pattern (*left*), $8.75 for the metallic paper (*center*), and $14.50 for the hand-screened, flocked design (*right*). (*Montgomery Ward; Denst & Soderlund; Sherle Wagner*)

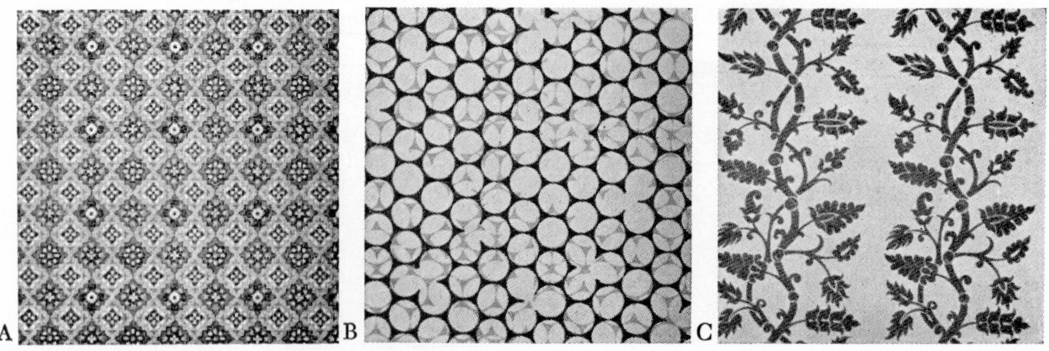

A B C

Window Treatments	Cost Per Window *40″ wide, 60″ high*
Venetian Blinds	$6.00 to $20.00
Roller Window Shades	2.00 to 7.00
Glass Curtains	
Celanese marquisette	$1.75 to $ 3.00
Dacron marquisette	2.50 to 5.00
Fiberglas marquisette	3.75 to 6.00
Nylon marquisette	1.80 to 4.00
Draw Curtains and Draperies	
Fiberglas	$5.00 to $15.00
Plastic	.90 to 2.00
Rayon and cotton (unlined)	4.00 to 15.00
Rayon and cotton (lined)	5.00 to 15.00
Woven bamboo, reed or wood	4.50 to 20.00

The price range of ready-made or custom-tailored curtains and draperies greatly exceeds the figures cited above, depending on the fiber and weave, distinctiveness of design, lining (if any), and quality of tailoring. Cost of material alone ranges from 30¢ per yard for good quality unbleached muslin to $10.00—or much more—for luxury fabrics. Considerable savings can be effected, however, by making draperies at home.

Furniture	*Cost*
Beds	
Foam-rubber mattress & box springs	$ 79.95 to $150.00
Innerspring mattress & box springs	45.00 to 150.00
Six wooden legs	3.50 to 8.00
Metal frame on casters	7.00 to 12.00
Headboards and footboards	9.00 to 200.00
Desks	$ 20.00 to $200.00
Sofas	
Studio couches	$ 50.00 to $200.00
Sofas	100.00 to 400.00

A

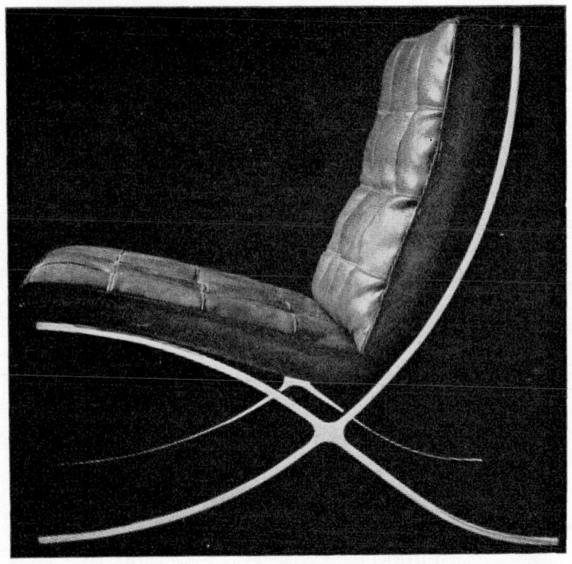
B

Left. Aluminum and webbing chairs, mass-produced in great quantities from inexpensive materials, sell for about $10. (*Troy Sunshade Co.*)

Right. The superbly designed, meticulously crafted chair of chromium-plated steel with leather cushions is almost a collector's item at about $600. Mies van der Rohe, designer. (*Kroll Associates*)

Chairs	
Upholstered, with springs and/or foam rubber	$ 30.00 to $200.00
Split cane or reed	5.00 to 20.00
Webbed	7.50 to 50.00
Padded	13.00 to 100.00
Utility—dining, games, work	6.00 to 30.00
Tables	
Dining	$ 40.00 to $200.00
Coffee and end	8.00 to 100.00
Storage	
Bookcases (small units)	$ 10.00 to $ 50.00
Chests of drawers	40.00 to 200.00
Cabinets (for dishes, etc.)	30.00 to 200.00

Upholstery Fabrics	*Cost Per Yard*
Slipcover materials (usually cotton, 36″ wide and equally suitable for draperies)	$ .75 to $ 3.00
Heavier upholstery materials (54″ wide, rayon-cotton blends, wool and long-wearing synthetics)	2.00 to 12.00
Plastic upholstery (also 54″ wide)	1.20 to 12.00

Lighting Fixtures

Floor lamps	$ 10.00 to $100.00
Table lamps	6.00 to 100.00
Pin-up wall lamps	6.00 to 100.00

Table Settings

Dinnerware	*Cost Per Five-piece Place Setting*
Bone China	$ 3.00 to $ 40.00
Earthenware	1.50 to 10.00
Plastic	1.50 to 9.00
Porcelain	13.00 to 50.00
Semiporcelain	1.50 to 10.00
Stoneware	4.00 to 10.00
Glassware	*Cost Per Piece*
Tumblers, goblets, etc.	$ .10 to $ 3.00
Silverware	*Cost Per Five-piece Place Setting*
Silver plate	$ 3.00 to $ 16.00
(24-piece sets may be bought for as little as $5.00)	
Stainless steel	.80 to 20.00
Sterling silver	22.50 to 65.00

Table Coverings

Place Mats	*Cost Per Mat*
Bamboo, grass, rush, etc.	$ .15 to $ 1.75
Cotton	.50 to 1.50
Linen	1.00 to 3.00
Plastic	.25 to 2.00
Table Cloths	*Cost*
Cotton or rayon, 54″ x 54″	$ 1.50 to $ 6.00
Linen, 54″ x 54″	3.00 to 10.00
Plastic, 54″ x 54″	1.00 to 6.00
Lace, 72″ x 90″	5.00 to 25.00
Linen damask, 72″ x 90″	5.00 to 50.00
Rayon damask, 72″ x 90″	4.00 to 25.00

Accessories

Handsome rocks and driftwood cost nothing if you seek them out. Beyond these, the tremendous diversity of kinds of accessories, to say nothing of the range within each type, makes it impossible to state any prices other than that accessories can be had for as little as 10¢ and for as much as hundreds of dollars.

	Cost
PAINTINGS	
Originals	$15.00 and up
Reproductions	1.00 to 15.00
GRAPHIC PRINTS—Originals	$ 5.00 and up
SCULPTURE	
Originals	$25.00 and up
Reproductions	5.00 to 75.00

This survey gives some of the raw data with which you can begin to think about planning your expenditures in a considered, budget-wise manner. If it has done no more than make you aware of price differences, it will have served a purpose. We hope, though, that it will have started you thinking about cost relationships of one item to another. Now we turn to budgets.

Budget planning—and saving—are family affairs. (*"Money Management—Your Budget," copyright by Household Finance Corporation*)

► BUDGETS

Budgeting is the art and science of planning your expenditures so that both ends meet with some left for savings. It is probably more a matter of emotions than of intellect, for it is remarkably easy to lay out a budget with a cool head but remarkably difficult to adhere to it when the heart warms toward an extravagance. Our concern is with wise planning for the expenses entailed by shelter and furnishings.

More than in any other part of this book there is need for caution in applying the material in this section of the book. These are the cautions:

- No ready-made budget will fit all families.
- No rule of thumb or suggested proportional expenditures can be applied to all situations.
- Each family has to decide, after thorough consideration of all factors, what percentage of its income will be used for the many items in a family budget.

Take them, then, for what they are—generalizations that work in typical cases. Do not assume that you should try to follow them if special circumstances indicate other ways of managing your money.

Budgeting for Your Shelter

How much of your weekly or annual income can you afford to spend for rent or your own home? What are the advantages of renting and of buying?

Proportions of Income. The answer to the first question depends on the amount, regularity, and dependability of your income; and on the size, ages, interests, and ideas of your family. If your income is large, regular, and dependable, and there is ample provision for emergencies, more of it *could* be used for shelter than would be advisable on a small, irregular income. Similarly, shelter costs can be increased if your family is small, the children have become financially independent, or the family prefers spending money on its home to other ways of enjoying its income. Typical families, though, spend from 15 to 25 percent of their income on housing.

On purchases, a long-held rule of thumb is that the total cost of the house you buy should not exceed from 1½ to 2½ times your annual income. In general, this is a good rule, but it is safer to limit the cost to not more than twice the income. In addition to all of the factors mentioned above, two others are important. First is the amount of savings the family has accumulated for a down payment, because the larger the down payment, the less you pay for interest on the mortgage, the smaller are the monthly payments, and the shorter the term the mortgage runs. The second factor is the resources you can call on in case of an emergency, chief of which are insurance and savings not invested in the house.

Although most of us want the best homes possible for our families, caution should be exerted to avoid becoming "house poor," no matter whether the poverty comes from payments on a purchase or payments of rent.

Owning versus Renting. Each has its special advantages, and although today there is a strong national urge toward owning one's own home, it may not be the most advisable way of getting shelter for you.

The financial advantages of owning are:

- Savings of several thousand dollars on a $15,000 house may accrue over a 25-year period.
- Interest paid on the mortgage and taxes paid on the house are deductible from taxable income.
- Owning your home is a reasonably safe investment.
- Monthly payments remain stable with no fluctuation such as may occur with rents. (This is advantageous during times of prosperity, may well be disadvantageous in depressions.)
- There is great incentive to save for your home.
- Savings can be made by doing some or much of the maintenance whereas in renting you invariably pay the landlord (through rent) for having it done. Maintenance costs on new houses usually run about 1 percent of the cost, 2 percent on old houses.

The monetary advantages of renting are:

- It costs up to $2,000 more the first year to buy a low-cost house than it does to rent one (because of down payment, fees for title-search and lawyers, etc.).
- There are no long-term commitments to hinder you from moving to a better situation.
- Renting gives you an opportunity to check the desirability of a community before investing money in a home.
- There are no unpredictable repair or replacement expenses.

Digressing from money matters for a sentence or two, the authors add that home-ownership has such compelling advantages as the satisfaction that comes from a permanent home with its uninterrupted social life for the whole family and schooling for children. It makes a family feel as though it belonged to the community rather than as though it were merely temporarily roosting there.

Budgeting for Landscape Development

Some part of the total cost of a house ought to be reserved for the development of the yard, but (as explained in the section on Landscaping) this is an extremely variable figure. A landscape developed as completely as is the typical house would easily come to a total of 10 to 20 percent of the cost of the house, but most families spend only a fraction of this. To cite an example, for a 1,200 square-foot house on a 60′ x 100′ lot costing $15,000, an average figure for the thorough development of the 4,800 square feet not covered by the house would be around $2,250 (15 percent of $15,000). Here, again, it is up to each family to decide for what necessities and pleasures they wish to spend their money. The cost of the landscaping should not be forgotten—but you may, wisely or otherwise, decide to reserve a very small amount for it.

Budgeting for Furnishings

In normal situations, these are general guides:

- Furnishings usually cost about one half of one year's income or one fourth of the value of the house.
- It is desirable to have one fourth of the total furnishings budget in cash to furnish the first apartment.
- Replacements for furnishings per year average around 3 to 4 percent of the annual income over a period of time but usually show conspicuous fluctuation from year to year. As income increases this percentage often increases.

  There is some advantage in concentrating replacement expenditures in certain years so that a sizable project is carried out at one time with a resulting unity as, for example, waiting until it is possible to do a thorough job on the living room or getting rugs for most or all the house.

Many factors determine the percentage of income available or needed for replacing furnishings.

- Family size.
- Stage of family cycle—usually there is less money available for this purpose from the time children arrive until they become independent than there is before or after.
- Amount and kind of entertaining.
- Durability of original furnishings.
- The kind of use and care given the furnishings.
- Amount of labor undertaken by family—repairing, refinishing, remodeling furniture; making draperies or slip covers; etc.

In general, furniture budgets tend to be divided as follows:

Living room	30 to 40%
Dining space	15 to 20%
Master bedroom	15 to 20%
Child's bedroom	10 to 15%
Child's bedroom or guest room	10 to 15%

The amount available for each room is likely to be apportioned as follows:

Furniture	60 to 70%
Floor covering	10 to 20%
Window treatment	5 to 10%
Accessories (including lamps)	2 to 7%

These percentages are based on a completely furnished home that usually is achieved only after some years of marriage. More often than not in the beginning, spending will be concentrated on a few good pieces of furniture for the living room and master bedroom, with the other rooms and planned-for rugs and draperies coming later. Then, of course, these figures do not hold.

Countless factors can alter these proportions:

- The money available for each room is in part determined by the number of rooms to be furnished.
- Good hard-surfaced flooring (asphalt, cork, or vinyl tile) minimizes the need for rugs.
- A separate dining room usually costs more to furnish than does dining space in the living room.
- One or two rooms unusually large or small in relationship to the others make a difference.
- Even a few pieces of inherited, cast-off, or bargain furniture affect the expenditures for the rooms in which they are used.

Costs and budgets are of the utmost importance in home planning and furnishing because the way in which a family handles its money is one of the primary sources of security or of frustration and worry. It is risky to give specific advice to others, but we can urge that you plan your expenditures at least as wisely as you plan your color schemes or furniture arrangements.

Concluding this book with a chapter on costs and budgets may seem to give finances an emphasis greater than they deserve. They are neither the beginning nor the end of home planning and furnishing, but constant factors in the process. They are seldom exhilarating, but they should not be depressing: they are simply ever-present problems that must be faced and solved. Remember, too, that money is only one factor in the economy of the home, and that economy takes its place along with use, beauty, and individuality as one of the goals of getting and keeping a good home.

Planning your home is an important challenge, for its shell, furnishings, and surroundings shape your living.

(Reproduced by Permission. Copyright 1946. The New Yorker Magazine, Inc.)

Index

(*Pages on which illustrations occur are italicized.*)